ANATOMY AND PHYSIOLOGY LABORATORY MANUAL

SECOND EDITION

Gerard J. Tortora

late, Nicholas P. Anagnostakos

Bergen Community College
Paramus, New Jersey

MACMILLAN PUBLISHING COMPANY
New York
COLLIER MACMILLAN PUBLISHERS
London

Macmillan Publishing Company
866 Third Avenue, New York, New York 10022

Collier Macmillan Canada, Inc.

Printing: 6 7 8 9 0 Year: 9 0

ISBN 0-02-421013-7

CONTENTS

PREFACE

Anatomy and Physiology Laboratory Manual, Second Edition,* has been written to guide students in the laboratory study of introductory anatomy and physiology. The manual was written to accompany most of the leading anatomy and physiology textbooks.

Comprehensiveness

This manual examines virtually every structure and function of the human body that is typically studied in an introductory anatomy and physiology course. Because of its detail, the need for supplemental handouts is minimized; the manual is a strong teaching device in itself.

Use of the Scientific Method

Anatomy and physiology cannot be understood without the practical experience of laboratory work. The exercises in this manual challenge students to understand the way scientists work by asking them to make microscopic examinations and evaluations of cells and tissues, to observe and interpret chemical reactions, to record data, to make gross examinations of organs and systems, to dissect, and to conduct physiological laboratory work and interpret and apply the results of this work.

Illustrations

The manual contains a large number and variety of illustrations. The illustrations of the body systems of the human have been carefully drawn to exhibit structures that are essential

---

*The First Edition appeared under the title *Laboratory Exercises in Anatomy and Physiology: Brief Edition.*

to students' understanding of anatomy and physiology. One hundred and seventy photographs, photomicrographs, and scanning electron micrographs are presented to show students how the structures of the body actually look. We feel that this laboratory manual has better and more complete illustrations than any other anatomy and physiology manual.

Important Features

Among the key features of this manual are (1) dissection of the white rat and selected mammalian organs, (2) numerous physiological experiments, (3) emphasis on the study of anatomy through histology, (4) lists of appropriate terms accompanying drawings and photographs to be labeled, (5) inclusion of numerous scanning electron micrographs and specimen photos, (6) a separate exercise on surface anatomy, (7) phonetic pronunciations for many anatomical and physiological terms, (8) diagrams of commonly used laboratory equipment, and (9) laboratory report questions at the back of the manual for each exercise that can be filled in, torn out, and turned in for grading if the instructor so desires. Many features in this manual are included in response to surveys made to determine the needs of instructors who teach college courses in anatomy and physiology.

New to Second Edition

Numerous changes have been made in the second edition of this manual in response to suggestions from students and instructors. We have added seven dissection exercises, many physiology experiments, and two new chapters on surface anatomy and genetics. We have also added over 135 new line drawings and photographs, including 15 new scanning electron photomicrographs. Line drawings now accompany the photomicrographs of cell division and epithelial and connective tissues. The additions and revisions in each exercise are described below.

Exercise 1, Microscopy, now contains a section on electron microscopy. Exercise 2, Introduction to the Human Body, has three new sections: levels of structural organization, abdominopelvic quadrants, and dissection of the white rat. Exercise 3, Cells, is expanded to include sections on modified plasma membranes, cell inclusions, and extracellular materials. In Exercise 4, Tissues, epithelium is reorganized into covering and lining and glandular epithelium, with new sections on membranes and the structural and functional classification of exocrine glands. New line art is added adjacent to the photomicrographs of epithelial and connective tissues. Sections on the skin and its glands are expanded in Exercise 5, Integumentary System, with new sections on skin color, hair, glands, and nails.

The skeletal system is now divided into two exercises: osseous tissue and bone. Exercise 6, Osseous Tissue, contains a new experiment on the chemistry of bone, and a table of bone markings, while Exercise 7, Bones, includes a table describing foramina of the skull. Exercise 8, Articulations, has an expanded section on synovial joints.

The muscular system is also divided into two exercises: muscle tissue and skeletal muscles. Exercise 9, Muscle Tissue, contains a revised section on the neuromuscular junction, and new tests on muscle contraction and Exercise 10, Skeletal Muscles, has four new tables that describe muscles of the pharynx, larynx, pelvic floor, and perineum.

A major change in this second edition is the addition of Exercise 11, Surface Anatomy. This new exercise can be studied before, in conjunction with, or after the study of various body systems as a review.

The nervous system is divided into two exercises: nervous tissue and physiology and nervous system. Exercise 12, Nervous Tissue and Physiology, contains new sections on the histology of neuroglia and spinal reflexes of the frog. Exercise 13, Nervous System, now contains an expanded discussion of spinal nerves, a new section on plexuses, a dissection

of the sheep brain, and a new section on the autonomic nervous system. The receptors for general senses have been reorganized in Exercise 14, Sensations, with new sections on the classification of sensations, use of the ophthalmoscope, dissection of a vertebrate eye, and the apparatus for equilibrium. Exercise 15, Endocrine System, contains revised discussions on the pituitary, thyroid, parathyroid, pancreas, pineal, and thymus glands, a new section on other endocrine tissues, experiments on basal metabolism using rats, and experiments demonstrating the effects of estrogens and testosterone on rats.

Exercise 16, Blood, has a new section on plasma. The heart, blood vessels, and lymphatic systems are now treated in separate exercises. Exercise 17, Heart, now contains expanded sections on the pericardial sac, heart wall, and heart chambers and a new section on dissection of a sheep heart. In Exercise 18, Blood Vessels, are expanded sections on the histology of blood vessels. Exercise 19, Cardiovascular Physiology, includes revised discussions of the cardiac cycle, heart sounds, pulse, electrocardiogram, and blood pressure and a new series of experiments on the physiology of the turtle heart.

Exercise 21, Respiratory System, has expanded discussions on the histology and gross anatomy of respiratory organs, a dissection of sheep pluck, revised pulmonary function tests, and a new section that combines respiratory and cardiovascular interactions. A new section on the physiology of intestinal smooth muscle as well as sections on teeth, dentitions, the esophagus, pancreas, liver, and gallbladder are included in Exercise 22, Digestive System. The Urinary System, Exercise 23, has revised discussions on histology and gross anatomy, new experiments on tubular secretion, and dissection of a sheep kidney.

The reproductive systems and development are now in separate exercises. In Exercise 24, Reproductive Systems, histology and gross anatomy are expanded, and sections on the menstrual cycle and dissection of a fetus-containing uterus of a pig are added. Exercise 25, Development, contains expanded discussions of gametogenesis and the embryonic and fetal periods.

Exercise 26, Genetics, is new to this edition. This exercise contains sections dealing with genotype and phenotype, Punnett squares, sex inheritance, *X*-linked inheritance, Mendelian laws, and multiple alleles.

Changes in Terminology

In recent years, the use of eponyms for anatomical terms has been minimized or eliminated. Anatomical eponyms are terms named after various individuals. Examples include fallopian tube (after Gabriello Fallopio) and eustachian tube (after Bartolommeo Eustachio).

Anatomical eponyms are often vague and nondescriptive and do not necessarily mean that the person whose name is applied contributed anything very original. For these reasons, we have also decided to minimize their use. However, because some still prevail, we have provided eponyms, in parentheses, after the first reference in each chapter to the more acceptable synonym. Thus, you will expect to see terms such as **uterine (fallopian) tube** or **auditory (eustachian) tube.**

Instructor Aids

A complimentary instructor's guide to accompany the manual is available from the publisher. This comprehensive guide contains: (1) a listing of materials needed to complete each exercise, (2) suggested audiovisual materials, (3) answers to illustrations and questions within the exercises, and (4) answers to laboratory report questions.

Acknowledgments

We wish to acknowledge the valuable contributions of Robert B. Tallitsch who is responsible for many of the additions and revisions to selected physiology sections. We also wish to thank Mary Dersch, whose outstanding medical illustrations have greatly improved the pedagogy and visual appeal of the manual. We also thank the instructors who reviewed the manuscript of this edition: Hope H. Adams, Sacred Heart University, Louis Debetaz, Angelina College, Jewett Dunham, Iowa State University, John C. Humphrey, Community College of Allegheny County, and R. Myles McCune, Crafton Hills College. To the reviewers and all the others who offered suggestions, we express our gratitude and our hope that the manual well reflects their contributions. A very special thanks is extended to Jan Richardson, Development Editor at Burgess Publishing, who coordinated every phase of the project and whose constant involvement and guidance have been major forces in its successful completion. Lastly, special thanks go to those who choose to use our manual. Your contribution will allow our manual to improve with time.

Related Manuals

For those courses that use the cat as a major dissection specimen, an alternate edition of this manual is available: *Laboratory Exercises in Anatomy and Physiology with Cat Dissections*, Second Edition, by Gerard J. Tortora, Nicholas P. Anagnostakos, and Robert B. Tallitsch. For anatomy courses, we recommend *Laboratory Exercises in Human Anatomy with Cat Dissections*, by Gerard J. Tortora.

G.J.T.

PRONUNCIATION KEY

One of the unique features of this revised manual is the addition of phonetic pronunciations for many anatomical and physiological terms. The pronunciations are given in parentheses immediately after the particular term is introduced. The following key explains the essential features of the pronunciations.

1. The syllable with the strongest accent appears in capital letters, for example, bilateral (bī-LAT-er-al) and diagnosis (dī-ag-NŌ-sis).

2. A secondary accent is noted by a single quote mark ('), for example, constitution (kon'-sti-TOO-shun) and physiology (fiz'-ē-OL-ō-jē). Additional secondary accents are also noted by a single quote mark, for example, decarboxylation (dē'-kar-bok'-si-LĀ-shun).

3. Vowels marked with a line above the letter are pronounced with the long sound as in the following common words:

ā as in *māke*   ī as in *īvy*
ē as in *bē*   ō as in *pōle*

4. Unmarked vowels are pronounced with the short sound, as in the following words:

e as in *bet*   o as in *not*
i as in *sip*   u as in *bud*

5. Other phonetic symbols are used to indicate the following sounds:

a as in *above*   yoo as in *cute*
oo as in *sue*   oy as in *oil*

COMMONLY USED LABORATORY EQUIPMENT

Beaker

Erlenmeyer Flask

Florence Flask

Funnel

Graduated Cylinder

Crucible Cover

Crucible

Evaporating Dish

Mortar and Pestle

Watch Glass

Stirring Rod

Test Tube

Test Tube Brush

Test Tube Holder

Test Tube Rack

Ring Stand and Ring

Pinch Clamp

Utility Clamp

Tripod

Clay Triangle

Wire Gauze

Crucible Tongs

Beaker Tongs

Forceps

Medicine Dropper

Nichrome Wire

Spatula

1 | MICROSCOPY

One of the most important instruments that you will use in your anatomy and physiology course is a compound light microscope. In this instrument, the lenses are arranged so that images of objects too small to be seen with the naked eye can become highly magnified, that is, apparent size can be increased, and their minute details revealed. Before you actually learn the parts of a compound light microscope and how to use it properly, discussion of some of the principles employed in light microscopy (mī-KROS-kō-pē) will be helpful. Later in this exercise, some of the principles used in electron microscopy will be discussed.

A. COMPOUND LIGHT MICROSCOPE

A **compound light microscope** uses two sets of lenses, ocular and objective, and employs light as its source of illumination. Magnification is achieved as follows: Light rays from an illuminator are passed through a condenser, which directs the light rays through the specimen under observation; from here, light rays pass into the objective lens, a magnifying lens that is closest to the specimen; the image of the specimen then forms on a mirror and is magnified again by the ocular lens.

A general principle of microscopy is that the shorter the wavelength of light used in the instrument, the greater the resolution. **Resolution,** or **resolving power,** is the ability of the lenses to distinguish fine detail and structure, that is, to distinguish between two points set at a specified distance apart. As an example, a microscope with a resolving power of 0.3 micrometers (mī-KROM-e-ters) symbolized by μm[1] is

capable of distinguishing two points as separate objects if they are at least 0.3 μm apart. The light used in a compound light microscope has a relatively long wavelength and cannot resolve structures smaller than 0.3 μm. This fact, as well as practical considerations, means that even the best compound light microscopes can magnify images only about 2000 times.

A **photomicrograph** (fō-tō-Mī-krō'-graf), a photograph of a specimen taken through a compound light microscope, is shown in Figure 4.1. In later exercises you will be asked to examine photomicrographs of various specimens of the body before you actually view them yourself through the microscope.

1. Parts of the Microscope

Carefully carry the microscope from the cabinet to your desk by placing one hand around the arm and the other hand firmly under the base. Gently place it on your desk, directly in front of you, with the arm facing you. Locate the following parts of the microscope and, as you read about each part, label Figure 1.1 by placing the correct numbers in the spaces next to the list of terms that accompanies the figure.

Base—The bottom portion on which the microscope rests.

Body tube—The portion that receives the ocular.

Arm—Angular or curved part of the frame.

Inclination joint—A movable hinge in some microscopes that allows the instrument to be tilted to a comfortable viewing position.

Stage—A platform on which slides or other objects to be studied are placed. The opening in the center allows light to pass from below through the object being examined. Some

---

[1]1μm = 0.000001 m or 10^{-6}m. See Appendix A.

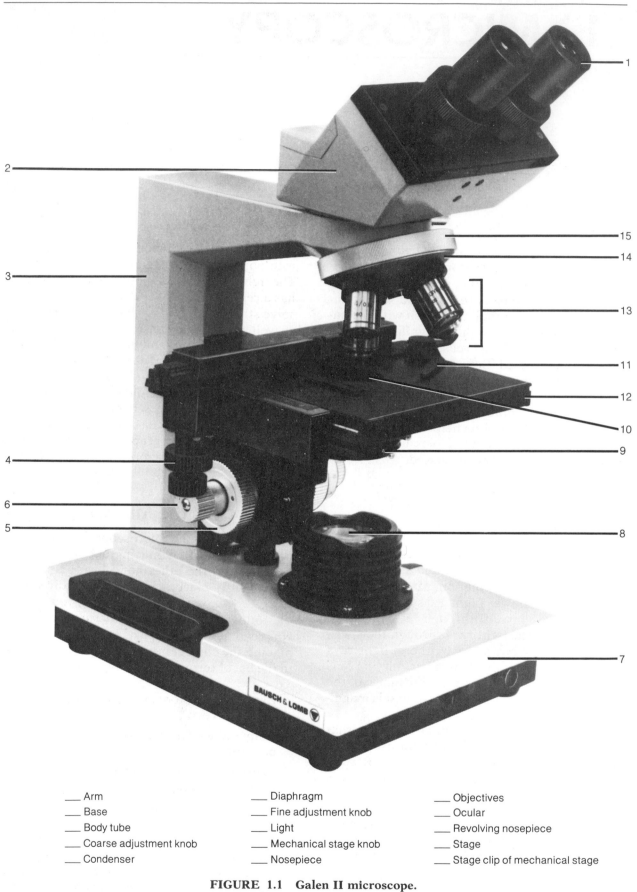

—— Arm   —— Diaphragm   —— Objectives
—— Base   —— Fine adjustment knob   —— Ocular
—— Body tube   —— Light   —— Revolving nosepiece
—— Coarse adjustment knob   —— Mechanical stage knob   —— Stage
—— Condenser   —— Nosepiece   —— Stage clip of mechanical stage

FIGURE 1.1 Galen II microscope.

microscopes have a **mechanical stage.** An adjustor knob below the stage moves the stage forward and backward and from side to side. With a mechanical stage, the slide and the stage move simultaneously.

Stage (spring) clips—Two clips mounted on the stage that hold slides securely in place.

Mirror—A feature found in some microscopes below the stage. The mirror directs light from its source through the stage opening and through the lenses. If the light source is built in, a mirror is not necessary.

Diaphragm (DĪ-a-fram)—A device located beneath the stage that regulates light intensity passing through the condenser and lenses to the observer's eyes. Such regulation is needed because transparent or very thin specimens cannot be seen in bright light. One of two types of diaphragms is usually used. An **iris diaphragm,** as found in cameras, is a series of sliding leaves that vary the size of the opening. A **disc diaphragm** consists of a plate with a graded series of holes, any of which can be rotated into position.

Condenser—A lens located beneath the stage opening that concentrates the light beam on the specimen.

Condenser adjustment knob—A knob that functions to raise and lower the condenser. In its highest position, it allows full illumination.

Coarse adjustment knob—When turned, functions to raise and lower the body tube for focusing the microscope.

Fine adjustment knob—Usually found below or external to the coarse adjustment knob and used for fine or final focusing. Some microscopes have both coarse and fine adjustment knobs combined into one.

Nosepiece—A plate, usually circular, at the bottom of the body tube.

Revolving nosepiece—The lower, movable part of the nosepiece that contains the various objective lenses.

Scanning objective—A lens, marked 5× on most microscopes.

Low-power objective—A lens, marked 10× on most microscopes.

High-power objective—A lens, marked 43× or 45× on most microscopes; also called a **high-dry objective.**

Oil-immersion objective—A lens, marked 100× on most microscopes and distinguished by an etched colored circle (special instructions for this objective are discussed later).

Ocular (eyepiece)—A removable lens at the top of the body tube, marked 10× on most microscopes.

2. Rules of Microscopy

You must observe certain basic rules at all times to obtain maximum efficiency and provide proper care for your microscope.

1. Keep all parts of the microscope clean, especially the lenses of the ocular, objectives, condenser, and mirror. You should use the special lens paper that is provided and never use paper towels or cloths, because these tend to scratch the delicate glass surfaces. When using lens paper, use the same area on the paper only once. As you wipe the lens, change the position of the paper as you go.

2. Do not permit the objectives to get wet, especially when observing a **wet mount.** You must use a **cover slip** when you examine a wet mount or the image becomes distorted.

3. Consult your instructor if any mechanical or optical difficulties arise. *Do not try to solve these problems yourself.*

4. Keep *both* eyes open at all times while observing objects through the microscope. This is difficult at first, but with practice becomes natural. This important technique will help you to draw and observe microscopic specimens without moving your head. Only your eyes will move.

5. Always use either the scanning or low-power objective first to locate an object; then, if necessary, switch to a higher power.

6. If you are using the high-power objectives, *never focus using the coarse adjustment knob.* The distance between these objectives and the slide is very small and you may break the cover slip and the slide and scratch the lens.

7. When looking through the microscope, *never focus downward.* By observing from one side you can see that the objectives do not make contact with the cover slip or slide.

8. Make sure that you raise the body tube before placing a slide on the stage or before removing a slide.

9. At the end of a laboratory session when you are to return the microscope to the cabinet, leave it with the scanning or low-power objective aligned, the diaphragm open, and the condenser raised to its highest fixed position. Also, be sure to clean all lenses with lens paper and remove all slides from the stage.

3. Setting up the Microscope

1. Place the microscope on the table with the arm toward you and with the back of the base at least 1 inch (in.) from the edge of the table.

2. Position yourself and the microscope so that you can look into the ocular comfortably.

3. Wipe the objectives, the top lens of the eyepiece, the condenser, and the mirror with lens paper. Clean the most delicate and the least dirty lens first. Apply xylol or ethanol to the lens paper only to remove grease and oil from the lenses and microscope slides.

4. Position the low-power objective in line with the body tube. When it is in its proper place, it will click. Lower the body tube using the coarse adjustment knob until the bottom of the lens is approximately ¼ in. from the stage.

5. Admit the maximum amount of light by opening the diaphragm, if it is an iris, or turning the disc to its largest opening.

6. Place your eye to the eyepiece (ocular), and adjust the light. When a uniform circle (the **microscopic field**) appears without any shadows, the microscope is ready for use.

4. Using the Microscope

1. Using the coarse adjustment knob, raise the body tube to its highest fixed position.

2. Make a temporary mount using a single letter of newsprint, or use a slide that has been specially prepared with a letter, usually the letter "e." If you prepare such a slide, cut a single letter—"a," "b," or "e"—from the smallest print available and place this letter in the correct position to be read with the naked eye. Your instructor will provide directions for preparing the slide.

3. Place the slide on the stage, making sure that the letter is centered over the opening in the stage, directly over the condenser. Secure the slide in place with the stage clips.

4. Align the low-power objective with the body tube.

5. Lower the body tube as far as it will go while you watch it from the side, taking care not to touch the slide. The tube will reach an automatic stop that prevents the low-power objective from hitting the slide.

6. While looking through the eyepiece, turn the coarse adjustment knob counterclockwise, raising the body tube. Watch for the object to suddenly appear in the microscopic field. If it is in proper focus, the low-power objective is about ½ in. above the slide. When focusing, always *raise* the body tube.

7. Use the fine adjustment knob to complete the focusing; you will usually use a counterclockwise motion once again.

8. Compare the orientation of the letter as originally seen with its appearance under the microscope.

Has the orientation of the letter been changed?

_____

9. While looking at the slide through the ocular, change the position of the slide by using your thumbs, or, if the microscope is equipped with them, the mechanical stage knobs. This exercise teaches you to move your material in various directions quickly and efficiently.

In which direction does the letter move when

you move the slide to the left? _____

This procedure, "scanning" a slide, will be useful for examining living objects and for entering objects so you can observe them easily.

Make a drawing of the letter as it appears under low power in the space to the left.

_____

Drawing of letter as seen under low power   *Drawing of letter as seen under high power*

10. Change your magnification from low to high power by carrying out the following steps:

a. Place the letter in the center of the field under low power. Centering is important because you are now focusing on a smaller area of the microscopic field. As you will see, microscopic field size decreases with higher magnification.

b. Make sure the illumination is at its maximum. Illumination must be increased at higher magnifications because the amount of light entering the lens increases as the size of the objective lens increases.

c. The letter should be in focus, and if the microscope is **parfocal** (meaning that when clear focus has been attained using any objective at random, revolving the nosepiece results in a change in magnification but leaves the specimen still in focus), the high-power objective can be switched into line with the body tube without changing focus. If it is not completely in focus after switching the lens, a slight turn of the fine adjustment knob will focus it.

d. If your microscope is not parfocal, observe the stage from one side and carefully switch the high-power objective in line with the body tube.

e. While still observing from the side and using the coarse adjustment knob, *carefully* lower the objective until it almost touches the slide.

f. Look through the ocular and focus up slowly. Finish focusing by turning the fine adjustment knob.

g. If your microscope has an oil-immersion objective, you must follow special procedures. Place a drop of special **immersion oil** on the microscope slide, and lower the oil-immersion objective until it just contacts the oil. If your microscope is parfocal, you do not have to raise or lower the objectives. For example, if you are using the high-power objective and the specimen is in focus, just switch the high-power objective out of line with the body tube. Then add the oil and switch the oil-immersion objective into position; the specimen should be in focus. The same holds true when you switch from low power to high power. The special light-transmitting properties of the oil are such that light is refracted (bent) toward the specimen, permitting the use of powerful objectives in a relatively narrow field of vi-

sion. This objective is extremely close to the slide being examined, so when it is in position take precautions *never to focus downward* while you are looking through the eyepiece. Whenever you finish using immersion oil, be sure to saturate a piece of lens paper with xylol or alcohol and clean the oil-immersion objective and the slide if it is to be used again.

Is as much of the letter visible under high power as under low power? Explain. _____

_____

Make a drawing of the letter as it appears under high power in the space provided following step 9.

11. Now select a prepared slide of three different colored threads. Examination will show that a specimen mounted on a slide has depth as well as length and width. At lower magnification the amount of depth of the specimen that is clearly in focus, the depth of field, is greater than that at higher magnification. You must focus at different depths to determine the position (depth) of each thread.

After you make your observation under low power and high power, answer the following questions about the location of the different threads:

What color is at the bottom, closest to the slide?

_____

On top, closest to the cover slip? _____

In the middle? _____

12. Your instructor might want you to prepare a wet mount as part of your introduction to microscopy. If so, the directions are given in Exercise 4, A.6.

5. Magnification

The total magnification of your microscope is calculated by multiplying the magnification of the ocular by the magnification of the objective used. Example: An ocular of $10\times$ used with an objective of $5\times$ gives a total magnification of $50\times$. Calculate the total magnification of each of the objectives on your microscope:

1. Ocular _____ × Objective _____ = _____

2. Ocular _____ × Objective _____ = _____

3. Ocular _____ × Objective _____ = _____

4. Ocular _____ × Objective _____ = _____

B. ELECTRON MICROSCOPE

Examination of specimens smaller than 0.3 μm requires an **electron microscope,** an instrument with a much greater resolving power than a compound light microscope. An electron microscope uses a beam of electrons instead of light. Electrons travel in waves just as light does. Instead of glass lenses, magnets are used in an electron microscope to focus a beam of electrons through a vacuum tube onto a specimen. Since the wavelength of electrons is about 1/100,000 that of visible light, the resolving power of very sophisticated transmission electron microscopes (described shortly) is close to 1 angstrom (Å[1]). Most electron microscopes have a working resolving power of about 10 Å and can magnify images up to 200,000×.

Two types of electron microscope are available. In a **transmission electron microscope,** a finely focused beam of electrons passes through a specimen, usually ultrathin sections of material. The beam is then refocused, and the image reflects what the specimen has done to the transmitted electron beam. The image may be used to produce what is called a **transmission electron micrograph** (see Figure 6.2a). The method is extremely valuable in providing details of the interior of specimens at different layers but does not give a three-dimensional effect. Such an effect can be obtained with a **scanning electron microscope.** With this instrument, a finely focused beam of electrons is directed over the specimen and then reflected from the surface of the specimen onto a televi-

_____

[1] Å = 0.000 000 000 1 m or 10^{-10} m. See Appendix A.

sion-like screen or photographic plate. The photograph produced from an image generated in this manner is called a **scanning electron micrograph** (see Figure 6.2b). Scanning electron micrographs commonly magnify specimens up to 10,000 times and are especially useful in studying surface features of specimens.

The one drawback of the electron microscope is the fact that specimens must be killed because they are placed in a vacuum. With a process called **microtomography,** three-dimensional images of *living* cells can be produced. Through microtomography, scientists hope to study how normal and abnormal cells move, reproduce, and grow. The process will also be used to follow developmental sequences in growing embryos. Other very important applications are observing the effects of drugs and cancer-causing substances on living cells.

LABORATORY REPORT QUESTIONS (PAGE 365)

Note: A section of **laboratory report questions** for each exercise is located at the back of this manual, starting on page 365. These questions can be answered by the student and handed in for grading at the direction of the instructor. Even if the instructor does not require you to answer these questions, we recommend that you do so anyway to check your understanding.

Some exercises have a section of **laboratory report results,** in which students can record results of laboratory exercises, in addition to laboratory report questions. As with the laboratory report questions, the laboratory report results are located at the back of the manual and can be handed in as the instructor directs. Instructions in the manual tell students when and where to record laboratory results.

2 | INTRODUCTION TO THE HUMAN BODY

In this exercise, you will be introduced to the organization of the human body through a study of its levels of structural organization, principal body systems, anatomical position, regional names, directional terms, planes of the body, body cavities, abdominopelvic regions, and abdominopelvic quadrants.

A. LEVELS OF STRUCTURAL ORGANIZATION

The human body is composed of several levels of structural organization associated with each other in various ways:

1. **Chemical level**—Composed of all atoms and molecules necessary to maintain life.

2. **Cellular level**—Consists of cells, the structural and functional units of the body.

3. **Tissue level**—Formed by tissues, groups of similarly specialized cells and their intercellular material.

4. **Organ level**—Consists of organs, structures of definite form and function composed of two or more different tissues.

5. **System level**—Formed by systems, associations of organs that have a common function. The systems together constitute an organism.

B. SYSTEMS OF THE BODY

Using an anatomy and physiology textbook, torso, wall chart, and any other materials that might be available to you, identify the principal organs that compose the following body systems.[1] In the spaces that follow, indicate the components and functions of the systems.

Integumentary

Components _____

_____

_____

_____

Functions _____

_____

_____

_____

Skeletal

Components _____

_____

_____

_____

Functions _____

_____

_____

_____

Muscular

Components _____

_____

_____

_____

[1]You will probably need other sources, plus any aids the instructor might provide, to label many of the figures and answer some questions in this manual. You are encouraged to use other sources as you find necessary.

Functions _____

_____

_____

_____

Cardiovascular

Components _____

_____

_____

_____

Functions _____

_____

_____

_____

Lymphatic

Components _____

_____

_____

_____

Functions _____

_____

_____

_____

Nervous

Components _____

_____

_____

_____

Functions _____

_____

_____

_____

Endocrine

Components _____

_____

_____

_____

Functions _____

_____

_____

_____

Respiratory

Components _____

_____

_____

_____

Functions _____

_____

_____

_____

Digestive

Components _____

_____

_____

_____

Functions _____

_____

_____

_____

Urinary

Components _____

_____

_____

_____

Functions _____

_____

_____

_____

Reproductive

Components _____

_____

_____

_____

Functions _____

_____

_____

_____

C. ANATOMICAL POSITION AND REGIONAL NAMES

Figure 2.1 shows anterior and posterior views of a subject in the **anatomical position**. The subject is erect and facing the observer, the arms are at the sides, and the palms of the hands are facing forward. The figure also shows the common names for various regions of the body. In the spaces next to the list of terms in Figure 2.1 write the number of each common term next to each corresponding anatomical term. For example, the skull (31) is cranial, so write the number *31* next to the term *Cranial.*

D. EXTERNAL FEATURES OF THE BODY

Referring to your textbook and human models, identify the following external features of the body:

1. **Head (caput)**—This is divided into the **cranium** (brain case) and **face.**

2. **Neck (collum)**—This region consists of an anterior **cervix**, two lateral surfaces, and a posterior **nucha** (NOO-ka).

3. **Trunk**—This region is divided into the **back** (dorsum), **chest** (thorax), **abdomen** (venter), and **pelvis.**

4. **Upper extremity**—This consists of the **armpit** (axilla), **shoulder** (omos), **arm** (brachium), **elbow** (cubitus), **forearm** (antebrachium), and **hand** (manus). The hand, in turn, consists of the **wrist** (carpus), **palm** (metacarpals), and **fingers** (digits or phalanges).

5. **Lower extremity**—This consists of the **buttocks** (gluteus), **thigh** (femoral region), **knee** (genu), **leg** (crus), and **foot** (pes). The foot includes the **ankle** (tarsus) and **toes** (digits or phalanges).

E. DIRECTIONAL TERMS

To explain exactly where a structure of the body is located, it is a standard procedure to use **directional terms.** Commonly used directional terms for humans are as follows:

1. **Superior (cephalad** or **cranial)**—Toward the head or the upper part of a structure; generally refers to structures in the trunk.

2. **Inferior (caudad)**—Away from the head or toward the lower part of a structure; generally refers to structures in the trunk.

3. **Anterior (ventral)**—Nearer to or at the front or belly surface of the body.

4. **Posterior (dorsal)**—Nearer to or at the back or backbone surface of the body.

5. **Medial**—Nearer the midline of the body or a structure.

6. **Lateral**—Farther from the midline of the body or a structure.

7. **Intermediate**—Between two structures, one medial and one lateral.

8. **Ipsilateral**—On the same side of the body.

9. **Contralateral**—On the opposite side of the body.

10. **Proximal**—Nearer the attachment of an extremity to the trunk.

11. **Distal**—Farther from the attachment of an extremity to the trunk.

12. **Superficial (external)**—Toward or on the surface of the body.

13. **Deep (internal)**—Away from the surface of the body.

14. **Parietal**—Pertaining to the outer wall of a body cavity.

15. **Visceral**—Pertaining to the covering of an organ (viscus).

Using a torso and an articulated skeleton, and consulting with your instructor as necessary, describe the location of the following by inserting the proper directional term.

1. The ulna is on the _____ side of the forearm.

2. The ascending colon is _____ to the urinary bladder.

3. The heart is _____ to the liver.

4. The muscles of the arm are _____ to the skin of the arm.

5. The sternum is _____ to the heart.

6. The humerus is _____ to the radius.

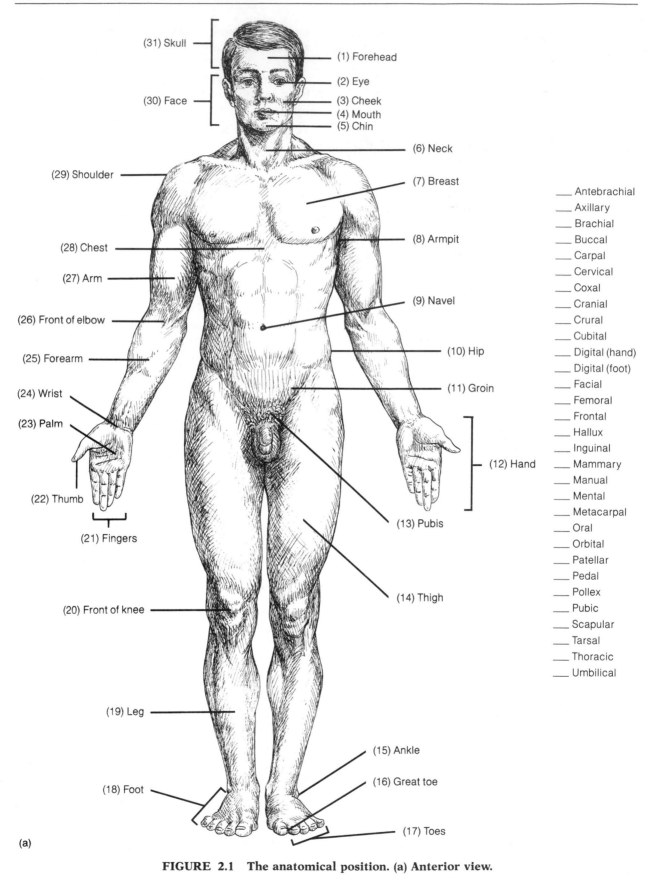

(31) Skull
(1) Forehead
(2) Eye
(30) Face
(3) Cheek
(4) Mouth
(5) Chin
(6) Neck
(29) Shoulder
(7) Breast
(8) Armpit
(28) Chest
(27) Arm
(9) Navel
(26) Front of elbow
(10) Hip
(25) Forearm
(11) Groin
(24) Wrist
(23) Palm
(12) Hand
(22) Thumb
(21) Fingers
(13) Pubis
(14) Thigh
(20) Front of knee
(19) Leg
(15) Ankle
(18) Foot
(16) Great toe
(17) Toes

___ Antebrachial
___ Axillary
___ Brachial
___ Buccal
___ Carpal
___ Cervical
___ Coxal
___ Cranial
___ Crural
___ Cubital
___ Digital (hand)
___ Digital (foot)
___ Facial
___ Femoral
___ Frontal
___ Hallux
___ Inguinal
___ Mammary
___ Manual
___ Mental
___ Metacarpal
___ Oral
___ Orbital
___ Patellar
___ Pedal
___ Pollex
___ Pubic
___ Scapular
___ Tarsal
___ Thoracic
___ Umbilical

(a)

FIGURE 2.1   The anatomical position. (a) Anterior view.

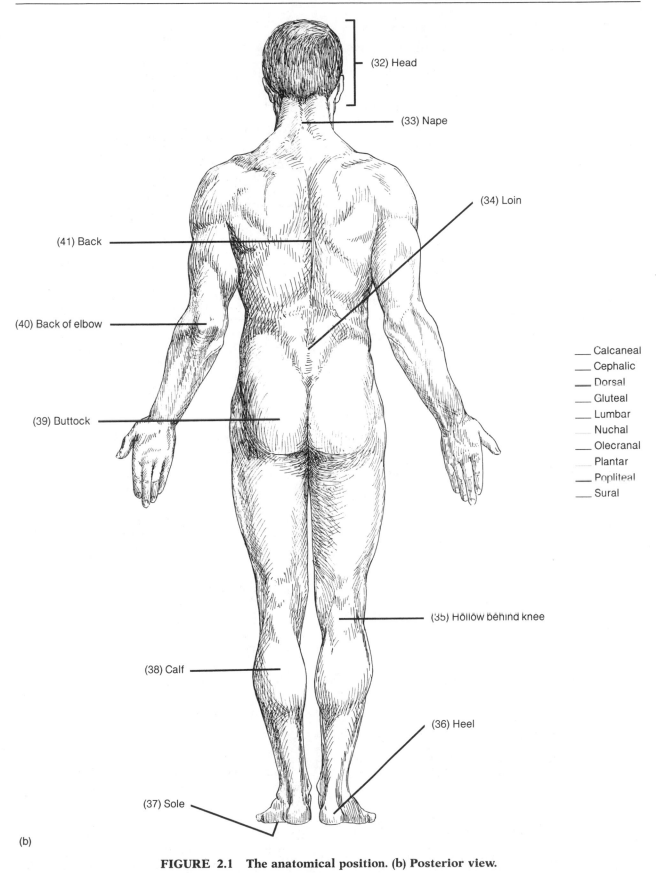

(32) Head

(33) Nape

(34) Loin

(41) Back

(40) Back of elbow

(39) Buttock

(35) Hollow behind knee

(38) Calf

(36) Heel

(37) Sole

___ Calcaneal
___ Cephalic
___ Dorsal
___ Gluteal
___ Lumbar
___ Nuchal
___ Olecranal
___ Plantar
___ Popliteal
___ Sural

(b)

FIGURE 2.1   The anatomical position. (b) Posterior view.

7. The stomach is _____ to the lungs.

8. The muscles of the thoracic wall are _____ to the viscera in the thoracic cavity.

9. The _____ pleura forms the outer layer of the pleural sacs that surround the lungs.

10. The esophagus is _____ to the trachea.

11. The phalanges are _____ to the carpals.

12. The _____ pleura forms the inner layer of the pleural sacs and covers the external surface of the lungs.

13. The ring finger is _____ between the little (medial) and middle (lateral) fingers.

14. The ascending colon of the large intestine and the gallbladder are _____.

15. The ascending and descending colons of the large intestine are _____.

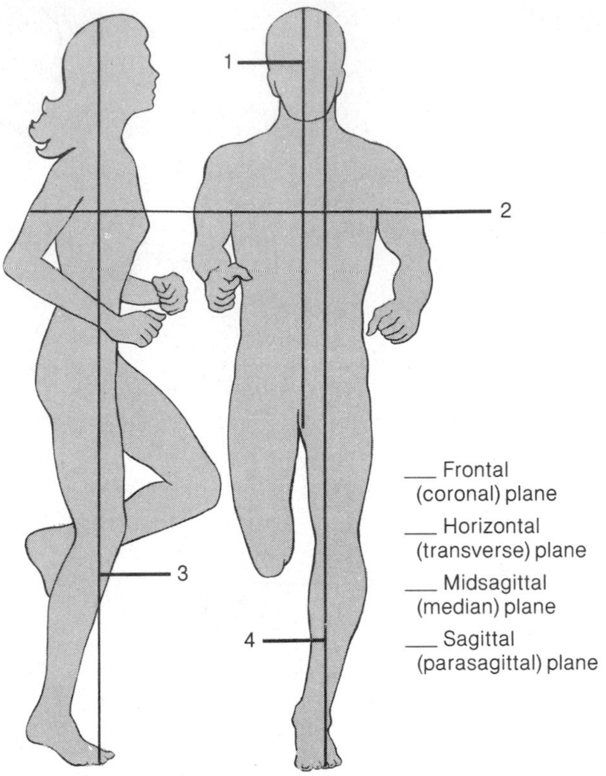

F. PLANES OF THE BODY

The structural plan of the human body may also be analyzed with respect to **planes** (sections) passing through it. Planes are frequently used to show the relationship of several structures in a region to one another.

Commonly used planes are:

1. **Midsagittal (median)**—Runs through the midline of the body or of an organ and divides the body or an organ into equal right and left sides.

2. **Sagittal (parasagittal)**—Runs parallel to the midsagittal plane and divides the body or an organ into unequal left and right portions.

3. **Frontal (coronal)**—Runs at right angles to the midsagittal and sagittal planes and divides the body or an organ into anterior and posterior portions.

4. **Horizontal (transverse)**—Divides the body or an organ into superior and inferior portions.

Refer to Figure 2.2 and label the planes shown.

___ Frontal (coronal) plane

___ Horizontal (transverse) plane

___ Midsagittal (median) plane

___ Sagittal (parasagittal) plane

FIGURE 2.2 Planes of the body.

G. BODY CAVITIES

Spaces within the body that contain various internal organs are called **body cavities.** One way of organizing the principal body cavities follows:

Dorsal body cavity
Cranial cavity
Vertebral (spinal) cavity
Ventral body cavity
Thoracic cavity
Right pleural
Left pleural
Pericardial
Abdominopelvic cavity
Abdominal
Pelvic

The space (actually a mass of tissue) between the pleurae of the lungs and extending from the sternum (breast bone) to the backbone is called the **mediastinum.** It contains the heart, thymus gland, esophagus, trachea, and many large blood vessels.

Label the body cavities shown in Figure 2.3. Then examine a torso or wall chart, or both,

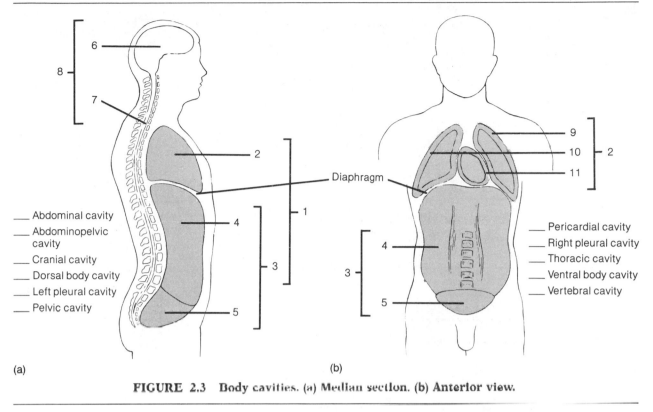

(a)

(b)

___ Abdominal cavity
___ Abdominopelvic cavity
___ Cranial cavity
___ Dorsal body cavity
___ Left pleural cavity
___ Pelvic cavity

Diaphragm

___ Pericardial cavity
___ Right pleural cavity
___ Thoracic cavity
___ Ventral body cavity
___ Vertebral cavity

FIGURE 2.3   Body cavities. (a) Median section. (b) Anterior view.

and determine which organs lie within each cavity.

H. ABDOMINOPELVIC REGIONS

To describe the location of viscera more easily, the abdominopelvic cavity may be divided into **nine regions** by using four imaginary lines: (1) an upper horizontal **transpyloric line** that passes through the pylorus (lower portion) of the stomach, (2) a lower horizontal line, the **transtubercular line,** that joins the iliac crests (top surfaces of the hipbones), (3) a **right lateral line** drawn slightly medial to the right nipple, and (4) a **left lateral line** drawn slightly medial to the left nipple.

The four imaginary lines divide the abdominopelvic cavity into the following nine regions: (1) **umbilical,** which is centrally located; (2) **left lumbar,** to the left of the umbilical region; (3) **right lumbar,** to the right of the umbilical region; (4) **epigastric region,** directly above the umbilical region; (5) **left hypochondriac** (hī′-pō-KON-drē-ak) **region,** to the left of the epigastric region; (6) **right hypochondriac region,** to the right of the epigastric region; (7) **hypogastric (pubic) region,** directly below the umbilical

region; (8) **left iliac (inguinal) region,** to the left of the hypogastric (pubic) region; and (9) **right iliac (inguinal) region,** to the right of the hypogastric (pubic) region.

Label Figure 2.4 by indicating the names of the four imaginary lines and the nine abdominopelvic regions.

Examine a torso and determine which organs or parts of organs lie within each of the nine abdominopelvic regions.

I. ABDOMINOPELVIC QUADRANTS

An easier way to divide the abdominopelvic cavity is into **four quadrants** by passing one horizontal line and one vertical line through the umbilicus. The two lines thus divide the abdominopelvic cavity into a **right upper quadrant (RUQ), left upper quadrant (LUQ), right lower quadrant (RLQ),** and **left lower quadrant (LLQ).** Quadrant names are frequently used by clinicians for locating the site of an abdominopelvic pain, tumor, or other abnormality.

Examine a torso or wall chart, or both, and determine which organs or parts of organs lie within each of the four abdominopelvic quadrants.

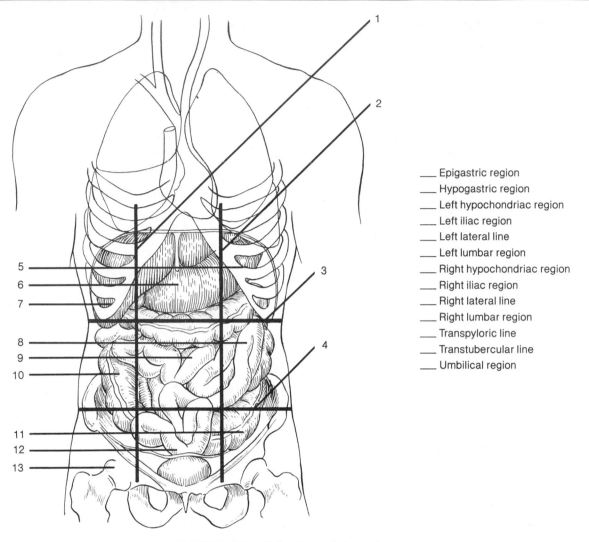

___ Epigastric region
___ Hypogastric region
___ Left hypochondriac region
___ Left iliac region
___ Left lateral line
___ Left lumbar region
___ Right hypochondriac region
___ Right iliac region
___ Right lateral line
___ Right lumbar region
___ Transpyloric line
___ Transtubercular line
___ Umbilical region

FIGURE 2.4   Abdominopelvic regions.

J. DISSECTION OF WHITE RAT

Now that you have some idea of the names of the various body systems and the principal organs that comprise each, you can actually observe some of these organs by dissecting a white rat. Dissect means "to separate." This procedure gives you an excellent opportunity to see the different sizes, shapes, locations, and relationships of organs and to compare the different textures and external features of organs.

1. Procedure

1. Place the rat on its backbone on a wax dissecting pan (tray). Using dissecting pins, anchor each of the four extremities to the wax (Figure 2.5a).

2. To expose the contents of the thoracic, abdominal, and pelvic cavities, you will have to first make a midline incision. This is done by lifting the abdominal skin with a forceps to separate the skin from the underlying connective tissue and muscle. While lifting the abdominal skin, cut through it with scissors and make an incision that extends from the lower jaw to the anus (Figure 2.5a).

3. Now make four lateral incisions that extend from the midline incision into the four extremities (Figure 2.5a).

4. Peel the skin back and pin the flaps to the wax to expose the superficial muscles (Figure 2.5b).

5. Next, lift the abdominal muscles with a forceps and cut through the muscle layer, being careful not to damage any underlying organs. Keep the scissors parallel to the rat's back-

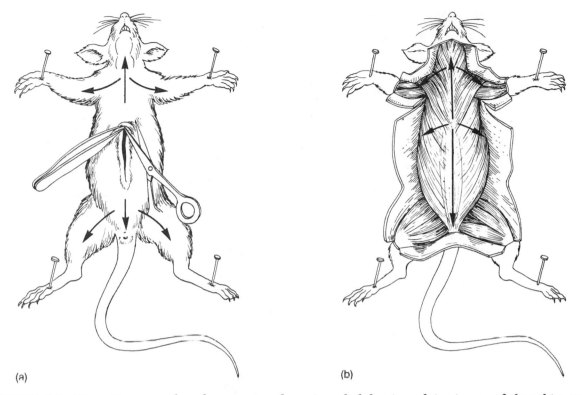

(a)   (b)

FIGURE 2.5   Dissection procedure for exposing thoracic and abdominopelvic viscera of the white rat for examination. (a) Lines of incision in skin. (b) Peeling back skin and lines of incision in muscles.

bone. Extend this incision from the anus to a point just below the bottom of the rib cage (Figure 2.5b). Make two lateral incisions just below the rib cage and fold back the muscle flaps to expose the abdominal and pelvic viscera (Figure 2.5b).

6. To expose the thoracic viscera, cut through the ribs on either side of the sternum. This incision should extend from the diaphragm to the neck (Figure 2.5b). The **diaphragm** is the thin muscular partition that separates the thoracic from the abdominal cavity. Again make lateral incisions in the chest wall so that you can lift the ribs to view the thoracic contents.

2. Examination of Thoracic Viscera

You will first examine the thoracic viscera. As you dissect and observe the various structures, palpate (feel with the hand) them so that you can compare their texture. Use Figure 2.6 as a guide.

a. **Thymus gland**—An irregular mass of glandular tissue superior to the heart and superficial to the trachea. Push the thymus gland aside or remove it.

b. **Heart**—A structure located in the midline, inferior to the thymus gland and between the lungs. The sac covering the heart is the *pericardium*, which may be removed. The large vein that returns blood to the heart from the lower regions of the body is the *inferior vena cava*, while the large vein that returns blood from the upper regions of the body is the *superior vena cava*. The large artery that carries blood from the heart to most parts of the body is the *aorta*.

c. **Lungs**—Reddish, spongy structures on either side of the heart. Note that the lungs are divided into regions called *lobes*.

d. **Trachea**—A tubelike passageway superior to the heart and deep to the thymus gland. Note that the wall of the trachea consists of rings of cartilage. Identify the **larynx** (voice box) at the superior end of the trachea and the **thyroid gland,** a bilobed structure on either side of the larynx. The lobes of the thyroid gland are connected by a band of thyroid tissue, the isthmus.

e. **Bronchial tubes**—Trace the trachea inferiorly and note that it divides into bronchial

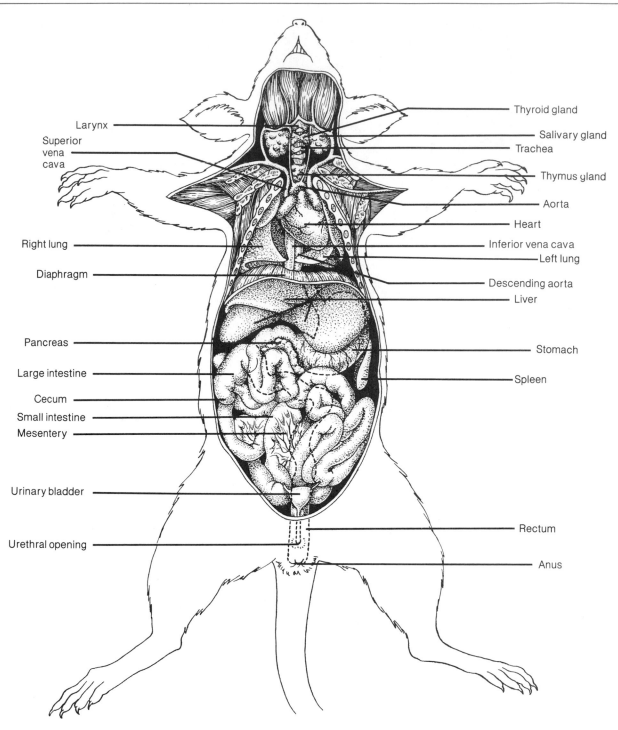

Thyroid gland
Larynx
Salivary gland
Superior vena cava
Trachea
Thymus gland
Aorta
Heart
Right lung
Inferior vena cava
Left lung
Diaphragm
Descending aorta
Liver
Pancreas
Stomach
Large intestine
Spleen
Cecum
Small intestine
Mesentery
Urinary bladder
Rectum
Urethral opening
Anus

FIGURE 2.6 **Superficial structures of the thoracic and abdominopelvic cavities of the white rat.**

tubes that enter the lungs and continue to divide within them.

f. **Esophagus**—A muscular tube posterior to the trachea that transports food from the throat into the stomach. Trace the esophagus inferiorly to see where it passes through the diaphragm to join the stomach.

3. Examination of Abdominopelvic Viscera

You will now examine the principal viscera of the abdomen and pelvis. As you do so, again refer to Figure 2.6.

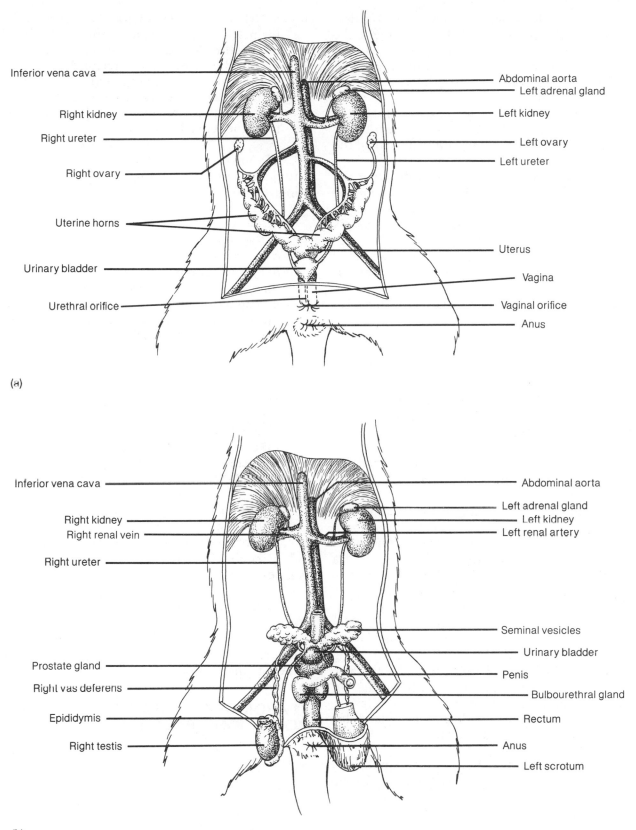

Inferior vena cava
Right kidney
Right ureter
Right ovary
Uterine horns
Urinary bladder
Urethral orifice

Abdominal aorta
Left adrenal gland
Left kidney
Left ovary
Left ureter
Uterus
Vagina
Vaginal orifice
Anus

(a)

Inferior vena cava
Right kidney
Right renal vein
Right ureter
Prostate gland
Right vas deferens
Epididymis
Right testis

Abdominal aorta
Left adrenal gland
Left kidney
Left renal artery
Seminal vesicles
Urinary bladder
Penis
Bulbourethral gland
Rectum
Anus
Left scrotum

(b)

FIGURE 2.7   Deep structures of the abdominopelvic cavity of the white rat. (a) Female. (b) Male.

a. **Stomach**—A viscus located on the left side of the abdomen and in contact with the liver. The digestive organs are attached to the posterior abdominal wall by a membrane called the *mesentery.* Note the blood vessels in the mesentery.

b. **Small intestine**—An extensively coiled tube that extends from the stomach to the first portion of the large intestine called the cecum.

c. **Large intestine**—A wider tube than the small intestine that begins at the cecum and ends at the rectum. The cecum is a large, saclike structure. In humans, the appendix is attached to the cecum.

d. **Rectum**—A muscular passageway, located on the midline in the pelvic cavity, that terminates in the anus.

e. **Anus**—Terminal opening of the digestive tract to the exterior.

f. **Pancreas**—A pale gray, glandular organ posterior and inferior to the stomach.

g. **Spleen**—A small, dark red organ lateral to the stomach.

h. **Liver**—A large, brownish-red organ directly inferior to the diaphragm. The rat does not have a gallbladder, a structure associated with the liver. To locate the remaining viscera, either move the superficial viscera aside or remove them. Use Figure 2.7 as a guide.

i. **Kidneys**—Bean-shaped organs embedded in fat and attached to the posterior abdominal wall on either side of the backbone. As will be explained later, the kidneys and a few other structures are behind the membrane that lines the abdomen (*peritoneum*). Such structures are referred to as *retroperitoneal* and are not actually within the abdominal cavity. See if you can find the *abdominal aorta*, the large artery located along the midline behind the inferior vena cava. Also, locate the *renal arteries* branching off the abdominal aorta to enter the kidneys.

j. **Adrenal (suprarenal) glands**—Glandular structures. One is located on top of each kidney.

k. **Ureters**—Tubes that extend from the medial surface of the kidney inferiorly to the urinary bladder.

l. **Urinary bladder**—A saclike structure in the pelvic cavity that stores urine.

m. **Urethra**—A tube that extends from the urinary bladder to the exterior. Its opening to the exterior is called the *urethral orifice.* In male rats, the urethra extends through the penis; in female rats, the tube is separate from the reproductive tract.

If your specimen is female (no visible scrotum anterior to the anus), identify the following:

n. **Ovaries**—Small, dark structures inferior to the kidneys.

o. **Uterus**—An organ located near the urinary bladder consisting of two sides (horns) that join separately into the vagina.

p. **Vagina**—A tube that leads from the uterus to the external vaginal opening, the *vaginal orifice.* This orifice is in front of the anus and behind the urethral orifice.

If your specimen is male, identify the following:

q. **Scrotum**—Large sac anterior to the anus that contains the testes.

r. **Testes**—Egg-shaped glands in the scrotum. Make a slit into the scrotum and carefully remove one testis. See if you can find a coiled duct attached to the testis (*epididymis*) and a duct that leads from the epididymis into the abdominal cavity (*vas deferens*).

s. **Penis**—Organ of copulation medial to the testes.

When you have finished your dissection, store or dispose of your specimen. Wash your dissecting pan and dissecting instruments with laboratory detergent, dry them, and return them to their storage areas.

LABORATORY REPORT QUESTIONS (PAGE 367)

3 | CELLS

A **cell** is the basic living structural and functional unit of the body. The study of cells is called **cytology** (sī-TOL-o-jē). The different kinds of cells (blood, nerve, bone, muscle, epithelial, and others) perform specific functions and differ from one another in shape, size, and structure. You will start your study of cytology by learning the important components of a theoretical, generalized cell.

A. CELL PARTS

Refer to Figure 3.1, a generalized cell based on electron micrograph studies. With the aid of your textbook and any other items made available by your instructor, label the parts of the cell indicated. In the spaces that follow, describe the function of the following cellular structures:

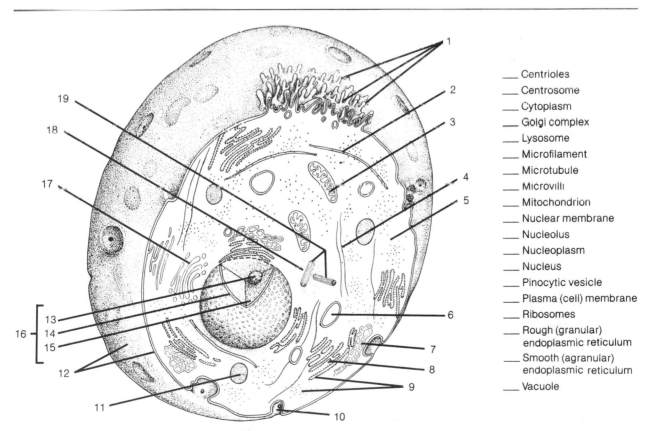

___ Centrioles
___ Centrosome
___ Cytoplasm
___ Golgi complex
___ Lysosome
___ Microfilament
___ Microtubule
___ Microvilli
___ Mitochondrion
___ Nuclear membrane
___ Nucleolus
___ Nucleoplasm
___ Nucleus
___ Pinocytic vesicle
___ Plasma (cell) membrane
___ Ribosomes
___ Rough (granular) endoplasmic reticulum
___ Smooth (agranular) endoplasmic reticulum
___ Vacuole

FIGURE 3.1 Generalized animal cell.

1. **Plasma (cell) membrane** _____

_____

2. **Cytoplasm** (SĪ-tō-plazm´) _____

_____

3. **Nucleus** (NOO-klē-us) _____

_____

4. **Endoplasmic reticulum (ER)** _____

_____

5. **Ribosome** _____

_____

6. **Golgi** (GOL-jē) **complex** _____

_____

7. **Mitochondria** (mī´-tō-KON-drē-a) _____

_____

8. **Lysosome** _____

_____

9. **Peroxisome** (pe-ROKS-i-sōm) _____

_____

10. **Microfilament** _____

_____

11. **Microtubule** _____

_____

12. **Centriole** _____

_____

13. **Cilium** (SIL-ē-um) _____

_____

14. **Flagellum** (fla-JEL-um) _____

_____

15. **Vacuole** (VAK-yoo-ōl) _____

_____

16. **Pinocytic vesicle** _____

_____

B. DIVERSITY OF CELLS

Now obtain prepared slides of the following types of cells and examine them under the magnifications suggested:

1. Ciliated columnar epithelial cells (high power)
2. Sperm cells (oil immersion)
3. Nerve cells (high power)
4. Muscle cells (high power)

After you have made your examination, draw an example of each of these kinds of cells in the spaces provided and under each cell indicate how each is adapted to its particular function.

_____

Ciliated columnar epithelial cell

Sperm cell

Nerve cell

Muscle cell

_____

C. MOVEMENT OF SUBSTANCES ACROSS PLASMA MEMBRANES

In general, substances move across plasma membranes by two principal kinds of processes—passive and active. In **passive** or **physical processes**, substances move because of differences in concentration (or pressure) from regions of higher concentration (or pressure) to regions of lower concentration (or pressure). The movement usually continues until an equilibrium or an even distribution of substances is accomplished. Passive processes are the result of the kinetic energy (energy of motion) of the substances themselves and the cell does not expend energy to move the substances. Examples of passive processes are diffusion, osmosis, filtration, and dialysis.

In **active** or **physiological processes**, substances may move from areas of lower to higher concentration. Moreover, cells must expend energy to carry on active processes. Examples of active processes are active transport, phagocytosis, and pinocytosis.

1. Passive Processes

a. DIFFUSION

Diffusion is the net (greater) movement of molecules or ions from a region of higher concentration to a region of lesser concentration until they are evenly distributed. An example of diffusion in the human body is the movement of oxygen and carbon dioxide between body cells and blood.

1. To demonstrate diffusion of a solid in a liquid, *using forceps, carefully* place a large crystal of potassium permanganate ($KMnO_4$) into a test tube filled with water.

2. Place the tube in a rack against a white background where it will not be disturbed.

3. Note the diffusion of the crystal material through the water at 15-minute intervals for 120 minutes (2 hours).

4. Record the diffusion of the crystal in millimeters (mm) per minute at 15-minute intervals. Simply measure the distance of diffusion using a millimeter ruler.

Time	Distance in mm
15 minutes	
30 minutes	
45 minutes	
60 minutes	
75 minutes	
90 minutes	
105 minutes	
120 minutes	

1. To demonstrate diffusion of a solid in a solid, *using forceps, carefully* place a large crystal of methylene blue on the surface of agar in the center of a petri plate.

2. Note the diffusion of the crystal through the agar at 15-minute intervals for 120 minutes (2 hours).

3. Record the diffusion of the crystal in millimeters (mm) per minute at 15-minute intervals, using a millimeter ruler.

Time	Distance in mm
15 minutes	
30 minutes	
45 minutes	
60 minutes	
75 minutes	
90 minutes	
105 minutes	
120 minutes	

b. OSMOSIS

Osmosis is the net movement of *water* through a selectively permeable membrane from a region of higher water (lower solute) concentration to a region of lower water (higher solute) concentration. In the body, fluids move between cells as a result of osmosis.

1. Refer to the osmosis apparatus in Figure 3.2.

2. Tie a knot very tightly at one end of a 4-in. piece of cellophane dialysis tubing that has been soaking in water and fill the tubing with a

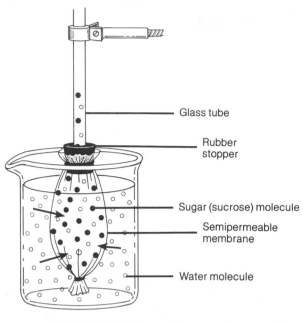

Glass tube

Rubber stopper

Sugar (sucrose) molecule

Semipermeable membrane

Water molecule

FIGURE 3.2 Osmosis apparatus.

10% sugar (sucrose) solution that has been colored with Congo red (red food coloring may also be used).

3. Close the open end of the tubing with a one-hole rubber stopper into which a glass tube has been carefully inserted.

4. Tie a piece of string tightly around the tubing to secure it to the cork.

5. Secure and suspend the glass tube and tubing by means of a clamp attached to a ring stand.

6. Insert the cellophane bag into a beaker or flask of water until the water comes up to the bottom of the rubber stopper.

7. As soon as the sugar solution becomes visible in the glass tubing, mark the tube with a wax pencil and note the time.

8. Mark the height of liquid in the tube after 10-, 20-, and 30-minute intervals by using your millimeter ruler.

Time	Height of liquid (mm)
10 minutes	_____
20 minutes	_____
30 minutes	_____

Explain what happened. _____

_____

c. HEMOLYSIS AND CRENATION

Osmosis can also be understood by noting the effects of different water concentrations on red blood cells. Red blood cells maintain their normal shape when placed in an **isotonic solution** (that is, one having the same salt concentration; 0.85% solution of NaCl [sodium chloride] is isotonic to red blood cells). If, however, red blood cells are placed in a **hypotonic solution** (concentration of NaCl lower than 0.85%), a net movement of water into the cells occurs, causing the cells to swell and possibly burst. The rupture of blood cells in this manner with the loss of hemoglobin into the surrounding liquid is called **hemolysis** (hē-MOL-i-sis). If, instead, red blood cells are placed in a **hypertonic solution** (concentration of NaCl higher than 0.85%), a net movement of water out of the cells occurs, causing them to shrink. This shrinkage is known as **crenation** (kre-NĀ-shun).

1. With a wax marking pencil, mark three microscope slides as follows: 0.85%, DW (distilled water), and 3%.

2. Place three drops of fresh (uncoagulated) human or ox blood on a microscope slide that contains 2 milliliters (ml) of a 0.85% NaCl solution (isotonic solution). Mix gently and thoroughly. (The procedure for cleaning your finger and using a lancet to draw blood is given in Exercise 16, D.1).

3. Place three drops of fresh blood on a microscope slide that contains 2 ml of distilled water (hypotonic solution). Mix gently and thoroughly.

4. Now add three drops of fresh blood to a microscope slide that contains 2 ml of a 3% NaCl solution (hypertonic solution). Mix gently and thoroughly.

5. Place two drops of the red blood cells in the isotonic solution on another microscope slide, cover with a cover slip, and examine the red blood cells under high power. Reduce your illumination.

What is the shape of the cells? _____

_____

Explain their shape. _____

_____

6. Place two drops of the red blood cells in the hypotonic solution on another microscope slide, cover with a cover slip, and examine the red blood cells under high power. Reduce your illumination.

What is the shape of the cells? _____

_____

Explain their shape. _____

_____

7. Place two drops of the red blood cells in the hypertonic solution on another microscope slide, cover with a cover slip, and examine the red blood cells under high power. Reduce your illumination.

What is the shape of the cells? _____

_____

Explain their shape. _____

_____

d. FILTRATION

Filtration is the movement, under the influence of gravity, of solvents and dissolved substances across a selectively permeable membrane from regions of higher pressure to regions of lower pressure. The pressure is called hydrostatic pressure and is the result of the solvent, usually water. In general, any substance having a molecular weight of less than 100 is filtered because the pores in the filter paper (membrane) are larger than the molecules of the substance. Filtration is one mechanism by which the kidneys regulate the chemical composition of the blood.

1. Refer to Figure 3.3, the filtration apparatus.

2. Fold a piece of filter paper in half and then in half again.

3. Open it into a cone, place it in a funnel, and place the funnel over the beaker.

4. Shake a mixture of a few particles of powdered wood charcoal (black), 1% copper sulfate (blue), boiled starch (white), and water and pour it into the funnel until the mixture almost reaches the top of the filter paper. Gravity will pull the particles through the pores of the membrane (that is, the filter paper).

5. Count the number of drops passing through the funnel for the following time intervals:

        10 seconds _____

        30 seconds _____

        60 seconds _____

        90 seconds _____

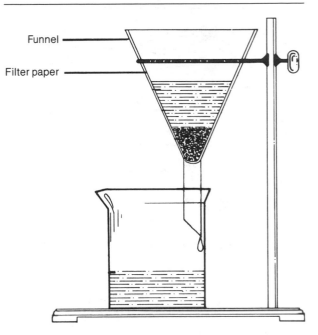

FIGURE 3.3 Filtration apparatus.

        120 seconds _____

6. Observe which substances passed through the filter paper by noting their color in the filtered fluid in the beaker.

7. Examine the filter paper to determine whether any colored particles were not filtered.

8. To determine if any starch is in the filtrate (liquid in the beaker), add several drops of 0.01 M IKI solution. A blue-black color reaction indicates the presence of starch.

e. DIALYSIS

Dialysis is the separation of smaller molecules from larger ones by using a selectively permeable membrane that permits diffusion of the smaller molecules but not the larger. The principle of dialysis is employed in artificial kidneys.

1. Refer to the dialysis apparatus in Figure 3.4.

2. Tie off one end of a piece of dialysis tubing that has been soaking in water. Place a prepared solution containing starch, sodium chloride, 5% glucose, and albumin into the dialysis tubing.

3. Tie off the other end of the tubing and immerse into a beaker of distilled water.

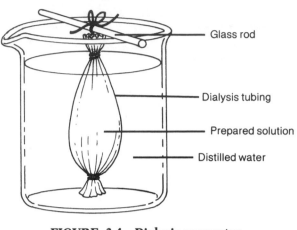

FIGURE 3.4   Dialysis apparatus.

4. After 1 hour, test the solution in the beaker for the presence of each of the substances in the tubing, as follows:

a. **Albumin**—*Carefully* add several drops of concentrated nitric acid to a test tube containing 2 ml of the solution in the beaker. *Be careful using nitric acid. It can severely damage your skin.* If it does make contact with your skin or eyes, immediately flush the area with water for several minutes and then seek medical attention. Positive reaction = white coagulate.

b. **Sugar**—Test 5 ml of the solution in the beaker in a test tube with 5 ml of Benedict's solution. Place the test tube, *with its mouth pointing away from you and your classmates,* in a boiling water bath for three minutes. Positive reaction = green, yellow, orange, or red precipitate.

c. **Starch**—Add several drops of IKI solution to 2 ml of the solution in the beaker in a test tube. Positive reaction = blue-black color.

d. **Sodium chloride**—Place 2 ml of the solution in the beaker in a test tube and add several drops of 1% silver nitrate. Positive reaction = white precipitate.

2. Active Processes

a. ACTIVE TRANSPORT

Active transport is a process by which substances, usually ions, are transported across a plasma membrane from an area of lower to one of higher concentration. An example is the movement of sodium (Na^+) and potassium (K^+) ions across nerve cell membranes during nerve impulse conduction. Because reliable results are difficult to demonstrate simply, you will not be asked to demonstrate active transport.

b. PHAGOCYTOSIS

Phagocytosis (fag'-ō-sī-TŌ-sis), or cell "eating," is the engulfment of solid particles or organisms by *pseudopodia* (temporary fingerlike projections of cytoplasm) of the cell. Once the particle is surrounded by the membrane, the membrane folds inward, pinches off from the rest of the plasma membrane, and forms a vacuole around the particle. Enzymes are secreted into the vacuole or the vacuole combines with a lysosome and the particle is digested.

Phagocytosis can be demonstrated by observing the feeding of an amoeba, a unicellular animal whose movement and ingestion are similar to those of human white blood cells (leucocytes).

1. Place a drop of culture containing amoebae that have been starved for 48 hours into the well of a depression slide and cover the well with a cover slip. Cultures containing *Chaos chaos* or *Amoeba proteus* should be used. (Your instructor may wish to use the hanging-drop method instead. If so, he or she will give you verbal instructions.)

2. Examine the amoebae under low power, and be sure that your light is reduced considerably.

3. Observe the locomotion of an amoeba for several minutes. Pay particular attention to the pseudopodia that appear to flow out of the cell.

4. To observe phagocytosis, add a drop containing small unicellular animals called *Tetrahymena pyriformis* to the culture containing the amoebae.

5. Examine under low power, and observe the ingestion of *Tetrahymena pyriformis* by an amoeba. Note the action of the pseudopodia and the formation of the vacuole around the ingested organism.

c. PINOCYTOSIS

Pinocytosis (pi'-nō-sī-TŌ-sis), or cell "drinking," is the engulfment of a liquid. The liquid is attracted to the surface of the membrane, and the membrane folds inward, surrounds the liquid, and detaches from the rest of the intact membrane.

D. MODIFIED PLASMA MEMBRANES

The plasma membranes of certain cells of the body may possess surface modifications that reflect specialized functions. Modified plasma membranes include:

1. **Microvilli**—Fingerlike projections of some cells that line the small intestine. Observe microvilli in Figure 3.1 and in your textbook or a histology textbook.

What is the function of microvilli? _____

_____

2. **Stereocilia**—Long, slender branching processes at the free surfaces of cells lining the ductus epididymis of the male reproductive system (see Figure 24.4). Observe stereocilia in a prepared slide, your textbook, or a histology textbook.

What is the function of stereocilia? _____

_____

3. **Myelin sheath**—Lipid covering around the long processes of certain nerve cells. Observe the myelin sheath in your textbook or a histology textbook.

What is the function of the myelin sheath? ___

_____

E. CELL INCLUSIONS

Cell inclusions are a diverse group of intracellular chemicals, principally organic, that may appear or disappear at various times in the life of a cell. Using your textbook as a reference, indicate the function of the following cell inclusions:

1. **Melanin** _____

2. **Glycogen** _____

3. **Lipids** _____

F. EXTRACELLULAR MATERIALS

Substances that lie outside the plasma membranes of body cells are referred to as **extracel-**

lular materials. They include body fluids, such as interstitial fluid and plasma, which provide a medium for dissolving, mixing, and transporting substances. Extracellular materials also include special substances that form the matrix in which some cells are embedded.

Matrix materials are produced by certain cells and deposited outside their plasma membranes where they support the cells, bind them together, and provide strength and elasticity. Some matrix materials have no definite shape and are referred to as *amorphous*. These include hyaluronic (hī'-a-loo-RON-ik) acid and chondroitin (kon-DROY-tin) sulfate. Other matrix materials are *fibrous*. Examples include collagenous, reticular, and elastic fibers.

Using your textbook as a reference, indicate the location and function for each of the following matrix materials:

Hyaluronic acid

Location _____

_____

_____

Function _____

_____

_____

Chondroitin sulfate

Location _____

_____

_____

_____

Function _____

_____

_____

Collagenous fibers

Location _____

_____

_____

_____

Function _____

_____

_____

_____

Reticular fibers

Location _____

_____

_____

_____

Function _____

_____

_____

_____

Elastic fibers

Location _____

_____

_____

_____

Function _____

_____

_____

_____

G. CELL DIVISION

Cell division, the basic mechanism by which cells reproduce themselves, may be of two types. The first type consists of mitosis (nuclear division) and cytokinesis (cytoplasmic division) and provides the body with a means of growth and of replacement of diseased or damaged cells. In the overall process, a single parent cell divides and produces two daughter cells, each exactly like the parent cell. The second type of cell division, called **meiosis,** is the mechanism by which sperm and eggs are produced (Exercise 25).

Obtain a prepared slide of a whitefish blastula and examine it under high power.

A cell that is carrying on every life process except division is said to be in **interphase** of the cell cycle. At this time, the cell is between divisions. One of the most important activities of interphase is the replication of DNA so that the two daughter cells that eventually form will each have the same kind and amount of DNA as the parent cell. Scan your slide and find a cell in interphase. Such a parent cell is characterized by a clearly defined nuclear membrane. Within the nucleus look for the nucleolus, the nucleoplasm (amorphous nuclear material), and DNA (which is associated with protein in the form of a granular substance called **chromatin**). Also locate a pair of centrioles. Make a labeled diagram of an interphase cell in the space provided under the photomicrograph in Figure 3.5.

Once a cell completes its interphase activities, mitosis begins. **Mitosis,** or nuclear division, also called **karyokinesis,** is the distribution of chromosomes into two separate and equal nuclei after replication of the chromosomes of the parent cell, an event that takes place in the interphase preceding mitosis. Although a continuous process, mitosis is divided into four stages for purposes of study: prophase, metaphase, anaphase, and telophase.

1. **Prophase**—The initial stage of mitosis takes about one-half the total time required for cell division and is characterized by a series of rather conspicuous events. The paired centrioles separate and move to opposite poles (ends) of the cell. Once in position they project a series of **continuous microtubules** that grow toward each other, connect, and thus extend from one pole of the cell to another. As this is happening, **chromosomal microtubules** grow out of each centriole and extend to both poles of the cell. Together, the continuous and chromosomal microtubules constitute the **mitotic spindle** and, with the centrioles, are referred to as the **mitotic apparatus.** At the same time the microtubules are forming, the chromatin shortens and thickens into distinct rod-shaped bodies, the **chromosomes;** nucleoli become less distinct; and the nuclear membrane disappears. Careful examination of prophase chromosomes reveals that each consists of two separate units called **chromatids,** joined at a point called a **centromere.** At the end of prophase, the chromatid pairs move toward the equatorial plane (center) of the cell. Isolate a cell in prophase, study it carefully, and draw a labeled diagram in the space provided under the photomicrograph in Figure 3.5.

2. **Metaphase**—In the second stage of mitosis, the centromeres of the chromatid pairs line up along the equatorial plane of the cell. The centromere of each chromatid pair forms chromosomal microtubules that associate each chro-

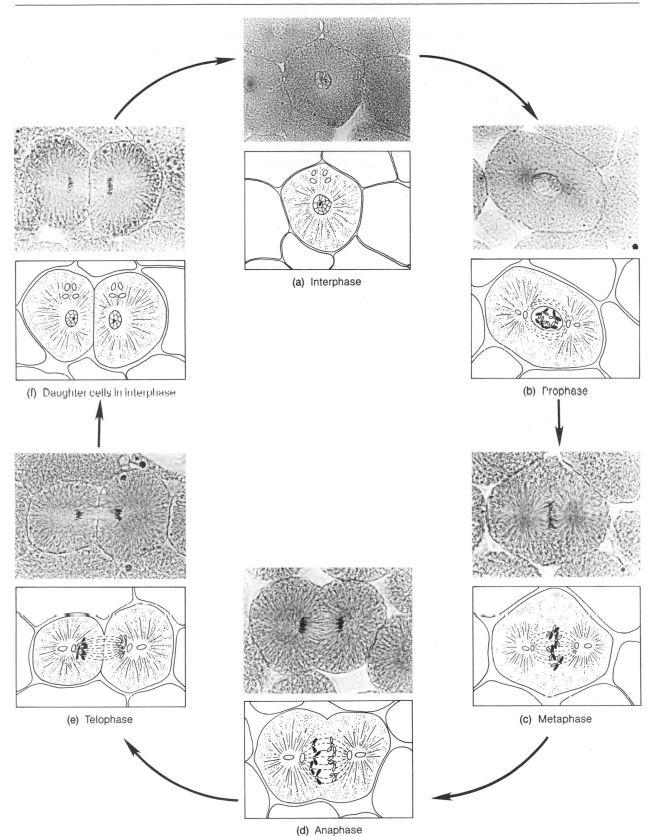

(a) Interphase

(b) Prophase

(c) Metaphase

(d) Anaphase

(e) Telophase

(f) Daughter cells in interphase

FIGURE 3.5 Cell division: mitosis and cytokinesis. Photomicrographs of the various stages of cell division in whitefish eggs.

matid pair with both poles of the cell. Next, the lengthwise separation of the chromatids takes place. After separation, each chromatid is referred to as a chromosome. Draw and label a cell in metaphase in the space provided under the photomicrograph in Figure 3.5.

3. **Anaphase**—The third stage of mitosis is characterized by the division of the centromeres and the movement of complete identical sets of chromosomes to opposite poles of the cell. During this movement, the centromeres attached to chromosomal microtubules lead, while the rest of the chromosome trails like a streamer. The mechanism of chromosome movement to opposite poles of the cell is not completely understood. According to one theory, chromosomes move by the assembly and disassembly of microtubules. That is, chromosomal microtubules shorten by the removal of component subunits pulling the chromosomes toward the poles. At the same time, continuous microtubules are lengthened by the addition of subunits, further contributing to chromosomal movement. Draw and label a cell in anaphase in the space provided under the photomicrograph in Figure 3.5.

4. **Telophase**—The final stage of mitosis consists of a series of events nearly the reverse of prophase. When the chromosome sets reach their respective poles, new nuclear membranes enclose them, chromosomes uncoil and lengthen into their chromatin form, nucleoli reappear, and the mitotic spindle disappears. The formation of two nuclei identical to those in cells of interphase terminates telophase and completes a mitotic cycle. Draw and label a cell in telophase in the space provided under the photomicrograph in Figure 3.5.

Cytokinesis (sī'-tō-ki-NĒ-sis), or division of the cytoplasm, begins in late anaphase and terminates in telophase. You can recognize cytokinesis in animal cells by the formation of a **cleavage furrow** that runs around the cell at the equator. The furrow spreads inward as a constricting ring and cuts completely through the cell, forming two portions of cytoplasm. At this point, two identical daughter cells are formed.

Following cytokinesis, each daughter cell returns to interphase. Each cell in most tissues of the body eventually grows and undergoes mitosis and cytokinesis, and a new divisional cycle begins. Examine your telophase cell again and be sure that it contains a cleavage furrow.

LABORATORY REPORT QUESTIONS (PAGE 371)

4 | TISSUES

A **tissue** is a group of similar cells and their intercellular substance operating together to perform a specific function. The cells constituting a tissue are generally all derived from the same embryological precursor and are usually found in proximity to one another. The study of tissues is called **histology.** The various body tissues can be categorized into four principal kinds: (1) epithelial, (2) connective, (3) muscular, and (4) nervous. In this exercise you will examine the structure and functions of epithelial and many connective tissues. Other tissues will be studied later as parts of the systems to which they belong.

A. COVERING AND LINING EPITHELIUM

Epithelial (ep'-i-THĒ-lē-al) **tissue** is avascular (without blood vessels) and covers and lines body surfaces, including hollow organs and body cavities. Epithelium also forms glands and is the tissue from which gametes (sperm and eggs) develop. Before you start your microscopic examination of epithelial tissues, refer to Figure 4.1. Study the tissues carefully to familiarize yourself with their general structural characteristics. For each of the types of epithelium listed, obtain a prepared slide and, unless otherwise specified by your instructor, examine each under high power. In conjunction with your examination, consult a textbook of anatomy.

1. **Simple squamous** (SKWĀ-mus)—This tissue consists of a single layer of flat, scalelike cells and is highly adapted for diffusion, osmosis, and filtration because of its thinness. Simple squamous tissue lines the air sacs of the lungs, glomerular capsule of the kidneys, inner surface of the wall of the membranous labyrinth of the inner ear, and inner surface of the tympanic membrane of the ear. Simple squamous tissue that lines the heart, blood vessels, and

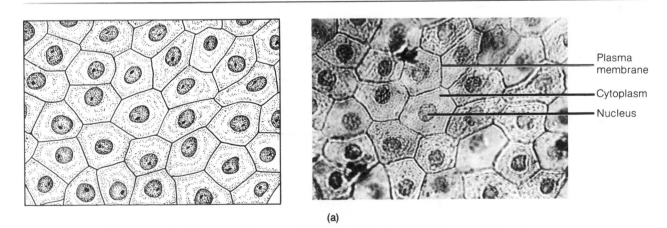

(a)

FIGURE 4.1   Epithelial tissues. (a) Simple squamous epithelium, surface view.

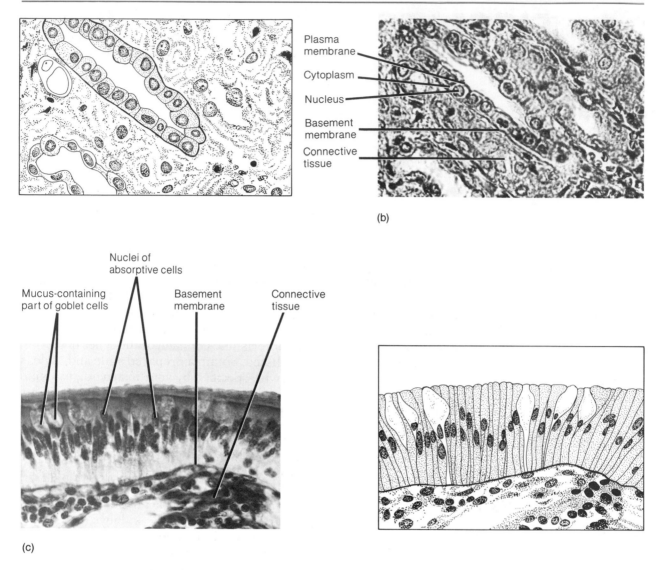

Plasma membrane

Cytoplasm

Nucleus

Basement membrane

Connective tissue

(b)

Nuclei of absorptive cells

Mucus-containing part of goblet cells

Basement membrane

Connective tissue

(c)

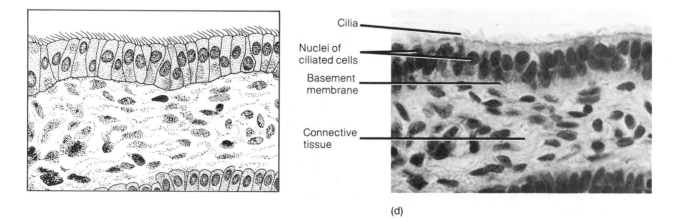

Cilia

Nuclei of ciliated cells

Basement membrane

Connective tissue

(d)

FIGURE 4.1 (*Continued*) **Epithelial tissues. (b) Simple cuboidal epithelium. (c) Simple columnar nonciliated epithelium. (d) Simple columnar ciliated epithelium.**

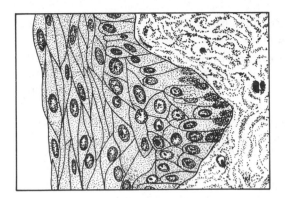

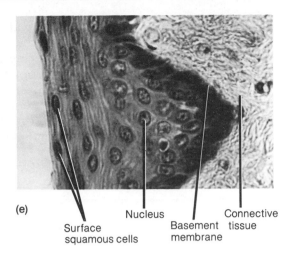

(e)

Surface squamous cells

Nucleus

Basement membrane

Connective tissue

Nuclei of transitional cells

Basement membrane

Connective tissue

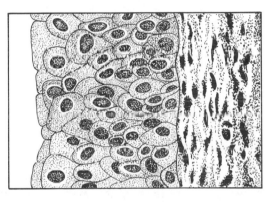

(f)

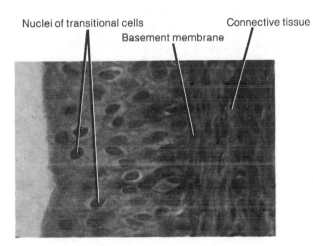

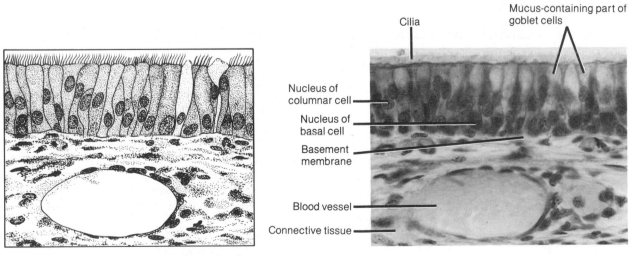

Cilia

Mucus-containing part of goblet cells

Nucleus of columnar cell

Nucleus of basal cell

Basement membrane

Blood vessel

Connective tissue

(g)

FIGURE 4.1 (*Continued*)   Epithelial tissues. (e) Stratified squamous epithelium. (f) Stratified transitional epithelium. (g) Pseudostratified epithelium.

lymphatic vessels and forms capillary walls is called **endothelium.** That lining the thoracic and abdominopelvic cavities and covering viscera within them as the epithelial layer of a serous membrane is called **mesothelium.**

After you make your microscopic examination, draw several cells in the space that follows and label plasma membrane, cytoplasm, and nucleus.

Simple squamous epithelium

2. **Simple cuboidal**—This tissue consists of a single layer of cube-shaped cells. When the tissue is sectioned at right angles, its cuboidal nature is obvious. Highly adapted for secretion and absorption, cuboidal tissue covers the surface of the ovaries; lines the smaller ducts of some glands and the anterior surface of the capsule of the lens of the eye; and forms the pigmented epithelium of the retina, part of the tubules of the kidneys, and the secreting units of other glands.

After you make your microscopic examination, draw several cells in the space that follows and label plasma membrane, cytoplasm,

Simple cuboidal epithelium

nucleus, basement membrane, and connective tissue layer.

3. **Simple columnar nonciliated**—This tissue consists of a single layer of columnar cells and, when sectioned at right angles, these cells appear as rectangles. Adapted for secretion and absorption, this tissue lines the gallbladder and the digestive tract from the cardia of the stomach to the anus and is found in the excretory ducts of many glands. In these locations, the cells protect underlying tissues. Some of the cells are modified in that the plasma membranes are folded into microvilli that increase the surface area for absorption. Other cells are modified as goblet cells that store and secrete mucus to protect the lining of the gastrointestinal tract.

After you make your microscopic examination, draw several cells in the space that follows and label plasma membrane, cytoplasm, nucleus, goblet cell, absorptive cell, basement membrane, and connective tissue layer.

Simple columnar nonciliated epithelium

4. **Simple columnar ciliated**—This type of columnar epithelium has a single layer of both goblet and ciliated cells. It lines some portions of the upper respiratory tract, uterine (fallopian) tubes, uterus, some paranasal sinuses, and the central canal of the spinal cord. Mucus produced by goblet cells forms a thin film over the surface of the tissue, and movements of the cilia propel substances over the surface of the tissue.

After you make your microscopic examination, draw several cells in the space that follows and label plasma membrane, cytoplasm, nucleus, cilia, goblet cell, basement membrane, and connective tissue layer.

Simple columnar ciliated epithelium

5. Stratified squamous—This tissue consists of several layers of cells. The superficial cells are flat whereas cells of the deep layers vary in shape from cuboidal to columnar. The basal (bottom) cells continually multiply by cell division. As surface cells are sloughed, new cells replace them from the basal layer. The surface cells of **keratinized stratified squamous** contain a waterproofing protein called **keratin** that also resists friction and bacterial invasion. The keratinized variety forms the outer layer of the skin. Surface cells of **nonkeratinized stratified squamous** do not contain keratin. The nonkeratinized variety lines wet surfaces such as the tongue, mouth, esophagus, part of the epiglottis, and vagina. Both varieties of stratified squamous afford considerable protection against friction.

After you make your microscopic examination, draw several cells in the space that follows and label plasma membrane, cytoplasm, nucleus, squamous surface cells, basal cells, basement membrane, and connective tissue layer.

6. Cheek cell smear—Before examining the next slide, prepare a smear of cheek cells from the epithelial lining of the mouth. As noted previously, epithelium that lines the mouth is nonkeratinized stratified squamous epithelium. However, you will be examining surface cells only, and these will appear similar to simple squamous epithelium.

a. Using the blunt end of a toothpick, *gently* scrape the lining of your cheek several times to collect some surface cells of the stratified squamous epithelium.

b. Now move the toothpick across a clean glass microscope slide until a thin layer of scrapings is left on the slide.

c. Allow the preparation to air dry.

d. Next, cover the smear with several drops of 1% methylene blue stain. After about 1 minute, gently rinse the slide in cold tap water or distilled water to remove excess stain.

e. Gently blot the slide dry using a paper towel.

f. Examine the slide under low and high power. See if you can identify the plasma membrane, cytoplasm, nuclear membrane, and nucleoli. Some bacteria are commonly found on the slide and usually appear as rods or spheres.

7. Stratified transitional—This tissue resembles nonkeratinized stratified squamous, except that the superficial cells are larger and more rounded. When stretched, the surface cells are drawn out into squamouslike cells. This drawing out permits the tissue to stretch without the outer cells breaking apart from one another. The tissue lines parts of the urinary system, such as the urinary bladder, that are subject to expansion from within.

After you have made your microscopic examination, draw several cells in the space that follows and label plasma membrane, cyto-

Stratified squamous epithelium

Stratified transitional epithelium

plasm, nucleus, surface cells, basement membrane, and connective tissue layer.

8. **Pseudostratified**—Nuclei of columnar cells in this tissue are at varying depths, and, although all of the cells are attached to the basement membrane in a single layer, some do not reach the surface. This arrangement gives the impression of multilayered tissue, thus the name pseudostratified. The nonciliated type lines large excretory ducts of many glands, parts of the male urethra, and parts of the auditory (eustachian) tubes. The ciliated type contains goblet cells and lines most of the upper respiratory tract, parts of the auditory tubes, and certain ducts of the male reproductive system. Ciliated tissue is highly adapted for secretion and movement of substances by ciliary action.

After you have made your microscopic examination, draw several cells in the space that follows and label plasma membrane, cytoplasm, nucleus, cilia, goblet cell, basement membrane, and connective tissue layer.

Pseudostratified epithelium

B. GLANDULAR EPITHELIUM

A **gland** may consist of a single epithelial cell or a group of highly specialized epithelial cells that secrete various substances. Glands that have no ducts (ductless), secrete hormones, and release their secretions into the blood are called **endocrine glands.** Examples include the pituitary, thyroid, and adrenals (Exercise 15). Glands that secrete their products into ducts are called **exocrine glands.** Examples include sweat glands and salivary glands.

1. Structural Classification of Exocrine Glands

Based on the shape of the secretory portion and the degree of branching of the duct, exocrine glands can be structurally classified as follows:

a. Unicellular—One-celled glands that secrete mucus. An example is the goblet cell (see Figure 4.1c). These cells line portions of the respiratory, digestive, and reproductive systems.

b. Multicellular—Many-celled glands that occur in several different forms (see Figure 4.2).

  1. **Simple**—Single, nonbranched duct.

    Tubular—Secretory portion is straight and tubular (intestinal glands).

    Branched tubular—Secretory portion is branched and tubular (gastric and uterine glands).

    Coiled tubular—Secretory portion is coiled (sudoriferous [soo-dor-IF-er-us], or sweat, glands).

    Acinar (AS-i-nar)—Secretory portion is flasklike (seminal vesicle glands).

    Branched acinar—Secretory portion is branched and flasklike (sebaceous [se-BĀ-shus], or oil, glands).

  2. **Compound**—Branched duct.

    Tubular—Secretory portion is tubular (bulbourethral glands, testes, liver).

    Acinar—Secretory portion is flasklike (sublingual and submandibular salivary glands).

    Tubuloacinar—Secretory portion is both tubular and flasklike (parotid salivary glands, pancreas).

Obtain a prepared slide of a representative of each of the types of multicellular exocrine glands just described. As you examine each slide, compare your observations to the diagrams of the glands in Figure 4.2.

2. Functional Classification of Exocrine Glands

Functional classification is based on how the gland releases its secretion. **Holocrine glands,** such as sebaceous glands, accumulate their secretory product in their cytoplasm. The cell then dies and is discharged with its contents as the glandular secretion; the discharged cell is replaced by a new one. **Apocrine glands,** such as the mammary glands, accumulate secretory products at the outer margins of the secreting cells. The margins pinch off as the secretion and the remaining portions of the cells are repaired so that the process can be repeated. **Merocrine glands,** such as the pancreas and salivary glands, produce secretions that are

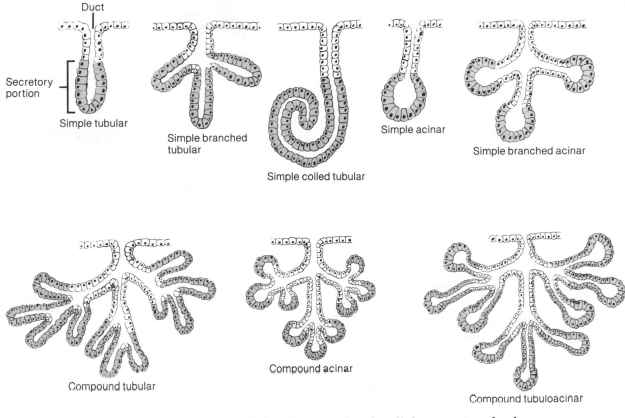

FIGURE 4.2 Structural classification of multicellular exocrine glands.

simply formed by the secretory cells and then discharged into a duct.

C. CONNECTIVE TISSUE

Connective tissue, the most abundant in the body, functions by protecting, supporting, and binding structures together. It is typically vascular, except for cartilage, which is avascular, and contains a large amount of intercellular substance that surrounds widely scattered cells. This tissue usually does not occur on free surfaces. Before you start your microscopic examination of connective tissues, refer to Figure 4.3. Study the tissues carefully to familiarize yourself with their general structural characteristics. For each type of connective tissue listed, obtain a prepared slide and, unless otherwise specified by your instructor, examine each under high power.

1. **Loose** or **areolar** (a-RĒ-ō-lar)—One of the most widely distributed connective tissues in the body, this type consists of a viscous intercellular substance containing hyaluronic acid,

three kinds of fibers, and several types of cells. Collagenous (white) fibers are synthesized from the protein collagen and often occur in parallel bundles and provide strength; elastic (yellow) fibers are smaller than collagenous, branch freely, have nonparallel construction, and provide elasticity; and reticular fibers are very thin, branch extensively, have nonparallel construction, and provide the framework of many soft organs. The cells in loose connective tissue include fibroblasts that form fibers and intercellular substance if the tissue is injured; macrophages (MAK-rō-fā-jez) that are capable of phagocytosis; plasma cells that produce antibodies; mast cells that form the anticoagulant heparin and the vasodilator histamine; melanocytes or pigment cells; and fat cells. Loose connective tissue is present in many mucous membranes, around blood vessels, nerves, and organs, and, together with adipose tissue, forms the subcutaneous (sub′-kyoo-TĀ-nē-us) layer of the skin or superficial fascia (FASH-ē-a).

After you make your microscopic examination, draw a small area of the tissue in the space that follows and label the elastic fibers, collagenous fibers, fibroblasts, and mast cells.

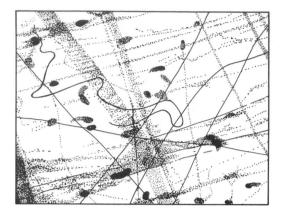
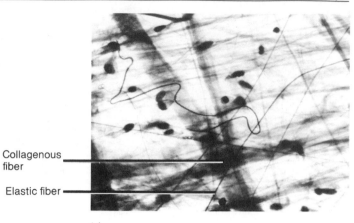

Collagenous fiber

Elastic fiber

(a)

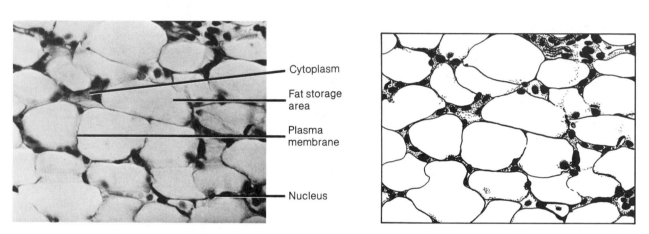

Cytoplasm

Fat storage area

Plasma membrane

Nucleus

(b)

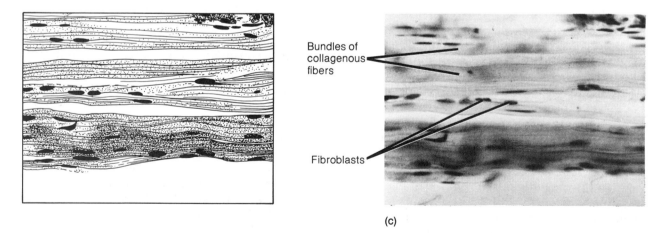

Bundles of collagenous fibers

Fibroblasts

(c)

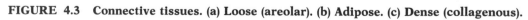

FIGURE 4.3 Connective tissues. (a) Loose (areolar). (b) Adipose. (c) Dense (collagenous).

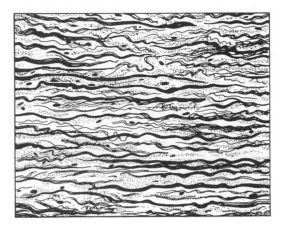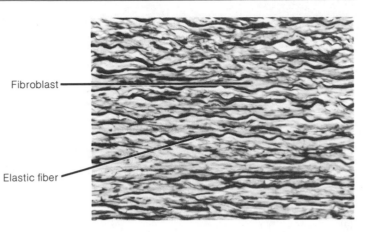

Fibroblast

Elastic fiber

(d)

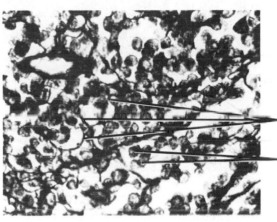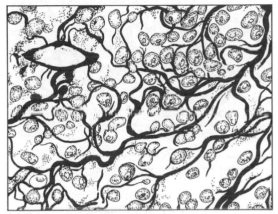

Reticular fibers

Cells of
particular organ

(e)

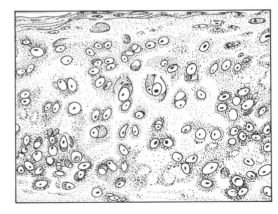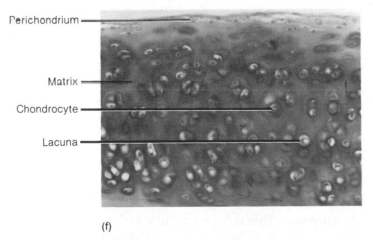

Perichondrium

Matrix

Chondrocyte

Lacuna

(f)

FIGURE 4.3 (*Continued*)   Connective tissues. (d) Elastic. (e) Reticular. (f) Hyaline cartilage.

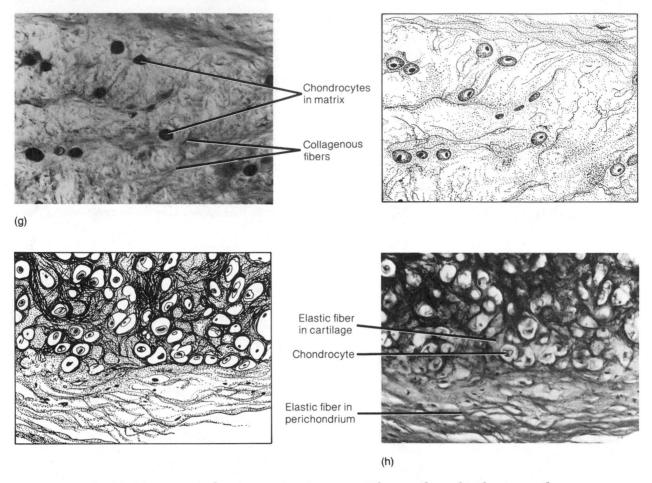

(g)

(h)

FIGURE 4.3 (*Continued*) Connective tissues. (g) Fibrocartilage. (h) Elastic cartilage.

After your microscopic examination, draw several cells in the space that follows and label the fat storage area, cytoplasm, nucleus, and plasma membrane.

Loose (areolar) connective tissue

2. **Adipose**—This is fat tissue in which cells derived from fibroblasts, called **adipocytes,** are modified for fat storage. Because the cytoplasm and nuclei of the cells are pushed to the side, the cells resemble signet rings. The tissue provides insulation, energy reserve, support, and protection, and, as noted previously, is often found together with loose connective tissue.

Adipose tissue

3. **Dense (collagenous)**—This tissue has a predominance of closely packed collagenous fibers with fibroblasts arranged between the bundles of fibers. Its principal function is strength. It forms the tendons, aponeuroses

(ap'-ō-noo-RŌ-sēz), and ligaments; the membrane capsules around the kidneys, heart, testes, liver, and lymph nodes; and, finally, the deep fasciae around muscles.

After you make your microscopic examination, draw a sample of the tissue in the space that follows and label the collagenous fibers and fibroblasts.

Dense (collagenous) connective tissue

---

4. Elastic—This tissue has a predominance of elastic fibers with fibroblasts in the spaces between fibers. It provides strength and elasticity and is found in the walls of elastic arteries, bronchial tubes, lungs, ligamenta flava of the vertebrae, suspensory ligament of the penis, and true vocal cords.

After you make your microscopic examination, draw a sample of the tissue in the space that follows and label the elastic fibers and fibroblasts.

Elastic connective tissue

---

5. Reticular—This tissue consists of interlacing reticular fibers in which the cells are interspersed between the fibers. It provides strength and support, forms the stroma (framework) of the liver, spleen, and lymph nodes, and binds smooth muscle cells together.

After you make your microscopic examination, draw a sample of the tissue in the space

that follows and label the reticular fibers and cells of the organ.

Reticular connective tissue

---

6. Hyaline cartilage—Cartilage consists of a dense network of collagenous and elastic fibers firmly embedded in a gel-like substance. The fibers are not usually visible in hyaline cartilage. The cells of cartilage are called **chondrocytes** (KON-drō-sīts) and occur singly or in groups in spaces called **lacunae** (la-KOO-nē) in the intercellular substance. The surface of cartilage is surrounded by a connective tissue membrane called the **perichondrium** (per'-i-KON-drē-um). Cartilage, like epithelium, is avascular.

Hyaline cartilage, also called gristle, is the most abundant cartilage in the body. It provides strength and support and is found at joints over the ends of long bones (articular cartilage) and at the ventral ends of the ribs (costal cartilage). It helps form the nose, larynx, trachea, bronchi, and bronchial tubes.

After you make your microscopic examination, draw a sample of the tissue in the space that follows and label the perichondrium, chondrocytes, lacunae, and intercellular substance (matrix).

Hyaline cartilage

---

7. **Fibrocartilage**—Unlike those in hyaline cartilage, collagenous fibers are visible in fibrocartilage. This tissue combines strength and rigidity. It is found in the symphysis pubis joint and in the discs between vertebrae.

After you make your microscopic examination, draw a sample of the tissue in the space that follows and label the chondrocytes, lacunae, intercellular substance, and collagenous fibers.

Fibrocartilage

8. **Elastic cartilage**—In this tissue, the chondrocytes are located in a threadlike network of elastic fibers. The tissue provides strength and maintains the shape of organs such as the epiglottis, larynx, external part of the ear, and auditory tubes.

After you make your microscopic examination, draw a sample of the tissue in the space that follows and label the perichondrium, chondrocytes, lacunae, intercellular substance, and elastic fibers.

Elastic cartilage

D. MEMBRANES

Mucous membranes, also called the **mucosa,** line body cavities that open directly to the exterior, such as the digestive, respiratory, urinary, and reproductive tracts. The surface tissue of a mucous membrane consists of epithelium and has a variety of functions, depending on location. Accordingly, the epithelial layer secretes mucus but may also secrete enzymes, filter dust, and have a protective and absorbent action. The underlying connective tissue layer of a mucous membrane, called the *lamina propria,* binds the epithelial layer in place, protects underlying tissues, provides the epithelium with nutrients and oxygen and removes wastes, and holds blood vessels in place.

Serous membranes, also called the **serosa,** line body cavities that do not open to the exterior and cover organs that lie within the cavities. Serous membranes consist of a surface layer of mesothelium and an underlying layer of loose connective tissue. The mesothelium secretes a lubricating fluid. Serous membranes are double-walled sacs. The part attached to the cavity wall is called the **parietal layer;** the part that covers the organs in the cavity is called the **visceral layer.** Examples of serous membranes are the pleurae, pericardium, and peritoneum.

Synovial membranes line joint cavities. They do not contain epithelium but rather consist of loose connective tissue, adipose tissue, and elastic fibers. Synovial membranes produce synovial fluid, which lubricates the ends of bones as they move at joints and nourishes the articular cartilage around the ends of bones.

The **cutaneous membrane** or skin is the principal component of the integumentary system, which will be considered in the next exercise.

**LABORATORY REPORT
QUESTIONS (PAGE 375)**

5 | INTEGUMENTARY SYSTEM

The skin and its derivatives (hair, nails, and glands), and several specialized receptors constitute the **integumentary** (in-teg-yoo-MEN-tar-ē) **system,** which you will study in this exercise. An **organ** is an aggregation of tissues of definite form that performs a definite function; a **system** is a group of organs that operate together to perform specialized functions.

A. SKIN

The **skin (cutis)** is one of the larger organs of the body in terms of surface area, occupying a surface area of about 19,355 cm² (3000 in.²). Among the functions performed by the skin are protection of underlying tissues against bacterial invasion, prevention of excessive water loss, protection against harmful light rays, maintenance of body temperature, storage of chemicals, excretion of water and salts and several organic compounds, synthesis of vitamin D in the presence of sunlight, and reception of stimuli for touch, pressure, pain, and temperature change sensations.

The skin consists of an outer, thinner **epidermis,** which is avascular, and an inner, thicker **dermis,** which is vascular. Below the dermis is the **subcutaneous layer (superficial fascia** or **hypodermis)** that attaches the skin to underlying tissues and organs.

1. Epidermis

Obtain a prepared slide of human skin and carefully examine the epidermis. Identify the following layers from the outside inward:

a. **Stratum corneum**—25 to 30 rows of flat, dead cells that are filled with keratin, a waterproofing protein.

b. **Stratum lucidum**—Several rows of clear, flat cells that contain eleidin (el-Ē-i-din), a precursor of keratin; found only in the palms and soles.

c. **Stratum granulosum**—3 to 5 rows of flat cells that contain keratohyalin (ker'-a-tō-HĪ-a-lin), a precursor of eleidin.

d. **Stratum spinosum**—8 to 10 rows of polyhedral (many-sided) cells that help in the production of a new epidermis.

e. **Stratum basale**—Single layer of cuboidal to columnar cells that constantly undergo division.

Label the epidermal layers in Figures 5.1 and 5.2.

2. Skin Color

The color of skin results from (1) **blood in capillaries** of the dermis (beneath the epidermis); (2) **carotene,** a yellow/orange pigment in the stratum corneum of the epidermis and fatty areas of the dermis; and (3) **melanin,** a pale yellow to black pigment found primarily in the stratum basale and spinosum of the epidermis. Whereas blood in capillaries imparts a pink color to Caucasian skin, carotene imparts the characteristic yellow color to Asian skin. Because the number of **melanocytes** (me-LAN-ō-sīts) or melanin-producing cells is about the same in all races, most differences in skin color are due to the amount of melanin that the melanocytes synthesize and disperse. Exposure to ultraviolet (UV) radiation increases melanin synthesis, resulting in darkening (tanning) of the skin to protect the body against further UV radiation.

An inherited inability of a person of any race to produce melanin results in **albinism** (AL-bi-nizm). The pigment is absent from the

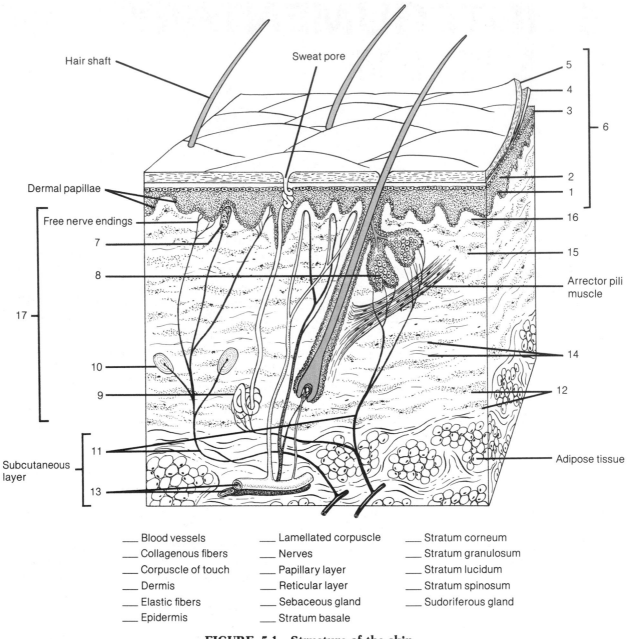

Hair shaft

Sweat pore

Dermal papillae

Free nerve endings

7

8

10

9

17

11

Subcutaneous
layer

13

5

4

3

6

2

1

16

15

Arrector pili
muscle

14

12

Adipose tissue

___ Blood vessels	___ Lamellated corpuscle	___ Stratum corneum
___ Collagenous fibers	___ Nerves	___ Stratum granulosum
___ Corpuscle of touch	___ Papillary layer	___ Stratum lucidum
___ Dermis	___ Reticular layer	___ Stratum spinosum
___ Elastic fibers	___ Sebaceous gland	___ Sudoriferous gland
___ Epidermis	___ Stratum basale	

FIGURE 5.1   Structure of the skin.

hair and eyes as well as from the skin, and the individual is referred to as an **albino.** In some people, melanin tends to form in patches called **freckles.** Others inherit patches of skin that lack pigment, a condition called **vitiligo** (vit-i-LĪ-gō).

3. Dermis

The dermis is divided into two regions and is composed of connective tissue containing col-

lagenous and elastic fibers embedded with a number of structures. The upper region of the dermis **(papillary layer)** is loose connective tissue containing collagenous and elastic fibers. This layer contains fingerlike projections, the **dermal papillae** (pa-PIL-ē). Some papillae enclose blood capillaries; others contain **corpuscles of touch (Meissner's corpuscles),** nerve endings sensitive to touch. The lower region of the dermis **(reticular layer)** consists of denser connective tissue with interlacing bundles of larger collagenous and coarse elastic fibers. Spaces be-

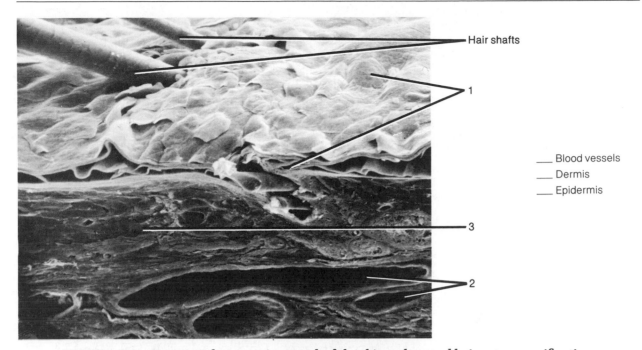

Hair shafts

1

___ Blood vessels
___ Dermis
___ Epidermis

3

2

FIGURE 5.2 Scanning electron micrograph of the skin and several hairs at a magnification of 260×. (From *Tissues and Organs: A Text-Atlas of Scanning Electron Microscopy* by Richard G. Kessel and Randy H. Kardon, W. H. Freeman and Company. Copyright © 1979.)

tween the fibers may be occupied by **hair follicles, sebaceous (oil) glands, bundles of smooth muscle (arrector pili muscle), sudoriferous (sweat) glands, blood vessels,** and **nerves.**

The reticular region of the dermis is attached to the underlying structures (bones and muscles) by the subcutaneous layer. This layer also contains nerve endings sensitive to deep pressure called **lamellated (pacinian) corpuscles.**

Carefully examine the dermis and subcutaneous layer on your microscope slide. Label the following structures in Figure 5.1: papillary layer, reticular layer, corpuscle of touch, blood vessels, nerves, elastic fibers, collagenous fibers, sebaceous gland, sudoriferous gland, and lamellated corpuscle. Also label the dermis and blood vessels in Figure 5.2.

If a model of the skin and subcutaneous layer is available, examine it to see the three-dimensional relationship of the structures to each other.

B. HAIR

Hairs (pili) develop from the epidermis and are variously distributed over the body. Each hair consists of a **shaft**, most of which is visible above the surface of the skin, and a **root**, the portion below the surface that penetrates deep into the dermis and even into the subcutaneous layer.

The shaft of a coarse hair consists of the following parts:

1. **Medulla**—Inner region composed of several rows of polyhedral cells containing eleidin; poorly developed or not present in fine hairs.

2. **Cortex**—Several rows of dark cells surrounding the medulla; contains pigment in dark hair and pigment and air in gray hair.

3. **Cuticle of the hair**—Outermost layer; consists of a single layer of flat, scalelike cells arranged like shingles on a house.

The root of a hair also contains a medulla, cortex, and cuticle of the hair along with the following associated parts:

1. **Hair follicle**—Structure surrounding the root that consists of an external root sheath, an internal root sheath, and a bulb. These three epidermally derived layers are surrounded by a dermal layer of connective tissue.

2. **External root sheath**—Downward continuation of strata basale and spinosum of the epidermis.

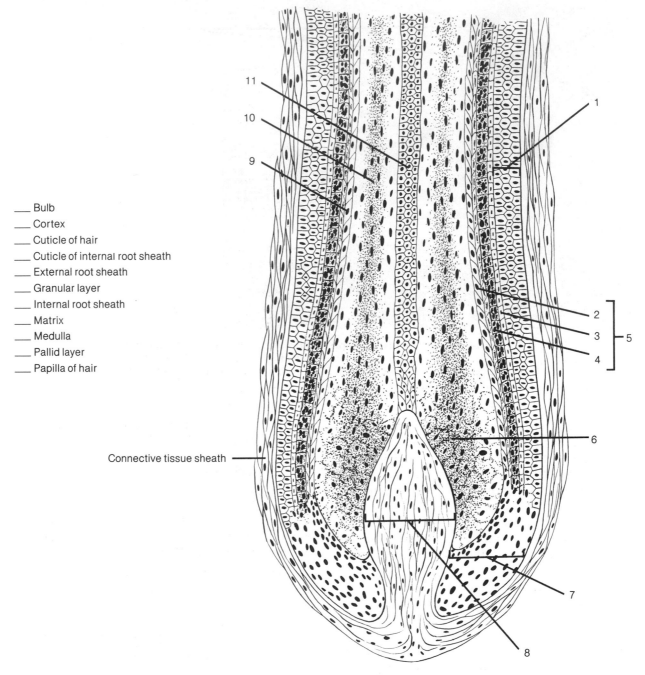

___ Bulb
___ Cortex
___ Cuticle of hair
___ Cuticle of internal root sheath
___ External root sheath
___ Granular layer
___ Internal root sheath
___ Matrix
___ Medulla
___ Pallid layer
___ Papilla of hair

Connective tissue sheath

FIGURE 5.3 Longitudinal section of a hair root.

3. Internal root sheath—Cellular tubular sheath that separates the hair from the external root sheath; consists of (1) the **cuticle of the internal root sheath,** an inner single layer of flattened cells with atrophied nuclei, (2) **granular (Huxley's) layer,** a middle layer of one to three rows of cells with flattened nuclei, and (3) **pallid (Henle's) layer,** an outer single layer of cuboidal cells with flattened nuclei.

4. Bulb—Enlarged, onion-shaped structure at the base of the hair follicle.

5. Papilla of the hair—Dermal indentation into the bulb; contains loose connective tissue and blood vessels to nourish the hair.

6. Matrix—Region of cells at the base of the bulb that divides to produce new hair.

7. **Arrector pili muscle**—Bundle of smooth muscle extending from the dermis of the skin to the side of the hair follicle; its contraction, under the influence of fright or cold, causes the hair to move into a vertical position, producing "goose bumps."

8. **Root hair plexus**—Nerve endings around each hair follicle that are sensitive to touch and respond when the hair shaft is moved.

Obtain a prepared slide of a cross section and a longitudinal section of a hair root and identify as many parts as you can. Using your textbook as a reference, label Figure 5.3. Also label the parts of a hair shown in Figure 5.4.

C. GLANDS

Sebaceous (se-BĀ-shus) or **oil glands,** with few exceptions, are connected to fair follicles (see Figures 5.1 and 5.4). They secrete an oily substance called **sebum,** a mixture of fats, cholesterol, proteins, and salts. Sebaceous glands are absent in the skin of the palms and soles but are numerous in the skin of the face, neck, upper chest, and breasts. Sebum helps prevent hair from drying and forms a protective film over the skin that prevents excessive evaporation and keeps the skin soft and pliable.

Sudoriferous (soo'-dor-IF-er-us) or **sweat glands** are separated into two principal types on the basis of structure, location, and secre-

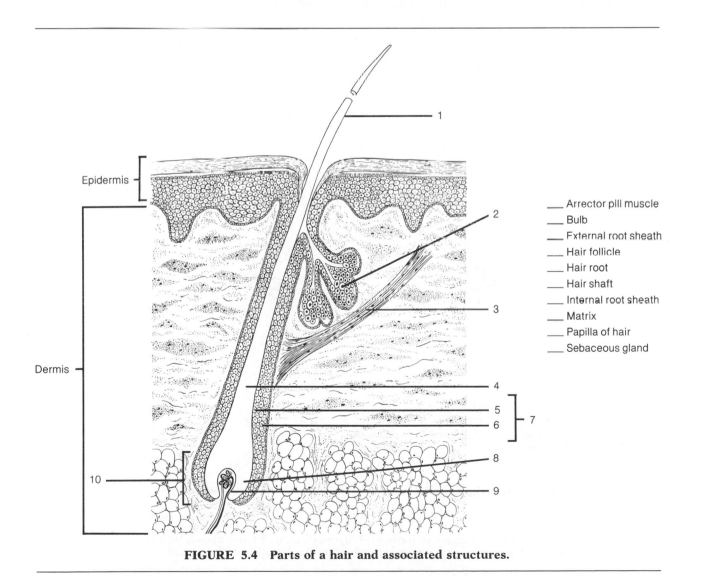

___ Arrector pili muscle
___ Bulb
___ External root sheath
___ Hair follicle
___ Hair root
___ Hair shaft
___ Internal root sheath
___ Matrix
___ Papilla of hair
___ Sebaceous gland

FIGURE 5.4 Parts of a hair and associated structures.

tion. **Apocrine sweat glands** are simple, branched tubular glands found primarily in the skin of the axilla, pubic region, and areolae (pigmented areas) of the breasts. Their secretory portion is located in the dermis; the excretory duct opens into hair follicles. Apocrine sweat glands begin to function at puberty and produce a more viscous secretion than the other type of sweat gland. **Eccrine sweat glands** are simple, coiled tubular glands found throughout the skin, except for the margins of the lips, nail beds of the fingers and toes, glans penis, glans clitoris, and eardrums. The secretory portion of these glands is in the subcutaneous layer; the excretory duct projects upward and terminates at a pore at the surface of the epidermis (see Figure 5.1). Eccrine sweat glands function throughout life and produce a more watery secretion than the apocrine glands. Sudoriferous glands produce **perspiration,** a mixture of water, salt, urea, uric acid, amino acids, ammonia, sugar, lactic acid, and ascorbic acid. The evaporation of perspiration helps to maintain normal body temperature.

Ceruminous (se-ROO-mi-nus) **glands** are modified sudoriferous glands in the external auditory meatus. The combined secretion of ceruminous and sudoriferous glands is called **cerumen** (earwax).

D. NAILS

Nails are hard, keratinized epidermal cells that form a clear covering over the dorsal surfaces of the terminal portions of the fingers and toes. Each nail consists of the following parts:

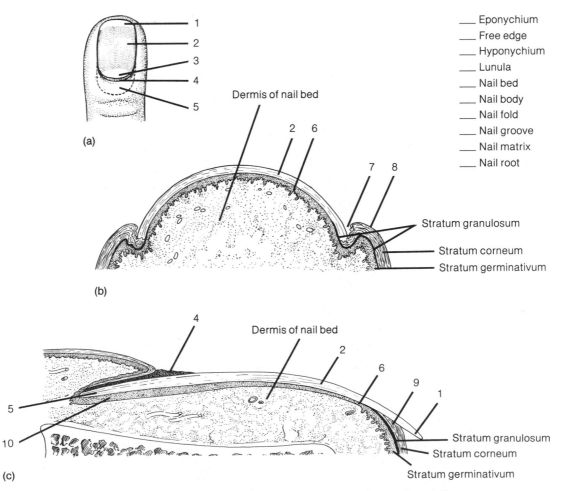

___ Eponychium
___ Free edge
___ Hyponychium
___ Lunula
___ Nail bed
___ Nail body
___ Nail fold
___ Nail groove
___ Nail matrix
___ Nail root

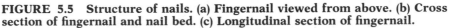

FIGURE 5.5 Structure of nails. (a) Fingernail viewed from above. (b) Cross section of fingernail and nail bed. (c) Longitudinal section of fingernail.

1. **Nail body**—Portion that is visible.

2. **Free edge**—Part that projects beyond the distal end of the digit.

3. **Nail root**—Portion hidden in nail groove.

4. **Lunula** (LOO-nyoo-la)—Whitish semilunar area at proximal end of body.

5. **Nail fold**—Fold of skin that extends around the proximal end and lateral borders of the nail.

6. **Nail bed**—Strata basale and spinosum of the epidermis beneath the nail.

7. **Nail groove**—Furrow between the nail fold and nail bed.

8. **Eponychium** (ep′ō-NIK-ē-um)—Cuticle; a narrow band of epidermis.

9. **Hyponychium**—Thickened area of stratum corneum below the free edge of the nail.

10. **Nail matrix**—Epithelium of the proximal part of the nail bed; division of the cells brings about growth of nails.

Using your textbook as a reference, label the parts of a nail shown in Figure 5.5. Also, identify the parts that are visible on your own nails.

LABORATORY REPORT QUESTIONS (PAGE 377)

6 | OSSEOUS TISSUE

Structurally, the **skeletal system** consists of two types of connective tissue: cartilage and bone. The microscopic structure of cartilage has been discussed in Exercise 4. In this exercise the gross structure of a typical bone and the histology of **osseous (bone) tissue** will be studied.

The skeletal system has the following basic functions:

1. **Support**—It provides a supporting framework for the soft tissues, maintaining the body's shape and posture.

2. **Protection**—It protects delicate structures such as the brain, spinal cord, heart, lungs, major blood vessels in the chest, and pelvic viscera.

3. **Movement**—When muscles contract, bones serve as levers to help produce body movements.

4. **Storage**—Bones store mineral salts, especially calcium and phosphorus.

5. **Blood cell production** or **hematopoiesis** (hē'-mat-ō-poy-Ē-sis)—Red marrow consists of primitive blood cells in immature stages, fat cells, and macrophages and is responsible for producing red blood cells, platelets, and some white blood cells.

A. GROSS STRUCTURE OF A LONG BONE

Examine the external features of a fresh long bone and locate the following structures:

1. **Periosteum** (per'-ē-OS-tē-um)—Dense white fibrous membrane covering the surface of the bone, except for areas covered by cartilage; the membrane contains blood vessels, lymphatics, nerves, and osteoblasts (bone-producing cells);

functions in bone growth, nutrition, and repair, and as an attachment site for tendons and ligaments.

2. **Articular cartilage**—Thin layer of hyaline cartilage covering the ends of the bone where joints are formed.

3. **Epiphysis** (e-PIF-i-sis)—End or extremity of a bone; the epiphyses are referred to as proximal and distal.

4. **Diaphysis** (dī-AF-i-sis)—Elongated shaft of a bone between the epiphyses.

5. **Metaphysis** (me-TAF-i-sis)—In mature bone, the region where the diaphysis joins the epiphysis; in growing bone, the region where calcified cartilage is replaced by bone as the bone lengthens.

Now examine a mature long bone that has been sectioned longitudinally and locate the following structures:

1. **Medullary** (MED-yoo-lar'-ē) or **marrow cavity**—Cavity within the diaphysis that contains yellow marrow (primarily fat cells and a few scattered cells that can produce blood cells).

2. **Endosteum**—Membrane that lines the medullary cavity and contains osteoblasts and scattered osteoclasts (bone resorption cells); it coats spongy bone and separates it from marrow.

3. **Compact (dense) bone**—Bone that forms the bulk of the diaphysis and covers the epiphyses.

4. **Spongy (cancellous) bone**—Bone that forms a small portion of the diaphysis at the ends of the medullary cavity and the bulk of the epiphysis; spongy bone contains red marrow.

Label the parts of a long bone indicated in Figure 6.1.

48

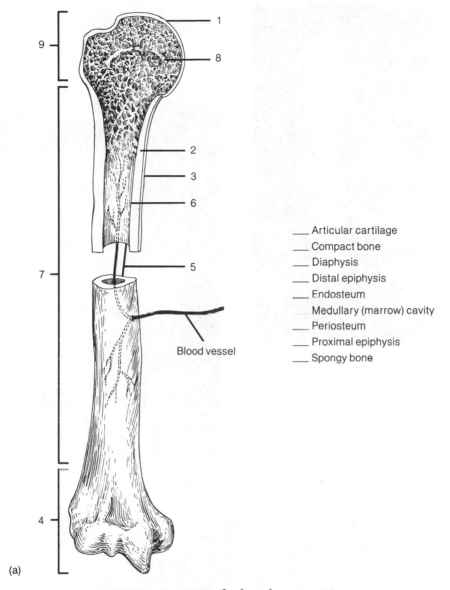

Blood vessel

___ Articular cartilage
___ Compact bone
___ Diaphysis
___ Distal epiphysis
___ Endosteum
___ Medullary (marrow) cavity
___ Periosteum
___ Proximal epiphysis
___ Spongy bone

(a)

FIGURE 6.1   Parts of a long bone. (a) Diagram.

B. CHEMISTRY OF BONE

Unlike other connective tissues, the intercellular substance of bone is very hard. This hardness results from the presence of mineral salts, mainly calcium phosphate ($Ca_3 (PO_4)_2 \cdot [OH]_2$) and some calcium carbonate ($CaCO_3$). Mineral salts comprise about 67% of the weight of bone. Despite its hardness, bone is also flexible, a characteristic that enables it to resist various forces. The flexibility of bone comes from organic substances in its intercellular substance, especially collagenous fibers. Organic materials comprise about 33% of the weight of bone.

1. Obtain a bone that has been baked. How does this bone compare to an untreated one?

_____

What substances does baking remove from the

bone (inorganic or organic)? _____

_____

2. Now obtain a bone that has been soaked in nitric acid. How does this bone compare to an

untreated one? _____
What substances does nitric acid treatment remove from the bone (inorganic or organic)?

_____

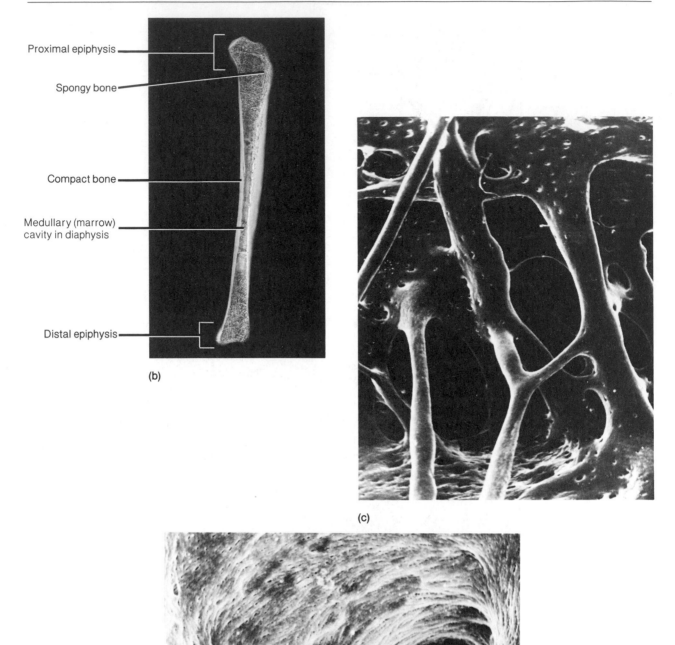

Proximal epiphysis

Spongy bone

Compact bone

Medullary (marrow) cavity in diaphysis

Distal epiphysis

(b)

(c)

(d)

FIGURE 6.1 (*Continued*) Parts of a long bone. (b) Photograph of a section through the tibia. (c) Scanning electron micrograph of spongy bone trabeculae at a magnification of 25×. (d) Scanning electron micrograph of a view inside a central (haversian) canal at a magnification of 250×.

C. HISTOLOGY OF BONE

Bone tissue, like other connective tissues, contains a large amount of intercellular substance that surrounds widely separated cells, or **osteocytes,** that are found in spaces called lacunae (la-KOO-nē). This intercellular substance consists of (1) collagenous fibers and (2) abundant mineral salts.

Depending on the size and distribution of spaces, bone may be categorized as spongy (cancellous) or compact (dense). **Spongy bone,** which contains many large spaces that store red marrow, composes most of the tissue of short, flat, and irregularly shaped bones and most of the epiphyses of long bones. **Compact bone,** which contains few spaces and is deposited in layers over spongy bone, is thicker in the diaphysis than in the epiphyses.

Obtain a prepared slide of compact bone in which several osteons (haversian systems) are shown in cross section. Observe under high power. Look for the following structures:

1. **Central (haversian) canal**—Circular canal in the center of an osteon that runs longitudinally through the bone; the canal contains blood vessels, lymphatics, and nerves.

2. **Lamellae** (la-MEL-ē)—Concentric layers of calcified intercellular substance.

3. **Lacunae**—Spaces or cavities that contain osteocytes; located between lamellae.

4. **Canaliculi** (kan'a-LIK-yoo-lē)—Minute canals that radiate in all directions from the lacunae and interconnect with each other; contain slender processes of osteocytes.

5. **Osteocyte**—Bone cell located within a lacuna.

6. **Osteon (haversian system)**—Central (haversian) canal plus its surrounding lamellae, lacunae, canaliculi, and osteocytes; structural unit of compact bone.

Label the parts of the osteon shown in Figure 6.2.

Now obtain a prepared slide of a longitudinal section of compact bone and examine under high power. Locate the following:

1. **Perforating (Volkmann's) canals**—Canals that extend obliquely or horizontally inward from the bone surface and contain blood vessels, lymphatics, and nerves; extend into central canals and medullary cavity.

2. **Endosteum**—Layer of osteoblasts and scattered osteoclasts lining medullary (marrow) cavity and spongy bone.

3. **Medullary (marrow) cavity**—Space within diaphysis that contains yellow marrow in adult.

4. **Lamellae**—Concentric rings of hard, calcified, intercellular substance.

5. **Lacunae**—Spaces that contain osteocytes.

6. **Canaliculi**—Minute canals that radiate from lacunae and contain slender processes of osteocytes.

7. **Osteocytes**—Mature osteoblasts in lacunae that are no longer capable of producing new bone tissue.

Label the parts indicated in the microscopic view of bone in Figure 6.3.

D. TYPES OF BONES

The 206 named bones of the body may be classified by shape into four principal types:

1. **Long**—Have greater length than width, consist of a diaphysis and two epiphyses, and have a marrow cavity; contain more compact than spongy bone. Example: humerus.

2. **Short**—Somewhat cube-shaped, and differences in length and width not significant; contain more spongy than compact bone. Example: wrist bones.

3. **Flat**—Generally thin and flat and composed of two more-or-less parallel plates of compact bone enclosing a layer of spongy bone. Example: sternum.

4. **Irregular**—Very complex shapes; cannot be grouped into any of the three categories just described. Example: vertebrae.

Other bones that are recognized, although not considered in the structural classification, include the following:

1. **Sutural (wormian)**—Small bones between certain cranial bones; variable in number.

2. **Sesamoid**—Small bones found in tendons; variable in number; the only constant sesamoid bones are the paired kneecaps; *sesamoid* means "resembling a grain of sesame."

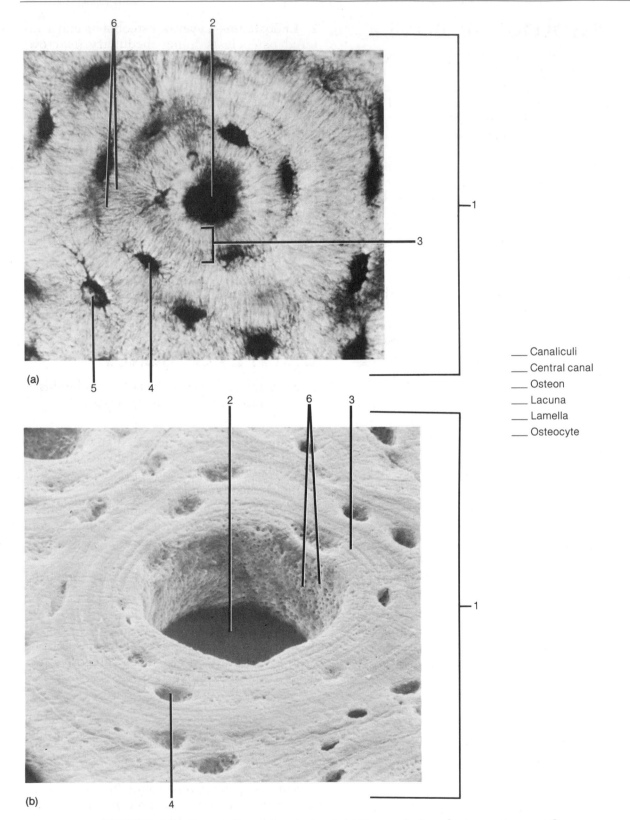

(a)

(b)

___ Canaliculi
___ Central canal
___ Osteon
___ Lacuna
___ Lamella
___ Osteocyte

FIGURE 6.2 Osteon (haversian system). (a) Transmission electron micrograph. (b) Scanning electron micrograph at a magnification of 1040×. ((b) from *Tissues and Organs: A Text-Atlas of Scanning Electron Microscopy* by Richard G. Kessel and Randy H. Kardon. W. H. Freeman and Company. Copyright © 1979.)

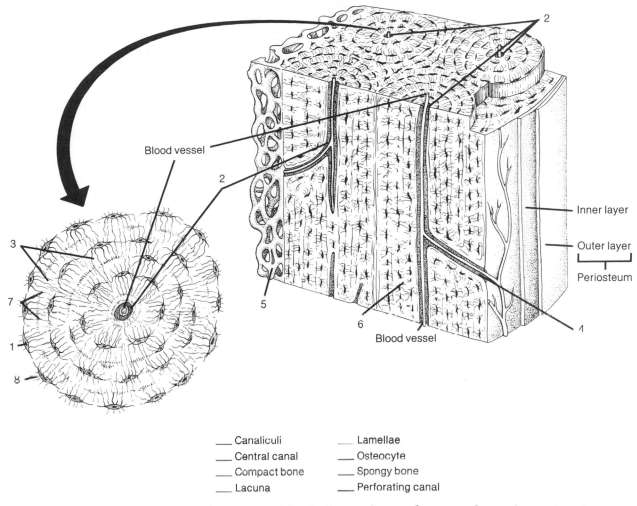

Blood vessel

Inner layer

Outer layer

Periosteum

Blood vessel

___ Canaliculi	___ Lamellae
___ Central canal	___ Osteocyte
___ Compact bone	___ Spongy bone
___ Lacuna	___ Perforating canal

FIGURE 6.3   Cross section and longitudinal section of several osteons (haversian systems).

Examine the disarticulated skeleton, Beau-chene (disarticulated) skull, and articulated skeleton and find several examples of long, short, flat, and irregular bones. List examples of each type you find.

1. **Long** _____

_____

_____

2. **Short** _____

_____

_____

_____

3. **Flat** _____

_____

_____

_____

4. **Irregular** _____

_____

_____

_____

E. BONE MARKINGS

The surfaces of bones contain various structural features that have specific functions. These

TABLE 6.1
BONE MARKINGS

MARKING	DESCRIPTION
DEPRESSIONS AND OPENINGS	
Fissure (FISH-ur)	A narrow, cleftlike opening between adjacent parts of bones through which blood vessels or nerves pass
Foramen (fō-RĀ-men; *foramen* = hole)	An opening through which blood vessels, nerves, or ligaments pass
Meatus (mē-Ā-tus; *meatus* = canal)	A tubelike passageway running within a bone
Paranasal sinus (*sin* = cavity)	An air-filled cavity within a bone connected to the nasal cavity
Groove or **sulcus** (*sulcus* = ditchlike groove)	A furrow or depression that accommodates a soft structure such as a blood vessel, nerve, or tendon
Fossa (*fossa* = basinlike depression)	A depression in or on a bone
PROCESSES (PROJECTIONS) THAT FORM JOINTS	
Condyle (KON-dīl; *condylus* = knucklelike process)	A large, rounded articular prominence
Head	A rounded, articular projection supported on the constricted portion (neck)
Facet	A smooth, flat surface
PROCESSES (PROJECTIONS) TO WHICH TENDONS, LIGAMENTS, AND OTHER CONNECTIVE TISSUES ATTACH	
Tubercle (TOO-ber-kul; *tube* = knob)	A small, rounded process
Tuberosity	A large, rounded, usually roughened process
Trochanter (trō-KAN-ter)	A large, blunt projection found only on the femur
Crest	A prominent border or ridge
Line	A less prominent ridge
Spinous process or **spine**	A sharp, slender process
Epicondyle (*epi* = above)	A prominence above a condyle

features are called **bone markings.** The bone markings are listed and described in Table 6.1. Knowledge of the bone markings will be very useful when you learn the bones of the body in Exercise 7.

LABORATORY REPORT
QUESTIONS (PAGE 379)

7 | BONES

The bones of the adult skeleton are grouped into two divisions: axial and appendicular. The **axial skeleton** consists of bones that compose the axis of the body. The axis is a straight line that runs along the center of gravity of the body, through the head, and down to the space between the feet. The **appendicular skeleton** consists of the bones of the extremities (upper and lower) and the girdles (pectoral and pelvic).

In this exercise you will study the names and locations of bones and their markings by examining various regions of the skeleton:

Region	Number of bones
Axial skeleton	
Skull	8
Cranium	14
Face	1
Hyoid (above the larynx)	
Auditory ossicles, 3 in each ear	6
Vertebral column	26
Thorax	
Sternum	1
Ribs	24
	80
Appendicular skeleton	
Pectoral (*shoulder*) *girdles*	
Clavicle	2
Scapula	2
Upper extremities	
Humerus	2
Ulna	2
Radius	2
Carpals	16
Metacarpals	10
Phalanges	28
Pelvic (*hip*) *girdle*	
Coxal, hip, or pelvic bone	2

Region	Number of bones
Appendicular skeleton (Continued)	
Lower extremities	
Femur	2
Fibula	2
Tibia	2
Patella	2
Tarsals	14
Metatarsals	10
Phalanges	28
	126

A. BONES OF ADULT SKULL

The **skull** is composed of two sets of bones—**cranial** and **facial**. The 8 cranial bones are 1 **frontal**, 2 **parietals** (pa-RĪ-i-talz), 2 **temporals**, 1 **occipital** (ok-SIP-i-tal), 1 **sphenoid** (SFĒ-noyd), and 1 **ethmoid.** The 14 facial bones include 2 **nasals**, 2 **maxillae** (mak-SIL-ē), 2 **zygomatics**, 1 **mandible**, 2 **lacrimals**, 2 **palatines**, 2 **inferior conchae** (KONG-kē), and 1 **vomer.** These bones are indicated by *arrows* in Figure 7.1. Using the series of photographs in Figure 7.1 for reference, locate the cranial and facial bones on both a Beauchene (disarticulated) and an articulated skull.

Obtain a Beauchene skull and an articulated skull and observe them in anterior view. Using Figure 7.1a for reference, locate the **frontal eminence, frontal squama (vertical plate), glabella, superciliary arch, supraorbital margin, superior orbital fissure, mental foramen** (fō-RĀ-men), **infraorbital foramen,** and **supraorbital foramen.**

Turn the Beauchene skull and articulated skull so that you are looking at the right side. Using Figure 7.1b for reference, locate the **zygomatic process, temporal process, mastoid**

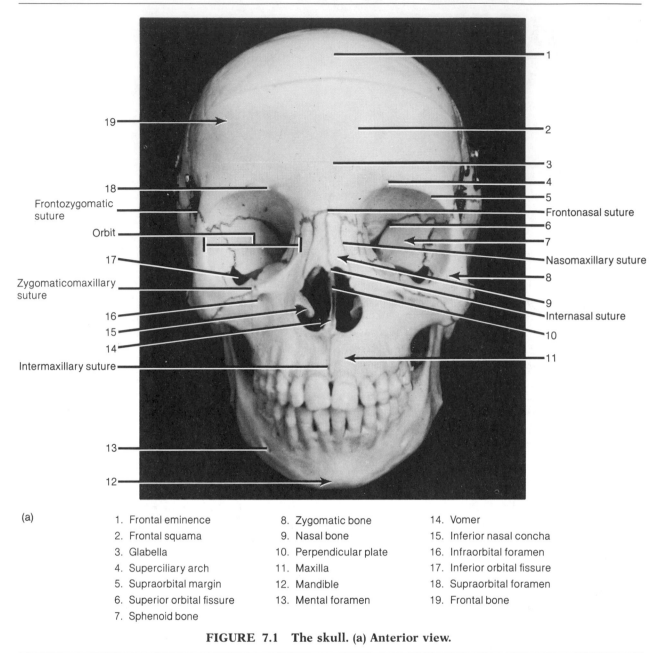

19 — Frontozygomatic suture

18 —

Frontozygomatic
suture

Orbit —

17 —

Zygomaticomaxillary
suture

16 —
15 —
14 —

Intermaxillary suture —

13 —

12 —

Frontonasal suture

Nasomaxillary suture

Internasal suture

(a)

1. Frontal eminence	8. Zygomatic bone	14. Vomer
2. Frontal squama	9. Nasal bone	15. Inferior nasal concha
3. Glabella	10. Perpendicular plate	16. Infraorbital foramen
4. Superciliary arch	11. Maxilla	17. Inferior orbital fissure
5. Supraorbital margin	12. Mandible	18. Supraorbital foramen
6. Superior orbital fissure	13. Mental foramen	19. Frontal bone
7. Sphenoid bone		

FIGURE 7.1   The skull. (a) Anterior view.

process, mastoid portion, external auditory meatus, and **temporal squama.**

If a skull in median section is available, use Figure 7.1c for reference and locate the **sella turcica** (TUR-si-ka), **frontal sinus, crista galli, cribriform plate, sphenoidal sinus, superior nasal concha** (KONG-ka), **middle nasal concha, inferior nasal concha, pterygoid** (TER-i-goyd) **process, styloid process, palatine process,** and **external occipital protuberance.** Note also the **hyoid bone** below the mandible. This is not a bone of the skull, but is noted here because of its proximity to the skull.

Take an articulated skull and turn it upside down so that you are looking at the inferior surface. Using Figure 7.1d for reference, locate the **palatine process, zygomatic arch, foramen spinosum, mandibular fossa, foramen lacerum, carotid foramen, mastoid process, stylomastoid foramen, foramen magnum, external occipital protuberance, condylar fossa, occipital condyle, jugular foramen, styloid process, foramen ovale, inferior orbital fissure, middle nasal concha, lesser palatine foramina, greater palatine foramen, horizontal plate,** and **incisive fossa.**

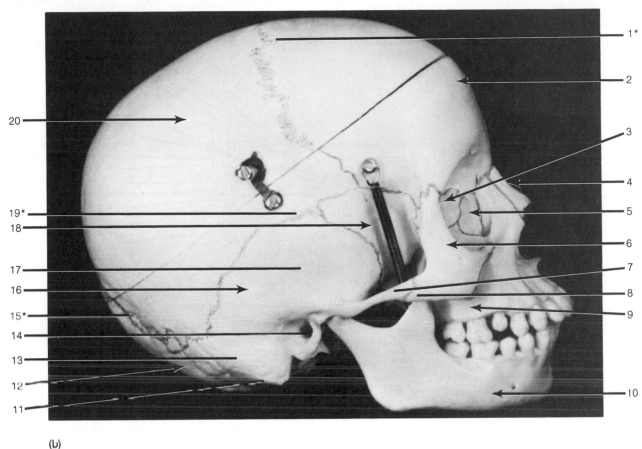

(b)

1. Coronal suture	11. Mastoid process
2. Frontal bone	12. Occipital bone
3. Ethmoid bone	13. Mastoid portion
4. Nasal bone	14. External auditory meatus
5. Lacrimal bone	15. Lambdoidal suture
6. Zygomatic bone	16. Temporal bone
7. Zygomatic process	17. Temporal squama
8. Temporal process	18. Sphenoid bone
9. Maxilla	19. Squamosal suture
10. Mandible	20. Parietal bone

FIGURE 7.1 (Continued) The skull. (b) Right lateral view.

Obtain an articulated skull with a removable crown. Using Figure 7.1e for reference, locate the **olfactory foramina, crista galli, lesser wing, optic foramen, greater wing, sella turcica, foramen ovale, foramen spinosum, foramen lacerum, petrous portion, foramen magnum, foramen rotundum, superior orbital fissure,** and **cribriform plate.**

Examine the right orbit of an articulated skull. Using Figure 7.2 for reference, locate the **frontal bone, nasal bone, ethmoid bone, lacrimal bone, maxilla, zygomatic bone, sphenoid bone, optic foramen, infra-**orbital foramen, supraorbital foramen, inferior orbital fissure,** and **superior orbital fissure.**

Obtain a mandible and, using Figure 7.3 for reference, identify the **body, ramus, angle, condylar process, coronoid process, mandibular notch, mental foramen, alveolar** (al-VĒ-ō-lar) **process,** and **mandibular foramen.**

Before you move on, examine Table 7.1, Summary of Foramina of the Skull. It will give you an understanding of the structures that pass through the various foramina you just studied.

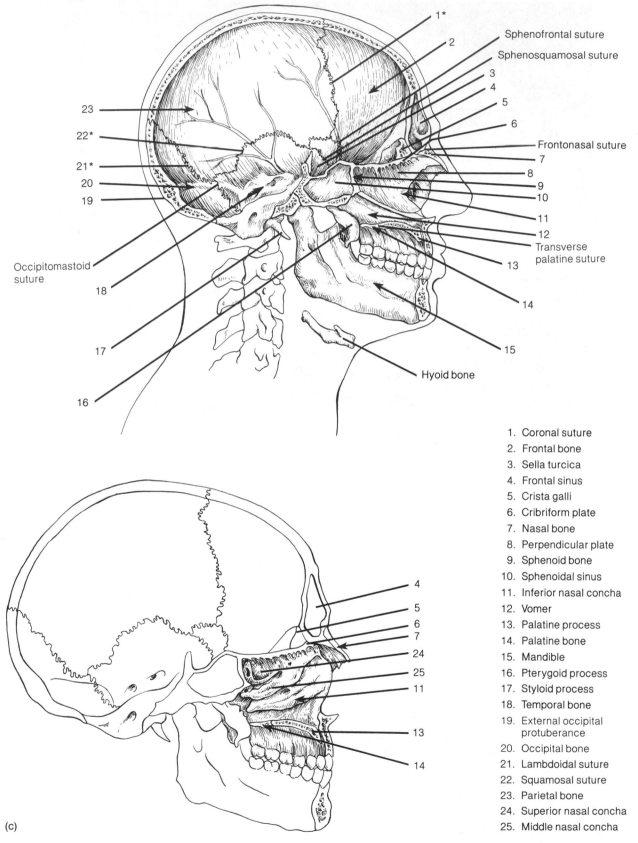

1*

2

Sphenofrontal suture

Sphenosquamosal suture

3
4
5
6

Frontonasal suture

7
8
9
10
11
12

Transverse palatine suture

13

14

23
22*
21*
20
19

Occipitomastoid suture

18

17

16

15

Hyoid bone

4
5
6
7
24
25
11

13

14

(c)

1. Coronal suture
2. Frontal bone
3. Sella turcica
4. Frontal sinus
5. Crista galli
6. Cribriform plate
7. Nasal bone
8. Perpendicular plate
9. Sphenoid bone
10. Sphenoidal sinus
11. Inferior nasal concha
12. Vomer
13. Palatine process
14. Palatine bone
15. Mandible
16. Pterygoid process
17. Styloid process
18. Temporal bone
19. External occipital protuberance
20. Occipital bone
21. Lambdoidal suture
22. Squamosal suture
23. Parietal bone
24. Superior nasal concha
25. Middle nasal concha

FIGURE 7.1 (*Continued*) The skull. (c) Median sections.

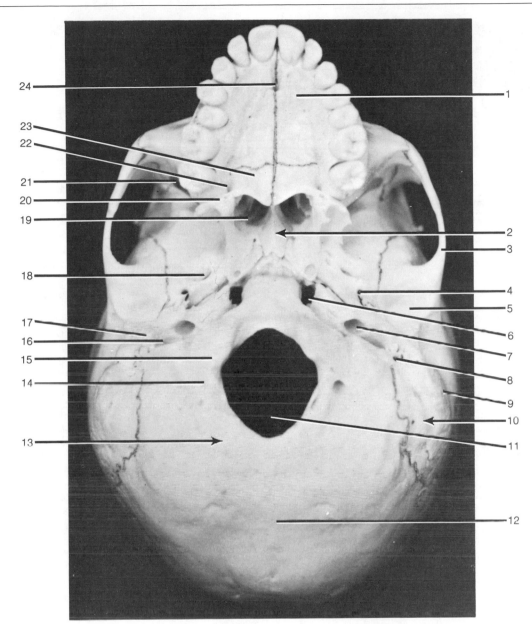

(d)

1. Patatine process
2. Vomer
3. Zygomatic arch
4. Foramen spinosum
5. Mandibular fossa
6. Foramen lacerum
7. Carotid foramen
8. Stylomastoid foramen
9. Mastoid process
10. Temporal bone
11. Foramen magnum
12. External occipital protuberance
13. Occipital bone
14. Condylar fossa
15. Occipital condyle
16. Jugular foramen
17. Styloid process
18. Foramen ovale
19. Middle nasal concha
20. Lesser palatine foramina
21. Inferior orbital fissure
22. Greater palatine foramen
23. Horizontal plate
24. Incisive fossa

FIGURE 7.1 (*Continued*) The skull. (d) Inferior view.

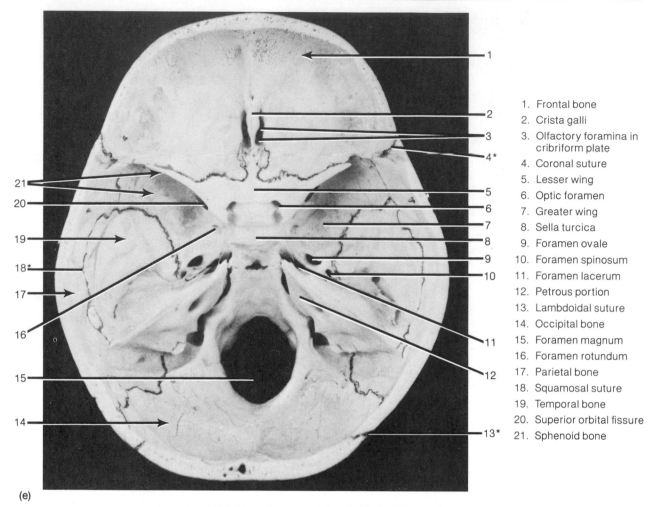

1. Frontal bone
2. Crista galli
3. Olfactory foramina in cribriform plate
4. Coronal suture
5. Lesser wing
6. Optic foramen
7. Greater wing
8. Sella turcica
9. Foramen ovale
10. Foramen spinosum
11. Foramen lacerum
12. Petrous portion
13. Lambdoidal suture
14. Occipital bone
15. Foramen magnum
16. Foramen rotundum
17. Parietal bone
18. Squamosal suture
19. Temporal bone
20. Superior orbital fissure
21. Sphenoid bone

FIGURE 7.1 (*Continued*)   The skull. (e) Floor of cranium.

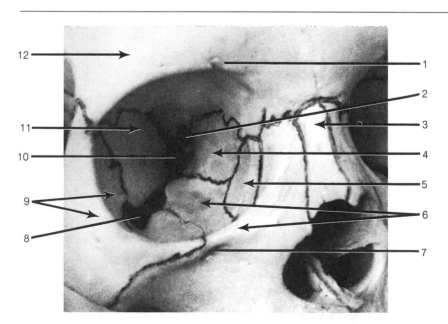

1. Supraorbital foramen
2. Superior orbital fissure
3. Nasal bone
4. Ethmoid bone
5. Lacrimal bone
6. Maxilla
7. Infraorbital foramen
8. Inferior orbital fissure
9. Zygomatic bone
10. Optic foramen
11. Sphenoid bone
12. Frontal bone

FIGURE 7.2   The right orbit.

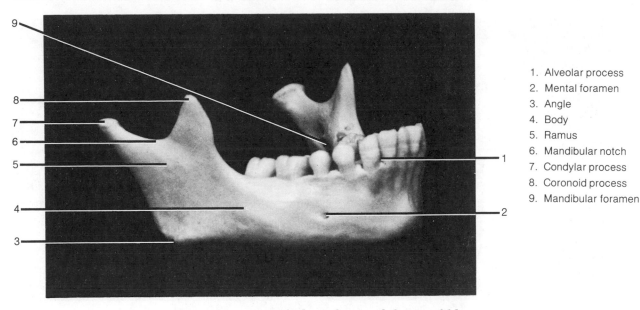

1. Alveolar process
2. Mental foramen
3. Angle
4. Body
5. Ramus
6. Mandibular notch
7. Condylar process
8. Coronoid process
9. Mandibular foramen

FIGURE 7.3 Right lateral view of the mandible.

TABLE 7.1
SUMMARY OF FORAMINA OF THE SKULL

FORAMEN	STRUCTURES PASSING THROUGH
Carotid	Internal carotid artery
Greater palatine	Greater palatine nerve and greater palatine vessels
Incisive	Branches of descending palatine vessels and nasopalatine nerve
Infraorbital	Infraorbital nerve and artery
Jugular	Internal jugular vein, glossopharyngeal (IX) nerve, vagus (X) nerve, accessory (XI) nerve, and sigmoid sinus
Lacerum	Internal carotid artery and branch of ascending pharyngeal artery
Lesser palatine	Lesser palatine nerves and artery
Magnum	Medulla oblongata and its membranes, the accessory (XI) nerve, and the vertebral and spinal arteries and meninges
Mandibular	Inferior alveolar nerve and vessels
Mental	Mental nerve and vessels
Olfactory	Olfactory (I) nerve
Optic	Optic (II) nerve and ophthalmic artery
Ovale	Mandibular branch of trigeminal (V) nerve
Rotundum	Maxillary branch of trigeminal (V) nerve
Spinosum	Middle meningeal vessels
Stylomastoid	Facial (VII) nerve and stylomastoid artery
Supraorbital	Supraorbital nerve and artery

B. SUTURES OF SKULL

A **suture** (SOO-chur) is an immovable joint between skull bones. The four prominent sutures are the **coronal, sagittal, lambdoidal** (lam-DOY-dal), and **squamosal.** The lines identifying these sutures are marked with *asterisks* in Figure 7.1. Using Figures 7.1 and 7.4 for reference, locate these sutures on an articulated skull.

C. FONTANELS OF SKULL

At birth, the skull bones are separated by membrane-filled spaces called **fontanels**

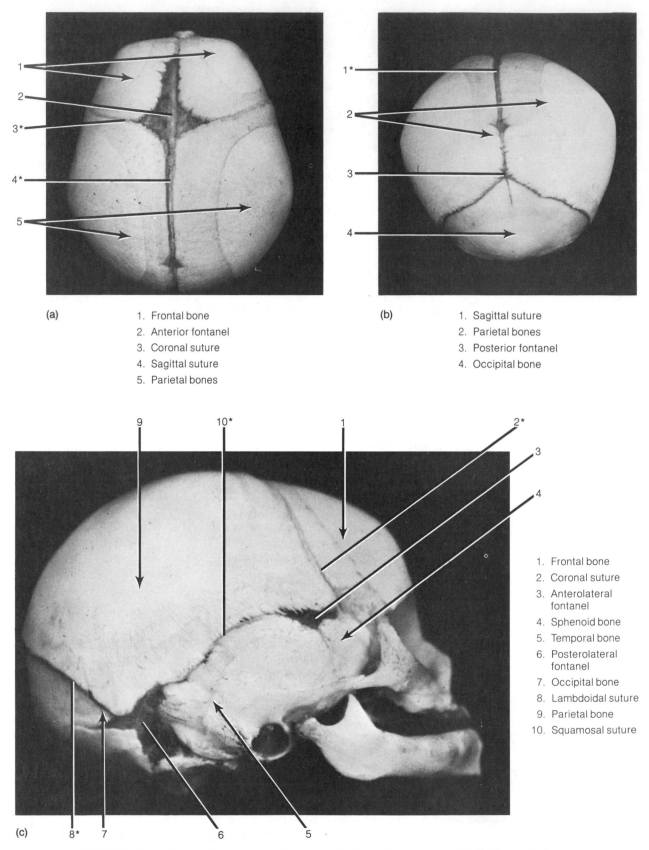

(a)

1. Frontal bone
2. Anterior fontanel
3. Coronal suture
4. Sagittal suture
5. Parietal bones

(b)

1. Sagittal suture
2. Parietal bones
3. Posterior fontanel
4. Occipital bone

1. Frontal bone
2. Coronal suture
3. Anterolateral fontanel
4. Sphenoid bone
5. Temporal bone
6. Posterolateral fontanel
7. Occipital bone
8. Lambdoidal suture
9. Parietal bone
10. Squamosal suture

(c)

FIGURE 7.4 **Fontanels. (a) Superior view. (b) Posterior view. (c) Right lateral view.**

(fon'-ta-NELZ). The principal fontanels are **anterior (frontal), posterior (occipital), anterolateral (sphenoidal),** and **posterolateral (mastoid).** Using Figure 7.4 for reference, locate the fontanels on the skull of a newborn infant.

D. PARANASAL SINUSES OF SKULL

A **paranasal sinus,** or just simply **sinus,** is a cavity in a bone located near the nasal cavity. Paired paranasal sinuses are found in the maxillae and the frontal, sphenoid, and ethmoid bones. Locate the paranasal sinuses on the Beauchene skull or other demonstration models that may be available. Label the paranasal sinuses shown in Figure 7.5.

E. VERTEBRAL COLUMN

The **vertebral column,** together with the sternum and ribs, constitutes the skeleton of the trunk. The **vertebrae** of the adult column are distributed as follows: 7 **cervical** (SER-vi-kal) (neck), 12 **thoracic** (thō-RAS-ik) (chest), 5 **lumbar** (lower back), 5 **sacral** (fused into one bone, the **sacrum** between the hipbones), and 3, 4, or 5 **coccygeal** (kok-SIJ-ē-al) (fused into one bone, the **coccyx** (KOK-six), forming the tail of the column). Locate each of these regions on the articulated skeleton. Label the same regions in Figure 7.6, the anterior view.

Examine the vertebral column on the articulated skeleton and identify the cervical, thoracic, lumbar, and sacral (sacrococcygeal) curves. Label the curves in Figure 7.6, the right lateral view.

F. VERTEBRAE

A typical **vertebra** consists of the following portions:

1. **Body**—Thick, disc-shaped anterior portion.

2. **Vertebral (neural) arch**—Posterior extension from the body that surrounds the spinal cord and consists of the following parts:

    a. **Pedicles** (PED-i-kuls)—Two short, thick processes that project posteriorly; each has a superior and inferior notch and, when successive vertebrae are fitted together, the opposing notches form an **intervertebral fora-**

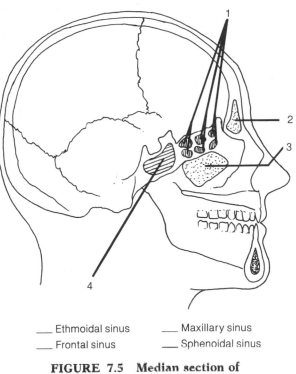

| ___ | Ethmoidal sinus | ___ | Maxillary sinus |
| ___ | Frontal sinus | ___ | Sphenoidal sinus |

FIGURE 7.5 Median section of skull showing paranasal sinuses.

men through which spinal nerves and blood vessels pass.

b. **Laminae** (LAM-i-nē)—Flat portions that form the posterior wall of the vertebral arch.

c. **Vertebral foramen**—Opening through which the spinal cord passes; when all the vertebrae are fitted together, the foramina form a canal, the **vertebral canal.**

3. **Processes**—Seven processes arise from the vertebral arch:

    a. Two **transverse processes**—Lateral extensions where the laminae and pedicles join.

    b. One **spinous process**—Posterior projection of the lamina.

    c. Two **superior articular processes**—Articulate with the vertebra above. Their top surfaces, called **superior articular facets,** articulate with the vertebra above.

    d. Two **inferior articular processes**—Articulate with the vertebra below. Their bottom surfaces, called **inferior articular facets,** articulate with the vertebra below.

Obtain a thoracic vertebra and locate each part just described. Now label the vertebra in Figure 7.7a. You should be able to distinguish

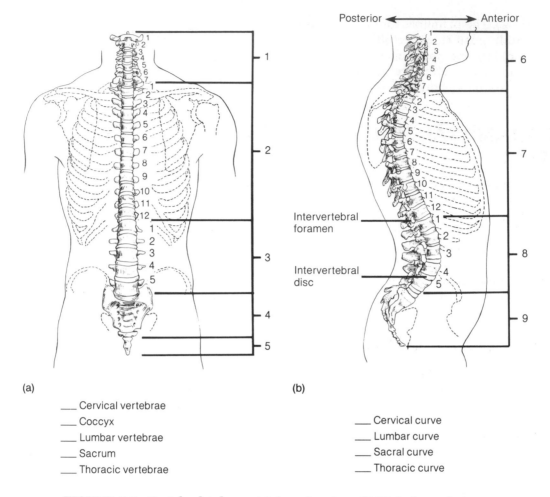

Posterior ⟵——⟶ Anterior

Intervertebral foramen

Intervertebral disc

(a)   (b)

___ Cervical vertebrae

___ Coccyx

___ Lumbar vertebrae

___ Sacrum

___ Thoracic vertebrae

___ Cervical curve

___ Lumbar curve

___ Sacral curve

___ Thoracic curve

FIGURE 7.6   Vertebral column. (a) Anterior view. (b) Right lateral view.

the general parts on all the different vertebrae that contain them.

Although vertebrae have the same basic design, those of a given region have special distinguishing features. Obtain examples of the following vertebrae and identify their distinguishing features.

1. **Cervical vertebrae**

   a. **Atlas**—First cervical vertebra (see Figure 7.7b)

   Transverse foramen—Opening in transverse process through which an artery, a vein, and a branch of a spinal nerve pass.

   Anterior arch—Anterior wall of vertebral foramen.

   Posterior arch—Posterior wall of vertebral foramen.

   Lateral mass—Side wall of vertebral foramen.

Label the other indicated parts.

   b. **Axis**—Second cervical vertebra (see Figure 7.7c)

   Dens—Superior projection of body that articulates with atlas.

Label the other indicated parts.

   c. **Cervicals 3 through 6** (see Figure 7.7d)

   Bifid spinous process—Cleft in spinous processes of cervical vertebrae 2 through 6.

Label the other indicated parts.

   d. **Vertebra prominens**—Seventh cervical vertebra; contains a nonbifid and long spinous process.

2. **Thoracic vertebrae** (see Figure 7.7e)

   a. **Facets**—For articulation with the tubercle and head of a rib; found on body and transverse processes.

   b. **Spinous processes**—Long, pointed, downward projection.

Label the other indicated parts.

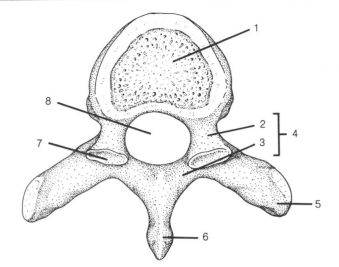

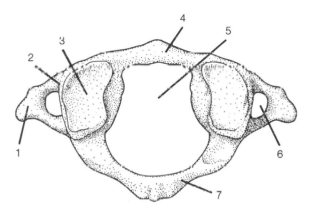

(a)

___ Body
___ Lamina
___ Pedicle
___ Spinous process
___ Superior articular facet
___ Transverse process
___ Vertebral arch
___ Vertebral foramen

(b)

Anterior arch
Lateral mass
___ Posterior arch
___ Superior articular facet
___ Transverse foramen
___ Transverse process
___ Vertebral foramen

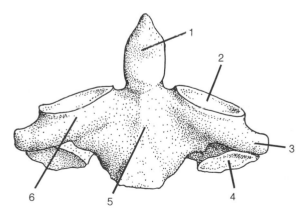

(c)

___ Body
___ Dens
___ Inferior articular facet
___ Lateral mass
___ Superior articular facet
___ Transverse process

FIGURE 7.7 Vertebrae. (a) Superior view of a typical vertebra.
(b) Superior view of the atlas. (c) Anterior view of the axis.

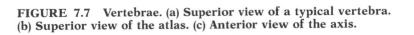

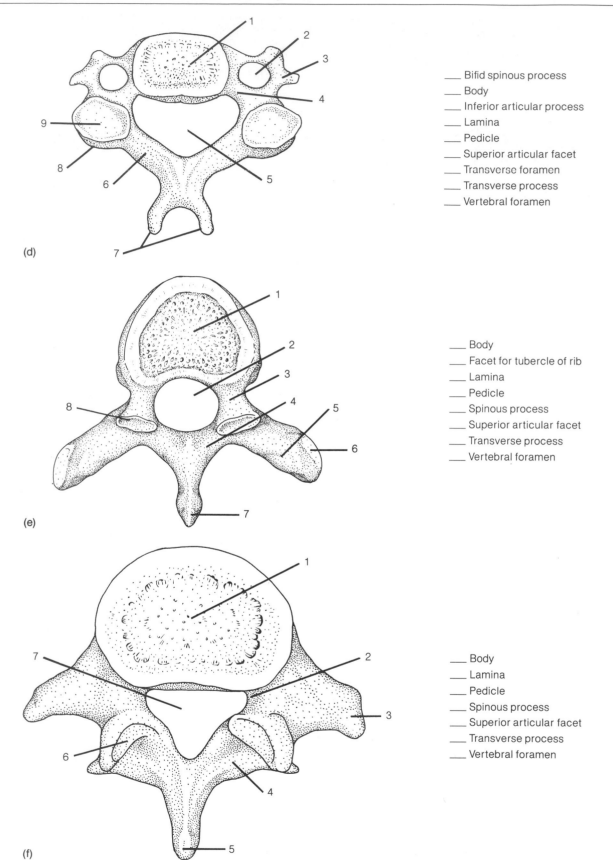

___ Bifid spinous process
___ Body
___ Inferior articular process
___ Lamina
___ Pedicle
___ Superior articular facet
___ Transverse foramen
___ Transverse process
___ Vertebral foramen

(d)

___ Body
___ Facet for tubercle of rib
___ Lamina
___ Pedicle
___ Spinous process
___ Superior articular facet
___ Transverse process
___ Vertebral foramen

(e)

___ Body
___ Lamina
___ Pedicle
___ Spinous process
___ Superior articular facet
___ Transverse process
___ Vertebral foramen

(f)

FIGURE 7.7 (*Continued*) Vertebrae. (d) Superior view of a cervical vertebra. (e) Superior view of a thoracic vertebra. (f) Superior view of a lumbar vertebra.

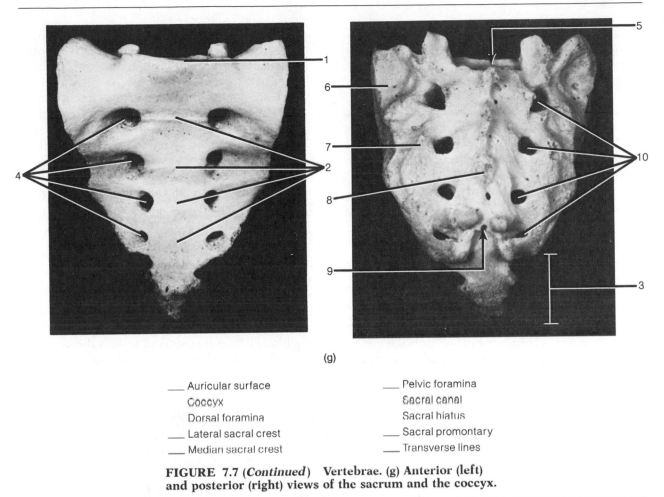

(g)

___ Auricular surface	___ Pelvic foramina
Coccyx	Sacral canal
Dorsal foramina	Sacral hiatus
___ Lateral sacral crest	___ Sacral promontary
___ Median sacral crest	___ Transverse lines

FIGURE 7.7 (*Continued*) Vertebrae. (g) Anterior (left) and posterior (right) views of the sacrum and the coccyx.

3. **Lumbar vertebrae** (see Figure 7.7f)
a. **Spinous processes**—Broad, blunt.
b. **Superior articular processes**—Directed medially, not superiorly.
c. **Inferior articular processes**—Directed laterally, not inferiorly.
Label the other indicated parts.

4. **Sacrum** (see Figure 7.7g)
a. **Transverse lines**—Points where bodies of vertebrae are joined.
b. **Pelvic foramina**—Four pairs of foramina that communicate with dorsal sacral foramina; passages for blood vessels and nerves.
c. **Median sacral crest**—Spinous processes of fused vertebrae.
d. **Lateral sacral crest**—Transverse processes of fused vertebrae.
e. **Dorsal foramina**—Four pairs of foramina that communicate with pelvic foramina; passages for blood vessels and nerves.
f. **Sacral canal**—Continuation of vertebral canal.

g. **Sacral promontory**—Superior, anterior projecting border.
h. **Auricular surface**—Articulates with ilium of coxal bone.
i. **Sacral hiatus**—Inferior entrance to sacral canal where laminae of S5, and sometimes S4, fail to meet.

5. **Coccyx** (see Figure 7.7g)

Label the coccyx and the parts of the sacrum in Figure 7.7g.

G. STERNUM AND RIBS

The skeleton of the **thorax** consists of the **sternum, costal cartilages, ribs,** and bodies of the **thoracic vertebrae.**

Examine the articulated skeleton and disarticulated bones and identify the following:

1. **Sternum**—Breastbone, flat bone in midline of anterior thorax.

a. **Manubrium**—Superior, triangular portion.

b. **Body**—Middle, largest portion.

c. **Xiphoid**—(ZĪ-foyd) **process**—Inferior, smallest portion.

d. **Jugular (suprasternal) notch**—Depression on the superior surface of the manubrium that may be palpated.

e. **Clavicular notches**—Articular surfaces for the clavicles.

f. **Costal notches**—Points at which ribs articulate.

2. **Costal cartilage**—Strip of hyaline cartilage that attaches a rib to the sternum.

3. **Ribs**—Parts of a typical rib (third through ninth) include:

a. **Body**—Shaft, main part of rib.

b. **Head**—Posterior projection.

c. **Neck**—Constricted portion behind head.

d. **Tubercle** (TOO-ber-kul)—Knoblike elevation just below neck; consists of a **nonarticu-**

lar part that affords attachment for a ligament and an **articular part** that articulates with an inferior vertebra.

e. **Costal groove**—Depression on the inner surface containing blood vessels and a nerve.

f. **Superior facet**—Articulates with facet on superior vertebra.

g. **Inferior facet**—Articulates with facet on inferior vertebra.

Label the parts of the sternum in Figure 7.8a and the parts of a rib in Figure 7.8b.

H. PECTORAL (SHOULDER) GIRDLES

Each **pectoral (shoulder) girdle** consists of two bones—**clavicle** (collar bone) and **scapula** (shoulder blade). Its purpose is to attach the bones of the upper extremity to the axial skeleton.

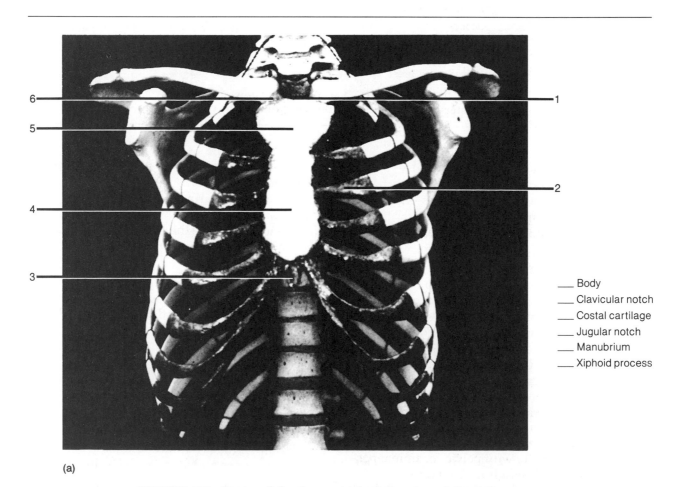

___ Body
___ Clavicular notch
___ Costal cartilage
___ Jugular notch
___ Manubrium
___ Xiphoid process

(a)

FIGURE 7.8   Bones of the thorax. (a) Anterior view of thoracic cage.

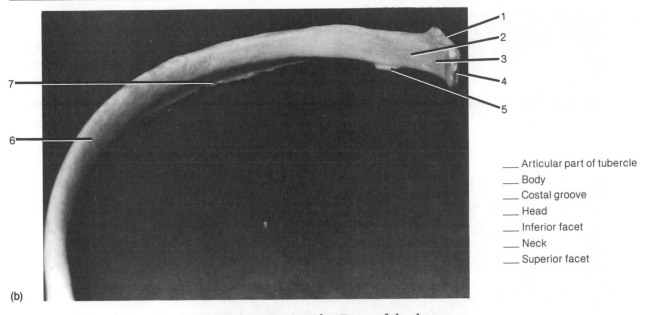

___ Articular part of tubercle
___ Body
___ Costal groove
___ Head
___ Inferior facet
___ Neck
___ Superior facet

(b)

FIGURE 7.8 (Continued) Bones of the thorax.
(b) Inner aspect of a portion of the fifth right rib.

Examine the articulated skeleton and disarticulated bones and identify the following:

1. **Clavicle**—Slender bone with a double curvature; lies horizontally in superior and anterior part of thorax.
   a. **Sternal extremity**—Rounded, medial end that articulates with manubrium of sternum.
   b. **Acromial** (a-KRŌ-mē-al) **extremity**—Broad, flat, lateral end that articulates with the acromion of the scapula.
   c. **Conoid tubercle**—Projection on the inferior, lateral surface for attachment of ligaments.

2. **Scapula**—Large, flat triangular bone in dorsal thorax between the levels of ribs 2 through 7.
   a. **Body**—Flattened, triangular portion.
   b. **Spine**—Ridge across posterior surface.
   c. **Acromion**—Flattened, expanded process of spine.
   d. **Medial (vertebral) border**—Edge of body near vertebral column.
   e. **Lateral (axillary) border**—Edge of body near arm.
   f. **Inferior angle**—Bottom of body where medial and lateral borders join.
   g. **Glenoid cavity**—Depression below acromion that articulates with head of humerus to form the shoulder joint.
   h. **Coracoid process**—Projection at lateral end of superior border.

   i. **Supraspinous** (soo'-pra-SPI-nus) **fossa**—Surface for muscle attachment above spine.
   j. **Infraspinous fossa**—Surface for muscle attachment below spine.
   k. **Superior border**—Superior edge of the body.
   l. **Superior angle**—Top of body where superior and medial borders join.

Label Figure 7.9.

I. UPPER EXTREMITIES

The skeleton of the **upper extremities** consists of a humerus in each arm, an ulna and radius in each forearm, carpals in each wrist, metacarpals in each palm, and phalanges in the fingers.

Examine the articulated skeleton and disarticulated bones and identify the following:

1. **Humerus**—Arm bone; longest and largest bone of the upper extremity.
   a. **Head**—Articulates with glenoid cavity of scapula.
   b. **Anatomical neck**—Oblique groove below head.
   c. **Greater tubercle**—Lateral projection below anatomical neck.
   d. **Lesser tubercle**—Anterior projection.
   e. **Intertubercular sulcus (groove)**—Between tubercles.

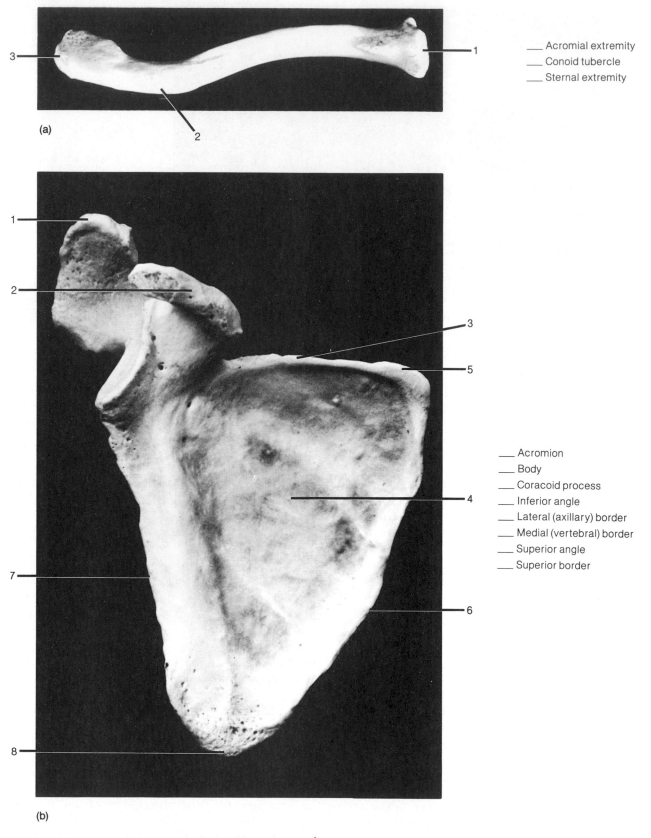

(a)

_____ Acromial extremity
_____ Conoid tubercle
_____ Sternal extremity

_____ Acromion
_____ Body
_____ Coracoid process
_____ Inferior angle
_____ Lateral (axillary) border
_____ Medial (vertebral) border
_____ Superior angle
_____ Superior border

(b)

FIGURE 7.9   The pectoral (shoulder) girdle. (a) Right clavicle viewed from below. (b) Anterior view of right scapula.

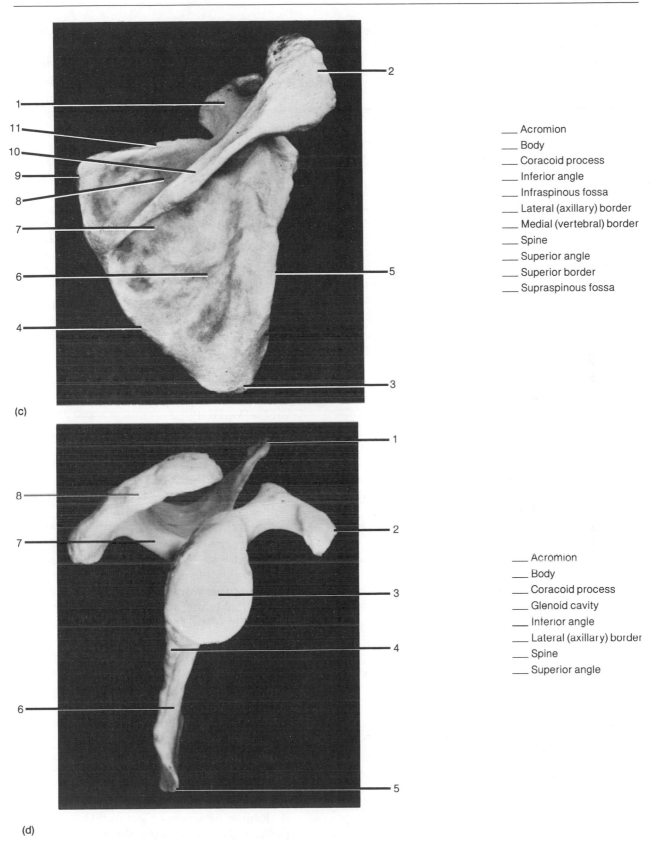

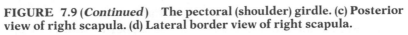

___ Acromion
___ Body
___ Coracoid process
___ Inferior angle
___ Infraspinous fossa
___ Lateral (axillary) border
___ Medial (vertebral) border
___ Spine
___ Superior angle
___ Superior border
___ Supraspinous fossa

(c)

___ Acromion
___ Body
___ Coracoid process
___ Glenoid cavity
___ Inferior angle
___ Lateral (axillary) border
___ Spine
___ Superior angle

(d)

FIGURE 7.9 (*Continued*) **The pectoral (shoulder) girdle. (c) Posterior view of right scapula. (d) Lateral border view of right scapula.**

f. **Surgical neck**—Constricted portion below tubercles.

g. **Body**—Shaft.

h. **Deltoid tuberosity**—V-shaped area about midway down the lateral surface of shaft.

i. **Capitulum** (ka-PIT-yoo-lum)—Rounded knob that articulates with head of radius.

j. **Radial Fossa**—Anterior lateral depression that receives head of radius when forearm is flexed.

k. **Trochlea** (TRŌK-lē-a)—Projection that articulates with the ulna.

l. **Coronoid fossa**—Anterior medial depression that receives part of the ulna when the forearm is flexed.

m. **Olecranon** (ō-LEK-ra-non) **fossa**—Posterior depression that receives the olecranon of the ulna when the forearm is extended.

n. **Medial epicondyle**—Projection on medial side of distal end.

o. **Lateral epicondyle**—Projection on lateral side of distal end.

2. **Ulna**—Medial bone of forearm.

a. **Olecranon**—Prominence of elbow at proximal end.

b. **Coronoid process**—Anterior projection that, with olecranon, receives trochlea of humerus.

c. **Trochlear (semilunar) notch**—Curved area between olecranon and coronoid process into which trochlea of humerus fits.

d. **Radial notch**—Depression lateral and inferior to trochlear notch that receives the head of the radius.

e. **Head**—Rounded portion at distal end.

f. **Styloid process**—Projection on posterior side of distal end.

3. **Radius**—Lateral bone of forearm.

a. **Head**—Disc-shaped process at proximal end.

b. **Radial tuberosity**—Medial projection for insertion of the biceps brachii muscle.

c. **Styloid process**—Projection on lateral side of distal end.

d. **Ulnar notch**—Medial, concave depression for articulation with ulna.

4. **Carpus**—Wrist, consists of eight small bones, called carpals, united by ligaments.

a. **Proximal row**—From medial to lateral are called **pisiform, triquetral, lunate,** and **scaphoid.**

b. **Distal row**—From medial to lateral are called **hamate, capitate, trapezoid,** and **trapezium.**

5. **Metacarpus**—Five bones in the palm of the hand, numbered as follows beginning with thumb side: I, II, III, IV, and V metacarpals.

6. **Phalanges** (fa-LAN-jēz)—Bones of the fingers; two in each thumb (proximal and distal) and three in each finger (proximal, middle, and distal). The singular of phalanges is phalanx.

Label Figure 7.10.

J. PELVIC (HIP) GIRDLES

The **pelvic (hip) girdles** consist of the two **coxal,** or **hip, bones.** They provide a strong and stable support for the lower extremities on which the weight of the body is carried and attach the lower extremities to the axial skeleton.

Examine the articulated skeleton and disarticulated bones and identify the following parts of the coxal bone:

1. **Ilium**—Superior flattened portion.

a. **Iliac crest**—Superior border of ilium.

b. **Anterior superior iliac spine**—Anterior projection of iliac crest.

c. **Anterior inferior iliac spine**—Projection under anterior superior iliac spine.

d. **Posterior superior iliac spine**—Posterior projection of iliac crest.

e. **Posterior inferior iliac spine**—Projection below posterior superior iliac spine.

f. **Greater sciatic** (sī-AT-ik) **notch**—Concavity under posterior inferior iliac spine.

g. **Iliac fossa**—Medial concavity for attachment of iliacus muscle.

h. **Iliac tuberosity**—Point of attachment for sacroiliac ligament posterior to iliac fossa.

i. **Auricular surface**—Point of articulation with sacrum.

j. **Posterior, anterior,** and **inferior gluteal lines**—Between these lines gluteal muscles are attached on the lateral surface.

2. **Ischium**—Lower, posterior portion.

a. **Ischial spine**—Posterior projection of ischium.

b. **Lesser sciatic notch**—Concavity under ischial spine.

c. **Ischial tuberosity**—Roughened projection.

d. **Ramus**—Portion of ischium that joins the pubis and surrounds the **obturator foramen.**

3. **Pubis**—Anterior, inferior portion.

a. **Superior ramus**—Upper portion of pubis.

b. **Inferior ramus**—Lower portion of pubis.

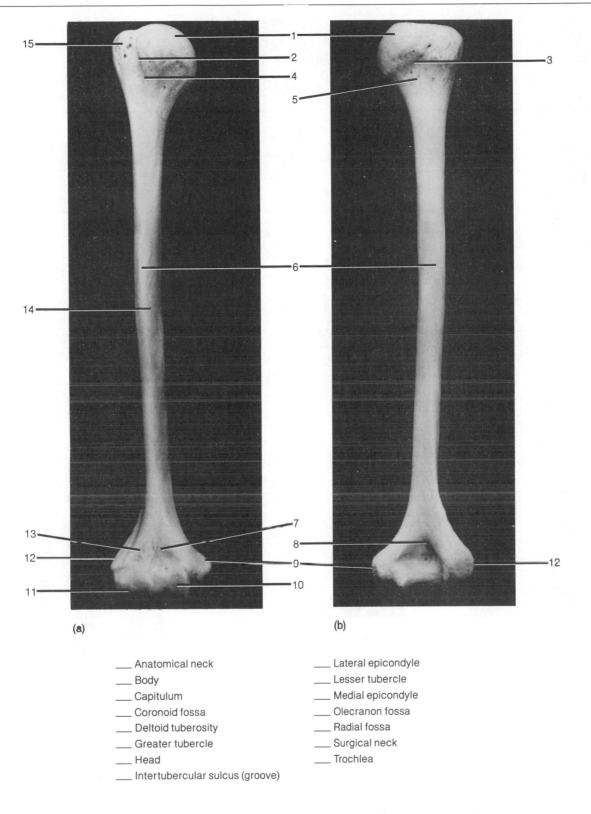

FIGURE 7.10 **Bones of upper extremity. (a) Anterior view of right humerus. (b) Posterior view of right humerus.**

___ Anatomical neck

___ Body

___ Capitulum

___ Coronoid fossa

___ Deltoid tuberosity

___ Greater tubercle

___ Head

___ Intertubercular sulcus (groove)

___ Lateral epicondyle

___ Lesser tubercle

___ Medial epicondyle

___ Olecranon fossa

___ Radial fossa

___ Surgical neck

___ Trochlea

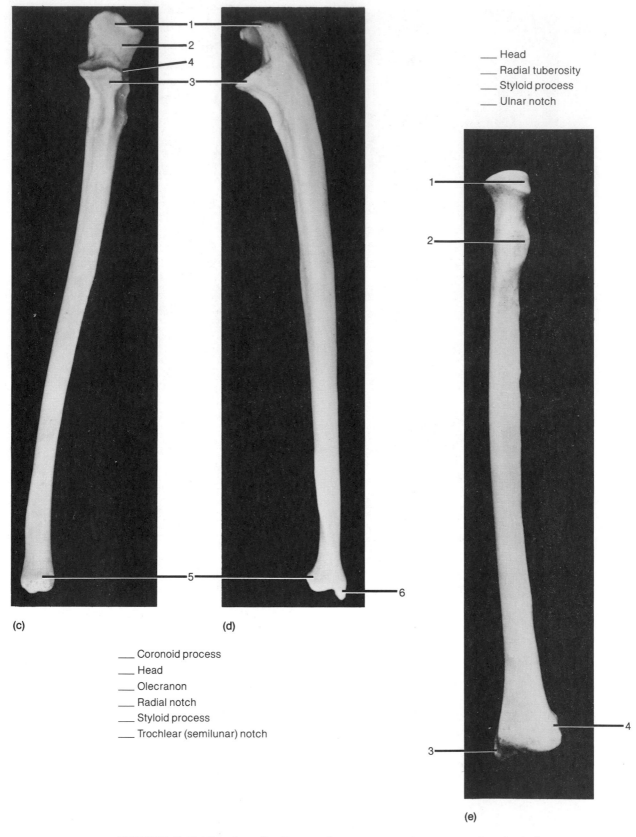

_____ Head
_____ Radial tuberosity
_____ Styloid process
_____ Ulnar notch

(c)

(d)

_____ Coronoid process
_____ Head
_____ Olecranon
_____ Radial notch
_____ Styloid process
_____ Trochlear (semilunar) notch

(e)

FIGURE 7.10 (*Continued*) **Bones of upper extremity. (c) Anterior view of right ulna. (d) Lateral view of right ulna. (e) Anterior view of right radius.**

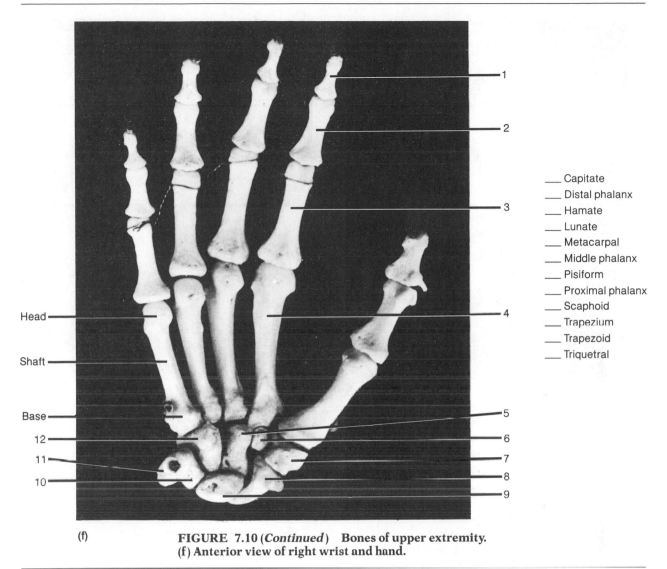

Head

Shaft

Base

12

11

10

___ Capitate
___ Distal phalanx
___ Hamate
___ Lunate
___ Metacarpal
___ Middle phalanx
___ Pisiform
___ Proximal phalanx
___ Scaphoid
___ Trapezium
___ Trapezoid
___ Triquetral

(f)   **FIGURE 7.10 (*Continued*)   Bones of upper extremity.**
(f) Anterior view of right wrist and hand.

c. **Symphysis** (SIM-fi-sis) **pubis**—Joint between left and right hipbones.

4. **Acetabulum** (as'-e-TAB-yoo-lum)—Socket that receives the head of the femur to form the hip joint; two-fifths of the acetabulum is formed by the ilium, two-fifths is formed by the ischium, and one-fifth is formed by the pubis.

Label Figure 7.11.
Again, examine the articulated skeleton. This time compare the male and female pelvis. The **pelvis** consists of the two hipbones, sacrum, and coccyx. Identify the following:

1. **Greater (false) pelvis**—Expanded portion situated above the brim of the pelvis; bounded laterally by the ilia and posteriorly by the upper sacrum.

2. **Lesser (true) pelvis**—Below and behind the brim of the pelvis; constructed of parts of the ilium, pubis, sacrum, and coccyx; contains an opening above, the **pelvic inlet,** and an opening below, the **pelvic outlet.**

K. LOWER EXTREMITIES

The bones of the **lower extremities** consist of a femur in each thigh, a patella in front of each knee joint, a tibia and fibula in each leg, tarsals in each ankle, metatarsals in each foot, and phalanges in the toes.
Examine the articulated skeleton and disarticulated bones and identify the following:

1. **Femur**—Thigh bone; longest and heaviest bone in the body.

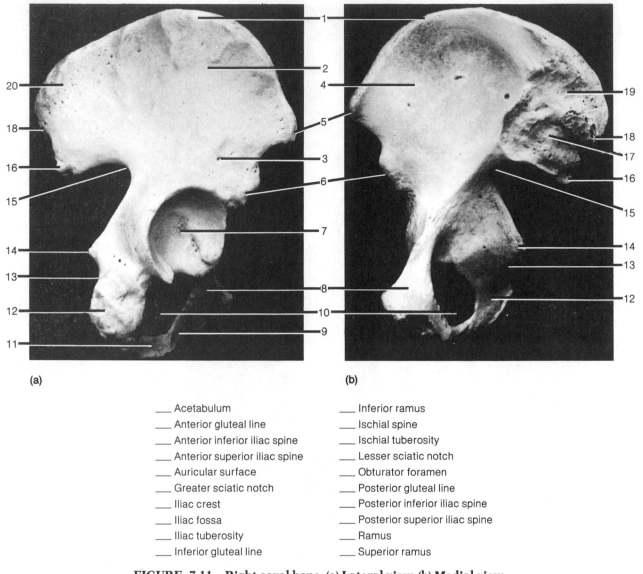

(a)   (b)

___ Acetabulum   ___ Inferior ramus
___ Anterior gluteal line   ___ Ischial spine
___ Anterior inferior iliac spine ___ Ischial tuberosity
___ Anterior superior iliac spine ___ Lesser sciatic notch
___ Auricular surface   ___ Obturator foramen
___ Greater sciatic notch   ___ Posterior gluteal line
___ Iliac crest   ___ Posterior inferior iliac spine
___ Iliac fossa   ___ Posterior superior iliac spine
___ Iliac tuberosity   ___ Ramus
___ Inferior gluteal line   ___ Superior ramus

FIGURE 7.11   Right coxal bone. (a) Lateral view. (b) Medial view.

a. **Head**—Rounded projection at proximal end that articulates with acetabulum of hip bone.

b. **Neck**—Constricted portion below head.

c. **Greater trochanter** (trō-KAN-ter)—Prominence on lateral side.

d. **Lesser trochanter**—Prominence on dorsomedial side.

e. **Intertrochanteric line**—Ridge on anterior surface.

f. **Intertrochanteric crest**—Ridge on posterior surface.

g. **Linea aspera**—Vertical ridge on posterior surface.

h. **Medial condyle**—Medial posterior projection on distal end that articulates with tibia.

i. **Lateral condyle**—Lateral posterior projection on distal end that articulates with tibia.

j. **Intercondylar fossa**—Depressed area between condyles on posterior surface.

k. **Medial epicondyle**—Projection above medial condyle.

l. **Lateral epicondyle**—Projection above lateral condyle.

m. **Patellar surface**—Between condyles on the anterior surface.

2. **Patella**—Kneecap in front of knee joint; develops in tendon of quadriceps femoris muscle.

a. **Base**—Broad superior portion.
b. **Apex**—Pointed inferior portion.
c. **Articular facets**—Articulating surfaces on posterior surface for medial and lateral condyles of femur.
3. **Tibia**—Shinbone; medial bone of leg.
a. **Lateral condyle**—Articulates with lateral condyle of femur.
b. **Medial condyle**—Articulates with medial condyle of femur.
c. **Intercondylar eminence**—Upward projection between condyles.
d. **Tibial tuberosity**—Anterior projection for attachment of patellar ligament.
e. **Medial malleolus** (mal-LĒ-ō-lus)—Distal projection that articulates with talus bone of ankle.
f. **Fibular notch**—Distal depression that articulates with the fibula.
4. **Fibula**—Lateral bone of leg.
a. **Head**—Proximal projection that articulates with tibia.
b. **Lateral malleolus**—Projection at distal end that articulates with the talus bone of ankle.
5. **Tarsus**—Seven bones of the ankle called tarsals.

a. **Posterior bones**—**Talus** and **calcaneus** (heel bone).
b. **Anterior bones**—**Cuboid, navicular (scaphoid),** and three **cuneiforms** called the first (medial), second (intermediate), and third (lateral) cuneiforms.
6. **Metatarsus**—Consists of five bones of the foot called metatarsals, numbered as follows, beginning on the medial (large toe) side: I, II, III, IV, and V metatarsals.
7. **Phalanges**—Bones of the toes, comparable to phalanges of fingers; two in each large toe (proximal and distal) and three in each small toe (proximal, middle, and distal).

Label Figure 7.12.

L. ARTICULATED SKELETON

Now that you have studied all of the bones of the body, label the entire articulated skeleton in Figure 7.13.

LABORATORY REPORT QUESTIONS (PAGE 381)

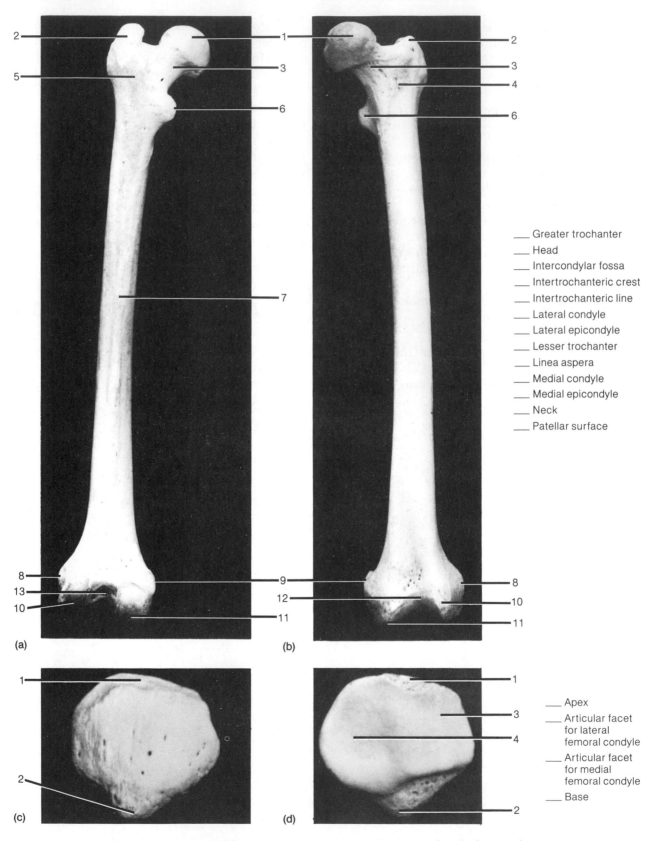

_____ Greater trochanter
_____ Head
_____ Intercondylar fossa
_____ Intertrochanteric crest
_____ Intertrochanteric line
_____ Lateral condyle
_____ Lateral epicondyle
_____ Lesser trochanter
_____ Linea aspera
_____ Medial condyle
_____ Medial epicondyle
_____ Neck
_____ Patellar surface

_____ Apex
_____ Articular facet for lateral femoral condyle
_____ Articular facet for medial femoral condyle
_____ Base

(a)　(b)　(c)　(d)

FIGURE 7.12 Bones of lower extremity. (a) Posterior view of right femur. (b) Anterior view of right femur. (c) Anterior view of right patella. (d) Posterior view of right patella.

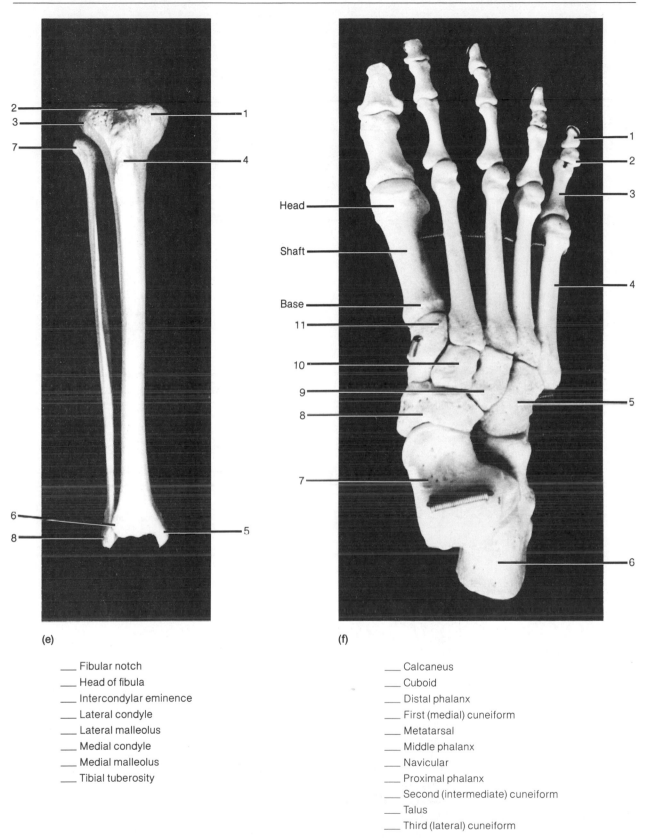

(e)

(f)

___ Fibular notch
___ Head of fibula
___ Intercondylar eminence
___ Lateral condyle
___ Lateral malleolus
___ Medial condyle
___ Medial malleolus
___ Tibial tuberosity

___ Calcaneus
___ Cuboid
___ Distal phalanx
___ First (medial) cuneiform
___ Metatarsal
___ Middle phalanx
___ Navicular
___ Proximal phalanx
___ Second (intermediate) cuneiform
___ Talus
___ Third (lateral) cuneiform

FIGURE 7.12 (*Continued*)   Bones of lower extremity. (e) Anterior view of right fibula (left side) and right tibia (right side). (f) Superior view of right foot.

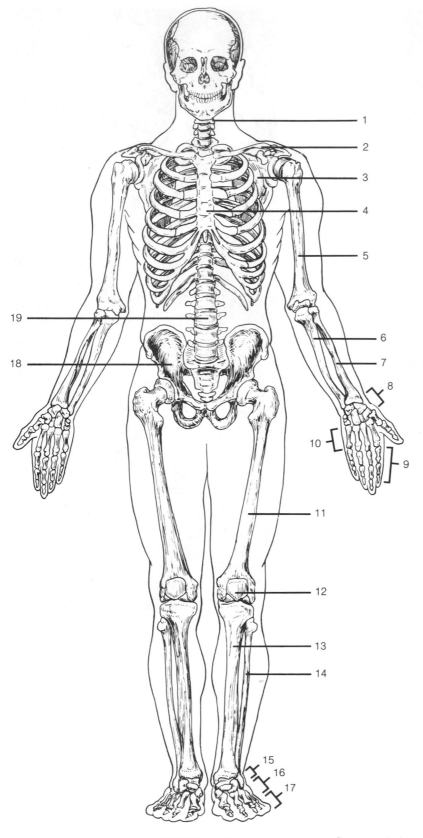

___ Carpals
___ Clavicle
___ Coxal bone
___ Femur
___ Fibula
___ Humerus
___ Hyoid bone
___ Metacarpals
___ Metatarsals
___ Patella
___ Phalanges of foot
___ Phalanges of hand
___ Radius
___ Scapula
___ Sternum
___ Tarsals
___ Tibia
___ Ulna
___ Vertebral column

FIGURE 7.13   Anterior view of entire skeleton.

8 | ARTICULATIONS

An **articulation** (ar-tik'-yoo-LĀ-shun), or **joint**, is a point of contact between bones. Some joints permit no movement, others permit a slight degree of movement, and still others permit free movement. In this exercise you will study the structure and action of joints.

A. KINDS OF JOINTS

The joints of the body may be classified into three principal kinds based on their function and structure.

The functional classification of joints is as follows:

1. **Synarthroses** (sin'-ar-THRŌ-sēz)—Immovable joints.

2. **Amphiarthroses** (am'-fē-ar-THRŌ-sēz)—Slightly movable joints.

3. **Diarthroses** (dī-ar-THRŌ-sēz)—Freely movable joints.

The structural classification of joints is as follows:

1. **Fibrous**—Allow little or no movement; do not contain synovial (joint) cavity; articulating bones held together by fibrous connective tissue.
   a. **Sutures**—Found between skull bones; bones separated by thin layer of fibrous tissue; synarthroses. Example: lambdoidal suture.
   b. **Syndesmosis** (sin'-dez-MŌ-sis)—Articulating bones united by dense fibrous tissue; amphiarthroses. Example: distal ends of tibia and fibula.

2. **Cartilaginous**—Allow little or no movement; do not contain synovial (joint) cavity; articulating bones held together by cartilage.

   a. **Synchondrosis** (sin'-kon-DRŌ-sis)—Connecting cartilage is hyaline cartilage; synarthroses. Example: epiphyseal plate.
   b. **Symphysis**—Connecting substance is a broad, flat disc of fibrocartilage; amphiarthroses. Example: intervertebral discs between vertebrae and symphysis pubis between anterior surfaces of hipbones.

3. **Synovial** (si NŌ-vē-al)—Diarthroses that contain a **synovial (joint) cavity,** a space between articulating bones (see Figure 8.1); articulating parts of the bones are covered by a thin layer of hyaline cartilage called **articular cartilage.** The synovial cavity and articulating surfaces of bones are surrounded by a sleevelike **articular capsule;** the outer layer of the articular capsule, the **fibrous capsule,** consists of collagenous connective tissue and forms ligaments that are attached to the periosteum of the articulating bones; the inner layer of the articular capsule is the **synovial membrane** that secretes synovial fluid to lubricate the joint and nourish the articular cartilage. Many synovial joints contain ligaments outside the articular capsule **(extracapsular ligaments),** such as the collateral ligament of the knee (see Figure 8.2), and ligaments within the articular capsule but outside the synovial cavity **(intracapsular ligaments),** such as the cruciate ligaments of the knee joint (see Figure 8.2). Some synovial joints contain **menisci (articular discs),** pads of fibrocartilage between articular surfaces of the bones that help to maintain the stability of the joint and direct the flow of synovial fluid to areas of greatest friction (see Figure 8.2). Some synovial joints are associated with fluid-filled connective tissue sacs called **bursae,** which cushion the movement of one part of the body over another (bursae are located between skin and bone, tendons and bone, muscles and bone,

and ligaments and bone, and between adjacent muscles [see Figure 8.2]).

The principal types of synovial joints include:

a. **Gliding**—Articulating surfaces usually flat; permits movement in two planes (biaxial movement), side to side and back and forth. Example: between carpals, tarsals, sacrum and ilium, sternum and clavicle, scapula and clavicle, and articular processes of vertebrae.

b. **Hinge**—Spool-like surface of one bone fits into the concave surface of another; movement in single plane (monaxial movement), usually flexion and extension. Example: elbow, knee, ankle, interphalangeal joints.

c. **Pivot**—Rounded, pointed, or conical surface of one bone articulates within a ring formed partly by bone and partly by a ligament; primary movement is rotation; joint is monaxial. Example: between atlas and axis and between proximal ends of radius and ulna.

d. **Ellipsoidal**—Oval-shaped condyle of one bone fits into an elliptical cavity of another bone; movement is biaxial, side to side and back and forth. Example: between radius and carpals.

e. **Saddle**—Surfaces of articulating bones are saddle-shaped, that is, concave in one direction and convex in the other; movement similar to that of an ellipsoidal joint. Example: between trapezium and metacarpal of thumb.

f. **Ball-and-socket**—Ball-like surface of one bone fits into cuplike depression of another bone; movement is in three planes (triaxial movement), flexion-extension, abduction-adduction, and rotation. Example: shoulder and hip joint.

Examine the articulated skeleton and find as many examples as you can of the joints just described. As part of your examination, be sure to note the shapes of the articular surfaces and the movements possible at each joint.

Label Figure 8.1, the principal parts of a synovial joint.

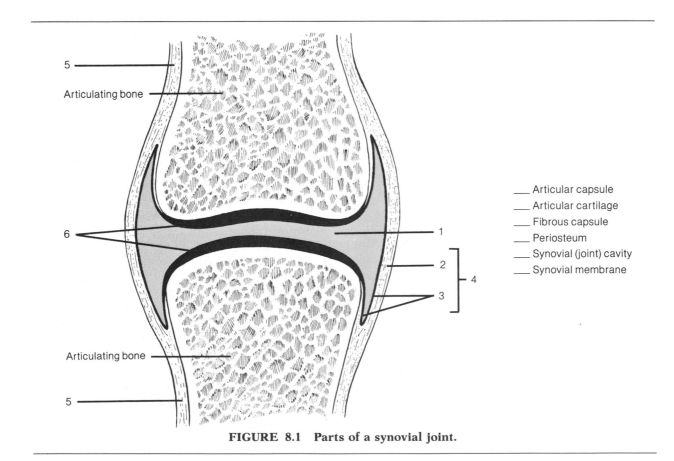

FIGURE 8.1 Parts of a synovial joint.

B. KNEE JOINT

The knee joint is one of the largest joints in the body and illustrates the basic structure of a synovial joint and the limitations on its movement. Some of the structures associated with the knee joint are as follows:

1. **Tendon of quadriceps femoris muscle**—Strengthens joint anteriorly and externally.

2. **Gastrocnemius muscle**—Strengthens joint posteriorly and externally.

3. **Patellar ligament**—Strengthens anterior portion of joint and prevents leg from being flexed too far backward.

4. **Fibular collateral ligament**—Between femur and fibula; strengthens the lateral side of the joint and prohibits side-to-side movement at the joint.

5. **Tibial collateral ligament**—Between femur and tibia; strengthens the medial side of the joint and prohibits side-to-side movement at the joint.

6. **Oblique popliteal ligament**—Starts in a tendon that lies over the tibia and runs upward and laterally to the lateral side of the femur; supports the back of the knee and prevents hyperextension.

7. **Anterior cruciate ligament**—Passes posteriorly and laterally from the tibia and attaches to the femur; strengthens the joint internally and may help stabilize the knee during its movements.

8. **Posterior cruciate ligament**—Passes anteriorly and medially from the tibia and attaches to the femur; strengthens the joint internally and may help stabilize the knee during its movements.

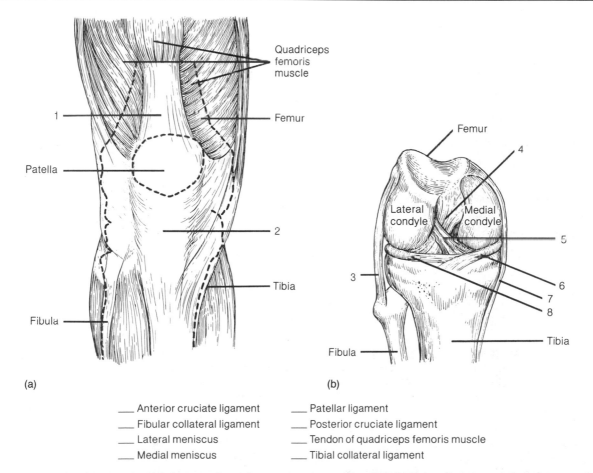

(a)   (b)

___ Anterior cruciate ligament

___ Fibular collateral ligament

___ Lateral meniscus

___ Medial meniscus

___ Patellar ligament

___ Posterior cruciate ligament

___ Tendon of quadriceps femoris muscle

___ Tibial collateral ligament

FIGURE 8.2 Ligaments, tendons, bursae, and menisci of right knee joint. (a) Anterior, superficial view. (b) Anterior view (flexed) with many superficial structures removed.

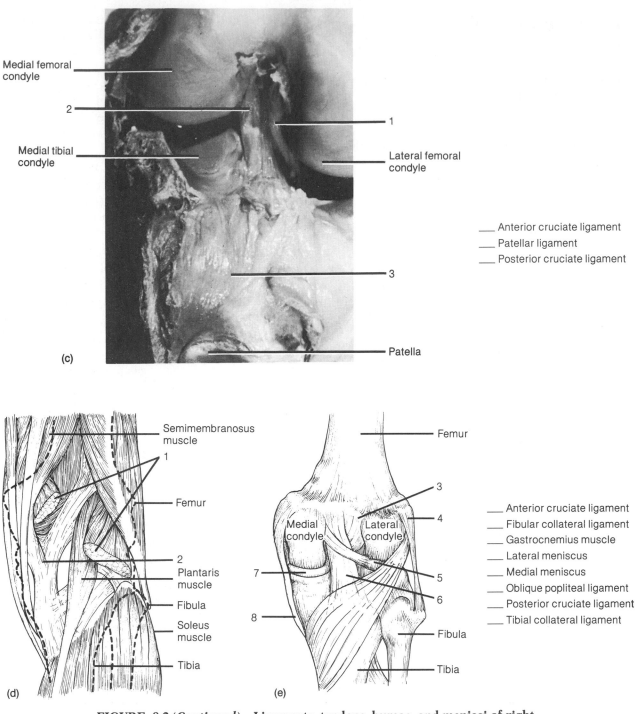

Medial femoral condyle

2

Medial tibial condyle

1

Lateral femoral condyle

___ Anterior cruciate ligament
___ Patellar ligament
___ Posterior cruciate ligament

3

Patella

(c)

Semimembranosus muscle

1

Femur

2

Plantaris muscle

Fibula

Soleus muscle

Tibia

(d)

Femur

3

4

Medial condyle

Lateral condyle

7

5

6

8

Fibula

Tibia

(e)

___ Anterior cruciate ligament
___ Fibular collateral ligament
___ Gastrocnemius muscle
___ Lateral meniscus
___ Medial meniscus
___ Oblique popliteal ligament
___ Posterior cruciate ligament
___ Tibial collateral ligament

FIGURE 8.2 (*Continued*) Ligaments, tendons, bursae, and menisci of right knee joint. (c) Photograph of internal structure. (d) Posterior, superficial view. (e) Posterior view with many superficial structures removed.

9. **Menisci**—Concentric wedge-shaped pieces of fibrocartilage between the femur and tibia; called **lateral meniscus** and the **medial meniscus**; provide support for the continuous weight placed on the knee joint.

Label the structures associated with a knee joint in Figure 8.2.

If a longitudinally sectioned knee joint of a cow or lamb is available, examine it and see how many structures you can identify.

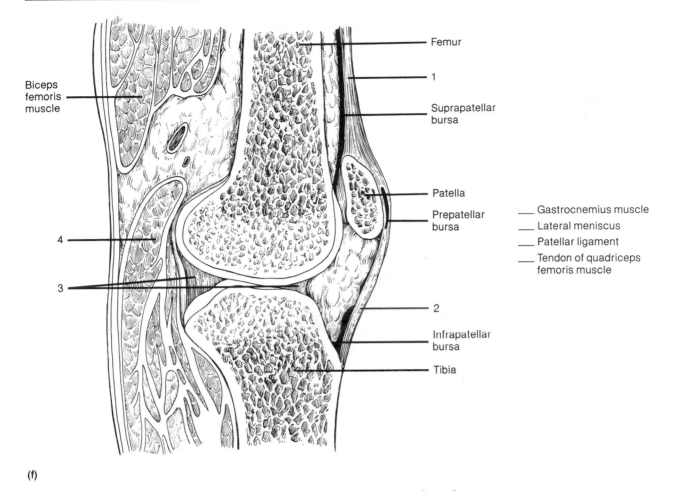

Biceps femoris muscle

Femur

1

Suprapatellar bursa

Patella

Prepatellar bursa

4

3

2

Infrapatellar bursa

Tibia

___ Gastrocnemius muscle
___ Lateral meniscus
___ Patellar ligament
___ Tendon of quadriceps femoris muscle

(f)

FIGURE 8.2 (*Continued*) Ligaments, tendons, bursae, and menisci of right knee joint. (f) Sagittal section.

C. MOVEMENTS AT SYNOVIAL JOINTS

Movements at synovial joints may be classified as follows:

1. **Gliding**—One surface moves back and forth and from side to side without any angular or rotary movement.

2. **Angular**—Increase or decrease the angle between bones.
    a. **Flexion**—Usually involves decrease in angle between anterior surfaces of articulating bones.
    b. **Dorsiflexion**—Flexion of foot at ankle joint.
    c. **Extension**—Usually involves increase in angle between anterior surfaces of articulating bones.

d. **Hyperextension**—Continuation of extension beyond the anatomical position.
    e. **Plantar flexion**—Extension of foot at ankle joint.
    f. **Abduction**—Movement of a bone away from midline.
    g. **Adduction**—Movement of a bone toward midline.

3. **Rotation**—Movement of a bone around its own longitudinal axis.

4. **Circumduction**—Movement in which the distal end of a bone moves in a circle while the proximal end remains relatively stable; bone describes a cone in the air.

5. **Special**—Found only at the joints indicated:
    a. **Inversion**—Movement of sole of foot inward at ankle joint.
    b. **Eversion**—Movement of sole of foot outward at ankle joint.

c. **Protraction**—Movement of mandible or clavicle forward on plane parallel to ground.

d. **Retraction**—Movement of protracted part of the body backward on plane parallel to ground.

e. **Supination**—Movement of forearm in which palm of hand is turned anteriorly or superiorly.

f. **Pronation**—Movement of forearm in which palm of hand is turned posteriorly or inferiorly.

g. **Depression**—Movement in which part of body moves inferiorly.

h. **Elevation**—Movement in which part of body moves superiorly.

Label the various movements illustrated in Figure 8.3.

LABORATORY REPORT QUESTIONS (PAGE 383)

(a)

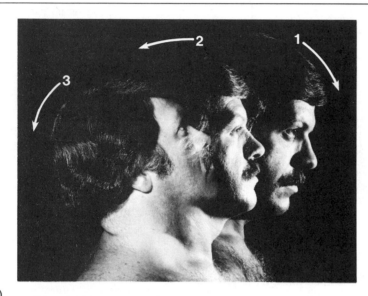

(b)

___ Abduction
___ Adduction
___ Circumduction
___ Depression
___ Extension
___ Extension
___ Eversion
___ Flexion
___ Flexion
___ Flexion
___ Hyperextension
___ Hyperextension
___ Plantar flexion
___ Protraction
___ Rotation

FIGURE 8.3 Movements at synovial joints.

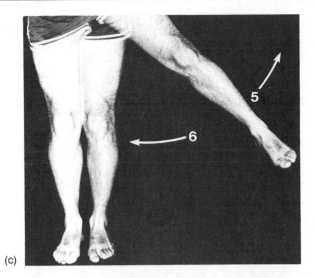

(c)

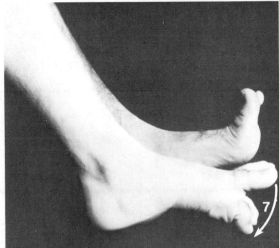

(d)

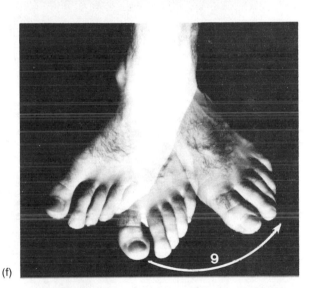

(e)

(f)

(g)

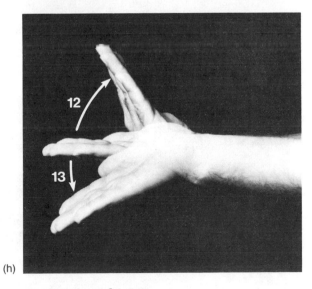

(h)

FIGURE 8.3 (*Continued*) Movements at synovial joints.

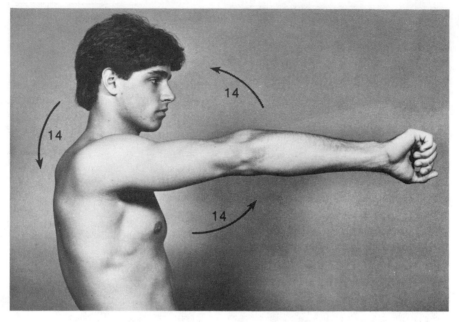

(i)

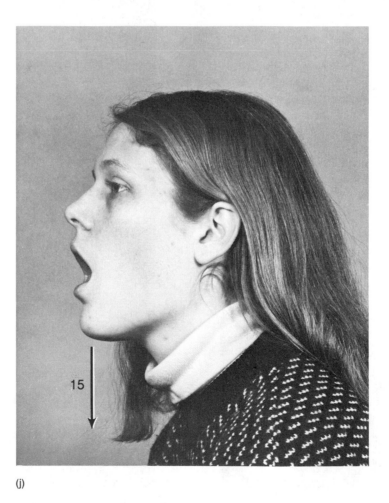

(j)

FIGURE 8.3 (*Continued*) **Movements at synovial joints.**

9 | MUSCLE TISSUE

Muscle tissue constitutes 40% to 50% of total body weight and is composed of cells that are highly specialized with respect to four characteristics: (1) **excitability,** or ability to receive and respond to stimuli; (2) **contractility,** or ability to contract (shorten and thicken); (3) **extensibility (extension),** or ability to stretch when pulled; and (4) **elasticity,** or ability to return to original shape after contraction or extension. Through contraction, muscle performs three basic functions: motion, maintenance of posture, and heat production. In this exercise you will examine the histological structure of muscle tissue and conduct exercises on the physiology of frog muscle.

A. KINDS OF MUSCLE TISSUE

Histologically, three kinds of muscle tissue are recognized:

1. **Skeletal muscle tissue**—Usually attached to bones; contains conspicuous striations when viewed microscopically; voluntary because it contracts under conscious control.

2. **Smooth muscle tissue**—Located in walls of viscera and blood vessels; referred to as nonstriated because it lacks striations; involuntary because it contracts without conscious control.

3. **Cardiac muscle tissue**—Found only in the wall of the heart; striated; involuntary.

B. SKELETAL MUSCLE TISSUE

Examine a prepared slide of skeletal muscle in longitudinal and cross section under high power. Look for the following:

1. **Sarcolemma**—Plasma membrane of the fiber (cell).

2. **Sarcoplasm**—Cytoplasm of the fiber.

3. **Nuclei**—Several in each fiber lying close to sarcolemma.

4. **Striations**—Cross stripes in each fiber.

5. **Endomysium** (en'-dō-MĪZ-ē-um)—Fibrous connective tissue between fibers.

6. **Perimysium** (per'-i-MĪZ-ē-um)—Fibrous connective tissue surrounding a bundle (fascicle) of fibers.

Refer to Figure 9.1 and label the structures indicated.

With the use of an electron microscope, additional details of skeletal muscle tissue may be noted. Among these are the following:

1. **Mitochondria**—Organelles that have smooth outer membrane and folded inner membrane.

2. **Sarcoplasmic reticulum**—Tubelike network of roughly parallel sacs.

3. **T tubules**—Run perpendicular to and connect with reticulum; open to outside of the fiber.

4. **Triad**—T tubule and the segments of sarcoplasmic reticulum on both sides.

5. **Myofibrils**—Threadlike structures that run longitudinally through a fiber and consist of **thin myofilaments** composed of the protein actin and **thick myofilaments** composed of the protein myosin.

6. **Sarcomere**—Compartments within a muscle fiber formed by separations of zones of dense material called **Z lines.**

7. **A band**—Dark region in a sarcomere where actin and myosin myofilaments overlap.

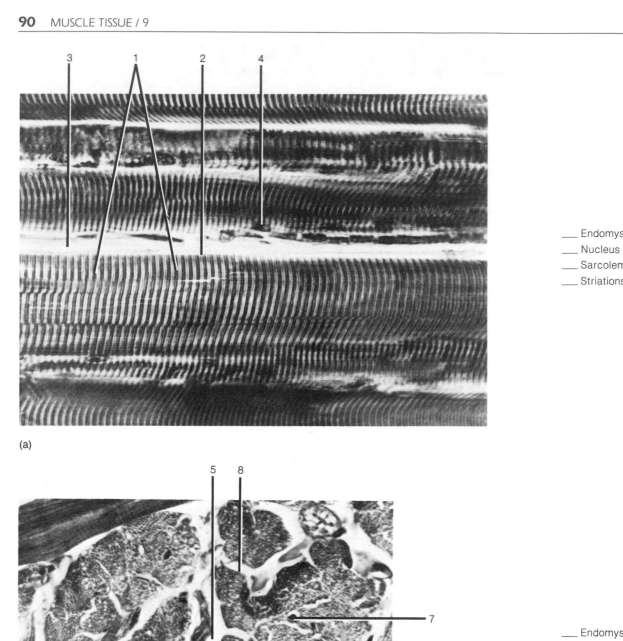

(a)

___ Endomysium
___ Nucleus
___ Sarcolemma
___ Striations

(b)

___ Endomysium
___ Nucleus
___ Perimysium
___ Sarcolemma

FIGURE 9.1   Histology of skeletal muscle tissue. (a) Photomicrograph of several muscle fibers in longitudinal section. (b) Photomicrograph of several muscle fibers in cross section.

8. **I band**—Light region in a sarcomere composed of actin myofilaments only.

9. **H zone**—Region in a sarcomere consisting of myosin myofilaments only.

10. **M line**—Series of fine threads in the center of the H zone that appear to connect the middle parts of adjacent thick myofilaments.

Figure 9.2 is a diagram of skeletal muscle tissue based on electron micrographic studies. Label the structures shown.

C. SMOOTH MUSCLE TISSUE

Examine a prepared slide of smooth muscle tissue in longitudinal and cross section under high power. Locate and label the following

structures in Figure 9.3: **sarcolemma, sarcoplasm, nucleus,** and **muscle fiber.**

D. CARDIAC MUSCLE TISSUE

Examine a prepared slide of cardiac muscle tissue in longitudinal and cross section under high power. Locate the following structures: **sarcolemma, endomysium, nuclei, striations,** and **intercalated discs** (transverse thickenings of the sarcolemma that separate individual fibers). Label Figure 9.4.

E. PHYSIOLOGY OF MUSCLE CONTRACTION

The process of skeletal muscle contraction involves a series of both electrical and chemical

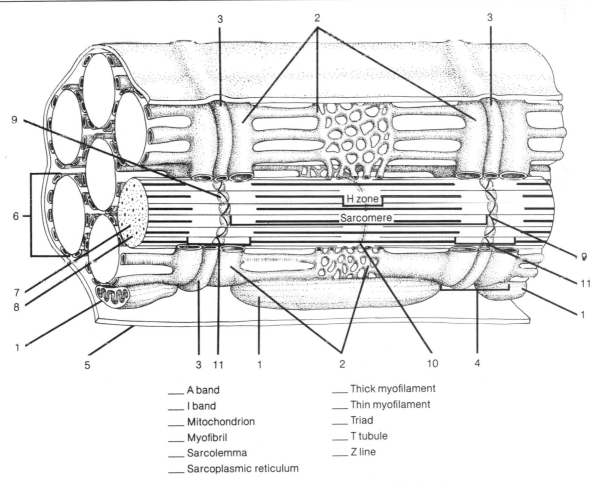

H zone

Sarcomere

___ A band	___ Thick myofilament
___ I band	___ Thin myofilament
___ Mitochondrion	___ Triad
___ Myofibril	___ T tubule
___ Sarcolemma	___ Z line
___ Sarcoplasmic reticulum	

FIGURE 9.2 Enlarged aspect of several myofibrils of skeletal muscle tissue based on an electron micrograph.

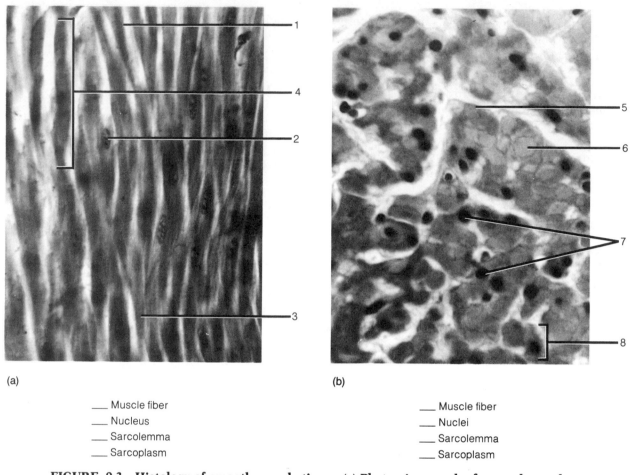

(a)   (b)

___ Muscle fiber   ___ Muscle fiber
___ Nucleus   ___ Nuclei
___ Sarcolemma   ___ Sarcolemma
___ Sarcoplasm   ___ Sarcoplasm

FIGURE 9.3   Histology of smooth muscle tissue. (a) Photomicrograph of several muscle fibers in longitudinal section. (b) Photomicrograph of several muscle fibers in cross section.

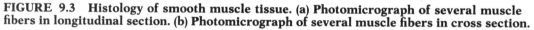

events. Muscle contraction occurs only if the muscle is properly stimulated. In the body this is accomplished by a nerve impulse transmitted via a nerve cell called a **motor neuron.** The portion of the motor neuron that extends from the nerve cell body to a muscle is called an **axon.** Upon entering a skeletal muscle, an axon branches into axon terminals (**telodendria**) that come into close approximation with the sarcolemma of a muscle fiber. Such an area of close approximation consisting of the axon terminal of a motor neuron and the portion of the sarcolemma near it is called a **neuromuscular (myoneural) junction** or **motor end plate** (see Figure 9.5).

Close examination of a neuromuscular junction reveals that the distal ends of the axon terminals are expanded into bulblike structures called **synaptic end bulbs.** The bulbs contain membrane-enclosed sacs, called **synaptic vesicles,** that store chemicals called neurotrans-

mitters. If these chemicals are released from the vesicles, they transmit a nerve impulse to a muscle, gland, or another nerve cell. The invaginated area of the sarcolemma under the axon terminal is referred to as a **synaptic gutter (trough);** the space between the axon terminal and sarcolemma is known as a **synaptic cleft.** Along the synaptic gutter are numerous folds of the sarcolemma, called **subneural clefts,** which greatly increase the surface area of the synaptic gutter.

In a skeletal neuromuscular junction, the nerve impulse reaches the end of an axon, causing synaptic vesicles in the axon terminal to release a neurotransmitter called **acetylcholine** (as'-ē-til-KŌ-lēn) or **ACh.** This substance transmits the nerve impulse from the axon terminal across the synaptic cleft to the sarcolemma of the muscle fiber. The nerve impulse travels along the sarcolemma and into the interior of the muscle fiber via the T tubules, causing the

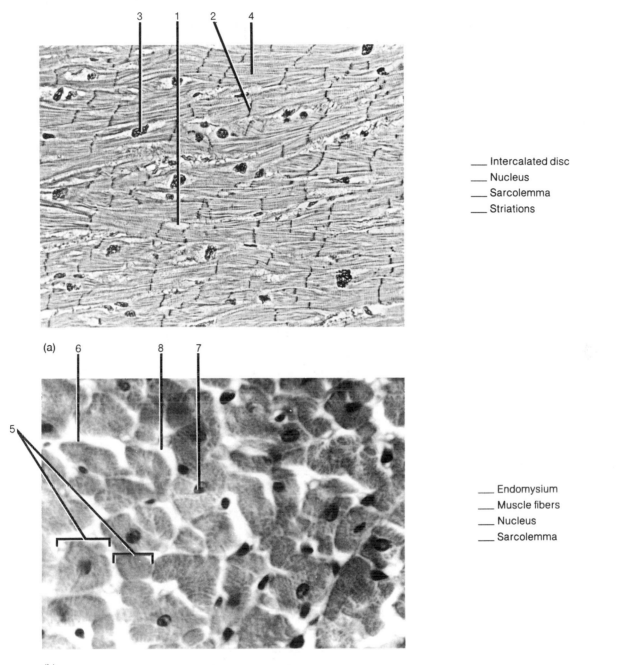

_____ Intercalated disc
_____ Nucleus
_____ Sarcolemma
_____ Striations

_____ Endomysium
_____ Muscle fibers
_____ Nucleus
_____ Sarcolemma

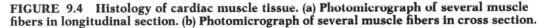

FIGURE 9.4 Histology of cardiac muscle tissue. (a) Photomicrograph of several muscle fibers in longitudinal section. (b) Photomicrograph of several muscle fibers in cross section.

sarcoplasmic reticulum to release calcium ions among thin myofilaments (actin) and thick myofilaments (myosin). As myosin cross-bridges of the thick myofilaments attach to receptors on the thin myofilaments, ATP is split. Energy thus released causes myosin cross-bridges to move, and thin myofilaments slide inward toward the H zone, causing the muscle fiber to shorten. This action is referred to as the **sliding filament theory** of muscle contraction (see Figure 9.6). After replacement of ATP on thick myofilaments and removal of calcium ions by sarcoplasmic reticulum, the cross-bridges release and relaxation occurs.

A contracting skeletal muscle fiber follows the **all-or-none principle.** Simply stated, this

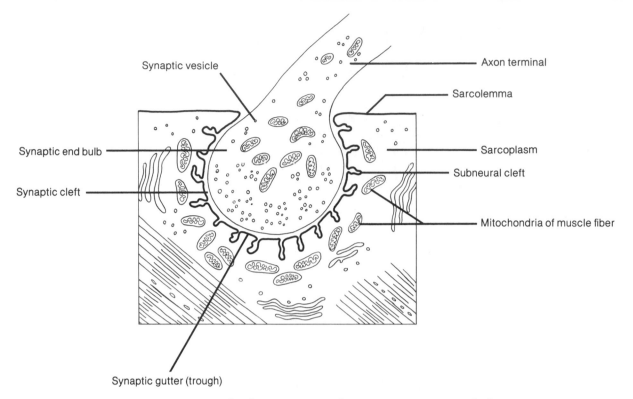

Synaptic vesicle

Axon terminal

Sarcolemma

Synaptic end bulb

Sarcoplasm

Subneural cleft

Synaptic cleft

Mitochondria of muscle fiber

Synaptic gutter (trough)

FIGURE 9.5   Details of a neuromuscular junction (motor end plate).

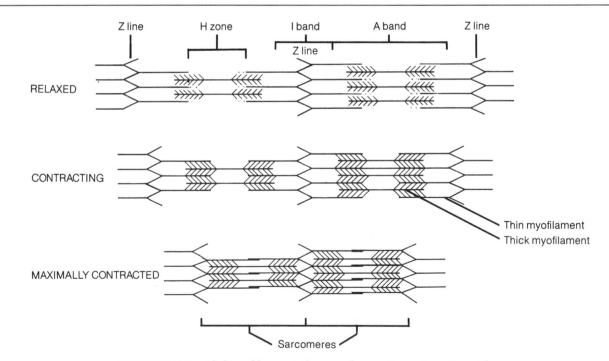

Z line   H zone   I band   A band   Z line

Z line

RELAXED

CONTRACTING

Thin myofilament
Thick myofilament

MAXIMALLY CONTRACTED

Sarcomeres

FIGURE 9.6   Sliding filament theory of muscle contraction. The positions of the various parts of two sarcomeres in relaxed, contracting, and maximally contracted states are shown. Note movement of thin myofilaments and relative size of H zone.

principle says that a properly stimulated skeletal muscle fiber will either contract maximally or not at all. This principle, however, does not imply that the entire muscle must be either fully relaxed or fully contracted because some of its many fibers will be contracting while others are relaxing. Thus, the muscle as a whole can have graded contractions.

With these facts in mind, you will now perform a few simple lab tests that will illustrate muscle contraction.

F. BIOCHEMISTRY OF MUSCLE CONTRACTION

You will examine the effect of the following solutions on the contraction of glycerinated muscle fibers:[1] (1) ATP solution, (2) mineral ion solution, and (3) ATP plus mineral ion solution.

1. Using $7\times$ to $10\times$ magnification and glass needles or clean stainless steel forceps, gently tease the muscle into very thin groups of myofibers, the muscle cells. Single cells or thin groups must be used because strands thicker than a silk thread curl when they contract.

2. Mount one strand in a drop of glycerol on a clean glass slide and cover the preparation with a cover slip. A Pasteur pipette or dropper is best for transferring the fibers. Examine the strand under low and high power and note the striations. Also note that each cell has several nuclei.

3. Transfer one of the thinnest strands to a drop of glycerol on a second microscope slide. Do not add a cover slip. If the amount of glycerol on the slide is more than a small drop, soak the excess into a piece of lens paper held at the edge of the glycerol farthest from the fibers. Using a dissecting microscope and a millimeter ruler held beneath the slide, measure the length of one of the fibers.

4. Now flood the fibers with the solution containing ATP only and observe their reaction. After 30 seconds or more, remeasure the same fiber.

How much did the fiber contract? ___ mm.

5. Using clean slides and pipettes, and being especially sure to use clean teasing needles or

forceps, transfer other fibers to a drop of glycerol on a slide. Again measure the length of one fiber. Next flood the fibers with a solution containing mineral ions, observe their reaction, and remeasure the fiber.

How much did the fiber contract? ___ mm.

6. Repeat the exercise, this time using a solution containing a combination of ATP and ions.

7. Observe a contracted fiber under low and high power, and look for differences in appearance between muscle in a contracted and that in a relaxed state (see Figure 9.6).

G. LABORATORY TESTS ON MUSCLE CONTRACTION[2]

Skeletal muscles produce different kinds of contractions depending on the stimulus applied. Among these contractions are isotonic, isometric, tonic, twitch, tetanic, and treppe. Twitch contractions do not occur in the body but are worth demonstrating because they show the different phases of muscle contraction quite clearly. Any record of a muscle contraction is called a **myogram.**

You may test muscle contraction through a team exercise or by observing a demonstration prepared by your instructor. Read the sections that follow on pithing a frog, preparing muscle or nerve-muscle preparations, and using a kymograph or a physiograph (whichever you have in your lab) *before* you do the exercise or observe the demonstration. Depending on the size of the class and the equipment available, you should work in teams of three to five students. One or two students should be assigned to assist the instructor to set up the physiologic apparatus, one or two other students should be assigned as "surgeons" to isolate, remove, and suspend the frog muscle, and another student should act as the recorder and coordinate the work.

1. Pithing of Frogs

By definition, *pithing* is destruction of the central nervous system by piercing the brain or

---

[1]Glycerinated muscle preparation and solutions are supplied by the Carolina Biological Supply Company, Burlington, North Carolina 27215.

[2]These tests involve skeletal muscle tissue only. Tests on cardiac muscle tissue are included in Exercise 19 (Cardiovascular Physiology) and tests on smooth muscle in Exercise 22 (Digestive System). At the discretion of the instructor, muscle tissue tests may be done in individual exercises or combined into a single exercise.

spinal cord. This procedure is used in animal experimentation to render the animal unconscious so that it feels no pain. A single-pithed frog is one in which only the brain is destroyed, whereas a double-pithed frog has its spinal cord destroyed too. Usually the double-pithing procedure is used.

1. Hold the frog in a paper towel with its dorsal side up and with the index finger pressing the nose down so that the head makes a right angle with the trunk.

2. Locate the slight depression formed by the first vertebra and the skull about 3 mm behind the line joining the posterior borders of the tympanic membrane. This groove represents the area of the foramen magnum.

3. To single-pith the frog, carefully insert a long sharp-tipped needle or probe into the foramen magnum and direct it forward and a little downward.

4. Exert a steady pressure and rotate it, moving it from side to side in the cranial cavity to destroy the brain.

5. To double-pith the frog, insert the needle into the vertebral canal, directing it downward until it has reached the end of the canal. Move the needle from side to side as you go (see Figure 9.7).

2. Physiograph

The **physiograph** (see Figure 9.8), more commonly called the polygraph, records physiological events. The machine works by receiving a signal from a sensing device, amplifying it, and changing it into a perceptible form. For example, a sensing device called a myograph transducer measures the force exerted by a contracting muscle and converts this mechanical force into an electrical signal. This signal is magnified by the amplifier and then changed into perceptible form by a writing pen that makes a permanent, visible record of the contraction. This method of recording an event resembles a phonograph system in which the needle receives the vibrations from the record and changes them into electrical signals, the amplifier magnifies these electrical signals, and the loudspeaker changes the electrical signals into perceptible form.

A physiograph usually has a number of recording channels. Each is used to record a par-

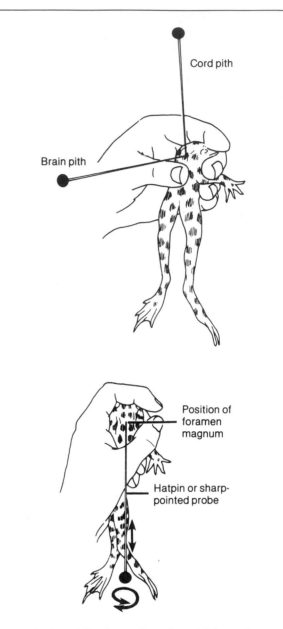

FIGURE 9.7 Procedure for pithing a frog.

ticular physiological event as it occurs. Different physiological events may be recorded simultaneously by using different channels. Each channel consists of a sensing device to detect the event, a coupler to join the sensing device to the amplifier, an amplifier, and a writing pen to make a record of what happened. A fifth pen, marked TIME AND EVENTS, is used to keep track of time and to mark the points at which stimuli are delivered. This time pen is the lowest pen on the instrument. The other pens are numbered to correspond to the recording channel with which they work.

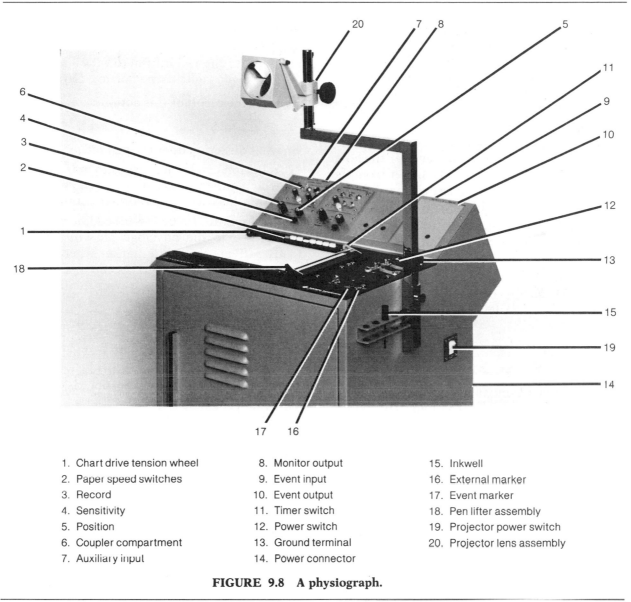

1. Chart drive tension wheel
2. Paper speed switches
3. Record
4. Sensitivity
5. Position
6. Coupler compartment
7. Auxiliary input

8. Monitor output
9. Event input
10. Event output
11. Timer switch
12. Power switch
13. Ground terminal
14. Power connector

15. Inkwell
16. External marker
17. Event marker
18. Pen lifter assembly
19. Projector power switch
20. Projector lens assembly

FIGURE 9.8 A physiograph.

Either electrodes or a transducer can serve as the sensing device for the physiograph. **Electrodes** are made of metal plates or small rods that can detect electrophysiological phenomena such as changes in electrical potential of the skin or nerves. Electrodes transmit the original electrical signal without change to the amplifier. In many cases a transducer must be used as the sensing device. The **transducer** converts nonelectrical signals into electrical signals: for example, the myograph transducer already mentioned converts mechanical force from a muscle contraction into an electrical signal; a heat transducer converts heat into an electrical signal; and a pressure transducer converts pressure changes into an electrical signal.

a. ORIENTATION TO THE PHYSIOGRAPH AND RELATED ACCESSORIES

Plug the physiograph into an electrical outlet. Turn on the master switch and the power switch on one of the amplifiers. (If you have a Model 7000 Amplifier, the amplifiers are on when the master switch is on.) The power switch is located at the bottom left corner of the amplifier.

Ink Supply

1. Check to see that the ink wells are no more than half full. Position the ink wells so that the ink level is even with the level of the flat paper table of the physiograph.

2. Send ink to the pens by placing a finger over the hole in the top of the ink bottle and squeezing very gently until a drop of ink appears at the pen point. You must remove your finger before you stop squeezing the bottle or the ink will not remain in the pen assembly.

3. At the conclusion of the exercise, empty the pens by reversing the above sequence, that is, squeeze the bottle, place a finger over the hole, stop squeezing, and remove the finger from the hole when the ink has been entirely withdrawn from the tubing assembly feeding the pens.

4. A watch glass containing water should be placed under the pen point when you empty the pens so that water will be drawn into the pen assembly as the ink is being withdrawn. Ink is fed by gravity pull. Therefore, if the ink is not flowing adequately (is too light), raise the ink well 3 mm.

Paper and Paper Controls

The paper drive control along the back edge of the flat paper table sets the paper in motion and lowers the pens.

1. Move the paper drive control to the left. Note that the paper will move only if the leading edge of the paper is under the turning wheel.

2. The speed of the paper can be controlled by the knob marked CM/SEC—PAPER SPEED. Change the settings and observe the speed. Reuse this paper in the next steps.

3. The paper can be pulled back into the body of the unit if the cabinet door below the flat paper table is opened.

4. While you have the cabinet door open, observe the manner in which the paper is guided through the slot onto the flat paper table of the physiograph.

5. Pull the paper all the way out and practice reloading. You should observe that the physiograph paper is ruled in metric units, usually in either 5-mm squares or 1-mm squares.

Time and Event Marker

A knob to the right of the paper speed knob controls the time and event marker.

1. Turn it on at the lowest setting, 1 SEC. Observe the fifth pen and determine how often the

pen deflects and in what direction the pen moves.

2. Depress the red button (EVENT MARKER) at the lower right corner of the physiograph.

What is the result of this action? _____

_____

In what direction does the pen move? _____
This button can be depressed to mark the time at which either an event occurred or an external stimulus was delivered to the subject.

3. A stimulator (to be discussed later) properly connected to the physiograph will automatically activate the event marker when each single stimulus is delivered. (Some models of stimulator also mark when continuous stimuli are delivered.)

4. The time marker can be set at intervals of 0 (time marker is off), 1, 5, 30, or 60 seconds. Every 60 seconds the time marker skips a mark, which indicates that a minute has passed during the recording of the experiment.

5. Practice using the timer and the external event marker.

Amplifiers

The amplifier units are located in the upper portion of the physiograph. Each amplifier controls one specific pen, which is numbered identically to the amplifier controlling it. Examples of solid state amplifiers are shown in Figure 9.8. Each amplifier has several switches.

1. The on-off switch (in lower left corner) must be ON for the unit to be operational. This will be indicated by the red signal light.

2. The record switch must be placed in RECORD phase to record data. When out of RECORD phase, the record switch disconnects the amplifier from the sensing device. *The record switch must be disengaged before any connections are made to the physiograph. Otherwise, fuses will blow and light bulbs will burn out.* The record switch must also be disengaged unless actual recording is taking place. In solid state models, engage the record switch by depressing the clear button; it will light.

3. The position control situates the pen on the paper. Rotate this control and observe the movement of the pen.

4. The sensitivity (amplitude) control determines the amount of amplification of the in-

coming signal. If the amplification is low, the magnitude of the pen deflection will be small. If the amplification is increased, the magnitude of the pen deflection will also increase. This control is the one used to calibrate the size of pen deflection when a known signal is presented. As you increase the sensitivity, you also increase the susceptibility of the system to outside disturbances.

5. The filter control (Model 7070 only) is generally only used in research work and should be left in the 10K position.

6. The polarity switch (Model 7070 only) should be set to positive (+) unless measuring electrophysiological events (for example, electrocardiography, electroencephalography). When measuring electrophysiological events, the switch should be set to the negative (−) position.

Preamplifiers and Couplers

A coupler is a module in a solid state system that links a sensing device to its amplifier. If preamplification is necessary, the coupler also acts in this capacity. In solid state systems the sensitivity control on the amplifier remains operational because the signal often must be amplified a second time.

Transducers

Transducers are elements of the system that convert nonelectrical signals into electrical signals. Transducers are usually connected to the amplifier by a cable; however, they are occasionally connected directly to the amplifier.

1. Look at the 9-pin cable and note that when the pins of the cable are aligned with the input socket, the yellow dot on the pin is aligned with the yellow dot on the socket.

2. If the yellow dots are not properly aligned, a broken connector may result.

b. CALIBRATION OF THE SYSTEM

1. Suspend a 100-g weight from the muscle transducer and adjust the sensitivity of the amplifier so that a 5-cm pen deflection is obtained.

2. If at any time this calibration proves unsatisfactory, change the sensitivity to best fit the situation. *Record the calibration factor* for future reference during this experiment.

3. Experimental Preparation

a. ISOLATED MUSCLE PREPARATION

The gastrocnemius muscle of the frog is commonly used in the laboratory to demonstrate muscle contraction.

1. After double-pithing the frog, cut the leg off two-thirds of the way up the thigh. Completely remove the skin at the ankle, and gently pull it loose up over the foot.

2. Cut the calcaneal (Achilles) tendon as far down over the ankle as possible and then gently pull the gastrocnemius free from the lower leg.

3. Cut through the lower leg so as to leave the gastrocnemius muscle attached to the femur, and carefully cut away the severed muscle of the upper leg.

4. The muscle preparation consists of the gastrocnemius muscle, with its calcaneal tendon, attached to the bare lower half of the femur. The other gastrocnemius muscle should not be removed until needed. The gastrocnemius muscle is shown in Figure 9.9.

5. Place the muscle preparation in the apparatus with the bone held firmly in a femur clamp and the tendon connected to a muscle trans-

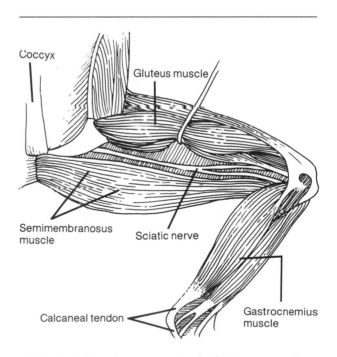

FIGURE 9.9 Structures in the lower extremity of the frog seen in posterior view.

ducer by means of an S-pin stuck through the tendon (see Figure 9.10).

6. Remember that an isolated skeletal muscle has no blood supply. Therefore moisten the muscle with Ringer's solution frequently and follow procedures carefully.

7. Adjust the height of the femur clamp so that the muscle has a slight amount of tension on it.

b. NERVE-MUSCLE PREPARATION

Another preparation that may be substituted for the isolated muscle preparation procedure is the nerve-muscle preparation. In this preparation the nerve innervating the gastrocnemius muscle is stimulated rather than directly stimulating the muscle.

1. Double-pith the frog and pin it down onto a frog board in the prone position. Remove the skin from the entire lower appendage by first making a cut around the upper leg and pulling the skin down over the ankle.

2. Cut the calcaneal tendon as far down over the ankle as possible and then gently pull the gastrocnemius free from the lower leg.

3. Cut through the lower leg so as to leave the gastrocnemius muscle attached to the femur. Gently spread the gluteus muscle from the semimembranosus muscle and expose the sciatic nerve (see Figure 9.9).

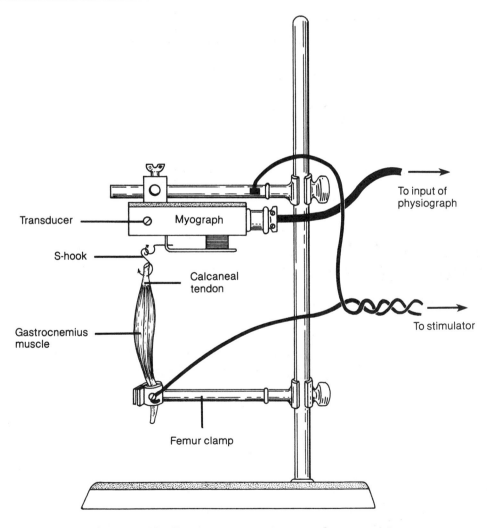

FIGURE 9.10 Frog gastrocnemius muscle preparation.

4. *Do not stretch the nerve, and avoid any unnecessary contact between the nerve, metal instruments, and other tissues.*

5. Gently place a ligature under the nerve. *Do not tie.* Utilize this ligature to place the stimulating electrodes under the nerve. Gently lower the nerve to lie over the electrode tips.

6. Attach the muscle to a transducer via an S-pin stuck through the calcaneal tendon. Periodically moisten the gastrocnemius muscle and sciatic nerve with Ringer's solution.

7. Adjust the height of the muscle transducer so that a slight amount of tension is placed upon the muscle.

4. Demonstration of Threshold Stimulus

1. With the physiograph set at its lowest paper speed and the stimulus intensity knob placed at its minimum setting, apply a single stimulus to the muscle by utilizing the single stimulus key.

2. Record the stimulus strength on the physiograph paper by the pen mark made by the event marker.

3. Soak the muscle preparation with Ringer's solution between each stimulus.

4. In a stepwise manner increase the stimulus intensity and determine when a threshold strength stimulus has been reached.

5. Once threshold has been determined, continue to increase the stimulus strength in a stepwise manner until a maximum strength contraction has been obtained.

6. If skeletal muscle obeys the all-or-none principle, are the results obtained in this procedure a contradiction to this principle?

7. Include your results and response in the Laboratory Report Results on page 385.

5. Single Muscle Twitch

1. With the physiograph set at its fastest paper speed, record a single muscle contraction resulting from a suprathreshold stimulus.

2. Calculate the latent period, contraction period, and relaxation period.

3. After rinsing the muscle with Ringer's solution, repeat this procedure several times.

4. Rinse the muscle after each procedure. Calculate the average for each value.

5. Place one tracing in the Laboratory Report Results and record the average values.

6. Effect of Fatigue on a Single Muscle Twitch

1. *Familiarize yourself with the entire procedure before starting.* Set the physiograph at its lowest paper speed. Using a frequency of 60 per second and the multiple stimulus setting, stimulate the muscle until it fatigues. (Fatigue is demonstrated when the contraction strength is reduced by 50% or more as compared to the initial contraction strength.)

2. Upon onset of fatigue, rapidly turn the stimulator off, set the paper speed at its highest level, and stimulate the muscle with a single suprathreshold stimulus.

3. *Do not* rinse the muscle with Ringer's solution.

4. Obtain several additional single muscle twitches, and calculate the average latent period, contraction period, and relaxation period.

5. Place one tracing in the Laboratory Report Results and record the average values.

6. Compare these values to those obtained in Section 5, Single Muscle Twitch. Explain any differences seen between the two tracings in the space provided in the Laboratory Report Results.

7. Before proceeding to the next section discard the muscle utilized up to this point and replace it with a fresh muscle. Quickly determine threshold for this new preparation.

7. Muscle Response to Variation of Stimulus Frequency

When a single threshold or suprathreshold stimulus is applied to either a single skeletal muscle fiber or a complete muscle, the contraction response follows the all-or-none principle. However, if two stimuli are applied in rapid succession so that the second stimulus is applied before complete relaxation from the first, one notices that the second contraction is greater than the first. Such a response is seen in either single skeletal muscle fibers or a whole muscle. The extent of the increased response to the second stimulus is dependent upon the interval between the successive stimuli, as long as the interval between the two stimuli is greater than the refractory period for that fiber or muscle. This response to increased stimulus frequency, termed **treppe** or **wave summation,** does not follow the all-or-none principle, and is due to increased amounts of calcium ions accumulating within the muscle fiber after successive stimuli. If you were to continue to increase the stimulus frequency you would note that the amount of relaxation between successive stimuli would progressively decrease until further stimuli would not increase the strength of contraction and no relaxation would be seen. This response would be termed **tetanus.** During tetanus the contraction strength may be three or four times that seen with a single contraction.

1. Set the paper speed at a medium value.

2. Turn the stimulus frequency knob to 1 per second and set the stimulator mode selector switch to repetitive stimuli.

3. Progressively increase the frequency in a stepwise manner until wave summation and tetany are observed. Record the frequencies at which summation and tetany occur.

4. Turn the stimulator off and bathe the muscle with Ringer's solution frequently.

5. Allow 2 to 3 minutes of recovery time before proceeding to the next section.

8. Effect of Resting Length Upon Contraction Strength

1. Adjust either the femur clamp or muscle transducer height (depending upon the preparation used) so that a minimal amount of resting tension is applied to the muscle.

2. With the paper drive set at its lowest speed, apply a single suprathreshold stimulus to the muscle. Observe the contraction strength.

3. Rinse the muscle with Ringer's solution after each stimulation.

4. Adjust the level of the femur clamp or transducer so that the resting tension is increased slightly. Stimulate again with a single stimulus and rinse. Observe the contraction strength at this new resting tension.

5. Repeat until the contraction strength has reached a maximum and started to decline.

6. Graph your results in the Laboratory Report Results. Explain your findings in the space provided.

LABORATORY REPORT QUESTIONS (PAGE 387)

10 | SKELETAL MUSCLES

In this exercise you will learn the names, locations, and actions of the principal skeletal muscles of the body.

A. NAMING SKELETAL MUSCLES

Most of the almost 700 skeletal muscles of the body are named on the basis of one or more distinctive criteria. If you understand these criteria, you will find it much easier to learn and remember the names of individual muscles. Some muscles are named on the basis of the **direction of the muscle fibers**, for example, *rectus* (meaning straight), *transverse*, and *oblique*. Rectus fibers run parallel to some imaginary line, usually the midline of the body, transverse fibers run perpendicular to the line, and oblique fibers run diagonal to the line. Muscles named according to the direction their fibers run include the rectus abdominis, transversus abdominis, and external oblique. Another criterion employed is **location.** For example, the temporalis is so named because of its proximity to the temporal bone, and the tibialis anterior is located near the tibia. **Size** is also commonly employed. For instance, *maximus* means largest, *minimus* means smallest, *longus* refers to long, and *brevis* refers to short. Examples include the gluteus maximus, gluteus minimus, adductor longus, and peroneus brevis.

Some muscles, such as biceps, triceps, and quadriceps, are named on the basis of the **number of origins** they have. For instance, the biceps has two origins, the triceps three, and the quadriceps four. Other muscles are named on the basis of **shape.** Common examples include the deltoid (meaning triangular) and trapezius (meaning trapezoid). Muscles may also be named after their **insertion** and their **origin.** Two such examples are the sternocleidomastoid (originates on sternum and clavicle and inserts at mastoid process of temporal bone), and the stylohyoid (originates on styloid process of temporal bone and inserts at the hyoid bone).

Still another basis for naming muscles is **action.** Listed here are the principal actions of muscles, their definitions, and examples of muscles that perform the actions.

Flexor—Usually decreases the anterior angle at a joint. Example: flexor carpi radialis.

Extensor—Usually increases the anterior angle at a joint. Example: extensor carpi ulnaris.

Abductor—Moves a bone away from the midline. Example: abductor hallucis longus.

Adductor—Moves a bone closer to the midline. Example: adductor longus.

Levator—Produces an upward or superiorly directed movement. Example: levator scapulae.

Depressor—Produces a downward or inferiorly directed movement. Example: depressor labii inferioris.

Supinator—Turns the palm upward or to the anterior. Example: supinator.

Pronator—Turns the palm downward or to the posterior. Example: pronator teres.

Plantar flexor—Extends the ankle joint. Example: plantaris.

Sphincter—Decreases the size of an opening. Example: external anal sphincter.

Tensor—Makes a body part more rigid. Example: tensor fasciae latae.

Rotator—Moves a bone around its longitudinal axis. Example: obturator.

B. CONNECTIVE TISSUE COMPONENTS

Skeletal muscles are protected, strengthened, and attached to other structures by several connective tissue components. For example, the entire muscle is usually wrapped with a fibrous connective tissue called the **epimysium** (ep′-i-MĪZ-ē-um). When the muscle is cut in cross section, invaginations of the epimysium divide the muscle into bundles called **fasciculi (fascicles).** These invaginations of the epimysium are called the **perimysium** (per′-i-MĪZ-ē-um). In turn, invaginations of the perimysium, called **endomysium** (en′-dō-MĪZ-ē-um), penetrate into the interior of each fascicle and separate individual muscle fibers from each other. The epimysium, perimysium, and endomysium are all extensions of deep fascia and are all continuous with the connective tissue that attaches the muscle to another structure, such as bone or other muscle. All three elements may be extended beyond the muscle cells as a **tendon**—a cord of connective tissue that attaches a muscle to the periosteum of bone. The connective tissue may also extend as a broad, flat band of tendons called an **aponeurosis.** Aponeuroses also attach to the coverings of a bone or another muscle. When a muscle contracts, the tendon and its corresponding bone or muscle are pulled toward the contracting muscle. In this way skeletal muscles produce movement.

In Figure 10.1, label the epimysium, perimysium, endomysium, fasciculus, and muscle fibers.

C. PRINCIPAL MUSCLES

In the pages that follow, a series of tables has been provided for you to learn the principal skeletal muscles by region.[1] Use each table as follows:

1. Take each muscle, in sequence, and study the **learning key** that appears in parentheses after the name of the muscle. The learning key is a list of prefixes, suffixes, and definitions

---

[1] A few of the muscles listed are not illustrated in the diagrams. Please consult your textbook to locate these muscles.

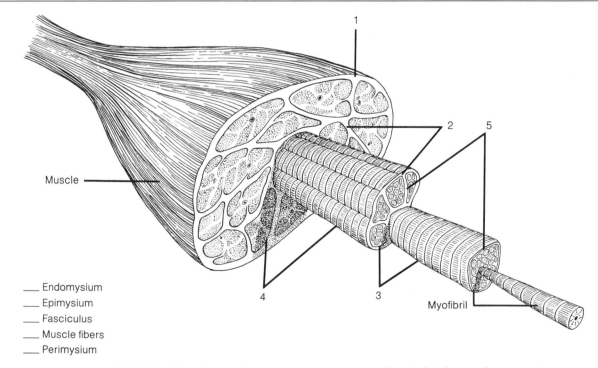

Muscle

___ Endomysium
___ Epimysium
___ Fasciculus
___ Muscle fibers
___ Perimysium

Myofibril

FIGURE 10.1 Connective tissue components of a skeletal muscle.

that explain the derivations of the muscles' names. It will help you to understand the reason for giving a muscle its name.

2. As you learn the name of each muscle, determine its origin, insertion, and action and write these in the spaces provided in the table. Consult your textbook if necessary.

3. Again, using your textbook as a guide, label the diagram referred to in the table.

4. Try to visualize what happens when the muscle contracts so that you will understand its action.

5. Do steps 1 through 4 for each muscle in the table. Before moving to the next table, examine a torso or chart of the skeletal system so that you can compare and approximate the positions of the muscles.

6. When possible, try to feel each muscle on your own body.

TABLE 10.1
MUSCLES OF FACIAL EXPRESSION (After completing the table, label Figure 10.2.)

MUSCLE	ORIGIN	INSERTION	ACTION
Epicranius (*epi* = over; *crani* = skull)	This muscle is divisible into two portions: the frontalis, over the frontal bone, and the occipitalis, over the occipital bone. The two muscles are united by a strong aponeurosis, the galea aponeurotica, which covers the superior and lateral surfaces of the skull.		
Frontalis (*front* = forehead)			
Occipitalis (*occipito* = base of skull)			
Orbicularis oris (*orb* = circular; *or* = mouth)			
Zygomaticus major (*zygomatic* = cheek bone; *major* = greater)			
Levator labii superioris (*levator* = raises or elevates; *labii* = lip; *superioris* = upper)			
Depressor labii inferioris (*depressor* = depresses or lowers; *inferioris* = lower)			
Buccinator (*bucc* = cheek)			

(Table 10.1 is continued on next page.)

TABLE 10.1 (*Continued*)

MUSCLE	ORIGIN	INSERTION	ACTION
Mentalis (*mentum* = chin)			
Platysma (*platy* = flat, broad)			
Risorius (*risor* = laughter)			
Orbicularis oculi (*ocul* = eye)			
Corrugator supercilii (*corrugo* = to wrinkle; *supercilium* = eyebrow)			
Levator palpebrae superioris (*palpebrae* = eyelids) (See Figure 10.4)			

TABLE 10.2
MUSCLES THAT MOVE THE LOWER JAW (After completing the table, label Figure 10.3.)

MUSCLE	ORIGIN	INSERTION	ACTION
Masseter (*masseter* = chewer)			
Temporalis (*tempora* = temples)			
Medial pterygoid (*medial* = closer to midline; *pterygoid* = like a wing)			
Lateral pterygoid (*lateral* = farther from midline)			

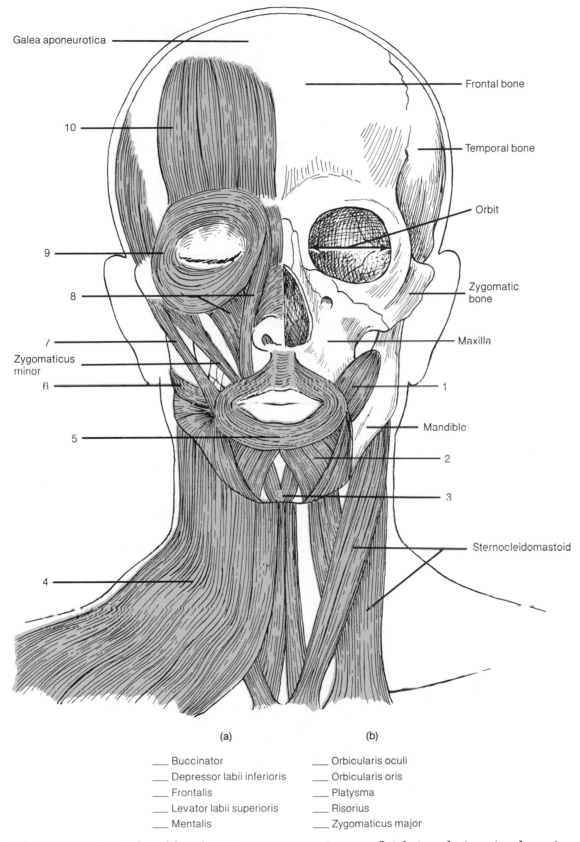

Galea aponeurotica

Frontal bone

Temporal bone

10

Orbit

9

Zygomatic bone

8

7

Maxilla

Zygomaticus minor

6

1

5

Mandible

2

3

Sternocleidomastoid

4

(a)   (b)

___ Buccinator   ___ Orbicularis oculi
___ Depressor labii inferioris   ___ Orbicularis oris
___ Frontalis   ___ Platysma
___ Levator labii superioris   ___ Risorius
___ Mentalis   ___ Zygomaticus major

FIGURE 10.2   Muscles of facial expression. (a) Anterior superficial view. (b) Anterior deep view.

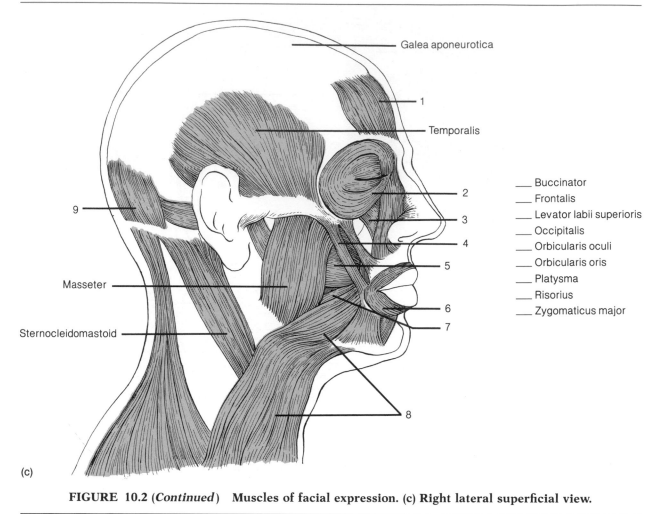

Galea aponeurotica

1

Temporalis

2

3

4

5

6

7

8

9

Masseter

Sternocleidomastoid

(c)

___ Buccinator
___ Frontalis
___ Levator labii superioris
___ Occipitalis
___ Orbicularis oculi
___ Orbicularis oris
___ Platysma
___ Risorius
___ Zygomaticus major

FIGURE 10.2 (*Continued*)   Muscles of facial expression. (c) Right lateral superficial view.

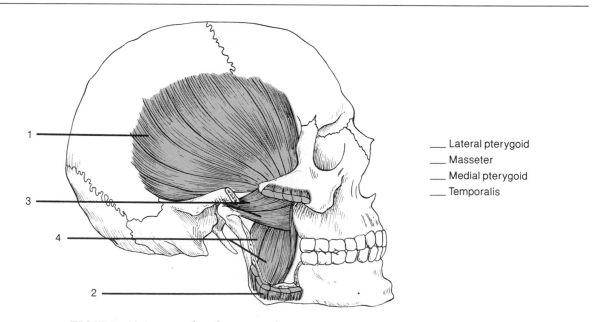

1

3

4

2

___ Lateral pterygoid
___ Masseter
___ Medial pterygoid
___ Temporalis

FIGURE 10.3   Muscles that move lower jaw seen in right lateral view.

TABLE 10.3
MUSCLES THAT MOVE THE EYEBALL—THE EXTRINSIC MUSCLES[1]
(After completing the table, label Figure 10.4.)

MUSCLE	ORIGIN	INSERTION	ACTION
Superior rectus (*superior* = above; *rectus* = in this case, muscle fibers running parallel to long axis of eyeball)			
Inferior rectus (*inferior* = below)			
Lateral rectus			
Medial rectus			
Superior oblique (*oblique* = in this case, muscle fibers running diagonally to long axis of eyeball)			
Inferior oblique			

[1]Muscles situated on the outside of the eyeball.

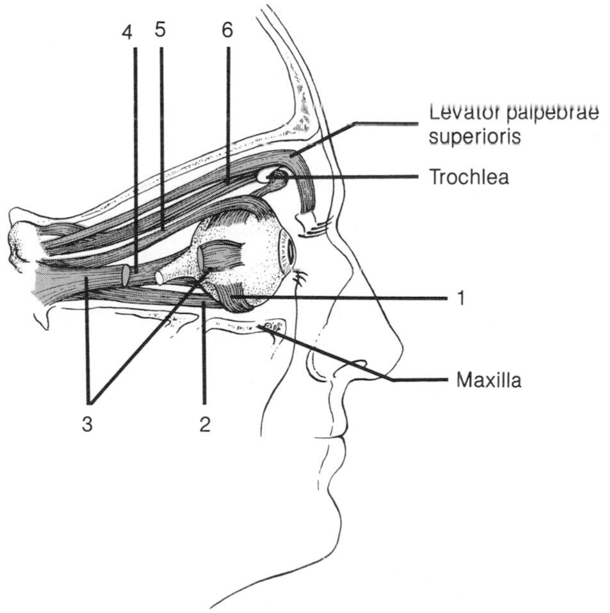

Levator palpebrae superioris

Trochlea

Maxilla

___ Inferior oblique
___ Inferior rectus
___ Lateral rectus
___ Medial rectus
___ Superior oblique
___ Superior rectus

FIGURE 10.4   Extrinsic muscles of eyeball seen in right lateral view.

TABLE 10.4
MUSCLES THAT MOVE THE TONGUE (After completing the table, label Figure 10.5.)

MUSCLE	ORIGIN	INSERTION	ACTION
Genioglossus (*geneion* = chin; *glossus* = tongue)			
Styloglossus (*stylo* = stake or pole)			
Stylohyoid (*hyoeides* = U-shaped)			
Palatoglossus (*palato* = palate)			
Hyoglossus			

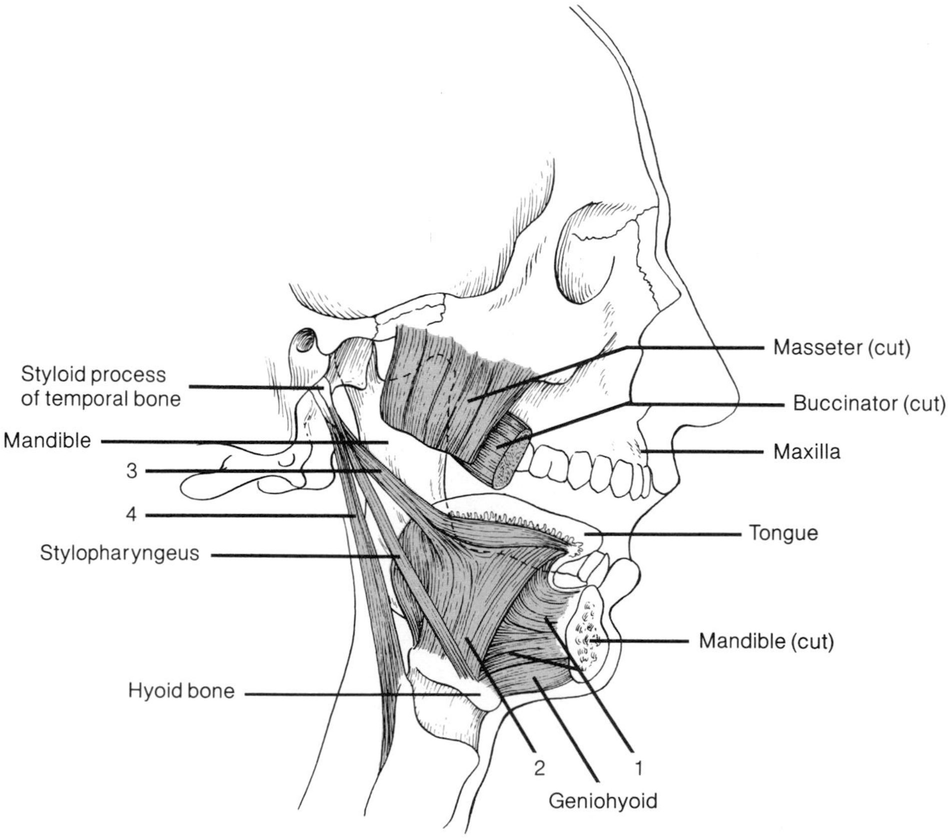

___ Genioglossus
___ Hyoglossus
___ Styloglossus
___ Stylohyoid

FIGURE 10.5 Muscles that move the tongue viewed from right side.

TABLE 10.5
MUSCLES OF THE PHARYNX (After completing the table, label Figure 10.6.)

MUSCLE	ORIGIN	INSERTION	ACTION
Inferior constrictor (*inferior* = below; *constrictor* = decreases diameter of lumen)			
Middle constrictor			
Superior constrictor (*superior* = above)			
Stylopharyngeus (*stylo* = stake or pole; *pharyngeus* = pharynx)			
Salpingopharyngeus (*salping* = pertaining to auditory tube or uterine tube)			
Palatopharyngeus (*palato* = palate)			

TABLE 10.6
MUSCLES OF THE LARYNX (After completing the table, label Figure 10.7.)

MUSCLE	ORIGIN	INSERTION	ACTION
Omohyoid (*omo* = relationship to shoulder; *hyoeides* = U-shaped)			
Sternohyoid (*sterno* = sternum)			
Sternothyroid (*thyro* = thyroid gland)			

(Table 10.6 is continued on next page.)

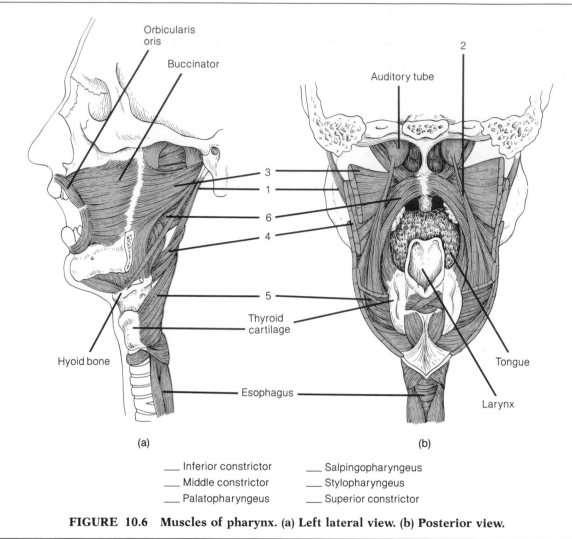

(a)

(b)

___ Inferior constrictor   ___ Salpingopharyngeus

___ Middle constrictor   ___ Stylopharyngeus

___ Palatopharyngeus   ___ Superior constrictor

FIGURE 10.6 Muscles of pharynx. (a) Left lateral view. (b) Posterior view.

TABLE 10.6 (*Continued*)

MUSCLE	ORIGIN	INSERTION	ACTION
Thyrohyoid			
Stylopharyngeus **Palatopharyngeus** **Inferior constrictor** **Middle constrictor**	See Table 10.5 and Figure 10.6		
Cricothyroid (*crico* = cricoid cartilage of larynx)			

(Table 10.6 is continued on next page.)

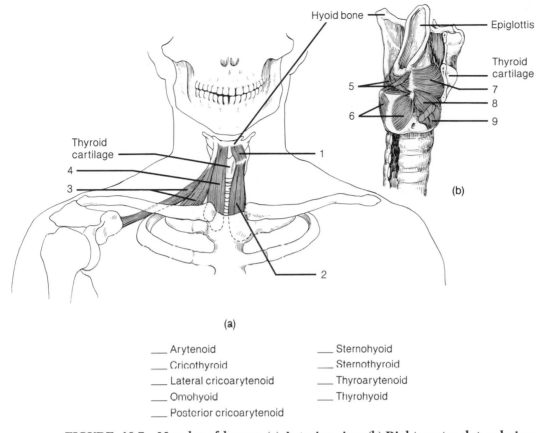

Hyoid bone — Epiglottis

Thyroid cartilage

5
6
7
8
9

(b)

Thyroid cartilage
4
3
1
2

(a)

___ Arytenoid   ___ Sternohyoid
___ Cricothyroid   ___ Sternothyroid
___ Lateral cricoarytenoid   ___ Thyroarytenoid
___ Omohyoid   ___ Thyrohyoid
___ Posterior cricoarytenoid

FIGURE 10.7   Muscles of larynx. (a) Anterior view. (b) Right posterolateral view.

TABLE 10.6 (*Continued*)

MUSCLE	ORIGIN	INSERTION	ACTION
Posterior cricoarytenoid (*arytaina* = shaped like a jug)			
Lateral cricoarytenoid			
Arytenoid			
Thyroarytenoid			

TABLE 10.7
MUSCLES THAT MOVE THE HEAD

MUSCLE	ORIGIN	INSERTION	ACTION
Sternocleidomastoid (*sternum* = breastbone; *mastoid* = mastoid process of temporal bone) (label this muscle in Figure 10.11a)			
Semispinalis capitis (*semi* = half; *spine* = spinous process; *caput* = head) (label this muscle in Figure 10.15)			
Splenius capitis (*splenion* = bandage) (label this muscle in Figure 10.15)			
Longissimus capitis (*longissimus* = longest) (label this muscle in Figure 10.15)			

TABLE 10.8
MUSCLES THAT ACT ON THE ANTERIOR ABDOMINAL WALL
(After completing the table, label Figure 10.8.)

MUSCLE	ORIGIN	INSERTION	ACTION
Rectus abdominis (*abdomino* = belly)			
External oblique (*external* = closer to the surface)			
Internal oblique (*internal* = farther from the surface)			
Transversus abdominis (*transverse* = muscle fibers run transversely to midline)			

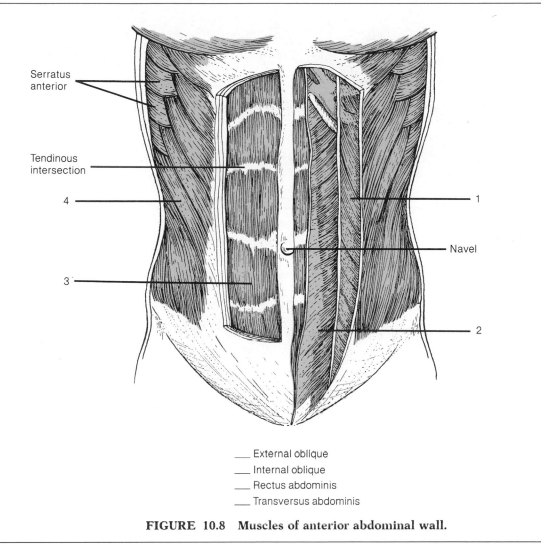

Serratus anterior

Tendinous intersection

4

3

Navel

1

2

___ External oblique
___ Internal oblique
___ Rectus abdominis
___ Transversus abdominis

FIGURE 10.8   Muscles of anterior abdominal wall.

TABLE 10.9
MUSCLES USED IN BREATHING (After completing the table, label Figure 10.9.)

MUSCLE	ORIGIN	INSERTION	ACTION
Diaphragm (*dia* = across, between; *phragma* = wall)			
External intercostals (*inter* = between; *costa* = rib)			
Internal intercostals			

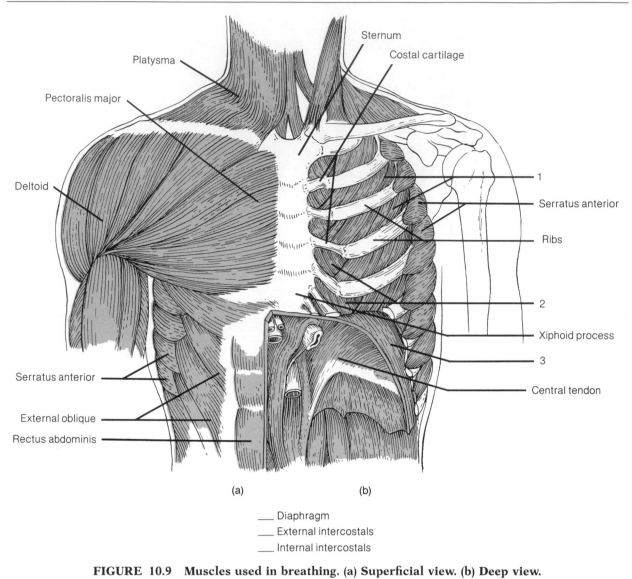

(a)   (b)

___ Diaphragm
___ External intercostals
___ Internal intercostals

FIGURE 10.9   Muscles used in breathing. (a) Superficial view. (b) Deep view.

TABLE 10.10
MUSCLES OF THE PELVIC FLOOR[1] (After completing the table, label Figure 10.10.)

MUSCLE	ORIGIN	INSERTION	ACTION
Pubococcygeus (*pubo* = pubis)			
Iliococcygeus (*ilio* = ilium)			
Coccygeus			

[1]The muscles of the pelvic floor, together with fasciae covering their internal and external surfaces, are collectively referred to as the **pelvic diaphragm.**

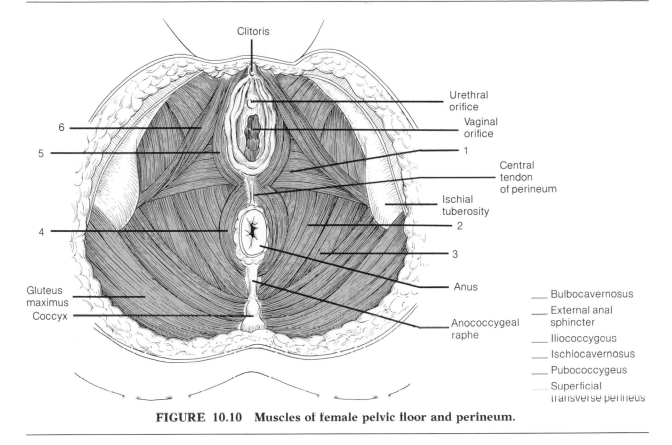

Clitoris

Urethral
orifice

Vaginal
orifice

6

5

1

Central
tendon
of perineum

Ischial
tuberosity

2

4

3

Anus

Gluteus
maximus

Coccyx

Anococcygeal
raphe

___ Bulbocavernosus

___ External anal
      sphincter

___ Iliococcygeus

___ Ischiocavernosus

___ Pubococcygeus

___ Superficial
      transverse perineus

FIGURE 10.10 Muscles of female pelvic floor and perineum.

**TABLE 10.11
MUSCLES OF THE PERINEUM[1] (After completing the table, label Figure 10.10.)**

MUSCLE	ORIGIN	INSERTION	ACTION
Superficial transverse perineus (*superficial* = near surface; *transverse* = across; *perineus* = perineum)			
Bulbocavernosus (*bulbus* = bulb; *caverna* = hollow space)			
Ischiocavernosus (*ischion* = hip)			
Deep transverse perineus[2] (*deep* = farther from surface)			

(Table 10.11 is continued on next page.)

[1]The **perineum** is a diamond-shaped area at the lower end of the trunk between the thighs and buttocks. The area is bordered anteriorly by the symphysis pubis, laterally by the ischial tuberosities, and posteriorly by the coccyx. A transverse line drawn between the two ischial tuberosities divides the perineum into an anterior **urogenital triangle** that contains the external genitals and a posterior **anal triangle** that contains the anus.

TABLE 10.11 (*Continued*)

MUSCLE	ORIGIN	INSERTION	ACTION
Urethral sphincter[2] (*urethral* = pertaining to urethra; *sphincter* = circular muscle that decreases the size of an opening)			
External anal sphincter			

[2]These muscles, together with a fibrous membrane, constitute the **urogenital diaphragm,** which surrounds the urogenital ducts and helps to strengthen the pelvic floor.

TABLE 10.12
MUSCLES THAT MOVE THE PECTORAL (SHOULDER) GIRDLE
(After completing the table, label Figure 10.11.)

MUSCLE	ORIGIN	INSERTION	ACTION
Subclavius (*sub* = under; *clavius* = clavicle)			
Pectoralis minor (*pectus* = breast, chest, thorax; *minor* = lesser)			
Serratus anterior (*serratus* = serrated; *anterior* = front)			
Trapezius (*trapezoides* = trapezoid-shaped)			
Levator scapulae (*levator* = raises; *scapulae* = scapula)			
Rhomboideus major (*rhomboides* = rhomboid-shaped or diamond-shaped)			
Rhomboideus minor			

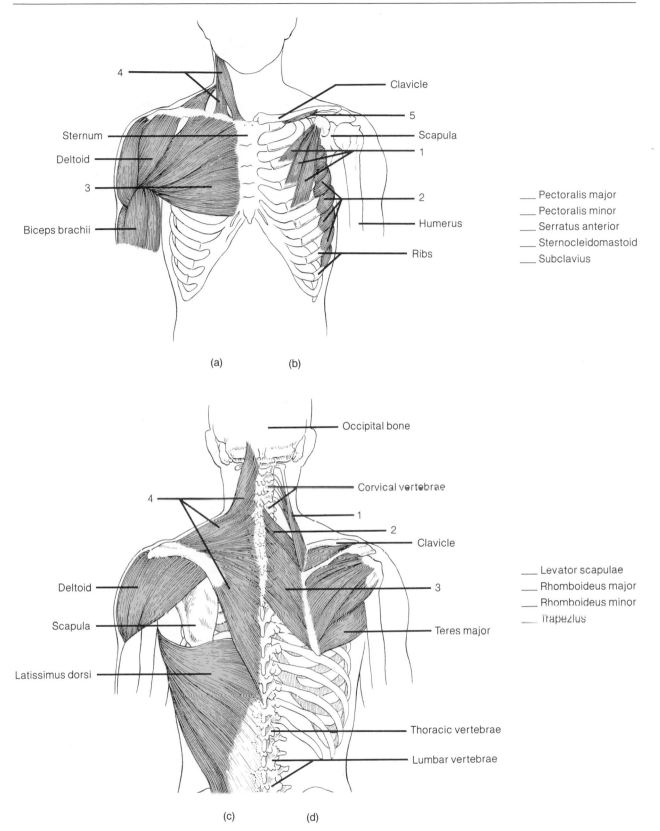

4

Clavicle

5

Sternum

Scapula

Deltoid

1

3

2

Biceps brachii

Humerus

Ribs

___ Pectoralis major
___ Pectoralis minor
___ Serratus anterior
___ Sternocleidomastoid
___ Subclavius

(a)   (b)

Occipital bone

Corvical vertebrae

4

1

2

Clavicle

Deltoid

3

Scapula

Teres major

Latissimus dorsi

___ Levator scapulae
___ Rhomboideus major
___ Rhomboideus minor
___ Trapezius

Thoracic vertebrae

Lumbar vertebrae

(c)   (d)

FIGURE 10.11 **Muscles that move the pectoral (shoulder) girdle. (a) Anterior superficial view. (b) Anterior deep view. (c) Posterior superficial view. (d) Posterior deep view.**

TABLE 10.13
MUSCLES THAT MOVE THE ARM (After completing the table, label Figure 10.12.)

MUSCLE	ORIGIN	INSERTION	ACTION
Pectoralis major (label this muscle in Figure 10.11)			
Latissimus dorsi (*dorsum* = back)			
Deltoid (*delta* = triangular- shaped)			
Supraspinatus (*supra* = above; *spinatus* = spine of scapula)			
Infraspinatus (*infra* = below)			
Teres major (*teres* = long and round)			
Teres minor			

TABLE 10.14
MUSCLES THAT MOVE THE FOREARM (After completing the table, label Figure 10.13.)

MUSCLE	ORIGIN	INSERTION	ACTION
Biceps brachii (*biceps* = two heads of origin; *brachion* = arm)			
Brachialis			
Brachioradialis (*radialis* = radius) (see Figure 10.14 also)			

(Table 10.14 is continued on next page.)

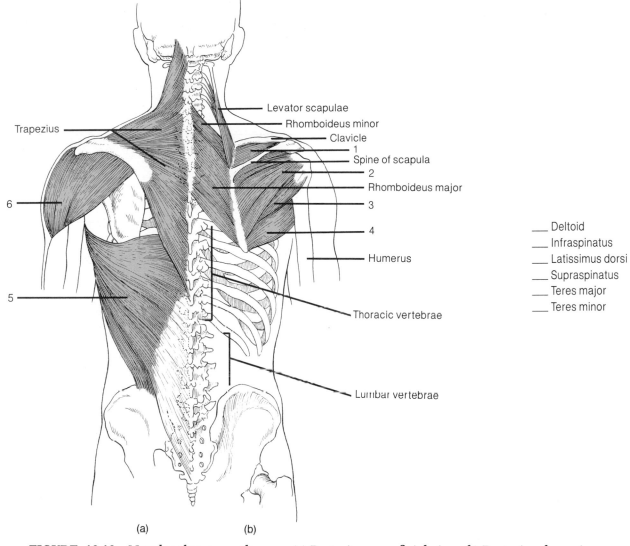

Trapezius

Levator scapulae
Rhomboideus minor
Clavicle
1
Spine of scapula
2
Rhomboideus major
3

6

4

Humerus

5

Thoracic vertebrae

Lumbar vertebrae

___ Deltoid
___ Infraspinatus
___ Latissimus dorsi
___ Supraspinatus
___ Teres major
___ Teres minor

(a)   (b)

FIGURE 10.12   Muscles that move the arm. (a) Posterior superficial view. (b) Posterior deep view.

TABLE 10.14 (*Continued*)

MUSCLE	ORIGIN	INSERTION	ACTION
Triceps brachii (*triceps* = three heads of origin)			
Coracobrachialis (*coraco* = coracoid process)			
Anconeus (*anconeal* = pertaining to the elbow)			

(Table 10.14 is continued on next page.)

TABLE 10.14 (*Continued*)

MUSCLE	ORIGIN	INSERTION	ACTION
Supinator (*supination* = turning palm upward or anteriorly)			
Pronator teres (*pronation* = turning palm downward or posteriorly)			
Pronator quadratus (*quadratus* = squared, four-sided)			

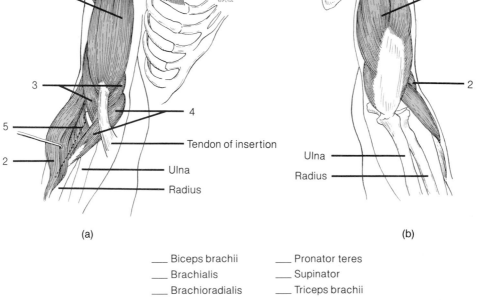

_____ Biceps brachii   _____ Pronator teres

_____ Brachialis   _____ Supinator

_____ Brachioradialis   _____ Triceps brachii

FIGURE 10.13 Muscles that move the forearm. (a) Anterior view. (b) Posterior view.

TABLE 10.15
MUSCLES THAT MOVE THE WRIST AND FINGERS (After completing the table, label Figure 10.14.)

MUSCLE	ORIGIN	INSERTION	ACTION
Flexor carpi radialis (*flexor* = decreases angle at a joint; *carpus* = wrist)			
Flexor carpi ulnaris (*ulnaris* = ulna)			
Palmaris longus (*palma* = palm)			
Extensor carpi radialis longus (*extensor* = increases angle at a joint; *longus* = long)			
Extensor carpi ulnaris			
Flexor digitorum profundus (*digit* = finger or toe; *profundus* = deep)			
Flexor digitorum superficialis (*superficialis* = superficial)			
Extensor digitorum			
Extensor indicis (*indicis* = index)			

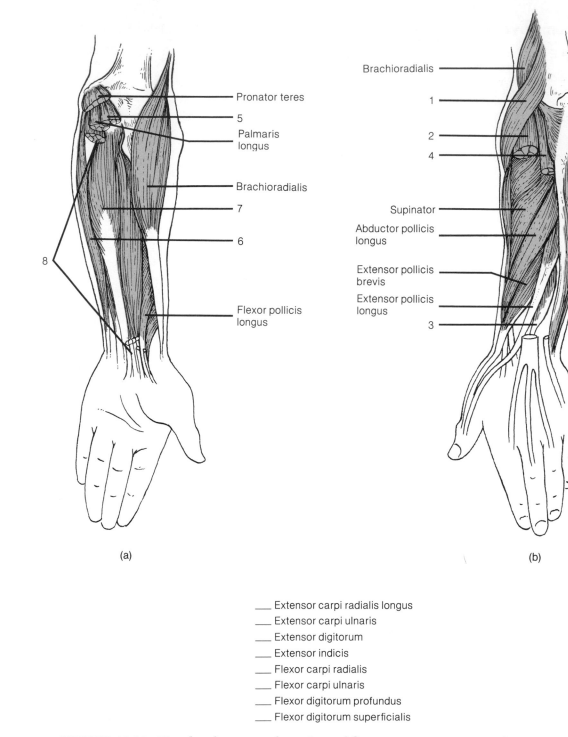

Pronator teres

5

Palmaris longus

Brachioradialis

7

6

8

Flexor pollicis longus

(a)

Brachioradialis

1

2

4

Supinator

Abductor pollicis longus

Extensor pollicis brevis

Extensor pollicis longus

3

(b)

___ Extensor carpi radialis longus
___ Extensor carpi ulnaris
___ Extensor digitorum
___ Extensor indicis
___ Flexor carpi radialis
___ Flexor carpi ulnaris
___ Flexor digitorum profundus
___ Flexor digitorum superficialis

FIGURE 10.14   Muscles that move the wrist and fingers. (a) Anterior view. (b) Posterior view.

TABLE 10.16
MUSCLES THAT MOVE THE VERTEBRAL COLUMN (After completing the table, label Figure 10.15.)

MUSCLE	ORIGIN	INSERTION	ACTION
Rectus abdominis (see Figure 10.8)			
Quadratus lumborum (*quad* = four; *lumb* = lumbar region)			
Sacrospinalis **(erector spinae)**	This muscle consists of three posterior groupings: **iliocostalis, longissimus,** and **spinalis.** These groups, in turn, consist of a series of overlapping muscles. The iliocostalis group is laterally placed, the longissimus group intermediately, and the spinalis medially.		
Lateral			
Iliocostalis **lumborum** (*ilium* = flank; *lumbus* = loin)			
Iliocostalis thoracis (*thorax* = chest)			
Iliocostalis cervicis (*cervix* = neck)			
Intermediate			
Longissimus thoracis			
Longissimus cervicis			
Longissimus capitis			
Medial			
Spinalis thoracis			

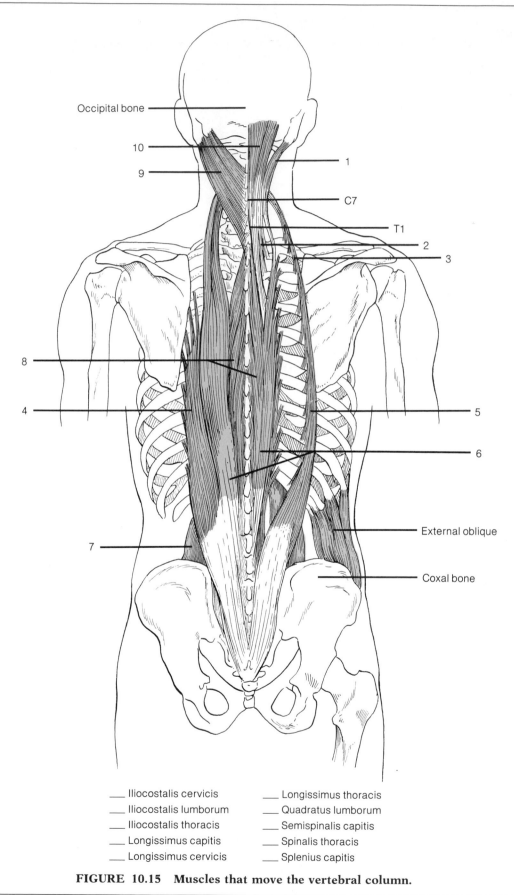

Occipital bone

10

9

1

C7

T1

2

3

8

4

5

6

External oblique

Coxal bone

7

___ Iliocostalis cervicis   ___ Longissimus thoracis
___ Iliocostalis lumborum   ___ Quadratus lumborum
___ Iliocostalis thoracis   ___ Semispinalis capitis
___ Longissimus capitis   ___ Spinalis thoracis
___ Longissimus cervicis   ___ Splenius capitis

FIGURE 10.15 Muscles that move the vertebral column.

TABLE 10.17
MUSCLES THAT MOVE THE THIGH (After completing the table, label Figure 10.16.)

MUSCLE	ORIGIN	INSERTION	ACTION
Psoas major (*psoa* = muscle of loin)			
Iliacus (*iliac* = ilium)			
Gluteus maximus (*gloutos* = buttock; *maximus* = largest)			
Gluteus medius (*media* = middle)			
Gluteus minimus (*minimus* = small)			
Tensor fasciae latae (*tensor* = makes tense; *fascia* = band; *latus* = broad, wide)			
Adductor longus (*adductor* = moves a part closer to the midline)			
Adductor brevis (*brevis* = short)			
Adductor magnus (*magnus* = large)			
Piriformis (*pirum* = pear; *forma* = shape)			
Obturator internus (*obturator* = closed because it arises over the obturator foramen, which is closed by a heavy membrane; *internus* = inside)			
Pectineus (*pecten* = comb-shaped)			

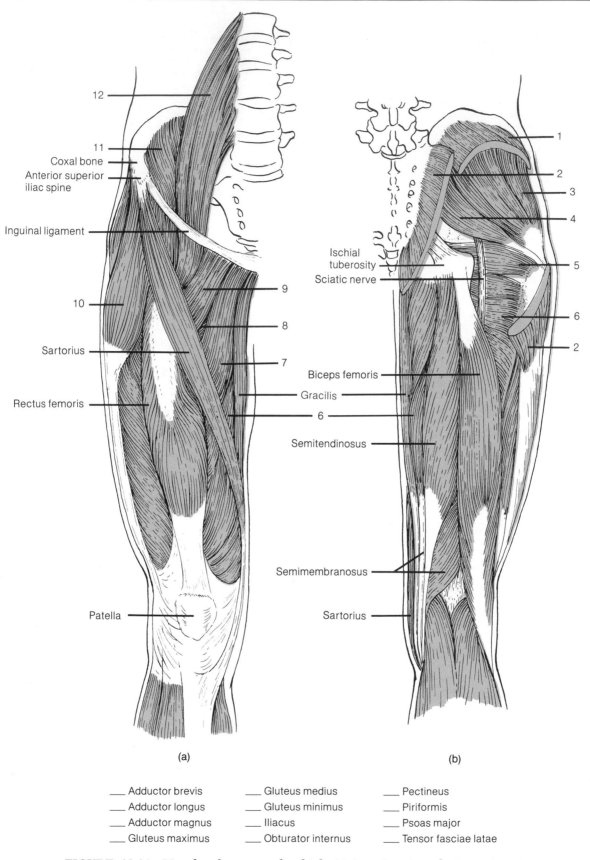

(a)

(b)

12

11

Coxal bone

Anterior superior
iliac spine

Inguinal ligament

10

Sartorius

Rectus femoris

Patella

9

8

7

Ischial
tuberosity

Sciatic nerve

Biceps femoris

Gracilis

6

Semitendinosus

Semimembranosus

Sartorius

1

2

3

4

5

6

2

___ Adductor brevis   ___ Gluteus medius   ___ Pectineus

___ Adductor longus   ___ Gluteus minimus   ___ Piriformis

___ Adductor magnus   ___ Iliacus   ___ Psoas major

___ Gluteus maximus   ___ Obturator internus   ___ Tensor fasciae latae

FIGURE 10.16   Muscles that move the thigh. (a) Anterior view. (b) Posterior view.

TABLE 10.18
MUSCLES THAT ACT ON THE LEG (After completing the table, label Figure 10.17.)

MUSCLE	ORIGIN	INSERTION	ACTION
Quadriceps femoris	A composite muscle that includes four distinct parts, usually described as four separate muscles. The common tendon from the patella to the tibial tuberosity is know as the patellar ligament.		
Rectus femoris (*rectus* = fibers parallel to midline; *femoris* = femur)			
Vastus lateralis (*vastus* = vast, large; *lateralis* = lateral)			
Vastus medialis (*medialis* = medial)			
Vastus intermedius (*intermedius* = middle)			
Hamstrings	A collective designation for three separate muscles		
Biceps femoris (*biceps* = two heads of origin)			
Semitendinosus (*scmi* = half; *tendo* = tendon)			
Semimembranosus (*membran* = membrane)			
Gracilis (*gracilis* = slender)			
Sartorius (*sartor* = tailor; refers to cross-legged position in which tailors sit)			

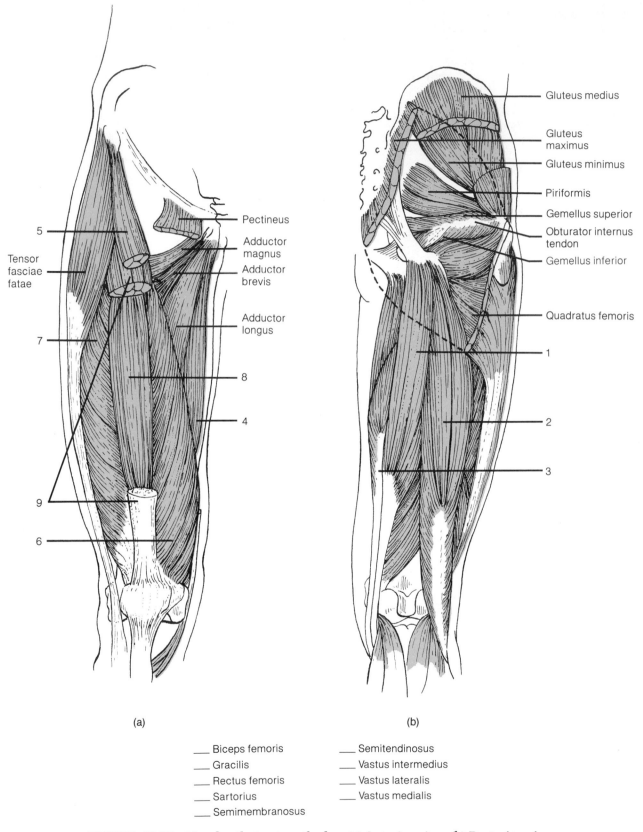

(a)

(b)

Tensor fasciae fatae

Pectineus

Adductor magnus

Adductor brevis

Adductor longus

Gluteus medius

Gluteus maximus

Gluteus minimus

Piriformis

Gemellus superior

Obturator internus tendon

Gemellus inferior

Quadratus femoris

___ Biceps femoris ___ Semitendinosus
___ Gracilis ___ Vastus intermedius
___ Rectus femoris ___ Vastus lateralis
___ Sartorius ___ Vastus medialis
___ Semimembranosus

FIGURE 10.17 Muscles that act on the leg. (a) Anterior view. (b) Posterior view.

TABLE 10.19
MUSCLES THAT MOVE FOOT AND TOES (After completing the table, label Figure 10.18.)

MUSCLE	ORIGIN	INSERTION	ACTION
Gastrocnemius (*gaster* = belly; *kneme* = leg)			
Soleus (*soleus* = sole of foot)			
Peroneus longus (*perone* = fibula)			
Peroneus brevis			
Flexor hallucis longus			
Tibialis anterior (*tibialis* = tibia)			
Tibialis posterior (*posterior* = back)			
Flexor digitorum longus (*digitorum* — digit, finger, or toe)			
Extensor digitorum longus			

D. COMPOSITE MUSCULAR SYSTEM

Now that you have studied the muscles of the body by region, label the composite diagram shown in Figure 10.19.

LABORATORY REPORT QUESTIONS (PAGE 389)

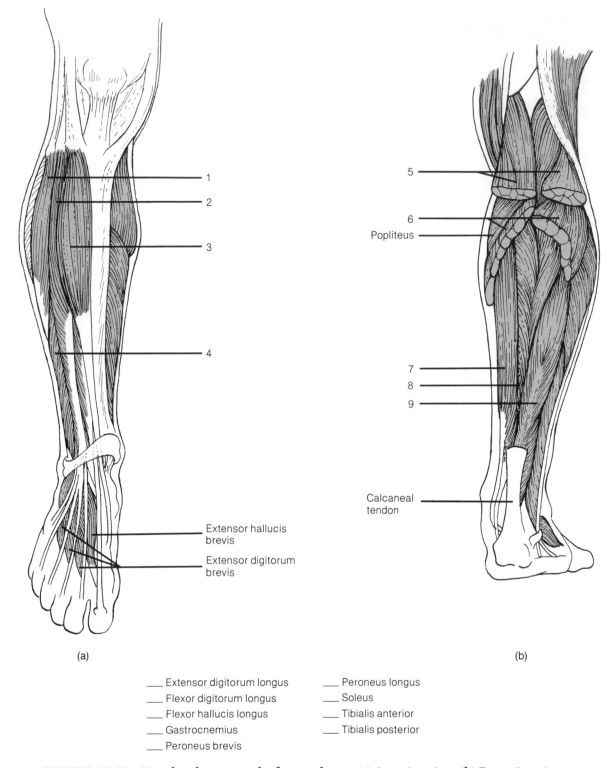

(a)   (b)

___ Extensor digitorum longus   ___ Peroneus longus
___ Flexor digitorum longus   ___ Soleus
___ Flexor hallucis longus   ___ Tibialis anterior
___ Gastrocnemius   ___ Tibialis posterior
___ Peroneus brevis

FIGURE 10.18   Muscles that move the foot and toes. (a) Anterior view. (b) Posterior view.

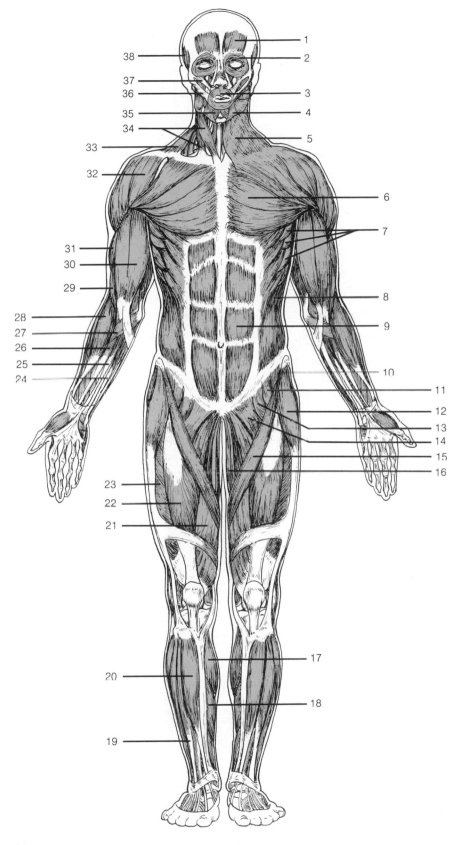

_____ Adductor longus
_____ Biceps brachii
_____ Brachialis
_____ Brachioradialis
_____ Deltoid
_____ Depressor labii inferioris
_____ External oblique
_____ Flexor carpi radialis
_____ Flexor carpi ulnaris
_____ Frontalis
_____ Gastrocnemius
_____ Gracilis
_____ Iliacus
_____ Mentalis
_____ Orbicularis oculi
_____ Orbicularis oris
_____ Palmaris longus
_____ Pectineus
_____ Pectoralis major
_____ Peroneus longus
_____ Platysma
_____ Pronator teres
_____ Psoas major
_____ Rectus abdominis
_____ Rectus femoris
_____ Sartorius
_____ Serratus anterior
_____ Soleus
_____ Sternocleidomastoid
_____ Temporalis
_____ Tensor fasciae latae
_____ Tibialis anterior
_____ Trapezius
_____ Triceps brachii
_____ Vastus lateralis
_____ Vastus medialis
_____ Zygomaticus major
_____ Zygomaticus minor

(a)

FIGURE 10.19 Principal superficial muscles. (a) Anterior view.

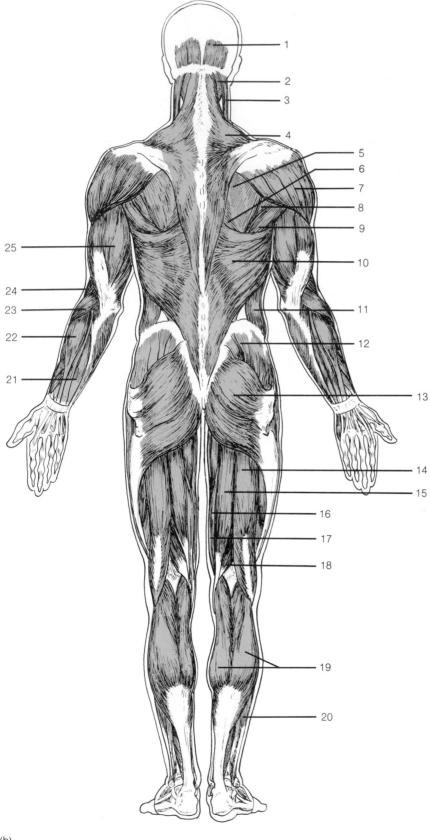

___ Biceps femoris

___ Brachioradialis

___ Deltoid

___ Extensor carpi radialis longus

___ Extensor carpi ulnaris

___ Extensor digitorum

___ External oblique

___ Gastrocnemius

___ Gluteus maximus

___ Gluteus medius

___ Gracilis

___ Infraspinatus

___ Latissimus dorsi

___ Occipitalis

___ Rhomboideus major

___ Sartorius

___ Semimembranosus

___ Semispinalis capitis

___ Semitendinosus

___ Soleus

___ Sternocleidomastoid

___ Teres major

___ Teres minor

___ Trapezius

___ Triceps brachii

(b)

FIGURE 10.19 (*Continued*) Principal superficial muscles. (b) Posterior view.

11 | SURFACE ANATOMY

Now that you have studied the skeletal and muscular systems, you will be introduced to a study of **surface anatomy,** in which you will study the form and markings of the surface of the body.[1] A knowledge of surface anatomy will help you to identify certain superficial structures by visual inspection or palpation (to feel with the hand).

A convenient way to study surface anatomy is first to divide the body into its principal regions: head, neck, trunk, and upper and lower extremities. These may be reviewed in Figure 2.1.

A. HEAD

The **head** (cephalic region or caput) is divisible into the cranium and face. Several surface features of the head are:

1. **Cranium** (brain case or skull)
   a. **Frontal region**—Front of skull (sinciput) that includes forehead.
   b. **Parietal region**—Crown of skull (vertex).
   c. **Temporal region**—Side of skull (tempora).
   d. **Occipital region**—Base of skull (occiput).
2. **Face** (Facies)
   a. **Orbital** or **ocular region**—Includes eyeballs (bulbi oculorum), eyebrows (supercilia), and eyelids (palpebrae).
   b. **Nasal region**—Nose (nasus).
   c. **Infraorbital region**—Inferior to orbit.
   d. **Oral region**—Mouth.
   e. **Mental region**—Anterior part of mandible.

f. **Buccal region**—Cheek.
g. **Parotid-masseteric region**—External to parotid gland and masseter muscle.
h. **Zygomatic region**—Inferolateral to orbit.
i. **Auricular region**—Ear.

Using your textbook as an aid, label Figure 11.1.

Using a mirror, examine the various surface features of the head just described. Working with a partner, be sure that you can identify the regions by both common *and* anatomical names.

The surface anatomy features of the eyeball and accessory structures are presented in Figure 14.6, of the ear in Figure 14.14, and of the nose in Figure 21.3.

B. NECK

The **neck** (collum) can be divided into an anterior cervical region, two lateral cervical regions, and a posterior (nuchal) region. Among the surface features of the neck are:

1. **Thyroid cartilage (Adam's apple)**—Triangular laryngeal cartilage in the midline of the anterior cervical region.

2. **Hyoid bone**—First resistant structure palpated in the midline below the chin, lying just above thyroid cartilage.

3. **Cricoid cartilage**—Inferior laryngeal cartilage that attaches larynx to trachea. This structure can be palpated by running your fingertip down from your chin over the thyroid cartilage. (After you pass the cricoid cartilage, your fingertip sinks in.)

---

[1]At the discretion of your instructor, surface anatomy may be studied either before or in conjunction with your study of various body systems. This exercise can be used as an excellent review of many topics already studied.

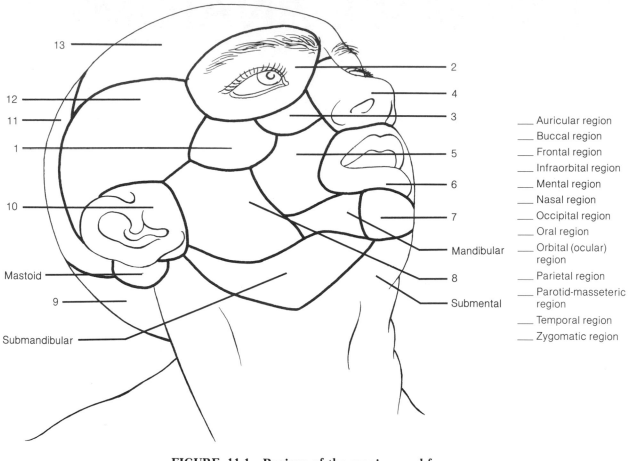

FIGURE 11.1 Regions of the cranium and face.

13

12

11

1

10

Mastoid

9

Submandibular

2

4

3

5

6

7

Mandibular

8

Submental

___ Auricular region
___ Buccal region
___ Frontal region
___ Infraorbital region
___ Mental region
___ Nasal region
___ Occipital region
___ Oral region
___ Orbital (ocular) region
___ Parietal region
___ Parotid-masseteric region
___ Temporal region
___ Zygomatic region

4. **Sternocleidomastoid muscles**—Form major portion of lateral cervical regions, extending from mastoid process of temporal bone (felt as bump behind pinna of ear) to sternum and clavicle. Each muscle divides the neck into an anterior and posterior (lateral) triangle.

5. **Trapezius muscles**—Form portion of lateral cervical region, extending downward and outward from base of skull. "Stiff neck" is frequently associated with inflammation of these muscles.

6. **Anterior triangle of neck**—Bordered superiorly by mandible, inferiorly by sternum, medially by cervical midline, and laterally by anterior border of sternocleidomastoid muscle.

7. **Posterior (lateral) triangle of neck**—Bordered inferiorly by clavicle, anteriorly by posterior border of sternocleidomastoid muscle, and posteriorly by anterior border of trapezius muscle.

8. **External jugular veins**—Prominent veins along lateral cervical regions, readily seen when a person is angry or a collar fits too tightly.

Using a mirror and working with a partner, use your textbook as an aid in identifying the surface features of the neck just described. Then label Figure 11.2.

C. TRUNK

The **trunk** is divided into the back, chest, abdomen, and pelvis. Its surface features include:

1. **Back (dorsum)**
   a. **Vertebral spines**—Dorsally pointed projections of vertebrae. Very prominent is the **vertebrae prominens,** the spine of C7, easily palpated when the head is flexed.

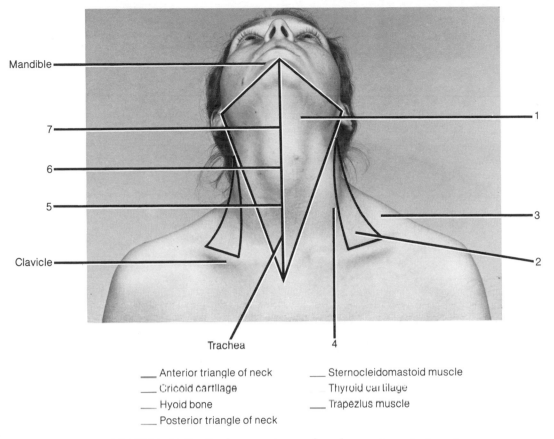

Mandible

7

6

5

Clavicle

Trachea

1

3

2

4

___ Anterior triangle of neck   ___ Sternocleidomastoid muscle
___ Cricoid cartilage   ___ Thyroid cartilage
___ Hyoid bone   ___ Trapezius muscle
___ Posterior triangle of neck

FIGURE 11.2 **Surface anatomy of neck seen in anterior view.**

b. **Scapula**—Shoulder blade. Several parts of the scapula, such as the medial (axillary) border, lateral (vertebral) border, inferior angle, spine, and acromion, may be observed or palpated.

c. **Ribs**—These may be seen in thin individuals.

d. **Muscles**—Among the visible superficial back muscles are the **latissimus dorsi** (covers lower half of back), **erector spinae** (on either side of vertebral column), **infraspinatus** (inferior to spine of scapula), **trapezius,** and **teres major** (inferior to infraspinatus).

Using your textbook as an aid, label Figure 11.3.

2. **Chest (thorax)**
   a. **Clavicles**—Collarbones. These lie in superior region of thorax and can be palpated along their entire length.
   b. **Sternum**—Breastbone, lies in midline of chest. The following parts of the sternum are important surface features:
      1. **Jugular notch**—Depression on superior surface of sternum between medial

ends of clavicles. The trachea can be palpated in the notch.
      2. **Sternal angle**—Formed by junction of manubrium and body of sternum. This is palpable under the skin and locates the sternal end of second rib.
      3. **Xiphoid process**—Inferior portion of sternum.
   c. **Ribs**
   d. **Costal margins**—Inferior edges of costal cartilages of ribs 7 through 10.
   e. **Muscles**—Among the superficial chest muscles that can be seen are the **pectoralis major** (principal upper chest muscle) and **serratus anterior** (inferior and lateral to pectoralis major).

Using your textbook as an aid, label Figure 11.4.

3. **Abdomen** and **Pelvis**
   a. **Umbilicus**—Also called navel, site of attachment of umbilical cord in fetus. Umbilicus is most obvious surface marking on the abdomen of most individuals.

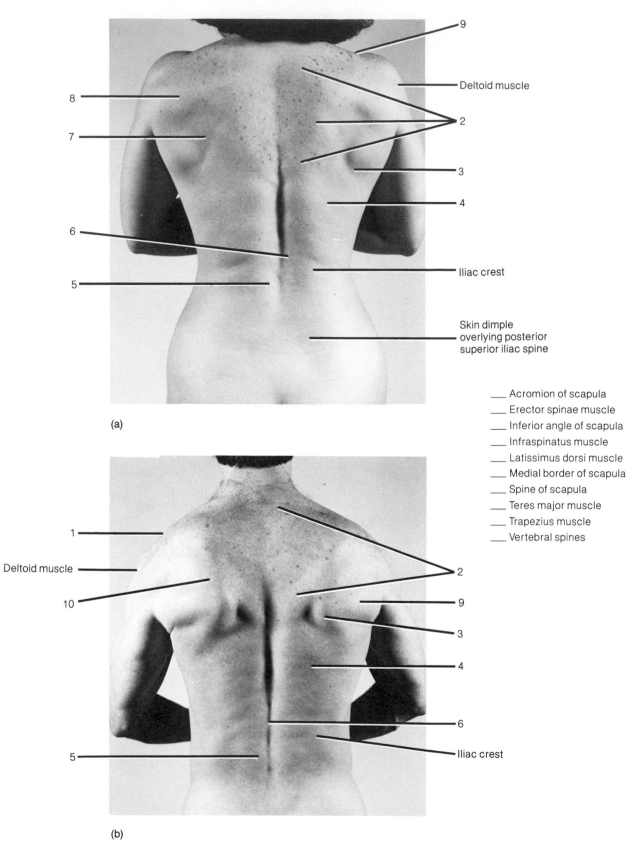

9

Deltoid muscle

8

2

7

3

4

6

Iliac crest

5

Skin dimple
overlying posterior
superior iliac spine

(a)

___ Acromion of scapula
___ Erector spinae muscle
___ Inferior angle of scapula
___ Infraspinatus muscle
___ Latissimus dorsi muscle
___ Medial border of scapula
___ Spine of scapula
___ Teres major muscle
___ Trapezius muscle
___ Vertebral spines

1

Deltoid muscle

2

10

9

3

4

6

5

Iliac crest

(b)

FIGURE 11.3   Surface anatomy of back. (a) Female. (b) Male.

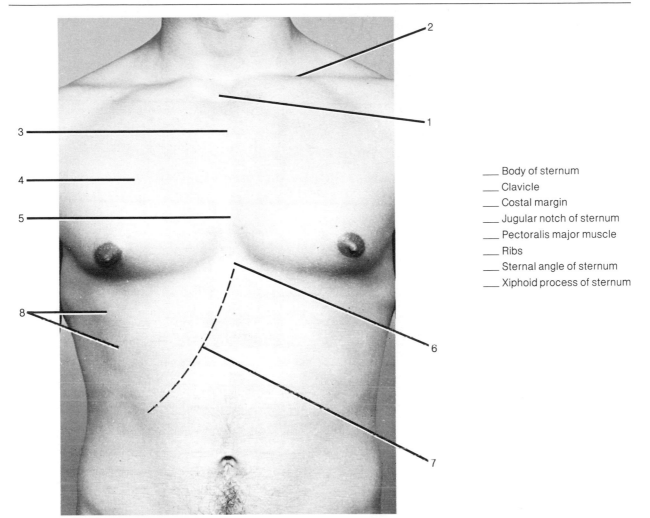

___ Body of sternum
___ Clavicle
___ Costal margin
___ Jugular notch of sternum
___ Pectoralis major muscle
___ Ribs
___ Sternal angle of sternum
___ Xiphoid process of sternum

FIGURE 11.4 **Surface anatomy of chest. (The serratus anterior muscle is shown in Figure 11.5.)**

b. **Linea alba**—Slight groove in midline extending from xiphoid process to symphysis pubis. This is particularly obvious in thin, muscular males.

c. **Tendinous intersections**—Fibrous bands that run transversely across the rectus abdominis muscle. Three or more are visible in muscular persons.

d. **Muscles**—Among the superficial abdominal muscles are the **external oblique** (inferior to serratus anterior) and **rectus abdominis** (just lateral to midline of abdomen).

e. **Symphysis pubis**—Anterior joint of hipbones. This structure is palpated as a firm resistance in the midline at the inferior portion of the anterior abdominal wall.

Using your textbook as an aid, label Figure 11.5.

D. UPPER EXTREMITY

The **upper extremity** consists of the armpit, arm, shoulder, elbow, forearm, wrist, and hand (palm and fingers).

1. Major surface features of the **shoulder (acromial)** are:

a. **Acromioclavicular joint**—Slight elevation at lateral end of clavicle.

b. **Acromion**—Expanded end of spine of scapula. This is clearly visible in some individuals and can be palpated about 2.5 cm (1 in.) distal to acromioclavicular joint (see Figure 11.3).

c. **Deltoid muscle**—Triangular muscle that forms rounded prominence of shoulder. This is a frequent site for intramuscular injections (see Figure 11.3).

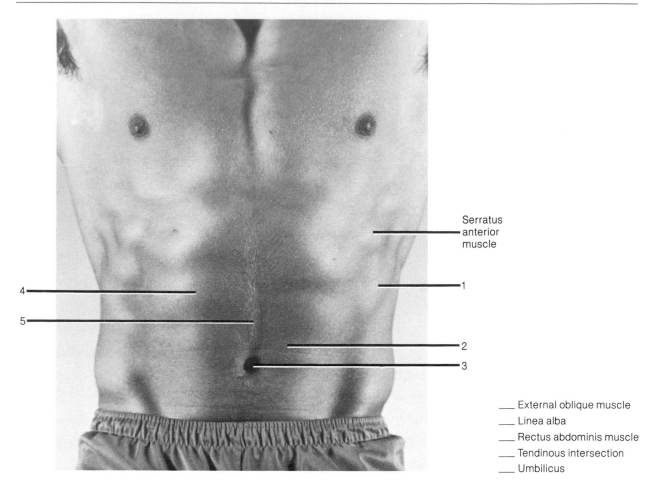

Serratus anterior muscle

1

4

5

2

3

___ External oblique muscle
___ Linea alba
___ Rectus abdominis muscle
___ Tendinous intersection
___ Umbilicus

FIGURE 11.5 Surface anatomy of abdomen.

2. Major surface features of the **arm (brachium)** and **elbow (cubitus)** are:

a. **Biceps brachii muscle**—Forms bulk of anterior surface of arm.

b. **Triceps brachii muscle**—Forms bulk of posterior surface of arm.

c. **Medial epicondyle**—Medial projection at distal end of humerus.

d. **Ulnar nerve**—Can be palpated as a rounded cord in a groove behind the medial epicondyle.

e. **Lateral epicondyle**—Lateral projection at distal end of humerus.

f. **Olecranon**—Projection of proximal end of ulna that lies between and slightly superior to epicondyles when forearm is extended; forms elbow.

g. **Cubital fossa**—Triangular space in anterior region of elbow. This area contains bi-

ceps brachii tendon, brachial artery and its terminal branches (radial and ulnar arteries), and parts of median and radial nerves.

h. **Median cubital vein**—Crosses cubital fossa obliquely. This vein is frequently selected for removal of blood.

Using your textbook as an aid, label Figure 11.6.

3. Major surface features of the **forearm (antebrachium)** and **wrist (carpus)** are:

a. **Styloid process of ulna**—Projection of distal end of ulna at medial side of wrist.

b. **Styloid process of radius**—Projection of distal end of radius at lateral side of wrist.

c. **Brachioradialis muscle**—Located at superior and lateral aspect of forearm.

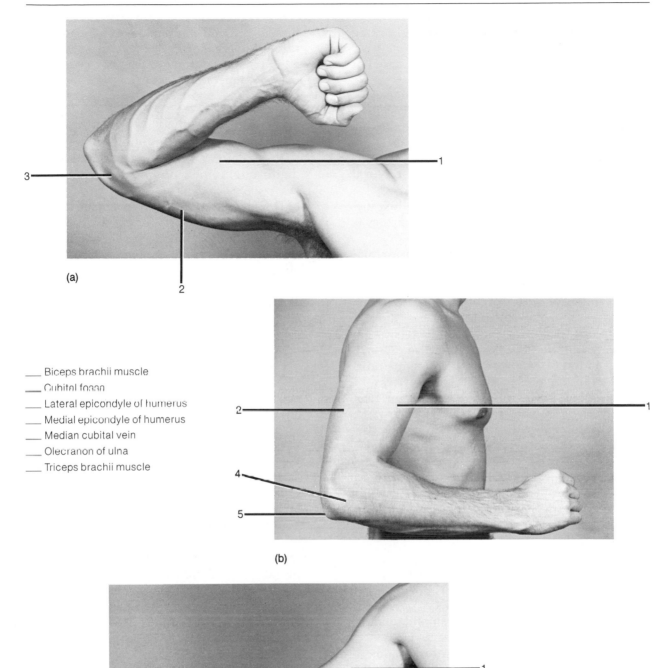

___ Biceps brachii muscle
___ Cubital fossa
___ Lateral epicondyle of humerus
___ Medial epicondyle of humerus
___ Median cubital vein
___ Olecranon of ulna
___ Triceps brachii muscle

Basilic vein

FIGURE 11.6 **Surface anatomy of arm and elbow. (a) Medial view. (b) Lateral view. (c) Anterior view.**

d. **Flexor carpi radialis muscle**—Located along midportion of forearm.

e. **Flexor carpi ulnaris muscle**—Located at medial aspect of forearm.

f. **Tendon of palmaris longus muscle**—Located on anterior surface of wrist near ulna. When you make a fist, you can see this tendon.

g. **Tendon of flexor carpi radialis muscle**—Tendon on anterior surface of wrist lateral to tendon of palmaris longus.

h. **Radial artery**—Can be palpated just medial to styloid process of ulna; this artery is frequently used to take pulse.

i. **Pisiform bone**—Medial bone of proximal carpals. The bone is easily palpated as a projection distal to styloid process of ulna.

j. **Tendon of extensor pollicis brevis muscle**—Tendon close to styloid process of radius along posterior surface of wrist, best seen when thumb is bent backward.

k. **Tendon of extensor pollicis longus muscle**—Tendon closer to styloid process of ulna along posterior surface of wrist, best seen when thumb is bent backward.

l. **"Anatomical snuffbox"**—Depression between tendons of extensor pollicis brevis and extensor pollicis longus muscles. Radial artery can be palpated in the depression.

m. **Bracelet flexure lines**—Several more or less constant lines on anterior aspect of wrist where skin is firmly attached to underlying deep fascia.

Using your textbook as an aid, label Figure 11.7.

4. Major surface features of the **hand (manus)** are:

a. **"Knuckles"**—Commonly refers to dorsal aspects of distal ends of metacarpals II, III, IV, and V. Term also includes dorsal aspects of metacarpophalangeal and interphalangeal joints.

b. **Thenar eminence**—Lateral rounded contour on anterior surface of hand formed by muscles of thumb.

c. **Hypothenar eminence**—Medial rounded contour on anterior surface of hand formed by muscles of little finger.

d. **Skin creases**—Several more or less constant lines on the anterior aspect of the palm and digits where skin is firmly attached to underlying deep fascia. These are generally divided into **palmar flexion creases** and **digital flexion creases.**

e. **Extensor tendons**—Besides the tendons of the extensor pollicis brevis and extensor pollicis longus muscles associated with the thumb, the following extensor tendons are also visible on the posterior aspect of the hand: **extensor digiti minimi tendon** in line with phalanx V (little finger) and **extensor digitorum** in line with phalanges II, III, and IV.

f. **Dorsal venous arch**—Superficial veins on posterior surface of hand; displayed by compressing the blood vessels at the wrist for a few moments as the hand is opened and closed.

With the aid of your textbook, label Figure 11.8.

E. LOWER EXTREMITY

The **lower extremity** consists of the buttocks, thigh, knee, leg, ankle, and foot.

1. Major surface features of the **buttocks (gluteal region)** and **thigh (femoral region)** are:

a. **Iliac crest**—Superior margin of ilium of hipbone, forming outline of superior border of buttock. When you rest your hands on your hips, they rest on the iliac crests.

b. **Posterior superior iliac spine**—Posterior termination of iliac crest; lies deep to a dimple (skin depression) about 4 cm (1.5 in.) lateral to midline. Dimple forms because skin and underlying fascia are attached to bone.

c. **Gluteus maximus muscle**—Forms major portion of prominence of buttock.

d. **Gluteus medius muscle**—Superolateral to gluteus maximus. This is a frequent site for intramuscular injections.

e. **Gluteal cleft**—Depression along midline that separates the buttocks.

f. **Gluteal fold**—Inferior limit of buttock formed by inferior margin of gluteus maximus muscle.

g. **Ischial tuberosity**—Bony prominence of ischium of hipbone, bears weight of body when seated.

h. **Greater trochanter**—Projection of proximal end of femur on lateral surface of thigh. This can be palpated about 20 cm (8 in.) inferior to iliac crest.

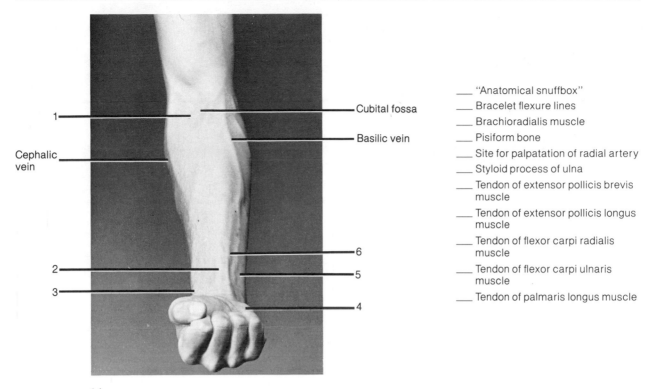

(a)

1 —
Cephalic vein
2 —
3 —

Cubital fossa
Basilic vein
6
5
4

___ "Anatomical snuffbox"
___ Bracelet flexure lines
___ Brachioradialis muscle
___ Pisiform bone
___ Site for palpatation of radial artery
___ Styloid process of ulna
___ Tendon of extensor pollicis brevis muscle
___ Tendon of extensor pollicis longus muscle
___ Tendon of flexor carpi radialis muscle
___ Tendon of flexor carpi ulnaris muscle
___ Tendon of palmaris longus muscle

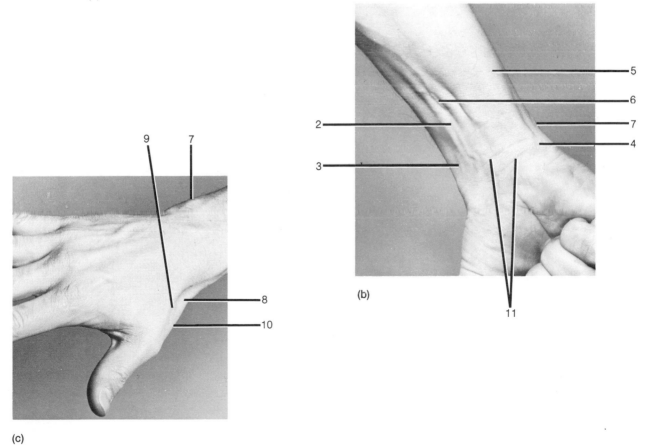

(b)

2 —
3 —

5
6
7
4

11

(c)

9   7

8
10

FIGURE 11.7   Surface anatomy of forearm and wrist. (a) and (b) Anterior views. (c) Posterolateral view.

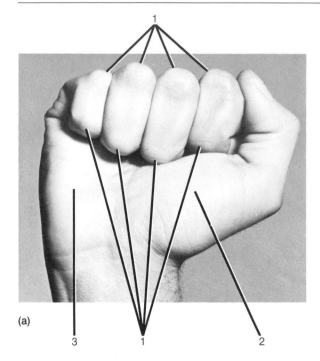

(a)

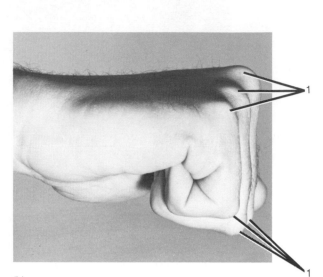

(b)

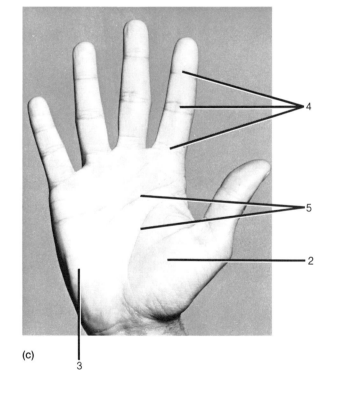

(c)

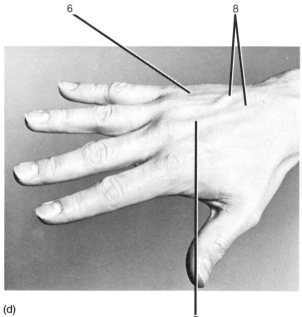

(d)

___ Digital flexion creases   ___ Palmar flexion creases

___ Dorsal venous arch   ___ Tendon of extensor digiti minimi muscle

___ Hypothenar eminence   ___ Tendon of extensor digitorum muscle

___ "Knuckles"   ___ Thenar eminence

**FIGURE 11.8   Surface anatomy of hand. (a) Anterior
view. (b) Medial view. (c) Anterior view. (d) Posterior view.**

i. **Anterior thigh muscles**—Include **sartorius** (runs obliquely across thigh) and **quadriceps femoris**, which consists of **rectus femoris** (midportion of thigh), **vastus lateralis** (anterolateral surface of thigh), **vastus medialis** (medial inferior portion of thigh), and **vastus intermedius** (deep to rectus femoris). Vastus lateralis is frequent injection site for diabetics.

j. **Posterior thigh muscles**—Include the **hamstrings (semitendinosus, semimembranosus**, and **biceps femoris).**

k. **Medial thigh muscles**—Include **adductor magnus, adductor brevis, adductor longus, gracilis, obturator externus**, and **pectineus.**

With the aid of your textbook, label Figure 11.9.

2. Major surface anatomy features of the **knee (genu)** are as follows:

a. **Patella**—Kneecap, located within quadriceps femoris tendon on anterior surface of knee along midline. Margins of condyles (described shortly) can be felt on either side of it.

b. **Patellar ligament**—Continuation of quadriceps femoris tendon inferior to patella.

c. **Popliteal fossa**—Diamond-shaped space on posterior aspect of knee visible when knee is flexed. Fossa is bordered superolaterally by the biceps femoris muscle, superomedially by the semimembranosus and semitendinosus muscles, and inferolaterally and inferomedially by the lateral and medial heads of the gastrocnemius muscle.

d. **Medial condyles of femur and tibia**—Medial projections just below patella. Upper part of projection belongs to distal end of femur, lower part of projection belongs to proximal end of tibia.

e. **Lateral condyles of femur and tibia**—Lateral projections just below patella. Upper part of projections belongs to distal end of femur, lower part of projections belongs to proximal end of tibia.

With the aid of your textbook, label Figure 11.10.

3. Major surface anatomy features of the **leg (crus)** and **ankle (tarsus)** are:

a. **Tibial tuberosity**—Bony prominence of tibia below patella into which patellar ligament inserts (see Figure 11.10a).

b. **Medial malleolus**—Projection of distal end of tibia that forms medial prominence of ankle.

c. **Lateral malleolus**—Projection of distal end of fibula that forms lateral prominence of ankle.

d. **Calcaneal (Achilles) tendon**—Tendon of insertion into calcaneus for gastrocnemius and soleus muscles.

e. **Tibialis anterior muscle**—Located on anterior surface of leg.

f. **Gastrocnemius muscle**—Forms bulk of middle and superior portions of posterior surface of leg.

g. **Soleus muscle**—Mostly deep to gastrocnemius, visible on either side of gastrocnemius below middle of leg.

With the aid of your textbook, label Figure 11.11.

4. Major surface anatomy features of the **foot (pes)** are:

a. **Calcaneus**—Heel bone to which calcaneal (Achilles) tendon inserts.

b. **Tendon of extensor hallucis longus muscle**—Visible in line with phalanx I (great toe).

c. **Tendons of extensor digitorum longus muscles**—Visible in line with phalanges II through V.

d. **Dorsal venous arch**—Superficial veins on dorsum of foot that unite to form small and great saphenous veins.

With the aid of your textbook, label Figure 11.12.

LABORATORY REPORT QUESTIONS (PAGE 391)

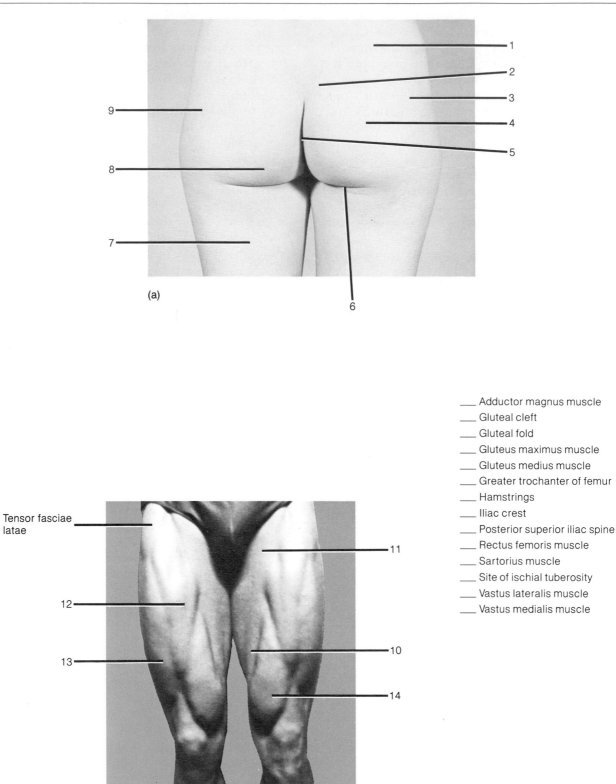

(a)

(b)

Tensor fasciae latae

_____ Adductor magnus muscle
_____ Gluteal cleft
_____ Gluteal fold
_____ Gluteus maximus muscle
_____ Gluteus medius muscle
_____ Greater trochanter of femur
_____ Hamstrings
_____ Iliac crest
_____ Posterior superior iliac spine
_____ Rectus femoris muscle
_____ Sartorius muscle
_____ Site of ischial tuberosity
_____ Vastus lateralis muscle
_____ Vastus medialis muscle

FIGURE 11.9 Surface anatomy of buttocks and thigh. (a) Posterior view. (b) Anterior view.

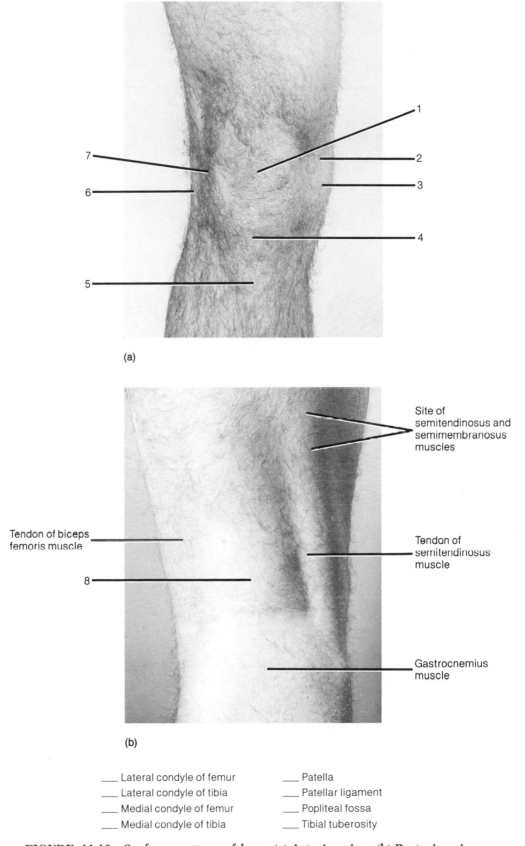

(a)

Site of
semitendinosus and
semimembranosus
muscles

Tendon of biceps
femoris muscle

Tendon of
semitendinosus
muscle

Gastrocnemius
muscle

(b)

___ Lateral condyle of femur   ___ Patella

___ Lateral condyle of tibia   ___ Patellar ligament

___ Medial condyle of femur   ___ Popliteal fossa

___ Medial condyle of tibia   ___ Tibial tuberosity

FIGURE 11.10   **Surface anatomy of knee. (a) Anterior view. (b) Posterior view.**

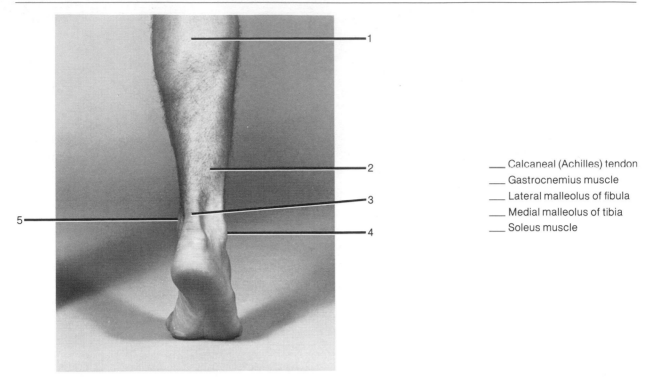

___ Calcaneal (Achilles) tendon
___ Gastrocnemius muscle
___ Lateral malleolus of fibula
___ Medial malleolus of tibia
___ Soleus muscle

FIGURE 11.11 Surface anatomy of leg seen in posterior view.

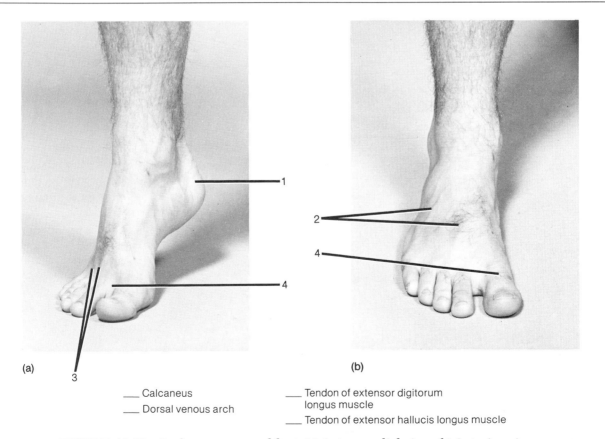

(a)

(b)

___ Calcaneus
___ Dorsal venous arch

___ Tendon of extensor digitorum longus muscle
___ Tendon of extensor hallucis longus muscle

FIGURE 11.12 Surface anatomy of foot. (a) Anteromedial view. (b) Anterior view.

12 | NERVOUS TISSUE AND PHYSIOLOGY

In this exercise you will identify the parts of a neuron and the components of a reflex arc. You will also perform several experiments on reflexes in the frog.

A. HISTOLOGY OF NERVOUS TISSUE

Despite its complexity, the nervous system consists of only two principal kinds of cells: neurons and neuroglia. **Neurons** (nerve cells) constitute the nervous tissue and are highly specialized for impulse conduction. **Neuroglia** (noo-ROG-lē-a) bind together nervous tissue, form myelin sheaths around axons within the central nervous system, and carry on phagocytosis. They do not transmit impulses.

A neuron consists of the following parts:

1. **Cell body (perikaryon)** (per′-i-KAR-ē-on)—Contains a nucleus, cytoplasm, mitochondria, Golgi apparatus, chromatophilic substance (Nissl bodies), and neurofibrils.

2. **Dendrites**—Usually short, highly branched extensions of the cell body that conduct impulses toward the cell body.

3. **Axon**—Single, usually relatively long process that conducts impulses away from the cell body. An axon, in turn, consists of the following:
   a. **Axon hillock**—The origin of an axon from the cell body represented as a small conical elevation.
   b. **Axoplasm**—Cytoplasm of an axon.
   c. **Axolemma**—Plasma membrane around the axoplasm.
   d. **Axon collateral**—Side branch of an axon.

e. **Telodendria** (tel′-ō-DEN-drē-a)—Fine, branching filaments of an axon or axon collateral.
f. **Synaptic end bulbs**—Bulblike structures at distal end of telodendria that contain storage sacs (synaptic vesicles) for neurotransmitters.
g. **Myelin sheath**—Phospholipid, segmented covering of many axons, especially large peripheral ones; the myelin sheath is produced by peripheral nervous system neuroglia called **neurolemmocytes (Schwann cells)**.
h. **Neurilemma (sheath of Schwann)**—Peripheral, nucleated cytoplasmic layer of the neurolemmocyte that encloses the myelin sheath.
i. **Neurofibral node (node of Ranvier)**—Unmyelinated gap between segments of the myelin sheath.

Using your textbook and models of neurons as a guide, label Figure 12.1.

Now obtain a prepared slide of an ox spinal cord (cross section), human spinal cord (cross and longitudinal sections), nerve endings in skeletal muscle, and a nerve trunk (cross and longitudinal sections). Examine each under high power and identify as many parts of the neuron as you can.

Neurons may be classified on the basis of structure and function. Structurally, neurons are **multipolar** (several dendrites and one axon), **bipolar** (one dendrite and one axon), and **unipolar** (a single process that branches into an axon and a dendrite). Functionally, neurons are classified as (1) **sensory (afferent)**, which carry impulses toward the central nervous system; (2) **motor (efferent)**, which carry impulses away from the central nervous system; and (3) **associ-**

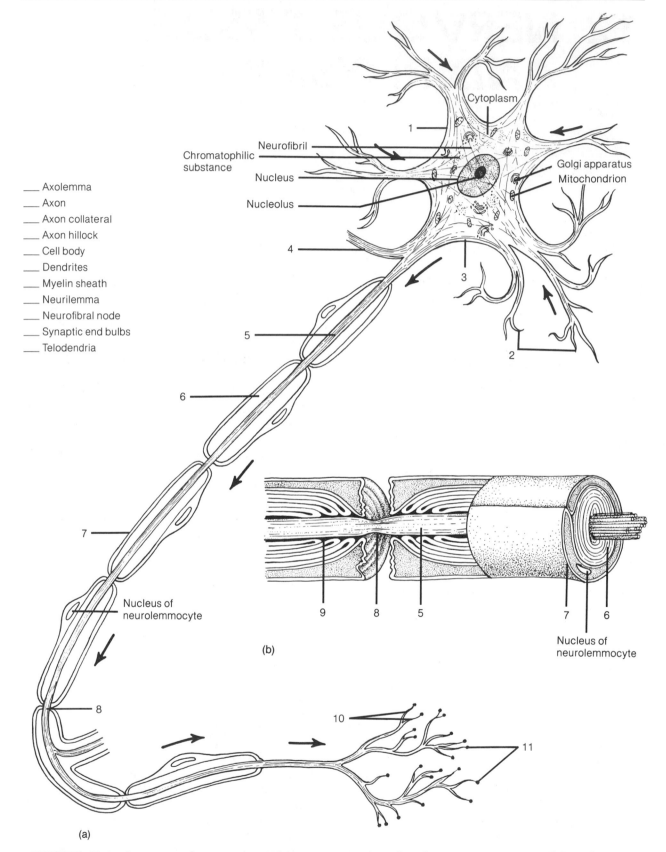

___ Axolemma
___ Axon
___ Axon collateral
___ Axon hillock
___ Cell body
___ Dendrites
___ Myelin sheath
___ Neurilemma
___ Neurofibral node
___ Synaptic end bulbs
___ Telodendria

Cytoplasm

Neurofibril

Chromatophilic substance

Nucleus

Nucleolus

Golgi apparatus

Mitochondrion

Nucleus of neurolemmocyte

(b)

Nucleus of neurolemmocyte

(a)

FIGURE 12.1 **Structure of a neuron. (a) Shown is an entire multipolar neuron. Arrows indicate direction in which the nerve impulse travels. (b) Cross section and longitudinal section through a myelinated fiber.**

ation (internuncial), which are located in the central nervous system and carry impulses between sensory and motor neurons.

The neuron you have already labeled in Figure 12.1 is a motor neuron.

B. HISTOLOGY OF NEUROGLIA

Among the types of neuroglial cells are the following:

1. **Astrocytes** (AS-trō-sīts)—Star-shaped cells having numerous processes; they twine around neurons to form a supporting network in the central nervous system and attach neurons to blood vessels.

    a. **Protoplasmic astrocytes** are found in the gray matter of the central nervous system.

    b. **Fibrous astrocytes** are found in the white matter of the central nervous system.

2. **Oligodendrocytes** (ol'-i-gō-DEN-drō-sīts)—Resemble astrocytes but with fewer and shorter processes; they provide support in the central nervous system and produce a myelin sheath on axons of neurons of the central nervous system.

3. **Microglia** (mī-KROG-lē-a)—Small cells with few processes; although normally stationary, they can migrate to damaged nervous tissue and there carry on phagocytosis; they are macrophages.

4. **Ependyma** (e-PEN-di-ma)—Epithelial cells arranged in a single layer that range from squamous to columnar in shape; many are ciliated; they form a continuous epithelial lining for the ventricles of the brain, spaces that form and circulate cerebrospinal fluid.

    Obtain prepared slides of astrocytes (protoplasmic and fibrous), oligodendrocytes, microglia, and ependyma. Using your textbook, Figure 12.2, and models of neuroglia as a guide, identify the various kinds of cells. In the spaces provided, draw each of the cells.

C. REFLEX ARC

Reflexes are rapid responses to changes in the internal or external environment that attempt to restore body functions to homeostasis. For a reflex to occur, a nerve impulse must travel

Protoplasmic astrocyte

Fibrous astrocyte

Oligodendrocyte

Microglial cell

Ependymal cell

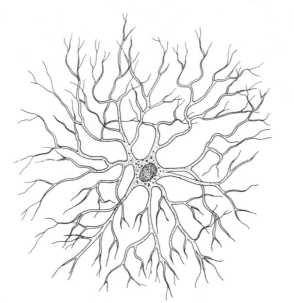

(a)

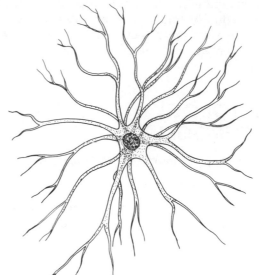

(b)

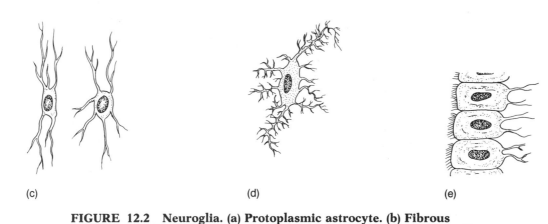

(c)   (d)   (e)

FIGURE 12.2   Neuroglia. (a) Protoplasmic astrocyte. (b) Fibrous
astrocyte. (c) Oligodendrocytes. (d) Microglial cell. (e) Ependymal cells.

over a neural pathway called a **reflex arc,**
which consists of the following components:

1. **Receptor**—The distal end of a dendrite or
sensory structure associated with the distal
end of a dendrite; it responds to a stimulus by
initiating a nerve impulse in a sensory neuron.

2. **Sensory neuron**—Nerve cell that carries the
impulse from the receptor to the central nervous system.

3. **Center**—Region within the central nervous
system where an incoming sensory impulse is
processed. The center may generate an outgo-
ing motor impulse; the center may also contain

an association neuron between the sensory
neuron and the motor neuron. The number of
synapses in the center is directly proportional
to the complexity of the reflex.

4. **Motor neuron**—Nerve cell that transmits
the impulse generated by the sensory neuron
or the association neuron in the center to the
part of the body that will respond.

5. **Effector**—The part of the body, either a
muscle or a gland, that responds to the motor
neuron impulse and thus the stimulus.

Label the components of a reflex arc in Figure 12.3.

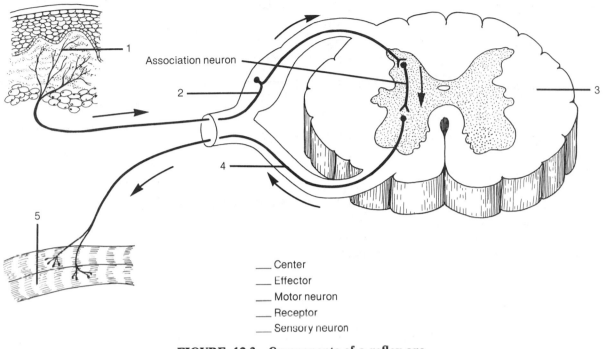

_____ Center
_____ Effector
_____ Motor neuron
_____ Receptor
_____ Sensory neuron

FIGURE 12.3   Components of a reflex arc.

D. SPINAL REFLEXES OF FROG

The following exercise will demonstrate the varying levels of complexity encountered in several common reflexes. Through the results obtained in this experiment you should be able to determine which reflexes involve synapses within the brain and which involve synapses within the spinal cord only. You should also be able to determine the relative complexities of the reflexes. Refer to Exercise 9 for pithing instructions and for the nerve-muscle preparation.

All test results should be recorded in the table provided in the Laboratory Report Results (page 395).

1. Place the frog on the lab bench and observe the position of the head and legs.

2. Rate of respiration can be determined by counting the number of times that the frog raises and lowers the floor of its mouth or opens and closes its nostrils per minute.

3. Place the frog on its back and see if it rights itself (righting reflex).

4. Place the frog on a turtle board and then slowly tilt the board and observe the animal's response (horizon reflex).

5. Place the frog in water and observe whether or not it stays afloat or swims.

6. Pinch the toes of the hind legs and observe if the frog withdraws its foot (withdrawal reflex).

7. Touch the frog's cornea and observe the presence or absence of a corneal reflex.

8. Slap the table sharply, close to the frog, and observe its response to this loud noise and table vibration.

Single-pith the frog and repeat the same 8 procedures. Upon completion of these procedures, the following tests should also be conducted on a single-pithed frog:

1. Insert a small wire through the anterior area of both jaws. Attach the wire so that the frog is suspended over a pan or sink with its legs hanging freely.

2. Using a piece of cotton that has been moistened with a 30% acetic acid solution, rub the lower portion of one leg. Observe the response. Rinse the frog with water.

3. Place the acid on the chest of the frog, observe the response, and wash the frog as before.

Repeat all 11 procedures with a double-pithed frog and record the observations.

1. Prepare the sciatic nerve and muscle preparation of one leg of the frog as outlined in Exercise 9.

2. Ascertain reactivity of the sciatic nerve by determining the threshold of the nerve. What response should you be observing in order to determine that threshold, and therefore an action potential, has been obtained in the nerve?

_____

_____

_____

If the sciatic nerve can be stimulated, what aspects of the reflex are functional and what aspects are not in a single- and double-pithed frog?

_____

_____

_____

_____

_____

_____

LABORATORY REPORT QUESTIONS (PAGE 397)

13 | NERVOUS SYSTEM

The nervous system has two principal divisions: central and peripheral. The **central nervous system (CNS)** consists of the brain and spinal cord and is the control center of the entire nervous system. The **peripheral nervous system (PNS)** consists of the various processes that connect the CNS with receptors, muscles, and glands. The PNS is divided into afferent and efferent systems. The **afferent system** consists of neurons that convey information from receptors to the CNS. The **efferent system** consists of nerve cells that convey information from the CNS to muscles and glands. Finally, the efferent system is subdivided into a somatic nervous system and an autonomic nervous system. The **somatic nervous system (SNS)** consists of efferent neurons that convey information from the CNS to skeletal muscles and is under conscious control. The **autonomic nervous system (ANS)** contains efferent neurons that convey information from the CNS to smooth muscle, cardiac muscle, and glands and is usually involuntary.

In this exercise, you will examine the principal structural features of the spinal cord and spinal nerves, perform several experiments on reflexes, identify the principal structural features of the brain, trace the course of cerebrospinal fluid, identify the cranial nerves, and perform several experiments designed to test for cranial nerve function. You will also dissect and study the sheep brain.

A. SPINAL CORD AND SPINAL NERVES

1. General Features

Obtain a model or preserved specimen of the spinal cord and identify the following general features:

a. **Cervical enlargement**—Between vertebrae C4 and T1; origin of nerves to upper extremities.

b. **Lumbar enlargement**—Between vertebrae T9 and T12; origin of nerves to lower extremities.

c. **Conus medullaris** (KŌ-nus med-yoo-LAR-is)—Tapered conical portion of spinal cord near vertebra L1 or L2.

d. **Filum terminale** (FĪ-lum ter-mi-NAL-e)—Nonnervous fibrous tissue arising from the conus medullaris and extending inferiorly to the coccyx.

e. **Cauda equina** (KAW-da ē-KWĪ-na)—Spinal nerves that angle inferiorly in the vertebral canal giving the appearance of wisps of coarse hair.

f. **Anterior median fissure**—Deep, wide groove on the anterior surface of the spinal cord.

g. **Posterior median sulcus**—Shallow, narrow groove on the posterior surface of the spinal cord.

After you have located the parts on a model or preserved specimen of the spinal cord, label the spinal cord in Figure 13.1.

2. Meninges

The **meninges** (me-NIN-jēz) are coverings that run continuously around the spinal cord and brain. They protect the central nervous system. The spinal meninges are:

a. **Dura mater** (DYOO-ra MĀ-ter)—The outer meninx composed of dense fibrous connective tissue. Between the wall of the vertebral canal and the dura mater is the **epidural space**, which is filled with fat, connective tissue, and blood vessels.

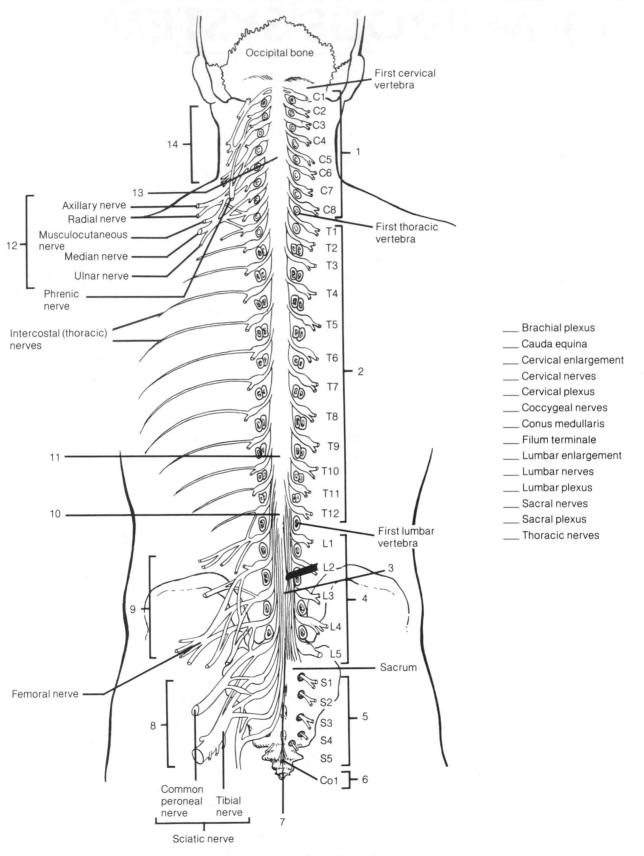

Occipital bone

First cervical
vertebra

C1
C2
C3
C4
C5
C6
C7
C8

1

14

13

Axillary nerve
Radial nerve
Musculocutaneous
nerve
Median nerve
Ulnar nerve

12

Phrenic
nerve

First thoracic
vertebra

T1
T2
T3
T4
T5
T6
T7
T8
T9
T10
T11
T12

Intercostal (thoracic)
nerves

2

11

10

First lumbar
vertebra

L1
L2
L3
L4
L5

3
4

9

Femoral nerve

Sacrum

S1
S2
S3
S4
S5

Co1

5

6

8

Common
peroneal
nerve

Tibial
nerve

7

Sciatic nerve

___ Brachial plexus
___ Cauda equina
___ Cervical enlargement
___ Cervical nerves
___ Cervical plexus
___ Coccygeal nerves
___ Conus medullaris
___ Filum terminale
___ Lumbar enlargement
___ Lumbar nerves
___ Lumbar plexus
___ Sacral nerves
___ Sacral plexus
___ Thoracic nerves

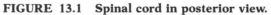

FIGURE 13.1 Spinal cord in posterior view.

b. **Arachnoid** (a-RAK-noyd)—The middle meninx composed of very delicate connective tissue. Between the arachnoid and the dura mater is a space called the **subdural space**.

c. **Pia mater** (PĒ-a MĀ-ter)—The inner meninx composed of a transparent fibrous membrane that contains blood vessels. Between the pia mater and the arachnoid is a space called the **subarachnoid space** where cerebrospinal fluid circulates. Extensions of the pia mater called **denticulate** (den-TIK-yoo-lāt) **ligaments** suspend the spinal cord and afford protection against shock and sudden displacement.

Label the meninges, subarachnoid space, and denticulate ligament in Figure 13.2.

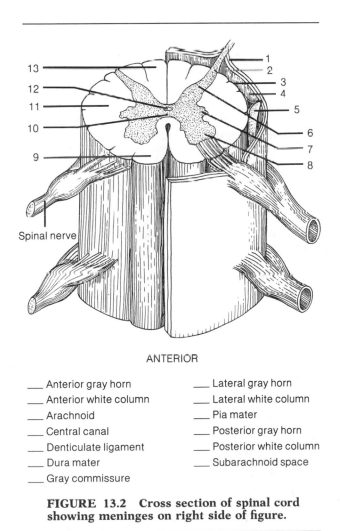

ANTERIOR

___ Anterior gray horn   ___ Lateral gray horn
___ Anterior white column   ___ Lateral white column
___ Arachnoid   ___ Pia mater
___ Central canal   ___ Posterior gray horn
___ Denticulate ligament   ___ Posterior white column
___ Dura mater   ___ Subarachnoid space
___ Gray commissure

FIGURE 13.2 Cross section of spinal cord showing meninges on right side of figure.

3. Cross Section of Spinal Cord

Obtain a model or specimen of the spinal cord in cross section and note the gray matter, shaped like a letter H or a butterfly. Identify the following parts:

a. **Gray commissure** (KOM-mi-shur)—Cross bar of the letter H.

b. **Central canal**—Small space in the center of the gray commissure that contains cerebrospinal fluid.

c. **Anterior gray horn**—Anterior region of the upright portion of the H.

d. **Posterior gray horn**—Posterior region of the upright portion of the H.

e. **Lateral gray horn**—Intermediate region between the anterior and posterior gray horns.

f. **Anterior white column**—Anterior region of white matter.

g. **Posterior white column**—Posterior region of white matter.

h. **Lateral white column**—Intermediate region of white matter between the anterior and posterior white columns.

Label these parts of the spinal cord in cross section in Figure 13.2.

If available, examine a slide of a spinal cord in cross section and see how many structures you can identify.

4. Spinal Nerve Attachments

Spinal nerves are the paths of communication between the spinal cord tracts and the periphery. The 31 pairs of spinal nerves are named and numbered according to the region of the spinal cord from which they emerge. The first cervical pair emerges between the atlas and occipital bone; all other spinal nerves leave the vertebral column from intervertebral foramina between adjoining vertebrae. There are 8 pairs of cervical nerves, 12 pairs of thoracic nerves, 5 pairs of lumbar nerves, 5 pairs of sacral nerves, and 1 pair of coccygeal nerves. Label the spinal nerves in Figure 13.1.

Each pair of spinal nerves is connected to the spinal cord by two points of attachment called roots. The **posterior (sensory) root** contains sensory nerve fibers only and conducts impulses from the periphery to the spinal cord.

Each posterior root has a swelling, the **posterior (sensory) root ganglion,** which contains the cell bodies of the sensory neurons from the periphery. Fibers extend from the ganglion into the posterior gray horn. The other point of attachment, the **anterior (motor) root,** contains motor nerve fibers only and conducts impulses from the spinal cord to the periphery. The cell bodies of the motor neurons are located in lateral or anterior gray horns.

Label the posterior root, posterior root ganglion, anterior root, spinal nerve, cell body of sensory neuron, axon of sensory neuron, cell body of motor neuron, and axon of motor neuron in Figure 13.3.

5. Structure of Spinal Nerves

The posterior and anterior roots unite to form a spinal nerve at the intervertebral foramen. Because the posterior root contains sensory nerve fibers and the anterior root contains motor nerve fibers, all spinal nerves are mixed nerves.

Individual nerve fibers within a nerve, whether myelinated or unmyelinated, are wrapped in a connective tissue covering called the **endoneurium** (en'-dō-NOO-rē-um). Groups of fibers with their endoneurium are arranged in bundles called fascicles, and each bundle is wrapped in a connective tissue covering called the **perineurium** (per'-i-NOO-rē-um). All the fascicles, in turn, are wrapped in a connective tissue covering called the **epineurium** (ep'-i-NOO-rē-um). This is the outermost covering around the entire nerve.

Obtain a prepared slide of a nerve in cross section and identify the fibers, endoneurium, perineurium, epineurium, and fascicles. Now label Figure 13.4.

6. Branches of Spinal Nerves

Shortly after leaving its intervertebral foramen, a spinal nerve divides into several branches called rami:

a. **Dorsal ramus** (RĀ-mus)—Innervates deep muscles and skin of the dorsal surface of the back.
b. **Ventral ramus**—Innervates superficial back muscles and all structures of the extremities and lateral and ventral trunk; except for thoracic nerves T2 to T11, the ventral rami of other spinal nerves form plexuses before innervating their structures.

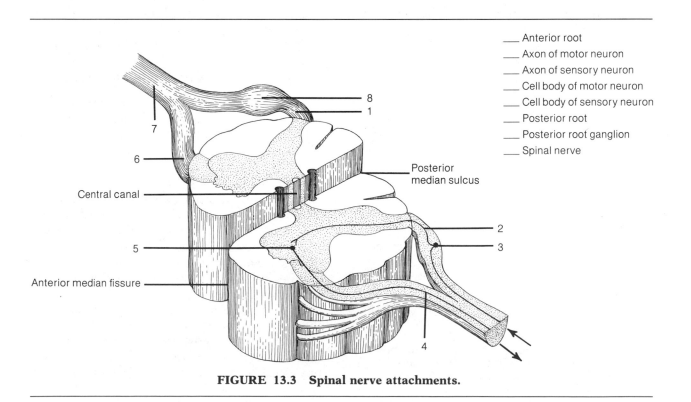

___ Anterior root
___ Axon of motor neuron
___ Axon of sensory neuron
___ Cell body of motor neuron
___ Cell body of sensory neuron
___ Posterior root
___ Posterior root ganglion
___ Spinal nerve

Posterior median sulcus

Central canal

Anterior median fissure

FIGURE 13.3 Spinal nerve attachments.

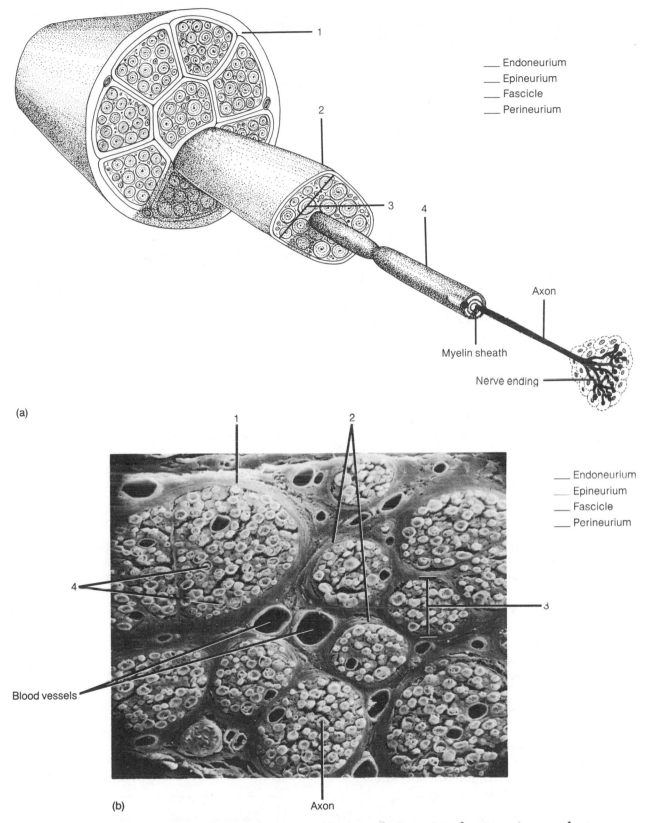

(a)

_____ Endoneurium
_____ Epineurium
_____ Fascicle
_____ Perineurium

Axon

Myelin sheath

Nerve ending

_____ Endoneurium
_____ Epineurium
_____ Fascicle
_____ Perineurium

Blood vessels

(b)

Axon

FIGURE 13.4   Coverings of a spinal nerve. (a) Diagram. (b) Scanning electron micrograph at a magnification of 900×. (From _Tissues and Organs: A Text-Atlas of Scanning Electron Microscopy_ by Richard G. Kessel and Randy H. Kardon. W. H. Freeman and Company. Copyright © 1979.)

c. **Meningeal branch**—Innervates vertebrae, vertebral ligaments, blood vessels of the spinal cord, and meninges.

d. **Rami communicantes** (RĀ-mē ko-myoo-nē-KAN-tēz)—Gray and white rami communicantes are components of the autonomic nervous system; they connect the ventral rami with sympathetic trunk ganglia.

7. Plexuses

The ventral rami of spinal nerves, except for T2-T11, join with adjacent nerves on either side of the body to form networks called **plexuses** (PLEK-sus-ēz).

a. **Cervical plexus** (PLEK-sus)—Formed by the ventral rami of the first four cervical nerves (C1-C4) with contributions from C5; one is located on each side of the neck alongside the first four cervical vertebrae; the plexus supplies the skin and muscles of the head, neck, and upper part of shoulders.

b. **Brachial plexus**—Formed by the ventral rami of spinal nerves C5-C8 and T1 with contributions from C4 and T2; each is located on either side of the last four cervical and first thoracic vertebrae and extends downward and laterally, over the first rib behind the clavicle, and into the axilla; the plexus constitutes the entire nerve supply for the upper extremities and shoulder region.

c. **Lumbar plexus**—Formed by the ventral rami of spinal nerves L1-L4; each is located on either side of the first four lumbar vertebrae posterior to the psoas major muscle and anterior to the quadratus lumborum muscle; the plexus supplies the anterolateral abdominal wall, external genitals, and part of the lower extremity.

d. **Sacral plexus**—Formed by the ventral rami of spinal nerves L4-L5 and S1-S4; each is located largely anterior to the sacrum; the plexus supplies the buttocks, perineum, and lower extremities.

Label the cervical, brachial, lumbar, and sacral plexuses in Figure 13.1. Also note the names of some of the major peripheral nerves that arise from the plexuses.

8. Reflex Experiments

In this section, you will determine the response obtained in various common human reflexes.

Reflexes that result in contraction of skeletal muscles are called **somatic reflexes.** Those that cause contraction of cardiac or smooth muscle or secretion by glands are known as **visceral (autonomic) reflexes.**

a. **Corneal reflex**—Approach, but *do not touch,* the cornea of your partner's eye very gently with lens paper.

What happens? _____

_____

What is the purpose of this reflex? _____

_____

b. **Light reflex (photopupil reflex)**—Have your partner close his or her eyes for about 2 minutes while facing a bright light. Now have your partner open his or her eyes and note the size of the pupils.

Describe the response. _____

_____

Which nerves and muscles act in this reflex? _____

What is the purpose of this reflex? _____

_____

c. **Accommodation pupil reflex**—Have your partner focus on an object at a distance of 20 ft or more.
Describe the size of the subject's pupils.

_____

Now have the subject focus on an object 10 in. away. Make sure that there has been no change in illumination. Note the size of the pupils again.

Has there been any change? _____

_____

_____

What is the purpose of this reflex? _____

_____

_____

What nerve and muscles act in this reflex?

_____

d. **Convergence reflex**—Observe the position of your partner's eyeballs while he or she looks at a distant object. Now have your partner look at a near object.

What changes do you observe in the eye-balls? _____

_____

_____

What is the purpose of this reflex? _____

_____

e. **Swallowing reflex**—Swallow the saliva in your mouth and immediately swallow again and again for 20 seconds. Swallow again for 20 seconds but this time drink a small amount of water each time you swallow. How do the results of the first and second

experiment compare? _____

_____

_____

What is the stimulus for the receptors to ini-

tiate swallowing? _____
What muscles are involved in swallowing?

_____

f. **Patellar reflex**—Have your partner sit on a table so that the leg hangs freely. Strike the patellar ligament just below the kneecap with the reflex hammer.

What is the response? _____

_____

_____

_____

Test the patellar reflex while the subject is adding a column of numbers. Test the reflex again while the subject interlocks his or her fingers and pulls one hand against the other. Compare the results of these two experi-

ments. _____

_____

_____

What is the purpose of the patellar reflex?

_____

_____

g. **Achilles reflex**—Have the subject kneel on a chair and let the feet hang freely over the edge of the chair. Bend one foot to in-crease the tension on the gastrocnemius muscle. Tap the calcaneal (Achilles) tendon with the reflex hammer.

What is the result? _____

_____

_____

h. **Plantar reflex**—Scratch the sole of your partner's foot by moving a blunt object along the sole toward the toes.

What is the response? _____

_____

What is the Babinski sign? _____

_____

Why is it normal in children under the age of

18 months? _____

_____

_____

What does the Babinski sign indicate in an

adult? _____

B. BRAIN

1. Parts

The brain may be divided into four principal parts: (1) **brain stem,** which consists of the medulla oblongata, pons, and midbrain; (2) **diencephalon** (dī-en-SEF-a-lon), which consists primarily of the thalamus and hypothalamus; (3) **cerebellum,** which is posterior to the brain stem; and (4) **cerebrum,** which is superior to the brain stem and comprises about seven-eighths of the total weight of the brain.

Examine a model and preserved specimen of the brain and identify the parts just described. Then refer to Figure 13.5 and label the parts of the brain.

2. Meninges

As is the spinal cord, the brain is protected by **meninges.** The cranial meninges are continuous with the spinal meninges. The cranial meninges are the outer **dura mater,** the middle **arachnoid,** and the inner **pia mater.** The cranial dura mater consists of two layers called the periosteal layer (adheres to the cranial bones and serves as a periosteum) and the meningeal layer (thinner, inner layer that corresponds to the spinal dura mater).

Refer to Figure 13.6 and label all of the meninges.

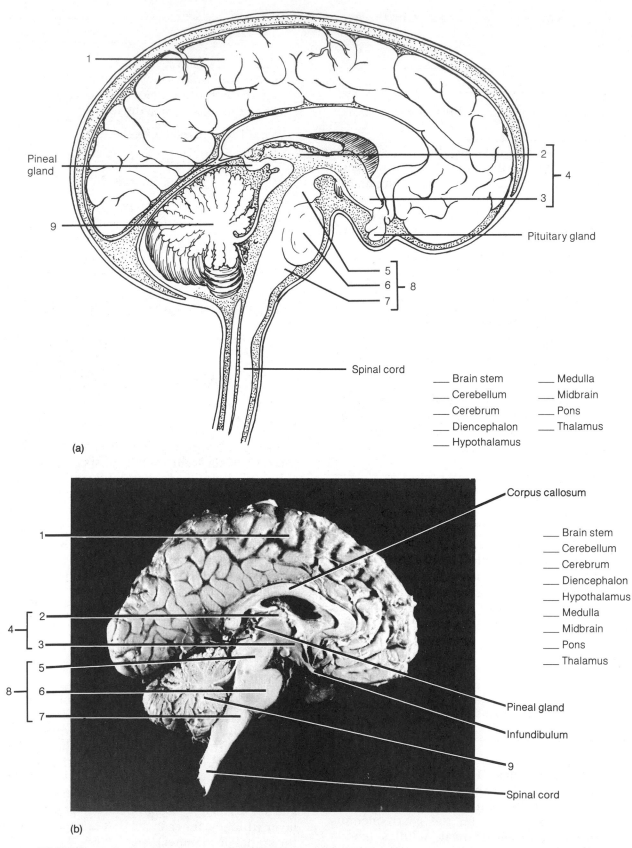

Pineal
gland

9

1

2

4

3

Pituitary gland

5
6
7
8

Spinal cord

___ Brain stem ___ Medulla
___ Cerebellum ___ Midbrain
___ Cerebrum   ___ Pons
___ Diencephalon ___ Thalamus
___ Hypothalamus

(a)

Corpus callosum

___ Brain stem
___ Cerebellum
___ Cerebrum
___ Diencephalon
___ Hypothalamus
___ Medulla
___ Midbrain
___ Pons
___ Thalamus

1

4

2

3

5

8

6

7

Pineal gland

Infundibulum

9

Spinal cord

(b)

FIGURE 13.5 Principal parts of the brain in midsagittal section. (a) Diagram. (b) Photograph.

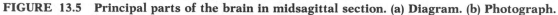

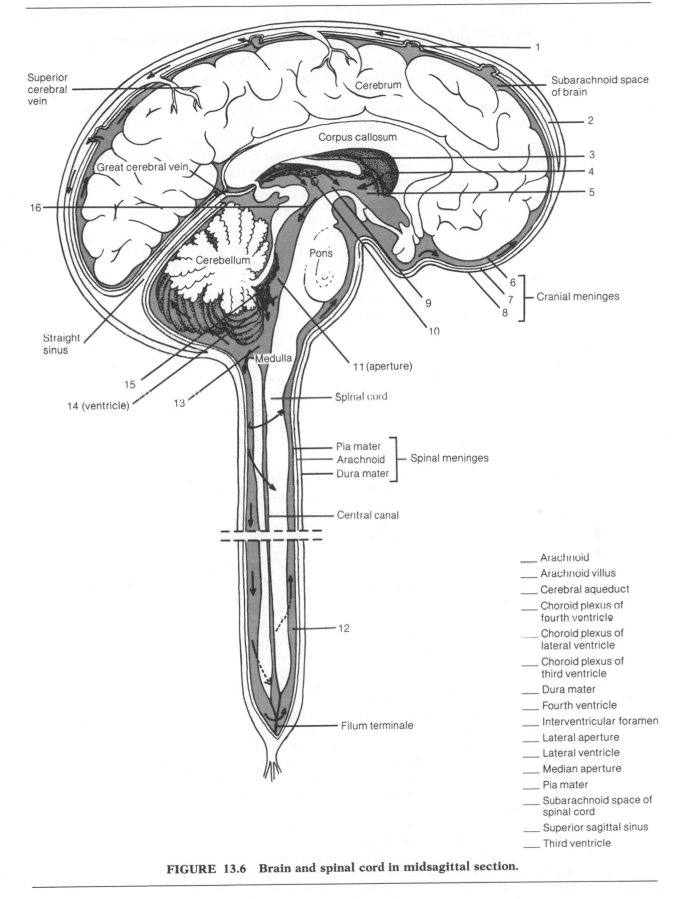

Superior cerebral vein

Cerebrum

Subarachnoid space of brain

1

2

Corpus callosum

3

4

5

Great cerebral vein

16

Cerebellum

Pons

6
7 } Cranial meninges
8

9

10

Straight sinus

Medulla

11 (aperture)

15

Spinal cord

14 (ventricle)

13

Pia mater
Arachnoid } Spinal meninges
Dura mater

Central canal

12

Filum terminale

___ Arachnoid
___ Arachnoid villus
___ Cerebral aqueduct
___ Choroid plexus of fourth ventricle
___ Choroid plexus of lateral ventricle
___ Choroid plexus of third ventricle
___ Dura mater
___ Fourth ventricle
___ Interventricular foramen
___ Lateral aperture
___ Lateral ventricle
___ Median aperture
___ Pia mater
___ Subarachnoid space of spinal cord
___ Superior sagittal sinus
___ Third ventricle

FIGURE 13.6 Brain and spinal cord in midsagittal section.

3. Cerebrospinal Fluid

The central nervous system is protected by **cerebrospinal fluid.** The fluid circulates through the subarachnoid space around the brain and spinal cord and through the ventricles of the brain. The ventricles are cavities in the brain that communicate with each other, with the central canal of the spinal cord, and with the subarachnoid space.

Cerebrospinal fluid is formed primarily by filtration and secretion from networks of capillaries, called **choroid** (KŌ-royd) **plexuses,** in the ventricles (see Figure 13.6). Each of the two **lateral ventricles** (VEN-tri-kuls) is located within a hemisphere (side) of the cerebrum under the corpus callosum. The fluid formed in the choroid plexuses of the lateral ventricles circulates through an opening called the **interventricular foramen** into the third ventricle. The **third ventricle** is a slit between and inferior to the right and left halves of the thalamus and between the lateral ventricles. More fluid is added by the choroid plexus of the third ventricle. Then the fluid circulates through an opening called the **cerebral aqueduct** (AK-we-dukt) into the fourth ventricle. The **fourth ventricle** lies between the inferior brain stem and the cerebellum. More fluid is added by the choroid plexus of the fourth ventricle. The roof of the fourth ventricle has three openings: one **median aperture** (AP-e-chur) and two **lateral apertures.** The fluid circulates through the apertures into the subarachnoid space around the back of the brain and downward through the central canal of the spinal cord to the subarachnoid space around the posterior surface of the spinal cord, up the anterior surface of the spinal cord, and around the anterior part of the brain. Most of the cerebrospinal fluid is absorbed into the superior sagittal sinus through its arachnoid villi.

Refer to Figure 13.6 and label the choroid plexus of the lateral ventricle, lateral ventricle, interventricular foramen, choroid plexus of third ventricle, third ventricle, cerebral aqueduct, choroid plexus of fourth ventricle, fourth ventricle, median aperture, lateral aperture, subarachnoid space of spinal cord, superior sagittal sinus, and arachnoid villus.

Note the arrows in Figure 13.6, which indicate the path taken by cerebrospinal fluid. With the aid of your textbook, starting at the choroid plexus of the lateral ventricle and ending at the superior sagittal sinus, see if you can follow the remaining path of the fluid.

4. Medulla Oblongata

The **medulla oblongata** (me-DULL-la ob'-long-GA-ta), or just simply medulla, is a continuation of the upper part of the spinal cord and forms the inferior part of the brain stem. The medulla contains all ascending and descending tracts that communicate between the spinal cord and various parts of the brain. On the ventral side of the medulla are two roughly triangular structures called **pyramids.** They contain the largest motor tracts that run from the cerebral cortex to the spinal cord. Most fibers in the left pyramid cross to the right side of the spinal cord and most fibers in the right pyramid cross to the left side of the spinal cord. The medulla contains three vital reflex centers called the cardiac center, respiratory center, and vasomotor center. The medulla also contains the nuclei of origin of four pairs of cranial nerves. These are the glossopharyngeal (IX) nerves, vagus (X) nerves, accessory (XI) nerves, and hypoglossal (XII) nerves.

Examine a model or specimen of the brain and identify the parts of the medulla. Then refer to Figure 13.5 and locate the medulla.

5. Pons

The **pons** lies directly above the medulla and anterior to the cerebellum. The pons contains fibers that connect parts of the cerebellum and medulla with the cerebrum. The pons contains the nuclei or origin of the following pairs of cranial nerves: trigeminal (V) nerves, abducens (VI) nerves, facial (VII) nerves, and vestibulocochlear (VIII) nerves.

Identify the pons on a model or specimen of the brain. Locate the pons in Figure 13.5.

6. Midbrain

The **midbrain** extends from the pons to the lower portion of the cerebrum. The ventral position of the midbrain contains the paired **cerebral peduncles** (pe-DUNG-kulz), which connect the upper parts of the brain to lower parts of the brain and spinal cord. The dorsal part of the midbrain contains four rounded eminences called **corpora quadrigemina** (KOR-po-ra kwad-ri-JEM-in-a). Two of the eminences, the **superior colliculi** (ko-LIK-yoo-lī), serve as reflex centers for movements of the eyeballs and the head in response to visual and other stimuli. The other two eminences, the **inferior colli-**

culi, serve as reflex centers for movements of the head and trunk in response to auditory stimuli. The midbrain contains the nuclei of origin for two pairs of cranial nerves: oculomotor (III) and trochlear (IV).

Identify the parts of the midbrain on a model or specimen of the brain. Locate the midbrain in Figure 13.5.

7. Thalamus

The **thalamus** (THAL-a-mus) is a large oval structure, located above the midbrain, that consists of two masses of gray matter covered by a layer of white matter. The two masses are joined by a bridge of gray matter called the **intermediate mass.** The thalamus contains numerous nuclei that serve as relay stations for all sensory impulses, except smell. The most prominent are

the **medial geniculate** (je-NIK-yoo-lāt) **nuclei** (hearing), **lateral geniculate nuclei** (vision), **ventral posterior nuclei** (general sensations and taste), **ventral lateral nuclei** (voluntary motor actions), and the **ventral anterior nuclei** (voluntary motor actions and arousal).

Identify the thalamic nuclei on a model or specimen of the brain. Then refer to Figure 13.7 and label the nuclei.

8. Hypothalamus

The **hypothalamus** is located inferior to the thalamus and forms the floor and part of the wall of the third ventricle. Among the functions served by the hypothalamus are control and integration of the autonomic nervous system and parts of the endocrine system, reception of sensory impulses from the viscera, secretion of

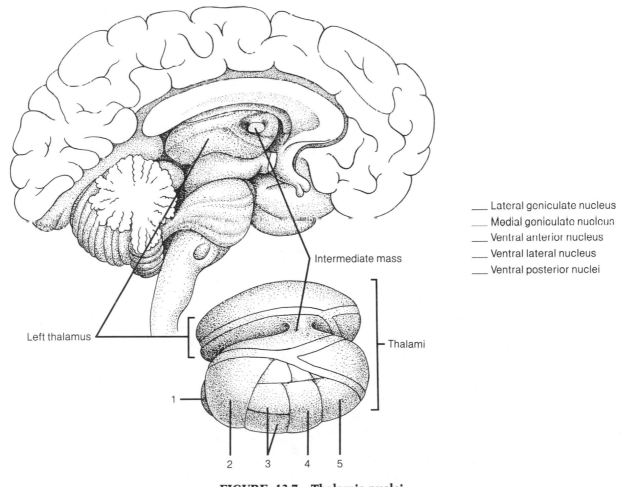

___ Lateral geniculate nucleus
___ Medial geniculate nucleus
___ Ventral anterior nucleus
___ Ventral lateral nucleus
___ Ventral posterior nuclei

Intermediate mass

Left thalamus

Thalami

1

2   3   4   5

FIGURE 13.7   Thalamic nuclei.

regulating factors, and control of body temperature. The hypothalamus also assumes a role in feelings of rage and aggression, food intake, thirst, the waking state and sleep patterns, and circadian rhythms.

Identify the hypothalamus on a model or specimen of the brain. Locate the hypothalamus in Figure 13.5.

9. Cerebrum

The **cerebrum** is the largest portion of the brain and is supported on the brain stem. Its outer surface consists of gray matter and is called the **cerebral cortex.** Beneath the cerebral cortex is the cerebral white matter. The upfolds of the cerebral cortex are termed **gyri (convolutions),** the deep downfolds are termed **fissures,** and the shallow downfolds are termed **sulci** (SUL-sī).

The **longitudinal fissure** separates the cerebrum into right and left halves called **hemispheres.** Each hemisphere is further divided into lobes by sulci or fissures. The **central sulcus** separates the **frontal lobe** from the **parietal lobe.** The **lateral cerebral sulcus** separates the frontal lobe from the **temporal lobe.** The **parietooccipital sulcus** separates the **parietal lobe** from the **occipital lobe.** Another prominent fissure, the **transverse fissure,** separates the cerebrum from the cerebellum. Another lobe of the cerebrum, the **insula,** lies deep within the lateral cerebral fissure under the parietal, frontal, and temporal lobes. It cannot be seen in external view. Two important gyri on either side of the **central sulcus** are the **precentral gyrus** and the **postcentral gyrus.** The olfactory (I) and optic (II) cranial nerves are associated with the cerebrum.

Examine a model of the brain and identify the parts of the cerebrum just described. Refer to Figure 13.8 and label the lobes.

10. Basal Ganglia

Basal ganglia (GANG-lē-a) or **cerebral nuclei** are paired masses of gray matter, with one member of each pair in each cerebral hemisphere. The largest of the basal ganglia is the **corpus striatum** (strī-Ā-tum), which consists of the **caudate nucleus** and the **lentiform nucleus.** The lentiform nucleus, in turn, is subdivided into a lateral **putamen** (pu-TĀ-men) and a medial **globus pallidus.** The basal ganglia control large, subconscious movement of skeletal muscles. An example is swinging the arms while walking.

Examine a model or specimen of the brain and identify the basal ganglia. Now refer to Figure 13.9 and label the basal ganglia.

11. Cerebellum

The **cerebellum** is inferior to the posterior portion of the cerebrum and separated from it by the transverse fissure. The central constricted area of the cerebellum is called the **vermis** and the lateral portions are referred to as **hemispheres.** The surface of the cerebellum, called the **cerebellar cortex,** consists of gray matter thrown into a series of slender parallel ridges called **folia.** Beneath the gyri are tracts of white matter called **arbor vitae.**

The cerebellum is attached to the brain stem by three paired bundles of fibers called **cerebellar peduncles.** The **inferior cerebellar peduncles** connect the cerebellum with the medulla at the base of the brain stem and with the spinal cord. The **middle cerebellar peduncles** connect the cerebellum with the pons. The **superior cerebellar peduncles** connect the cerebellum with the midbrain.

The cerebellum is a motor area of the brain that coordinates certain subconscious movements in skeletal muscles required for coordination, posture, and balance.

Examine a model or specimen of the brain and locate the parts of the cerebellum. Identify the cerebellum in Figure 13.5.

12. Determination of Cerebellar Function

Working with your lab partner, perform the following tests to determine cerebellar function:

1. While looking straight ahead, walk heel to toe for 20 ft without losing your balance.

2. Stand with your feet together and your eyes closed without losing your balance.

3. While looking straight ahead, touch your outstretched hand with the tip of the corresponding foot.

4. While looking straight ahead, move the heel of one foot down the shin of your other leg.

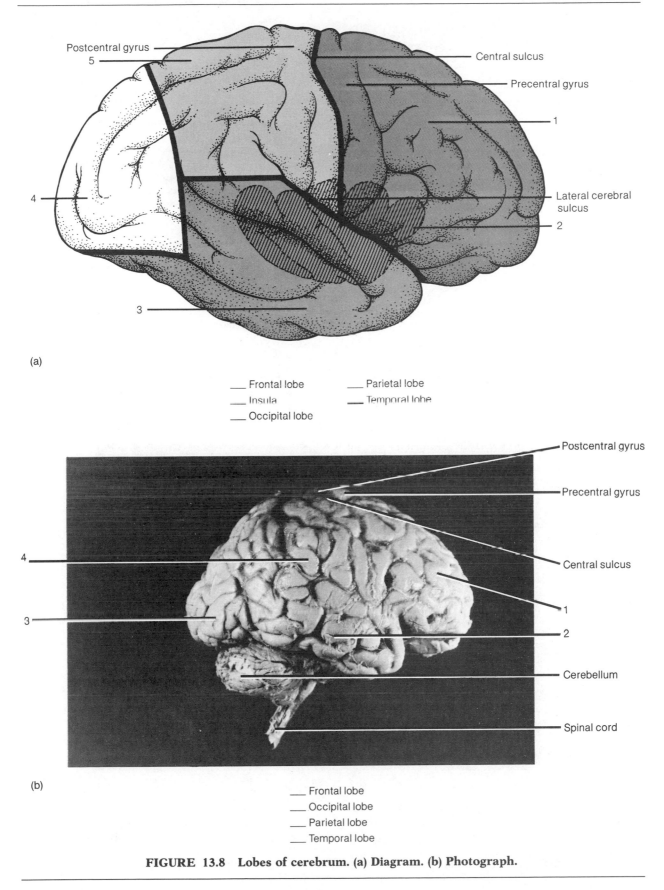

(a)

___ Frontal lobe   ___ Parietal lobe
___ Insula   ___ Temporal lobe
___ Occipital lobe

(b)

___ Frontal lobe
___ Occipital lobe
___ Parietal lobe
___ Temporal lobe

FIGURE 13.8 Lobes of cerebrum. (a) Diagram. (b) Photograph.

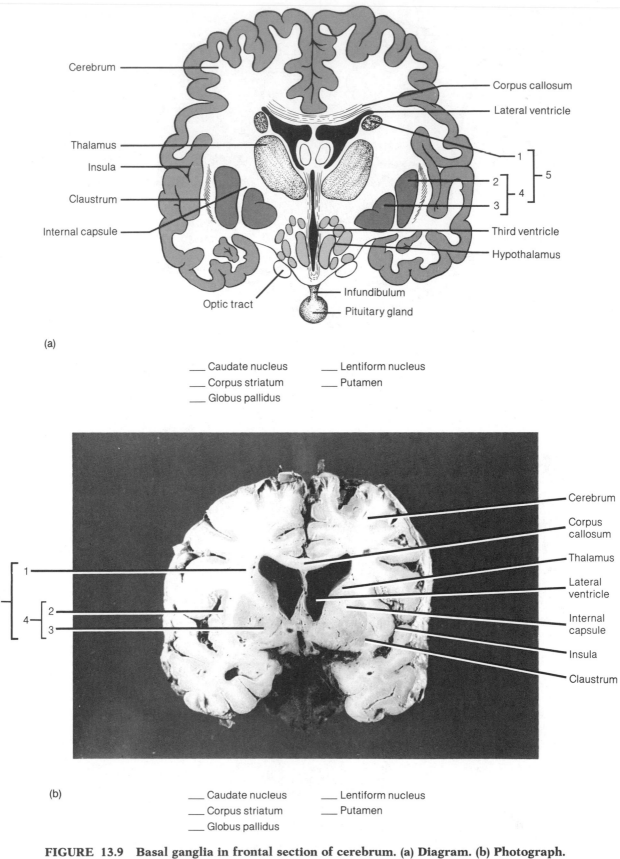

(a)

___ Caudate nucleus   ___ Lentiform nucleus
___ Corpus striatum   ___ Putamen
___ Globus pallidus

(b)

___ Caudate nucleus   ___ Lentiform nucleus
___ Corpus striatum   ___ Putamen
___ Globus pallidus

FIGURE 13.9 Basal ganglia in frontal section of cerebrum. (a) Diagram. (b) Photograph.

5. Move your hands and fingers as quickly as you can.

6. With your eyes open, touch your partner's fingers.

7. With your eyes closed, touch your nose with the index finger of each hand.

C. CRANIAL NERVES

Of the 12 pairs of **cranial nerves,** 10 originate from the brain stem, but all 12 pairs leave the skull through foramina in the base of the skull. The cranial nerves are designated by Roman numerals and names. The Roman numerals indicate the order in which the nerves arise from the brain, from front to back. The names indicate the distribution or function of the nerves.

Obtain a model of the brain and, using your text and any other aids available, identify the 12 pairs of cranial nerves. Now refer to Figure 13.10 and label the cranial nerves.

D. TESTS OF CRANIAL NERVE FUNCTION

The following simple tests may be performed to determine cranial nerve function. Although they provide only superficial information, they will help you to understand how the various cranial nerves function. Perform each of the tests with your partner.

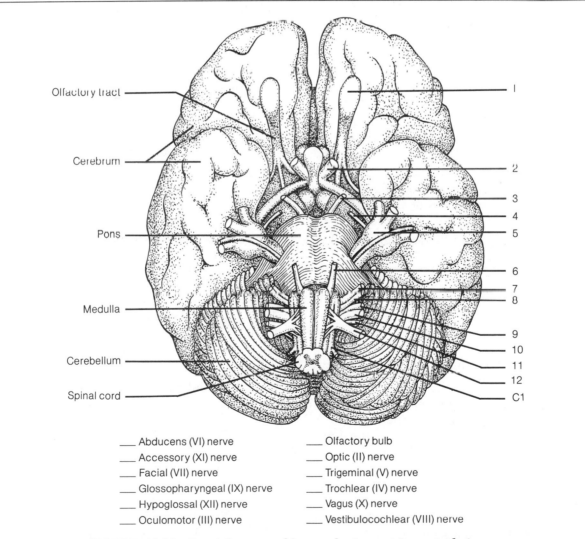

Label	Nerve
Olfactory tract	
Cerebrum	
Pons	
Medulla	
Cerebellum	
Spinal cord	

___ Abducens (VI) nerve
___ Accessory (XI) nerve
___ Facial (VII) nerve
___ Glossopharyngeal (IX) nerve
___ Hypoglossal (XII) nerve
___ Oculomotor (III) nerve
___ Olfactory bulb
___ Optic (II) nerve
___ Trigeminal (V) nerve
___ Trochlear (IV) nerve
___ Vagus (X) nerve
___ Vestibulocochlear (VIII) nerve

FIGURE 13.10 Cranial nerves of human brain seen in ventral view.

1. **Olfactory (I) nerve**—Have your partner smell several familiar substances such as spices, first using one nostril and then the other. Your partner should be able to distinguish the odors equally well with each nostril.

What structures could be malfunctioning if the ability to smell is lost? _____

_____

_____

_____

2. **Optic (II) nerve**—Have your partner read a portion of a printed page using each eye. Do the same while using a Snellen chart at a distance of 20 ft.

Describe the visual pathway from the optic nerve to the cerebral cortex. _____

_____

_____

_____

3. **Oculomotor (III), Trochlear** (TROK-lē-ar) **(IV),** and **Abducens** (ab-DOO-sens) **(VI) nerves**—To test the motor responses of these nerves, have your partner follow your finger with his or her eyes without moving the head. Move your finger up, down, medially, and laterally.

Which nerves control which movements of the eyeball? _____

_____

Look for signs of ptosis (drooping of one or both eyelids).

Which cranial nerve innervates the upper eyelid? _____

To test for pupillary light reflex, shine a small flashlight into each eye from the side. *Do not make contact with the eyes.* Observe the pupil.

What cranial nerve controls this reflex? _____

_____

4. **Trigeminal** (trī-JEM-i-nal) **(V) nerve**—To test the motor responses of this nerve, have your partner close his or her jaws tightly.

What muscles are used? _____

Now while holding your hand under your partner's lower jaw to provide resistance, ask your partner to open his or her mouth. To test the sensory responses of this nerve, have your partner close his or her eyes and lightly whisk a piece of dry cotton over the mandibular, maxillary, and ophthalmic areas on each side of the face. Do the same with cotton that has been moistened with cold water.

What cranial nerves bring about the response?

_____

5. **Facial (VII) nerve**—To test the motor responses of this nerve, ask your partner to bring the corners of the mouth straight back, smile while showing his or her teeth, whistle, puff his or her cheeks, frown, raise his or her eyebrows, and wrinkle his or her forehead.

Define Bell's palsy. _____

_____

To test the sensory responses of this nerve, touch the tip of your partner's tongue with an applicator that has been dipped into a salt solution. Rinse the mouth out with water and now place an applicator dipped into a sugar solution along the anterior surface of the tongue.

What are the four basic tastes that can be distinguished? _____

_____

_____

6. **Vestibulocochlear** (ves-tib′-yoo-lō-KŌK-lē-ar) **(VIII) nerve**—To test for the functioning of the vestibular portion of this nerve, have your partner sit on a swivel stool and turn him or her *slowly and very carefully* about 10 times. Stop the stool suddenly and look for nystagmus (rapid movement or quivering of the eyeballs). This is a normal response when a person is dizzy.

What cranial nerves would be affected if nystagmus occurs when the person is not dizzy?

_____

To test for the functioning of the cochlear portion of the nerve, have your partner close his or her eyes and determine his or her ability to hear a ticking watch.

Measure the distance at which sound can no longer be heard for each ear. _____

_____

7. **Glossopharyngeal** (glos'-ō-fa-RIN-jē-al) **(IX)** and **Vagus (X) nerves**—The palatal (gag) reflex can be used to test the functioning of both of these nerves. Using a cotton-tipped applicator, *very slowly and gently* touch your partner's uvula.

What is the purpose of this reflex? _____

_____

_____

To test the sensory responses of these nerves, have your partner swallow. Does swallowing occur easily? Now *gently* hold your partner's tongue down with a tongue depressor and ask him or her to say "ah." Does the uvula move? Are the movements on both sides of the soft palate the same? The sensory function of the glossopharyngeal nerve may be tested by applying a cotton-tipped applicator dipped in quinine to the tip, sides, and back of the tongue.

In which area of the tongue was the quinine tasted? _____

What taste sensation is located there? _____

_____

8. **Accessory (XI) nerve**—The strength and muscle tone of the sternocleidomastoid and trapezius muscles indicate the proper functioning of the accessory nerve. To ascertain the strength of the sternocleidomastoid muscle, have your partner turn his or her head from side to side against *slight* resistance that you supply by placing your hands on either side of your partner's head. To ascertain the strength of the trapezius muscle, place your hands on your partner's shoulders and while *gently* pressing down firmly ask him or her to shrug his or her shoulders.

Do both muscles appear to be reasonably strong? _____

9. **Hypoglossal (XII) nerve**—Have your partner protrude his or her tongue. It should protrude without deviation. Now have your partner protrude his or her tongue and move it from side to side while you attempt to resist the movements with a tongue depressor.

E. DISSECTION OF SHEEP BRAIN

The brains of the fetal pig, sheep, and human show many similarities. They possess the pro-

tective membranes called the **meninges,** which can easily be seen as you proceed with the dissections. The outermost layer is the **dura mater.** It is the toughest, protective one, and may have been removed from the preserved sheep brain. The middle membrane is the **arachnoid,** and the inner one containing blood vessels and adhering closely to the surface of the brain itself is the **pia mater.**

Use Figures 13.11 through 13.14 as references for this dissection.

The most prominent external parts of the brain are the pair of large **cerebral hemispheres** and the posterior **cerebellum** on the dorsal surface. These large hemispheres are separated from each other by the **longitudinal fissure.** The **transverse fissure** separates the hemispheres from the cerebellum. The surfaces of these hemispheres form many **gyri,** or raised ridges, that are separated by grooves, or **sulci.** If you spread the hemispheres gently apart you can see, deep in the longitudinal fissure, thick bundles of white transverse fibers. These bundles form the **corpus callosum,** which connects the hemispheres.

Spreading the cerebral hemispheres and the cerebellum apart reveals the roof of the midbrain (mesencephalon), which is seen as two pairs of round swellings collectively called the **corpora quadrigemina.** The larger, more anterior pair are the **superior colliculi.** The smaller posterior pair are the **inferior colliculi.** The **pineal gland (body)** is seen directly between the superior colliculi. Just posterior to the inferior colliculus, appearing as a thin white strand, is the **trochlear (IV) nerve.**

The cerebellum is connected to the brain stem by three prominent fiber tracts called **peduncles.** The **superior cerebellar peduncle** connects the cerebellum with the midbrain, the **inferior cerebellar peduncle** connects the cerebellum with the medulla, and the **cerebellar peduncle** connects the cerebellum with the pons.

Most of the following parts can be located on the ventral surface of the intact brain.

Just beneath the cerebral hemispheres are two **olfactory bulbs,** which continue posteriorly as two **olfactory tracts.** Posterior to these tracts, the **optic (II) nerves** undergo a crossing (decussation) known as the **optic chiasma.** Locate the **pituitary gland (hypophysis)** just posterior to the chiasma. This gland is connected to the **hypothalamus** portion of the diencephalon by a stalk called the **infundibulum.** The **mammillary body** appears immediately poste-

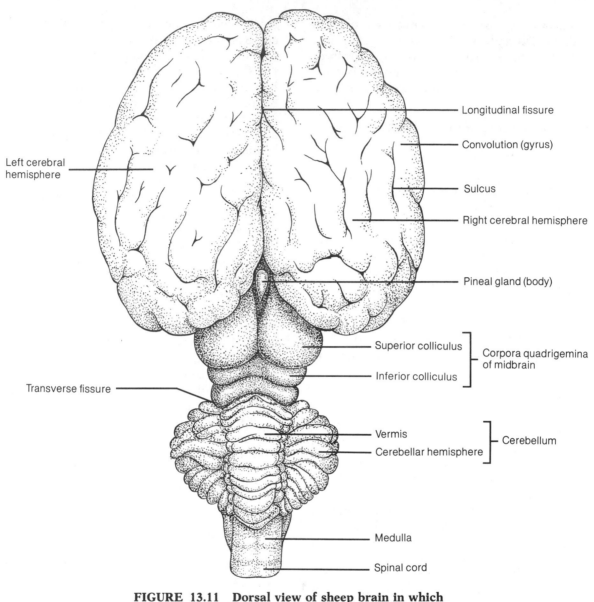

Longitudinal fissure

Convolution (gyrus)

Sulcus

Right cerebral hemisphere

Pineal gland (body)

Left cerebral hemisphere

Superior colliculus

Inferior colliculus

Corpora quadrigemina of midbrain

Transverse fissure

Vermis

Cerebellar hemisphere

Cerebellum

Medulla

Spinal cord

FIGURE 13.11   Dorsal view of sheep brain in which cerebellum has been spread apart from the cerebrum.

rior to the infundibulum. Just posterior to this body are the paired **cerebral peduncles,** from which arise the large **oculomotor (III) nerves.** They may be partially covered by the pituitary gland. The **pons** is a posterior extension of the hypothalamus and the **medulla oblongata** is a posterior extension of the pons. The **cerebral aqueduct** dorsal to the peduncles runs posteriorly and connects the third ventricle with the **fourth ventricle,** which is located dorsal to the medulla and ventral to the cerebellum.

The medulla merges with the **spinal cord,** and is separated by the **ventral median fissure.** The **pyramids** are the longitudinal bands of tissue on either side of this fissure.

Identify the remaining **cranial nerves** on the ventral surface of the brain. They are the trigeminal (V), abducens (VI), facial (VII), vestibulocochlear (VIII), glossopharyngeal (IX), vagus (X), accessory (XI), and hypoglossal (XII). The previously identified cranial nerves are the olfactory (I), optic (II), oculomotor (III), and trochlear (IV), for a total of twelve.

Most of the following structures can be identified by examining a midsagittal section of the sheep brain, or by cutting an intact brain along the longitudinal fissure completely through the corpus callosum. If you break through the thin ventral wall, the **septum pellucidum** of the corpus callosum, you can see part

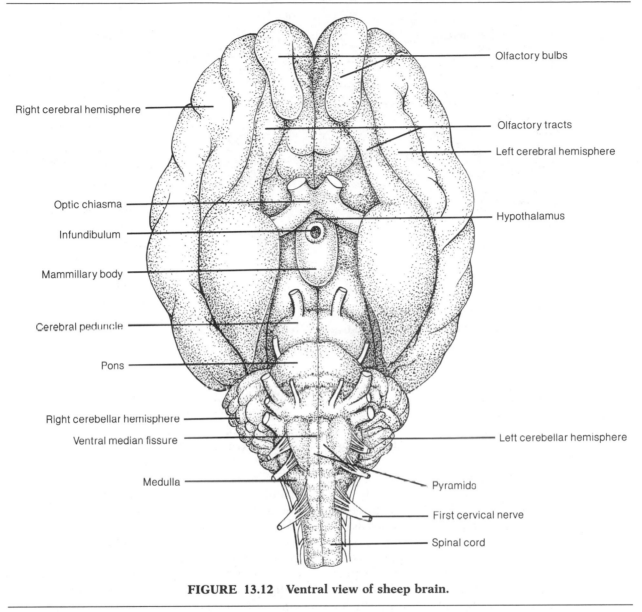

FIGURE 13.12 Ventral view of sheep brain.

Labels on figure:
- Olfactory bulbs
- Right cerebral hemisphere
- Olfactory tracts
- Left cerebral hemisphere
- Optic chiasma
- Hypothalamus
- Infundibulum
- Mammillary body
- Cerebral peduncle
- Pons
- Right cerebellar hemisphere
- Ventral median fissure
- Left cerebellar hemisphere
- Medulla
- Pyramids
- First cervical nerve
- Spinal cord

of a large chamber, the **lateral ventricle,** inside the hemisphere.

Each hemisphere has one of these ventricles. Ventral to the septum pellucidum, locate a smaller band of white fibers called the **fornix.** Close by where the fornix disappears is a small, round bundle of fibers called the **anterior commissure.** The **third ventricle** and the **thalamus** are located ventral to the fornix. The third ventricle is outlined by its shiny epithelial lining, and the thalamus forms the lateral walls of this ventricle. This ventricle is crossed by a large circular mass of tissue, the **intermediate mass,** which connects the two sides of the thalamus. Each lateral ventricle communicates with the third ventricle through an opening, the **inter-**

ventricular foramen, which lies in a depression anterior to the intermediate mass and can be located with a dull probe. A midsagittal section through the cerebellum reveals a treelike arrangement of gray and white matter called the **arbor vitae** (tree of life).

Make several cross sections through the cerebral hemispheres about ½ in. apart, starting from front to back. Identify the **gray matter** near the surface of the **cerebral cortex** and the **white matter** beneath this layer. See if you can also find the **lateral ventricles, third ventricle, corpus callosum, thalamus, hypothalamus,** and **fornix.**

A cross section through the spinal cord reveals the fourth ventricle. It contains **cerebrospinal fluid.**

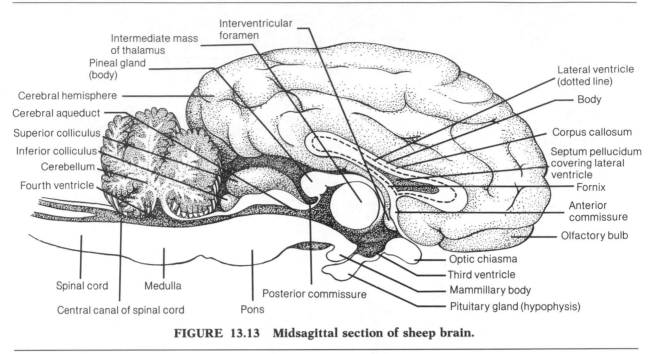

FIGURE 13.13 Midsagittal section of sheep brain.

F. AUTONOMIC NERVOUS SYSTEM

The **autonomic nervous system (ANS)** regulates the activities of smooth muscle, cardiac muscle, and glands, usually involuntarily. In the somatic nervous system (SNS), which is voluntary, the cell bodies of the efferent (motor) neurons are in the CNS, and their axons extend all the way to skeletal muscles in spinal nerves. The ANS always has two efferent neurons in the pathway. The first efferent neuron, the preganglionic neuron, has its cell body in the CNS. Its axon leaves the CNS and synapses in an autonomic ganglion with the second neuron called the postganglionic neuron. The cell body of the postganglionic neuron is inside an autonomic ganglion, and its axon terminates in a visceral effector (muscle or gland).

Label the components of the autonomic pathway shown in Figure 13.15.

The ANS consists of two divisions: sympathetic and parasympathetic. Most viscera are innervated by both divisions. In general, impulses from one division stimulate a structure, whereas impulses from the other division decrease its activity (Figure 13.16).

In the **sympathetic division,** the cell bodies of the preganglionic neurons are located in the lateral gray horns of the spinal cord in the thoracic and first two lumbar segments. The ax-

ons of preganglionic neurons are myelinated and leave the spinal cord through the ventral root of a spinal nerve. Each axon travels briefly in a ventral ramus and then through a small branch called a white ramus communicans to enter a sympathetic trunk ganglion. These ganglia lie in a vertical row, on either side of the vertebral column, from the base of the skull to the coccyx. In the ganglion, the axon may synapse with a postganglionic neuron, travel upward or downward through the sympathetic trunk ganglia to synapse with postganglionic neurons at different levels, or pass through the ganglion without synapsing to form part of the splanchnic nerves. If the preganglionic axon synapses in a sympathetic trunk ganglion, it reenters the ventral or dorsal ramus of a spinal nerve via a small branch called a gray ramus communicans. If the preganglionic axon forms part of the splanchnic nerves, it passes through the sympathetic trunk ganglion but synapses with a postganglionic neuron in a prevertebral (collateral) ganglion. These ganglia are anterior to the vertebral column close to large abdominal arteries from which their names are derived (celiac, superior mesenteric, and inferior mesenteric).

In the **parasympathetic division,** the cell bodies of the preganglionic neurons are located in nuclei in the brain stem and lateral gray horn of the second through fourth sacral seg-

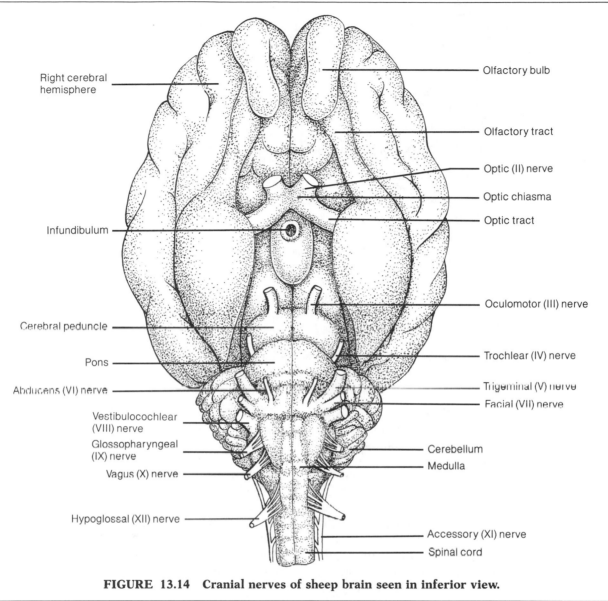

FIGURE 13.14 Cranial nerves of sheep brain seen in inferior view.

Labels:
- Right cerebral hemisphere
- Olfactory bulb
- Olfactory tract
- Optic (II) nerve
- Optic chiasma
- Optic tract
- Infundibulum
- Oculomotor (III) nerve
- Cerebral peduncle
- Trochlear (IV) nerve
- Pons
- Trigeminal (V) nerve
- Abducens (VI) nerve
- Facial (VII) nerve
- Vestibulocochlear (VIII) nerve
- Glossopharyngeal (IX) nerve
- Cerebellum
- Medulla
- Vagus (X) nerve
- Hypoglossal (XII) nerve
- Accessory (XI) nerve
- Spinal cord

ments of the spinal cord. The axons emerge as part of cranial or spinal nerves. The preganglionic axons synapse with postganglionic neurons in terminal ganglia, near or within visceral effectors.

The sympathetic division is primarily concerned with processes that expend energy. During stress, the sympathetic division sets into operation a series of reactions collectively called the **fight-or-flight response,** designed to help the body counteract the stress and return to homeostasis. During the fight-or-flight response, the heart and breathing rates increase and the blood sugar level rises, among other things.

The parasympathetic division is primarily concerned with activities that restore and conserve energy. It is thus called the **rest-repose system.** Under normal conditions, the parasympathetic division dominates the sympathetic division in order to maintain homeostasis.

Autonomic fibers, like other axons of the nervous system, release neurotransmitters at synapses as well as at points of contact with visceral effectors **(neuroeffector junctions).** On the basis of the neurotransmitter produced, autonomic fibers may be classified as either cholinergic or adrenergic. **Cholinergic** (kō'-lin-ER-jik) **fibers** release **acetylcholine (ACh)** and include the following: (1) all sympathetic and

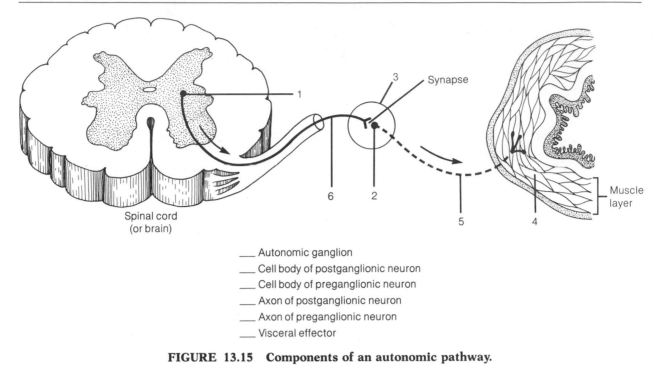

___ Autonomic ganglion
___ Cell body of postganglionic neuron
___ Cell body of preganglionic neuron
___ Axon of postganglionic neuron
___ Axon of preganglionic neuron
___ Visceral effector

FIGURE 13.15 Components of an autonomic pathway.

parasympathetic preganglionic axons, (2) all parasympathetic postganglionic axons, and (3) some sympathetic postganglionic axons. **Adrenergic** (ad'-ren-ER-jik) **fibers** produce **norepinephrine** (NE). Most sympathetic postganglionic axons are adrenergic.

The actual effects produced by ACh are determined by the type of receptor with which it intereacts. The two types of receptors are known as nicotinic receptors and muscarinic receptors. **Nicotinic receptors** are found on both sympathetic and parasympathetic postganglionic neurons. These receptors are so named because the actions of ACh on them are similar to those produced by nicotine. **Muscarinic receptors** are found on effectors innervated by parasympathetic postganglionic axons. These receptors are so named because the actions of ACh on them are similar to those produced by muscarine, a toxin produced by a mushroom.

The effects of NE and epinephrine, like those of ACh, are also determined by the type of receptor with which they intereact. Such receptors are found on visceral effectors innervated by most sympathetic postganglionic axons and are referred to as **alpha receptors** and **beta receptors.** Although cells of most effectors contain either alpha or beta receptors, some effector cells contain both. NE, in general, stimulates alpha receptors to a greater extent than beta receptors, and epinephrine, in general, stimulates both alpha and beta receptors.

Using your textbook as a reference, write in the sympathetic and parasympathetic responses for the visceral effectors listed in Table 13.1.

LABORATORY REPORT QUESTIONS (PAGE 399)

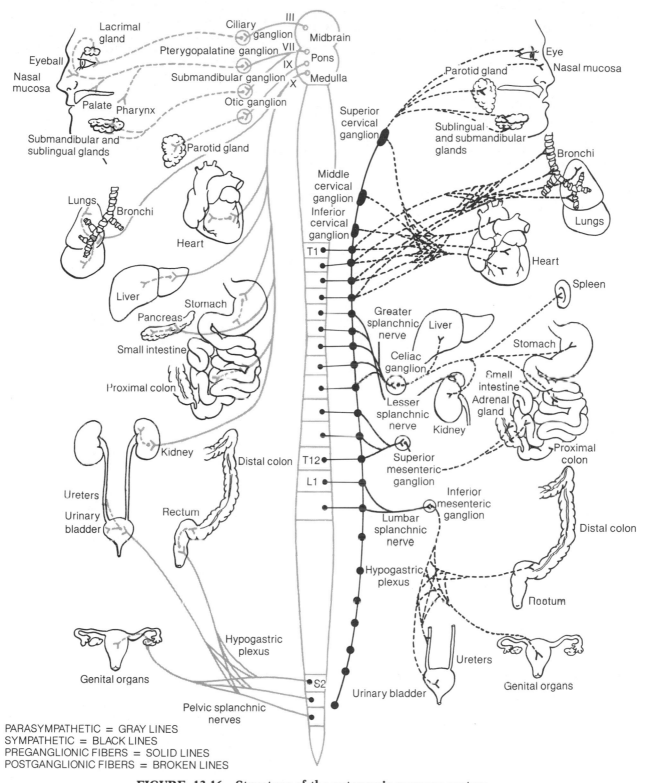

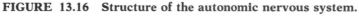

PARASYMPATHETIC = GRAY LINES
SYMPATHETIC = BLACK LINES
PREGANGLIONIC FIBERS = SOLID LINES
POSTGANGLIONIC FIBERS = BROKEN LINES

FIGURE 13.16 Structure of the autonomic nervous system.

TABLE 13.1
ACTIVITIES OF THE AUTONOMIC NERVOUS SYSTEM

VISCERAL EFFECTOR	SYMPATHETIC RESPONSE	PARASYMPATHETIC RESPONSE
Iris of eye		
Sweat glands		
Salivary glands		
Gastric and intestinal glands		
Adrenal cortex		
Adrenal medulla		
Lungs		
Blood vessels of skin and viscera		
Blood vessels of skeletal muscles		
Heart		
Liver		
Stomach and intestines		
Kidney		
Pancreas		
Spleen		
Urinary bladder		
Arrector pili of hair follicle		
Uterus		
Sex organs Clitoris (female) Penis (male)		

14 | SENSATIONS

Now that you have studied the nervous system, you will study sensations, which are closely related to and integrated with this system. In its broadest context, the term **sensation** refers to the state of awareness of external or internal conditions of the body. Sensations are picked up by sensory receptors that change stimuli into nerve impulses.

A. CHARACTERISTICS OF SENSATIONS

For a sensation to occur, four prerequisites must be met: (1) a **stimulus,** or changing input of energy in the environment, capable of initiating a response by the nervous system, must be present; (2) a **sensory receptor** or **sense organ** must receive the stimulus and convert it to a nerve impulse (a sensory receptor or sense organ may be viewed as specialized nervous tissue that exhibits a high degree of sensitivity to specific internal or external conditions); (3) the impulse must be **conducted** along a nervous pathway from the sensory receptor or sense organ to the brain; (4) a **region** of the brain must **translate** the impulse into a sensation.

A sensory receptor might be very simple, such as the dendrites of a single neuron, or it may be a complex organ, such as the eye, that contains highly specialized neurons, epithelium, and connective tissues. All sensory receptors contain the dendrites of sensory neurons, exhibit a high degree of excitability, and possess a low threshold stimulus. Furthermore, the majority of sensory impulses are conducted to the sensory areas of the cerebral cortex, for it is in this region of the body that a stimulus produces conscious feeling.

We see with our eyes, hear with our ears, and feel pain in an injured part of our body only because the cortex interprets the sensation as coming from the stimulated sensory receptor. One characteristic of sensations, that of **projection,** describes the process by which the brain refers sensations to their point of learned origin of the stimulation. A second characteristic of many sensations is **adaptation,** that is, disappearance of a sensation even though a stimulus is still being applied. For example, when you first get into a tub of hot water, you might feel an intense burning sensation. But after a brief period of time the sensation decreases to one of comfortable warmth, even though the stimulus (hot water) is still present. Another characteristic is **after images,** that is, the persistence of a sensation after the stimulus has been removed. One common example of after image occurs when you look at a bright light and then look away. You will still see the light for several seconds afterward. The fourth characteristic of sensations is **modality,** that is, the possession of distinct properties by which one sensation may be distinguished from another. For example, pain, pressure, touch, body position, equilibrium, hearing, vision, smell, and taste are all distinctive because the body perceives each differently.

B. CLASSIFICATION OF SENSATIONS

One convenient method of classifying sensations is by location of the receptor:

1. **Exteroceptors** (eks'-ter-ō-SEP-tors), located near the surface of the body, provide information about the external environment. They receive stimuli from outside the body, and transmit sensations of hearing, sight, touch, pressure, temperature, and pain on the skin.

2. **Visceroceptors** (vis-er-ō-SEP-tors) or **entero-ceptors**, located in blood vessels and viscera, provide information about the internal environment. This information arises from within the body and may be felt as pain, taste, fatigue, hunger, thirst, and nausea.

3. **Proprioceptors** (prō'-prē-ō-SEP-tors), located in muscles, tendons, and joints, allow us to feel sensations of position, movement, equilibrium, and tension of muscles and joints through the stretching or movement of parts where these receptors are located.

Another classification is based on the type of stimuli receptors receive:

1. **Mechanoreceptors** detect mechanical deformation of the receptors themselves or in adjacent cells. Sensations such as touch, pressure, vibration, proprioception, hearing, equilibrium, and blood pressure result from stimulation of mechanoreceptors.

2. **Thermoreceptors** detect changes in temperature.

3. **Nociceptors** (no-sē-SEP-tors) detect pain, usually as a result of physical or chemical damage to tissues.

4. **Electromagnetic (photo) receptors** detect light on the retina of the eye.

5. **Chemoreceptors** detect certain molecules in the mouth and nose (sense of taste and smell, respectively) and changes in oxygen, carbon dioxide, water, and glucose concentrations in body fluids.

Sensations may also be classified according to the simplicity or complexity of the receptor and the neural pathway involved:

1. **General senses** involve simple receptors and neural pathways. Taken together, a, b, and c below are referred to as **cutaneous sensations.**
   a. **Tactile** (TAK-tīl) **sensations** (touch, pressure, vibration).
   b. **Thermoreceptive sensations** (hot and cold).
   c. **Pain sensations.**
   d. **Proprioceptive** (prō'-prē-ō-SEP-tiv) **sensations** (awareness of the activities of muscles, tendons, and joints, and equilibrium).

2. **Special senses** involve complex receptors and neural pathways.
   a. **Olfactory** (ol-FAK-tō-rē) **sensations** (smell).
   b. **Gustatory** (GUS-ta-tō-rē) **sensations** (taste).

   c. **Visual sensations** (sight).
   d. **Auditory sensations** (hearing).
   e. **Equilibrium** (ē'-kwi-LIB-rē-um) **sensations** (orientation of the body).

C. RECEPTORS FOR GENERAL SENSES

1. Tactile Receptors

Although touch, pressure, and vibration are classified as separate sensations, all are detected by the same type of receptor, that is, one that responds to tissue deformation.

Touch sensations generally result from stimulation of tactile receptors in the skin or in tissues immediately beneath the skin. Receptors for touch include corpuscles of touch, tactile discs, root hair plexuses, and free nerve endings. **Corpuscles of touch (Meissner's corpuscles)** are found in dermal papillae. They have already been discussed in Exercise 5 (see Figure 5.1). **Tactile (Merkel's) discs** consist of disc-like formations of dendrites attached to deeper layers of the epidermis. **Root hair plexuses** are dendrites arranged in networks around the roots of hairs. **Free nerve endings** are found everywhere in the skin and in many other tissues (see Figure 5.1).

Receptors for touch are variously distributed throughout the surface of the skin and are most numerous in fingertips, palms of hands, and soles of feet. They are also abundant in the eyelids, tip of the tongue, lips, nipples, clitoris, and tip of the penis.

Examine prepared slides of corpuscles of touch, tactile discs, root hair plexuses, and free nerve endings. With the aid of your textbook, draw each of the receptors in the spaces that follow.

Corpuscles of touch

Examine prepared slides of lamellated corpuscles and type II cutaneous mechanoreceptors. With the aid of your textbook, draw the receptors in the spaces that follow.

Tactile discs

Lamellated corpuscles

Root hair plexuses

Type II cutaneous mechanoreceptors

Free nerve endings

Pressure sensations generally result from deformation of deeper tissues and are longer lasting and have less variation in intensity than touch sensations. Moreover, whereas touch is felt in a small "pinprick" area, pressure is felt over a much larger area. Receptors for pressure sensations include free nerve endings (discussed under touch sensations), lamellated corpuscles, and type II cutaneous mechanoreceptors. **Lamellated (pacinian) corpuscles** are found in the subcutaneous layer and have already been discussed in Exercise 5 (see Figure 5.1). **Type II cutaneous mechanoreceptors (end organs of Ruffini)** are deeply embedded in the dermis.

Pressure receptors are found in the subcutaneous tissue under the skin, in the deep subcutaneous tissues that lie under mucous membranes, around joints and tendons, in the perimysium of muscles, in the mammary glands, in the external genitals of both sexes, and in some viscera.

Vibration sensations result from rapidly repetitive sensory signals. Receptors for vibration include corpuscles of touch and lamellated corpuscles.

2. Thermoreceptors

The cutaneous receptors for the sensation of cold are widely distributed in the dermis and subcutaneous connective tissue, and are also located in the cornea of the eye, tip of the tongue, and external genitals. They consist of myelinated nerve endings (and possibly free nerve endings). The cutaneous receptors for heat are deeply embedded in the dermis and are less abundant than cold receptors. Cutaneous receptors for heat have not yet been identified histologically.

3. Pain Receptors

Receptors for **pain** are free nerve endings (see Figure 5.1). Pain receptors are found in practically every tissue of the body and adapt only slightly or not at all. They may be excited by any type of stimulus. Excessive stimulation of any sense organ causes pain. For example, when stimuli for other sensations such as touch, pressure, heat, and cold reach a certain threshold, they stimulate pain receptors as well. Pain receptors, because of their sensitivity to all stimuli, have a general protective function of informing us of changes that could be potentially dangerous to health or life. Adaptation to pain does not readily occur. This lack of adaptation is important, because pain indicates disorder or disease. If we became used to it and ignored it, irreparable damage could result.

4. Proprioceptive Receptors

An awareness of the activities of muscles, tendons, and joints is provided by the **proprioceptive (kinesthetic) sense.** It informs us of the degree to which tendons are tensed and muscles are contracted. The proprioceptive sense enables us to recognize the location and rate of movement of one part of the body in relation to other parts. It also allows us to estimate weight and to determine the muscular work necessary to perform a task. With the proprioceptive sense, we can judge the position and movements of our limbs without using our eyes when we walk, type, play a musical instrument, or dress in the dark.

Proprioceptive receptors are located in skeletal muscles and tendons, in and around joints, and in the internal ear. Proprioceptors adapt only slightly. This slight adaptation is beneficial because the brain must be appraised of the status of different parts of the body at all times so that adjustments can be made to ensure coordination.

Receptors for proprioception are as follows. The **joint kinesthetic** (kin'-es-THET-ik) **receptors** are located in the articular capsules of joints and ligaments about joints. These receptors provide feedback information on the degree and rate of angulation (change of position) of a joint. **Muscle spindles** consist of the endings of sensory neurons that are wrapped around specialized muscle fibers. They are located in nearly all skeletal muscles and are more numerous in the muscles of the extremities. Muscle spindles provide feedback information on the degree of muscle stretch. This information is relayed to the central nervous system to assist in the coordination and efficiency of muscle contraction. **Tendon organs (Golgi tendon organs)** are located at the junc-

tion of skeletal muscle and tendon. They function by sensing the tension applied to a tendon. The degree of tension is related to the degree of muscle contraction and is translated by the central nervous system.

Proprioceptors in the internal ear are the maculae and cristae that function in equilibrium. These are discussed at the end of the exercise.

Examine prepared slides of joint kinesthetic receptors, muscle spindles, and tendon organs. With the aid of your textbook, draw the receptors in the spaces that follow.

Joint kinesthetic receptors

Muscle spindles

Tendon organs

D. TESTS FOR GENERAL SENSES

Cutaneous receptors are not randomly distributed over the body surface; some parts of the skin are densely populated with receptors and other parts contain only a few widely separated ones. Areas of the body that have few cutaneous receptors are relatively insensitive, whereas those regions that contain large numbers of cutaneous receptors are quite sensitive. This difference can be demonstrated by the **two-point discrimination test** for touch. In the following tests, students can work in pairs, with one acting as subject and the other as experimenter. The subject will keep his or her eyes closed during the experiments.

1. Two-Point Discrimination Test

In this test, the two points of a measuring compass are applied to the skin and the distance in millimeters between the two points is varied. The subject indicates when he or she feels two points and when he or she feels only one.

1. Place the compass on the tip of the tongue, an area where receptors are very densely packed.

2. Narrow the distance between the two points to 1.4 mm. At this distance, the points are able to stimulate two different receptors, and the subject feels that he or she is being touched by two objects.

3. Decrease the distance to less than 1.4 mm. The subject feels only one point, even though both points are touching the tongue because the points are so close together that they reach only one receptor.

4. Now place the compass on the back of the neck, where receptors are relatively few and far between. Here the subject feels two distinctly different points only if the distance between them is 36.2 mm or more.

5. The two-point discrimination test shows that the more sensitive the area, the closer the compass points can be placed and still be felt separately.

6. The following order, from greatest to least sensitivity, has been established from the test: tip of tongue, tip of finger, side of nose, back of hand, and back of neck.

7. Test the tip of finger, side of nose, and back of hand and record your results.

2. Identifying Touch Receptors

1. Using a water-soluble colored felt marking pen, draw a 1-in. square on the back of the fore-

Part of body	Least distance at which two points can be detected
Tip of tongue	1.4 mm
Tip of finger	
Side of nose	
Back of hand	
Back of neck	36 mm

arm and divide the square into 16 smaller squares.

2. With the subject's eyes closed, press a Von Frey hair or bristle against the skin, just enough to cause the hair to bend, once in each of the 16 squares. The pressure should be applied in the same manner each time.

3. The subject should indicate when he or she experiences the sensation of touch, and the experimenter should make dots in Square 1 at the places corresponding to the points at which the subject feels the sensations.

4. The subject and the experimenter switch roles and repeat the test.

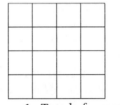

Square 1. Touch, forearm.

The pair of students working as a team should examine their 1-in. squares after the test is done. They should compare the number of positive and negative responses in each of the 16 small squares, and see how uniformly the touch receptors are distributed throughout the entire 1-in. square. Other general areas used for locating touch receptors are the arm and the back of the hand.

3. Identifying Pressure Receptors

1. The experimenter touches the skin of the subject (whose eyes are closed) with the point of a piece of colored chalk.

2. With eyes still closed, the subject then tries to touch the same spot with a piece of differently colored chalk. The distance between the two points is then measured.

3. Proceed using various parts of the body, such as palm of hand, arm, forearm, and back of neck.

4. Record your results below.

Part of body	Distance between points touched by chalk
Palm of hand	_____
Arm	_____
Forearm	_____
Back of neck	_____

4. Identifying Thermoreceptors

1. Draw a 1-in. square on the back of the wrist.

2. Place a forceps or other metal probe in ice-cold water for a minute, dry it quickly, and, with the *dull* point, explore the area in the square for the presence of cold spots.

3. Keep the probe cold and, using ink, mark the position of each spot that you find.

4. Mark each corresponding place in Square 2 with the letter "c."

5. Immerse the forceps in hot water so that it will give a sensation of warmth when removed and applied to the skin, but *avoid having it too hot.*

6. Proceeding as before, locate the position of the warm spots in the same area of the skin.

7. Mark these spots with ink of a different color, and then mark each corresponding place in Square 2 with the letter "h."

8. Repeat the entire procedure, using both cold forceps and warm forceps on the back of the hand and the palm of the hand, respectively, and mark Squares 3 and 4 as you did Square 2.

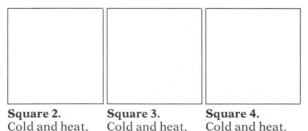

Square 2. Cold and heat, back of wrist. **Square 3.** Cold and heat, back of hand. **Square 4.** Cold and heat, palm of hand.

5. Identifying Pain Receptors

1. Using the same 1-in. square of the forearm that was previously used for the touch test in Section D.2, perform the following experiment.

2. Apply a piece of absorbent cotton soaked with water to the area of the forearm for 5 minutes to soften the skin.

3. Add water to the cotton as needed.

4. Place the blunt end of a probe to the surface of the skin and press enough to produce a sensation of pain. Explore the marked area systematically.

5. Using dots, mark the places in Square 5 that correspond to the points that give pain sensation when stimulated.

6. Distinguish between sensations of pain and touch. Are the areas for touch and pain identical? _____

7. At the end of the test, compare your squares as you did in Section D.2.

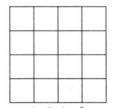

Square 5. Pain, forearm.

Perform the following test to demonstrate the phenomenon of **referred pain**. Place your elbow in a large shallow pan of ice water, and note the progression of sensation that you experience. At first, you will feel some discomfort in the region of the elbow. Later, pain sensations will be felt elsewhere.

Where do you feel the referred pain? _____

6. Identifying Proprioceptors

1. Face a blackboard close enough so that you can easily reach to mark it. Mark a small X on the board in front of you and keep the chalk on the X for a moment. Now close your eyes, raise your right hand above your head and then, with your eyes still closed, mark a dot as near as possible to the X. Repeat the procedure by placing your chalk on the X, closing your eyes, raising your arm above your head, and then marking another dot as close as possible to the X. Repeat the procedure a third time. Record your results by estimating or measuring how far you missed the X for each trial.

First trial _____   Second trial _____

Third trial _____

2. Write the word "physiology" on the left line that follows. Now, with your *eyes closed*, write the same word immediately to the right. How do the samples of writing compare?

_____   _____

Explain your results. _____

_____

_____

_____

3. The following experiments demonstrate that kinesthetic sensations facilitate repetition of certain acts involving muscular coordination.

Students work in pairs for these experiments.

a. The experimenter asks the subject to carry out certain movements with his or her eyes closed, for example, point to the middle finger of the subject's left hand with the index finger of the subject's right hand.

b. With his or her eyes closed, the subject extends the right arm as far as possible behind the body, and then brings the index finger quickly to the tip of his or her nose.

How accurate is the subject in doing this?

_____

c. Ask the subject, with eyes shut, to touch the named fingers of one hand with the index finger of the other hand.

How well does the subject carry out the directions? _____

_____

_____

E. OLFACTORY SENSATIONS

1. Olfactory Receptors

The receptors for the **olfactory sense** are found in the nasal epithelium in the superior portion of the nasal cavity on either side of the nasal septum. The nasal epithelium consists of two principal kinds of cells. The **supporting cells** are columnar epithelial cells of the mucous membrane that lines the nose. The **olfactory cells** are bipolar neurons. Their cell bodies lie between the supporting cells. The distal (free) end of each olfactory cell contains six to eight dendrites, called **olfactory hairs.** The unmyelinated axons of the olfactory cells unite to form the **olfactory (I) nerves,** which pass through foramina in the cribriform plate of the ethmoid bone. The olfactory nerves terminate in paired masses of gray matter, the **olfactory bulbs.** They lie beneath the frontal lobes of the cerebrum on either side of the crista galli of the ethmoid bone. The first synapse of the olfactory neural pathway occurs in the olfactory bulbs between the axons of the olfactory nerves and the dendrites of neurons inside the olfactory bulbs. Axons of these neurons run posteriorly to form the **olfactory tract.** From here, impulses are conveyed to the olfactory area of the cerebral cortex. In the cortex, the impulses are interpreted as odor and give rise to the sensation of smell.

Adaptation happens quickly, especially adaptation to odors. For this reason, we become accustomed to some odors and are also able to endure unpleasant ones. Rapid adaptation also accounts for the failure of a person to detect gas that accumulates slowly in a room.

Label the structures associated with olfaction in Figure 14.1.

Now examine a slide of the olfactory epithelium under high power. Identify the olfactory cells and supporting cells and label Figure 14.2.

2. Olfactory Adaptation

1. The subject should close his or her eyes after plugging one nostril with cotton.

2. Hold a bottle of oil of cloves, or other substance having a distinct odor, under the open nostril.

3. The subject breathes in through the open nostril, and exhales through the mouth. Note the time required for the odor to disappear, and repeat with the other nostril.

4. As soon as **olfactory adaptation** has occurred, test an entirely different substance.

5. Compare results for the various materials tested.

Olfactory stimuli, such as pepper, onions, ammonia, ether, and chloroform, are irritating and may cause tearing because they stimulate the receptors of the trigeminal (V) nerve as well as the olfactory neurons.

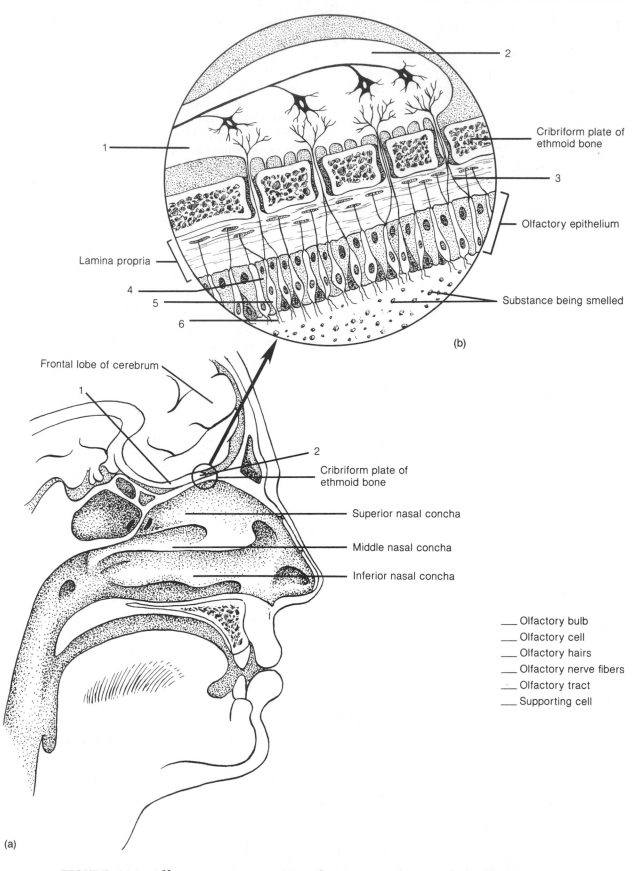

Cribriform plate of ethmoid bone

Olfactory epithelium

Substance being smelled

Lamina propria

(b)

Frontal lobe of cerebrum

Cribriform plate of ethmoid bone

Superior nasal concha

Middle nasal concha

Inferior nasal concha

(a)

___ Olfactory bulb
___ Olfactory cell
___ Olfactory hairs
___ Olfactory nerve fibers
___ Olfactory tract
___ Supporting cell

FIGURE 14.1 Olfactory receptors. (a) In relation to nasal cavity. (b) Enlarged aspect.

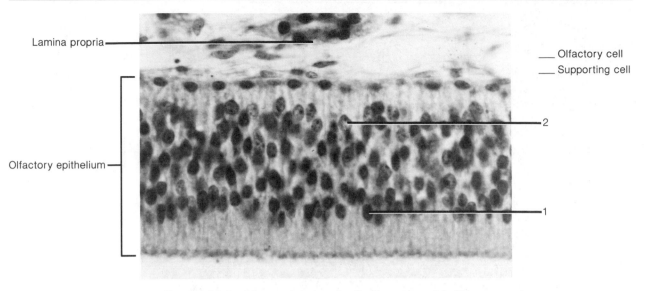

Lamina propria

Olfactory epithelium

___ Olfactory cell
___ Supporting cell

2

1

FIGURE 14.2   Photomicrograph of olfactory epithelium.

F. GUSTATORY SENSATIONS

1. Gustatory Receptors

The receptors for **gustatory sensations**, or sensations of taste, are located in the taste buds. Although taste buds are most numerous on the tongue, they are also found on the soft palate and in the pharynx. **Taste buds** are oval bodies consisting of two kinds of cells. The **supporting cells** are a specialized epithelium that forms a capsule. Inside each capsule are 4 to 20 **gustatory cells.** Each gustatory cell contains a hairlike process **(gustatory hair)** that projects to the surface through an opening in the taste bud called the **taste pore.** Gustatory cells make contact with taste stimuli through the taste pore.

Examine a slide of taste buds and label the structures associated with gustation in Figure 14.3.

Taste buds are located in some connective tissue elevations on the tongue called **papillae** (pa-PILL-ē). They give the upper surface of the tongue its rough texture and appearance. **Circumvallate (vallate) papillae** are circular and form an inverted V-shaped row at the posterior portion of the tongue. **Fungiform papillae** are knoblike elevations found primarily on the tip and sides of the tongue. All circumvallate and most fungiform papillae contain taste buds. **Filiform papillae** are threadlike structures that cover the anterior two-thirds of the tongue.

Have your partner protrude his or her tongue and examine its surface with a hand lens to identify the shape and position of the papillae.

2. Identifying Taste Zones

For gustatory cells to be stimulated, substances tasted must be in solution in the saliva in order to enter the taste pores in the taste buds. Despite the many substances tasted, there are basically only four taste sensations: sour, salty, bitter, and sweet. Each taste is due to a different response to different chemicals. Some regions of the tongue react more strongly than others to particular taste sensations.

To identify the taste zones for the four taste sensations, perform the following steps and record the results in Table 14.1 by inserting a " + " (taste detected) or a " – " (taste not detected) where appropriate.

1. The subject thoroughly dries his or her tongue (use a clean paper towel). The experimenter places some granulated sugar on the tip of the tongue and notes the time. The subject indicates when he or she tastes sugar by raising his or her hand. The experimenter notes the time again and records how long it takes for the subject to taste the sugar.

2. Repeat the experiment, but this time use a drop of sugar solution. Again record how long it takes for the subject to taste the sugar. How do you explain the difference in time periods?

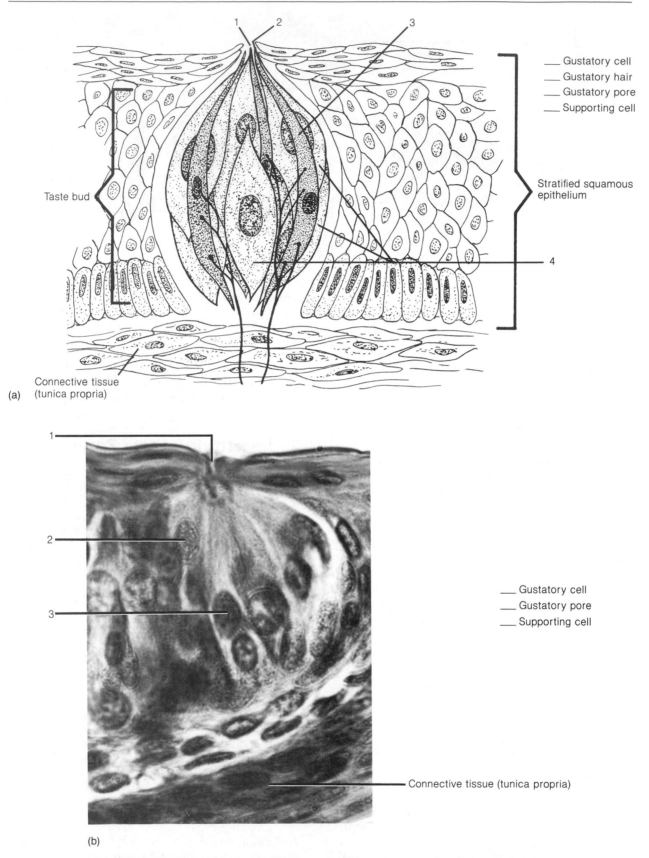

___ Gustatory cell
___ Gustatory hair
___ Gustatory pore
___ Supporting cell

Stratified squamous epithelium

Taste bud

Connective tissue (tunica propria)

(a)

1

___ Gustatory cell
___ Gustatory pore
___ Supporting cell

Connective tissue (tunica propria)

(b)

FIGURE 14.3   Structure of a taste bud. (a) Diagram. (b) Photograph.

TABLE 14.1
AREAS OF TONGUE IN WHICH BASIC TASTES ARE DETECTED

	SWEET	BITTER	SALTY	SOUR
Tip of tongue				
Back of tongue				
Sides of tongue				

3. The subject rinses his or her mouth again. The experiment is then repeated using the quinine solution (bitter taste), and then the salt solution.

4. After rinsing yet again, the experiment is repeated using the acetic acid solution or vinegar (sour) placed on the tip and *sides* of the tongue.

3. Taste and Inheritance

Taste for certain substances is inherited, and geneticists for many years have been using the chemical **phenylthiocarbamide (PTC)** to test taste. To some individuals this substance tastes bitter, to others it is sweet, and some cannot taste it at all.

1. Place a few crystals of PTC on the subject's tongue. Does he or she taste it? If so, describe the taste.

2. Special paper that is flavored with this chemical may be chewed and mixed with saliva and tested in the same manner.

3. Record on the blackboard your response to the PTC test. Usually about 70% of the people tested can taste this compound; 30% cannot. Compare this percentage with the class results.

4. Taste and Smell

This test combines the effect of smell on the sense of taste.

1. Obtain small cubes of carrot, onion, potato, and apple.

2. The subject dries the tongue, closes the eyes, and pinches the nostrils shut. The experimenter places the cubes, one by one, on the subject's tongue.

3. The subject attempts to identify each cube in the following sequences: (1) immediately, (2) after chewing (nostrils closed), and (3) after opening the nostrils.

4. Record your results in Table 14.2.

G. VISUAL SENSATIONS

Structures related to **vision** are the eyeball (which is the receptor organ for visual sensations), optic (II) nerve, brain, and accessory structures. The extrinsic muscles of the eyeball may be reviewed in Figure 10.4.

1. Accessory Structures

Among the **accessory structures** are the eyebrows, eyelids, eyelashes, and lacrimal, or

TABLE 14.2
TASTE SENSATION

	SENSATIONS WHEN PLACED ON DRY TONGUE	SENSATIONS WHILE CHEWING (NOSTRILS CLOSED)	SENSATIONS WITH NOSTRILS OPENED
Carrot			
Onion			
Potato			
Apple			

tearing, apparatus. **Eyebrows** protect the eyeball from falling objects, prevent perspiration from getting into the eye, and shade the eye from the direct rays of the sun. **Eyelids (palpebrae)** (PAL-pe-brē) consist primarily of muscle covered externally by skin. The underside of the muscle is lined by a mucous membrane called the **conjunctiva** (kon-junk-TĪ-va), which also covers the surface of the eyeball. Also within eyelids are **tarsal (meibomian) glands,** modified sebaceous glands whose oily secretion keeps the eyelids from adhering to each other. Infection of these glands produces a **chalazion** (cyst) in the eyelid. Eyelids shade the eye during sleep, protect the eye from light rays and foreign objects, and spread lubricating secretions over the surface of the eyeball. Projecting from the border of each eyelid is a row of short, thick hairs, the **eyelashes.** Sebaceous glands at the base of the hair follicles of the eyelashes, called **sebaceous ciliary glands (glands of Zeis),** pour a lubricating fluid into the follicles. An infection of these glands is called a **sty.**

The **lacrimal** (LAK-ri-mal) **apparatus** consists of a group of structures that manufactures and drains tears. Each **lacrimal gland** is located at the superior lateral portion of both orbits. Leading from the lacrimal glands are 6 to 12 **excretory lacrimal ducts** that empty tears onto the surface of the conjunctiva of the upper lid. From here, the tears pass medially and enter two small openings called **puncta lacrimalia** that appear as two small pores, one in each papilla of the eyelid, at the medial commissure of the eye. The tears then pass into two ducts, the **lacrimal canals,** and are next conveyed into the lacrimal sac. The **lacrimal sac** is the superior expanded portion of the **nasolacrimal duct,** a canal that carries the tears into the inferior meatus of the nose. Tears clean, lubricate, and moisten the external surface of the eyeball.

Label the parts of the lacrimal apparatus in Figure 14.4.

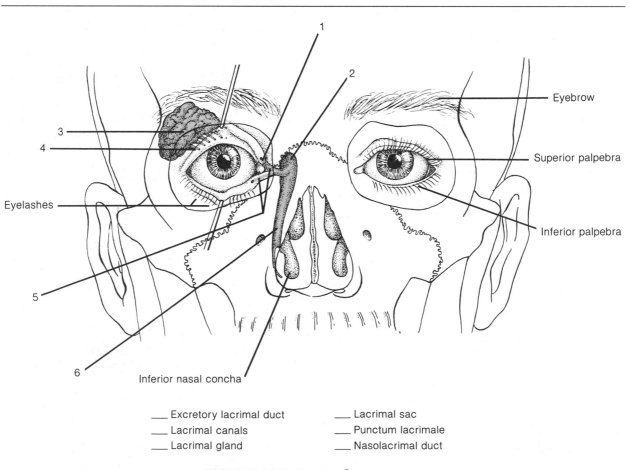

_____ Excretory lacrimal duct _____ Lacrimal sac
_____ Lacrimal canals _____ Punctum lacrimale
_____ Lacrimal gland _____ Nasolacrimal duct

FIGURE 14.4 Lacrimal apparatus.

2. Structure of the Eyeball

The eyeball can be divided into three principal layers: (1) fibrous tunic, (2) vascular tunic, and (3) nervous tunic (retina). See Figure 14.5.

The **fibrous tunic** is the outer coat. It is divided into the posterior sclera and the anterior cornea. The **sclera** (SKLE-ra), called the "white of the eye," is a white coat of fibrous tissue that covers all the eyeball except the anterior portion. The sclera gives shape to the eyeball and protects its inner parts. The anterior portion of the fibrous tunic is known as the **cornea**. This nonvascular, transparent fibrous coat covers the iris, which is the colored part of the eye. The cornea is also composed of fibrous tissue. The outer surface of the cornea contains epithelium that is continuous with the epithelium of the bulbar conjunctiva. At the junction of the sclera and cornea is the **scleral venous sinus (canal of Schlemm).**

The **vascular tunic** is the middle layer of the eyeball and consists of three portions: posterior choroid, anterior ciliary body, and iris. The **choroid** (KŌ-royd) is a thin, dark brown membrane that lines most of the internal surface of the sclera and contains blood vessels and pigment. The choroid absorbs light rays so they are not reflected back out of the eyeball and maintains the nutrition of the retina. The anterior portion of the choroid is the **ciliary** (SIL-ē-ar′-ē) **body**, the thickest portion of the vascular tunic. It extends from the **ora serrata** (Ō-ra ser-RĀ-ta) of the retina (inner tunic) to a point just behind the sclerocorneal junction. The ora serrata is simply the jagged margin of the retina. The ciliary body contains the **ciliary muscle,** a smooth muscle that alters the shape of the lens for near or far vision. The **iris**, the third portion of the vascular tunic, consists of circular and radial smooth muscle fibers arranged to form a doughnut-shaped structure. The black hole in the center of the iris is the **pupil**, through which light enters the eyeball. One function of the iris is to regulate the amount of light entering the eyeball.

The third and inner coat of the eye, the **nervous tunic (retina)** is found only in the posterior portion of the eye. Its primary function is image formation. It consists of a nervous tissue layer and pigmented layer. The outer pigmented layer consists of epithelial cells in contact with the choroid. The inner nervous layer is composed of three zones of neurons. Named in the order in which they conduct impulses, these are the photoreceptor neurons, bipolar neurons, and ganglion neurons. Structurally, the photoreceptor layer is just internal to the pigmented layer, which lies adjacent to the choroid. The zone of ganglion neurons is the innermost of the neuronal layers.

The dendrites of the photoreceptor neurons are called rods and cones because of their respective shapes. **Rods** are specialized for vision in dim light. In addition, they allow discrimination between different shades of dark and light and permit discernment of shapes and movement. **Cones** are specialized for color vision and for sharpness of vision, that is, **visual acuity.** Cones are stimulated only by bright light and are most densely concentrated in the **central fovea,** a small depression in the center of the macula lutea. The **macula lutea** (MAK-yoo-la LOO-tē-a), or yellow spot, is situated in the exact center of the posterior portion of the retina and corresponds to the visual axis of the eye. The fovea is the area of sharpest vision because of the high concentration of cones. Rods are absent from the fovea and macula but increase in density toward the periphery of the retina.

When light stimulates photoreceptor neurons, impulses are conducted across synapses to the bipolar neurons in the intermediate zone of the nervous layer of the retina. From there, the impulses pass to the ganglion neurons. Axons of the ganglion neurons extend posteriorly to a small area of the retina called the **optic disc (blind spot).** This region contains openings through which fibers of the ganglion neurons exit as the **optic (II) nerve.** Because this area contains neither rods nor cones, and only nerve fibers, no image is formed on it. For this reason it is called the blind spot.

The eyeball itself also contains the lens, just behind the pupil and iris. The **lens** is constructed of numerous layers of protein fibers arranged like the layers of an onion. Normally, the lens is perfectly transparent and is enclosed by a clear capsule and held in position by the **suspensory ligament.** An opacity of the lens is called a **cataract.**

The interior of the eyeball contains a large cavity divided into two smaller cavities. These are called the anterior cavity and the posterior cavity and are separated from each other by the lens. The **anterior cavity,** in turn, has two subdivisions known as the anterior chamber and the posterior chamber. The **anterior chamber** lies posterior to the cornea and anterior to the iris. The **posterior chamber** lies posterior to the iris and anterior to the suspensory ligaments and lens. The anterior cavity is filled with a clear, watery fluid known as the **aqueous humor.** From the posterior chamber, the fluid permeates the posterior cavity and then passes forward between the iris and the lens, through the pupil into the anterior chamber. From the anterior chamber, the aqueous humor is drained off into the scleral venous sinus and passes into the blood. Pressure in the eye, called **intraocular pressure,** is produced mainly by the aqueous humor. Intraocular pressure keeps the retina smoothly applied to the choroid so that the retina may form clear images. Abnormal elevation of intraocular pressure, called **glaucoma** (glow-KŌ-ma), results in degeneration of the retina and blindness.

The second, larger cavity of the eyeball is the **posterior cavity.** It is located between the lens and retina and contains a soft, jellylike substance called the **vitreous humor.** This substance contributes to intraocular pressure, helps to prevent the eyeball from collapsing, and holds the retina flush against the internal portions of the eyeball.

Label the parts of the eyeball in Figure 14.5.

3. Surface Anatomy

Refer to Figure 14.6 for a summary of several surface anatomy features of the eyeball and accessory structures of the eye.

4. Dissection of Vertebrate Eye (Beef or Sheep)

a. EXTERNAL EXAMINATION

1. Note any **fat** on the surface of the eyeball that protects the eyeball from shock in the orbit. Remove the fat.

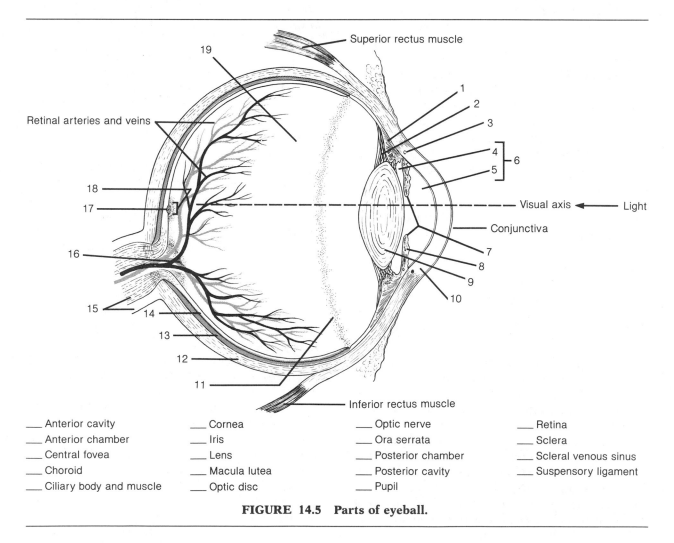

FIGURE 14.5 Parts of eyeball.

___ Anterior cavity   ___ Cornea   ___ Optic nerve   ___ Retina

___ Anterior chamber   ___ Iris   ___ Ora serrata   ___ Sclera

___ Central fovea   ___ Lens   ___ Posterior chamber   ___ Scleral venous sinus

___ Choroid   ___ Macula lutea   ___ Posterior cavity   ___ Suspensory ligament

___ Ciliary body and muscle   ___ Optic disc   ___ Pupil

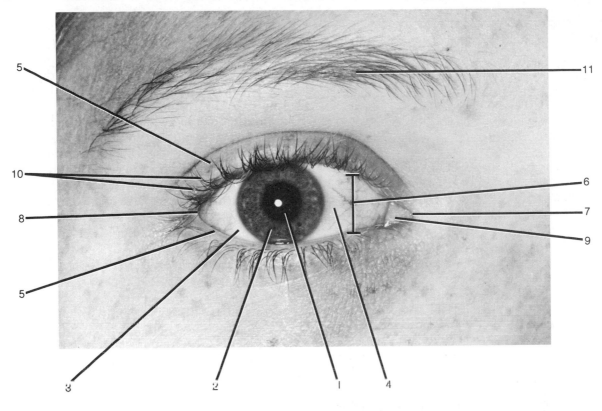

1. **Pupil.** Opening of center of iris of eyeball for light transmission.
2. **Iris.** Circular pigmented muscular membrane behind cornea.
3. **Sclera.** "White" of eye, a coat of fibrous tissue that covers entire eyeball except for cornea.
4. **Conjunctiva.** Membrane that covers exposed surface of eyeball and lines eyelids.
5. **Palpebrae** (eyelids). Folds of skin and muscle lined by conjunctiva.
6. **Palpebral fissure.** Space between eyelids when they are open.

7. **Medial commissure.** Site of union of upper and lower eyelids near nose.
8. **Lateral commissure.** Site of union of upper and lower eyelids away from nose.
9. **Lacrimal caruncle.** Fleshy, yellowish projection of medial commissure that contains modified sweat and sebaceous glands.
10. **Eyelashes.** Hairs on margins of eyelids, usually arranged in two or three rows.
11. **Eyebrows.** Several rows of hairs superior to upper eyelids.

FIGURE 14.6 **Surface anatomy of eyeball and accessory structures.**

2. Locate the **sclera,** the tough external white coat, and the **conjunctiva,** a delicate membrane that covers the anterior surface of the eyeball and is attached near the edge of the cornea. The **cornea** is the anterior, transparent portion of the sclera. It is probably opaque in your specimen due to the preservative.

3. Locate the **optic (II) nerve,** a solid, white cord of nerve fibers on the posterior surface of the eyeball.

4. If possible, identify the six **extrinsic eye muscles** that appear as flat bands near the posterior part of the eyeball.

b. INTERNAL EXAMINATION

1. With a sharp scalpel, make an incision about ¼ in. lateral to the cornea (Figure 14.7).

2. Insert scissors into the incision and carefully and slowly cut all the way around the corneal region. The eyeball contains fluid, so take care that is does not squirt out when you make your first incision. Examine the inside of the anterior part of the eyeball.

3. The **lens** can be seen held in position by **suspensory ligaments,** which are delicate fibers. Around the outer margin of the lens, with a

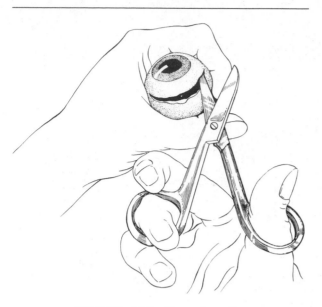

FIGURE 14.7 Procedure for dissecting a vertebrate eye.

pleated appearance, is the black **ciliary body,** which also functions to hold the lens in place. Free the lens and notice how hard it is.

4. The **iris** can be seen just anterior to the lens and is also heavily pigmented or black.

5. The **pupil** is the circular opening in the center of the iris.

6. Examine the inside of the posterior part of the eyeball, identifying the thick **vitreous humor** that fills the space between the lens and retina.

7. The **retina** is the white inner coat beneath the choroid coat and is easily separated from it.

8. The **choroid coat** is a dark, iridescent-colored tissue that gets its iridescence from a special structure called the **tapetum lucidum.** The tapetum lucidum, which is not present in the human eye, functions to reflect some light back onto the retina.

9. Finally, identify the **blind spot,** the point at which the retina is attached to the back of the eyeball.

5. Ophthalmoscopic Examination of the Eyeball

Examinations of the eye include inspection of the fundus (interior) of the eyeball. This is ac-

complished by using an instrument called an **ophthalmoscope** (of-THAL-mō-skōp). It consists of a light source, a set of mirrors or prism arranged to reflect light so that the fundus of the eyeball is illuminated, and a set of lenses arranged on a rotating disc. Ophthalmoscopic examination of the eyeball permits examination of the nervous tunic (retina), optic disc, macula lutea, and blood vessels and is useful in detecting changes associated with conditions such as diabetes mellitus, atherosclerosis, and cataracts. Without using eye drops to dilate the pupil, a physician can see about 15% of the retina; if the pupil is dilated, about half of the retina can be visualized.

The procedure for using the ophthalmoscope is as follows:

1. In a dimly lit or dark room, seat your partner comfortably and have her or him look straight ahead at an object at eye level.

2. To examine your partner's right eye, hold the ophthalmoscope in your right hand and use your right eye. Reverse hands and eyes when viewing your partner's left eye.

3. With your index finger on the edge of the lens selection disc, rotate the disc so that the "O" is in position.

4. Hold the instrument about 6 in. from the subject's eye and direct light *toward the edge of the pupil* rather than directly in its center. You should now see a red circular area in the fundus of the eyeball.

5. Now move to within 2 in. of the subject and, while still directing the beam of light toward the edge of the pupil, rotate the disc to lens numbers of higher value until the optic disc is in sharp focus (Figure 14.8). Examine the optic disc carefully and note its blood vessels. The disc should have a sharp outline.

6. Examine the macula lutea lateral to the optic disc. It lacks blood vessels and should be darker than the optic disc. Locate the central fovea, a slightly lighter area in the center of the macula lutea.

6. Testing for Visual Acuity

The acuteness of vision may be tested by means of a **Snellen Chart.** It consists of letters of different sizes which are read at a distance normally designated at 20 ft. If the subject reads to the line that is marked "50," he or she is said

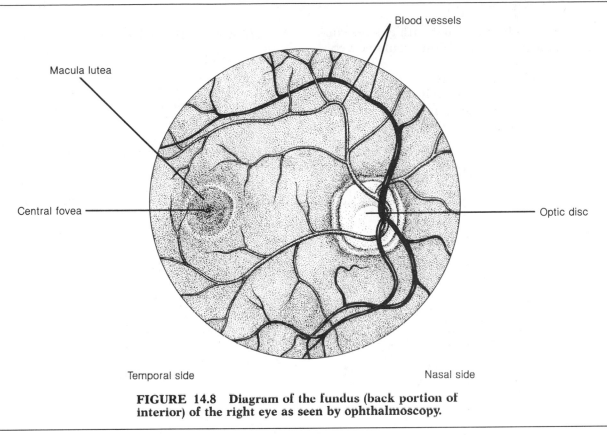

Blood vessels

Macula lutea

Central fovea

Optic disc

Temporal side

Nasal side

FIGURE 14.8 Diagram of the fundus (back portion of interior) of the right eye as seen by ophthalmoscopy.

to possess 20/50 vision in that eye, meaning that he or she is reading at 20 ft what a person who has normal vision can read at 50 ft. If he or she reads to the line marked "20," he or she has 20/20 vision in that eye. The normal eye can sufficiently refract light rays from an object 20 ft away to focus a clear object on the retina. Therefore, if you have 20/20 vision, your eyes are perfectly normal. The higher the bottom number, the larger the letter must be for you to see it clearly, and of course the worse or weaker your eyes are.

1. Have the subject stand 20 ft from the Snellen Chart and cover the right eye with a 3″ × 5″ card.

2. Instruct the subject to slowly read down the chart until he or she can no longer focus the letters.

3. Record the number of the last line (20/20, 20/30, or whichever) that can be successfully read.

4. Repeat this procedure covering the left eye.

5. Now the subject should read the chart using both eyes.

6. Record your results and change places.

Visual acuity, left eye   _____

Visual acuity, right eye   _____

Visual acuity, both eyes   _____

7. Abnormalities Related to Refraction

The eye, with normal ability to refract light, is referred to as an **emmetropic** (em′-e-TROP-ik) eye. It can sufficiently refract light rays from an object 20 ft away to focus a clear object on the retina. If the lens is normal, objects as far away as the horizon and as close as about 20 ft will form images on the sensitive part of the retina. When objects are closer than 20 ft, however, the lens has to sharpen its focus by using the ciliary muscles. Many individuals, however, have abnormalities related to improper refraction. Among these are **myopia** (mī-Ō-pē-a) (nearsightedness), **hypermetropia** (hī′-per-mē-TRO-pē-a) (farsightedness), and **astigmatism** (a-STIG-ma-tizm) (irregularities in the surface of the lens or cornea). Why do you think nearsightedness can be corrected with glasses containing biconcave lenses? How would you correct farsightedness?

In order to determine the presence of astigmatism, remove any corrective lenses if you are wearing them and look at the center of the following astigmatism test chart, first with one eye, then the other:

If all the radiating lines appear equally sharp and equally black, there is no astigmatism. If some of the lines are blurred or less dark than others, astigmatism is present. If you wear corrective lenses, try the test with them on.

8. Testing for the Blind Spot

1. Hold this page about 20 in. from your face with the cross in the following diagram directly in front of your right eye. You should be able to see the cross and the circle when you close you left eye.

2. Now, keeping the left eye closed, slowly bring the page closer to your face while fixing the right eye on the cross.

3. At a certain distance the circle will disappear from your field of vision because its image falls on the blind spot.

9. Image Formation

Formation of an image on the retina requires four basic processes, all concerned with focusing light rays. These are: (1) refraction of light rays, (2) accommodation of the lens, (3) constriction of the pupil, and (4) convergence of the eyes.

When light rays traveling through a transparent medium (such as air) pass into a second transparent medium with a different density (such as water), the rays bend at the surface of the two media. This is called **refraction.** The eye has four such media of refraction—the cornea, aqueous humor, lens, and vitreous humor.

The lens of the eye has the unique ability to change the focusing power of the eye by becoming moderately curved at one moment and greatly curved the next. When the eye is focusing on a close object, the lens curves greatly in order to bend the rays toward the central fovea of the eye. This increase in the curvature of the lens is called **accommodation.**

a. TESTING FOR NEAR-POINT ACCOMMODATION

The following test determines your **near-point accommodation:**

1. Using any card that has a letter printed on it, close one eye and focus on the letter.

2. Measure the distance of the card from the eye using a ruler or a meter stick.

3. Now slowly bring the card as close to your open eye as possible, and stop when you no longer see a clear, detailed letter.

4. Measure and record this distance. This value is your near-point accommodation.

5. Repeat this procedure three times and then test your other eye.

6. Check Table 14.3 to see whether the near point for your eyes corresponds with that recorded for your age group. (**Note:** Use a letter that is the size of typical newsprint.)

**TABLE 14.3
CORRELATION OF AGE AND
NEAR-POINT ACCOMMODATION**

AGE	INCHES	CENTIMETERS
10	2.95	7.5
20	3.54	9.0
30	4.53	11.5
40	6.77	17.2
50	20.67	52.5
60	32.80	83.3

b. TESTING FOR CONSTRICTION OF THE PUPIL

1. Place a 3″ × 5″ card on the side of the nose so that a light shining on one side of the face will not affect the eye on the other side.

2. Shine the light from a lamp or a flashlight on one eye, 6 in. away (approximately 15 cm), for about 5 seconds. Note the change in the size of the pupil of this eye.

3. Remove the light, wait about 3 minutes, and repeat, but this time observe the pupil of the opposite eye.

4. Wait a few minutes, and repeat the test observing the pupils of both eyes.

c. TESTING FOR CONVERGENCE

In humans, both eyes focus on only one set of objects—a characteristic called **single binocular vision**. The term **convergence** refers to a medial movement of the two eyeballs so that they are both directed toward the object being viewed. The nearer the object, the greater the degree of convergence necessary to maintain single binocular vision.

1. Hold a pencil or pen about 2 ft from your nose and focus on its point. Now slowly bring the pencil toward your nose.

2. At some moment you should suddenly see two pencil points, or a blurring of the point.

3. Observe your partner's eyes when he or she does this test.

Images are actually focused upside down on the retina. They also undergo mirror reversal. That is, light reflected from the right side of an object hits the left side of the retina and vice versa. Reflected light from the top of the object crosses light from the bottom of the object and strikes the retina below the central fovea. Reflected light from the bottom of the object crosses light from the top of the object and strikes the retina above the central fovea.

The reason why we do not see a topsy-turvy world is that the brain learns early in life to coordinate visual images with the exact location of objects. The brain stores memories of reaching and touching objects and automatically turns visual images right-side up and right-side around.

10. Visual Pathway

From the rods and cones, impulses are transmitted through bipolar neurons to ganglion cells. The cell bodies of the ganglion cells lie in the retina and their axons leave the eye via the **optic (II) nerve.** The axons pass through the **optic chiasma** (kī-AZ-ma), a crossing point of the optic nerves. Fibers from the medial retina cross to the opposite side. Fibers from the lateral retina remain uncrossed. Upon passing through the optic chiasma, the fibers, now part of the **optic tract,** enter the brain and terminate in the thalamus. Here the fibers synapse with the neurons whose axons pass to the visual centers located in the occipital lobes of the cerebral cortex.

Label the visual pathway in Figure 14.9.

H. AUDITORY SENSATIONS AND EQUILIBRIUM

In addition to containing receptors for sound waves, the **ear** also contains receptors for equilibrium. The ear is subdivided into three principal regions: (1) external or outer ear, (2) middle ear, and (3) internal or inner ear.

1. Structure of Ear

The **external (outer ear)** collects sound waves and directs them inward. Its structure consists of the pinna, external auditory canal, and tympanic membrane. The **pinna (auricle)** is a trumpet-shaped flap of elastic cartilage covered by thick skin. The rim of the pinna is called the helix, and the inferior portion is referred to as the lobe. The pinna is attached to the head by ligaments and muscles. The **external auditory canal (meatus)** is a tube, about 2.5 cm (1 in.) in length that leads from the pinna to the eardrum. The walls of the canal consist of

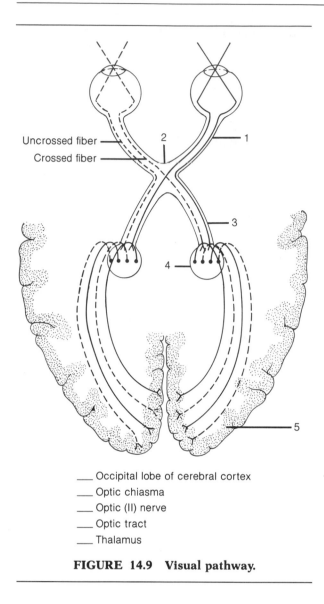

Uncrossed fiber
Crossed fiber

___ Occipital lobe of cerebral cortex
___ Optic chiasma
___ Optic (II) nerve
___ Optic tract
___ Thalamus

FIGURE 14.9 Visual pathway.

bone lined with cartilage that is continuous with the cartilage of the pinna. Near the exterior opening, the canal contains a few hairs and specialized sebaceous glands called **ceruminous** (se-ROO-me-nus) **glands,** which secrete **cerumen** (earwax). The combination of hairs and cerumen prevents foreign objects from entering the ear. The **tympanic** (tim-PAN-ik) **membrane (eardrum)** is a thin, semitransparent partition of fibrous connective tissue located between the external auditory meatus and the middle ear.

Examine a model or charts and label the parts of the external ear in Figure 14.10.

The **middle ear (tympanic cavity)** is a small, epithelium-lined, air-filled cavity hollowed out

of the temporal bone. The area is separated from the external ear by the eardrum and from the internal ear by a very thin bony partition that contains two small membrane-covered openings, called the oval window and the round window. The posterior wall of the cavity communicates with the mastoid cells of the temporal bone through a chamber called the **tympanic antrum.** The anterior wall of the cavity contains an opening that leads into the **auditory (eustachian) tube.** The auditory tube connects the middle ear with the nose and nasopharynx. The function of the tube is to equalize air pressure on both sides of the tympanic membrane. Any sudden pressure changes against the eardrum may be equalized by deliberately swallowing.

Extending across the middle ear are three exceedingly small bones called **auditory ossicles** (OS-si-kuls). These are known as the malleus, incus, and stapes. Based on their shape, they are commonly named the hammer, anvil, and stirrup, respectively. The "handle" of the **malleus** is attached to the internal surface of the tympanic membrane. Its head articulates with the base of the **incus,** the intermediate bone in the series, which articulates with the stapes. The base of the **stapes** fits into a small opening between the middle and inner ear called the **fenestra vestibuli** (fe-NES-tra ves-TIB-yoo-lī) **(oval window).** Directly below the oval window is another opening, the **fenestra cochlea** (KŌK-lē-a) **(round window).** This opening, which separates the middle and inner ears, is enclosed by a membrane called the **secondary tympanic membrane.**

Examine a model or charts and label the parts of the middle ear in Figures 14.10 and 14.11.

The **internal (inner) ear** is also known as the **labyrinth.** Structually, this consists of two main divisions: (1) a bony labyrinth and (2) a membranous labyrinth that fits within the bony labyrinth. The **bony labyrinth** (LAB-i-rinth) is a series of cavities within the petrous portion of the temporal bone that can be divided into three portions, named on the basis of shape. These areas are the vestibule, cochlea, and semicircular canals. The bony labyrinth is lined with periosteum and contains a fluid called the **perilymph.** This fluid surrounds the **membranous labyrinth,** a series of sacs and tubes lying inside and having the same general form as the bony labyrinth. Epithelium lines the membra-

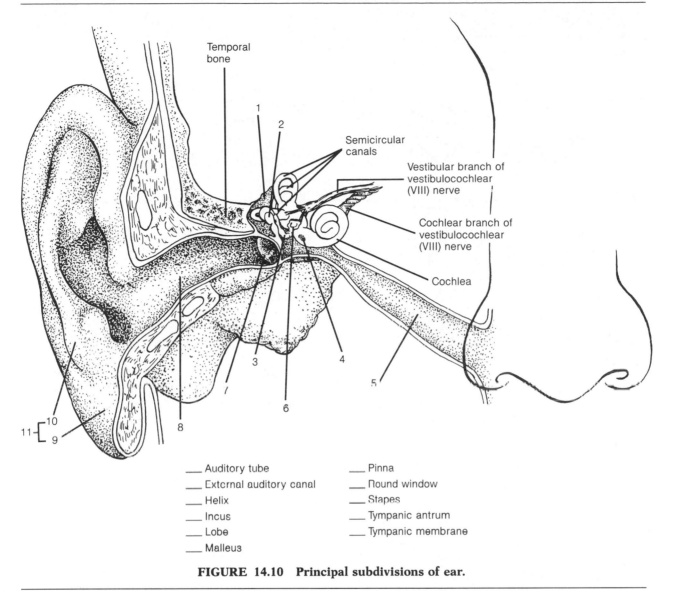

___ Auditory tube   ___ Pinna

___ External auditory canal   ___ Round window

___ Helix   ___ Stapes

___ Incus   ___ Tympanic antrum

___ Lobe   ___ Tympanic membrane

___ Malleus

FIGURE 14.10 Principal subdivisions of ear.

nous labyrinth, which is filled with a fluid called the **endolymph.**

The **vestibule** is the oval, central portion of the bony labyrinth (see Figure 14.11). The membranous labyrinth within the vestibule consists of two sacs called the **utricle** (YOO-tre-k′l) and **saccule** (SAK-yool). These sacs are connected to each other by a small duct.

Projecting superiorly and posteriorly from the vestibule are the three bony **semicircular canals** (see Figure 14.11). Each is arranged at approximately right angles to the other two. They are called the superior, posterior, and lateral canals. One end of each canal enlarges into a swelling called the **ampulla** (am-POOL-la). Inside the bony semicircular canals lie portions of the membranous labyrinth, the **semicircular**

ducts **(membranous semicircular canals).** These structures communicate with the utricle of the vestibule. Label these structures in Figure 14.12.

Anterior to the vestibule is the **cochlea** (label it in Figure 14.11), which resembles a snail's shell. The cochlea consists of a bony spiral canal that makes about 2¾ turns around a central bony core called the **modiolus.** A cross section through the cochlea shows that the canal is divided by partitions into three separate channels resembling the letter Y lying on its side. The stem of the Y is a bony shelf that protrudes into the canal. The wings of the Y are composed of the vestibular and basilar membranes. The channel above the partition is called the **scala vestibuli.** The channel below is known as the **scala tympani.** The cochlea ad-

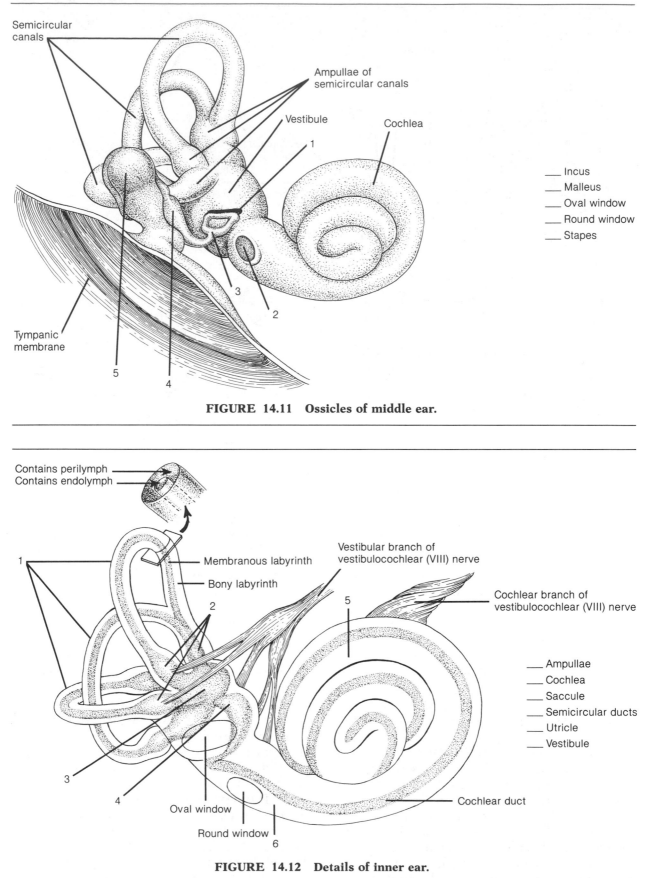

Semicircular canals

Ampullae of semicircular canals

Vestibule

Cochlea

1

___ Incus
___ Malleus
___ Oval window
___ Round window
___ Stapes

3

2

Tympanic membrane

5

4

FIGURE 14.11   Ossicles of middle ear.

Contains perilymph
Contains endolymph

1

Membranous labyrinth

Bony labyrinth

2

Vestibular branch of vestibulocochlear (VIII) nerve

5

Cochlear branch of vestibulocochlear (VIII) nerve

___ Ampullae
___ Cochlea
___ Saccule
___ Semicircular ducts
___ Utricle
___ Vestibule

3

4

Oval window

Round window

6

Cochlear duct

FIGURE 14.12   Details of inner ear.

joins the wall of the vestibule, into which the scala vestibuli opens. The scala tympani terminates at the round window. The perilymph of the vestibule is continuous with that of the scala vestibuli. The third channel (between the wings of the Y) is the membranous labyrinth, the **cochlear duct.** This duct is separated from the scala vestibuli by the **vestibular membrane** and from the scala tympani by the **basilar membrane.** Resting on the basilar membrane is the **spiral organ (organ of Corti),** the organ of hearing. Label these structures in Figure 14.13.

The spiral organ is a series of epithelial cells on the inner surface of the basilar membrane. This structure is composed of supporting cells and hair cells, which are receptors for auditory sensations. The hair cells have long hairlike processes at their free ends that extend into the endolymph of the cochlear duct. The basal ends of the hair cells are in contact with fibers of the cochlear branch of the vestibulocochlear (VIII) nerve. Projecting over and in contact with the hair cells of the spiral organ is the **tectorial membrane,** a very delicate and flexible gelatinous membrane. Label the tectorial membrane in Figure 14.13.

Obtain a prepared microscope slide of the spiral organ and examine under high power. Now label Figure 14.14.

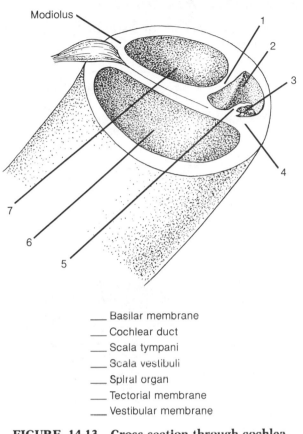

____ Basilar membrane
____ Cochlear duct
____ Scala tympani
____ Scala vestibuli
____ Spiral organ
____ Tectorial membrane
____ Vestibular membrane

FIGURE 14.13   Cross section through cochlea.

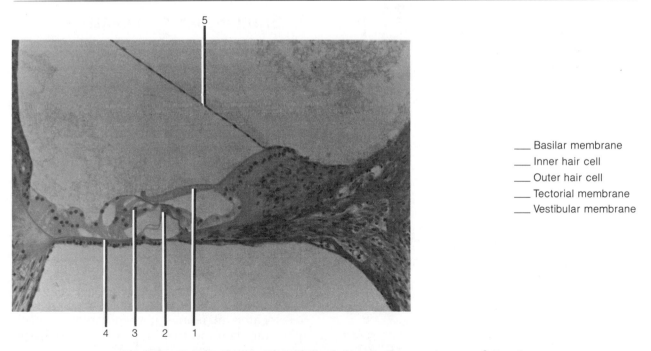

____ Basilar membrane
____ Inner hair cell
____ Outer hair cell
____ Tectorial membrane
____ Vestibular membrane

FIGURE 14.14   Photomicrograph of the spiral organ (organ of Corti).

2. Surface Anatomy

Refer to Figure 14.15 for a summary of several surface anatomy features of the ear.

3. Tests for Hearing Impairment

1. To test for hearing impairment, the subject places a cotton plug in one ear and closes the eyes.

2. The student partner then holds a watch next to the other ear and slowly moves it away.

3. The subject indicates when he or she can no longer hear the watch. Measure and record this distance.

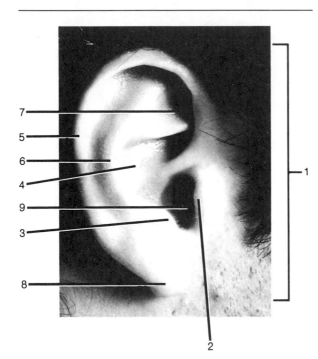

1. **Pinna (auricle).** Portion of external ear not contained in head, also called auricle or trumpet.
2. **Tragus.** Cartilaginous projection anterior to external opening of ear.
3. **Antitragus.** Cartilaginous projection opposite tragus.
4. **Concha.** Hollow of auricle.
5. **Helix.** Superior and posterior free margin of auricle.
6. **Antihelix.** Semicircular ridge posterior and superior to concha.
7. **Triangular fossa.** Depression in superior portion of antihelix.
8. **Lobule.** Inferior portion of auricle devoid of cartilage.
9. **External auditory meatus.** Canal extending from external ear to eardrum.

FIGURE 14.15   Surface anatomy of ear.

4. Repeat this test three times and calculate the average of the distances.

5. The other ear is tested in a similar manner. Compare your results with those of your partner.

Left ear

(1) _____   (2) _____

(3) _____   (Average) _____

Right ear

(1) _____   (2) _____

(3) _____   (Average) _____

The inner ear is located within the temporal bone of the cranium. Therefore, if the stimulus has a high enough intensity, any bone of the cranium can conduct sound to the cochlea.

1. Strike a tuning fork with a rubber mallet and place the vibrating fork upon the following bones: (1) temporal, (2) parietal, (3) frontal, (4) occipital.

2. Keep the vibrating fork on these bones until you can barely hear it, and then put the fork next to your ear. Notice whether sound is conducted better in bone, or in air.

4. Equilibrium Apparatus

The term **equilibrium** has two meanings. One kind of equilibrium, called **static equilibrium,** refers to the orientation of the body (mainly the head) relative to the ground. The second kind of equilibrium, called **dynamic equilibrium,** is the maintenance of the position of the body (mainly the head) in response to sudden movements (rotation, acceleration, and deceleration) or to a change in the rate or direction of movement. The receptor organs for equilibrium are the maculae in the saccule and utricle and the cristae in the semicircular ducts.

The **maculae** (MAK-yoo-lē) in the walls of the **utricle** and **saccule** are the receptors concerned with static equilibrium. The maculae are small, flat, plaquelike regions that resemble the spiral organ microscopically. Maculae are located in planes perpendicular to each other and contain two kinds of cells: **hair (receptor) cells** and **supporting cells.** The hair cells project **stereocilia** (microvilli) and a **kinocilium** (conventional cilium). The supporting cells are scattered among the hair cells. Floating over the hair cells is a thick, gelatinous glycoprotein layer, the **otolithic membrane.** A layer of calcium carbonate crystals, called **otoliths,** extends over the entire surface of the otolithic membrane. When the head is tilted, the membrane slides over the hair cells in the direction determined by the tilt of the head. This sliding causes the membrane to pull on the stereocilia, thus initiating a nerve impulse that is conveyed via the vestibular branch of the vestibulocochlear (VIII) nerve to the brain (cerebellum). The cerebellum sends continuous impulses to the motor areas of the cerebral cortex in response to input from the maculae in the utricle and saccule, causing the motor system to increase or decrease its impulses to specific skeletal muscles to maintain static equilibrium.

Label the parts of the macula in Figure 14.16a.

Now consider the role of the cristae in the semicircular ducts in maintaining dynamic equilibrium. The three semicircular ducts are positioned at right angles to each other in three planes: frontal (superior duct); sagittal (posterior duct); and lateral (lateral duct). This positioning permits correction of an imbalance in three planes. In the ampulla, the dilated portion of each duct, is a small elevation called the **crista.** Each crista is composed of a group of **hair (receptor) cells** and **supporting cells** covered by a mass of gelatinous material called the **cupula.** When the head moves, endolymph in the semicircular ducts flows over the hairs and bends them as water in a stream bends the plant life growing at its bottom. Movement of the hairs stimulates sensory neurons, and impulses pass over the vestibular branch of the vestibulocochlear (VIII) nerve. The impulses follow the same pathway as those involved in static equilibrium and are eventually sent to the muscles that must contract to maintain body balance in the new position.

Label the parts of the crista in Figure 14.16b.

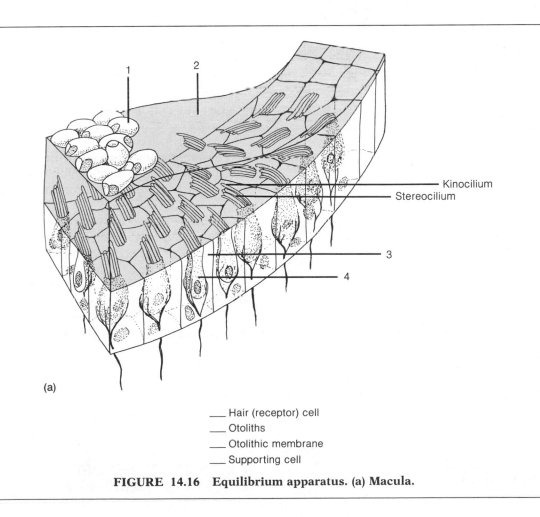

Kinocilium
Stereocilium

(a)

___ Hair (receptor) cell
___ Otoliths
___ Otolithic membrane
___ Supporting cell

FIGURE 14.16 Equilibrium apparatus. (a) Macula.

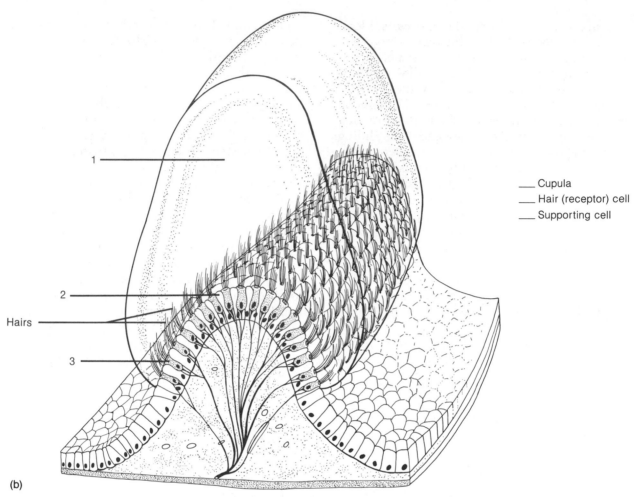

1 _____

2 _____

Hairs _____

3 _____

___ Cupula
___ Hair (receptor) cell
___ Supporting cell

(b)

FIGURE 14.16 (*Continued*)   Equilibrium apparatus. (b) Crista.

5. Tests for Equilibrium

You can test equilibrium by using a few simple procedures.

1. Test balance by having the subject stand perfectly still with his or her hands at his or her sides and the feet close together. Note any swaying movements.

2. If the subject stands in front of a light, swaying movements are more easily detected by observing the subject's shadow.

3. Have the subject repeat this test with the eyes closed. Note any swaying movements.

The next test evaluates the semicircular canals.

1. The subject sits firmly anchored on a stool, legs up on the stool rung, and the stool is *very carefully* revolved for a few seconds and suddenly stopped.

2. The subject will experience the sensation that the stool is still rotating, which means that the semicircular canals are functioning properly.

A cold test also evaluates the semicircular canals. A cold swab placed in one ear increases the density of the endolymph of the semicircular canal adjacent to that ear. This increased density stimulates the hair cells within the semicircular canals, causing a sensation of rotation characterized by **nystagmus** (involuntary rapid movement of the eyeball).

1. Place a cotton swab in an ice bath for several minutes and then *carefully* insert in one of your ears, noting the results.

2. Test your other ear using a second cooled swab.

LABORATORY REPORT QUESTIONS (PAGE 401)

15 | ENDOCRINE SYSTEM

You have learned how the nervous system controls the body through nerve impulses that are delivered over neurons. Now you will study the body's other great control system, the **endocrine system.** The endocrine organs affect bodily activities by releasing chemical messengers, called **hormones,** into the bloodstream. The nervous and endocrine systems coordinate their activities as an interlocking supersystem. Certain parts of the nervous system stimulate or inhibit the release of hormones. The hormones, in turn, are quite capable of stimulating or inhibiting the flow of particular nerve impulses.

The body contains two different kinds of glands: exocrine and endocrine. **Exocrine glands** secrete their products into ducts. The ducts then carry the secretions into body cavities, into the lumens of various organs, or to the external surface of the body. Examples are sweat, sebaceous, mucous, and digestive glands. **Endocrine glands,** by contrast, secrete their products (hormones) into the extracellular space around the secretory cells. The secretion passes through the membranes of cells lining blood vessels and into the blood. Because they have no ducts, endocrine glands are also called **ductless glands.**

A. ENDOCRINE GLANDS

The endocrine glands of the body are the pituitary (hypophysis), thyroid, parathyroids, adrenals (suprarenals), pancreas, testes, ovaries, pineal (epiphysis cerebri), and thymus. Other endocrine tissues include the kidneys, stomach, small intestine, and placenta. The endocrine glands are organs that together form the **endocrine system.** Locate the endocrine glands on a torso, and, using your textbook or charts for reference, label Figure 15.1.

All hormones maintain homeostasis by changing the physiological activities of cells (the term **hormone** means "to set in motion"). A hormone may stimulate changes in the cells of an organ or in groups of organs. Or, the hormone may directly affect the activities of all the cells in the body. The cells that respond to the effects of a hormone are called **target cells.**

B. PITUITARY GLAND (HYPOPHYSIS)

The hormones of the **pituitary gland,** also called the **hypophysis** (hī-POF-i-sis), regulate so many body activities that the pituitary has been nicknamed the "master gland." This gland lies in the sella turcica of the sphenoid bone and is attached to the hypothalamus of the brain via a stalklike structure, the **infundibulum.**

The pituitary is divided structurally and functionally into an anterior lobe called the **adenohypophysis** (ad'-i-nō-hī-POF-i-sis) and a posterior lobe called the **neurohypophysis** (noo'-rō-hī-POF-i-sis), both of which are connected to the hypothalamus. The anterior lobe contains many glandular epithelium cells and forms the glandular part of the pituitary. The posterior lobe contains neurons, which form the neural part of the pituitary. Between the two lobes is a small, relatively avascular zone, the **pars intermedia** whose role in humans is obscure.

1. Histology of Pituitary Gland

The adenohypophysis releases hormones that regulate a whole range of body activities, from growth to reproduction. However, the release of these hormones is either stimulated or in-

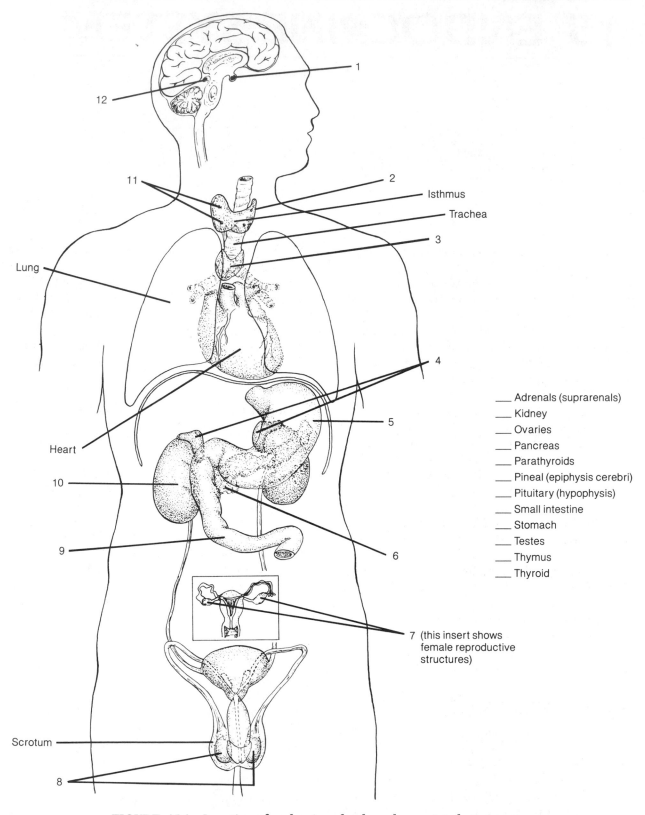

1

12

11

2

Isthmus

Trachea

3

Lung

Heart

4

5

10

9

6

___ Adrenals (suprarenals)

___ Kidney

___ Ovaries

___ Pancreas

___ Parathyroids

___ Pineal (epiphysis cerebri)

___ Pituitary (hypophysis)

___ Small intestine

___ Stomach

___ Testes

___ Thymus

___ Thyroid

7 (this insert shows female reproductive structures)

Scrotum

8

FIGURE 15.1 Location of endocrine glands and associated structures.

hibited by chemical secretions (**regulating factors**) that are produced by the hypothalamus of the brain. This is one interaction between the nervous system and the endocrine system. The hypothalamic regulating factors reach the adenohypophysis via a network of blood vessels referred to as the **hypothalamic-hypophyseal** (hī-pō-FIZ-ē-al) **portal system.**

When the adenohypophysis receives proper stimulation from the hypothalamus via regulating factors, its glandular cells secrete any one of seven hormones. Recently, special staining techniques have established the division of glandular cells into five principal types:

1. **Somatotroph cells** produce **growth hormone (GH),** which controls general body growth.

2. **Lactotroph cells** synthesize **prolactin (PRL),** which initiates milk production by the mammary glands.

3. **Thyrotroph cells** manufacture **thyroid-stimulating hormone (TSH),** which controls the thyroid gland.

4. **Gonadotroph cells** produce **follicle-stimulating hormone (FSH),** which stimulates the production of eggs and sperm in the ovaries and testes, respectively, and **luteinizing hormone (LH),** which stimulates other sexual and reproductive activities.

5. **Cortico-lipotroph cells** synthesize **adrenocorticotropic** (ad-rē-nō-kor'-ti-kō-TRŌ-pik) **hormone (ACTH),** which stimulates the adrenal cortex to secrete its hormones and **melanocyte-stimulating hormone (MSH),** which is related to skin pigmentation.

Except for growth hormone (GH), melanocyte-stimulating hormone (MSH), and prolactin (PRL), all the secretions are referred to as **tropic hormones,** which means that their target organs are other endocrine glands. Follicle-stimulating hormone (FSH) and luteinizing hormone (LH) are also called **gonadotropic** (gō-nad-ō-TRŌ-pik) **hormones** because they regulate the functions of the gonads. The gonads (ovaries and testes) are the endocrine glands that produce sex hormones.

Identify somatotroph cells, lactotroph cells, thyrotroph cells, gonadotroph cells, and cortico-lipotroph cells with the aid of your textbook or a histology textbook.

The posterior lobe (neurohypophysis) of the pituitary is not really an endocrine gland. Instead of synthesizing hormones, the lobe stores hormones synthesized by cells of the hypothalamus. The posterior lobe consists of (1) cells called **pituicytes** (pi-TOO-i-sītz), which are similar in appearance to the neuroglia of the nervous system, and (2) axon terminations of secretory nerve cells of the hypothalamus. The cell bodies of the neurons, called **neurosecretory cells,** originate in nuclei in the hypothalamus. The fibers project from the hypothalamus, form the **hypothalamic-hypophyseal tract,** and terminate on blood capillaries in the neurohypophysis. The cell bodies of the neurons produce the hormones **oxytocin** (ok'-sē-TŌ-sin), or **OT,** and **antidiuretic hormone (ADH).** These hormones are transported in the neuron fibers into the neurohypophysis and are stored in the axon terminals resting on the capillaries. When properly stimulated, the hypothalamus sends impulses over the neurons. The impulses cause release of hormones from the axon terminals into the blood.

Examine a prepared slide of the neurohypophysis under high power. Identify the pituicytes and axon terminations of neurosecretory cells with the aid of your textbook.

2. Hormones of Pituitary Gland

Using your textbook as a reference, give the major functions for the hormones listed below.

a. PITUITARY HORMONES SECRETED BY ADENOHYPOPHYSIS

Growth hormone (GH). Also called somatotropin and somatotropic hormone (STH) _____

_____

_____

_____

Thyroid-stimulating hormone (TSH). Also called thyrotropin _____

_____

_____

Adrenocorticotropic hormone (ACTH) _____

_____

_____

_____

Follicle-stimulating hormone (FSH)

In female. _____

_____

_____

In male. _____

_____

_____

Luteinizing hormone (LH)

In female. _____

_____

In male. _____

_____

_____

Prolactin (PRL). Also called lactogenic hormone _____

_____

_____

Melanocyte-stimulating hormone (MSH) _____

_____

_____

_____

b. PITUITARY HORMONES STORED BY NEUROHYPOPHYSIS

Oxytocin (OT) _____

_____

_____

Antidiuretic hormone (ADH) _____

_____

_____

_____

C. THYROID GLAND

The **thyroid gland** is the endocrine gland located just below the larynx. The **right and left lateral lobes** lie on either side of the trachea and are connected by a mass of tissue called an **isthmus** (IS-mus) that lies in front of the trachea just below the cricoid cartilage. The **pyramidal lobe,** when present, extends upward from the isthmus.

1. Histology of Thyroid Gland

Histologically, the thyroid consists of spherical sacs called **thyroid follicles.** The walls of each follicle consist of epithelial cells that reach the surface of the lumen of the follicle (**follicular cells**) and epithelial cells that do not reach the lumen (**parafollicular cells**). The follicular cells manufacture the hormones **thyroxine** (thī-ROX-sēn) (**T_4** or **tetraiodothyronine**) and **triiodothyronine** (trī-ī′-od-ō-THĪ-rō-nēn) (**T_3**). Together these hormones are referred to as the **thyroid hormones.** Thyroxine is considered to be the principal hormone produced by follicular cells. The parafollicular cells produce the hormone **calcitonin** (kal-si-TŌ-nin) (**CT**). Each thyroid follicle is filled with **thyroid colloid,** consisting partially of a stored form of the thyroid hormones.

Examine a prepared slide of the thyroid gland under high power. Identify the thyroid follicles, epithelial cells forming the follicle, and thyroid colloid. Now label the photomicrograph in Figure 15.2.

2. Hormones of Thyroid Gland

Using your textbook as a reference, give the major functions of the hormones listed below.

Thyroxine (T_4) and **triiodothyronine (T_3)** _____

_____

_____

_____

Calcitonin (CT) _____

_____

_____

D. PARATHYROID GLANDS

Embedded on the posterior surfaces of the lateral lobes of the thyroid are small, round masses of tissue called the **parathyroid glands.**

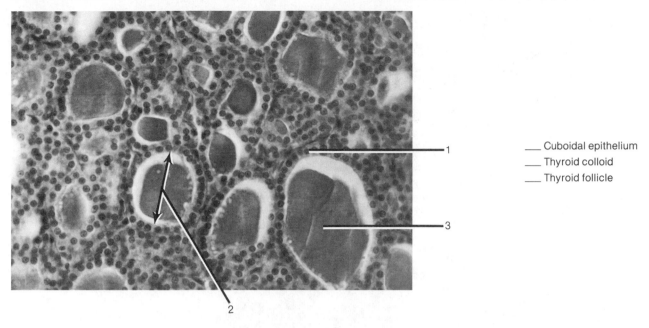

_____ Cuboidal epithelium
_____ Thyroid colloid
_____ Thyroid follicle

FIGURE 15.2 Histology of thyroid gland.

Typically two parathyroids, superior and inferior, are attached to each lateral thyroid lobe.

1. Histology of Parathyroid Glands

Histologically, the parathyroids contain two kinds of epithelial cells. The first, a larger cell called a **principal (chief) cell,** is believed to be the major synthesizer of **parathyroid hormone (PTH).** The second, a smaller cell called an **oxyphil cell,** may serve as a reserve cell for hormone synthesis.

Examine a prepared slide of the parathyroid glands under high power. Identify the principal and oxyphil cells. Now label the photomicrograph in Figure 15.3.

2. Hormone of Parathyroid Glands

Using your textbook as a reference, complete the following table by writing the major functions of the hormone listed:

Parathyroid hormone (PTH). Also called parathormone. _____

_____

_____

E. ADRENAL (SUPRARENAL) GLANDS

The two **adrenal (suprarenal) glands** are superior to each kidney and each is structurally and functionally differentiated into two regions: the outer **adrenal cortex,** which forms the bulk of the gland, and the inner **adrenal medulla.** Covering the gland are a thick layer of fatty connective tissue and an outer, thin fibrous capsule.

1. Histology of Adrenal Cortex

Histologically, the adrenal cortex is subdivided into three zones, each of which has a different cellular arrangement and secretes different steroid hormones. The outer zone, directly underneath the connective tissue capsule, is called the **zona glomerulosa.** Its cells, arranged in arched loops or round balls, primarily secrete a group of hormones called **mineralocorticoids** (min'-er-al-ō-KŌR-ti-koyds). The middle zone, or **zona fasciculata,** is the widest of the three zones and consists of cells arranged in long, straight cords. The zona fasciculata secretes mainly **glucocorticoids** (gloo'-kō-KŌR-ti-koyds). The inner zone, the **zona reticularis,** contains cords of cells that branch freely. This zone synthesizes minute amounts of **gonadocorticoids** (gō-na-dō-KŌR-ti-koyds) or sex hormones, chiefly male hormones (androgens).

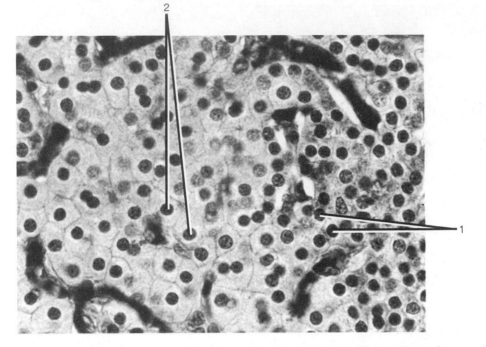

_____ Oxyphil cells
_____ Principal cells

FIGURE 15.3 Histology of parathyroids.

Examine a prepared slide of the adrenal cortex under high power. Identify the capsule, zona glomerulosa, zona fasciculata, and zona reticularis. Now label Figure 15.4.

2. Hormones of Adrenal Cortex

Using your textbook as a reference, give the major functions of the hormones listed below:

a. MINERALOCORTICOIDS

Aldosterone (only one of three mineralocorticoids, but responsible for 95% of their activity)

_____

_____

_____

_____

b. GLUCOCORTICOIDS

Cortisol (hydrocortisone), **corticosterone,** and

cortisone _____

_____

_____

_____

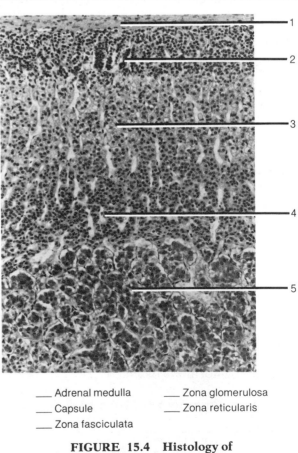

_____ Adrenal medulla   _____ Zona glomerulosa
_____ Capsule   _____ Zona reticularis
_____ Zona fasciculata

FIGURE 15.4 Histology of adrenal (suprarenal) gland.

c. GONADOCORTICOIDS

Estrogens (in female). See Estrogens under Hormones of Ovaries.

Androgens (in male). See Testosterone under Hormones of Testes.

3. Histology of Adrenal Medulla

The adrenal medulla consists of hormone-producing cells called **chromaffin cells.** These cells develop from the same source as the postganglionic cells of the sympathetic division of the nervous system. They are directly innervated by preganglionic cells of the sympathetic division of the autonomic nervous system and may be regarded as postganglionic cells that are specialized to secrete. In all other visceral effectors, preganglionic sympathetic fibers first synapse with postganglionic neurons before innervating the effector. In the adrenal medulla, however, the preganglionic fibers pass directly into the chromaffin cells of the gland. Secretion of hormones from the chromaffin cells is directly controlled by the autonomic nervous system, and innervation by the preganglionic fibers allows the gland to respond extremely rapidly to a stimulus. The adrenal medulla secretes the hormones **epinephrine** and **norepinephrine (NE).**

Examine a prepared slide of the adrenal medulla under high power. Identify the chromaffin cells. Now locate the cells in Figure 15.4.

4. Hormones of Adrenal Medulla

Using your textbook as a reference, give the major functions of the hormones listed below.

Epinephrine and **norepinephrine (NE)** _____

_____

_____

_____

F. PANCREAS

The **pancreas** is classified as both an endocrine and an exocrine gland. We shall discuss only its endocrine functions now. The pancreas is a flattened organ located posterior and slightly inferior to the stomach. The adult pancreas consists of a head, body, and tail.

1. Histology of Pancreas

The endocrine portion of the pancreas consists of clusters of cells called **pancreatic islets (islets of Langerhans).** They contain three kinds of cells: (1) **alpha cells,** which have more distinguishable plasma membranes, are usually peripheral in the islet, and secrete the hormone **glucagon;** (2) **beta cells,** which generally lie deeper within the islet and secrete the hormone **insulin;** and (3) **delta cells,** which secrete **somatostatin** or **growth hormone-inhibiting factor (GHIF),** a substance that inhibits the secretion of growth hormone (GH), glucagon, and insulin. The pancreatic islets are surrounded by blood capillaries and by the cells called **acini** that form the exocrine part of the gland.

Examine a prepared slide of the pancreas under high power. Identify the alpha cells, beta cells, delta cells, and acini (clusters of cells that secrete digestive enzymes) around the pancreatic islets. Now label Figure 15.5.

2. Hormones of Pancreas

Using your textbook as a reference, give the major functions of the hormones listed below.

Glucagon _____

_____

_____

Insulin _____

_____

_____

Somatostatin _____

_____

_____

G. TESTES

The **testes** (male gonads) are paired oval glands enclosed by the scrotum. They are covered by a dense layer of white fibrous tissue, the **tunica albuginea** (al'-byoo-JIN-ē-a), which extends in-

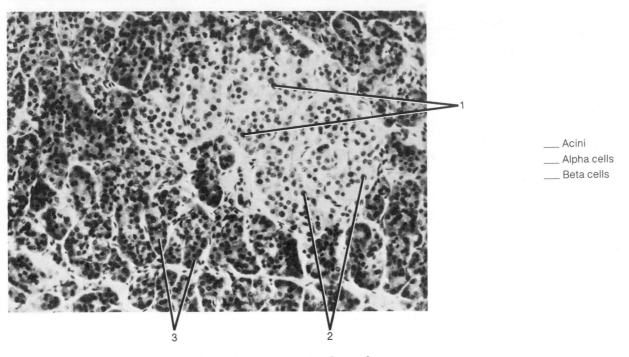

_____ Acini
_____ Alpha cells
_____ Beta cells

FIGURE 15.5 Histology of pancreas.

ward and divides each testis into a series of internal compartments called **lobules.** Each lobule contains one to three tightly coiled tubules, the convoluted **seminiferous tubules,** which produce sperm by a process called **spermatogenesis** (sper′-ma-tō-JEN-e-sis).

1. Histology of Testes

A cross section through a seminiferous tubule reveals that it is packed with sperm cells in various stages of development. The most immature cells, called **spermatogonia** (sper′-ma-tō-GŌ-nē-a), are located near the basement membrane. Toward the lumen in the center of the tube, layers of progressively more mature cells can be observed. In order of advancing maturity, these are **primary spermatocytes** (SPER-ma-tō-sīts), **secondary spermatocytes,** and **spermatids.** By the time a **sperm cell (spermatozoon)** (sper′-ma-tō-ZŌ-on) has reached full maturity, it is in the lumen of the tubule and begins to be moved through a series of ducts. Between the developing sperm cells in the tubules are **sustentacular** (sus′-ten-TAK-yoo-lar) **cells (Sertoli cells).** They produce secretions that supply nutrients to the spermatozoa and secrete the hormone **inhibin.** Between the seminiferous tubules are clusters of **interstitial endo-**

crinocytes (interstitial cells of Leydig) that secrete the primary male hormone **testosterone.**

Examine a prepared slide of the testes under high power. Identify the basement membrane, spermatogonia, spermatids, spermatozoa, sustentacular cells, interstitial endocrinocytes, and lumen of the seminiferous tubule. Now label Figure 15.6.

2. Hormones of Testes

Using your textbook as a reference, give the major functions of the hormones listed below.

Testosterone _____

_____

_____

Inhibin _____

_____

_____

H. OVARIES

The **ovaries** (female gonads) are paired glands resembling unshelled almonds in size and shape. They are positioned in the superior pelvic cav-

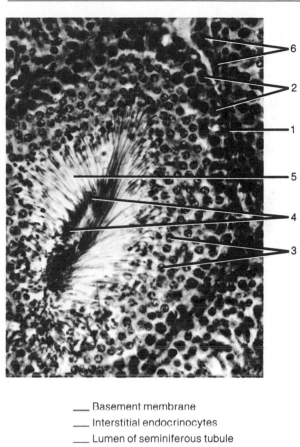

___ Basement membrane
___ Interstitial endocrinocytes
___ Lumen of seminiferous tubule
___ Spermatids
___ Spermatogonia
___ Spermatozoa

FIGURE 15.6 Histology of testes.

ity, one on each side of the uterus, and are maintained in position by a series of ligaments. They are (1) attached to the **broad ligament** of the uterus, which is itself part of the parietal peritoneum, by a fold of peritoneum called the **mesovarium;** (2) anchored to the uterus by the **ovarian ligament;** and (3) attached to the pelvic wall by the **suspensory ligament.** Each ovary also contains a **hilus,** which is the point of entrance for blood vessels and nerves.

1. Histology of Ovaries

Histologically, each ovary consists of the following parts:

1. **Germinal epithelium**—A layer of simple cuboidal epithelium that covers the free surface of the ovary.

2. **Tunica albuginea**—A capsule of collagenous connective tissue immediately deep to the germinal epithelium.

3. **Stroma**—A region of connective tissue deep to the tunica albuginea. This tissue is composed of an outer, dense layer called the **cortex** and an inner, loose layer known as the **medulla.** The cortex contains ovarian follicles.

4. **Ovarian follicles**—Ova and their surrounding tissues in various stages of development. Primary follicles are smaller and secondary follicles are larger.

5. **Vesicular ovarian follicle (graafian follicle)**—An endocrine structure composed of a mature ovum and its surrounding tissues. The vesicular ovarian follicle secretes hormones called **estrogens.**

6. **Corpus luteum**—A glandular body that develops from a vesicular ovarian follicle after extrusion of an ovum (ovulation). It produces the hormones **progesterone,** the **estrogens,** and **relaxin.**

Examine a prepared slide of the ovary under high power. Identify the germinal epithelial cells, tunica albuginea, cortex, medulla, primary follicle, secondary follicle, vesicular ovarian follicle, and corpus luteum. Label Figure 15.7.

2. Hormones of Ovaries

Using your textbook as a reference, give the major functions of the hormones listed below.

Estrogens _____

_____

_____

_____

Progesterone _____

_____

_____

_____

Relaxin _____

_____

_____

_____

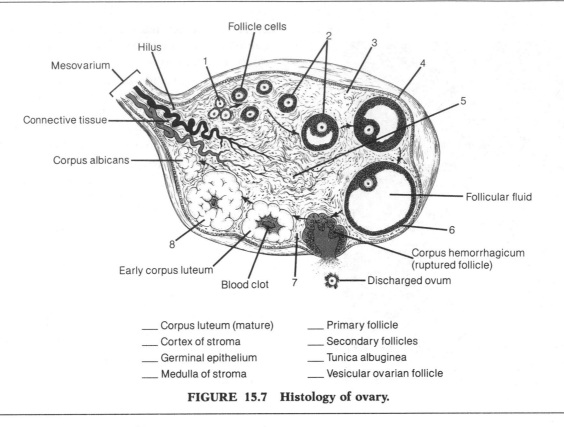

FIGURE 15.7 Histology of ovary.

___ Corpus luteum (mature)   ___ Primary follicle
___ Cortex of stroma   ___ Secondary follicles
___ Germinal epithelium   ___ Tunica albuginea
___ Medulla of stroma   ___ Vesicular ovarian follicle

I. PINEAL GLAND (EPIPHYSIS CEREBRI)

The cone-shaped endocrine gland attached to the roof of the third ventricle is known as the **pineal gland (epiphysis cerebri).**

1. Histology of Pineal Gland

The gland is covered by a capsule formed by the pia mater and consists of masses of neuroglial cells and parenchymal cells called **pinealocytes.** Around the cells are scattered preganglionic sympathetic fibers. The pineal gland starts to calcify at about the time of puberty. Such calcium deposits are called **brain sand.** Contrary to a once widely held belief, no evidence suggests that the pineal atrophies with age and that the presence of brain sand indicates atrophy. Rather, brain sand may denote increased secretory activity.

The physiology of the pineal gland is still somewhat obscure. The gland secretes **melatonin** and may secrete (1) **adrenoglomerulotropin** (which may stimulate the adrenal cortex to secrete aldosterone), (2) **serotonin** (which influ-ences brain functioning), and (3) a **growth-inhibiting hormone.**

2. Hormones of Pineal Gland

Using your textbook as a reference, give the major functions of the hormones listed below.

Melatonin _____

_____

_____

Adrenoglomerulotropin _____

_____

_____

J. THYMUS GLAND

The **thymus gland** is a bilobed lymphatic gland located in the upper mediastinum posterior to the sternum and between the lungs. The gland is conspicuous in infants and, during puberty, reaches maximum size. After puberty, thymic tissue, which consists primarily of **lympho-**

cytes, is replaced by fat. By the time a person reaches maturity, the gland has atrophied.

1. Histology of Thymus Gland

Lymphoid tissue of the body consists primarily of lymphocytes that may be distinguished into two kinds: B cells and T cells. Both are derived originally in the embryo from lymphocytic stem cells in bone marrow. Before migrating to their positions in lymphoid tissue, the descendants of the stem cells follow two distinct pathways. About half of them migrate to the thymus gland, where they are processed to become thymus-dependent lymphocytes, or **T cells.** The thymus gland confers on them the ability to destroy antigens (foreign microbes and substances) directly. The remaining stem cells are processed in some as yet undetermined area of the body, possibly the fetal liver and spleen, and are known as **B cells.** These cells, perhaps under the influence of hormones produced by the thymus gland—**thymosin, thymic humoral factor (THF), thymic factor (TF),** and **thymopoietin**—differentiate into plasma cells. Plasma cells, in turn, produce antibodies against antigens.

2. Hormones of Thymus Gland

Using your textbook as a reference, complete the following table by writing the major functions of the hormones listed:

Thymosin, thymic humoral factor (THF), thymic factor (TF), and thymopoietin _____

_____

_____

K. OTHER ENDOCRINE TISSUES

Body tissues other than endocrine glands also secrete hormones. The gastrointestinal tract synthesizes several hormones that regulate digestion in the stomach and small intestine. Among these hormones are **stomach gastrin, intestinal gastrin, secretin, cholecystokinin (CCK), enterocrinin,** and **gastric inhibitory peptide (GIP).**

The placenta produces **human chorionic gonadotropin (HCG), estrogens, progesterone, relaxin,** and **human chorionic somatomammotroph (HCS),** all of which are related to pregnancy.

Finally, when the kidneys (and liver, to a lesser extent) become hypoxic, it is believed that they release an enzyme called **renal erythropoietic factor.** This is secreted into the blood to act on a plasma protein and bring about the production of a hormone called **erythropoietin** (ē-rith′-rō-POY-ē-tin), which stimulates red blood cell production. **Vitamin D,** produced by the skin in the presence of sunlight, is converted to its active hormonal form in the kidneys.

L. PHYSIOLOGY OF THE ENDOCRINE SYSTEM

1. Determination of Basal Metabolic Rate in Normal, Hyperthyroid, and Hypothyroid Rats

As was mentioned previously, the thyroid gland produces two hormones related to metabolism, thyroxine (T_4) and triiodothyronine (T_3). This laboratory exercise will help you to determine the effect of a normally functioning, hyperactive, or hypoactive thyroid gland upon a rat's basal metabolic rate (BMR).

a. PREPARATION OF RATS

1. Hyperthyroid rat: Animals should be injected with 25 μg of L-thyroxine interperitoneally every third day for a two-week period.

2. Hypothyroid rat: Rats should be fed *either* 0.5% thiouracil in their rat chow *or* 0.02% propylthiouracil *or* 1% potassium perchlorate in their drinking water. (**Note:** If tetany appears in this group of animals, 1% lactate or gluconate should be given in their drinking water.) Maintain this dosage for two weeks.

b. CALIBRATION OF SYSTEM

1. Before starting the experiment, the system must be calibrated.

2. Place an object of approximately the same volume as the rat in the system (four or five No.

10 stoppers is approximately the same volume as a 3-month-old rat).

3. Completely seal the chamber, *making sure that the syringe is set at 0.*

4. Withdraw 40 ml of air from the system via the syringe and mark the new water level (Figure 15.8).

c. EXPERIMENTAL PROCEDURE

1. Remove the syringe from the rubber tubing and clamp the tube.

2. Weigh the rat.

3. Remove the stoppers from the system and replace them with an experimental animal.

4. Seal the system and record the time and temperature.

5. As the animal utilizes oxygen, it produces carbon dioxide. The carbon dioxide will be removed by the soda lime, causing the fluid to rise in the tubing as a result of decreased air volume within the chamber.

6. Record the time required for the water to rise to the calibration mark.

7. Also record the temperature within the system at this time.

8. After recording your calculations, repeat the procedure with another experimental animal until all three classes of animals are utilized.

9. Complete calculations as outlined with the example below. Compute average values for each class of animals.
Sample calculations:

Rat weight = 150 g
40 ml oxygen consumed in 10 min

$$\text{Oxygen consumption} = \frac{40\,\text{ml}}{10\,\text{min}} = 4\,\text{ml/min}$$

Reduced to standard conditions:
    Temperature = 27°C
    Barometric pressure = 731 mm Hg

$$4 \times \frac{731}{760} \times \frac{273}{300} = 3.5\,\text{ml/min}$$

(3.5 ml/min)/0.150 kg = 23.33 ml/kg/min

10. Record all calculations in the table provided in the Laboratory Report Results (page 405).

2. Demonstrations on Effects of Estrogens and Testosterone

Review the physiology of the male and female sex hormones upon the function and structure of the accessory sex organs as outlined in your textbook. These accessory organs are very sensitive to the effects of these hormones. The rats used in this demonstration have been prepared as follows:

Females	**Males**
Control	Control
Ovariectomized	Castrated
Ovariectomized and injected with estrogen	Castrated and injected with testosterone
Estrogen injection only	Testosterone injection only

Compare the size of uterus in females to the size of seminal vesicles in males.

Record your observations in the Laboratory Report Results.

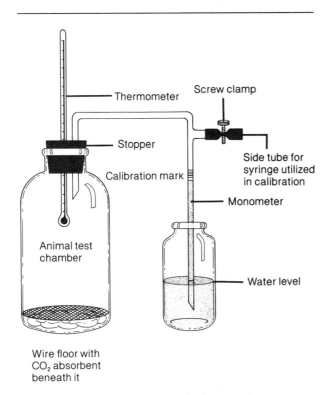

FIGURE 15.8 **Experimental setup for measuring basal metabolic rate (BMR) in rats.**

LABORATORY REPORT QUESTIONS (PAGE 407)

16 | BLOOD

The blood, heart, and blood vessels constitute the **cardiovascular system.** In this exercise you will examine the characteristics of **blood,** a connective tissue also known as **vascular tissue.**

A. COMPONENTS OF BLOOD

Microscopically, blood is composed of two portions: (1) **plasma,** a liquid that contains dissolved substances, and (2) **formed elements,** cells and cell-like bodies suspended in the plasma. In clinical practice, the most common classification of the formed elements of the blood is the following:

> **Erythrocytes (red blood cells)**
> **Leucocytes (white blood cells)**
>   *Granular leucocytes (granulocytes)*
>   Neutrophils
>   Eosinophils
>   Basophils
>   *Agranular leucocytes (agranulocytes)*
>   Lymphocytes
>   Monocytes
> **Thrombocytes (platelets)**

The origin and subsequent development of these formed elements can be seen in Figure 16.1. Blood cells are formed by a process called **hematopoiesis** (hē-ma-tō-poy-Ē-sis), and the process by which erythrocytes are formed is called **erythropoiesis** (e-rith'-rō-poy-Ē-sis). The immature cells that are eventually capable of developing into mature blood cells are called **hemocytoblasts** (hē-mō-SĪ-tō-blasts) (see Figure 16.1). Mature blood cells are constantly being replaced, so special cells called **reticuloendothelial cells** have the responsibility of clearing away the dead, disintegrating cell bodies so that small blood vessels are not clogged.

The shapes of the nuclei, staining characteristics, and color of cytoplasmic granules are all useful in differentiation and identification of the various white blood cells. Red cells are biconcave discs without nuclei and can be identified easily.

B. PLASMA

When cellular elements are removed from blood, a straw-colored liquid called **plasma** is left. This liquid consists of about 92% water and about 8% solutes. Among the solutes are proteins (albumins, globulins, and fibrinogen), nonprotein nitrogen (NPN) substances (urea, uric acid, and creatine), foods (amino acids, glucose, fatty acids, and glycerol), regulatory substances (enzymes and hormones), respiratory gases (oxygen and carbon dioxide), and electrolytes (Na^+, K^+, Ca^{2+}, Mg^{2+}, Cl^-, HCO_3^-, SO_4^{2-}, and PO_4^{3-}).

C. ERYTHROCYTES

Erythrocytes (e-RITH-rō-sīts) (red blood cells, RBCs) are biconcave in appearance, have no nucleus, and can neither reproduce nor carry on extensive metabolic activities (Figure 16.2a). The interior of the cell contains a red pigment called hemoglobin, which is responsible for the red color of blood. Erythrocytes function to combine with oxygen and, to a lesser extent, carbon dioxide and transport them through the blood vessels. A red blood cell becomes nonfunctional in about 120 days. A healthy male

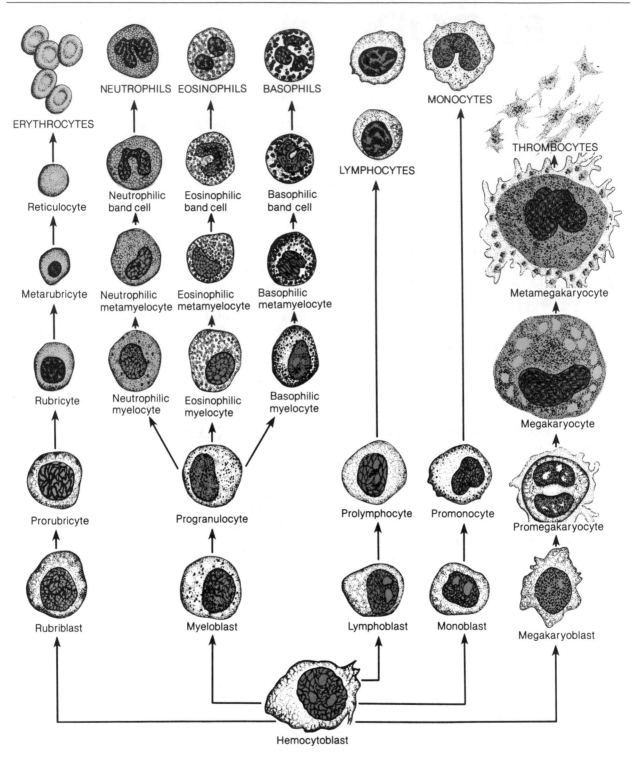

ERYTHROCYTES

NEUTROPHILS EOSINOPHILS BASOPHILS

MONOCYTES

THROMBOCYTES

LYMPHOCYTES

Reticulocyte

Neutrophilic band cell

Eosinophilic band cell

Basophilic band cell

Metarubricyte

Neutrophilic metamyelocyte

Eosinophilic metamyelocyte

Basophilic metamyelocyte

Metamegakaryocyte

Rubricyte

Neutrophilic myelocyte

Eosinophilic myelocyte

Basophilic myelocyte

Megakaryocyte

Prorubricyte

Progranulocyte

Prolymphocyte

Promonocyte

Promegakaryocyte

Rubriblast

Myeloblast

Lymphoblast

Monoblast

Megakaryoblast

Hemocytoblast

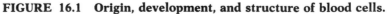

FIGURE 16.1 Origin, development, and structure of blood cells.

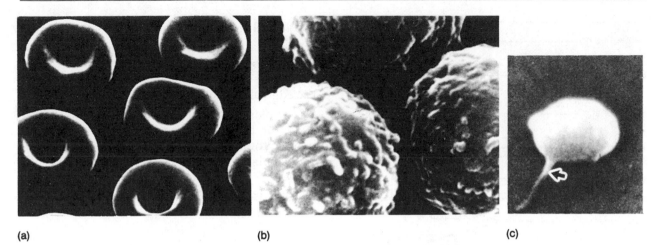

(a)　　　　　　　　　　　　　(b)　　　　　　　　　　　　　(c)

FIGURE 16.2 Scanning electron micrographs of blood cells.
(a) Erythrocytes (5000 ×). (b) Leucocytes (10,000 ×). (c) Platelet (10,000 ×).

has about 5.4 million red blood cells per cubic millimeter (cu mm) of blood, a healthy female, about 4.8 million. Erythropoiesis and red cell destruction normally proceed at the same pace. A diagnostic test that informs the physician about the rate of erythropoiesis is the **reticulocyte** (re-TIK-yoo-lō-sīt) **count.** The immature red blood cells called **reticulocytes** (Figure 16.1) appear in the blood in a certain concentration. An abnormally low or abnormally high concentration of reticulocytes indicates disease.

The different laboratory blood tests performed and evaluated by physicians are invaluable in their search for the causes of bodily malfunction, and are very useful tools in medicine. The following practical routine tests give us a clear insight on important characteristics of blood.

D. RED BLOOD CELL TESTS

1. Finger Puncture Procedure

Blood for various tests is obtained by finger puncture as follows:

1. Obtain 70% alcohol, a lancet, and cotton.

2. To enhance your chances for a successful finger puncture the first time, warm your finger if it is cold, shake your finger several times to dry the alcohol and force more blood into it, and gently milk blood toward the puncture site.

3. *Thoroughly* cleanse the end of the third or fourth finger with alcohol.

4. Holding your finger firmly, take the lancet and puncture the finger using a quick, jabbing motion. The puncture is made toward the side of the finger rather than in the full fleshy part. (Do not begin the motion from a great distance away from the finger. The closer you are and the quicker the motion, the less the discomfort that results.)

5. If the puncture is made properly, the blood should flow freely from the wound. If not, squeeze the finger at its base and move toward the tip.

6. If an additional puncture is required, discard the first lancet and use a new sterile one. **Note:** *Make sure the used lancets are discarded properly* to prevent subsequent injury, and to prevent passage of diseases such as hepatitis from one person to another.

7. Do not use the first drop, which usually coagulates fast.

8. Finally, place a piece of cotton between the finger and the thumb and press them together firmly.

When using red and white cell pipettes for counting, you must measure the blood accurately. The procedure for using pipettes and tubing (see Figure 16.3) is as follows:

1. Attach the aspirator tube to the top of the pipette and hold the other end in the mouth to draw the blood into the pipette.

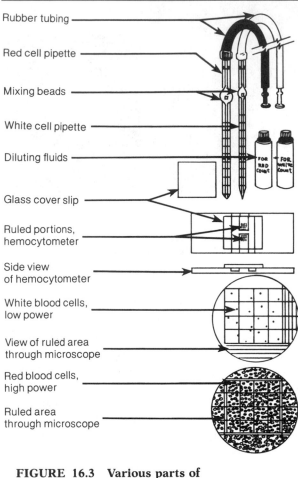

Rubber tubing

Red cell pipette

Mixing beads

White cell pipette

Diluting fluids

Glass cover slip

Ruled portions, hemocytometer

Side view of hemocytometer

White blood cells, low power

View of ruled area through microscope

Red blood cells, high power

Ruled area through microscope

FIGURE 16.3 Various parts of hemocytometer (counting chamber) and red and white blood cell pipettes used for blood counts.

2. When you have successfully drawn the blood up to the specified mark, place the tongue against the end of the tube to prevent the blood from draining out of the pipette.

3. Do not allow any of the sample to leak out into the diluting fluid, because any count performed afterward would be inaccurate. The count would be too low because the blood is too diluted.

2. Filling of Hemocytometer (Counting Chamber)

The procedure for filling the hemocytometer is as follows:

1. Obtain a hemocytometer and cover slip.

2. Clean the hemocytometer thoroughly and carefully with alcohol.

3. Place the cover slip on the hemocytometer.

4. Using a pipette filled with the proper dilution of blood, place the tip of the pipette on the polished surface of the hemocytometer next to the edge of the cover slip.

5. Deposit a drop of diluted blood, but do not leave the tip of the pipette in contact with the hemocytometer for more than an instant because this will cause the chamber to overfill. The diluted blood must not overflow the moat; overfilling the moat results in an inaccurate cell count (see Figure 16.4).

3. Red Blood Cell Count

The purpose of a red blood cell count is to determine the number of circulating red blood cells in the body. Red blood cells carry oxygen to all tissues; thus a drastic change in the red cell count will cause immediate reduction in available oxygen.

A decrease in red cells can result from a variety of conditions, including impaired cell production, increased cell destruction, and acute blood loss. When the red cell count is increased above normal limits, a condition called **polycythemia** results.

The procedure for determining the number of red blood cells per cubic millimeter (cu mm) of blood is as follows:[1]

1. Fill the pipette exactly to the 0.5 mark with blood from a finger puncture.

2. Wipe excess blood from the tip of the pipette without disturbing the column of blood. Recheck the column.

3. Fill the pipette to the 101 mark with diluting fluid.

4. Cover each end of the pipette with a finger and shake pipette for 3 minutes.

5. Discard one-third of the fluid in the pipette.

6. Fill the hemocytometer as just described previously (Section D.2).

7. Allow the cells to settle in the hemocytometer (approximately 1 minute).

---

[1]If UNOPETTE tests are available, follow the procedure outlined in UNOPETTE test No. 5851, "RBC Determination for Manual Methods," for the red blood cell count.

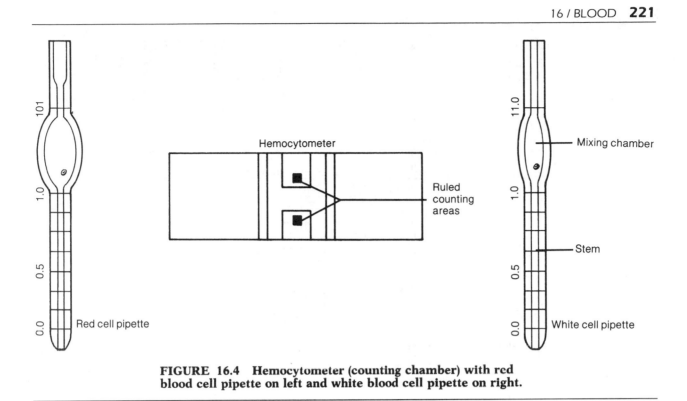

FIGURE 16.4 Hemocytometer (counting chamber) with red blood cell pipette on left and white blood cell pipette on right.

8. Using the 45× lens (high power), count the cells in each of the five squares (E, F, G, H, I) as shown in Figure 16.5. As you count, move up and down in a systematic manner. **Note:** To avoid overcounting cells at the boundaries, cells that touch the lines on the left and top sides of the hemocytometer should be counted, but not the ones that touch the boundary lines on the right and bottom sides.

9. Multiply the results by 10,000 to obtain the number of red blood cells in 1 cu mm of blood. Record your value in the Laboratory Report Results (page 409).

10. The pipette should be rinsed with acid, water, alcohol, or acetone (pipette cleaning solutions).

4. Red Blood Cell Volume (Hematocrit)

The packed cell volume (PCV) measurement is a good routine test for anemia. The percentage of blood volume occupied by the red blood cells is called the **hematocrit** or **packed cell volume**. When a tube of blood is centrifuged, the erythrocytes pack into the bottom part of the tube with the plasma on top. The white blood cells and platelets are found in a thin area, the buffy layer, above the column of red cells.

The Readacrit centrifuge (Figure 16.6) incorporates a built-in hematocrit scale and tube-holding compartments which, when used with special precalibrated capillary tubes, permit direct reading of the hematocrit value by measuring the length of the packed red cell column. Readacrit centrifuges present the final hematocrit value without requiring computation by the operator. If the Readacrit centrifuge or tube reader is not used for direct reading, measure the total length of blood volume, divide this quantity into length of packed red cells, and multiply by 100 for percentage. The calculation is as follows:

$$\frac{\text{length of packed red cells}}{\text{total length of blood volume}} \times 100 =$$

% volume of whole blood occupied by red cells (hematocrit)

In males the normal range is between 40% and 54%, with an average of 47%. In females the normal range is between 37% and 47%, with an average of 42%.

The following procedure for testing red blood cell volume is a micromethod requiring only a drop of blood:

1. Produce a free flow of blood from the tip of the finger.

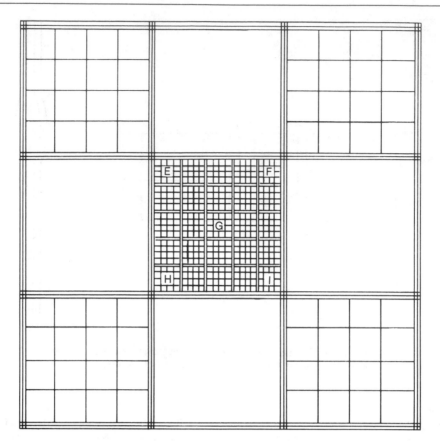

FIGURE 16.5 Hemocytometer (counting chamber). Areas E, F, G, H, and I are all counted in red blood cell count. The large square containing the smaller squares E, F, G, H, and I is seen in microscopic field under 10 × magnification. To count the smaller squares (E, F, G, H, and I), the 45 × lens is used and therefore E, F, G, H, and I each encompass the entire microscopic field.

2. Place the marked end (red) of the capillary tube into the drop of blood (see Figure 16.7). Draw blood two-thirds of the way into the tube. The tube fills rapidly if you hold the open end downward from the source of blood. Do not allow air bubbles in the tube. If bubbles appear, a new tube must be filled.

3. Seal the blood end of the tube with Seal-ease.

4. Place the tube into the centrifuge, making sure that the sealed end is against the ring of rubber at the circumference. Properly balance the tubes in the centrifuge.

5. Secure the inside cover and fasten down the outside cover.

6. Turn on the centrifuge and set the timer for 4 minutes.

7. Determine the hematocrit value by reading the length of packed red cells directly on the centrifuge scale, or by placing the tube in the tube reader (see Figure 16.8) and following instructions on the reader, or by calculation using the equation mentioned previously (page 221).

Record your results in the Laboratory Report Results.

5. Sedimentation Rate

If citrated blood is allowed to stand vertically in a tube, the red blood cells fall to the bottom of the tube and leave clear plasma in the upper portion. The distance that the cells fall in 1 hour can be measured and is called the sedimentation rate. This rate is greater than normal during menstruation, pregnancy, and most infections. A high rate may indicate tissue destruction in some part of the body; therefore, sedimentation rate is considered a valuable nonspecific diagnostic tool. The normal rate for adults is 0 to 6 mm per hour, for children 0 to 8 mm per hour.

The following method for determining sedimentation rate requires only one drop of blood and is called the Landau micromethod:

1. Using the mechanical suction device, draw the sodium citrate up to the first line that completely encircles the pipette.

2. Draw free-flowing blood up into the pipette to the second line. Care must be taken to avoid air bubbles. (If air bubbles are drawn into the blood, carefully expel the mixture onto a clean microscope slide and draw it up again.)

3. Draw the fluids up into the bulb and mix by expelling them into the lumen of the tube. Draw and mix the fluids six times. If any air bubbles appear, use the procedure described in step 2.

4. Adjust the top level of the blood as close to zero as possible. (Exactly zero is very difficult to get.)

5. Remove the suction device by placing the lower end of the pipette on the index finger of the left hand before removing the device from the other end. The blood is pulled out of the pipette if the lower end is not completely sealed.

6. Place the lower end of the pipette on the base of the pipette rack and the opposite end at

FIGURE 16.6 Centrifuge used for spinning blood to determine hematocrit.

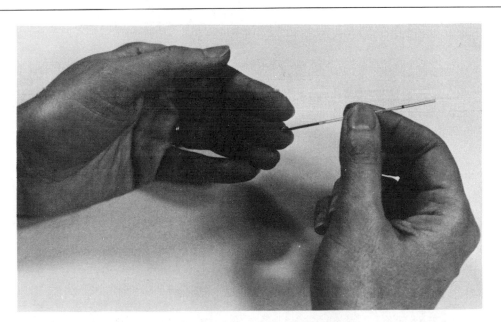

FIGURE 16.7 A heparinized capillary tube is filled with blood from freely flowing finger puncture. The tube is used for hematocrit determination.

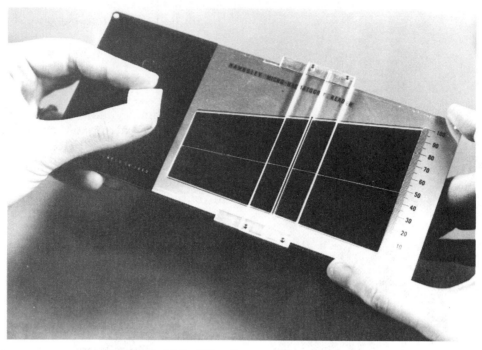

FIGURE 16.8 Microhematocrit tube reader.

the top of the rack. The tube must be exactly perpendicular. Record the time at which it is put in the rack (see Figure 16.9).

7. One hour later, measure the distance from the top of the plasma to the top of the red blood cells with an accurate millimeter scale, and record your results in the Laboratory Report Results.

8. Rinse the pipette with cleaning solution.

FIGURE 16.9 One type of sedimentation tube rack.

6. Hemoglobin Estimation[1]

A normal RBC count is possible with anemia if each cell is deficient in hemoglobin. Because the amount of hemoglobin in a given volume of blood is an accurate indication of the oxygen-carrying potential of the blood, various methods have been developed for its measurement. The procedure outlined here is the Sahli-Adams method. This method compares an acid-tested sample of blood with a color standard called a hemoglobinometer. The hemoglobin content of blood is expressed in terms of g per 100 ml of blood.

The procedure for measuring hemoglobin is as follows:

1. Fill the graduated tube to the 2-g mark with 1% hydrochloric acid.

2. Produce a free flow of blood and draw it into the pipette to the 20-cu mm mark. Wipe off the tip of the pipette and blow the contents of the pipette into the acid solution in the test tube. Draw the solution up into the pipette two or three times, expelling all fluid into the tube. Use the pipette cleaning solution to get it completely clean.

3. Place the tube in the hemoglobinometer and let stand for 10 minutes.

4. Compare the color of your test sample with the color standard. If the mixture is darker, add distilled water, drop by drop, mixing the solution after each addition. Keep adding water until both colors are identical. While mixing, care should be taken that no solution is lost.

5. When the two colors are identical, read the g of hemoglobin per 100 ml of blood on the side of the tube. The normal range for both men and women is between 13.5 and 17.5 g. Record your results in the Laboratory Report Results.

E. LEUCOCYTES

Leucocytes (LOO-kō-sīts) (white blood cells, WBCs) are different from red blood cells in that they have nuclei and do not contain hemoglobin (see Figures 16.1 and 16.2b). They are less numerous than red blood cells, averaging from 5000 to 9000 cells per cubic millimeter of blood. The ratio, therefore, of red blood cells to white blood cells is about 700:1.

As Figure 16.1 shows, leucocytes can be differentiated by their appearance. They are divided into two major groups, granular leucocytes and agranular leucocytes. **Granular leucocytes,** which are formed from red bone marrow, have granules in the cytoplasm and possess lobed nuclei. The three types of granular leucocytes are **neutrophils, eosinophils,** and **basophils. Agranular leucocytes,** which are formed from lymphoid and myeloid tissue, do not possess cytoplasmic granules and usually have spherical nuclei. The two types of agranular leucocytes are **lymphocytes** and **monocytes.**

Leucocytes as a group function in phagocytosis, producing antibodies, and combating allergies. The life span of a leucocyte ranges from a few hours to a few months.

F. WHITE BLOOD CELL TESTS

1. White Blood Cell Count[2]

This procedure determines the number of circulating white blood cells in the body. Because white blood cells are a vital part of the body's immune defense system, any abnormalities in the white cell count must be carefully noted.

An increase in number (leucocytosis) may result from such conditions as bacterial or viral infection, metabolic disorders, chemical and drug poisoning, and acute hemorrhage. A decrease in number (leucopenia) may result from typhoid infection, measles, infectious hepatitis, tuberculosis, or cirrhosis of the liver.

The procedure for determining the number of white blood cells per cu mm of blood is as follows:

1. Fill the pipette exactly to the 0.5 mark with blood from a finger puncture.

2. Wipe excess blood from tip of pipette without disturbing the column of blood.

---

[1]If UNOPETTE tests are available, follow the procedure outlined in UNOPETTE test Nos. 5857/5858, "Cyanmethemoglobin Determination for Manual Methods," for hemoglobin estimation.

[2]If UNOPETTE tests are available, follow the procedure outlined in UNOPETTE test No. 5855, "WBC/Platelet Determination for Manual Methods," for the white blood cell count.

3. Fill the pipette up to the 11 mark with diluting fluid.

4. Shake pipette for 2 minutes.

5. Discard two to three drops to clear the stem of the pipette of diluting fluid.

6. Fill the hemocytometer as described previously (Section D.2, page 220).

7. Using the 10× lens, count the cells in each of the four corner squares (A, B, C, D in Figure 16.10) of the hemocytometer.

Note: To avoid overcounting of cells at the boundaries, the cells that touch the lines on the left and top sides of the hemocytometer should be counted, but not the ones that touch the boundary lines on the right and bottom sides.

8. Multiply the results by 50 to obtain the amount of circulating white blood cells per cu mm of blood and record your results in the Laboratory Report Results.

9. The factor of 50 is the dilution factor, or 2.5 × 20 = 50. The volume correction factor of 2.5 is arrived at in this manner: each of the corner areas (A, B, C, and D) is exactly 1 sq mm by 0.1 mm deep (see Figure 16.10). Therefore, the volume of each of these corner areas is 0.1 cu mm. Because four of them are counted, the total volume of diluted blood examined is 0.4 cu mm. However, because we want to know the number of cells in 1 cu mm instead of 0.4 cu mm, we must multiply our count by 2.5 (0.4 × 2.5 = 1.0).

2. Differential White Cell Count

The purpose of a differential white cell count is to determine the *percentages* of each of the five

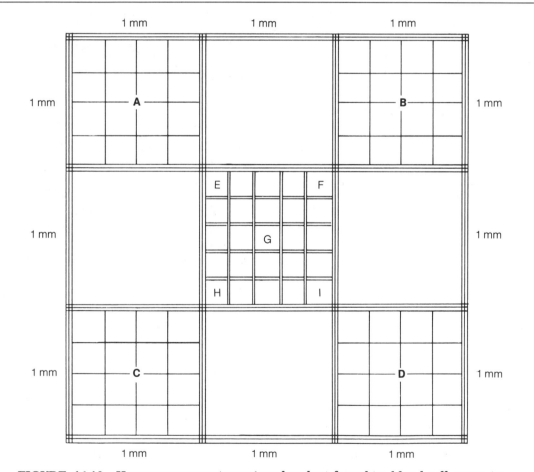

FIGURE 16.10 Hemtocytometer (counting chamber) for white blood cell count (as seen through scanning lens). A, B, C, and D are areas counted in white blood cell count (when viewed through 10× lens, 1 sq mm is seen in microscopic field). Areas A, B, C, and D each equal 1 sq mm; therefore, a total of 4 sq mm is counted in white cell count.

normally circulating types of white cells in a total count of 100 white blood cells. A normal differential count might appear as follows:

	Normal	Your Count
Neutrophils	60% to 70%	_____
Eosinophils	2% to 4%	_____
Basophils	0.5% to 1%	_____
Lymphocytes	20% to 25%	_____
Monocytes	3% to 8%	_____

Significant elevations of different types of white blood cells usually indicate specific pathological conditions. For example, a high neutrophil count indicates tissue destruction by invading bacteria. Lymphocytes predominate in specific leukemias and in infectious mononucleosis. An increase in eosinophils may be seen in allergic reactions. An elevated percentage of monocytes may result from parasitic infections and leukemia. An increase in basophils is rare and denotes a specific type of leukemia.

The procedure for making a differential white blood cell count is as follows:

1. Place one drop of blood on a glass slide.

2. Use a second slide as a spreader (see Figure 16.11).

3. Draw the spreader toward the drop of blood (in this direction →) until it touches the drop. The blood should fan out to the edges of the spreader slide.

4. Keeping the spreader at a 25° angle, press the edge of the spreader firmly against the slide and push the spreader rapidly over the entire length of the slide (in this direction ←). The drop of blood will thin out toward the end of the slide.

5. Let the smear dry.

6. To stain the slide follow this procedure:
   a. Place the slide on staining rack.
   b. Cover the entire slide with Wright's stain.
   c. Let stain stand for 1 minute.
   d. Add 25 drops of buffer solution and mix completely with Wright's stain.
   e. Let mixture stand for 8 minutes.
   f. Wash mixture off completely with distilled water.

7. Let the slide dry before counting.

8. To proceed with counting the cells, use area of slide where blood is thinnest. Count cells under an oil-immersion lens. Count a total of 100 white cells.

G. THROMBOCYTES

Thrombocytes (THROM-bo-sits) (platelets) are formed from fragments of the cytoplasm of megakaryocytes (see Figures 16.1 and 16.2c). The fragments become enclosed in pieces of cell membrane from the megakaryocytes and develop into platelets. Platelets are very small, disc-shaped cell fragments without nuclei. Between 250,000 and 400,000 are found in each cubic millimeter of blood. They function to prevent fluid loss by starting a chain of reactions that results in blood clotting. They have a short life span, probably only one week, because they are expended in clotting and are just too simple to carry on extensive metabolic activity.

Examine a prepared slide of a stained smear of blood cells using the oil immersion objective. With the aid of your textbook, identify red blood cells, neutrophils, basophils, eosinophils, lymphocytes, monocytes, and thrombocytes. Using colored crayons or pencil crayons, draw and label all of the different blood cells in

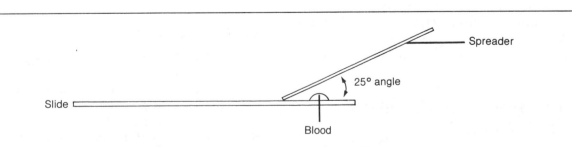

FIGURE 16.11 Procedure to prepare a blood smear.

the Laboratory Report Results. Be very accurate in drawing and coloring the granules and the nuclear shapes, because both of these are used to identify the various types of cells.

H. CLOTTING TESTS

Blood normally remains in a liquid state in the vessels but thickens and forms a jelly, or gel, when drawn from the body. The gel eventually separates from the liquid portion and produces the **clot**, which consists of insoluble fibers in which the formed elements of the blood are trapped. The straw-colored liquid portion, called **serum**, is plasma without its clotting proteins.

The process of clotting is called **coagulation.** Its function is to prevent blood loss when a blood vessel is ruptured. Clotting is a complex process requiring many coagulation factors and pathways, but basically occurs in three stages. In stage 1, thromboplastin forms. In stage 2, thromboplastin combines with prothrombin, a plasma protein, to form thrombin, an enzyme. In stage 3, thrombin catalyzes the conversion of fibrinogen, another plasma protein, into fibrin.

The time required for blood to coagulate when exposed to air, usually from 5 to 15 minutes, is known as **clotting time.** This time is used as an index of a person's blood-clotting properties. Record all results in the Laboratory Report Results.

1. Clotting Time (Slide Method)

The procedure for testing clotting time by the slide method is as follows:

1. Place a few drops of blood on a glass slide (start stopwatch when bleeding begins).
2. Pass an applicator stick or needle through the blood until a fibrin strand appears on the needle.
3. Stop the watch when the strand appears.

2. Clotting Time (Capillary Tube Method)

In the time that it takes for blood to clot, **fibrin,** the essential substance of a blood clot, is produced. The simplest way to determine one's clotting time is to fill a capillary tube with blood and break the tube at intervals to see the length of time necessary for fibrin to form.

1. Puncture the finger to expose a free flow of blood and *record the time immediately.* Place one end of the capillary tube into the drop of blood, holding the open end below the drop of blood so that the force of gravity aids capillary action.
2. At approximately 1-minute intervals, break off small portions of the tubing after first scratching the glass capillary with a file. **Note:** *Separate the broken ends slowly and gently when looking for fibrin.* Coagulation has occurred when threads of fibrin span the gap between the broken ends. Record the time as the interval from the blood's first appearance on the finger to the formation of fibrin.

I. BLOOD GROUPINGS

The plasma membranes of red blood cells contain genetically determined antigens called **agglutinogens** (ag'-loo-TIN-ō-jens). The plasma of blood contains genetically determined antibodies called **agglutinins** (a-GLOO-ti-nins). The antibodies cause the **agglutination (clumping)** of the red blood cells carrying the corresponding antigen.

These proteins, agglutinogens and agglutinins, are responsible for the two major classifications of blood groups: the ABO group and the Rh system. In addition to the ABO group and the Rh system, other human blood groups include: MNSs, P, Lutheran, Kell, Lewis, Duffy, Kidd, Diego, and Sutter. Fortunately these different antigenic factors do not exhibit extreme degrees of antigenicity and, therefore, usually cause very weak transfusion reactions or no reaction at all.

1. ABO Group

This major blood grouping is based on two agglutinogens symbolized as A and B (Figure 16.11). Individuals whose red blood cells produce only agglutinogen A have blood type A, whereas those who produce only agglutinogen B have blood type B. If both A and B agglutinogens are produced, the result is type AB, whereas the absence of both A and B agglutinogens results in the so-called type O.

The antibodies are antibody a (anti-A), which attacks agglutinogen A, and antibody b (anti-B), which attacks B. The antigens and antibodies formed by each of the four blood types and the various agglutination reactions that occur when whole blood samples are mixed with serum are shown in Figure 16.12. You do not have antibodies that attack the agglutinogens of your own erythrocytes. For example, a type A person has agglutinogen A but not antibody a. In practice, only matching blood types are used for transfusions. The danger in an unmatched blood transfusion lies in an individual's antibodies agglutinating (clumping) the donated erythrocytes, not only undoing the value of the transfusion, but causing a possible clogging of blood vessels and even possibly leading to death.

Because the cells of group O blood contain neither of the two agglutinogens, small quantities of this blood can be transfused into almost any recipient without immediate agglutination. For this reason, group O blood is sometimes called **universal donor** blood. However, transfusion of large amounts of group O blood into a mismatched recipient can cause either immediate or delayed agglutination of the recipient's own cells because the infused agglutinins then are not diluted sufficiently to prevent the reaction.

Group AB persons are sometimes called **universal recipients** because their plasma contains neither a nor b antibodies. Small quantities of all other blood groups can be infused without causing a transfusion reaction. However, here again, if large quantities of these

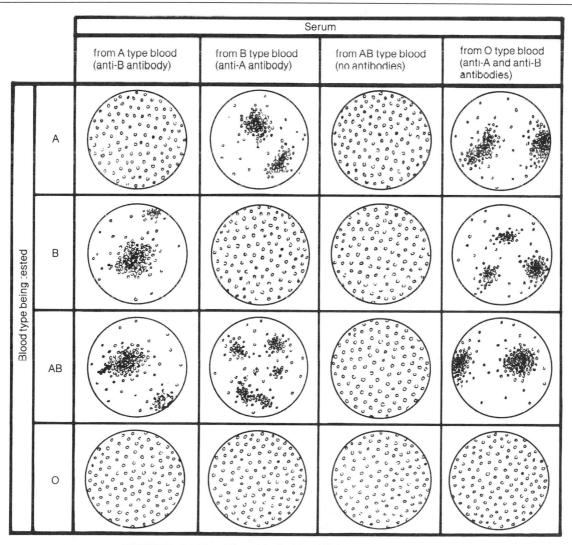

FIGURE 16.12 Chart to show agglutination reactions.

mismatched bloods are administered, the agglutinins in the donor's blood might accumulate in sufficient quantities to agglutinate the recipient's type AB cells.

Table 16.1 summarizes the various interreactions of the four blood types. Table 16.2 lists the incidence of these different blood types in the United States, comparing some races.

2. Rh System

The Rh factor is the other major classification of blood grouping. This group was designated Rh because the blood of the rhesus monkey was used in the first research and development. As is the ABO grouping, this classification is based on agglutinogens that lie on the surfaces of erythrocytes. The designation Rh$^+$ (positive) is given to those that have the agglutinogen, and Rh$^-$ (negative) is for those that lack the agglutinogen. The estimation is that 85% of whites and 88% of blacks in the United States are Rh$^+$, whereas 15% of whites and 12% of blacks are Rh$^-$.

Rh factor is extemely important in pregnancy and childbirth. Under normal circumstances, human plasma does not contain anti-Rh antibodies. If, however, a woman who is Rh$^-$ becomes pregnant with an Rh$^+$ child, her blood may produce antibodies that will react with the blood of a subsequent child.[1] The first child is unaffected because the mother's body has not yet produced these antibodies. This is a serious reaction and an antigen-antibody response called **hemolysis** may occur in the fetal blood. Hemolysis is a breakage of erythrocytes resulting in the liberation of hemoglobin. The hemolysis produced by this fetal-maternal incompatibility is called **hemolytic disease of newborn (erythroblastosis fetalis)** and could be fatal for the newborn infant. A drug called Rho-GAM, given to Rh$^-$ mothers immediately after delivery or abortion, prevents the production of antibodies by the mother so that the fetus of the next pregnancy is protected.

3. ABO Blood Grouping Test

The purpose of these exercises is to accurately type blood samples according to the ABO and Rh blood group systems.

---

[1]Be sure to note the important difference in the production of antibodies in the ABO and Rh systems. An Rh$^-$ person can *produce antibodies in response to the stimulus of invading Rh antigen;* by contrast, any antibodies of the ABO system that exist in the blood of a person *occur naturally and are present regardless of whether or not ABO antigens are introduced.*

TABLE 16.1
INTERREACTIONS OF CELLS AND PLASMA OF ABO SYSTEM

BLOOD TYPE	AGGLUTINOGEN	AGGLUTININ	PLASMA CAUSES AGGLUTINATION OF	CELLS AGGLUTINATED BY PLASMA OF
A	A	b	B, AB	B, O
B	B	a	A, AB	A, O
AB	AB	None	None	A, B, O
O	None	a, b	A, B, AB	None

TABLE 16.2
INCIDENCE OF HUMAN BLOOD GROUPS IN THE UNITED STATES

	BLOOD GROUPS (PERCENTAGES)			
	O	A	B	AB
Caucasians	45	41	10	4
Blacks	48	27	21	4
Japanese	31	38	22	9
Chinese	36	28	23	13
American Indians	23	76	0	1
Hawaiians	37	61	1.5	0.5

The procedure for ABO sampling is as follows:

1. Divide a glass slide in half using a marker and label the left side A and the right side B.

2. On the left side, place one drop of anti-A serum, and on the right side place one drop of anti-B serum.

3. Next to the drops of antisera, place one drop of blood obtained by finger puncture, being careful not to mix samples on the left and right sides.

4. Using an applicator stick or a toothpick, mix the blood on the left side with the anti-A serum, and then, using a different toothpick or the opposite end of the first one, mix the blood on the right side with the anti-B.

5. Gently tilt the slide back and forth and observe it for 1 minute.

6. Record your results, using " + " for clumping (agglutination) and " − " for no clumping.

Identify your own ABO system blood type based on your observations and record it in the Laboratory Report Results. You can also summarize the results obtained by your class in the table provided there if your instructor so directs.

4. Rh Blood Grouping Test

The procedure for Rh grouping is as follows:

1. Place one drop of anti-D serum on a slide.[1]

2. Add one drop of blood and mix using a toothpick.

3. Place the slide on a preheated warming box, and gently rock the box back and forth for 2 minutes. (Unlike ABO typing, Rh typing is better done on a heated warming box.)

4. Record your results, using " + " for clumping and " − " for no clumping. Record whether you are Rh+ or Rh− in the Laboratory Report Results. You can also summarize your class's results in the table provided there.

**LABORATORY REPORT
QUESTIONS (PAGE 411)**

---

[1]The Rh antigen is more specifically termed the D antigen after the Fisher-Race nomenclature, which is based on genetic concepts or theories of inheritance.

17 | HEART

The **heart** is a hollow, muscular organ that pumps blood through miles and miles of blood vessels. This organ is located in the mediastinum, between the lungs, with two-thirds of its mass lying to the left of the body's midline. Its pointed end, the **apex,** projects downward to the left, and its broad end, the **base,** projects upward to the right. The main parts of the heart and associated structures to be discussed here are the parietal pericardium, the wall, chambers, great vessels, and valves.

A. PARIETAL PERICARDIUM

A loose-fitting serous membrane called the **parietal pericardium (pericardial sac)** encloses the heart (see Figure 17.1). The membrane is composed of two layers, the fibrous layer and the serous layer. The **fibrous pericardium** forming the outer layer is tough connective tis-

sue that adheres to the parietal pleura and anchors the heart in the mediastinum. The inner layer, the **serous pericardium,** is a delicate membrane that is continuous with the visceral pericardium (outer layer of the heart wall) at the base of the heart and around the large blood vessels. Between the serous pericardium and visceral pericardium is a potential space, the **pericardial cavity,** which contains pericardial fluid and functions to prevent friction between the membranes as the heart beats. Identify these structures using a specimen, model, or chart of a heart and label Figure 17.1.

B. HEART WALL

Three layers of tissue compose the heart: the visceral pericardium (external layer), the myocardium (middle layer), and the endocardium (inner layer). The **visceral pericardium (epicar-**

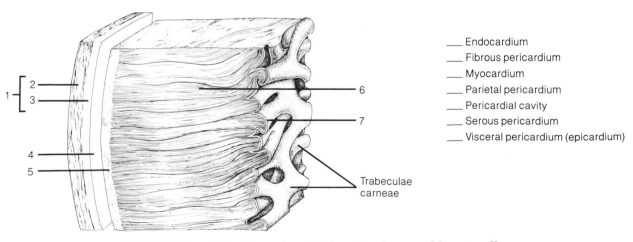

_____ Endocardium
_____ Fibrous pericardium
_____ Myocardium
_____ Parietal pericardium
_____ Pericardial cavity
_____ Serous pericardium
_____ Visceral pericardium (epicardium)

Trabeculae carneae

FIGURE 17.1 Structure of parietal pericardium and heart wall.

dium) is the thin transparent outer layer of the heart wall. The **myocardium,** which is composed of cardiac muscle tissue, forms the bulk of the heart and is responsible for contraction. The **endocarium** is a thin layer of endothelium that lines the inside of the myocardium and covers the heart valves and the tendons that hold them open. Label the layers of the heart in Figure 17.1.

C. CHAMBERS OF HEART

The interior of the heart is divided into four cavities called **chambers,** which receive circulating blood. The two superior chambers are known as **right** and **left atria** and are separated internally by a partition called the **interatrial septum.** A prominent feature of this septum is an oval depression, the **fossa ovalis,** which corresponds to the site of the **foramen ovale,** an opening in the interatrial septum of the fetal heart that helps blood bypass the nonfunctioning lungs. Each atrium has an appendage called an **auricle** (AWR-i-kul), so named because its shape resembles a dog's ear. The auricles increase the surface area of the atria. The lining of the atria is smooth, except for the anterior walls and linings of the auricles, which contain projecting muscle bundles called **musculi pectinati** (MUS-kyoo-lē pek-ti-NA-tē).

The two inferior and larger chambers, called the **right** and **left ventricles,** are separated internally by a partition called the **interventricular septum.** Externally, a groove known as the **coronary sulcus** (SUL-kus) separates the atria from the ventricles. The groove encircles the heart and houses the coronary sinus (a large cardiac vein) and the circumflex branch of the left coronary artery. The **anterior interventricular sulcus** and **posterior interventricular sulcus** separate the right and left ventricles externally. They also contain coronary blood vessels and a variable amount of fat.

Label the chambers and associated structures of the heart in Figures 17.2 and 17.3.

D. GREAT VESSELS AND VALVES OF HEART

The right atrium receives blood from every area of the body except the lungs. The blood enters through three veins: the **superior vena cava** bringing blood from the upper body, the **inferior vena cava** bringing blood from the lower body, and the **coronary sinus** bringing blood from most of the vessels supplying the heart wall.

The blood is passed from the right atrium into the right ventricle through the atrioventricular valve called the **tricuspid valve,** which consists of three cusps (flaps). The right ventricle then pumps the blood through the **pulmonary semilunar valve** into the **pulmonary trunk.** The pulmonary trunk divides into a **right** and **left pulmonary artery,** each of which carries blood to the lungs where the blood releases its carbon dioxide and takes on oxygen. It returns to the heart via four **pulmonary veins** that empty freshly oxygenated blood into the left atrium. The blood is then passed into the left ventricle through another atrioventricular valve called the **bicuspid (mitral) valve,** which consists of two cusps. The cusps of the tricuspid and bicuspid valves are connected to cords called **chordae tendineae,** which in turn attach to projections in the ventricular walls called **papillary muscles.** The left ventricle pumps the blood through the **aortic semilunar valve** into the **ascending aorta.** From this vessel, aortic blood is passed into the **coronary arteries, arch of the aorta, thoracic aorta,** and **abdominal aorta.** These blood vessels transport the blood to all areas of the body except the lungs. The function of the heart valves is to permit the blood to flow in only one direction.

Label the great vessels and valves of the heart in Figures 17.2 and 17.3a and b.

E. BLOOD SUPPLY OF HEART

Because of its importance in myocardial infarction (heart attack), the blood supply of the heart will be described briefly at this point. The arterial supply of the heart is provided by the right and left coronary arteries. The **right coronary artery** originates as a branch of the ascending aorta, descends in the coronary sulcus, and gives off a **marginal branch** that supplies the right ventricle. The right coronary artery continues around the posterior surface of the heart in the posterior interventricular sulcus. This portion of the artery is known as the **posterior interventricular branch** and supplies

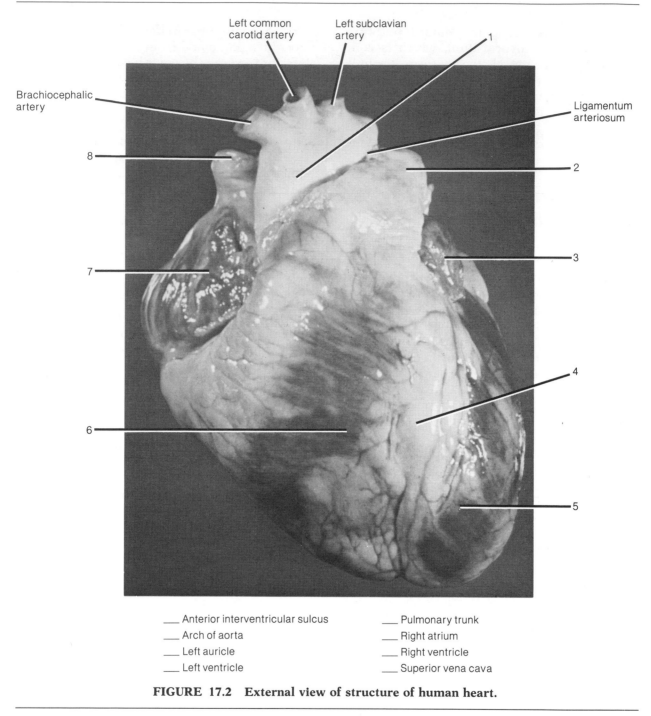

Left common carotid artery

Left subclavian artery

Brachiocephalic artery

Ligamentum arteriosum

1

8

2

7

3

6

4

5

___ Anterior interventricular sulcus

___ Arch of aorta

___ Left auricle

___ Left ventricle

___ Pulmonary trunk

___ Right atrium

___ Right ventricle

___ Superior vena cava

FIGURE 17.2   External view of structure of human heart.

the right and left ventricles. The **left coronary artery** also originates as a branch of the ascending aorta. Between the pulmonary trunk and left auricle, the left coronary artery divides into two branches: anterior interventricular and circumflex. The **anterior interventricular branch** passes in the anterior interventricular sulcus and supplies the right and left ventricles. The **circumflex branch** circles toward the posterior surface of the heart in the coronary sulcus and distributes blood to the left ventricle and left atrium.

Most blood from the heart drains into the **coronary sinus,** a venous channel in the posterior portion of the coronary sulcus between the left atrium and left ventricle. The principal tributaries of the coronary sinus are the **great cardiac vein,** which drains the anterior aspect of the heart, and the **middle cardiac vein,** which drains the posterior aspect of the heart.

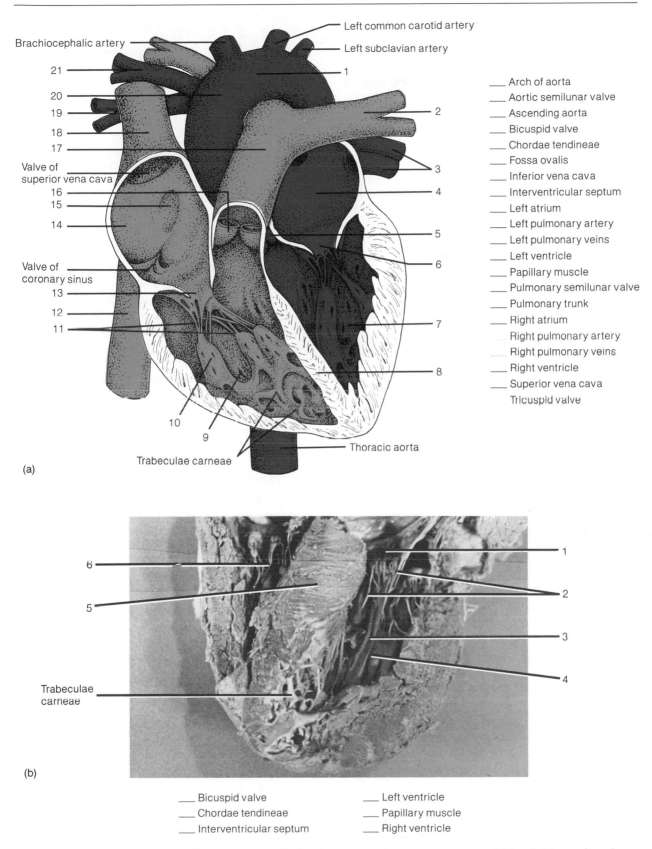

(a)

Left common carotid artery
Left subclavian artery
Brachiocephalic artery
Valve of superior vena cava
Valve of coronary sinus
Trabeculae carneae
Thoracic aorta

___ Arch of aorta
___ Aortic semilunar valve
___ Ascending aorta
___ Bicuspid valve
___ Chordae tendineae
___ Fossa ovalis
___ Inferior vena cava
___ Interventricular septum
___ Left atrium
___ Left pulmonary artery
___ Left pulmonary veins
___ Left ventricle
___ Papillary muscle
___ Pulmonary semilunar valve
___ Pulmonary trunk
___ Right atrium
___ Right pulmonary artery
___ Right pulmonary veins
___ Right ventricle
___ Superior vena cava
___ Tricuspid valve

(b)

Trabeculae carneae

___ Bicuspid valve   ___ Left ventricle
___ Chordae tendineae   ___ Papillary muscle
___ Interventricular septum   ___ Right ventricle

FIGURE 17.3 Structure of human heart. Red-colored vessels carry oxygenated blood; blue-colored vessels carry deoxygenated blood. (a) Diagram of internal view. (b) Photograph of internal view.

F. DISSECTION OF SHEEP HEART

The anatomy of the sheep heart closely resembles that of the human heart. Use Figures 17.4 and 17.5 as references for this dissection. In addition, models of human hearts can also be used as references.

First examine the **pericardium,** a fibroserous membrane that encloses the heart, which may have already been removed in preparing the sheep heart for preservation. The **myocardium** is the middle layer and constitutes the main muscle portion of the heart. The **endocardium** (the third layer) is the inner lining of the heart. Use the figures to determine which is the ventral surface of the heart and then identify the **pulmonary trunk** emerging from the anterior ventral surface, near the midline, and medial to the **left auricle.** A longitudinal depression on the ventral surface, called the **anterior longitudinal sulcus,** separates the right ventricle from the left ventricle. Locate the **coronary blood vessels** lying in this sulcus.

1. Remove any fat or pulmonary tissue that is present.

2. In cutting the sheep heart open to examine the chambers, valves, and vessels, the anterior longitudinal sulcus is used as a guide.

3. Carefully make a shallow incision through the ventral wall of the pulmonary trunk and the right ventricle, trying not to cut the dorsal surface of either structure.

4. The incision is best made *less than an inch to the right of, and parallel to,* the previously mentioned anterior longitudinal sulcus.

5. If necessary, the incision can be continued to where the pulmonary trunk branches into a **right pulmonary artery,** which goes to the right lung, and a **left pulmonary artery,** which goes to the left lung. The **pulmonary semilunar valve** of the pulmonary artery can be clearly seen upon opening it. In any of these internal dissections of the heart, any coagulated blood or latex should be immediately removed so that all important structures can be located and identified.

6. Keeping the cut still parallel to the sulcus, extend the incision around and through the dorsal ventricular wall until you reach the **interventricular septum.**

7. Now examine the dorsal surface of the heart and locate the thin-walled **superior vena cava** directly above the **right auricle.** This vein proceeds posteriorly straight into the right atrium.

8. Make a second longitudinal cut, this time through the superior vena cava (dorsal wall).

9. Extend the cut posteriorly through the right atrium on the left of the right auricle. Proceed posteriorly to the dorsal right ventricle wall and join your first incision.

10. The entire internal right side of the heart should now be clearly seen when carefully spread apart. The interior of the superior vena cava, right atrium, and right ventricle will now be examined. Start with the right auricle and locate the **musculi pectinati,** the large opening of the **inferior vena cava** on the left side of the right atrium, and the opening of the **coronary sinus** just below the opening of the inferior vena cava. By using a dull probe and gentle pressure, most of these vessels can be traced to the dorsal surface of the heart.

11. Now find the wall that separates the two atria, the **interatrial septum.** Also find the **fossa ovalis,** an oval-shaped depression ventral to the entrance of the inferior vena cava.

12. The **tricuspid valve** between the right atrium and the right ventricle should be examined to locate the three cusps as its name indicates. From the cusps of the valve itself, and tracing posteriorly, the **chordae tendineae,** which hold the valve in place, should be identified. Still tracing posteriorly, the chordae are seen to originate from the **papillary muscles,** which themselves originate from the wall of the right ventricle itself.

13. Look carefully again at the dorsal surface of the left atrium and locate as many **pulmonary veins** (normally, four) as possible.

14. Make your third longitudinal cut through the most lateral of the pulmonary veins that you have located.

15. Continue posteriorly through the left atrial wall and the left ventricle to the **apex** of the heart.

16. Compare the difference in the thickness of the wall between the right and left ventricle. Explain your answer.

17. Examine the **bicuspid (mitral) valve,** again counting the cusps. Determine if the left side of

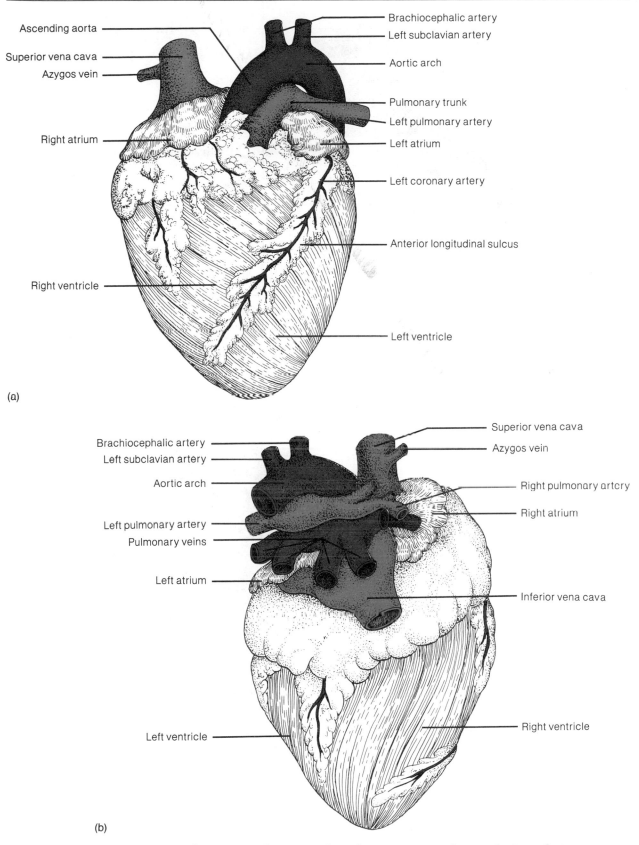

Ascending aorta

Superior vena cava

Azygos vein

Right atrium

Right ventricle

Brachiocephalic artery

Left subclavian artery

Aortic arch

Pulmonary trunk

Left pulmonary artery

Left atrium

Left coronary artery

Anterior longitudinal sulcus

Left ventricle

(a)

Brachiocephalic artery

Left subclavian artery

Aortic arch

Left pulmonary artery

Pulmonary veins

Left atrium

Left ventricle

Superior vena cava

Azygos vein

Right pulmonary artery

Right atrium

Inferior vena cava

Right ventricle

(b)

FIGURE 17.4 External structure of a cat or sheep heart. (a) Ventral view. (b) Dorsal view.

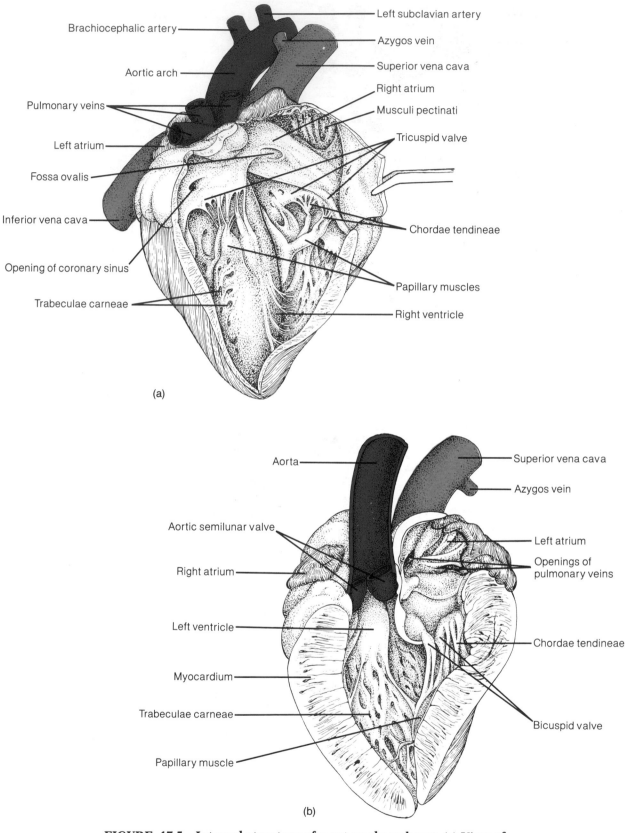

Brachiocephalic artery

Aortic arch

Pulmonary veins

Left atrium

Fossa ovalis

Inferior vena cava

Opening of coronary sinus

Trabeculae carneae

Left subclavian artery

Azygos vein

Superior vena cava

Right atrium

Musculi pectinati

Tricuspid valve

Chordae tendineae

Papillary muscles

Right ventricle

(a)

Aorta

Aortic semilunar valve

Right atrium

Left ventricle

Myocardium

Trabeculae carneae

Papillary muscle

Superior vena cava

Azygos vein

Left atrium

Openings of pulmonary veins

Chordae tendineae

Bicuspid valve

(b)

FIGURE 17.5   Internal structure of a cat or sheep heart. (a) View of right atrium and right ventricle. (b) View of left atrium and left ventricle.

the heart has basically the same structures as studied on the right side.

18. Probe from the left ventricle to the **aorta** as it emerges from the heart, examining the **aortic semilunar valve.** Find the openings of the right and left main coronary arteries.

19. Locate now the **brachiocephalic artery,** which is one of the first branches from the arch of the aorta. This artery continues branching and terminates by supplying the arms and head as its name indicates.

Connecting the aorta with the pulmonary artery is the remnant of the **ductus arteriosus,** called the **ligamentum arteriosum.** It may not be present in your sheep heart.

LABORATORY REPORT QUESTIONS (PAGE 413)

18 | BLOOD VESSELS

Blood vessels are networks of tubes that carry blood throughout the body. Blood vessels are called arteries, arterioles, capillaries, venules, or veins. In this exercise, you will study the histology of blood vessels and identify the principal arteries and veins of the human cardiovascular system.

A. ARTERIES AND ARTERIOLES

Arteries are blood vessels that carry blood away from the heart to body tissues. Arteries are constructed of three coats of tissue called **tunics** and a hollow core, called a **lumen,** through which blood flows (see Figure 18.1). The inner coat is called the **tunica interna** and consists of a lining of endothelium in contact with the blood and a layer of elastic tissue called the **internal elastic membrane.** The middle coat, or **tunica media,** is the thickest layer and consists of elastic fibers and smooth muscle. This tunic is responsible for two major properties of arteries: **elasticity** and **contractility.** The outer coat, or **tunica externa,** is composed principally of elastic and collagenous fibers.

Obtain a prepared slide of a cross section of an artery and identify the tunics using Figure 18.1 as a guide.

As arteries approach various tissues of the body, they become smaller and are known as **arterioles.** When arterioles enter a tissue, they branch into countless microscopic blood vessels called capillaries. Arterioles play a key role in regulating blood flow from arteries into capillaries.

B. CAPILLARIES

Capillaries are microscopic blood vessels that connect arterioles and venules. Their function is to permit the exchange of nutrients and wastes between blood and body tissues. This function is related to the fact that capillaries consist of only a single layer of endothelium.

C. VENULES AND VEINS

When several capillaries unite, they form small veins called **venules.** They collect blood from capillaries and drain it into veins.

Veins are composed of the same three tunics as arteries, except they have considerably less elastic tissue and smooth muscle and more white fibrous tissue. Veins also contain valves. In general, arteries are thicker and stronger than veins (Figure 18.1). Functionally, veins return blood from tissues to the heart.

Obtain a prepared slide of a cross section of an artery and its accompanying vein and compare them, using Figure 18.1 as a guide.

D. PRINCIPAL ARTERIES

The principal arteries and veins are described and illustrated in Figures 18.2 through 18.10 and Tables 18.1 through 18.8. Study these tables and, using your textbook, charts, models, dissection specimens, or projector slides for reference, identify the major blood vessels and label the figures.

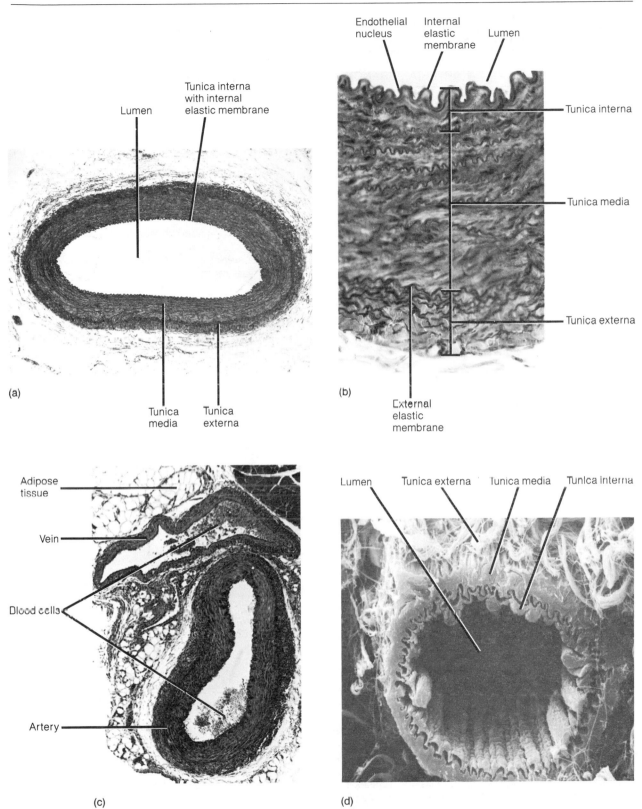

FIGURE 18.1 Histology of blood vessels. (a) Cross section of an artery. (b) Enlarged aspect of an arterial wall. (c) Comparison of structure of an artery and its accompanying vein. (d) Scanning electron micrograph of an artery at a magnification of 5170×. ((d) from *Tissues and Organs: A Text-Atlas of Scanning Electron Microscopy* by Richard G. Kessel and Randy H. Kardon. W. H. Freeman and Company. Copyright © 1979.)

TABLE 18.1
AORTA AND ITS BRANCHES

DIVISION OF AORTA	ARTERIAL BRANCH	REGION SUPPLIED
Ascending aorta	Right and left coronary	Heart
Arch of aorta	Brachiocephalic < Right common carotid / Right subclavian	Right side of head and neck / Right upper extremity
	Left common carotid	Left side of head or neck
	Left subclavian	Left upper extremity
Thoracic aorta	Intercostals	Intercostal and chest muscles, pleurae
	Superior phrenics	Posterior and superior surfaces of diaphragm
	Bronchials	Bronchi of lungs
	Esophageals	Esophagus
Abdominal aorta	Inferior phrenics	Inferior surface of diaphragm
	Celiac < Common hepatic / Left gastric / Splenic	Liver / Stomach and esophagus / Spleen, pancreas, stomach
	Superior mesenteric	Small intestine, cecum, ascending and transverse colons
	Suprarenals	Adrenal (suprarenal) glands
	Renals	Kidneys
	Gonadals < Testiculars / Ovarians	Testes / Ovaries
	Inferior mesenteric	Transverse, descending, sigmoid colons; rectum
	Common iliacs < External iliacs / Internal iliacs (hypogastrics)	Lower extremities / Uterus, prostate, muscles of buttocks, urinary bladder

TABLE 18.2
ARCH OF AORTA (FIGURES 18.2, 18.3, and 18.4)

BRANCH	DESCRIPTION AND REGION SUPPLIED
Brachiocephalic	**Brachiocephalic artery** is the first branch off arch of aorta. Divides to form right subclavian artery and right common carotid artery. **Right subclavian artery** extends from brachiocephalic to first rib, passes into armpit, or axilla, and supplies arm, forearm, and hand. This artery is a good example of the same vessel having different names as it passes through different regions. Continuation of right subclavian into axilla is called **axillary artery.** From here, it continues into arm as **brachial artery.** At bend of elbow, brachial artery divides into medial **ulnar** and lateral **radial arteries.** These vessels pass down to palm, one on each side of forearm. In palm, branches of two arteries anastomose to form two palmar arches—**superficial palmar arch** and **deep palmar arch.** From these arches arise **digital arteries,** which supply fingers and thumb (see Figure 18.2).

(Table 18.2 is continued on next page.)

TABLE 18.2 (*Continued*)

BRANCH	DESCRIPTION AND REGION SUPPLIED
Brachiocephalic (*continued*)	Before passing into axilla, right subclavian gives off major branch to brain called **vertebral artery.** Right vertebral artery passes through foramina of transverse processes of cervical vertebrae and enters skull through foramen magnum to reach undersurface of brain. Here it unites with left vertebral artery to form **basilar artery** (see Figures 18.3 and 18.4).
Right common carotid	**Right common carotid artery** passes upward in neck. At upper level of larynx, it divides into **right external** and **right internal carotid arteries.** External carotid supplies right side of thyroid gland, tongue, face, ear, scalp, and dura mater. Internal carotid supplies brain, right eye, and right sides of forehead and nose (Figure 18.3). Anastomoses of left and right internal carotids along with basilar artery form arterial circle at base of brain called **cerebral arterial circle (circle of Willis).** From this anastomosis arise arteries supplying brain. Essentially, cerebral arterial circle is formed by union of **anterior cerebral arteries** (branches of internal carotids) and **posterior cerebral arteries** (branches of basilar artery). Posterior cerebral arteries are connected with internal, carotids by **posterior communicating arteries.** Anterior cerebral arteries are connected by **anterior communicating arteries.** Cerebral arterial circle equalizes blood pressure to brain and provides alternate routes for blood to brain should arteries become damaged.
Left common carotid	**Left common carotid** branches directly from arch of aorta. Corresponding to right common carotid, it divides into basically same branches with same names—except that arteries are now labeled "left" instead of "right."
Left subclavian	**Left subclavian artery** is third branch off arch of aorta. It distributes blood to left vertebral artery and vessels of left upper extremity. Arteries branching from left subclavian are named like those of right subclavian.

Label Figures 18.2, 18.3, and 18.4.

TABLE 18.3
THORACIC AORTA (FIGURE 18.2)

BRANCH	DESCRIPTION AND REGION SUPPLIED
	Thoracic aorta runs from fourth to twelfth thoracic vertebrae, sending off numerous small arteries to viscera and skeletal muscles of the chest. Branches of an artery that supply viscera are called **visceral branches.** Those that supply body wall structures are **parietal branches.**
VISCERAL Pericardial	Several minute **pericardial arteries** supply blood to dorsal aspect of pericardium.
Bronchial	One **right** and two **left bronchial arteries** supply the bronchial tubes, areolar tissue of the lungs, and bronchial lymph nodes.
Esophageal	Four or five **esophageal arteries** supply the esophagus.
Mediastinal	Numerous small **mediastinal arteries** supply blood to structures in the posterior mediastinum.
PARIETAL Posterior intercostal	Nine pairs of **posterior intercostal arteries** supply (1) the intercostal, pectoral, and abdominal muscles; (2) overlying subcutaneous tissue and skin; (3) mammary glands; and (4) vertebral canal and its contents.
Subcostal	The **left** and **right subcostal arteries** have a distribution similar to that of the posterior intercostals.
Superior phrenic	Small **superior phrenic arteries** supply the superior surface of the diaphragm.

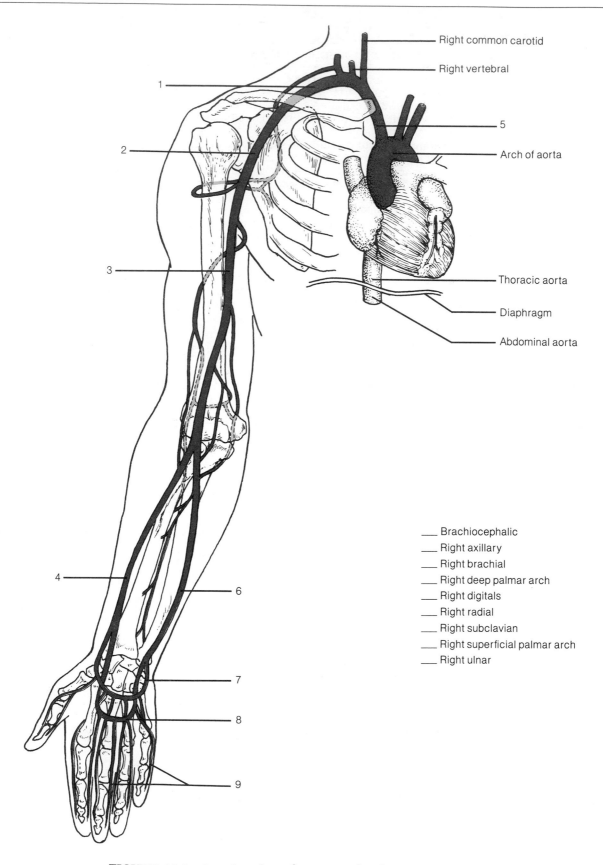

Right common carotid

Right vertebral

5

Arch of aorta

Thoracic aorta

Diaphragm

Abdominal aorta

___ Brachiocephalic
___ Right axillary
___ Right brachial
___ Right deep palmar arch
___ Right digitals
___ Right radial
___ Right subclavian
___ Right superficial palmar arch
___ Right ulnar

FIGURE 18.2 **Anterior view of arteries of right upper extremity.**

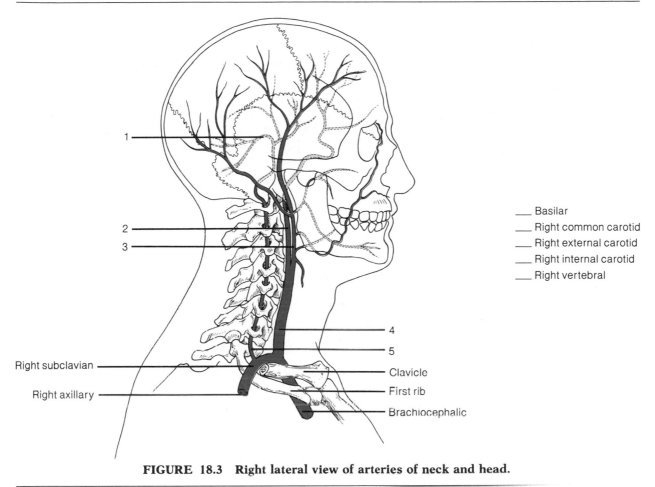

1
2
3

___ Basilar
___ Right common carotid
___ Right external carotid
___ Right internal carotid
___ Right vertebral

4
5

Right subclavian
Right axillary

Clavicle
First rib
Brachiocephalic

FIGURE 18.3   Right lateral view of arteries of neck and head.

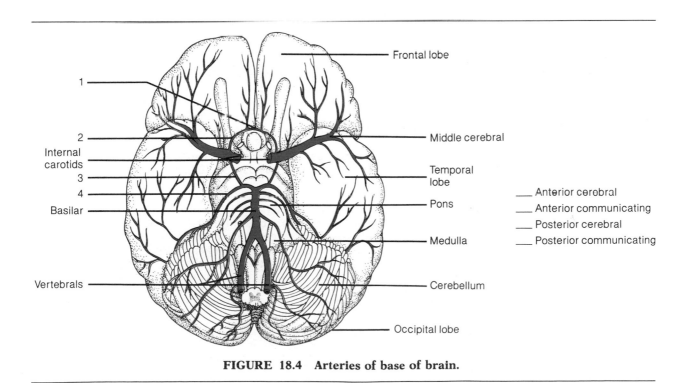

1
2
Internal
carotids
3
4
Basilar

Vertebrals

Frontal lobe

Middle cerebral

Temporal
lobe
Pons

Medulla

Cerebellum

Occipital lobe

___ Anterior cerebral
___ Anterior communicating
___ Posterior cerebral
___ Posterior communicating

FIGURE 18.4   Arteries of base of brain.

TABLE 18.4
ABDOMINAL AORTA (FIGURE 18.5)

BRANCH	DESCRIPTION AND REGION SUPPLIED
VISCERAL	Supply viscera.
Celiac	**Celiac artery (trunk)** is first visceral aortic branch below diaphragm. The artery has three branches: (1) **common hepatic artery,** which supplies tissues of liver; (2) **left gastric artery,** which supplies stomach; and (3) **splenic artery,** which supplies spleen, pancreas, and stomach.
Superior mesenteric	**Superior mesenteric artery** distributes blood to small intestine and part of large intestine.
Suprarenals	Right and left **suprarenal arteries** supply blood to adrenal (suprarenal) glands.
Renals	Right and left **renal arteries** carry blood to kidneys.
Gonadals (testiculars or ovarians)	Right and left **testicular arteries** extend into scrotum and terminate in testes. Right and left **ovarian arteries** are distributed to ovaries.
Inferior mesenteric	**Inferior mesenteric artery** supplies major part of large intestine and rectum.
PARIETAL	Supply structures of body wall.
Inferior phrenics	**Inferior phrenic arteries** are distributed to undersurface of diaphragm.
Lumbars	**Lumbar arteries** supply spinal cord and its meninges and muscles and skin of lumbar region of back.
Middle sacral	**Middle sacral artery** supplies sacrum, coccyx, gluteus maximus muscles, and rectum.

Label Figure 18.5.

TABLE 18.5
ARTERIES OF PELVIS AND LOWER EXTREMITIES (FIGURE 18.6)

BRANCH	DESCRIPTION AND REGION SUPPLIED
Common iliacs	At about level of fourth lumbar vertebra, abdominal aorta divides into right and left **common iliac arteries.** Each passes downward about 5 cm (2 in.) and gives rise to two branches: internal iliac and external iliac.
Internal iliacs	**Internal iliac (hypogastric) arteries** form branches that supply psoas major, quadratus lumborum, medial side of each thigh, urinary bladder, rectum, prostate gland, uterus, ductus deferens, and vagina.
External iliacs	**External iliac arteries** diverge through pelvis, enter thighs, and become right and left **femoral arteries.** Both femorals send branches back up to genitals and wall of abdomen. Other branches run to muscles of thigh. Femoral continues down medial and posterior side of thigh at back of knee joint, where it becomes **popliteal artery.** Between knee and ankle, popliteal runs down back of leg and is called **posterior tibial artery.** Below knee, **peroneal artery** branches off posterior tibial to supply structures on medial side of fibula and calcaneus. In calf, **anterior tibial artery** branches off popliteal and runs along front of leg. At ankle, it becomes **dorsalis pedis artery.** At ankle, posterior tibial divides into **medial** and **lateral plantar arteries.** These arteries anastomose with dorsalis pedis and supply blood to foot.

Label Figure 18.6.

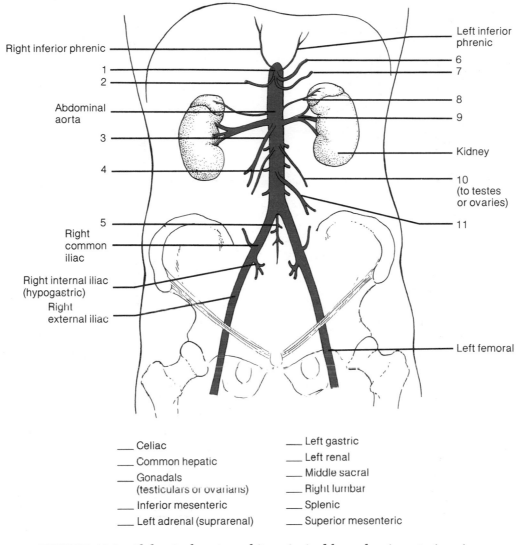

___ Celiac

___ Common hepatic

___ Gonadals
(testiculars or ovarians)

___ Inferior mesenteric

___ Left adrenal (suprarenal)

___ Left gastric

___ Left renal

___ Middle sacral

___ Right lumbar

___ Splenic

___ Superior mesenteric

FIGURE 18.5 Abdominal aorta and its principal branches in anterior view.

E. PRINCIPAL VEINS

**TABLE 18.6
VEINS OF SYSTEMIC CIRCULATION (FIGURE 18.9)**

VEIN	DESCRIPTION AND REGION DRAINED
	All systemic and cardiac veins return blood to the right atrium of the heart through one of three large vessels. Return flow in coronary circulation is taken up by **cardiac veins,** which empty into the large vein of the heart, the **coronary sinus.** From here, the blood empties into the right atrium of the heart. Return flow in systemic circulation empties into the superior vena cava or inferior vena cava.
Superior vena cava	Veins of the head and neck, upper extremities, and some from thorax empty into the **superior vena cava.**
Inferior vena cava	Veins of the abdomen, pelvis, and lower extremities and some from thorax empty into the **inferior vena cava.**

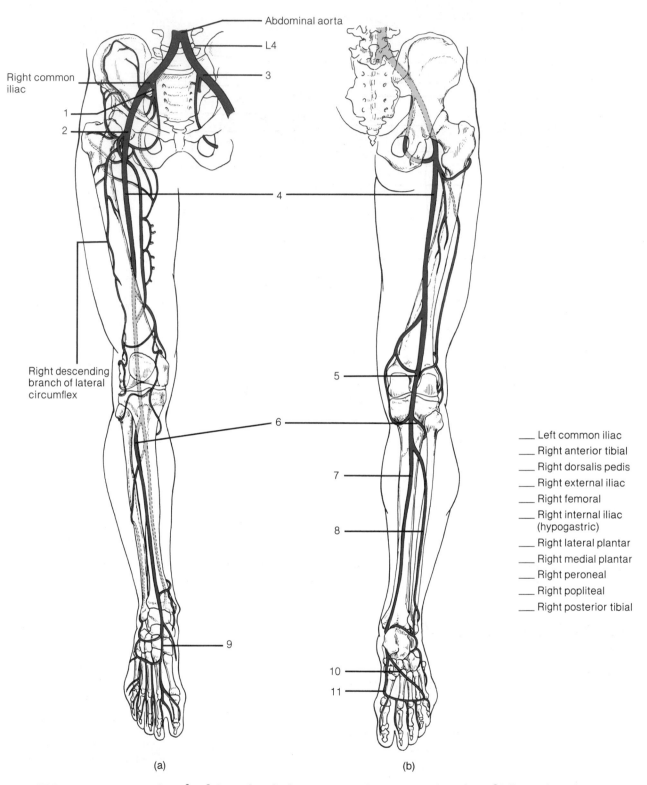

Abdominal aorta

L4

Right common iliac

3

1

2

Right descending branch of lateral circumflex

4

5

6

7

8

9

10

11

_____ Left common iliac
_____ Right anterior tibial
_____ Right dorsalis pedis
_____ Right external iliac
_____ Right femoral
_____ Right internal iliac (hypogastric)
_____ Right lateral plantar
_____ Right medial plantar
_____ Right peroneal
_____ Right popliteal
_____ Right posterior tibial

(a)   (b)

FIGURE 18.6   Arteries of pelvis and right lower extremity. (a) Anterior view. (b) Posterior view.

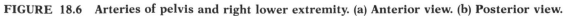

TABLE 18.7
VEINS OF HEAD AND NECK (FIGURE 18.7)

VEIN	DESCRIPTION AND REGION DRAINED
Internal jugulars	Right and left **internal jugular veins** arise as continuation of **sigmoid sinuses** at base of skull. Intracranial vascular sinuses are located between layers of dura mater and receive blood from brain. Other sinuses that drain into internal jugular include **superior sagittal sinus, inferior sagittal sinus, straight sinus,** and **transverse (lateral) sinuses.** Internal jugulars descend on either side of neck. They receive blood from face and neck and pass behind clavicles, where they join with right and left **subclavian veins.** Unions of internal jugulars and subclavians form right and left **brachiocephalic veins.** From here blood flows into **superior vena cava.**
External jugulars	Left and right **external jugular veins** run down neck along outside of internal jugulars. They drain blood from parotid (salivary) glands, facial muscles, scalp, and other superficial structures into **subclavian veins.**

Label Figure 18.7.

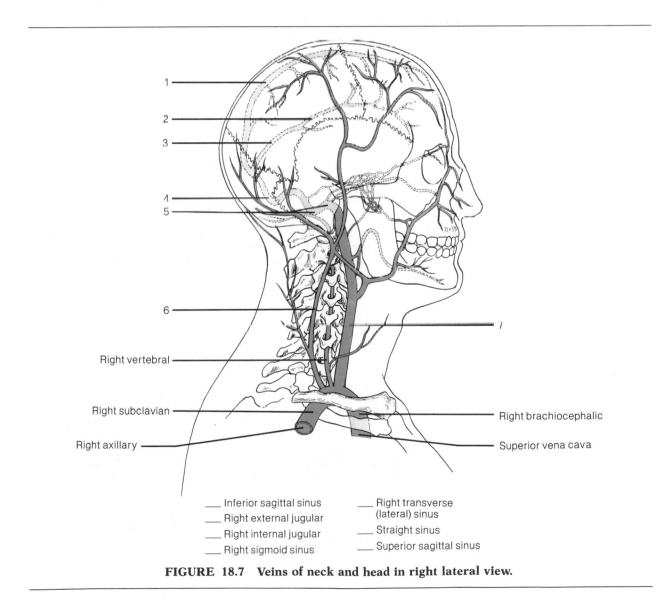

_____ Inferior sagittal sinus
_____ Right external jugular
_____ Right internal jugular
_____ Right sigmoid sinus

_____ Right transverse (lateral) sinus
_____ Straight sinus
_____ Superior sagittal sinus

FIGURE 18.7   Veins of neck and head in right lateral view.

TABLE 18.8
VEINS OF UPPER EXTREMITIES (FIGURES 18.8 and 18.9)

VEIN	DESCRIPTION AND REGION DRAINED
	Blood from each upper extremity is returned to heart by deep and superficial veins. Both sets of veins contain valves.
SUPERFICIAL VEINS	Superficial veins are just below skin and anastomose extensively with each other and with deep veins.
Cephalics	**Cephalic vein** of each upper extremity begins in the medial part of **dorsal arch** of hand and winds upward around radial border of forearm. Just below elbow, vein unites with **accessory cephalic vein** to form cephalic vein of upper extremity and eventually empties into **axillary vein.**
Basilics	**Basilic vein** of each upper extremity originates in ulnar part of dorsal arch. It extends along posterior surface of ulna to point below elbow where it receives **median cubital vein.** If a vein must be punctured for an injection, transfusion, or removal of a blood sample, median cubitals are preferred. The median cubital joins the basilic vein to form the **axillary vein.**
Median antebrachials	**Median antebrachial veins** drain venous plexus on palmar surface of hand, ascend on ulnar side of anterior forearm, and end in median cubital veins.
DEEP	Located deep in the body, usually accompany arteries, and bear same names as corresponding arteries.
Radials	**Radial veins** receive dorsal metacarpal veins.
Ulnars	**Ulnar veins** receive tributaries from deep palmar arch. Radial and ulnar veins unite in bend of elbow to form brachial veins.
Brachials	Located on either side of brachial artery, **brachial veins** join into axillary veins.
Axillaries	**Axillary veins** are a continuation of brachials and basilics. Axillaries end at first rib, where they become subclavians.
Subclavians	**Right** and **left subclavian veins** unite with internal jugulars to form **brachiocephalic veins.** Thoracic duct of lymphatic system delivers lymph into left subclavian vein at junction with internal jugular. Right lymphatic duct delivers lymph into right subclavian vein at corresponding junction.

Label Figure 18.8.

TABLE 18.9
VEINS OF THORAX (FIGURE 18.9)

VEIN	DESCRIPTION AND REGION DRAINED
	Principal thoracic vessels that empty into superior vena cava are brachiocephalic and azygos veins.
Brachiocephalic	Right and left **brachiocephalic veins,** formed by union of subclavians and internal jugulars, drain blood from head, neck, upper extremities, mammary glands, and upper thorax. Brachiocephalics unite to form **superior vena cava.**
Azygos	**Azygos veins,** besides collecting blood from thorax, serve as bypass for inferior vena cava that drains blood from lower body. Several small veins directly link azygos veins with inferior vena cava. Large veins that drain lower extremities and abdomen may drain blood into azygos. If inferior vena cava or hepatic portal vein becomes obstructed, azygos veins can return blood from lower body to superior vena cava.

(Table 18.9 is continued on next page.)

TABLE 18.9 (*Continued*)

VEIN	DESCRIPTION AND REGION DRAINED
Azygos	**Azygos vein** lies in front of vertebral column, slightly right of midline. The vein begins as continuation of right ascending lumbar vein and connects with inferior vena cava, right common iliac, and lumbar veins. Azygos receives blood from (1) right intercostal veins that drain chest muscles; (2) hemiazygos and accessory hemiazygos veins; (3) several esophageal, mediastinal, and pericardial veins; and (4) right bronchial vein. Vein ascends to fourth thoracic vertebra, arches over right lung, and empties into superior vena cava.
Hemiazygos	**Hemiazygos vein** is in front of vertebral column and slightly left of midline, beginning as continuation of left ascending lumbar vein. The vein receives blood from lower four or five intercostal veins and some esophageal and mediastinal veins. At level of ninth thoracic vertebra, it joins azygos vein.
Accessory hemiazygos	**Accessory hemiazygos vein** is also in front and to left of vertebral column. It receives blood from three or four intercostal veins and left bronchial vein and joins azygos at level of eighth thoracic vertebra.

Label Figure 18.9, using Figure 18.5 for reference, if necessary.

TABLE 18.10
VEINS OF THE ABDOMEN AND PELVIS (FIGURE 18.9)

VEIN	DESCRIPTION AND REGION DRAINED
Inferior vena cava	**Inferior vena cava,** the largest vein of the body, is formed by union of two common iliac veins that drain lower extremities and abdomen. Inferior vena cava extends upward through abdomen and thorax to right atrium. Numerous small veins enter the inferior vena cava. Most carry return flow from branches of abdominal aorta and names correspond to names of arteries.
Common iliacs	**Common iliac veins** are formed by union of internal (hypogastric) and external iliac veins and represent distal continuation of inferior vena cava at its bifurcation.
Internal iliacs (hypogastrics)	Tributaries of **internal iliac (hypogastric) veins** basically correspond with branches of external iliac arteries. Internal iliacs drain gluteal muscles, medial side of thigh, urinary bladder, rectum, prostate gland, ductus deferens, uterus, and vagina.
External iliacs	**External iliac veins** are continuation of femoral veins and receive blood from lower extremities and inferior part of anterior abdominal wall.
Renals	**Renal veins** drain kidneys.
Gonadals (testiculars and ovarians)	**Testicular veins** drain testes (left testicular vein empties into left renal vein) and **ovarian veins** drain ovaries (left ovarian vein empties into left renal vein).
Suprarenals	**Suprarenal veins** drain adrenal (suprarenal) glands (left suprarenal vein empties into left renal vein).
Inferior phrenics	**Inferior phrenic veins** drain diaphragm (left inferior phrenic vein sends tributary to left renal vein).
Hepatics	**Hepatic veins** drain liver.
Lumbars	A series of parallel **lumbar veins** drain blood from both sides of posterior abdominal wall. Lumbars connect at right angles with right and left ascending lumbar veins, which form origin of corresponding azygos or hemiazygos vein. Lumbars drain blood into ascending lumbars and then run to inferior vena cava, where they release remainder of flow.

Label Figure 18.9.

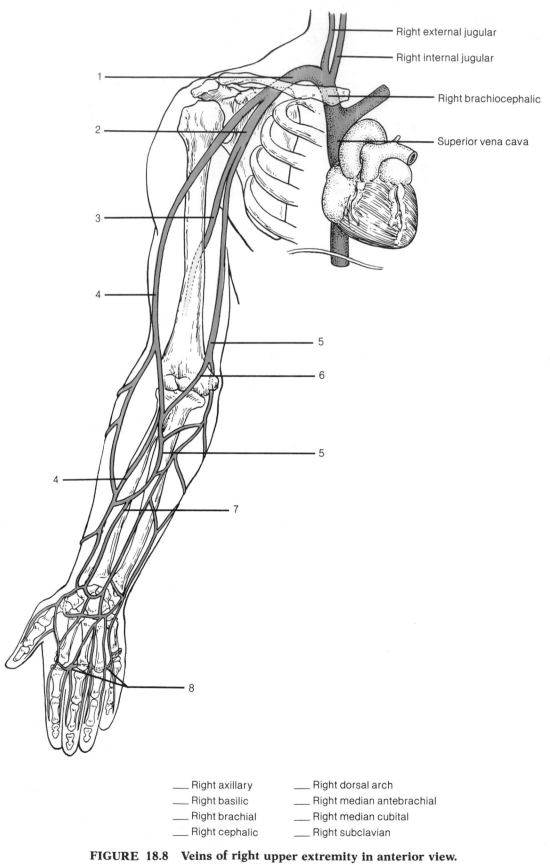

Right external jugular

Right internal jugular

Right brachiocephalic

Superior vena cava

___ Right axillary ___ Right dorsal arch
___ Right basilic ___ Right median antebrachial
___ Right brachial ___ Right median cubital
___ Right cephalic ___ Right subclavian

FIGURE 18.8   Veins of right upper extremity in anterior view.

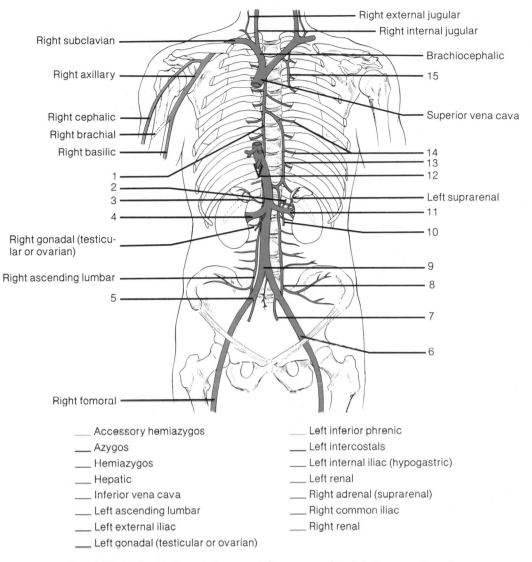

Right external jugular
Right internal jugular
Right subclavian
Brachiocephalic
Right axillary
15
Right cephalic
Superior vena cava
Right brachial
Right basilic
14
13
1
12
2
3
Left suprarenal
4
11
10
Right gonadal (testicular or ovarian)
9
Right ascending lumbar
8
5
7
6
Right femoral

___ Accessory hemiazygos
___ Azygos
___ Hemiazygos
___ Hepatic
___ Inferior vena cava
___ Left ascending lumbar
___ Left external iliac
___ Left gonadal (testicular or ovarian)

___ Left inferior phrenic
___ Left intercostals
___ Left internal iliac (hypogastric)
___ Left renal
___ Right adrenal (suprarenal)
___ Right common iliac
___ Right renal

FIGURE 18.9   Veins of thorax, abdomen, and pelvis in anterior view.

TABLE 18.11
VEINS OF LOWER EXTREMITIES (FIGURE 18.10)

VEIN	DESCRIPTION AND REGION DRAINED
	Blood from each lower extremity is returned by superficial set and deep set of veins. Superficials are formed from extensive anastomoses close to surface. Deep veins follow large arterial trunks. Both sets have valves.
SUPERFICIAL VEINS	Main superficial veins are great saphenous and small saphenous. Both, especially great saphenous, may become varicosed.
Great saphenous	**Great saphenous vein,** longest vein in body, begins at medial end of **dorsal venous arch** of foot. The vein passes in front of medial malleolus and then upward along medial aspect of leg and thigh. It receives tributaries from superficial tissues, connects with deep veins, and empties into femoral vein in groin.
Small saphenous	**Small saphenous vein** begins at lateral end of dorsal venous arch of foot. The vein passes behind lateral malleolus and ascends under skin of back of leg. It receives blood from foot and posterior portion of leg and empties into popliteal vein behind knee.

(Table 18.11 is continued on next page.)

TABLE 18.11 (Continued)

VEIN	DESCRIPTION AND REGION DRAINED
DEEP VEINS	
Posterior tibial	**Posterior tibial vein** is formed by union of **medial** and **lateral plantar veins** behind medial malleolus. The vein ascends deep in muscle at back of leg, receives blood from **peroneal vein,** and unites with anterior tibial vein just below knee. These veins begin in the **plantar arch** under the bones of the foot.
Anterior tibial	**Anterior tibial vein** is upward continuation of **dorsalis pedis** veins in foot. The vein runs between tibia and fibula and unites with posterior tibial to form popliteal vein.
Popliteal	**Popliteal vein,** just behind knee, receives blood from anterior and posterior tibials and small saphenous vein.
Femoral	**Femoral vein** is upward continuation of popliteal just above knee. Femorals run up posterior of thighs and drain deep structures of thighs. After receiving great saphenous veins in groin, they continue as right and left **external iliac veins.** Right and left **internal iliac veins** receive blood from pelvic wall and viscera, external genitals, buttocks, and medial aspect of thigh. Right and left **common iliac veins** are formed by union of internal and external iliacs. Common iliacs unite to form inferior vena cava.

Label Figure 18.10.

F. BLOOD VESSEL EXERCISE

For each vessel listed, indicate the region supplied (if an artery) or the region drained (if a vein):

1. **Coronary artery** _____

2. **Internal iliac veins** _____

3. **Lumbar arteries** _____

4. **Renal artery** _____

5. **Left gastric artery** _____

6. **External jugular vein** _____

7. **Left subclavian artery** _____

8. **Axillary vein** _____

9. **Brachiocephalic veins** _____

10. **Transverse sinuses** _____

11. **Hepatic artery** _____

12. **Inferior mesenteric artery** _____

13. **Suprarenal artery** _____

14. **Inferior phrenic artery** _____

15. **Great saphenous vein** _____

16. **Popliteal vein** _____

17. **Azygos vein** _____

18. **Internal iliac artery** _____

19. **Internal carotid artery** _____

20. **Cephalic vein** _____

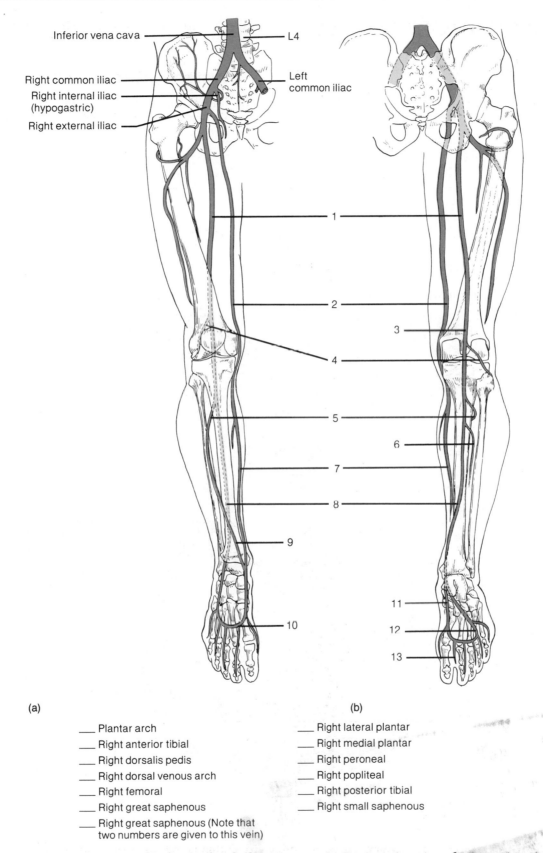

Inferior vena cava

L4

Right common iliac

Left common iliac

Right internal iliac (hypogastric)

Right external iliac

(a)

(b)

___ Plantar arch

___ Right anterior tibial

___ Right dorsalis pedis

___ Right dorsal venous arch

___ Right femoral

___ Right great saphenous

___ Right great saphenous (Note that two numbers are given to this vein)

___ Right lateral plantar

___ Right medial plantar

___ Right peroneal

___ Right popliteal

___ Right posterior tibial

___ Right small saphenous

FIGURE 18.10   Veins of pelvis and right lower extremity. (a) Anterior view. (b) Posterior view

G. CIRCULATORY ROUTES

The three basic circulatory routes are the systemic, hepatic portal, and pulmonary (Figure 18.11). Other circulatory routes include the coronary (cardiac) circulation, fetal circulation, and cerebral arterial circle (circle of Wil-

lis). The latter is found at the base of the brain (Table 18.2).

1. Systemic Circulation

The largest route is the **systemic circulation** (see Tables 18.2 through 18.11). This route in-

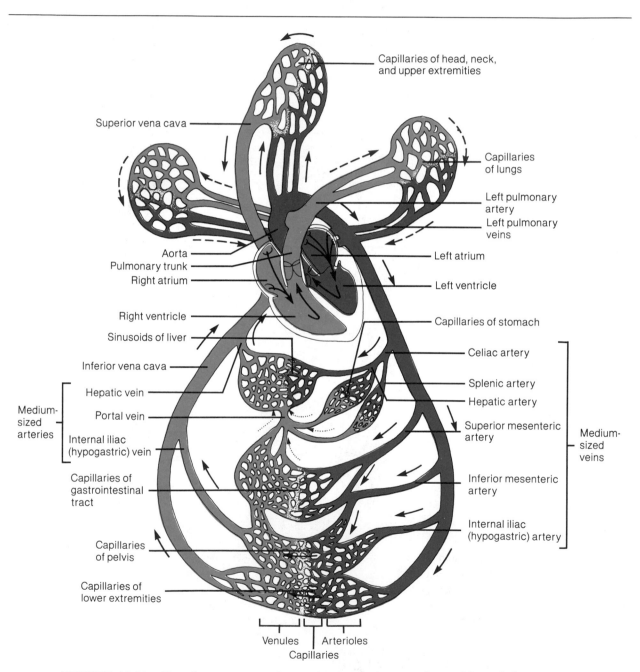

FIGURE 18.11 Circulatory routes. Systemic circulation is indicated by solid arrows; pulmonary circulation by broken arrows; and hepatic portal circulation by dotted arrows.

cludes the flow of blood from the left ventricle to all parts of the body except the lungs. The function of the systemic circulation is to carry oxygen and nutrients to all body tissues and to remove carbon dioxide and other wastes from the tissues. All systemic arteries branch from the **aorta,** and all the systemic veins that return blood to the heart flow into either the **superior** or **inferior venae cavae** or the **coronary sinus.**

2. Hepatic Portal Circulation

Hepatic portal circulation refers to the flow of venous blood from the digestive organs to the liver before it is returned to the heart (Figure 18.12). The blood vessels contained in this circulatory route include the **hepatic portal vein, superior mesenteric vein, splenic vein, gastric vein, pyloric vein, gastroepiploic vein, pancre-** atic veins, inferior mesenteric veins, and **cystic vein.** Ultimately, blood leaves the liver through the hepatic veins, which enter the inferior vena cava.

Using your textbook, charts, or models for reference, label Figure 18.12.

3. Pulmonary Circulation

Pulmonary circulation refers to the flow of deoxygenated blood from the right ventricle to the lungs and the return of oxygenated blood from the lungs to the left atrium (see Figure 18.13). The **right** and **left pulmonary arteries** are the only postnatal arteries that carry deoxygenated blood, and the **pulmonary veins** are the only postnatal veins that carry oxygenated blood.

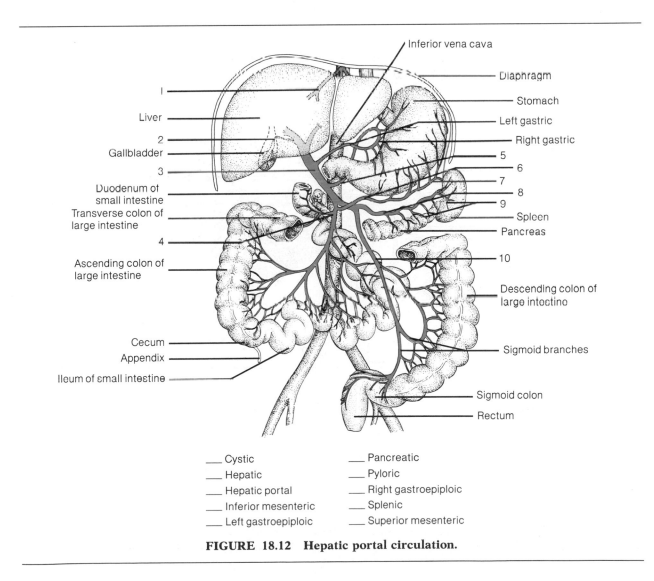

____ Cystic
____ Hepatic
____ Hepatic portal
____ Inferior mesenteric
____ Left gastroepiploic

____ Pancreatic
____ Pyloric
____ Right gastroepiploic
____ Splenic
____ Superior mesenteric

FIGURE 18.12 Hepatic portal circulation.

Study a chart or model of the pulmonary circulation, trace the path of blood through it, and label Figure 18.13.

4. Fetal Circulation

The developing fetus has nonfunctional lungs and a nonfunctional digestive tract, and this difference from an adult's circulatory system produces the **fetal circulation** (see Figure 18.14). The lungs of the fetus are not active in respiration because the fetus derives its oxygen and nutrients and eliminates its carbon dioxide and wastes through the maternal blood. An opening, the **foramen ovale,** is found between the right and left atria. Most blood leaving the right atrium passes through this opening into the left atrium rather than into the right ventricle. Blood that does enter the right ventricle is pumped into the pulmonary trunk, but little of this blood reaches the lungs. Most is conveyed from the pulmonary trunk to the aorta via a small vessel, the **ductus arteriosus,** which closes shortly after birth.

A highly specialized structure called the **placenta** accomplishes the exchange of substances between maternal and fetal circulation. Other special blood vessels include two **umbilical arteries** and an **umbilical vein,** which extend through the **umbilical cord,** and the **ductus venosus** in the liver.

Label Figure 18.14.

LABORATORY REPORT QUESTIONS (PAGE 415)

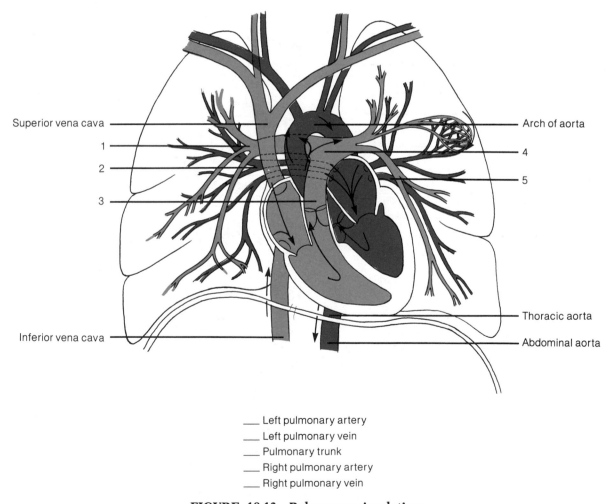

Superior vena cava

1

2

3

Inferior vena cava

Arch of aorta

4

5

Thoracic aorta

Abdominal aorta

___ Left pulmonary artery
___ Left pulmonary vein
___ Pulmonary trunk
___ Right pulmonary artery
___ Right pulmonary vein

FIGURE 18.13 Pulmonary circulation.

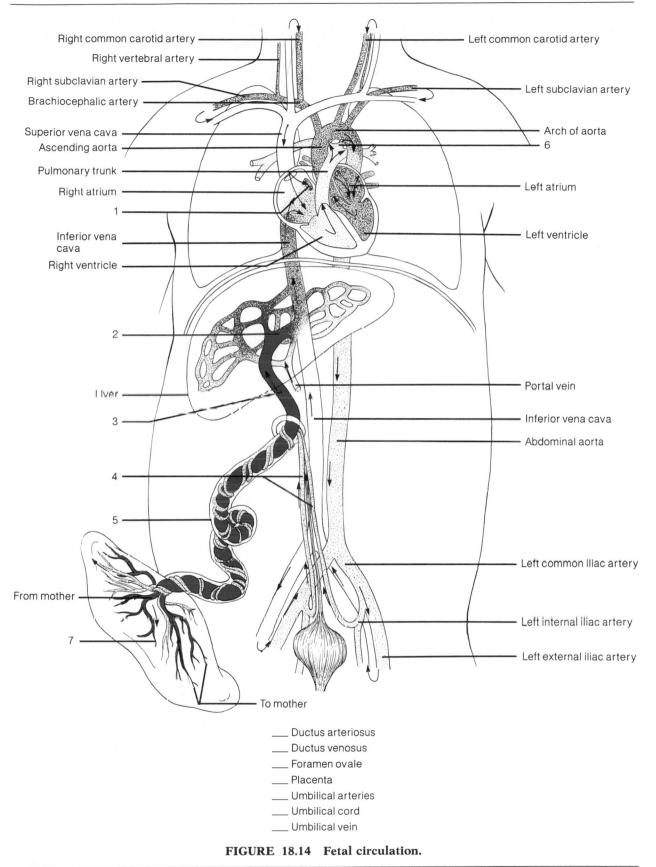

Right common carotid artery

Right vertebral artery

Right subclavian artery

Brachiocephalic artery

Superior vena cava

Ascending aorta

Pulmonary trunk

Right atrium

1

Inferior vena cava

Right ventricle

2

Liver

3

4

5

From mother

7

To mother

Left common carotid artery

Left subclavian artery

Arch of aorta

6

Left atrium

Left ventricle

Portal vein

Inferior vena cava

Abdominal aorta

Left common iliac artery

Left internal iliac artery

Left external iliac artery

___ Ductus arteriosus
___ Ductus venosus
___ Foramen ovale
___ Placenta
___ Umbilical arteries
___ Umbilical cord
___ Umbilical vein

FIGURE 18.14 Fetal circulation.

19 | CARDIOVASCULAR PHYSIOLOGY

A. CARDIAC CYCLE

In reference to the heart, the term **systole** (SIS-tō-lē) refers to the phase of contraction and **diastole** (dī-AS-tō-lē) refers to the phase of relaxation. A **cardiac cycle,** or complete heartbeat, consists of the systole and diastole of the atria plus the systole and diastole of the ventricles (see Figure 19.1a). In a complete cardiac cycle, the atria are in systole 0.1 second and in diastole 0.7 second. By contrast, the ventricles are in systole 0.3 second and in diastole 0.5 second. If we assume an average heartbeat of 75 times per minute, each cardiac cycle requires about 0.8 second.

The normal cardiac cycle is usually subdivided into four phases (see Figure 19.1a). The first is referred to as the period of **ventricular filling.** Ventricular filling starts with the opening of the atrioventricular valves (see Figure 19.1b). The initial filling of the ventricles is very fast and is accomplished via gravity. The latter filling of the ventricles is slower and only accounts for 15% of the ventricles' final volume. It is due to atrial contraction.

The second phase of the cardiac cycle is **isovolumic ventricular contraction.** During this phase the ventricles start to contract, thereby increasng ventricular pressure. The rising pressure within the ventricules causes the atrioventricular valves to close. The semilunar valves are still closed due to the pressure gradient between the ventricles and the aorta and pulmonary artery.

Ventricular ejection, the third phase of the cycle, starts when the pressure within the ventricles exceeds aortic pressure and pulmonary artery pressure, thereby causing the semilunar valves to open and blood to leave the ventricles. Pressure within the aorta and pulmonary artery are together referred to as arterial pressure. Initially blood leaves the ventricles at a very high velocity. As the ventricular pressure decreases, the rate of blood flow out of the ventricles decreases considerably.

When the ventricular pressure falls below that within the aorta and pulmonary artery, the respective semilunar valves close, initiating the period of **isovolumic ventricular relaxation,** the fourth phase of the cycle. Since ventricular pressure is still greater than intraatrial pressure, the pressure within the atria, the atrioventricular valves are still closed. As intraventricular pressure becomes less than atrial pressure, the atrioventricular valves open, thereby initiating ventricular filling again. The atria are constantly filling throughout the entire cardiac cycle due to the absence of valves between the venae cavae and right atrium and between the pulmonary veins and left atrium.

Blood flow through the heart is controlled by several factors, including opening and closing of the valves, the strength of contraction of the myocardium, speed of the cardiac cycle, and venous return to the heart.

B. ISOLATED TURTLE HEART EXPERIMENTS

Before beginning these experiments, review the procedure for pithing in Exercise 9, Section G.1 and proper use of the physiograph and stimulator in Exercise 9, Section G.2.

1. Double-pith the turtle and remove the ventral shell.
2. Carefully remove the mediastinum and pericardial sac.

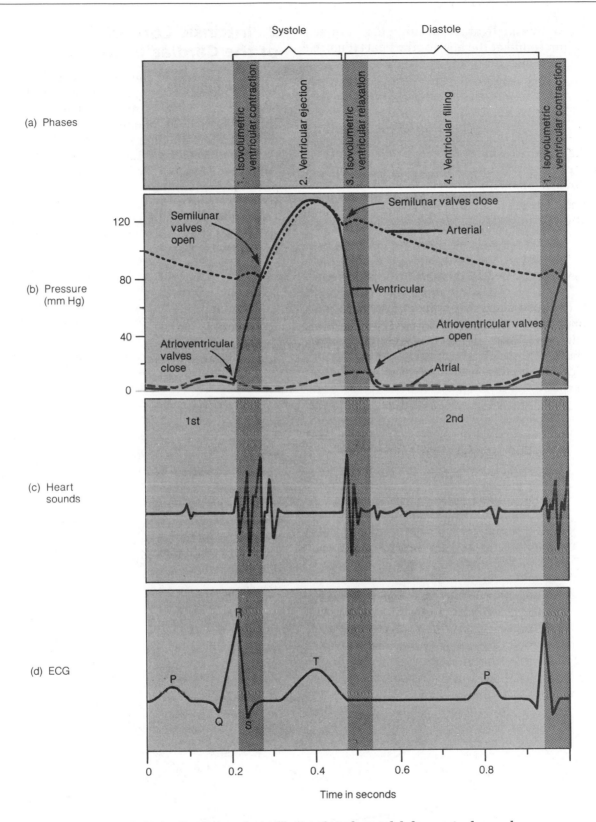

FIGURE 19.1 **Cardiac cycle. (a) Phases. (b) Left atrial, left ventricular, and arterial (aortic) pressure changes along with opening and closure of valves during cardiac cycle. (c) Heart sounds related to cardiac cycle. (d) Tracing of the lead II electrocardiogram (ECG) recording related to cardiac cycle.**

3. Tie a thread ligature around the cardiac frenulum found at the apex of the heart (Figure 19.2) and connect it to a force transducer.

4. Keep just enough tension on the thread to have a force tracing on the physiograph.

5. Cut the frenulum *distal to* the thread.

6. Tie a second thread ligature to either atrium on the posterior side of the heart and connect it to a second transducer. Again regulate the tension in a manner similar to that for the ventricle.

7. Keep the heart moist with Krebs-Ringer's solution throughout the experiment.

1. Cardiac Cycle

Note the normal cardiac cycle. Observe the relationship of atrial systole and diastole to ventricular systole and diastole. Attach the tracing on the physiograph in the space provided in Section B.1 of the Laboratory Report Results and explain the tracing.

2. Intrinsic Control of the Cardiac Cycle

Intrinsic control of the cardiac cycle refers to control mechanisms arising totally within the heart, devoid of any influence from nerves or hormones or both. The major intrinsic control mechanism is **Starling's Law of the Heart.** Simply stated Starling's Law says that the heart will pump out all of the blood it receives, within physiological limits.

1. Place minimal tension on the ventricle by regulating the tension of the ligature tied to the cardiac frenulum.

2. While continuously recording, increase the tension on the ventricle in stepwise increments by raising the height of the transducer on its stand. Allow several beats at each tension setting.

3. Return the heart to its original tension setting when the contraction strength starts to diminish.

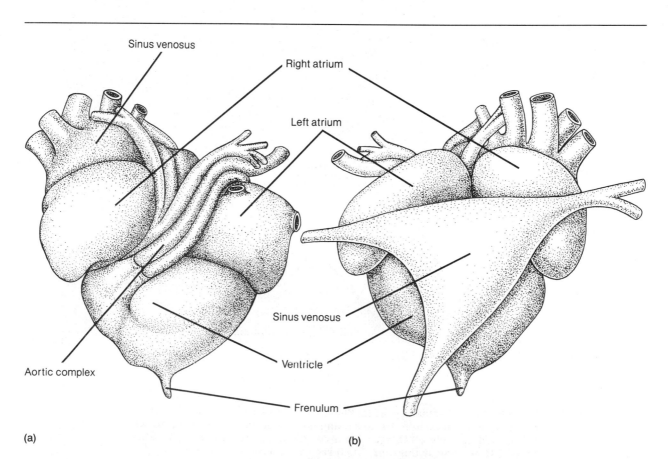

(a)   (b)

FIGURE 19.2 Turtle heart. (a) Ventral view. (b) Dorsal view.

4. Graph the relationship between resting tension and developed tension in Section B.2 of the Laboratory Report Results and explain your observations.

3. Extrinsic Control of the Cardiac Cycle

Extrinsic control of the cardiac cycle is accomplished through the influences of hormones of the adrenal medulla and the autonomic nervous system. The parasympathetic nervous system innervates the heart through the vagus nerves, while the sympathetic nervous system innervates the heart through branches of the stellate and cervical ganglia.

1. Expose the right and left vagus nerves in the neck of the turtle. Place a ligature under each nerve. *Do not tie.*

2. While continuously recording, stimulate the right vagus with varying strengths of stimuli at a frequency of 25 per second and a duration of 2 milliseconds (msec). Stimulate for approximately 30 seconds at each strength.

3. Repeat the above procedure with the left vagus after allowing a period of 2 to 3 minutes for recovery.

4. Attach the tracings in the space provided in Section B.3a of the Laboratory Report Results and explain your observations.

5. After allowing several minutes for recovery, apply a 1:1000 solution of acetylcholine to the surface of the heart.

6. Monitor the changes, if any, in the cardiac cycle for 2 to 3 minutes and then rinse with Krebs-Ringer's solution. Allow several minutes for recovery.

7. Attach the tracing in the space provided in Section B.3b of the Laboratory Report Results and explain your observations.

8. After recovery, apply a 1:1000 solution of atropine sulfate to the surface of the heart. Note any changes in the cardiac cycle.

9. Attach the tracing in the space provided in Section B.3c of the Laboratory Report Results and explain your observations.

10. Reapply atropine sulfate and immediately follow it with an external application of 1:1000 acetylcholine solution.

11. Note the effects, if any, of acetylcholine after application of atropine.

12. Attach the tracing in the space provided in Section B.3d of the Laboratory Report Results and explain your observations.

13. After another application of atropine sulfate, restimulate the right and left vagi, as previously outlined. Note the changes, if any.

14. Rinse the heart with Krebs-Ringer's solution.

15. Attach the tracing in the space provided in Section B.3e of the Laboratory Report Results and explain your observations.

16. After allowing several minutes for recovery, apply a 1:1000 solution of epinephrine to the external surface of the heart. Note the changes, if any, in the cardiac cycle.

17. Rinse with Krebs-Ringer's solution and allow several minutes for recovery before proceeding to the next section.

18. Attach the tracing in the space provided in Section B.3f of the Laboratory Report Results and explain your observations.

4. Demonstration of Refractory Period

The concept of refractory period in cardiac muscle is the same as that discussed in conjunction with nerve action potential propagation and skeletal muscle contraction. Simply stated a **refractory period** is the period during which a stimulus, regardless of strength, cannot elicit a response.

1. Set the paper drive on the physiograph at one of its highest speeds.

2. While continuously recording, stimulate the ventricle with a single stimulus at each of the points of the contraction curve shown below.

3. Utilize a suprathreshold stimulus and allow several contractions between stimuli.

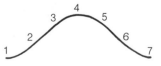

4. Note if an *extrasystole* occurs at any or all of the above points.

5. If an extrasystole does occur, note the relationship between the contraction of the beat

that was stimulated, the extrasystole, and successive beats.

6. Note the points at which a stimulus did not elicit a response.

7. Attach the tracing in the space provided in Section B.4 of the Laboratory Report Results and explain your observations.

C. HEART SOUNDS

The beating of a human heart consists of two well-defined sounds during each cardiac cycle. These two sounds can be easily heard by using an ordinary **stethoscope.** The first sound is created by the closure of the atrioventricular valves soon after ventricular systole begins (see Figure 19.1c). The second sound is created as the semilunar valves close near the end of ventricular systole.

Heart sounds provide valuable information about the valves. Peculiar sounds may be called **murmurs**. Some murmurs are caused by the noise made by a little blood flowing back in an atrium because of improper closure of an atrioventricular valve. Murmurs do not always indicate that the valves are not functioning properly, and many have no clinical significance.

1. Use of Stethoscope

1. The stethoscope should be used in a quiet room.

2. The earpieces of the stethoscope should be cleaned with alcohol just before using and should also be pointed slightly forward when placed in the ears. They will be more comfortable in this position, and it will be easier to hear through them.

3. Listen to the heart sounds of your laboratory partner with the stethoscope at several positions on the chest wall.

4. The first sound is best heard at the apex of the heart, which is located approximately at

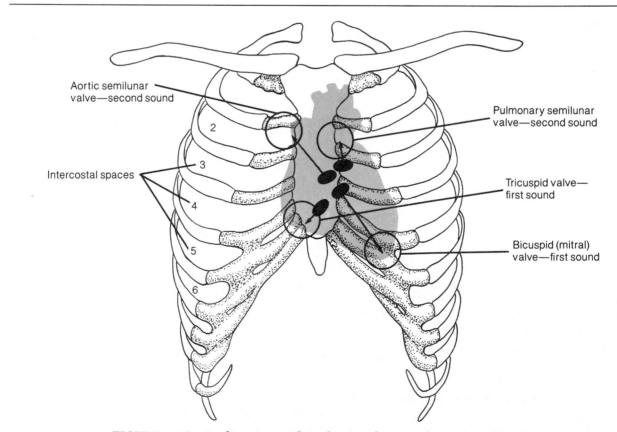

FIGURE 19.3 Surface areas where heart valve sounds are best heard.

the fifth intercostal space at the midline of the clavicles (Figure 19.3).

5. The second sound is best heard over the area between the second right costal cartilage and the second intercostal space on the left side (Figure 19.3).

6. Have your laboratory partner exercise by running in place about 25 steps. Listen to his or her heart sounds again.

7. Answer all questions pertaining to Section C in the Laboratory Report Results.

D. PULSE RATE

During ventricular systole, a wave of pressure, called **pulse**, is produced in the arteries due to ventricular contraction. The pulse rate and heart rate are essentially the same. The pulse can be felt readily where an artery is near the surface of the skin and over the surface of a bone. Pulse rates vary considerably in individuals because of time of day, temperature, emotions, stress, and other factors. The normal adult pulse rate of the heart at rest is within a range of 72 to 80 beats per minute. With practice you can learn to take accurate pulse rates by counting the beats per 15 seconds and multiplying by 4 to obtain beats per minute. The term **tachycardia** (tak′-ē-KAR-dē-a) is applied to a rapid heart rate or pulse rate. **Bradycardia** (brād-ē-KAR-dē-a) indicates a slow heart rate or pulse rate.

Although the pulse may be detected in most surface arteries, the pulse rate is usually determined on the **radial artery** of the wrist.

1. Radial Pulse

1. Using your index and middle fingers palpate your laboratory partner's radial artery.

2. The thumb should never be used because it has its own prominent pulse.

3. Palpate the area behind your partner's thumb just inside the bony prominence on the lateral aspect of the wrist.

4. Do not apply too much pressure.

5. Count the pulse, change positions, and record your results in Section D in the Laboratory Report Results.

6. Calculate the **median pulse rate** of the entire class.

2. Carotid Pulse

1. Using the same fingers that you used for the radial pulse, place them on either side of your partner's larynx.

2. *Gently* press downward and toward the back until you feel the pulse. You must feel the pulse clearly with at least two fingers, so adjust your hand accordingly.

3. The radial and carotid pulse can be compared under the following conditions: (a) sitting quietly, (b) standing quietly, (c) right after walking 60 steps, (d) right after running in place 60 steps. Notice how long it takes the pulse to return to normal after the walking and running exercises.

4. Record your results in Section D in the Laboratory Report Results.

5. Compare you radial and carotid pulses in the table provided.

E. CONDUCTION SYSTEM AND ELECTROCARDIOGRAM

The heart is innervated by the autonomic nervous system (ANS) which modulates, but does not initiate, the cardiac cycle. The heart can continue to contract if separated from the ANS. This is possible because the heart has an intrinsic pacemaker termed the **sinoatrial (SA) node.** The sinoatrial node is connected to a series of specialized muscle cells termed the **cardiac conduction system.** This distributes the electrical impulses that stimulate the cardiac muscle cells to contract.

The sinoatrial node is located in the right atrial wall, inferior to the opening of the superior vena cava. Once an action potential is initiated by this node, the impulse spreads out over both atria, causing them to contract and, at the same time, depolarizing the **atrioventricular (AV) node** near the inferior portion of the interatrial septum. From the atrioventricular node, a tract of conducting fibers called the **atrioventricular (AV) bundle** extends to the top of the interventricular septum and continues down both sides of the septum as the **right** and **left bundle branches.** The atrioventricular bundle distributes the electrical impulses over the medial surfaces of the ventricles. Actual contraction of the ventricles is stimulated by **conduc-**

tion myofibers (**Purkinje fibers**) that emerge from the bundle branches and pass into the cells of the ventricular myocardium.

Label the components of the conduction system in Figure 19.4.

These impulses generate electrical currents that may be detected on the surface of the body. An **electrocardiogram (ECG** or **EKG)** is a recording of the electrical changes accompanying each cardiac cycle. An **electrocardiograph** is the instrument used to record these changes. As the electrical impulses are transmitted throughout the cardiac conduction system and myocardial cells, a different electrical impulse is generated. These impulses are transmitted from the electrodes to a recording needle that graphs the impulses as a series of up-and-down waves called **deflection waves** (see Figure 19.5).

1. Electrocardiogram Readings

In a typical record (Figure 19.5), three clearly recognizable waves accompany each cardiac cycle. The electrocardiogram recording represents only the electrical events of the cardiac

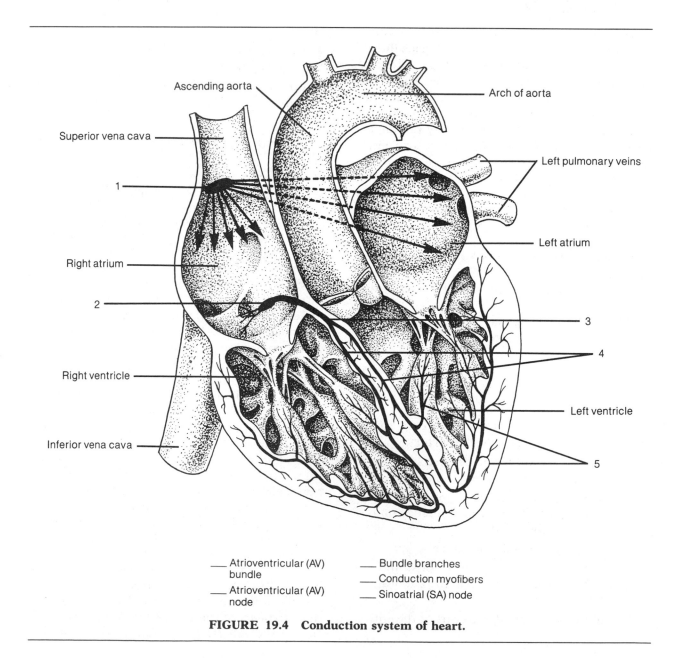

Ascending aorta
Arch of aorta
Superior vena cava
Left pulmonary veins
1
Left atrium
Right atrium
2
3
4
Right ventricle
Left ventricle
Inferior vena cava
5

___ Atrioventricular (AV) bundle
___ Atrioventricular (AV) node
___ Bundle branches
___ Conduction myofibers
___ Sinoatrial (SA) node

FIGURE 19.4 Conduction system of heart.

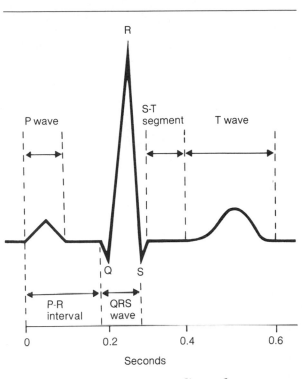

FIGURE 19.5 Recordings of a normal electrocardiogram (ECG).

cycle, *not the mechanical events.* The first wave, the **P wave,** indicates depolarization of the atria. A deflection wave, called the **QRS complex,** represents atrial repolarization and ventricular depolarization. The time interval between the P wave and the QRS complex, termed the *P-R interval,* represents the time needed for electrical impulses to pass from the sinoatrial node to the ventricular myocardium. The third deflection is the **T wave,** indicating ventricular repolarization. No deflection appears for atrial repolarization because depolarization of the ventricles masks this event.

In reading and interpreting an electrocardiogram, you must note the *lead* from which the electrocardiogram was recorded, the size of the deflection waves, and certain time intervals. An attempt will not be made to interpret an electrocardiogram, but only to become familiar with a normal ECG. The ECG is invaluable in diagnosing abnormal cardiac rhythms and conducting patterns, detecting the presence of fetal life, determining the presence of more than one fetus, and following the course of recovery from a heart attack.

In the following procedure a physiograph-type polygraph is used, but an electrocardiograph or oscilloscope may also be used (Figure 19.6a).

2. Use of Physiograph

In recording the electrocardiogram, we will utilize only the standard *three limb leads.* A **lead** is defined as two electrodes working in pairs. **Electrodes** are sensing devices that are made of sensitive metal plates or small rods that can detect electrophysiological phenomena such as changes in electrical potential of the skin or nerves (see Exercise 9). Usually only two electrodes will be in actual use at any one time. The third electrode will be automatically switched off by the **lead-selector switch** of the physiograph. The three standard limb leads most commonly used in electrocardiography are:

Lead	Electrodes Used
I	Right wrist and left wrist
II	Right wrist and left ankle
III	Left wrist and left ankle

For most general purposes three leads are usually used. However, electrocardiologists use additional leads, including several chest wall electrodes (see Figure 19.6b). These leads are positioned around the chest, and encircle the heart so that there are six intersecting lines on a horizontal plane through the atrioventricular node.

The procedure for recording electrocardiograms using the physiograph is as follows:

1. Either you or your laboratory partner should lie on a table or cot, roll down long stockings or socks to the ankles, and remove all wristwatches, rings, and bracelets.

2. Electrode cream, jelly, or saline paste is applied to the skin only where the electrode will make contact, such as to the inner forearm just above the wrists and to the inside of the legs just above the ankles.

3. The cream is then applied on the surface of the electrode plates, which are then fastened securely to the limb area surfaces with rubber straps.

4. Firmly connect the proper end of the electrode cables to the electrode plates and con-

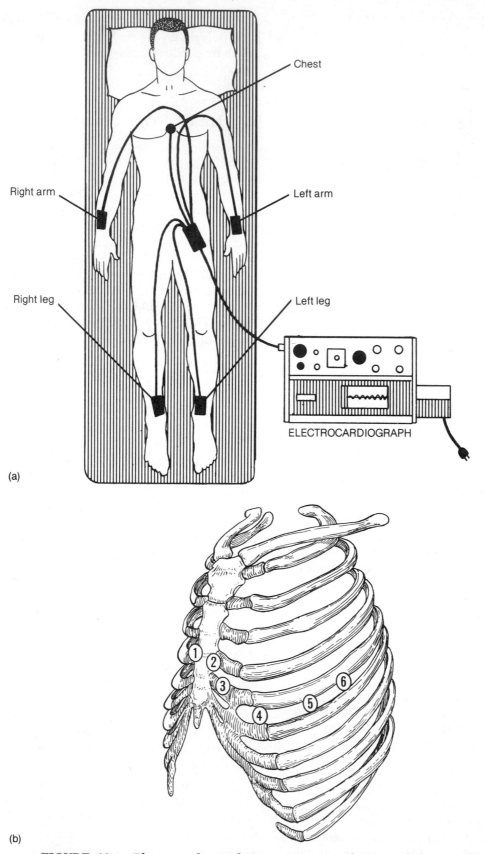

(a)

(b)

FIGURE 19.6 Electrocardiograph. (a) Connections. (b) Normal chest wall leads.

nect the other end to a cardiac preamplifier or to a self-contained electrocardiograph.

5. After you apply the electrodes and connect the instrument to the subject, ascertain the following before actually recording:

    a. Recording power switch is on.

    b. Paper is sufficient for the entire recording, and the pen is centered properly on the paper with ink flowing freely.

    c. Preamplifier sensitivity has been set at 10 mm per millivolt.

    d. Subject is lying quietly and is relaxed.

Note: Usually five or six ECG complex recordings from each lead are sufficient. All electrocardiographers have chosen a standard paper speed of 25 mm per second.

6. When the recording is finished, disconnect the leads from the subject and remove the electrodes, cleaning off the excess cream or paste.

7. Identify and letter the P, QRS, and T waves, and compare the waves with those shown in Figure 19.5.

8. Calculate the duration of the waves and the P-R interval. Attach this recording to Section E in the Laboratory Report Results.

F. BLOOD PRESSURE (AUSCULTATION METHOD)

Blood pressure, clinically, refers to the pressure only in the large arteries even though the term blood pressure may be defined as the pressure exerted by the blood on the walls of any blood vessel. Blood pressure is normally taken in the brachial artery and is measured by an instrument called a **sphygmomanometer** (sfig'-mō-ma-NOM-e-ter) (*sphygmo* = pulse).

    A commonly used sphygmomanometer (see Figure 19.7) consists of an inflatable rubber cuff attached by a rubber tube to a compressible hand pump or bulb. Another tube attaches to a cuff and to a mercury column marked off in millimeters that measures the pressure in millimeters of mercury (mm Hg).

    Stethoscopes are used in conjunction with the sphygmomanometers to locate the pulse. Pulse sounds are difficult to hear if the room is noisy.

    The procedure for determining blood pressure using the sphygmomanometer is as follows:

FIGURE 19.7 Use of sphygmomanometer.

1. Either you or your laboratory partner should be comfortably seated, at ease, with your arm bared, slightly flexed, abducted, and perfectly relaxed.

2. Wrap the deflated cuff of the sphygmomanometer around the arm with the lower edge about 1 in. above the antecubital space. Close the valve on the neck of the rubber bulb.

3. Clean the earpieces of the stethoscope with alcohol before using it. Using the bell of the stethoscope, find the pulse in the brachial artery just above the bend of the elbow, on the inner margin of the biceps brachii muscle.

4. Inflate the cuff by squeezing the bulb until the air pressure within it just exceeds 170 mm Hg. At this point the wall of the brachial artery is compressed tightly, and no blood can flow through.

5. Place the ball of the stethoscope firmly over the brachial artery and, while watching the pressure gauge, slowly turn the valve, releasing air from the cuff. Listen carefully as you watch the pressure fall and note the pressure on the gauge when you hear a loud, rapping noise. This is the **systolic pressure** reading. These rapping or thumping sounds that are heard are clinically called **Korotkoff** (kō-ROT-kof) **sounds.** Continue listening as the pressure

falls. The pressure recorded on the mercury column when the sounds become faint or disappear is the **diastolic pressure** reading. It measures the force of blood in arteries during ventricular relaxation and specifically reflects the peripheral resistance of the arteries.

6. Repeat this procedure for both readings two or three times to see if you get consistent results. Allow a few minutes between readings. Record all results in Section F in the Laboratory Report Results.

7. Have your partner stand and record his or her blood pressure several times for each arm. Record all results in the table provided in Section F in the Laboratory Report Results.

8. Now have your partner do some exercise, such as running in place 40 or 50 steps, and measure the blood pressure again. Have your partner run in place again and measure his or her blood pressure using the other arm. Record all results in the table provided in Section F in the Laboratory Report Results.

The average blood pressure of a young adult is about 120 mm Hg systolic and 80 mm Hg diastolic, abbreviated to 120/80. The difference between systolic and diastolic pressure is called **pulse pressure,** which averages 40 mm Hg and indicates whether or not the arteries are functioning properly. The normal ratio of systolic pressure to diastolic pressure to pulse pressure is 3:2:1. Record the pulse pressure in the table provided in Section F in the Laboratory Report Results.

LABORATORY REPORT QUESTIONS (PAGE 423)

20 | LYMPHATIC SYSTEM

The **lymphatic** (lim-FAT-ik) **system** is composed of lymph, lymphatics, small masses of lymphoid tissue called lymph nodes, and three organs: tonsils, thymus gland, and spleen.

A. STRUCTURE

The lymphatic system consists of tiny blind-ended vessels called **lymph capillaries** that originate in interstitial spaces and converge and enlarge to become lymph vessels called **lymphatics.** Lymphatics have thinner walls and more valves than veins, and all lymphatics eventually merge into two main channels, the **thoracic duct** and the **right lymphatic duct.** Lying along the length of the lymphatics are oval or bean-shaped structures called **lymph nodes.** The lymph circulates through these nodes and is processed by fixed phagocytic cells that line the sinuses of the nodes. These cells, called macrophages, filter the lymph of microorganisms, dirt, and cellular debris. The nodes also produce lymphocytes, plasma cells, or both. The plasma cells produce antibodies.

The lymphatic system and its relationship to the cardiovascular system can be seen in Figure 20.1. Using your textbook or charts for reference, label Figure 20.2.

Lymphangiography (lim-fan-jē-OG-ra-fē) is the X-ray examination of lymphatic vessels and lymph organs after they are filled with a radiopaque substance. The X ray, called a **lymphangiogram,** is useful for detecting edema and carcinomas and for localizing lymph nodes for surgical treatment or radiotherapy. A normal lymphangiogram is shown in Figure 20.3.

B. FUNCTIONS

The major function of the lymphatic system is to recover valuable proteins that escape from blood capillaries, thereby maintaining osmotic balance between blood and tissue cells. In addition, the system functions to transport fats from the digestive tract to the blood and fight foreign invasion by producing phagocytes and antibody-producing cells.

LABORATORY REPORT QUESTIONS (PAGE 425)

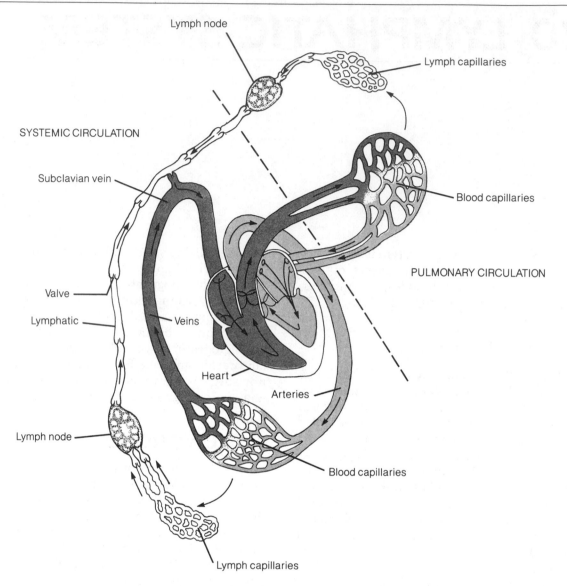

FIGURE 20.1 Relationship of lymphatic system to cardiovascular system.

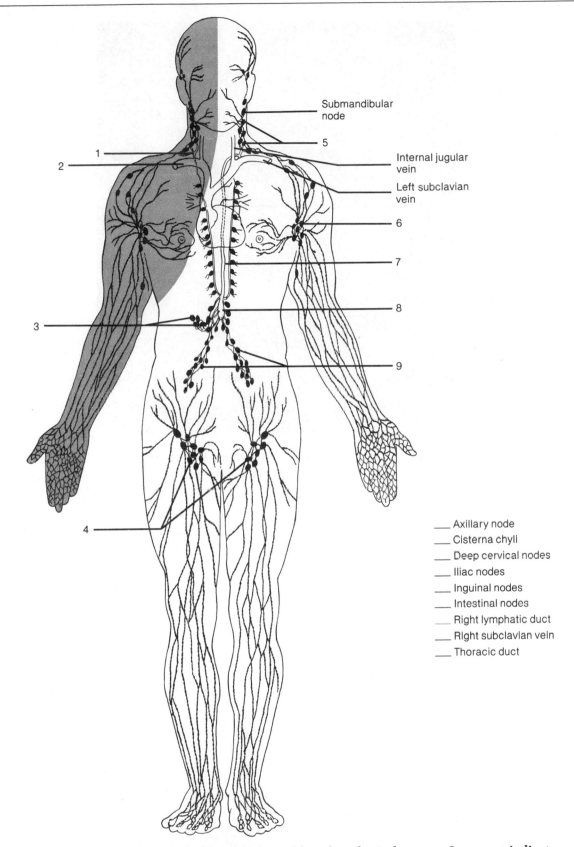

Submandibular
node

5

Internal jugular
vein

Left subclavian
vein

6

7

8

9

___ Axillary node
___ Cisterna chyli
___ Deep cervical nodes
___ Iliac nodes
___ Inguinal nodes
___ Intestinal nodes
___ Right lymphatic duct
___ Right subclavian vein
___ Thoracic duct

FIGURE 20.2 Location of principal lymphatics and lymph nodes in humans. Gray area indicates portions of body drained by right lymphatic duct. All other areas of body are drained by thoracic duct.

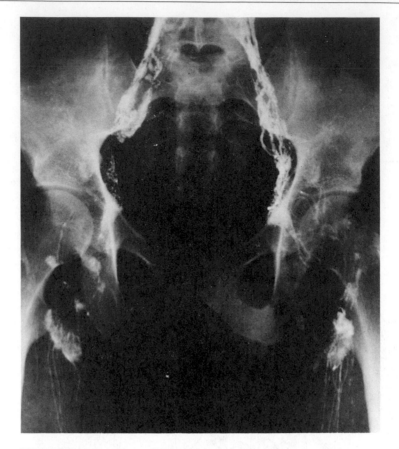

**FIGURE 20.3   Normal lymphangiogram of upper thighs
and pelvis. Can you identify the lymphatics and lymph nodes?**

21 | RESPIRATORY SYSTEM

The **respiratory system** consists of organs that exchange gases between the atmosphere and blood. These organs are the nose, pharynx, larynx, trachea, bronchi, and lungs (Figure 21.1). The blood then transports these gases between the lungs and the cells. **Respiration** is the overall exchange of gases between the atmosphere, blood, and cells.

Using your textbook, charts, or models for reference, label Figure 21.1.

A. ORGANS OF RESPIRATORY SYSTEM

1. Nose

The **nose** has an external portion and an internal portion found inside the skull. Both the external and internal nose are divided internally by a vertical partition called the **nasal septum.** The undersurface of the external nose contains two openings called the **nostrils (external nares)** (NA-rēz). The internal nose is formed by the ethmoid, maxillae, inferior conchae, and palatine bones and communicates with the paranasal sinuses. Sometimes the palatine and maxillary bones fail to fuse completely during embryonic life and the condition called **cleft palate** results. The interior of the nose is the **nasal cavity,** which communicates with the throat through two openings, the **internal nares (choanae).** The nasal cavity is separated from the **oral cavity** below it by the palate, which is composed of the anterior, bony **hard palate** and the posterior muscular **soft palate.** The anterior portion of the nasal cavity, just inside the nostrils, is called the **vestibule,** which is lined with coarse hairs. Three shelves formed by

projections of the **superior, middle,** and **inferior nasal conchae** (KON-kē) extend out of the lateral wall of each nasal cavity. The conchae almost reach the nasal septum and subdivide each nasal cavity into a series of groovelike passageways called the **superior, middle,** and **inferior meatuses.**

The interior structures of the nose are specialized for three functions: (1) incoming air is warmed, moistened, and filtered; (2) olfactory stimuli are received; and (3) large hollow resonating chambers are provided for speech sounds. In addition, mucous membranes trap dust particles and, with the help of cilia, move unwanted particles to the throat for elimination.

Label the hard palate, inferior meatus, inferior nasal concha, internal naris, middle meatus, middle nasal concha, nasal cavity, oral cavity, soft palate, superior meatus, superior nasal concha, and vestibule in Figure 21.2.

The surface anatomy of the nose is shown in Figure 21.3.

2. Pharynx

The **pharynx** (FAR-inks) (throat) is a somewhat funnel-shaped tube about 13 cm (5 in.) long. Lying in back of the nasal and oral cavities and just in front of the cervical vertebrae, the pharynx is a passageway for air and food and a resonating chamber for speech sounds.

The pharynx is composed of a superior portion, called the **nasopharynx,** a middle portion, the **oropharynx,** and an inferior portion, the **laryngopharynx** (la-rin'-gō-FAR-inks). The nasopharynx consists of **pseudostratified epithelium** and has four openings in its wall: two **internal nares** plus two openings into the **auditory (eustachian) tubes.** The nasopharynx

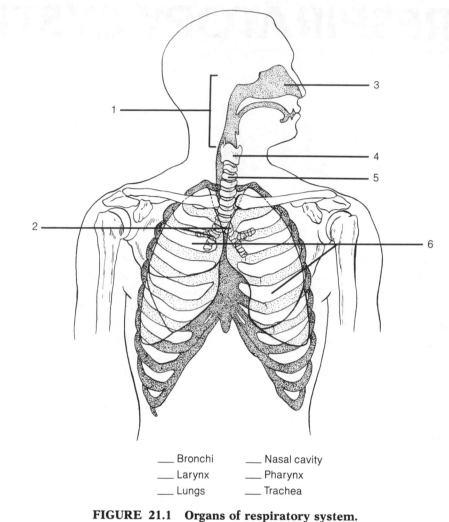

___ Bronchi   ___ Nasal cavity

___ Larynx   ___ Pharynx

___ Lungs   ___ Trachea

FIGURE 21.1   Organs of respiratory system.

also contains the **pharyngeal tonsil (adenoid).** The oropharynx is lined by **stratified squamous epithelium** and receives one opening: the **fauces (FAW-sēz).** The oropharynx contains the **palatine** and **lingual tonsils.** The laryngopharynx is also lined by **stratified squamous epithelium** and becomes continuous with the esophagus posteriorly and the larynx anteriorly.

Label the laryngopharynx, nasopharynx, oropharynx, palatine tonsil, and pharyngeal tonsil in Figure 21.2.

3. Larynx

The **larynx** (voice box) is a short passageway connecting the laryngopharynx with the trachea. Its wall is supported by nine pieces of cartilage.

a. **Thyroid cartilage (Adam's apple)**—Large anterior piece that gives larynx its triangular shape.

b. **Epiglottis**—Leaf-shaped cartilage on top of larynx that closes off the larynx so that foods and liquids are routed into the esophagus and kept out of the respiratory system.

c. **Cricoid** (KRĪ-koyd) **cartilage**—Ring of cartilage forming the inferior portion of the larynx that is attached to the first ring of tracheal cartilage.

d. **Arytenoid** (ar-i-TĒ-noyd) **cartilage**—Paired, pyramid-shaped cartilages at superior border of cricoid cartilage that attach vocal folds to pharyngeal muscles.

e. **Corniculate** (kor-NIK-yoo-lāt) **cartilages**—Paired, cone-shaped cartilages at apex of arytenoid cartilages.

f. **Cuneiform** (kyoo-NĒ-i-form) **cartilages**—Paired, rod-shaped cartilages in the mucous

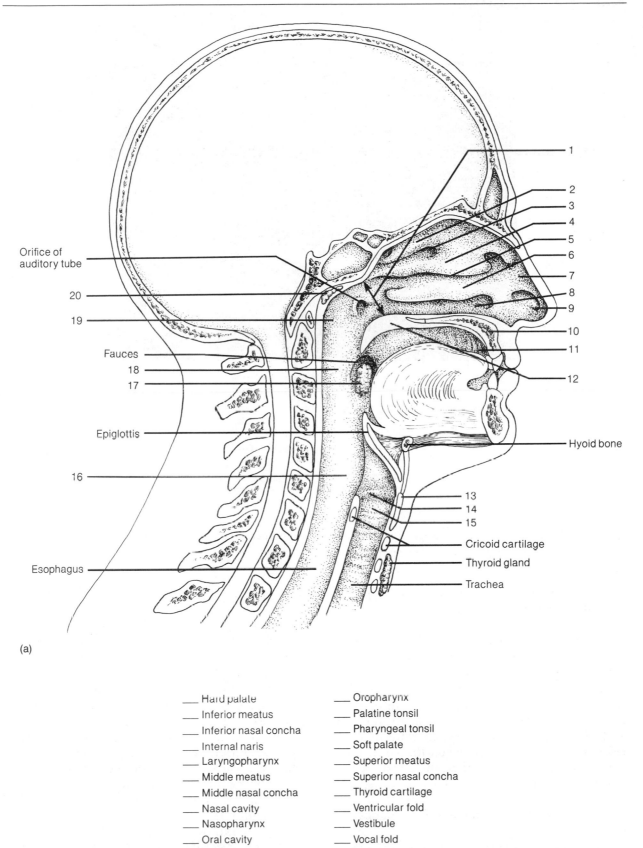

Orifice of
auditory tube

Fauces

Epiglottis

Esophagus

Hyoid bone

Cricoid cartilage

Thyroid gland

Trachea

(a)

___ Hard palate
___ Inferior meatus
___ Inferior nasal concha
___ Internal naris
___ Laryngopharynx
___ Middle meatus
___ Middle nasal concha
___ Nasal cavity
___ Nasopharynx
___ Oral cavity

___ Oropharynx
___ Palatine tonsil
___ Pharyngeal tonsil
___ Soft palate
___ Superior meatus
___ Superior nasal concha
___ Thyroid cartilage
___ Ventricular fold
___ Vestibule
___ Vocal fold

FIGURE 21.2 Upper respiratory system as seen in midsagittal section. (a) Diagram.

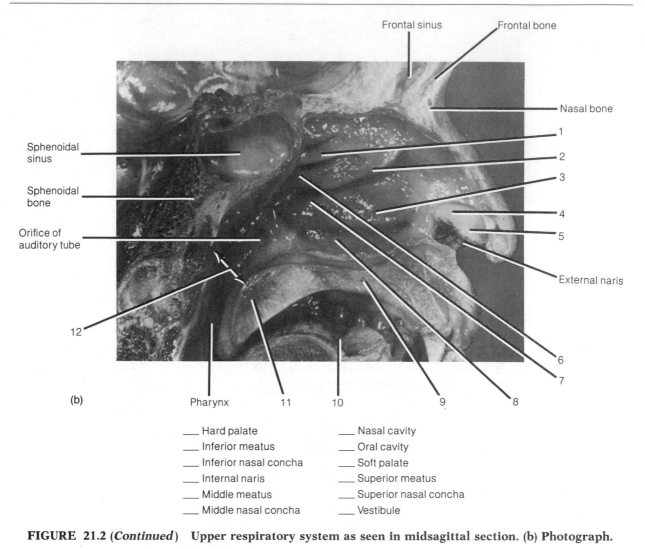

Frontal sinus
Frontal bone
Nasal bone
1
2
3
4
5
External naris
6
7

Sphenoidal sinus
Sphenoidal bone
Orifice of auditory tube
12

(b)
Pharynx   11   10   9   8

___ Hard palate
___ Inferior meatus
___ Inferior nasal concha
___ Internal naris
___ Middle meatus
___ Middle nasal concha

___ Nasal cavity
___ Oral cavity
___ Soft palate
___ Superior meatus
___ Superior nasal concha
___ Vestibule

FIGURE 21.2 (*Continued*)   Upper respiratory system as seen in midsagittal section. (b) Photograph.

membrane fold that connects the epiglottis to the arytenoid cartilages.

With the aid of your textbook, label the laryngeal cartilages shown in Figure 21.4. Also label the thyroid cartilage in Figure 21.2.

The mucous membrane of the larynx is arranged into two pairs of folds, an upper pair called the **ventricular folds (false vocal cords)** and a lower pair called the **vocal folds (true vocal cords).** The space between the vocal folds when they are apart is called the **glottis.** Movement of the vocal folds produces sounds; variations in pitch result from (1) varying degrees of tension and (2) varying lengths in males and females.

With the aid of your textbook, label the ventricular folds, vocal folds, and glottis in Figure 21.5. Also label the ventricular and vocal folds in Figure 21.2.

4. Trachea

The **trachea** (TRĀ-kē-a) (windpipe) is a tubular air passageway about 12 cm (4½ in.) in length and 2.5 cm (1 in.) in diameter. It lies in front of the esophagus and, at its inferior end (T5), divides into right and left primary bronchi (Figure 21.6). The epithelium of the trachea consists of **pseudostratified epithelium.** This epithelium consists of ciliated columnar cells, goblet cells, and basal cells. The epithelium offers the same protection against dust as the membrane lining the larynx.

Obtain a prepared slide of pseudostratified epithelium from the trachea, and, with the aid of your textbook, label the ciliated columnar cells, cilia, goblet cells, and basal cells in Figure 21.7.

The trachea consists of smooth muscle, elastic connective tissue, and incomplete **rings**

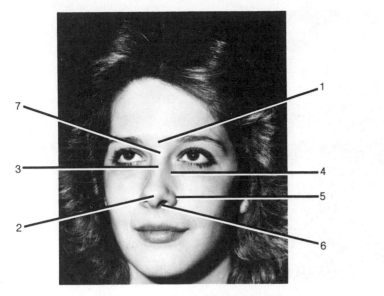

1. **Root.** Superior attachment of nose at forehead located between eyes.
2. **Apex.** Tip of nose.
3. **Dorsum nasi.** Rounded anterior border connecting root and apex; in profile, may be straight, convex, concave, or wavy.
4. **Nasofacial angle.** Point at which side of nose blends with tissues of face.
5. **Ala.** Convex flared portion of inferior lateral surface; unites with upper lip.
6. **External nares.** External openings into nose.
7. **Bridge.** Superior portion of dorsum nasi, superficial to nasal bones.

FIGURE 21.3 Surface anatomy of nose.

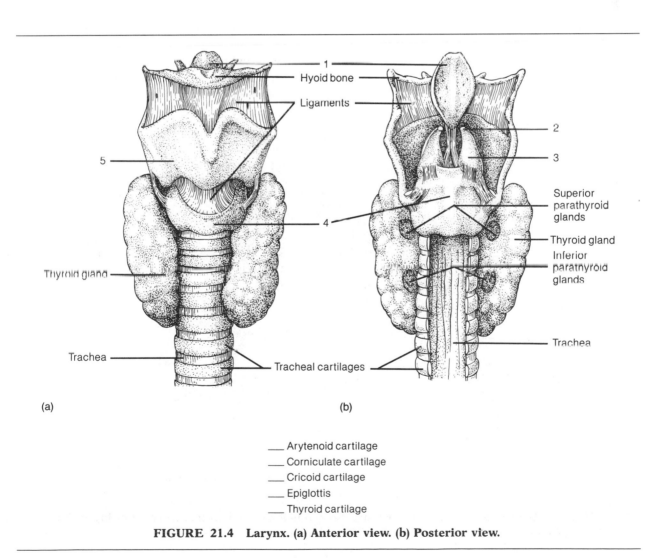

(a)   (b)

___ Arytenoid cartilage
___ Corniculate cartilage
___ Cricoid cartilage
___ Epiglottis
___ Thyroid cartilage

FIGURE 21.4 Larynx. (a) Anterior view. (b) Posterior view.

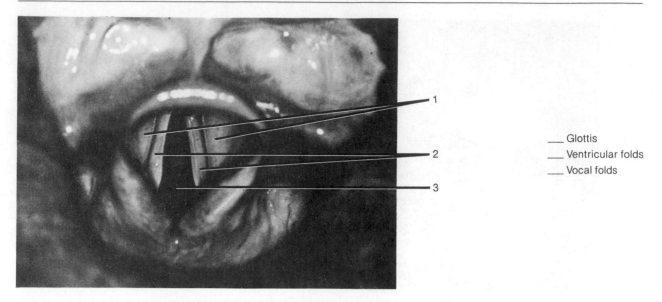

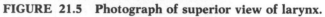

___ Glottis
___ Ventricular folds
___ Vocal folds

FIGURE 21.5   Photograph of superior view of larynx.

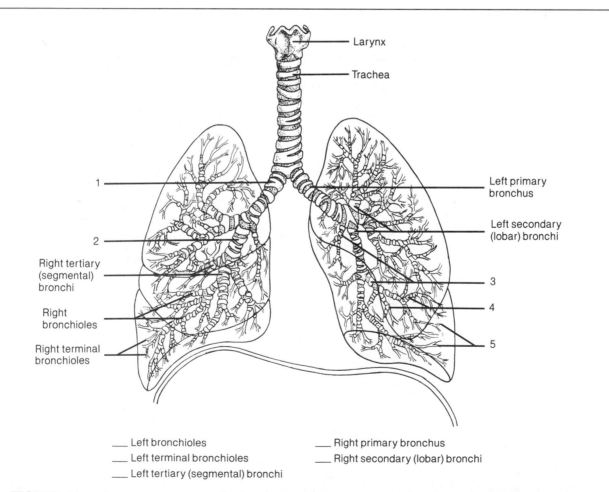

Larynx

Trachea

1

2

Right tertiary
(segmental)
bronchi

Right
bronchioles

Right terminal
bronchioles

Left primary
bronchus

Left secondary
(lobar) bronchi

3

4

5

___ Left bronchioles   ___ Right primary bronchus
___ Left terminal bronchioles   ___ Right secondary (lobar) bronchi
___ Left tertiary (segmental) bronchi

FIGURE 21.6   Air passageways to the lungs. Shown is the bronchial tree in relationship to lungs.

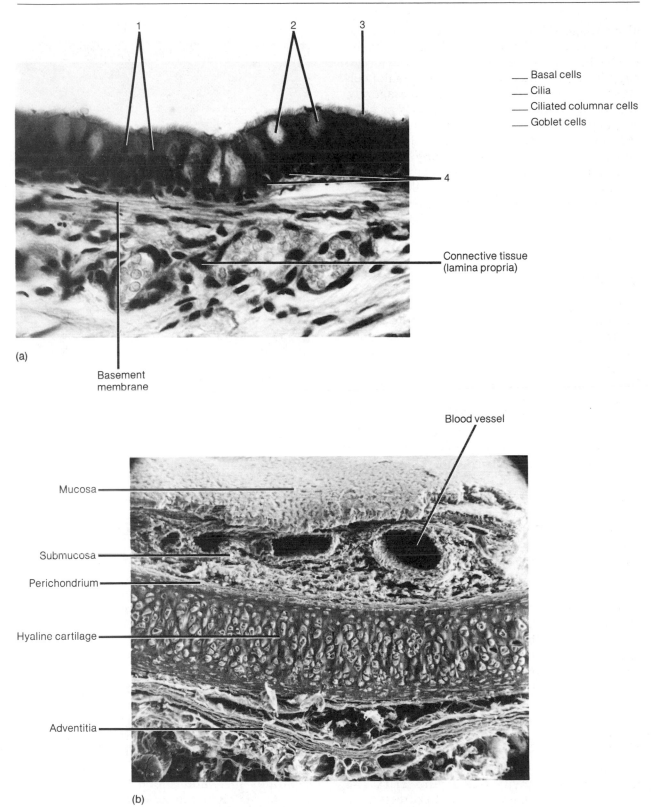

_____ Basal cells
_____ Cilia
_____ Ciliated columnar cells
_____ Goblet cells

Connective tissue
(lamina propria)

(a)

Basement
membrane

Blood vessel

Mucosa

Submucosa

Perichondrium

Hyaline cartilage

Adventitia

(b)

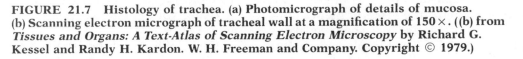

FIGURE 21.7 **Histology of trachea. (a) Photomicrograph of details of mucosa.
(b) Scanning electron micrograph of tracheal wall at a magnification of 150×. ((b) from
Tissues and Organs: A Text-Atlas of Scanning Electron Microscopy by Richard G.
Kessel and Randy H. Kardon. W. H. Freeman and Company. Copyright © 1979.)**

of cartilage shaped like a series of letter Cs. The open ends of the Cs are held together by the **trachealis muscle.** The cartilage provides a rigid support so that the tracheal wall does not collapse inward and obstruct the air passageway, and, because the open parts of the Cs face the esophagus, the latter can expand into the trachea during swallowing. If the trachea should become obstructed, a **tracheostomy** (trā-kē-OS-tō-mē) may be performed. Another method of opening the air passageway is called **intubation,** in which a tube is passed into the mouth and down through the larynx and the trachea.

5. Bronchi

The trachea terminates by dividing into a **right primary bronchus** (BRON-kus), going to the right lung, and a **left primary bronchus,** going to the left lung. They continue dividing in the lungs into smaller bronchi, the **secondary (lobar) bronchi** (BRON-kē), one for each lobe of the lung. These bronchi, in turn, continue dividing into still smaller bronchi called **tertiary (segmental) bronchi,** which divide into **bronchioles.** The next division is into even smaller tubes called **terminal bronchioles.** This entire branching structure of the trachea is commonly referred to as the **bronchial tree.**

Label Figure 21.6.

Bronchography (brong-KOG-ra-fē) is a technique for examining the bronchial tree. With this procedure, an intratracheal catheter is passed transorally or transnasally through the glottis into the trachea. Then an iodinated medium is introduced, by means of gravity, into the trachea and distributed through the bronchial branches. Roentgenograms of the chest in various positions are taken and the developed film, called a **bronchogram,** provides a picture of the bronchial tree (Figure 21.8).

6. Lungs

The **lungs** are paired, cone-shaped organs lying in the thoracic cavity (see Figure 21.1). The **pleural membrane** encloses and protects each lung. Whereas the **parietal pleura** lines the wall of the thoracic cavity, the **visceral pleura** covers the lungs; the potential space between parietal and visceral pleurae, the **pleural cavity,** contains a lubricating fluid to reduce friction as the lungs expand and recoil.

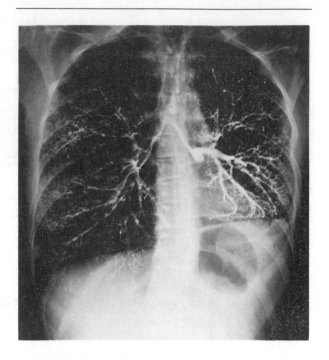

FIGURE 21.8   Bronchogram of lungs.

Major surface features of the lungs include:

a. **Base**—Broad inferior portion resting on diaphragm.
b. **Apex**—Narrow superior portion just above clavicles.
c. **Costal surface**—Surface lying against ribs.
d. **Mediastinal surface**—Medial surface.
e. **Hilus**—Vertical slit in mediastinal surface through which bronchial tubes, blood vessels, lymphatics, and nerves enter and exit the lung.
f. **Cardiac notch**—Medial concavity in left lung in which heart lies.

Each lung is divided into **lobes** by one or more **fissures.** The right lung has three lobes, **superior, middle,** and **inferior;** the left lung has two lobes, **superior** and **inferior.** The **horizontal fissure** separates the superior lobe from the middle lobe in the right lung; an **oblique fissure** separates the middle lobe from the inferior lobe in the right lung and the superior lobe from the inferior lobe in the left lung.

Using your textbook as a reference, label Figure 21.9a.

Each lobe of a lung is divided into many small compartments called **lobules.** Each lobule is wrapped in elastic connective tissue and

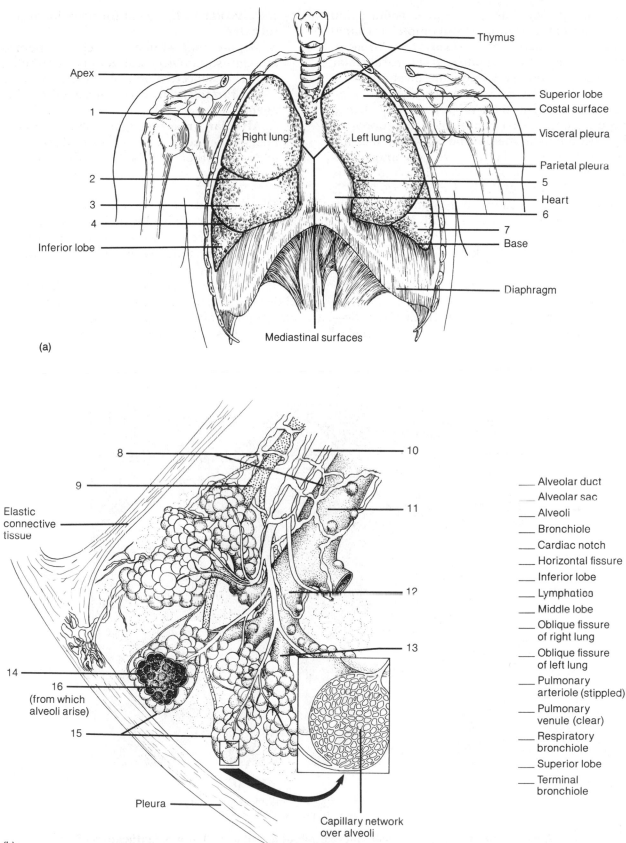

(a)

Thymus

Apex

Superior lobe

Costal surface

1

Right lung

Left lung

Visceral pleura

Parietal pleura

2

5

3

Heart

4

6

Inferior lobe

7

Base

Diaphragm

Mediastinal surfaces

(b)

8

10

9

11

Elastic
connective
tissue

12

13

14

16
(from which
alveoli arise)

15

Pleura

Capillary network
over alveoli

___ Alveolar duct

___ Alveolar sac

___ Alveoli

___ Bronchiole

___ Cardiac notch

___ Horizontal fissure

___ Inferior lobe

___ Lymphatics

___ Middle lobe

___ Oblique fissure
of right lung

___ Oblique fissure
of left lung

___ Pulmonary
arteriole (stippled)

___ Pulmonary
venule (clear)

___ Respiratory
bronchiole

___ Superior lobe

___ Terminal
bronchiole

FIGURE 21.9   Lungs. (a) Coverings and external anatomy. (b) Lobule of lung.

contains a lymphatic, arteriole, venule, and branch from a terminal bronchiole. Terminal bronchioles divide into **respiratory bronchioles,** which, in turn, divide into several **alveolar** (al-VĒ-ō-lar) **ducts.** Around the circumference of alveolar ducts are numerous alveoli and alveolar sacs. **Alveoli** (al-VĒ-ō-lī) are cup-shaped outpouchings lined by epithelium and supported by a thin elastic membrane. **Alveolar sacs** are two or more alveoli that share a common opening. Over the alveoli, an arteriole and venule disperse into a network of capillaries. Gas is exchanged between the lungs and blood by diffusion across the alveoli and the capillary walls.

Using your textbook as a reference, label Figure 21.9b.

The alveolar wall (Figure 21.10) consists of:

a. **Squamous pulmonary epithelial cells—** Large cells that form a continuous lining of the alveolar wall, except for occasional septal cells.

b. **Septal cells—**Cuboidal cells dispersed among squamous pulmonary epithelial cells that secrete a phospholipid substance called *surfactant,* a surface tension-lowering agent.

c. **Alveolar macrophages (dust cells)—** Phagocytic cells that remove dust particles and other debris from the alveolar spaces.

Obtain a slide of normal lung tissue and examine it under high power. Using your textbook as a reference, see if you can identify a terminal bronchiole, respiratory bronchiole, alveolar duct, alveolar sac, and alveoli.

If available, examine several pathological slides of lung tissue, such as slides that show emphysema and lung cancer. Compare your observations to the normal lung tissue.

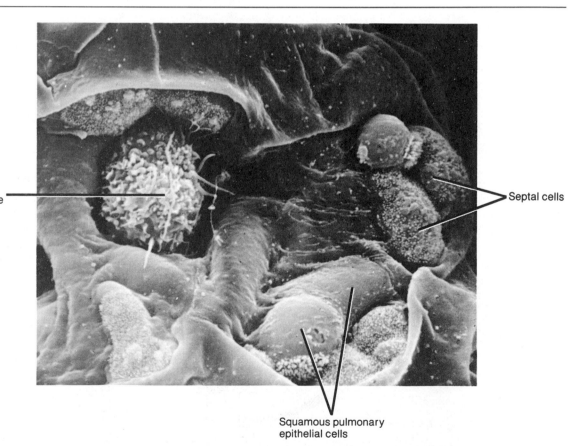

Alveolar macrophage

Septal cells

Squamous pulmonary epithelial cells

FIGURE 21.10   Scanning electron micrograph of alveolar wall at a magnification of 3430×. (From *Tissues and Organs: A Text-Atlas of Scanning Electron Microscopy* by Richard G. Kessel and Randy H. Kardon. W. H. Freeman and Company. Copyright © 1979.)

B. DISSECTION OF SHEEP PLUCK

Preserved sheep pluck consists mainly of a **trachea, bronchi, lungs, heart,** and **great vessels,** and a small portion of the **diaphragm.** It is a good demonstration because it is large and shows the close anatomical correlation between these structures and the systems to which they belong, namely, the respiratory and the cardiovascular systems.

The heart and its great blood vessels have been described in detail in Exercise 17. Pluck can also be used to examine in great detail the trachea and its relationship to the development of the bronchi until they branch into each lung. In addition, this specimen is sufficiently large that the bronchial tree can be exposed by careful dissection. This dissection is done by starting at the primary and secondary bronchi and slowly and carefully removing lung tissue as the tree forms even smaller branches into the lungs.

1. Place the sheep pluck on a dissecting tray and identify the heart, lungs, larynx, trachea, and diaphragm. If a pericardium is present, remove it so that you can examine the surface of the heart.

2. Now examine the larynx, if present. Using Figure 21.4 as a guide, note the large anterior thyroid cartilage, the superior epiglottis, and the inferior cricoid cartilage. See if you can find the vocal folds and glottis.

3. Below the cricoid cartilage, note the trachea, which terminates by bifurcating into the primary bronchi. Note the tracheal cartilages

How many can you count? _____ Are the cartilaginous rings complete from front to

back? _____

Explain. _____

_____

4. Each lung is covered by a pleural membrane that makes the surface appear smooth and glistening. How many lobes are in the right

lung? _____ How many lobes are in the

left lung? _____ Compare the number of

lobes in each lung to human lungs. _____

_____

Palpate a section of lung tissue and palpate the heart. How do they compare in texture? _____

_____

_____

5. Find the pulmonary trunk and note where it divides into right and left pulmonary arteries. Trace each pulmonary artery a short distance into the substance of the lungs. In a similar manner, trace the four pulmonary veins into the lungs.

6. Note where the trachea bifurcates into a right and left primary bronchus. How do the bronchi compare structurally to the trachea?

_____

_____

Continue your dissection into the one lung by following the continuous branching of the secondary and tertiary bronchi and bronchioles until you have exposed the bronchial tree. Note the blood vessels that parallel the bronchial tree.

7. Place a straw into the trachea and blow into it to note the expansion of the lungs.

C. AIR VOLUMES EXCHANGED

The word **respiration** means one inspiration plus one expiration. A normal adult has 14 to 18 respirations in a minute, during which the lungs exchange specific volumes of air with the atmosphere. Pulmonary malfunction usually produces lower-than-normal exchange volumes. A **respirometer (spirometer)** is the instrument commonly used to measure volumes of air exchanged in breathing. Several different respirometers are shown in Figure 21.11.

The Collins respirometer consists of a weighted drum, containing air, inverted over a chamber of water. The air-filled chamber is connected to the subject's mouth by a tube. When the subject inspires, air is removed from the chamber, causing the drum to sink and producing an upward deflection. This deflection is recorded by the stylus on the graph paper on the kymograph (rotating drum). When the subject expires, air is added, causing the drum to rise and producing a downward deflection. These deflections are recorded as a **spirogram** (see Figure 21.12). These spirometric studies measure lung capacities and rates and depths

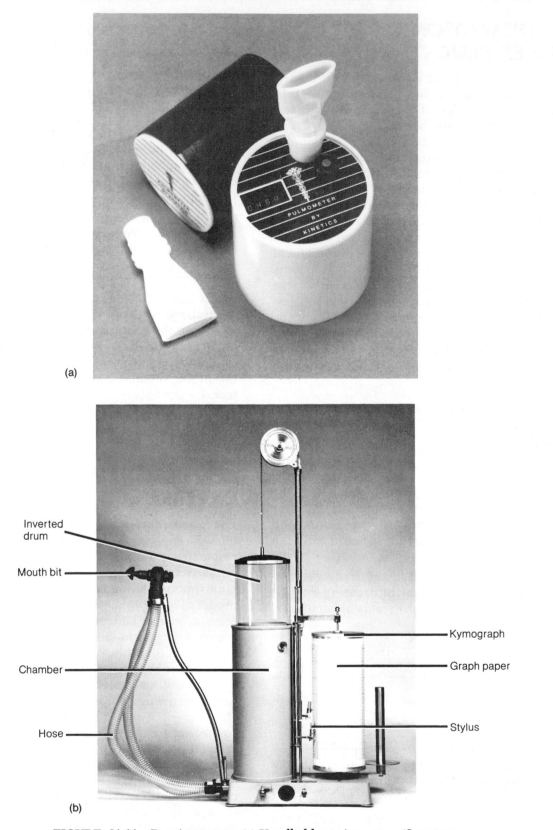

(a)

(b)

FIGURE 21.11 Respirometers. (a) Handheld respirometer. (Courtesy of Kinetics, Upper Saddle River, N.J.) (b) Collins respirometer. This type is commonly used in college biology laboratories.

of ventilation for diagnostic purposes. Spirometry is indicated for individuals with labored breathing, and is used to diagnose respiratory disorders such as bronchial asthma and emphysema.

As the following respiratory volumes and capacities are discussed, keep in mind that the values given vary with age, height, and sex. Each inspiration of normal, quiet breathing pulls about 500 ml (cc) of air into the respiratory passageways. The same amount moves out with each expiration, and this volume of air inspired (or expired) is called **tidal volume** (Figure 21.12). Only about 350 ml of this tidal volume reaches the alveoli. The other 150 ml is called **dead air volume** because it remains in the dead spaces of the nose, pharynx, larynx, trachea, and bronchi.

If we take a very deep breath, we can inspire much more than 500 ml. The additional inhaled air, called the **inspiratory reserve volume,** averages 3100 ml above the 500 ml of tidal volume. Thus, our respiratory system can pull in as much as 3600 ml of air. If we inspire normally and then expire as forcibly as possible, we can push out 1200 ml of air in addition to the 500-ml tidal volume. This extra 1200 ml is called **expiratory reserve volume.** Even after the expiratory reserve volume is expelled, a considerable amount of air still remains in the lungs because the lower intrapleural pressure keeps the alveoli slightly inflated. This air, the **residual volume,** amounts to about 1200 ml. When the chest cavity is opened, the intrapleural pressure equals the atmospheric pressure, which forces out the residual volume. The lungs still contain a small amount of air called **minimal volume,** which can be demonstrated by placing a piece of lung in water and watching it float.

Lung capacity can be calculated by combining various lung volumes. **Inspiratory capacity,** the total inspiratory ability of the lungs, is the sum of tidal volume plus inspiratory reserve volume (3600 ml). **Functional residual capacity** is the sum of residual volume plus expiratory reserve volume (2400 ml). **Vital capacity** is the sum of inspiratory reserve volume, tidal volume, and expiratory reserve volume (4800 ml). Finally, **total lung capacity** is the sum of all volumes (6000 ml).

D. LABORATORY TESTS ON RESPIRATION

1. Respiratory Sounds

Air flowing through the respiratory tract creates characteristic sounds that can be detected through the use of a stethoscope. Perform the following exercises.

1. Place the bell portion of the stethoscope just below the larynx and listen for bronchial sounds during both inspiration and expiration.

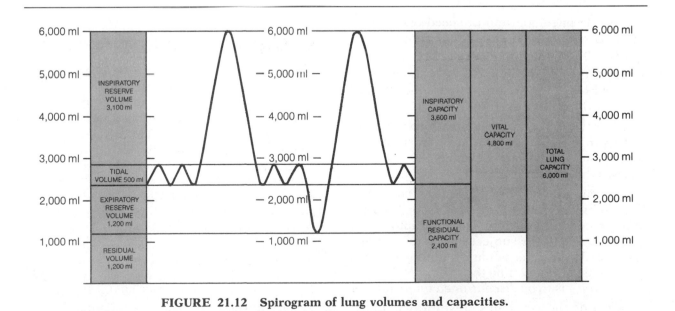

FIGURE 21.12 **Spirogram of lung volumes and capacities.**

2. Move the stethoscope slowly downward toward the bronchial tubes until the sounds are no longer heard.

3. Place the stethoscope under the scapula, under the clavicle, and over different intercostal spaces on the chest, and listen for any sound during inspiration and expiration. (The sound may be a rumbling or rustling murmur.)

2. Use of Pneumograph

The **pneumograph** is an instrument that records variations in breathing patterns caused by various physical or chemical factors. The chest pneumograph is a coiled rubber hose that fits around the chest. One end of this instrument is equipped with a thin tube that is attached to a recorder. As the subject breathes, chest movements cause changes in the air pressure within the pneumograph that are transmitted to the recorder. Normal inspiration and expiration can thus be recorded, and the effects of a wide range of physical and chemical factors on these movements can be studied.

Place the coiled rubber hose around the chest at the level of the sixth rib and attach it at the back. Connect the thin rubber tube to the recorder. As the subject breathes normally, the needle should deflect. If it does not, adjust the pneumograph.

Perform the following exercises and record your values in Section D.1 of the Laboratory Report Results.

1. Set the pneumograph at speed one and record normal, quiet breathing for about 30 seconds.

2. Have the subject inhale deeply and hold his or her breath for as long as possible. Record the breathing after this time interval.

3. After the subject is again breathing normally, have him or her hyperventilate (breathe deeply and rapidly) for approximately 30 seconds. Record the breathing after this period.

4. The subject then breathes into a paper bag for 2 minutes, and breathing is recorded after this procedure. **Caution!** The instructor *must carefully watch* the subject in this test for any untoward reactions while breathing into the paper bag. If at any time the *subject feels dizzy,* the exercise is to be *discontinued immediately.*

5. Record the student's respiratory movements during the following activities and at-

tach examples of your recordings to the Laboratory Report Results sheet.

Reading and talking	Yawning
Swallowing water	Coughing
Laughing	Sniffing

3. Measurement of Chest and Abdomen in Respiration

Consult your textbook regarding the relationship between inspiration and expiration as correlated with chest and abdomen expansion and contraction. With this relationship in mind, perform the following exercises and record your results in Section D.2 of the Laboratory Report Results.

1. Using a tape measure at about the level of the fifth rib, determine the size of the chest during normal inspiration and expiration.

2. Measure the chest in the same way after both a deep or forced inspiration and expiration.

3. Repeat steps 1 and 2, but measure the chest using chest calipers instead of a measuring tape.

4. Calculate the changes occurring at the abdomen in both normal and forced respiration, using both the measuring tape and the chest calipers.

4. Use of Collins Respirometer

The different volumes of air exchanged may be measured by each student using the Collins respirometer. The disposable mouthpiece is discarded, and the hose is then detached and rinsed with 70% alcohol. This procedure is repeated with every student using the equipment. Students should work in pairs, with one student operating the respirometer while the other student is tested. Before starting the recording, a little practice may be necessary to learn to inhale and exhale only through your mouth and into the hose. A nose clip may be used to prevent leakage from the nose.

Perform the following exercises and record your values in Section D.3 of the Laboratory Report Results. In each case, * indicates the placement of the mouth on the mouthpiece.

1. Inspire normally, then * exhale normally. This volume is your **tidal volume.** Repeat two more times and average and record the values.

2. Expire normally, then * exhale as much air as possible, recording this volume. This value is your **expiratory reserve volume.** Repeat two more times and record the values.

3. After taking a deep breath, * exhale as much air as possible. This volume is your **vital capacity.** Repeat two more times and record the values. Compare your vital capacity to the normal value shown in Tables 21.1 and 21.2.

4. Because your vital capacity consists of tidal volume, inspiratory reserve volume, and expiratory reserve volume, and because you have already measured tidal volume in step 1 and expiratory reserve volume in step 2, you can calculate your **inspiratory reserve volume** by subtracting tidal volume and expiratory reserve volume from vital capacity. Inspiratory reserve volume = (vital capacity) − (tidal volume + expiratory reserve volume). Record this value.

In some cases, an individual with a pulmonary disorder has a nearly normal vital capacity. If the rate of expiration is timed, however, the extent of the pulmonary disorder becomes apparent. In order to do this, an individual expels air into a Collins respirometer as fast as possible and the expired volume is measured per unit of time. Such a test is called **Forced Expiratory Volume (FEV_T).** The T indicates that the volume of air is timed. FEV_1 is the volume of air forcefully expired in 1 second, FEV_2 is the volume expired in 2 seconds, and so on. A normal individual should be able to expel 83% of the total capacity during the first second, 94% in 2 seconds, and 97% in 3 seconds. For individuals with disorders such as emphysema and asthma, the percentage can be considerably lower, depending on the extent of the problem.

FEV_1 is determined according to the following procedure:

1. Apply a noseclip to prevent leakage of air through the nose.

2. Turn on the kymograph.

3. Before placing the mouthpiece in your mouth, inhale as deeply as possible.

4. Expel all the air you can into the mouthpiece.

5. Turn off the kymograph.

6. Draw a vertical line on the spirogram at the starting point of exhalation. Mark this A.

7. Using the Collins VC timed interval ruler, draw a vertical line to the left of line A and label it line B. The time between lines A and B is 1 second.

8. The FEV_1 is the point where the spirogram tracing crosses line B.

9. Record your value here _____ .

10. Now read your vital capacity from the spirogram and record the value here _____ .

11. In order to adjust for differences in the temperature in the respirometer, use Table 21.3 as a guide. Determine the temperature in the respirometer, find the appropriate conversion factor and multiply the conversion factor by your vital capacity.

12. If, for example, the temperature of the respirometer is 75.2 °F (24 °C), the conversion factor is 1.080. And, if your vital capacity is 5600 ml, then

$$1.080 \times 5600 \text{ ml} = 6048 \text{ ml}$$

13. Use the same conversion factor and multiply it by your FEV_1. If your FEV_1 is 4000 ml, then

$$1.080 \times 4000 \text{ ml} = 4320 \text{ ml}$$

14. To calculate FEV_1, divide 4320 by 6048.

$$FEV_1 = \frac{4320}{6048} = 71\%$$

15. Repeat the procedure three times and record your FEV_1 in Section D.3 of the Laboratory Report Results.

5. Use of Handheld Respirometer

Several different handheld respirometers are available that measure different pulmonary functions. One such instrument is the Pulmometer (Figure 21.11a). It measures and provides a direct digital display of vital capacity, FEV_1, and maximum breathing capacity.

Following the instructions provided with the Pulmometer, determine your vital capacity, FEV_1, and maximum breathing capacity. Record your results in Section D.4.

Compare your results using the handheld respirometer with those using the Collins respirometer.

TABLE 21.1
PREDICTED VITAL CAPACITIES FOR FEMALES

HEIGHT IN CENTIMETERS AND INCHES

Age	cm 152 / in. 59.8	154 / 60.6	156 / 61.4	158 / 62.2	160 / 63.0	162 / 63.7	164 / 64.6	166 / 65.4	168 / 66.1	170 / 66.9	172 / 67.7	174 / 68.5	176 / 69.3	178 / 70.1	180 / 70.9	182 / 71.7	184 / 72.4	186 / 73.2	188 / 74.0
16	3,070	3,110	3,150	3,190	3,230	3,270	3,310	3,350	3,390	3,430	3,470	3,510	3,550	3,590	3,630	3,670	3,715	3,755	3,800
17	3,055	3,095	3,135	3,175	3,215	3,255	3,295	3,335	3,375	3,415	3,455	3,495	3,535	3,575	3,615	3,655	3,695	3,740	3,780
18	3,040	3,080	3,120	3,160	3,200	3,240	3,280	3,320	3,360	3,400	3,440	3,480	3,520	3,560	3,600	3,640	3,680	3,720	3,760
20	3,010	3,050	3,090	3,130	3,170	3,210	3,250	3,290	3,330	3,370	3,410	3,450	3,490	3,525	3,565	3,605	3,645	3,695	3,720
22	2,980	3,020	3,060	3,095	3,135	3,175	3,215	3,255	3,290	3,330	3,370	3,410	3,450	3,490	3,530	3,570	3,610	3,650	3,685
24	2,950	2,985	3,025	3,065	3,100	3,140	3,180	3,220	3,260	3,300	3,335	3,375	3,415	3,455	3,490	3,530	3,570	3,610	3,650
26	2,920	2,960	3,000	3,035	3,070	3,110	3,150	3,190	3,230	3,265	3,300	3,340	3,380	3,420	3,455	3,495	3,530	3,570	3,610
28	2,890	2,930	2,965	3,000	3,040	3,070	3,115	3,155	3,190	3,230	3,270	3,305	3,345	3,380	3,420	3,460	3,495	3,535	3,570
30	2,860	2,895	2,935	2,970	3,010	3,045	3,085	3,120	3,160	3,195	3,235	3,270	3,310	3,345	3,385	3,420	3,460	3,495	3,535
32	2,825	2,865	2,900	2,940	2,975	3,015	3,050	3,090	3,125	3,160	3,200	3,235	3,275	3,310	3,350	3,385	3,425	3,460	3,495
34	2,795	2,835	2,870	2,910	2,945	2,980	3,020	3,055	3,090	3,130	3,165	3,200	3,240	3,275	3,310	3,350	3,385	3,425	3,460
36	2,765	2,805	2,840	2,875	2,910	2,950	2,985	3,020	3,060	3,095	3,130	3,165	3,205	3,240	3,275	3,310	3,350	3,385	3,420
38	2,735	2,770	2,810	2,845	2,880	2,915	2,950	2,990	3,025	3,060	3,095	3,130	3,170	3,205	3,240	3,275	3,310	3,350	3,385
40	2,705	2,740	2,775	2,810	2,850	2,885	2,920	2,955	2,990	3,025	3,060	3,095	3,135	3,170	3,205	3,240	3,275	3,310	3,345
42	2,675	2,710	2,745	2,780	2,815	2,850	2,885	2,920	2,955	2,990	3,025	3,060	3,100	3,135	3,170	3,205	3,240	3,275	3,310
44	2,645	2,680	2,715	2,750	2,785	2,820	2,855	2,890	2,925	2,960	2,995	3,030	3,060	3,095	3,130	3,165	3,200	3,235	3,270
46	2,615	2,650	2,685	2,715	2,750	2,785	2,820	2,855	2,890	2,925	2,960	2,995	3,030	3,060	3,095	3,130	3,165	3,200	3,235
48	2,585	2,620	2,650	2,685	2,715	2,750	2,785	2,820	2,855	2,890	2,925	2,960	2,995	3,030	3,060	3,095	3,130	3,160	3,195
50	2,555	2,590	2,625	2,655	2,690	2,720	2,755	2,785	2,820	2,855	2,890	2,925	2,955	2,990	3,025	3,060	3,090	3,125	3,155
52	2,525	2,555	2,590	2,625	2,655	2,690	2,720	2,755	2,790	2,820	2,855	2,890	2,925	2,955	2,990	3,020	3,055	3,090	3,125
54	2,495	2,530	2,560	2,590	2,625	2,655	2,690	2,720	2,755	2,790	2,820	2,855	2,885	2,920	2,950	2,985	3,020	3,050	3,085
56	2,460	2,495	2,525	2,560	2,590	2,625	2,655	2,690	2,720	2,755	2,790	2,820	2,855	2,885	2,920	2,950	2,980	3,015	3,045
58	2,430	2,460	2,495	2,525	2,560	2,590	2,625	2,655	2,690	2,720	2,750	2,785	2,815	2,850	2,880	2,920	2,945	2,975	3,010
60	2,400	2,430	2,460	2,495	2,525	2,560	2,590	2,625	2,655	2,685	2,720	2,750	2,780	2,810	2,845	2,875	2,915	2,940	2,970
62	2,370	2,405	2,435	2,465	2,495	2,525	2,560	2,590	2,620	2,655	2,685	2,715	2,745	2,775	2,810	2,840	2,870	2,900	2,935
64	2,340	2,370	2,400	2,430	2,465	2,495	2,525	3,555	2,585	2,620	2,650	2,680	2,710	2,740	2,770	2,805	2,835	2,865	2,895
66	2,310	2,340	2,370	2,400	2,430	2,460	2,495	2,525	2,555	2,585	2,615	2,645	2,675	2,705	2,735	2,765	2,800	2,825	2,860
68	2,280	2,310	2,340	2,370	2,400	2,430	2,460	2,490	2,520	2,550	2,580	2,610	2,640	2,670	2,700	2,730	2,760	2,795	2,820
70	2,250	2,280	2,310	2,340	2,370	2,400	2,425	2,455	2,485	2,515	2,545	2,575	2,605	2,635	2,665	2,695	2,725	2,755	2,780
72	2,220	2,250	2,280	2,310	2,335	2,365	2,395	2,425	2,455	2,480	2,510	2,540	2,570	2,600	2,630	2,660	2,685	2,715	2,745
74	2,190	2,220	2,245	2,275	2,305	2,335	2,360	2,390	2,420	2,450	2,475	2,505	2,535	2,565	2,590	2,620	2,650	2,680	2,710

From: *Archives of Environmental Health*, February, 1966, Vol. 12, pp. 146–189, E. A. Gaensler, MD and G. W. Wright, MD

TABLE 21.2
PREDICTED VITAL CAPACITIES FOR MALES

HEIGHT IN CENTIMETERS AND INCHES

Age	cm 152	154	156	158	160	162	164	166	168	170	172	174	176	178	180	182	184	186	188
	in. 59.8	60.6	61.4	62.2	63.0	63.7	64.6	65.4	66.1	66.9	67.7	68.5	69.3	70.1	70.9	71.7	72.4	73.2	74.0
16	3,920	3,975	4,025	4,075	4,130	4,180	4,230	4,285	4,335	4,385	4,440	4,490	4,540	4,590	4,645	4,695	4,745	4,800	4,850
18	3,890	3,940	3,995	4,045	4,095	4,145	4,200	4,250	4,300	4,350	4,405	4,455	4,505	4,555	4,610	4,660	4,710	4,760	4,815
20	3,860	3,910	3,960	4,015	4,065	4,115	4,165	4,215	4,265	4,320	4,370	4,420	4,470	4,520	4,570	4,625	4,675	4,725	4,775
22	3,830	3,880	3,930	3,980	4,030	4,080	4,135	4,185	4,235	4,285	4,335	4,385	4,435	4,485	4,535	4,585	4,635	4,685	4,735
24	3,785	3,835	3,885	3,935	3,985	4,035	4,085	4,135	4,185	4,235	4,285	4,330	4,380	4,430	4,480	4,530	4,580	4,630	4,680
26	3,755	3,805	3,855	3,905	3,955	4,000	4,050	4,100	4,150	4,200	4,250	4,300	4,350	4,395	4,445	4,495	4,545	4,595	4,645
28	3,725	3,775	3,820	3,870	3,920	3,970	4,020	4,070	4,115	4,165	4,215	4,265	4,310	4,360	4,410	4,460	4,510	4,555	4,605
30	3,695	3,740	3,790	3,840	3,890	3,935	3,985	4,035	4,080	4,130	4,180	4,230	4,275	4,325	4,375	4,425	4,470	4,520	4,570
32	3,665	3,710	3,760	3,810	3,855	3,905	3,950	4,000	4,050	4,095	4,145	4,195	4,240	4,290	4,340	4,385	4,435	4,485	4,530
34	3,620	3,665	3,715	3,760	3,810	3,855	3,905	3,950	4,000	4,045	4,095	4,140	4,190	4,225	4,285	4,330	4,380	4,425	4,475
36	3,585	3,635	3,680	3,730	3,775	3,825	3,870	3,920	3,965	4,010	4,060	4,105	4,155	4,200	4,250	4,295	4,340	4,390	4,435
38	3,555	3,605	3,650	3,695	3,745	3,790	3,840	3,885	3,930	3,980	4,025	4,070	4,120	4,165	4,210	4,260	4,305	4,350	4,400
40	3,525	3,575	3,620	3,665	3,710	3,760	3,805	3,850	3,900	3,945	3,990	4,035	4,085	4,130	4,175	4,220	4,270	4,315	4,360
42	3,495	3,540	3,590	3,635	3,680	3,725	3,770	3,820	3,865	3,910	3,955	4,000	4,050	4,095	4,140	4,185	4,230	4,280	4,325
44	3,450	3,495	3,540	3,585	3,630	3,675	3,725	3,770	3,815	3,860	3,905	3,950	3,995	4,040	4,085	4,130	4,175	4,220	4,270
46	3,420	3,465	3,510	3,555	3,600	3,645	3,690	3,735	3,780	3,825	3,870	3,915	3,960	4,005	4,050	4,095	4,140	4,185	4,230
48	3,390	3,435	3,480	3,525	3,570	3,615	3,655	3,700	3,745	3,790	3,835	3,880	3,925	3,970	4,015	4,060	4,105	4,150	4,190
50	3,345	3,390	3,430	3,475	3,520	3,565	3,610	3,650	3,695	3,740	3,785	3,830	3,870	3,915	3,960	4,005	4,050	4,090	4,135
52	3,315	3,353	3,400	3,445	3,490	3,530	3,575	3,620	3,660	3,705	3,750	3,795	3,835	3,880	3,925	3,970	4,010	4,055	4,100
54	3,285	3,325	3,370	3,415	3,455	3,500	3,540	3,585	3,630	3,670	3,715	3,760	3,800	3,845	3,890	3,930	3,975	4,020	4,060
56	3,255	3,295	3,340	3,385	3,425	3,465	3,510	3,550	3,595	3,640	3,680	3,725	3,765	3,810	3,850	3,895	3,940	3,980	4,025
58	3,210	3,250	3,290	3,335	3,375	3,420	3,460	3,530	3,545	3,585	3,630	3,670	3,715	3,755	3,800	3,840	3,880	3,925	3,965
60	3,175	3,220	3,260	3,300	3,345	3,385	3,430	3,470	3,500	3,555	3,595	3,635	3,680	3,720	3,760	3,805	3,845	3,885	3,930
62	3,150	3,190	3,230	3,270	3,310	3,350	3,390	3,440	3,480	3,520	3,560	3,600	3,640	3,680	3,730	3,770	3,810	3,850	3,890
64	3,120	3,160	3,200	3,240	3,280	3,320	3,360	3,400	3,440	3,490	3,530	3,570	3,610	3,650	3,690	3,730	3,770	3,810	3,850
66	3,070	3,110	3,150	3,190	3,230	3,270	3,310	3,350	3,390	3,430	3,470	3,510	3,550	3,600	3,640	3,680	3,720	3,760	3,800
68	3,040	3,080	3,120	3,160	3,200	3,240	3,280	3,320	3,360	3,400	3,440	3,480	3,520	3,560	3,600	3,640	3,680	3,720	3,760
70	3,010	3,050	3,090	3,130	3,170	3,210	3,250	3,290	3,330	3,370	3,410	3,450	3,480	3,520	3,560	3,600	3,640	3,680	3,720
72	2,980	3,020	3,060	3,100	3,140	3,180	3,210	3,250	3,290	3,330	3,370	3,410	3,450	3,490	3,530	3,570	3,610	3,650	3,680
74	2,930	2,970	3,010	3,050	3,090	3,130	3,170	3,200	3,240	3,280	3,320	3,360	3,400	3,440	3,470	3,510	3,550	3,590	3,630

From: *Archives of Environmental Health.* February, 1966, Vol. 12, pp. 146–189, E. A. Gaensler, MD and G. W. Wright, MD

TABLE 21.3
TEMPERATURE VARIATION
CONVERSION FACTORS

TEMPERATURE °C(°F)	CONVERSION FACTOR
20 (68.0)	1.102
21 (69.8)	1.096
22 (71.6)	1.091
23 (73.4)	1.085
24 (75.2)	1.080
25 (77.0)	1.075
26 (78.8)	1.068
27 (80.6)	1.063
28 (82.4)	1.057
29 (84.2)	1.051
30 (86.0)	1.045
31 (87.8)	1.039
32 (89.6)	1.032
33 (91.4)	1.026
34 (93.2)	1.020
35 (95.0)	1.014
36 (96.8)	1.007
37 (98.6)	1.000

E. LABORATORY TESTS COMBINING RESPIRATORY AND CARDIOVASCULAR INTERACTIONS

1. **Experimental setup**—Review earlier explanations on recording the following:
   Respiratory movements with a pneumograph.
   Blood pressure with sphygmomanometer and stethoscope.
   Radial pulse.

Ask for a volunteer from your experimental group who acknowledges that he or she is physically fit to serve as a subject. Attach the various pieces of apparatus in order to record respiratory movements and blood pressure.

2. **Experimental procedure**—Some form of regulated exercise is necessary for this experiment. Choose one of the following forms of exercise to have your subject participate in:
   a. *Riding exercise cycle*—If this form is chosen, set the resistance to be felt while riding the cycle, but not so high that the subject cannot complete the 4-minute exercise period without difficulty.
   b. *Harvard Step Test*—In this form of exercise the subject is to step up onto a 20-in. platform (a chair will substitute quite well)

with one foot at a time. The subject is to bring *both* feet up onto the platform before stepping back down to the floor. The subject is also to remain erect at all times, and to do 30 complete cycles (up onto the platform and back down) per minute.

3. **Experimental protocol**—Record respiratory movements, blood pressure, and pulse during each of the procedures listed. Record your data in the table provided in Section E of the Laboratory Report Results. All data should be recorded *simultaneously,* thereby requiring participation of all members of the experimental group.
   a. *Basal readings*—Have the subject sit erect and quiet for 3 minutes. Obtain readings for:

Respiratory rate and depth.
Systolic and diastolic blood pressure.
Pulse rate.

When the above readings have been recorded, obtain additional readings after (1) sitting quietly on the exercise cycle for 3 mintues, if this form of exercise is to be utilized, or (2) standing quietly for 3 minutes in front of the platform that is to be utilized for the Harvard Step Test.

   b. *Readings after 1 minute of exercise*—After the subject has exercised for 1 minute, obtain additional readings.
   c. *Readings after 2 and 3 minutes of exercise*—Again, obtain additional readings after the subject has completed 2 and 3 minutes of exercise.
   d. *Readings upon completion of exercise*—When the subject has completed 4 minutes of exercise, obtain readings for respiratory rate, respiratory depth, heart rate, and systolic and diastolic blood pressure immediately upon completion *while the subject remains seated on the exercise cycle or stands erect on the floor*, depending upon the type of exercise utilized.
   e. *Readings 1, 2, 3, and 5 minutes after completion of exercise*—With the subject *still sitting on the exercise cycle or still standing erect on the floor* obtain additional readings at the above time intervals after completion of the exercise period.

**LABORATORY REPORT
QUESTIONS (PAGE 429)**

22 | DIGESTIVE SYSTEM

Digestion occurs basically as two events—mechanical digestion and chemical digestion. **Mechanical digestion** consists of various movements that help chemical digestion. These movements include physical breakdown of food by the teeth and complete churning and mixing of this food with enzymes by the smooth muscles of the stomach and small intestine. **Chemical digestion** consists of a series of catabolic reactions that break down the large nutrient molecules that we eat, such as carbohydrates, lipids, and proteins, into much smaller molecules that are usable by body cells.

A. GENERAL ORGANIZATION OF DIGESTIVE SYSTEM

Digestive organs are usually divided into two main groups. The first is the **gastrointestinal (GI) tract,** or **alimentary canal,** a continuous tube running from the mouth to the anus, and measuring about 9 m (30 ft) in length. This tract is composed of the mouth, pharynx, esophagus, stomach, small intestine, and large intestine. The small intestine has three regions: duodenum, jejunum, and ileum. The large intestine has four regions: cecum, colon, rectum, and anal canal. The colon is divided into ascending colon, transverse colon, descending colon, and sigmoid colon. The second group of organs composing the digestive system consists of the **accessory structures** such as the teeth, tongue, salivary glands, liver, gallbladder, and pancreas (see Figure 22.1).

Using your textbook, charts, or models for reference, label Figure 22.1.

The wall of the GI tract, especially from the esophagus to the anal canal, has the same basic arrangement of tissues. The four coats (tunics) of the tract, from the inside to the outside, are the **mucosa, submucosa, muscularis,** and **serosa,** or **adventitia** (see Figures 22.6 and 22.8).

The outermost layer of the GI tract is a serous membrane composed of connective tissue and epithelium, and is called the **tunica serosa** or **visceral peritoneum** (per'-i-tō-NĒ-um). The **parietal peritoneum** lines the wall of the abdominal cavity, and the **visceral peritoneum** covers some of the organs. The space between the parietal and visceral portions of the peritoneum is called the **peritoneal cavity.** Unlike the two other serous membranes of the body, the pericardium and the pleura, the peritoneum contains large folds that weave in between the viscera. The important extensions of the peritoneum are the **mesentery** (MEZ-en-ter'-ē) **mesocolon, falciform** (FAL-si-form) **ligament, lesser omentum** (ō-MENT-um), and **greater omentum.**

Inflammation of the peritoneum, called **peritonitis,** is a serious condition because the peritoneal membranes are continuous with each other, enabling the infection to spread to all the organs in the cavity.

B. ORGANS OF DIGESTIVE SYSTEM

1. Mouth (Oral Cavity)

The **mouth,** also called the **oral** or **buccal** (BUK-al) **cavity,** is formed by the cheeks, hard and soft palates, and tongue. The **hard palate** forms the anterior portion of the roof of the mouth and the **soft palate** forms the posterior portion. The **tongue** forms the floor of the oral cavity and is composed of skeletal muscle covered by

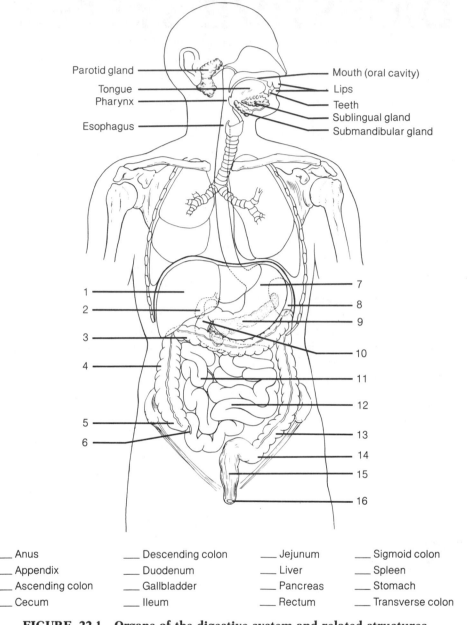

Parotid gland
Tongue
Pharynx
Esophagus

Mouth (oral cavity)
Lips
Teeth
Sublingual gland
Submandibular gland

1
2
3
4
5
6

7
8
9
10
11
12
13
14
15
16

___ Anus   ___ Descending colon   ___ Jejunum   ___ Sigmoid colon
___ Appendix   ___ Duodenum   ___ Liver   ___ Spleen
___ Ascending colon   ___ Gallbladder   ___ Pancreas   ___ Stomach
___ Cecum   ___ Ileum   ___ Rectum   ___ Transverse colon

FIGURE 22.1   **Organs of the digestive system and related structures.**

mucous membrane. Partial digestion of carbohydrates is the only chemical digestion that occurs in the mouth.

    a. **Cheeks**—Lateral walls of oral cavity. Muscular structures covered by skin and lined by stratified squamous epithelium; anterior portions terminate in the **superior** and **inferior labia** (lips).

    b. **Vermilion** (ver-MIL-yon)—Transition zone of lips where outer skin and inner mucous membranes meet.

    c. **Labial frenulum** (LĀ-bē-al FREN-yoo-lum)—Midline fold of mucous membrane

that attaches the inner surface of each lip to its corresponding gum.

    d. **Vestibule**—Space bounded externally by cheeks and lips and internally by gums and teeth.

    e. **Oral cavity proper**—Space extending from the vestibule to the **fauces** (FAW-sēz), opening of oral cavity proper with pharynx. Area is enclosed by the dental arches.

    f. **Hard palate**—Formed by maxillae and palatine bones and covered by mucous membrane.

    g. **Soft palate**—Arch-shaped muscular partition between oropharynx and nasopharynx. Hanging from free border of soft palate is a conical muscular process, the **uvula** (OO-vyoo-la).

h. **Palatoglossal arch**—Muscular fold that extends inferiorly, laterally, and anteriorly to the side of the base of tongue.

i. **Palatopharyngeal arch** (PAL-a-tō-fa-rin´- jē-al)—Muscular fold that extends inferiorly, laterally, and posteriorly to the side of pharynx. **Palatine tonsils** are between arches and **lingual tonsil** is at base of tongue.

j. **Tongue**—Movable, muscular organ on floor of mouth. **Extrinsic muscles** originate outside tongue, insert into it, and move tongue from side to side and in and out to maneuver food for chewing and swallowing; **intrinsic muscles** originate and insert within the tongue and alter shape and size of tongue for speech and swallowing.

k. **Lingual frenulum**—Midline fold of mucous membrane on undersurface of tongue that helps restrict its movement posteriorly.

l. **Papillae** (pa-PIL-ē)—Projections of lamina propria on surface of tongue covered with epithelium; **filiform papillae** are conical projections in parallel rows over anterior two-thirds of tongue; **fungiform papillae** are mushroomlike elevations distributed among filiform papillae and more numerous near tip of tongue (appear as red dots and most contain taste buds); **circumvallate (vallate) papillae** are arranged in the form of an inverted V on the posterior surface of tongue (all contain taste buds).

Using a mirror and tongue depressor, examine your mouth or your partner's and locate as many of the structures (a through l) as you can.

2. Salivary Glands

Most saliva is secreted by the **salivary glands,** which lie outside the mouth and pour their contents into ducts that empty into the oral cavity. The carbohydrate-digesting enzyme in saliva is salivary amylase. The three pairs of salivary glands are: the **parotid glands** (in front of and under the ears), **submandibular glands** (deep to the base of the tongue in the posterior part of the floor of the mouth), and **sublingual glands** (anterior to the submandibular glands).

Label Figure 22.2.

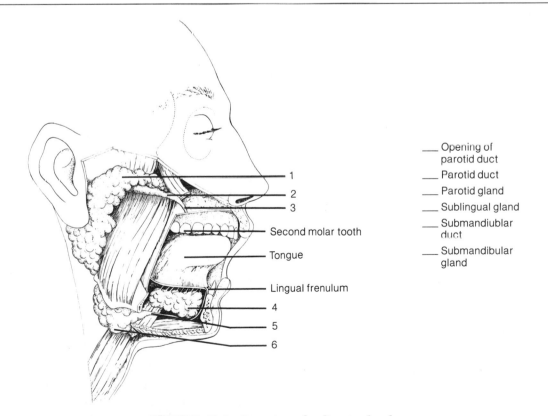

1

2

3

Second molar tooth

Tongue

Lingual frenulum

4

5

6

___ Opening of parotid duct

___ Parotid duct

___ Parotid gland

___ Sublingual gland

___ Submandiublar duct

___ Submandibular gland

FIGURE 22.2 Location of salivary glands.

The parotid glands are compound tubuloacinar glands, whereas the submandibulars and sublinguals are compound acinar glands (see Figure 22.3).

Examine prepared slides of the three different types of salivary glands and compare your observations to Figure 22.3.

3. Teeth

Teeth (dentes) are located in the sockets of the alveolar processes of the mandible and maxilla. The alveolar processes are covered by **gingivae** (jin-JĪ-vē) or gums, which extend slightly into each socket, forming a **gingival sulcus.** The sockets are lined by a dense fibrous connective tissue called a **periodontal ligament,** which anchors the teeth in position and helps dissipate the forces of chewing.

a. **Crown**—Portion above level of gums.
b. **Root**—One to three projections embedded in socket.
c. **Cervix**—Constricted junction line of the crown and root.
d. **Dentin**—Bonelike substance that gives teeth their basic shape.
e. **Pulp cavity**—Enlarged part of cavity in crown within dentin.
f. **Pulp**—Connective tissue containing blood vessels, lymphatics, and nerves.
g. **Root canal**—Narrow extension of pulp cavity in root.
h. **Apical foramen**—Opening in base of root canal through which blood vessels, lymphatics, and nerves enter tooth.
i. **Enamel**—Covering of crown that consists primarily of calcium phosphate and calcium carbonate.
j. **Cementum**—Bonelike substance that covers and attaches root to periodontal ligament.

With the aid of your textbook, label the parts of a tooth shown in Figure 22.4.

4. Dentitions

Dentitions (sets of teeth) are of two types: **deciduous** (baby) and **permanent.** Deciduous teeth begin to erupt at about 6 months of age, and one pair appears at about each month thereafter until all 20 are present. The deciduous teeth are:

a. **Incisors**—Central incisor closest to midline, with lateral incisor on either side. Incisors are chisel-shaped, adapted for cutting into food, have only one root.
b. **Cuspids (canines)**—Posterior to incisors. Cuspids have pointed surfaces (cusps) for tearing and shredding food, have only one root.
c. **Molars**—First and second molars posterior to canines. Molars crush and grind food. Upper molars have four cusps and three roots, lower molars have four cusps and two roots.

All deciduous teeth are usually lost between 6 and 12 years of age and replaced by permanent dentition consisting of 32 teeth that appear between age 6 and adulthood. The permanent teeth are:

a. **Incisors**—Central incisor and lateral incisor replace those of deciduous dentition.
b. **Cuspids (canines)**—These replace those of deciduous dentition.
c. **Premolars (bicuspids)**—First and second premolars replace deciduous molars. Premolars crush and grind food, have two cusps and one root (upper first premolars have two roots).
d. **Molars**—These erupt behind premolars as jaw grows to accommodate them and do not replace any deciduous teeth. First molars erupt at age 6, second at age 12, and third (wisdom teeth) after age 18.

Using a mirror and tongue depressor, examine your mouth or your partner's and locate as many teeth of the permanent dentition as you can.

With the aid of your textbook, label the deciduous and permanent dentitions in Figure 22.5.

5. Esophagus

The **esophagus** (e-SOF-a-gus) is a muscular, collapsible tube posterior to the trachea (see Figure 21.2a). The structure is 23 to 25 cm (10 in.) long and extends from the laryngopharynx through the mediastinum and esophageal hiatus in the diaphragm and terminates in the superior portion of the stomach. The esophagus conveys food from the pharynx to the stomach by peristalsis.

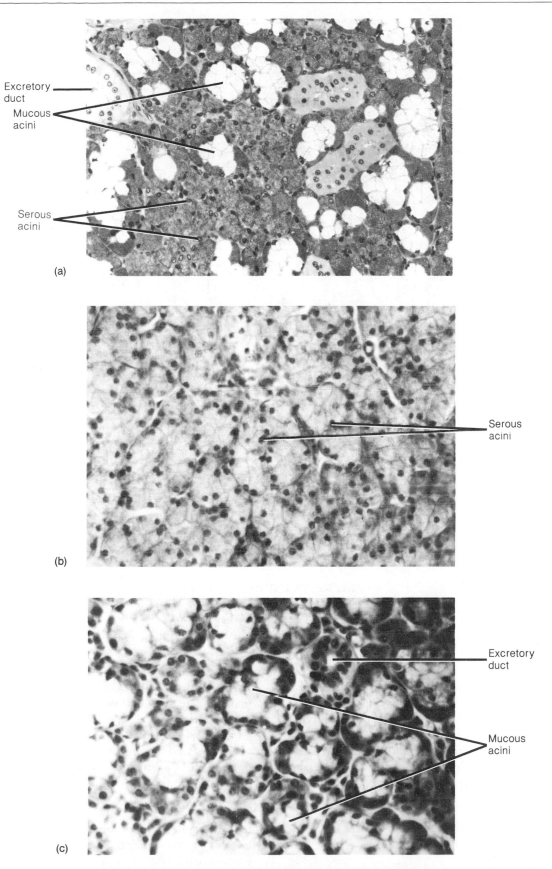

Excretory duct

Mucous acini

Serous acini

(a)

Serous acini

(b)

Excretory duct

Mucous acini

(c)

FIGURE 22.3 Histology of salivary glands. (a) Submandibular. (b) Parotid. (c) Sublingual.

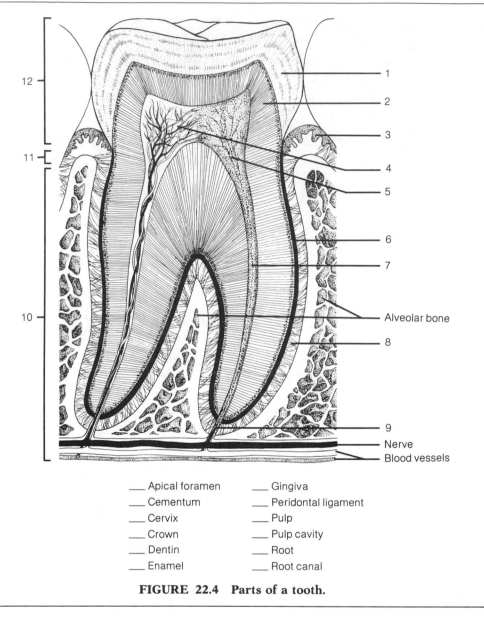

12
11
10

1
2
3
4
5
6
7
Alveolar bone
8
9
Nerve
Blood vessels

___ Apical foramen   ___ Gingiva
___ Cementum   ___ Peridontal ligament
___ Cervix   ___ Pulp
___ Crown   ___ Pulp cavity
___ Dentin   ___ Root
___ Enamel   ___ Root canal

FIGURE 22.4 Parts of a tooth.

Histologically, the esophagus consists of a **mucosa** (stratified squamous epithelium, lamina propria, muscularis mucosae), **submucosa** (connective tissue, blood vessels), **muscularis** (upper third striated, middle third striated and smooth, lower third smooth), and **tunica adventitia** (esophagus not covered by peritoneum).

Examine a prepared slide of a cross section of the esophagus that shows its various coats. With the aid of your textbook, label Figure 22.6.

6. Stomach

The **stomach** is a J-shaped enlargement of the GI tract under the diaphragm in the epigastric,

umbilical, and left hypochondriac regions of the abdomen (see Figure 22.1). The superior part is connected to the esophagus; the inferior part empties into the duodenum of the small intestine. The stomach is divided into four areas: cardia, fundus, body, and pylorus. The **cardia** surrounds the lower esophageal sphincter, a physiological sphincter in the esophagus just above the diaphragm. The rounded portion above and to the left of the cardia is the **fundus.** Below the fundus, the large central portion of the stomach is called the **body.** The narrow, inferior region is the **pylorus.** The concave medial border of the stomach is called the **lesser curvature,** and the convex lateral border is the **greater curvature.** The pylorus communicates with the duodenum of the small intestine via a

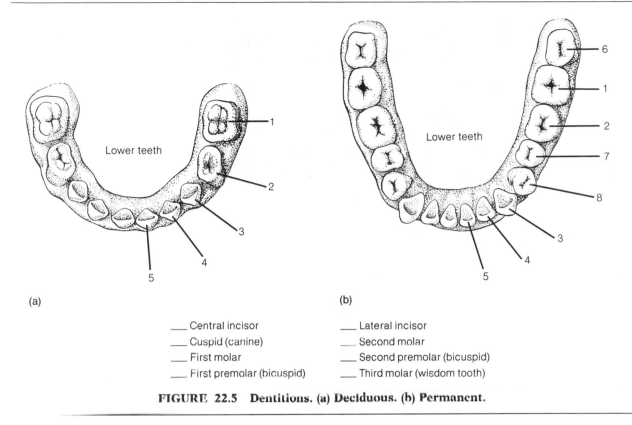

Lower teeth

(a)

Lower teeth

(b)

___ Central incisor
___ Cuspid (canine)
___ First molar
___ First premolar (bicuspid)

___ Lateral incisor
___ Second molar
___ Second premolar (bicuspid)
___ Third molar (wisdom tooth)

FIGURE 22.5 Dentitions. (a) Deciduous. (b) Permanent.

sphincter called the **pyloric sphincter (valve).** The main chemical activity of the stomach is to begin the digestion of proteins.

Label Figure 22.7.

The **mucosa** of the stomach contains large folds called **rugae** (ROO-jē). The columnar epithelium of the mucosa contains many narrow openings that extend down into the lamina propria. These openings are called **gastric glands (pits)** and are lined with three kinds of cells: (1) **zymogenic (chief) cells** that secrete inactive pepsinogen, which is converted to active pepsin, a protein-digesting enzyme; (2) **parietal cells** that secrete hydrochloric acid; and (3) **mucous cells** that secrete mucus and possibly the intrinsic factor (see Figure 22.8). The **submucosa** consists of areolar connective tissue. The **muscularis** has three layers of smooth muscle (outer longitudinal, middle circular, inner oblique). The **serosa** is part of the parietal peritoneum.

Examine a prepared slide of a section of the stomach that shows its various layers. With the aid of your textbook, label Figure 22.8.

7. Pancreas

The **pancreas** is a soft, oblong, tubuloacinar gland posterior to the greater curvature of the stomach (see Figure 22.1). The gland consists of a **head** (expanded portion near duodenum), **body** (central portion), and **tail** (terminal tapering portion).

Histologically, the pancreas consists of **pancreatic islets (islets of Langerhans)** that contain (1) glucagon-producing **alpha cells,** (2) insulin-producing **beta cells,** and (3) somatostatin-producing **delta cells** (see Figure 15.5). The pancreas also consists of **acini** that produce pancreatic juice (see Figure 15.5). Pancreatic juice contains enzymes that assist in the chemical breakdown of carbohydrates, proteins, and lipids.

Pancreatic juice is delivered from the pancreas to the duodenum by a large main tube, the **pancreatic duct.** This duct unites with the common bile duct from the liver and pancreas and enters the duodenum in a common duct called the **hepatopancreatic ampulla (ampulla of Vater).** The ampulla opens on an elevation of the duodenal mucosa, the **duodenal papilla.** An **accessory pancreatic duct** may also lead from the pancreas and empty into the duodenum about 2.5 cm (1 in.) above the hepatopancreatic ampulla.

With the aid of your textbook, label the structures associated with the pancreas in Figure 22.9.

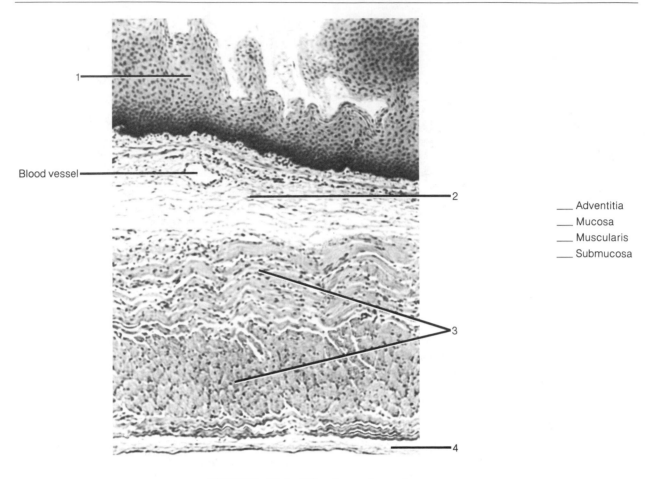

1

Blood vessel

2

3

4

____ Adventitia
____ Mucosa
____ Muscularis
____ Submucosa

FIGURE 22.6 Histology of esophagus.

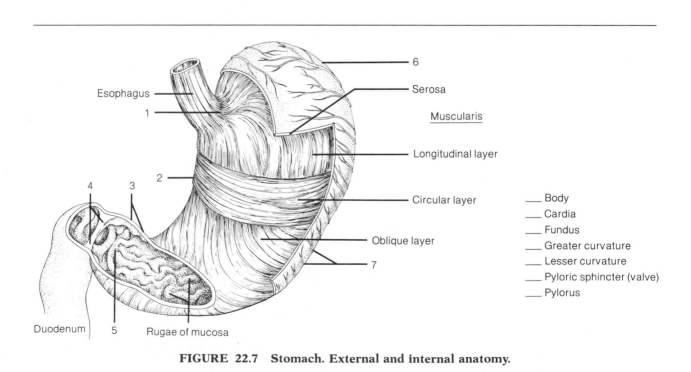

6

Esophagus

1

Serosa

Muscularis

Longitudinal layer

2

Circular layer

Oblique layer

7

4   3

Duodenum   5   Rugae of mucosa

____ Body
____ Cardia
____ Fundus
____ Greater curvature
____ Lesser curvature
____ Pyloric sphincter (valve)
____ Pylorus

FIGURE 22.7 Stomach. External and internal anatomy.

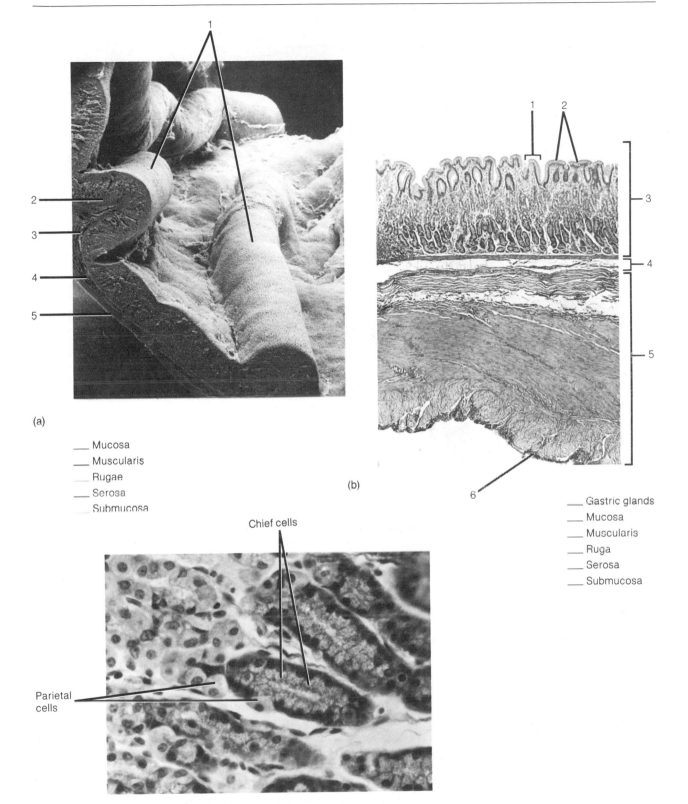

(a)

___ Mucosa
___ Muscularis
___ Rugae
___ Serosa
___ Submucosa

(b)

6

___ Gastric glands
___ Mucosa
___ Muscularis
___ Ruga
___ Serosa
___ Submucosa

Chief cells

Parietal
cells

(c)

FIGURE 22.8 **Histology of stomach. (a) Scanning electron micrograph at magnification of 55×. (b) Photomicrograph of fundic wall. (c) Photomicrograph of parietal and chief cells. ((a) from *Tissues and Organs: A Text-Atlas of Scanning Electron Microscopy* by Richard G. Kessel and Randy H. Kardon. W. H. Freeman and Company. Copyright © 1979.)**

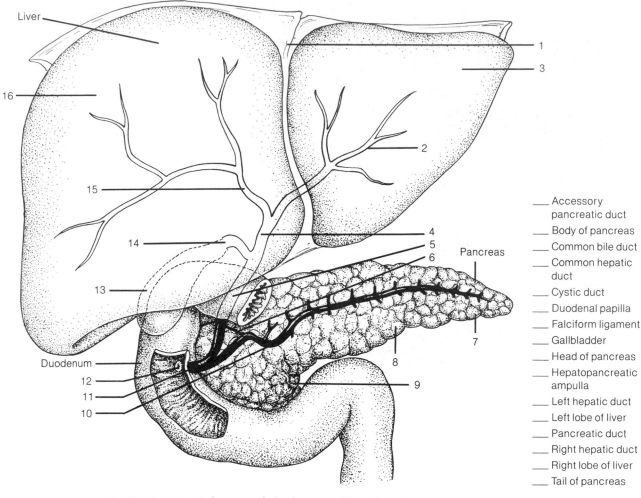

Liver

16

15

14

13

Duodenum

12

11

10

1

3

2

4

5

6

Pancreas

7

8

9

___ Accessory
  pancreatic duct
___ Body of pancreas
___ Common bile duct
___ Common hepatic
  duct
___ Cystic duct
___ Duodenal papilla
___ Falciform ligament
___ Gallbladder
___ Head of pancreas
___ Hepatopancreatic
  ampulla
___ Left hepatic duct
___ Left lobe of liver
___ Pancreatic duct
___ Right hepatic duct
___ Right lobe of liver
___ Tail of pancreas

FIGURE 22.9   Relations of the liver, gallbladder, duodenum, and pancreas.

8. Liver

The **liver** is located inferior to the diaphragm, occupying most of the right hypochondriac and part of the epigastric regions of the abdomen (see Figure 22.1). The gland is divided into two principal lobes, the **right lobe** and **left lobe,** separated by the **falciform ligament.** The falciform ligament attaches the liver to the anterior abdominal wall and diaphragm. The right lobe also has associated with it an inferior **quadrate lobe** and a posterior **caudate lobe.**

Each lobe is composed of microscopic functional units called **lobules.** Among the structures in a lobule are cords of **hepatic (liver) cells** arranged in a radial pattern around a **central vein; sinusoids,** endothelial lined spaces between hepatic cells through which blood flows; and **stellate reticuloendothelial (Kupffer)**

cells that destroy bacteria and worn-out blood cells by phagocytosis.

Examine a prepared slide of several liver lobules. Compare your observations with Figure 22.10.

Bile is manufactured by hepatic cells and functions in the emulsification of fats in the small intestine. The liquid is passed to the small intestine as follows: Hepatic cells secrete bile into **bile capillaries** that empty into small ducts. The small ducts merge into larger **right** and **left hepatic ducts,** one in each principal lobe of the liver. The right and left hepatic ducts unite outside the liver to form a single **common hepatic duct.** This duct joins the **cystic duct** from the gallbladder to become the **common bile duct,** which empties into the duodenum at the hepatopancreatic ampulla. When fats are not being digested, a valve around

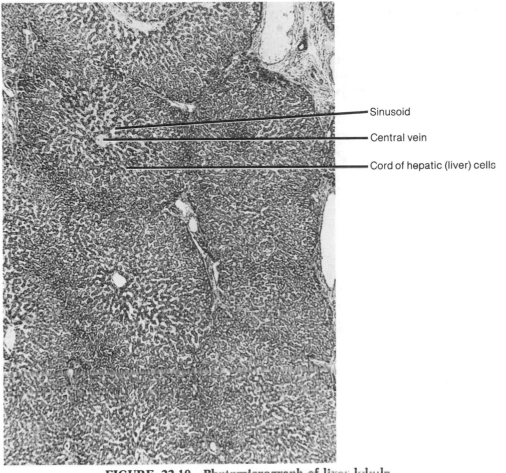

Sinusoid

Central vein

Cord of hepatic (liver) cells

FIGURE 22.10 Photomicrograph of liver lobule.

the hepatopancreatic ampulla, the **sphincter of the hepatopancreatic ampulla (sphincter of Oddi),** closes, and bile backs up into the gall-bladder via the cystic duct. In the gallbladder, bile is stored and concentrated.

With the aid of your textbook, label the structures associated with the liver in Figure 22.9.

9. Gallbladder

The **gallbladder** is a pear-shaped sac in a fossa along the undersurface of the liver (see Figure 22.1). The gallbladder stores and concentrates bile. The cystic duct of the gallbladder and common hepatic duct of the liver merge to form the common bile duct. The **mucosa** of the gallbladder contains rugae. The **muscularis** consists of smooth muscle and the outer coat consists of visceral peritoneum.

With the aid of your textbook, label the structures associated with the gallbladder in Figure 22.9.

10. Small Intestine

The bulk of digestion and absorption occurs in the **small intestine,** which begins at the pyloric sphincter (valve) of the stomach, coils through the central and lower part of the abdomen, and joins the large intestine at the ileocecal valve (see Figure 22.1). The mesentery attaches the small intestine to the posterior abdominal wall. The small intestine is about 6.35 m (21 ft) long and is divided into three segments: **duode-num** (doo′-ō-DĒ-num), which begins at the stom-ach; **jejunum** (jē-JOO-num), the middle segment, and **ileum** (IL-ē-um), which terminates at the large intestine.

Histologically, the **mucosa** contains many pits lined with glandular epithelium called **intestinal glands;** they secrete enzymes that digest carbohydrates, proteins, and nucleic acids (see Figure 22.11). Some of the simple columnar cells of the mucosa are **goblet cells** that secrete mucus (see Figure 22.11); others contain **microvilli** to increase the surface area for absorption (see Figure 3.1). The mucosa contains a series of fingerlike projections, the **villi** (see Figure 22.11). Each villus contains a blood capillary and a lymphatic vessel called a **lacteal;**

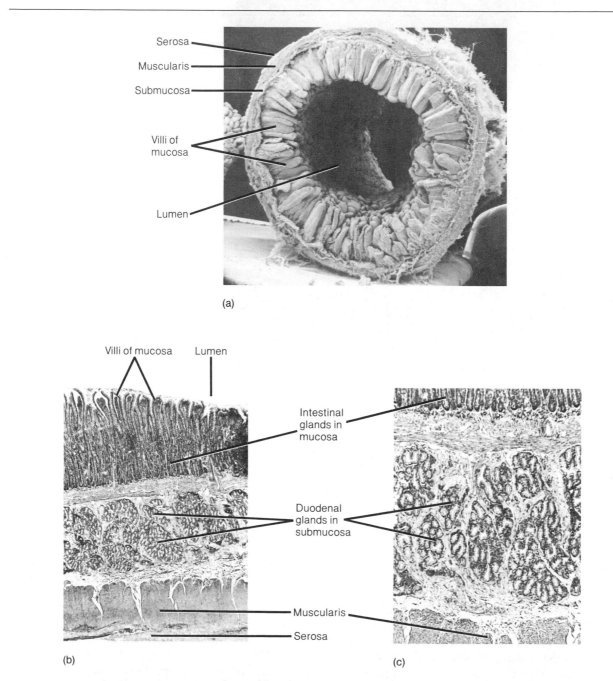

FIGURE 22.11 Histology of small intestine. (a) Scanning electron micrograph at magnification of 45×. (From *Tissues and Organs: A Text-Atlas of Scanning Electron Microscopy* by Richard G. Kessel and Randy H. Kardon. W. H. Freeman and Company. Copyright © 1979.) (b) Photomicrograph of portion of wall of duodenum. (c) Photomicrograph of enlarged aspect of intestinal glands.

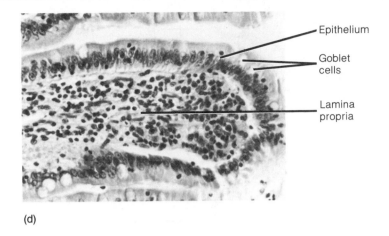

Epithelium

Goblet cells

Lamina propria

(d)

FIGURE 22.11 (*Continued*) Histology of small intestine. (d) Photomicrograph of enlarged aspect of a villus.

these absorb digested nutrients. The 4 million to 5 million villi in the small intestine greatly increase the surface area for absorption. The mucosa and **submucosa** also contain deep permanent folds, the **plicae circulares** (PLĪ-kē SER-kyoo-lar-es), which also help to increase the area for absorption. In the submucosa of the duodenum are **duodenal (Brunner's) glands,** which secrete an alkaline mucus to protect the mucosa from excess acid and the action of digestive enzymes. The **muscularis** of the small intestine consists of an outer longitudinal layer and an inner circular layer of smooth muscle. Except for a major portion of the duodenum, the **serosa** (visceral peritoneum) completely covers the small intestine.

Obtain prepared slides of the small intestine (section through its tunics and villi) and identify as many structures as you can, using Figure 22.11 and your textbook as references.

11. Large Intestine

The **large intestine** functions in the completion of absorption of water that leads to the formation of feces, and in the expulsion of feces from the body. Bacteria residing in the large intestine manufacture certain vitamins. The large intestine is about 1½ m (5 ft) long and extends from the ileum to the anus (see Figure 22.1). It is attached to the posterior abdominal wall by an extension of visceral peritoneum called **mesocolon.** The large intestine is divided into four principal regions: cecum, colon, rectum, and anal canal.

The opening from the ileum into the large intestine is guarded by a fold of mucous membrane, the **ileocecal sphincter (valve).** Hanging below the valve is a blind pouch, the **cecum,** to which is attached the **vermiform appendix** by an extension of visceral peritoneum called the **mesoappendix.** Inflammation of the vermiform appendix is called **appendicitis.** The open end of the cecum merges with the **colon.** The first division of the colon is the **ascending colon,** which ascends on the right side of the abdomen and turns abruptly to the left at the undersurface of the liver **(right colic [hepatic] flexure).** The **transverse colon** continues across the abdomen, curves beneath the spleen **(left colic [splenic] flexure),** and passes down the left side of the abdomen as the **descending colon.** The **sigmoid colon** begins at the iliac crest, projects inward toward the midline, and terminates at the rectum at S3. The **rectum** is the last 20 cm (7 to 8 in.) of the GI tract. Its terminal 2 to 3 cm is known as the **anal canal.** The opening of the anal canal to the exterior is the **anus.**

With the aid of your textbook, label the parts of the large intestine in Figure 22.12.

The **mucosa** of the large intestine consists of simple columnar epithelium with numerous **goblet cells** (Figure 22.13). The **submucosa** is similar to that in the rest of the GI tract. The **muscularis** consists of an outer longitudinal layer and an inner circular layer of smooth muscle. However, the longitudinal layer is not continuous; it is broken up into three flat bands, the **taeniae coli** (TĒ-ni-ē KŌ-lī), which gather the colon into a series of pouches called **haustra** (HAWS-tra) (see Figure 22.12). The **serosa** of the large intestine is visceral peritoneum.

Examine a prepared slide of the large intestine showing its tunics. Compare your observations to Figure 22.13.

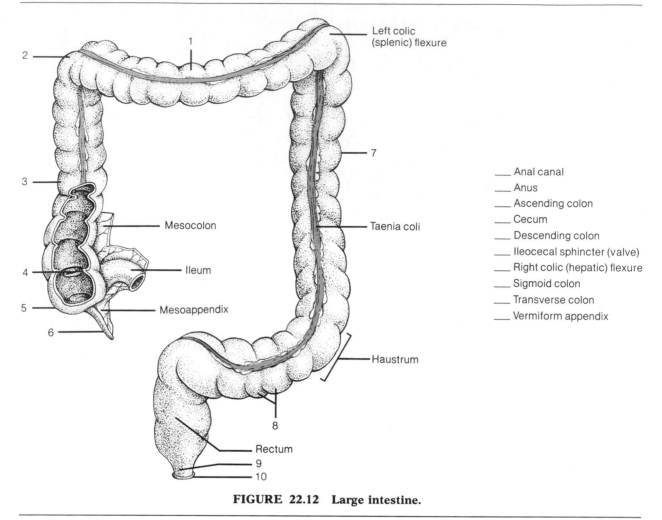

Left colic
(splenic) flexure

7

Mesocolon

Taenia coli

Ileum

Mesoappendix

Haustrum

8

Rectum

___ Anal canal
___ Anus
___ Ascending colon
___ Cecum
___ Descending colon
___ Ileocecal sphincter (valve)
___ Right colic (hepatic) flexure
___ Sigmoid colon
___ Transverse colon
___ Vermiform appendix

FIGURE 22.12   Large intestine.

C. PHYSIOLOGY OF INTESTINAL SMOOTH MUSCLE

Contraction of smooth muscle in the wall of the intestine is responsible for propelling foods through the tube and mixing the food with digestive enzymes. In these experiments you will have an opportunity to observe some of the factors that affect intestinal smooth muscle contraction. You will also be able to compare the physiology of intestinal smooth muscle to that of skeletal muscle (Exercise 9) and cardiac muscle (Exercise 19).

1. Isolation of the Intestinal Segment

Under light ether anesthesia make a center line incision and expose the abdominal cavity of a rabbit or rat. Remove a segment of jejunum and *immediately* immerse in 37 °C Locke's solution. Cut the intestinal segment into 1-in. pieces and rinse until all luminal contents are removed. Immerse the rinsed segments in clear Locke's solution warmed to 37 °C.

2. Experimental Setup

1. Tie a small length of thread to each end of the intestinal segment (Figure 22.14).

2. Attach one thread to a bent glass tube connected to an air supply. Attach the other thread to the myograph. (**Note:** Depending upon the model of the myograph utilized, either turn up the sensitivity or attach the thread to the most sensitive arm of the transducer.)

3. Adjust the tension on the myograph so that the string is taut but the intestinal segment is not overly stretched. Too much tension will cause the preparation to fall.

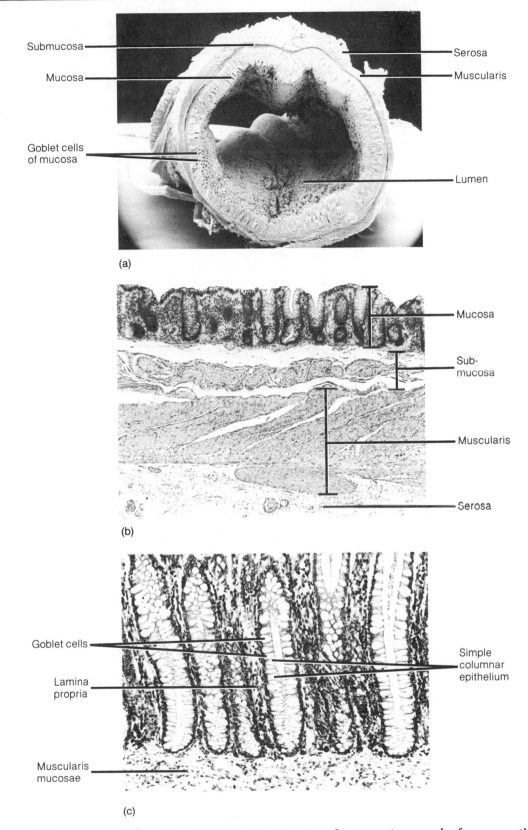

(a)

(b)

(c)

FIGURE 22.13 Histology of large intestine. (a) Scanning electron micrograph of cross section at magnification of 31×. (b) Photomicrograph of portion of wall. (c) Photomicrograph of enlarged aspect of mucosa. ((a) from *Tissues and Organs: A Text-Atlas of Scanning Electron Microscopy* by Richard G. Kessel and Randy H. Kardon. W. H. Freeman and Company. Copyright © 1979.)

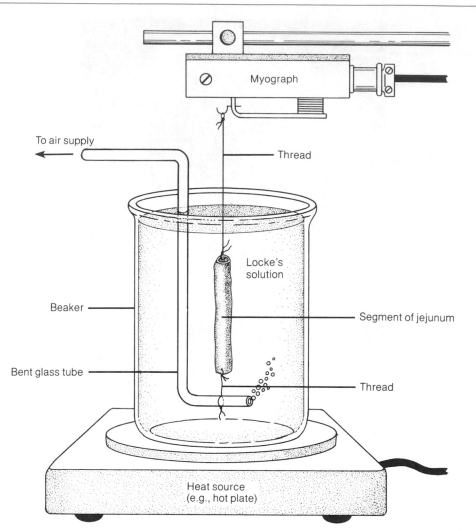

FIGURE 22.14 **Experimental setup for the physiology of intestinal smooth muscle.**

4. Adjust the air flow so that a continuous, light stream of air bubbles passes through the center of the intestinal segment.

3. Experimental Procedures

a. INHERENT CONTRACTILE ACTIVITY

After allowing an initial 5 to 10 minutes for the intestinal segment to stabilize, observe its basal activity while recording with the physiograph. Is the segment quiescent or does it exhibit intrinsic contractile activity? _____

_____ Is the extent of relaxation consistent, or does the preparation exhibit changes? _____

Does the preparation resemble skeletal or cardiac muscle with respect to inherent contractile activity? _____
Based upon your knowledge of the physiology of skeletal and cardiac muscle, explain your observation. _____

_____

_____

_____

_____

_____

b. EFFECT OF TEMPERATURE

1. Lower the temperature of Locke's solution to 20 °C by adding ice to it.

2. Record the contractile activity for about 2 minutes by turning on the physiograph. Mark the temperature on the paper.

3. Place a Bunsen burner or alcohol burner under the beaker and warm Locke's solution. *Keep the burner flame low.*

4. Turn on the physiograph and control the heat so that the temperature of the solution rises about 2 °C each 2 minutes, up to 40 °C.

5. Mark the temperature on the paper each 2 minutes as the temperature rises at 2 °C intervals. Turn off the physiograph.

Describe the changes that occurred in the intestinal segment with regard to strength and frequency of contraction as temperature increased. _____

_____

_____

_____

_____

_____

_____

At what temperature are the contractions strongest? _____

At what temperature is the frequency of contractions greatest? _____

Explain your observations. _____

_____

_____

_____

c. EFFECT OF NOREPINEPHRINE

1. Place 5 to 8 drops of a 1:50,000 norepinephrine solution into Locke's solution.

2. Observe any changes in the following: basal tone, strength of contraction, frequency of contraction, and speed of contraction.

3. How do each of these responses compare with those seen when norepinephrine was added to cardiac muscle in Exercise 19? Explain in the spaces provided.

Basal tone _____

_____

_____

Strength of contraction _____

_____

_____

Frequency of contraction _____

_____

_____

Speed of contraction _____

_____

_____

d. EFFECT OF ACETYLCHOLINE

1. Before performing this experiment, drain Locke's solution containing norepinephrine and add fresh solution. Wait 5 minutes before proceeding.

2. Now place 1 to 5 drops of a 1:1000 acetylcholine solution, one drop at a time, into Locke's solution.

3. Observe any changes in the following: basal tone, strength of contraction, frequency of contraction, and speed of contraction.

4. How do each of these responses compare with those seen when acetylcholine was added to cardiac muscle in Exercise 19? Explain in the spaces provided.

Basal tone _____

_____

_____

Strength of contraction _____

_____

_____

Frequency of contraction _____

_____

_____

Speed of contraction _____

_____

_____

Does acetylcholine modify the contractile properties of skeletal muscle? _____
Does the autonomic nervous system play a role in skeletal muscle contractions? _____

e. EFFECT OF ATROPINE

1. Before performing this experiment, drain Locke's solution containing acetylcholine and add a fresh solution. Wait 5 minutes before proceeding.

2. Place 5 to 10 drops of a 1:50,000 atropine solution into Locke's solution.

3. Explain the effects of atropine on the following:

Basal tone _____

_____

_____

Strength of contraction _____

_____

_____

Frequency of contraction _____

_____

_____

Speed of contraction _____

_____

_____

f. EFFECT OF ATROPINE AND ACETYLCHOLINE

1. Add 1 to 5 drops of a 1:1000 solution of acetylcholine to Locke's solution already containing atropine.

2. Wait 3 to 5 minutes and compare the effect of acetylcholine in the presence of atropine on the following:

Basal tone _____

_____

_____

Strength of contraction _____

_____

_____

Frequency of contraction _____

_____

_____

Speed of contraction _____

_____

_____

Based upon your observations, what type of acetylcholine receptors does the smooth muscle segment possess? _____

_____

g. EFFECT OF ATROPINE, ACETYLCHOLINE, AND NOREPINEPHRINE

1. Add 5 to 8 drops of a 1:50,000 solution of norepinephrine to Locke's solution already containing atropine and acetylcholine.

2. Wait 3 to 5 minutes and compare the effect of norepinephrine in the presence of atropine and acetylcholine on the following:

Basal tone _____

_____

_____

Strength of contraction _____

_____

_____

Frequency of contraction _____

_____

_____

Speed of contraction _____

_____

_____

h. EFFECT OF CALCIUM REMOVAL

1. Before performing this experiment, drain Locke's solution containing atropine, acetylcholine, and norepinephrine and fill the beaker with fresh Locke's solution. Allow 5 minutes before proceeding.

2. To determine whether the intestinal segment has completely recovered, record about 3

minutes of activity and then compare your observations to those recorded in Section 3a.

3. Now replace Locke's solution with Locke's solution containing O[Ca]$_e$.

4. Explain the effects of Locke's solution containing O[Ca]$_e$ on the following:

Basal tone _____

_____

_____

Strength of contraction _____

_____

_____

Frequency of contraction _____

_____

_____

Speed of contraction _____

_____

_____

Would you expect similar results if you were to expose cardiac muscle to Locke's solution containing O[Ca]$_e$? _____

_____

_____

Would you expect similar results if you were to expose skeletal muscle to Locke's solution containing O[Ca]$_e$? _____

_____

_____

D. CHEMISTRY OF DIGESTION

You have learned how food is digested and absorbed. Now you will learn what happens to the food after it reaches the cells of the body. You also will learn what nutrients are needed for survival and why.

Nutrients are chemical substances in food that provide energy, act as building blocks to form new body components, or assist body processes. The six major classes of nutrients are: carbohydrates, lipids, proteins, minerals, vitamins, and water. Cells break down carbohydrates, lipids, and proteins to release energy or use them to build new structures and new regulatory substances, such as hormones and enzymes.

Enzymes are proteins produced by living cells to catalyze or speed many of the reactions in the body. Enzymes act as **catalysts** to speed reactions without being permanently altered by the reaction. Digestive enzymes function as catalysts to speed chemical reactions in the digestive tract.

Because digestive enzymes function outside the cells that produce them, they are capable of also reacting within a test tube and therefore provide an excellent means of studying enzyme activity.

Caution! As you perform the following tests *use extreme care in working with all reagents. Should any of them make contact with your eyes or skin, flush with water for several minutes and then seek immediate medical attention.*

1. Positive Tests for Sugar and Starch

Salivary amylase is an enzyme produced by the salivary glands. This enzyme starts starch digestion and **hydrolyzes** (splits using water) it into maltose. We measure the amount of starch and sugar present before and after enzymatic activity. It is expected that the amount of starch should *decrease* and the sugar level should *increase* as a result of salivary amylase activity.

a. TEST FOR SUGAR

Benedict's test is commonly used to detect sugars. Glucose (monosaccharide), maltose (disaccharide), or any other reducing sugars react with **Benedict's solution,** forming insoluble red cuprous oxide. The precipitate of cuprous oxide can usually be seen in the bottom of the tube when standing. Benedict's solution turns green, yellow, orange, or red depending on the amount of reducing sugar present.

Test for the presence of sugar (maltose) as follows:

1. Place 2 ml of maltose and 2 ml of Benedict's solution in a test tube.

2. Place the test tube in a boiling water bath and heat for 5 minutes. *Make sure that the mouth of the test tube is pointed away from you and all other persons in the area.* Note the color change from blue to red; the more sugar present, the redder the solution.

3. Repeat the same procedure using starch solution instead of maltose. Notice that the color does not change, because the solution contains no sugar. Now you have a method for detecting sugar.

b. TEST FOR STARCH

Lugol's solution is a special iodine solution used to test certain polysaccharides, especially starch. Starch, for example, gives a **deep blue** to **black** color with Lugol's solution (the black is really a concentrated blue color). Cellulose, monosaccharides, and disaccharides do not react. A negative test is indicated by a yellow to brown color of the solution itself, or possibly some other color (other than blue to black) resulting from pigments present in the substance being tested.

1. Place a drop of starch solution on a spot plate and then add a drop of Lugol's solution to it. Notice the black color that forms as the starch-iodine complex develops.

2. Repeat the test using a maltose solution in place of the starch solution. Note that there is no color change, because Lugol's solution and maltose do not combine. Now you have a method for detecting starch.

c. DIGESTION OF STARCH

Salivary amylase from freshly collected saliva is used in this procedure to show digestion of starch.

1. Rinse your mouth thoroughly with distilled water two or three times.

2. Chew a piece of paraffin wax or sugarless gum to stimulate saliva flow, collecting 4 to 5 ml of saliva in a small container.

3. Add an equal amount of tap water carefully, so that you have diluted saliva that contains the enzyme to be studied. You may also use commercially prepared amylase.

4. Transfer 5 ml of a starch solution to a small beaker, add 5 ml of the saliva solution (or a pinch of amylase powder), and mix thoroughly.

5. Wait 1 minute, record the time, remove one drop of the mixture with a glass rod to the depression of a spot plate, and then test for starch with Lugol's solution.

6. At 1-minute intervals, test one-drop samples of the mixture until you no longer note a positive test for starch. Keep the glass rod in the mixture, stirring it from time to time.

7. After the starch test is seen to be negative, test the remaining mixture for the presence of glucose. Do this by adding 2 ml of the mixture to 2 ml of the Benedict's solution and heat in a boiling water bath. Answer questions a through c in Section D.1 of the Laboratory Report Results.

2. Effect of Temperature on Starch Digestion

In the following procedure, you will test starch digestion at five different temperatures to determine how temperature influences enzyme activity. Lugol's solution is again used for presence or absence of starch.

A fresh enzyme solution (salivary amylase) should be prepared as before. Five constant temperature water baths should be available. Starting with the lowest temperature, these are: 1 °C or cooler, 10 °C, 40 °C, 60 °C, and boiling.

1. Prepare 10 test tubes, 5 containing 1 ml each of enzyme solution and 5 containing 1 ml each of starch solution.

2. Pair the tubes (i.e., a tube containing enzyme with one containing starch) and place one pair into each water bath. *Make sure that the mouth of the test tube is pointed away from you and all other persons in the area.*

3. Permit the tubes to adapt to the bath temperatures for about 5 minutes, then mix the enzyme and starch solutions of each pair together, replacing the single test tube in its respective water bath.

4. After 30 seconds, test all five tubes for starch on a spot plate using Lugol's solution.

5. Repeat every 30 seconds until you have determined the time required for the starch to disappear (that is, to be digested).

6. Record your results in Section D.2 of the Laboratory Report Results.

3. Effect of pH on Starch Digestion

You can demonstrate the effectiveness of salivary amylase digestion at different pH readings.

1. Prepare three buffer solutions as follows:

Solution A—pH 4.0

Solution B—pH 7.0

Solution C—pH 9.0

2. Once again a fresh enzyme solution (salivary amylase) should be prepared.

3. Mix 4 ml of a starch solution with 2 ml of buffer solution A in a test tube.

4. Repeat this procedure with buffer solutions B and C.

5. You now have three test tubes of a starch-buffer solution, each at a different pH (4.0, 7.0, and 9.0).

6. Place one drop of starch-buffer solution A on a spot plate and immediately add one drop of the saliva.

7. Test for starch disappearance using Lugol's solution, and record the time when starch first disappears completely.

8. Repeat this test for the other two starch buffers (solutions B and C) and record the time when starch is no longer present at each pH.

9. Record and explain your results in Section D.3 of the Laboratory Report Results.

4. Digestion of Fats

You can demonstrate the effect of pancreatic juice on fat by the use of pancreatin, which contains all the enzymes present in pancreatic juice. Because the optimum pH of the pancreatic enzymes ranges from 7.0 to 8.8, the pancreatin is prepared in sodium carbonate. The enzyme activity in this test is **lipase,** which digests fat to fatty acids and glycerol. The fatty acid produced changes the color of **blue** litmus to **red.**

1. Place 5 ml of litmus cream (heavy cream to which powdered litmus has been added to give

it a blue color) in a test tube, and put it in a 40 °C water bath.

2. Repeat the procedure with another 5-ml portion in a second tube, but put it in an ice bath.

3. When the tubes have adapted to their respective temperatures (in about 5 minutes), add 5 ml of pancreatin to each tube and replace them in their water baths until a color change occurs in one tube.

4. Summarize your results and your explanation in Section D.4 of the Laboratory Report Results.

5. Action of Bile on Fats

Bile is important in the process of digestion because of its emulsifying effect (breaking down of large globules to smaller, uniformly distributed particles) on fats and oils. *Bile does not contain any enzymes.* Emulsification of lipids by means of bile serves to increase the surface area of the lipid that will be exposed to the action of lipase.

1. Place 5 ml of water into one test tube and 5 ml of bile solution into a second.

2. Add one drop of vegetable oil that has been colored with a fat-soluble dye, such as Sudan B, into each tube.

3. Shake both tubes *vigorously,* then let them stand in a test tube rack undisturbed for 10 minutes. Fat or oil that is broken into sufficiently small droplets will remain suspended in water in the form of an **emulsion.**

4. Answer questions i and j in Section D.5 of the Laboratory Report Results.

6. Digestion of Protein

Here you demonstrate the effect of pepsin on protein and the factors affecting the rate of action of pepsin. **Pepsin,** a proteolytic enzyme secreted by the chief cells in the lining of the stomach, digests proteins (fibrin in this experiment) to peptides. The efficiency of pepsin activity depends on the pH of the solution, the optimum being 1.5 to 2.5. Pepsin is almost completely inactive in neutral or alkaline solutions.

1. Prepare and number the following five test tubes. For this test, the quantity of each solution must be measured carefully.

>   Tube 1—5 ml of 0.5% pepsin; 5 ml of 0.8% HCl
>
>   Tube 2—5 ml of pepsin; 5 ml of water
>
>   Tube 3—5 ml of pepsin, boiled for 10 minutes in a water bath; 5 ml of 0.8% HCl
>
>   Tube 4—5 ml of pepsin; 5 ml of 0.5% NaOH
>
>   Tube 5—5 ml of water; 5 ml of 0.8% HCl

2. First determine the approximate pH of each test tube using Hydrion paper (range 1 to 11) and put the values in the table provided in the Laboratory Report Results.

3. Place a small amount of fibrin (the protein) in each test tube. An amount near the size of a pea will be sufficient. Put the tubes in a 40 °C water bath and *carefully* shake occasionally. Maintain 40 °C temperature closely. The tubes should remain in the water bath for *at least 1½ hours.*

4. Watch the changes that the fibrin undergoes. The swelling that occurs in some tubes should not be confused with digestion. Digested fibrin becomes transparent and disappears (dissolves) as the protein is digested to soluble peptides.

5. Finish the experiment when the fibrin is digested in one of the five tubes.

6. Record all your observations in the table provided in Section D.6 of the Laboratory Report Results.

LABORATORY REPORT QUESTIONS (PAGE 433)

23 | URINARY SYSTEM

The **urinary system** functions to keep the body in homeostasis by controlling the composition and volume of the blood. The system accomplishes these functions by removing and restoring selected amounts of water and various solutes. The kidneys also excrete selected amounts of various wastes, assume a role in erythropoiesis by forming renal erythropoietic factor, help control blood pH, help regulate blood pressure by secreting renin, and participate in the activation of vitamin D.

The urinary system consists of two kidneys, two ureters, one urinary bladder, and a single urethra (see Figure 23.1). Other systems that help in waste elimination are the respiratory, integumentary, and digestive systems.

Using your textbook, charts, or models for reference, label Figure 23.1.

A. ORGANS OF URINARY SYSTEM

1. Kidneys

The paired **kidneys,** which resemble kidney beans in shape, are found just above the waist between the parietal peritoneum and the posterior wall of the abdomen. Because they are external to the peritoneal lining of the abdominal cavity, they are referred to as **retroperitoneal** (re'-trō-per-i-to-NĒ-al). The kidneys are positioned between T12 and L3, with the right kidney slightly lower than the left because of the position of the liver. Near the center of the kidney's concave border, which faces the vertebral column, is an indentation called the **hilus,** through which the ureter leaves the kidney and blood vessels, lymph vessels, and nerves enter and exit the kidney. The hilus is the entrance to

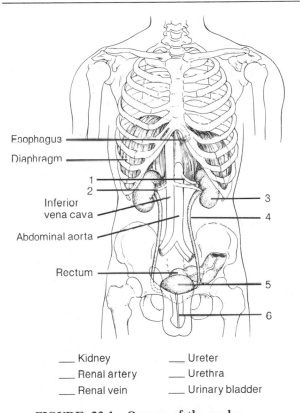

Esophagus
Diaphragm
1
2
Inferior vena cava
Abdominal aorta
Rectum
3
4
5
6

___ Kidney   ___ Ureter
___ Renal artery   ___ Urethra
___ Renal vein   ___ Urinary bladder

FIGURE 23.1 Organs of the male urinary system and associated structures.

a cavity in the kidney called the **renal sinus.** Three layers of tissue surround each kidney: the **renal capsule, adipose capsule,** and **renal fascia.** They function to protect the kidney and hold it firmly in place.

If a coronal (frontal) section is made through a kidney, the following structures can be seen:

a. **Cortex**—Outer, narrow, reddish area.

b. **Medulla**—Inner, wide, reddish-brown area.

315

c. **Renal (medullary) pyramids**—Striated triangular structures, 8 to 18 in number, in the medulla. The bases of the pyramids face the cortex, and the apices, called **renal papillae,** are directed toward the center of the kidney.

d. **Renal column**—Cortical substance between renal pyramids.

e. **Renal pelvis**—Large cavity in the renal sinus, enlarged proximal portion of ureter.

f. **Major calyces** (KĀ-li-sēz)—Consist of 2 or 3 cuplike extensions of the renal pelvis.

g. **Minor calyces**—Consist of 7 to 13 cuplike extensions of the major calyces.

Within the cortex and renal pyramids of each kidney are more than 1,000,000 microscopic units called nephrons, the functional units of the kidneys. As a result of their activity in regulating the volume and chemistry of the blood, they produce urine. Urine passes from the nephrons to the minor calyces, major calyces, renal pelvis, ureter, urinary bladder, and urethra.

Examine a specimen, model, or chart of the kidney and with the aid of your textbook, label Figure 23.2.

2. Nephrons

Basically, a **nephron** (NEF-ron) is a renal tubule and its vascular component. A nephron begins as a double-walled cup, called a **glomerular (Bowman's) capsule,** lying in the cortex of the kidney. The inner wall of the capsule, the **visceral layer,** consists of epithelial cells called **podocytes** and surrounds a capillary network called the **glomerulus** (glō-MER-yoo-lus). A space separates the visceral layer from the outer wall of the capsule, the **parietal layer,** which is composed of simple squamous epithelium. Together the glomerular capsule and enclosed glomerulus constitute the **renal corpuscle** (KŌR-pus-sul).

The visceral layer of the glomerular capsule and endothelium of the glomerulus form an **endothelial-capsular membrane,** a very effective filter. Electron microscopy has determined that the membrane consists of the following components, given in the order in which substances are filtered (Figure 23.3).

a. **Endothelium of glomerulus**—Single layer of endothelium with pores averaging 500 to 1000 Å in diameter.

b. **Basement membrane of glomerulus**—Nonporous glycoprotein beneath the endothelium that serves as a dialyzing membrane.

c. **Epithelium of visceral layer of the glomerular capsule**—Epithelial cells are called **podocytes** and consist of footlike structures called **pedicels** (PED-i-sels) arranged parallel to the circumference of the glomerulus. Pedicels cover the basement membrane of the glomerulus, except for spaces between them called **filtration slits (slit pores).**

The endothelial-capsular membrane filters blood passing through the kidney. Blood cells and large molecules, such as proteins, are retained by the filter and eventually are recycled into the blood. The filtered substances pass through the membrane and into the space between the parietal and visceral layers of the glomerular capsule, and then enter the next component of a nephron, the proximal convoluted tubule.

As the filtered fluid (filtrate) passes through the remaining parts of a nephron, substances are selectively added and removed. The waste product of these activities is urine. After the filtrate leaves the glomerular capsule, it passes through the following structures:

a. **Proximal convoluted tubule**—Coiled tubule in the cortex that originates at the glomerular capsule; consists of simple cuboidal epithelium with microvilli.

b. **Descending limb**—Extension of the proximal convoluted tubule that dips down into medulla; consists of simple squamous epithelium.

c. **Loop of the nephron (loop of Henle)**—U-shaped tubule in medulla connecting descending and ascending limbs.

d. **Ascending limb**—Extension of loop of the nephron that ascends in medulla and approaches cortex; consists of simple cuboidal epithelium, simple columnar epithelium, or both; wider in diameter than the descending limb.

e. **Distal convoluted tubule**—Coiled extension of ascending limb in cortex; consists of simple cuboidal epithelium with fewer microvilli than in proximal convoluted tubule.

Distal convoluted **tubules** terminate by merging with straight **collecting ducts.** In the medulla, collecting ducts receive distal convo-

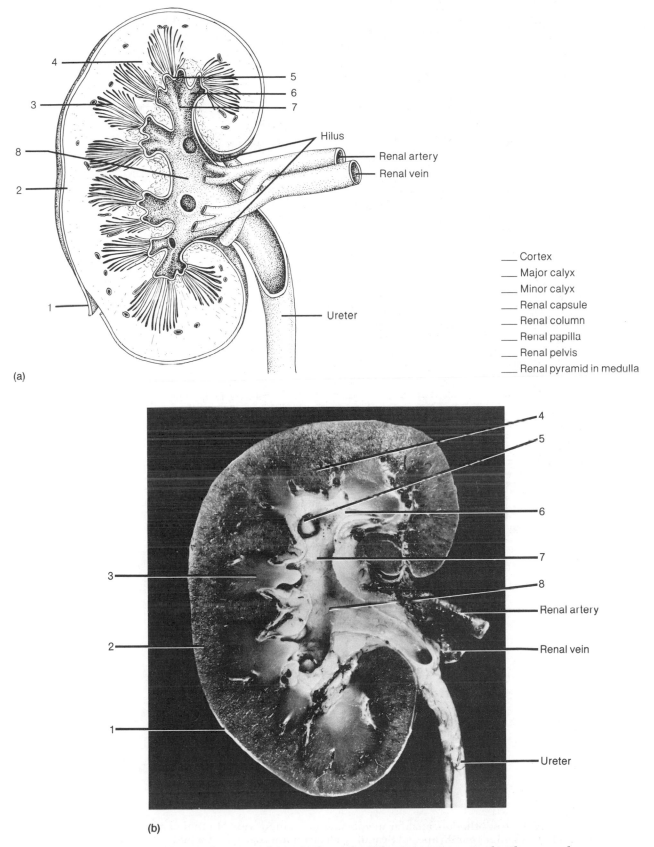

(a)

___ Cortex
___ Major calyx
___ Minor calyx
___ Renal capsule
___ Renal column
___ Renal papilla
___ Renal pelvis
___ Renal pyramid in medulla

Hilus

Renal artery

Renal vein

Ureter

(b)

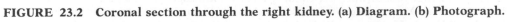

FIGURE 23.2   Coronal section through the right kidney. (a) Diagram. (b) Photograph.

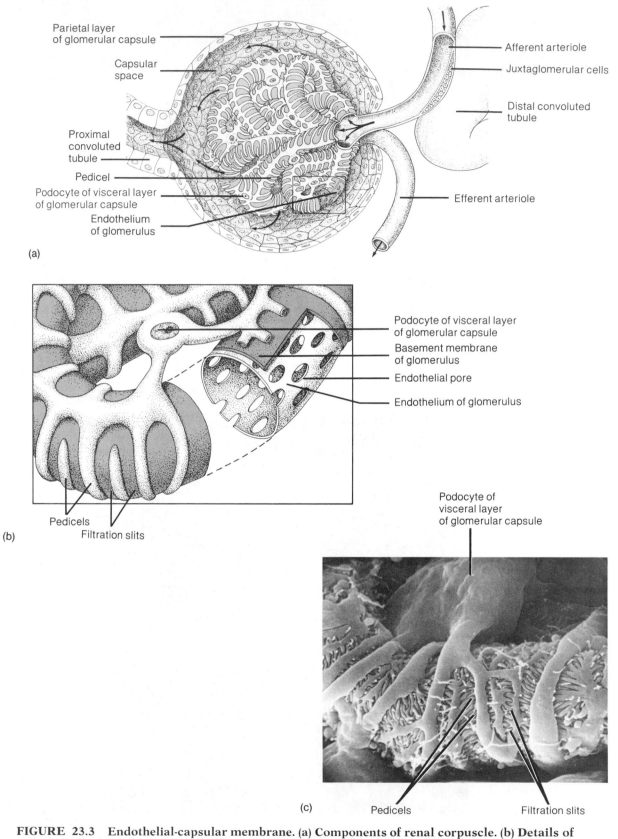

(a)

(b)

(c)

FIGURE 23.3 **Endothelial-capsular membrane. (a) Components of renal corpuscle. (b) Details of endothelial-capsular membrane. (c) Scanning electron micrograph of a podocyte at magnification of 7800×. ((c) from *Tissues and Organs: A Text-Atlas of Scanning Electron Microscopy* by Richard G. Kessel and Randy H. Kardon. W. H. Freeman and Company. Copyright © 1979.)**

luted tubules from several nephrons, pass through the renal pyramids, and open at the renal papillae into minor calyces through a number of large **papillary ducts.** The processed filtrate, called urine, passes from the collecting ducts to papillary ducts, minor calyces, major calyces, renal pelvis, ureter, urinary bladder, and urethra.

With the aid of your textbook, label the parts of a nephron and associated structures in Figure 23.4.

Examine prepared slides of various components of nephrons, and compare your observations to Figure 23.5.

3. Blood and Nerve Supply

The nephrons are abundantly supplied with blood vessels, and the kidneys actually receive around one-fourth the total cardiac output, or approximately 1200 ml, every minute. The blood

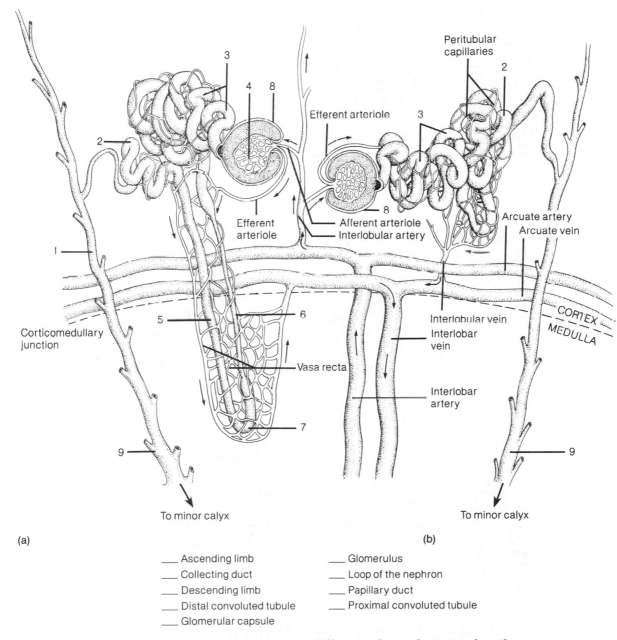

(a)

(b)

___ Ascending limb	___ Glomerulus
___ Collecting duct	___ Loop of the nephron
___ Descending limb	___ Papillary duct
___ Distal convoluted tubule	___ Proximal convoluted tubule
___ Glomerular capsule	

FIGURE 23.4 Nephrons. (a) Juxtamedullary nephron. (b) Cortical nephron.

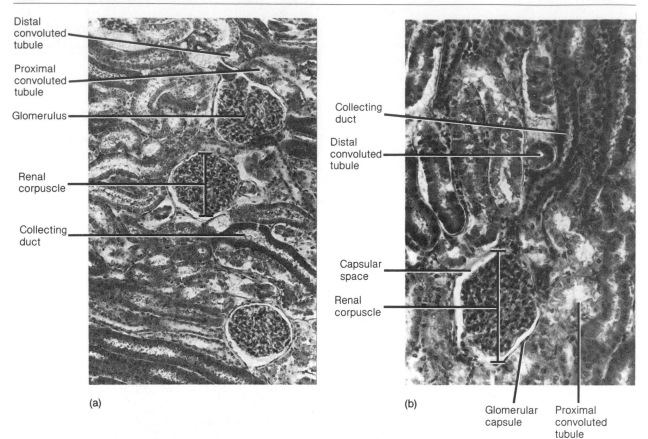

(a)

Distal convoluted tubule

Proximal convoluted tubule

Glomerulus

Renal corpuscle

Collecting duct

(b)

Collecting duct

Distal convoluted tubule

Capsular space

Renal corpuscle

Glomerular capsule

Proximal convoluted tubule

(c)

FIGURE 23.5 **Nephrons. (a) and (b) Microscopic appearance of components. (c) Scanning electron micrograph of renal tubules.**

supply originates in each kidney with the **renal artery,** which divides into many branches, eventually supplying the nephron and its complete tubule.

Before or immediately after entering the hilus, the renal artery divides into several branches, the **interlobar arteries,** which pass between the renal pyramids in the renal columns. At the bases of the pyramids, the interlobar arteries arch between the medulla and cortex and here are known as **arcuate arteries.** Branches of the arcuate arteries, called **interlobular arteries,** enter the cortex. **Afferent arterioles,** branches of the interlobular arteries, are distributed to the **glomeruli.** Blood leaves the glomeruli via **efferent arterioles.**

The next sequence of blood vessels depends on the type of nephron. A **cortical nephron** usually has its glomerulus in the cortex, and the remainder of the nephron rarely penetrates into the medulla (see Figure 23.4b). A **juxtamedullary nephron** usually has its glomerulus close to the corticomedullary junction, and other parts of the nephron penetrate deeply into the medulla (see Figure 23.4a). Around convoluted tubules, efferent arterioles of cortical nephrons divide to form capillary networks called **peritubular capillaries.** Efferent arterioles of juxtamedullary nephrons also form peritubular capillaries and, in addition, form long loops of blood vessels around medullary structures called **vasa recta.** Peritubular capillaries eventually reunite to form **interlobular veins.** Blood then drains into **arcuate veins** and **interlobar veins.** Blood leaves the kidney through the **renal vein** that exits at the hilus. (The vasa recta pass blood into the interlobular veins, arcuate veins, interlobar veins, and renal veins.)

As the afferent arteriole approaches the renal corpuscle, the smooth muscle cells of the tunica media become more rounded and granular and are known as **juxtaglomerular cells.** The cells of the distal convoluted tubule adjacent to the afferent and efferent arterioles become narrower and are known as the **macula densa.** Together the juxtaglomerular cells and macula densa constitute the **juxtaglomerular apparatus.** The juxtaglomerular apparatus responds to low renal blood pressure by secreting a substance (renin) that begins a sequence of responses that raises renal pressure back to normal.

Using Figures 23.4 and 23.6 as guides, trace a drop of blood from its entrance into the renal artery to its exit through the renal vein. As you do so, name in sequence each blood vessel through which blood passes for both cortical and juxtaglomerular nephrons.

The nerve supply to the kidneys comes from the **renal plexus** of the autonomic system. The nerves are vasomotor because they regulate the circulation of blood in the kidney by regulating the diameters of the small blood vessels.

4. Ureters

The body has two retroperitoneal **ureters** (YOO-rē-ters), one for each kidney; each ureter is a continuation of the renal pelvis and runs to the urinary bladder (see Figure 23.1). Urine is carried through the ureters mostly by peristaltic contractions of the muscular layer of the ureters. Each ureter extends 25 to 30 cm (10 to 12 in.) and enters the urinary bladder at the superior lateral angle of its base.

Histologically, the ureters consist of an inner **mucosa** of transitional epithelium and connective tissue, a middle **muscularis** (inner longitudinal and outer circular smooth muscle), and an outer **fibrous coat.**

Examine a prepared slide of the wall of the ureter showing its various layers. With the aid of your textbook, label Figure 23.7.

5. Urinary Bladder

The **urinary bladder** is a hollow muscular organ located in the pelvic cavity posterior to the symphysis pubis (see Figure 23.1). In the male, the bladder is directly anterior to the rectum; in the female, it is anterior to the vagina and inferior to the uterus.

At the base of the interior of the urinary bladder is the **trigone** (TRĪ-gōn), a triangular area bounded by the opening to the urethra and ureteral openings into the bladder. The **mucosa** of the urinary bladder consists of transitional epithelium and connective tissue that form **rugae.** The **muscularis,** also called the **detrusor** (de-TROO-ser) **muscle,** consists of an inner longitudinal, middle circular, and outer longitudinal smooth muscle layer. In the region around the opening to the urethra, the circular muscle fibers form an **internal sphincter.** Below this is the **external sphincter** composed of skeletal muscle. The **serosa** is formed by visceral peritoneum and covers the superior surface of the urinary bladder.

Urine is expelled from the bladder by an act called **micturition** (mik'-too-RISH-un), com-

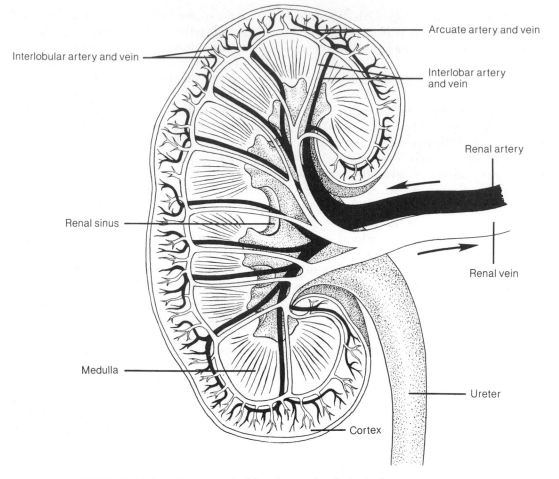

FIGURE 23.6 Macroscopic blood vessels of the kidney.
Macroscopic and microscopic blood vessels are shown in Figure 23.4.

monly known as urination or voiding. The average capacity of the urinary bladder is 700 to 800 ml.

Using your textbook as a guide, label the external sphincter, internal sphincter, ureteral openings, and ureters in Figure 23.8.

Examine a prepared slide of the wall of the urinary bladder. With the aid of your textbook, label Figure 23.9.

6. Urethra

The **urethra** is a small tube leading from the floor of the urinary bladder to the exterior of the body. In females, this tube is posterior to the symphysis pubis and is embedded in the anterior wall of the vagina; its length is approximately 3.8 cm (1½ in.). The opening of the urethra to the exterior, the **urethral orifice**, is between the clitoris and vaginal orifice. In males, its length is around 20 cm (8 in.), and it follows a different route than that of the female. Immediately below the urinary bladder, the urethra passes through the prostate gland, pierces the urogenital diaphragm, and traverses the penis. The urethra is the terminal portion of the urinary system, and serves as the passageway for discharging urine from the body. In addition, in the male, the urethra serves as the duct through which reproductive fluid (semen) is discharged from the body.

Label the urethra and urethral orifice in Figure 23.9.

B. TUBULAR SECRETION

The glomeruli of the kidneys form a filtrate through a simple filtration process. The material thus formed will pass through the remainder of the nephron and will be modified by sev-

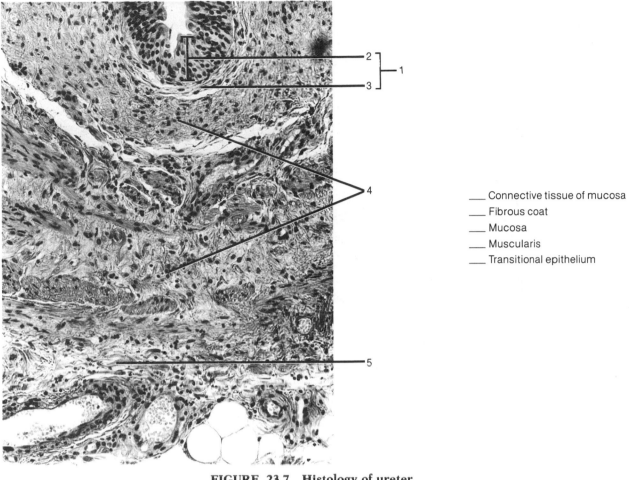

FIGURE 23.7   Histology of ureter.

___ Connective tissue of mucosa
___ Fibrous coat
___ Mucosa
___ Muscularis
___ Transitional epithelium

eral processes involving both active transport and passive diffusion. Movement of a substance from the tubular lumen into the peritubular capillaries is termed **tubular reabsorption.** This process can occur via either passive diffusion or active transport. Movement of a substance from the peritubular capillaries through the tubular cells and into the tubular lumen is termed **tubular secretion.** Like reabsorption, this process can occur via either passive diffusion or active transport. Typically materials secreted by the nephron are compounds that are incompletely metabolized or not metabolized at all, weak acids or bases, or a substance foreign to the body. Secretion may occur in both the proximal and distal convoluted tubules.

A very simple technique to demonstrate tubular secretion utilizes isolated goldfish renal tubules. The fish kidney is ideally suited because the lack of supportive connective tissue between the tubules allows easy and rapid dis-section of single tubules. Tubules suspended in Ringer's solution remain viable for several hours and readily demonstrate the secretion of several substances.

1. Isolation of Renal Tubules

1. After decapitating the fish, make a midline ventral incision and expose the kidneys. Identification of the kidneys is aided by their location lateral to the vertebral column and by their reddish-brown color.

2. Gently remove the kidneys and place them in a dish containing Ringer's solution.

3. Utilizing dissection needles, break the kidneys into progressively smaller pieces until the renal tubules are separated. If additional separation is necessary, gently pass some of the tubules into and out of a wide bore medicine dropper.

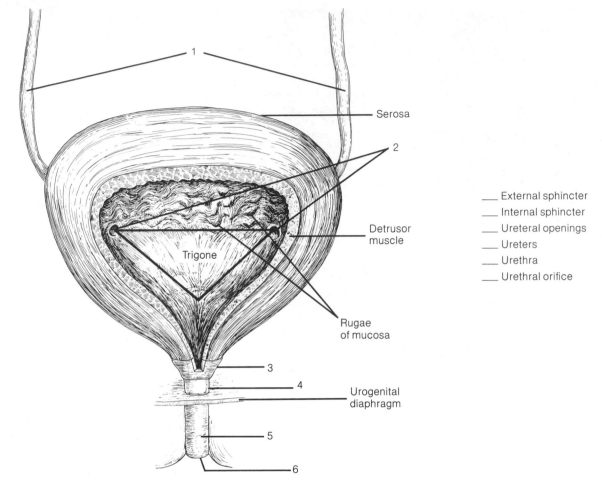

FIGURE 23.8 Urinary bladder and female urethra.

___ External sphincter
___ Internal sphincter
___ Ureteral openings
___ Ureters
___ Urethra
___ Urethral orifice

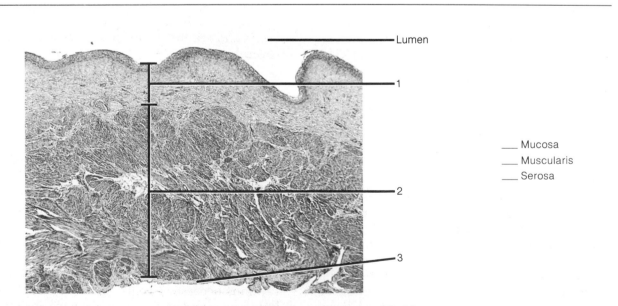

FIGURE 23.9 Histology of urinary bladder.

___ Mucosa
___ Muscularis
___ Serosa

2. Experimental Procedure

a. SECRETION OF PHENOL RED

1. Place several drops of Ringer's solution onto a depression slide and place one or two renal tubules into the depression via the dropper.

2. Observe the tubules under a microscope and become familiar with their anatomy. Be able to locate the lumen of the tubules.

3. Now place several drops of Ringer's solution containing phenol red (0.05 M) into the depression of another slide, and add one or two tubules to this solution.

4. Immediately place the slide under the microscope and determine (a) time required for the *first* appearance of phenol red within the lumen of the tubule and (b) time required for the *maximum concentration* of dye within the lumen of the tubule.

5. Record your results in Section B.1 of the Laboratory Report Results.

b. INHIBITION OF SECRETION

Several substances are secreted by similar or identical tubular carrier mechanisms. Therefore, if two substances are competing for the same carrier, the substance that has a higher concentration or greater affinity for the carrier will inhibit the secretion of the second substance. Such is the case with phenol red and penicillin G.

1. Place several tubules in a depression slide containing 0.05 M phenol red and 1 M penicillin G.

2. Determine the values for the time required for phenol red to first appear in the lumen of the tubule, and the time required for maximum concentration of the dye within the tubular lumen.

3. Record your results in Section B.2 of the Laboratory Report Results.

4. What type of inhibitory mechanism does this experiment demonstrate? _____

_____

_____

_____

c. METABOLIC REQUIREMENTS FOR SECRETION

Phenol red is secreted via active transport, that is, movement of a substance against a concentration gradient, utilizing a carrier and involving expenditure of energy. The energy in this process is obtained by splitting ATP into ADP and P.

1. To demonstrate that the secretion of phenol red requires energy, suspend several tubules in a solution containing 0.05 M phenol red and either 1 mM trichlorophenol or 0.2 mM 2,4 dinitrophenol.

2. Record the times required for dye transport in Section B.3 of the Laboratory Report Results.

3. Look up the actions of the chemical you utilized, and discuss how this would affect the transport process in the secretion of phenol

red. _____

_____

_____

C. DISSECTION OF SHEEP KIDNEY

The sheep kidney is very similar to both human and cat kidney. You may use Figure 23.2 as a reference for this dissection.

1. Examine the intact kidney and notice the hilus and fatty tissue that normally surrounds the kidney. Strip away the fat.

2. As you peel the fat off, look carefully for the **adrenal suprarenal gland.** This gland is usually found attached to the superior surface of the kidney, as it is in the human. Most preserved kidneys do not have this gland. If it is present, remove it, cut it in half, and note its distinct outer **cortex** and inner **medulla.**

3. Look at the **hilus,** which is the concave area of the kidney. From here the **ureter, renal artery,** and **renal vein** enter and exit.

4. Differentiate these blood vessels by examining the thickness of their walls. Which vessel has the thicker wall?

5. With a sharp scalpel *carefully* make a longitudinal (coronal) section through the kidney.

6. Identify the **renal capsule** as a thin, tough layer of connective tissue completely surrounding the kidney.

7. Immediately beneath this capsule is an outer light-colored area called the **renal cortex.** The inner dark-colored area is the **renal medulla.**

8. The **renal pelvis** is the large chamber formed by the expansion of the ureter inside the kidney. This renal pelvis divides into many smaller areas called **renal calyces,** each of which has a dark tuft of kidney tissue called a **renal pyramid.**

9. The bases of these pyramids face the cortical area. Their apices, called **renal papillae,** are directed toward the center of the kidney.

10. The calyces collect urine from collecting ducts and drain it into the renal pelvis and out through the ureter.

11. The renal artery divides into several branches that pass between the renal pyramids. These vessels are small and delicate and may be too difficult to dissect and trace through the renal medulla.

D. URINE

The kidneys perform their homeostatic functions of controlling the concentration and volume of blood and adjusting pH. The by-product of these functions is the fluid called **urine.** Urine contains a high concentration of solutes. In a healthy person its volume, pH, and solute concentration vary with the needs of the internal environment. In certain pathological conditions, the characteristics of urine may change drastically. An analysis of the volume and physical and chemical properties of urine tells us much about the state of the body.

1. Physical Characteristics

Normal urine is usually a straw yellow to amber transparent liquid with a characteristic odor. Urine color varies considerably according to the ratio of solutes to water and according to the diet.

Cloudy urine sometimes reflects the secretion of mucin from the urinary tract lining and is not necessarily pathological. The pH of urine is usually slightly acid, ranging between 5.0 and 7.8. The pH of urine is also strongly affected by diet with a high protein diet increasing acidity and a mostly vegetable diet increasing alkalinity.

Specific gravity is the ratio of the weight of a volume of a substance to the weight of an equal volume of distilled water. Water has a specific gravity of 1.000. The specific gravity of urine depends on the amount of solids in solution and normally ranges from 1.008 to 1.030. The greater the concentration of solutes, the higher the specific gravity.

2. Abnormal Constituents

When the body's metabolism is not working efficiently, many substances not normally found in urine may appear in trace amounts. In addition, normal constituents may appear in abnormal amounts. **Urinalysis** is the analysis of the physical and chemical properties of urine, and is a vital tool in diagnosing pathological conditions.

a. **Albumin—Albumin** is normally a part of plasma, but it usually does not appear in urine because the particles are too large to pass through the pores in the capillaries. When albumin is found in the urine, the condition is called **albuminuria.**

b. **Glucose**—Urine normally contains such small amounts of **glucose** that clinically glucose is considered absent. Its presence in significant amounts is called **glycosuria,** and the most common cause is a high blood sugar level.

c. **Erythrocytes—Hematuria** is the condition when red blood cells are found in the urine in appreciable amounts, and usually indicates a pathological condition.

d. **Leucocytes—Pyuria** is the condition when white blood cells and other components of pus are found in the urine, and usually indicates a pathological condition.

e. **Ketone bodies**—Normal urine contains small amounts of **ketone (acetone)** bodies. Their appearance in large quantities in urine produces the conditions called **ketosis (acetonuria)** and may indicate abnormalities.

f. **Casts—Casts** are tiny masses of various substances that have hardened and assumed the shape of the lumens of the nephron tubules. They are microscopic and are composed of many different substances.

g. **Calculi**—Insoluble **calculi** (stones) are various salts that have solidified in the urinary tract. They are found anywhere from the kidney tubules to the external opening.

E. URINALYSIS

In this exercise you will determine some of the characteristics of urine and perform tests for some abnormal constituents that may be present in urine. Some of these tests may be used in determining unknowns in urine specimens.

Caution! As you perform the following tests, *use extreme care in working with all reagents. Should any of them make contact with your eyes or skin, flush with water for several minutes and then seek immediate medical attention.*

A specimen of urine may be collected at any time for routine tests; urine voided within 3 hours after meals, however, may contain abnormal constituents. For this reason the first voiding in the morning is preferred.

Both males and females should collect a midstream sample of urine in a sterile container. A midstream sample is essential to avoid contamination from the external genitalia, and to avoid the presence of pus cells and bacteria that are normally found in the urethra. If not examined immediately, the specimen should be refrigerated to prevent unnecessary bacterial growth.

Before testing *always* mix urine by swirling, inverting the container, or stirring with a wooden swab stick. *Keep all containers clean!* Wrap all papers and sticks and put them in the garbage pail. Rinse all test tubes and glass containers carefully with *cold water* after they have cooled. Flush sinks well with cold water.

Obtain either your own freshly voided urine sample or a provided sample if one is available.

Alternate methods can be employed for several of the tests you are about to perform. One alternate method is the use of plastic strips to which are attached paper squares impregnated with various reagents. These strips display a color reaction when dipped into urine with any abnormal constituents.

At this point, you should take a Chemstrip and test your urine sample for the following: pH, protein, glucose, ketones, bilirubin, and blood (hemoglobin). Record your results below.

1. Dip the test strip into your urine sample for no longer than 1 second, being sure that all reagents on the strip are immersed.

2. Remove any excess urine from the strip by drawing the edge of the strip along the rim of the container holding your urine sample.

3. After the appropriate time, as indicated on the Chemstrip vial, hold the strip close to the color blocks on the vial.

4. Make sure that the strip blocks are properly lined up with the color chart on the vial.

Test	Chemstrip result
pH	_____
Protein	_____
Glucose	_____
Ketones	_____
Bilirubin	_____
Blood	_____

1. Physical Analysis

a. COLOR

Normal urine varies in color from straw yellow to amber because of the pigment **urochrome**, a by-product of hemoglobin destruction. Observe the color of your urine sample, which may show variations as follows:

Color	Possible cause
Colorless	Reduced concentration
Silvery, milky	Pus, bacteria, epithelial cells
Smoky brown	
Port wine	Blood
Yellow foam	Porphyrins
Orange, green, blue, red	Bile or medications Medications
Dark brown or black	Increase of melanin pigment

Record the color of your urine in the Laboratory Report Results, E.1.a.

b. TRANSPARENCY

A fresh urine sample should be clear. Cloudy urine may be due to substances such as phosphates, urates, fat, pus, mucus, microbes, crystals, and epithelial cells.

To determine transparency, shake your urine sample and observe the degree of cloudiness. Record your observations in the Laboratory Report Results, E.1.b.

c. pH

The pH of urine varies with several factors already indicated. You can test the pH of your urine by using either a Chemstrip or pH paper. Because you have already determined the pH of your urine by using a Chemstrip, you might want to verify the results using pH paper.

1. Place a strip of pH paper into your urine sample three consecutive times.

2. Shake off any excess urine.

3. Let the pH paper sit for 1 minute and then compare it to a color chart provided.

4. Record your observations in the Laboratory Report Results, E.1.c.

d. SPECIFIC GRAVITY

The specific gravity is easily determined using a urinometer (hydrometer). The urinometer is a float with a numbered scale near the top that indicates specific gravity directly.

1. Mix the urine and pour it into the urinometer cylinder.

2. Place the urinometer in the urine, spinning it slightly to make sure that it floats free.

3. Take your reading when the urinometer float is at rest.

4. Record your results in the Laboratory Report Results, E.1.d.

2. Chemical Analysis

a. GLUCOSE

Glycosuria (the presence of glucose in the urine) occurs in patients with diabetes mellitus or other disorders. Traces of glucose may occur in normal urine, but detection of these small amounts requires special tests.

Benedict's test. Benedict's solution is commonly used to detect reducing sugars in urine and is not specific for just glucose.

1. In a Pyrex test tube, combine 10 drops of urine with 5 ml of Benedict's solution. Mix the solution.

2. Place the test tube in a boiling water bath for 5 minutes. *Make sure that the mouth of the test tube is pointed away from you and all other persons in the area.*

3. Remove it from the heat and read the results according to the following chart.

4. Record your results in the Laboratory Report Results, E.2.a.

Color	Results
Blue	Negative
Greenish yellow	1 + (0.5 g/100 ml)
	2 + (1 g/100 ml)
Olive green	3 + (1.5 g/100 ml)
Orange-yellow	4 + (more than 2 g/
Brick red (with precipitate)	100 ml)

Clinitest reagent method. An alternative method is to use Clinitest reagent tablets.

1. Place 10 drops of water and 5 drops of urine in a test tube.

2. Add one Clinitest tablet. The concentrated sodium hydroxide in the tablet generates enough heat to make the liquid in the test tube boil.

3. The color of the solution is graded as in Benedict's test.

4. Record your results in the Laboratory Report Results, E.2.a.

Chemstrip method. Record your results in the Laboratory Report Results, E.2.a.

b. PROTEIN

Normal urine contains traces of proteins that are hard to detect through regular laboratory procedures. Albumin is the most abundant serum protein and is the one usually detected. Because tests for albumin are determined by precipitating the protein either by heat (coagulation) or by adding a reagent, the urine sample should either be filtered or centrifuged (see Figure 23.10). The test for protein will be done by either the sulfosalicylic acid method or the albutest reagent method and the Chemstrip method.

Sulfosalicylic acid method. Sulfosalicylic acid will precipitate protein in urine with a turbidity (cloudiness) that is approximately proportional to the concentration of protein present.

1. Place 3 ml of clear urine (supernatant of filtered or centrifuged urine) in a test tube and check its pH with litmus paper.

2. If the pH is already acidic, proceed with the next step. If the pH is alkaline, *carefully* add 10% acetic acid drop by drop until the specimen is just acidic.

3. Check the pH after each drop using litmus paper.

4. *Carefully* add 3 ml of 20% sulfosalicylic acid. Layer it carefully on top of the urine already in the test tube.

5. If proteins are present, a cloudy precipitate will appear at the junction of the two fluids.

6. Using the following table record your results in the Laboratory Report Results, E.2.b.

Appearance	Result
Clear (no cloudiness)	Negative
Cloudiness or ring barely perceptible	Very faint trace
Faint cloudiness; very fine ring	Trace
Dense or granular turbidity	1+
Flocculated cloudiness; thick, heavy ring	2+
Curdy cloud; curdy ring	3+
Solid coagulation; solid ring	4+

Albutest reagent method. An alternative method is to use Albutest reagent tablets containing bromphenol blue.

1. Place the tablet on a clean surface, and add one drop of urine.

2. After the drop has been absorbed, add two drops of water and allow these to penetrate before reading.

3. Compare the color (in daylight or fluorescent light) on top of the tablet with the color chart provided in lab.

4. If the test is negative, the original color of the tablet will not be changed much at the completion of the test.

5. If protein is present in the urine, a *blue-green* spot will remain on the surface of the tablet after the water is added. The amount of protein is indicated by the intensity of the blue-green color.

6. Record your results in the Laboratory Report Results, E.2.b.

Chemstrip method. Record your results in the Laboratory Report Results, E.2.b.

c. KETONE (ACETONE) BODIES

The presence of ketone (acetone) bodies in urine is a result of abnormal fat catabolism. Reagents such as sodium nitroprusside, ammonium sulfate, and ammonium hydroxide are available in the form of tablets. Ketones turn purple when added to these chemicals.

Acetest tablet method.

1. Place an Acetest tablet on a piece of white paper, and place one drop of urine on the tablet.

2. If acetone or ketone is present, a *lavender-purple* color develops within 30 seconds. Compare results with the color chart that comes with the reagent.

3. Record your results in the Laboratory Report Results, E.2.c.

Sodium nitroprusside method.

1. Dissolve a crystal of sodium nitroprusside in 5 ml of urine. (**Caution!** *Do not handle the sodium nitroprusside with your fingers.*)

2. *Carefully* add 5 drops of acetic acid to this mixture.

3. With an eyedropper, *carefully* place one drop of sodium hydroxide on the side of the tube, permitting it to run down to the mixture.

4. A *reddish-purple* ring indicates the presence of acetone.

5. Record your results in the Laboratory Report Results, E.2.c.

Chemstrip method. Record your results in the Laboratory Report Results, E.2.c.

d. BILE PIGMENTS

Bile pigments, biliverdin and bilirubin, are not normally present in urine. The presence of large quantities of bilirubin in the extracellular fluids produces jaundice, a yellowish tint to the body tissues, including yellowness of the skin and deep tissues.

Shaken tube test for bile pigments.

1. Fill a test tube halfway with urine and shake it vigorously.

2. A yellow color of foam indicates the presence of bile pigments.

3. Record your results in the Laboratory Report Results, E.2.d.

Rosenbach test for biliverdin.

1. Place some filter paper in a funnel and moisten the paper with a small amount of urine.

2. Add one drop of *concentrated nitric acid* to the tip of the paper cone. **Note:** *Use extreme caution in dispensing the concentrated nitric acid.*

3. A *greenish* color indicates a positive test for biliverdin.

4. Record your results in the Laboratory Report Results, E.2.d.

Icotest for bilirubin.

1. Place a drop of urine on one square of the special mat provided in the Icotest kit.

2. Place one Icotest reagent tablet in the center of the moistened area.

3. Add two drops of water directly to the tablet and observe the color. The presence of bilirubin will turn the mat *blue* or *purple*.

4. Record your results in the Laboratory Report Results, E.2.d.

Chemstrip method. Record your results in the Laboratory Report Results, E.2.d.

e. HEMOGLOBIN

Hemoglobin is not normally found in urine.

Weber test.

1. Combine and mix 10 ml of urine, 1 ml of glacial acetic acid, and 10 ml of ether in a test tube and shake vigorously. **Note:** *Use extreme caution with ether because it is very flammable.*

2. Allow the liquids to separate and remove 5 ml of the upper ether layer with a pipette.

3. To this 5-ml portion, *carefully* add 1 ml of a saturated solution of benzidene in alcohol, and 1 ml of 3% hydrogen peroxide.

4. A positive test for hemoglobin will produce a *greenish-blue* color.

5. Record your results in the Laboratory Report Results, 2.d.

Chemstrip method. Record your results in the Laboratory Report Results, E.2.d.

f. UREA

1. Place two drops of urine on a clean slide and carefully add two drops of concentrated nitric acid. **Note:** *Use extreme caution in dispensing the concentrated nitric acid.*

2. Gently place the slide on a hot plate using forceps and *slowly* warm the mixture.

3. Examine the slide under a microscope after the mixture has dried. Look for crystals of urea nitrate, which should be quite abundant because urea is a major portion of urine.

g. CREATININE

1. Place 5 ml of urine in a test tube and, using a syringe, *carefully* add 2 ml of picric acid solution.

2. Warm this mixture very *slowly* and *gently* in a water bath. *Make sure that the mouth of the test tube is pointed away from you and all other persons in the area.*

3. A positive test for creatinine is a *reddish* color. Creatinine is nearly as abundant as urea and should be present.

3. Microscopic Analysis

If you allow a urine specimen to stand undisturbed for a few hours, many suspended materials will settle to the bottom. A much faster method is to centrifuge a urine sample for approximately 10 minutes (see Figure 23.10). Pour off the supernatant fluid, leaving only the sediment at the bottom for microscopic examination. Place a drop of the sediment on a clean glass slide, add one drop of Sedi-Stain, and place a cover glass over the specimen.

Starting with low power, examine the urinary sediment for any of the following: red cells, white cells, epithelial cells, bacteria, vegetable fibers, and crystals of many types. Crystals can be identified as follows (see Figure 23.11).

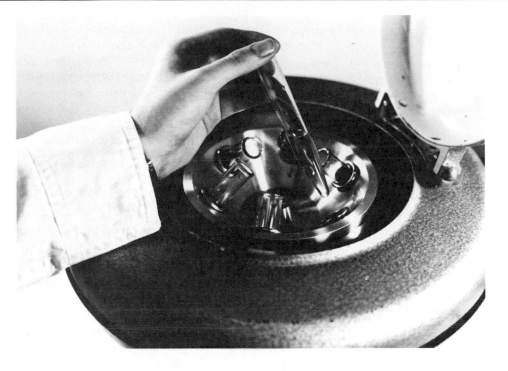

FIGURE 23.10 Tabletop centrifuge used for spinning urine samples to obtain sediment for microscopic analysis.

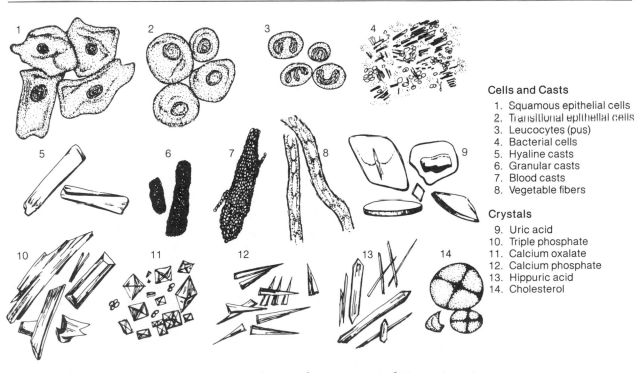

Cells and Casts

1. Squamous epithelial cells
2. Transitional epithelial cells
3. Leucocytes (pus)
4. Bacterial cells
5. Hyaline casts
6. Granular casts
7. Blood casts
8. Vegetable fibers

Crystals

9. Uric acid
10. Triple phosphate
11. Calcium oxalate
12. Calcium phosphate
13. Hippuric acid
14. Cholesterol

FIGURE 23.11 Diagram of microscopic elements in urine.

Calcium oxalate—Dumbbell and octahedral shapes.

Calcium phosphate—Very pointed, wedge-shaped formations that may occur as individual crystals or grouped together to form rosettes.

Cholesterol—Spherical crystals that have a crosslike configuration inside.

Hippuric acid—Long, needlelike crystals.

Triple phosphates—Prisms or feathery forms.

Uric acid—Rhombic prisms, wedges, dumbbells, rosettes, irregular crystals. These are pigmented in sediment, and the color varies from yellow to dark reddish brown.

Note: Crystals are usually much smaller than the other substances found in the urinary sediment, so it might be necessary to examine them under high-power or oil-immersion magnification.

Draw the results of your observation in the Laboratory Report Results, E.3.

4. Unknown Specimens

a. UNKNOWNS PREPARED BY INSTRUCTOR

When the composition of a substance has not been defined, it is called an **unknown.** In this exercise, the unknowns will be urine specimens to which the instructor has added glucose, albumin, or any other detectable substance. Each unknown contains only one added substance. Perform the previously outlined tests until you identify the substance in your unknown.

Record your results in the Laboratory Report Results, E.4.a.

b. UNKNOWNS PREPARED BY CLASS (OPTIONAL)

The class should be divided into two groups. Each group adds certain substances, such as glucose, protein, starch, or fat, to normal, freshly voided urine, keeping accurate records as to what was added to each sample. The two groups then exchange samples, and each group does the basic chemical tests on urine to detect which substances were added. Each student should add one substance to one urine sample and see if another student can detect what was added. Record your results in the Laboratory Report Results, E.4.b.

LABORATORY REPORT QUESTIONS (PAGE 439)

24 | REPRODUCTIVE SYSTEMS

In this exercise, you will study the structure of the male and female reproductive organs and associated structures.

A. ORGANS OF MALE REPRODUCTIVE SYSTEM

The **male reproductive system** includes (1) the testes, or male gonads, which produce sperm, (2) some ducts that either transport or store sperm, (3) accessory glands, whose secretions contribute to semen, and (4) several supporting structures, including the penis.

1. Testes

The **testes** are paired oval glands that lie in the pelvic cavity for most of fetal life. They usually begin to enter the scrotum by 32 weeks; full descent is not complete until just before birth. If the testes do not descend, the condition is called **cryptorchidism** (krip-TOR-ki-dizm). Cryptorchidism results in sterility, because the cells that stimulate the initial development of sperm cells are destroyed by the higher temperature of the pelvic cavity.

Each testis is covered by a dense layer of white fibrous tissue, the **tunica albuginea** (al'-byoo-JIN-ē-a), which extends inward and divides the testis into a series of about 250 internal compartments called **lobules.** Each lobule contains one to three tightly coiled **seminiferous tubules** where sperm production (**spermatogenesis**) occurs.

Label the structures associated with the testes in Figure 24.1.

Examine a microscope slide of a testis in cross section. Using oil immersion, note the developing reproductive cells in the seminiferous tubules. From the edge of the tubules inward, these cells are **spermatogonia, primary spermatocytes, secondary spermatocytes, spermatids,** and mature tailed **spermatozoa (sperm cells).** Distinguish between these cells and the **sustentacular (Sertoli) cells** which nourish the reproductive cells and secrete the hormone inhibin. Locate, in the tissue surrounding the seminiferous tubules, the clusters of **interstitial endocrinocytes (interstitial cells of Leydig),** which secrete the male hormone testosterone. Because they produce both sperm and hormones, the testes are both exocrine and endocrine glands.

Using your textbook, charts, or models as reference, label Figure 24.2.

Spermatozoa (sper'-ma-tō-ZŌ-a) are produced at the rate of about 300 million per day. Once ejaculated, they usually live about 48 hours in the female reproductive tract. The parts of a spermatozoon are as follows:

a. **Head**—Contains the **nucleus** and **acrosome** (produces hyaluronic acid to effect penetration of egg).
b. **Midpiece**—Contains numerous mitochondria in which the energy for locomotion is generated.
c. **Tail**—Typical flagellum used for locomotion.

With the aid of your textbook, label Figure 24.3.

2. Ducts

As spermatozoa mature, they are moved through seminiferous tubules into tubes called **straight tubules,** from which they are transported into a network of ducts, the **rete** (RĒ-tē) **testis.** The spermatozoa are next transported out of the

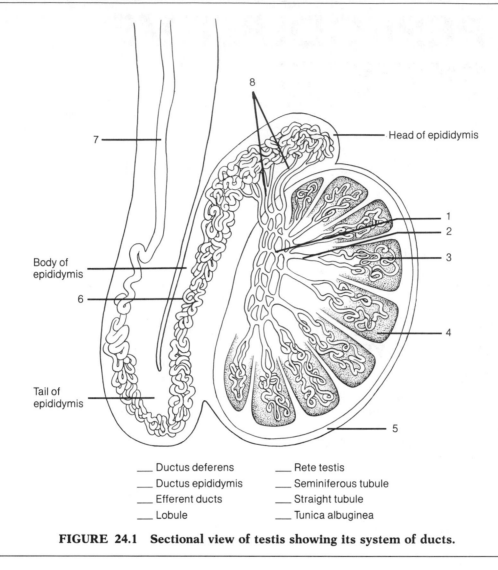

8

7

Head of epididymis

Body of epididymis

6

Tail of epididymis

1
2
3

4

5

___ Ductus deferens ___ Rete testis

___ Ductus epididymis ___ Seminiferous tubule

___ Efferent ducts ___ Straight tubule

___ Lobule ___ Tunica albuginea

FIGURE 24.1 Sectional view of testis showing its system of ducts.

testes through a series of coiled **efferent ducts** that empty into a single **ductus epididymis** (ep'-i-DID-i-mis). From there, they are passed into the **ductus (vas) deferens,** which ascends along the posterior border of the testis, penetrates the inguinal canal, enters the pelvic cavity, and loops over the side and down the posterior surface of the urinary bladder. The ductus deferens and duct from the seminal vesicle (gland) together form the **ejaculatory duct,** which propels the spermatozoa into the **urethra,** the terminal duct of the system. The male urethra is divisible into (1) a *prostatic portion,* which passes through the prostate gland; (2) a *membranous portion,* which passes through the urogenital diaphragm; and (3) a *spongy (cavernous) portion,* which passes through the corpus spongiosum of the penis (see Figure 24.6). The **epididymis** is a comma-shaped organ that is di-

visible into a head, body, and tail. The head is the superior portion that contains the efferent ducts; the body is the middle portion that contains the ductus epididymis; and the tail is the inferior portion in which the ductus epididymis continues as the ductus deferens.

Label the various ducts of the male reproductive system in Figure 24.1.

The ductus epididymis is lined with **pseudostratified epithelium.** The free surfaces of the cells contain long, branching microvilli called **stereocilia.** The muscularis deep to the epithelium consists of smooth muscle. Functionally, the ductus epididymis is the site of sperm maturation. It stores spermatozoa and propels them toward the urethra during ejaculation by peristaltic contractions of the muscularis. After about four weeks of storage, spermatozoa are reabsorbed.

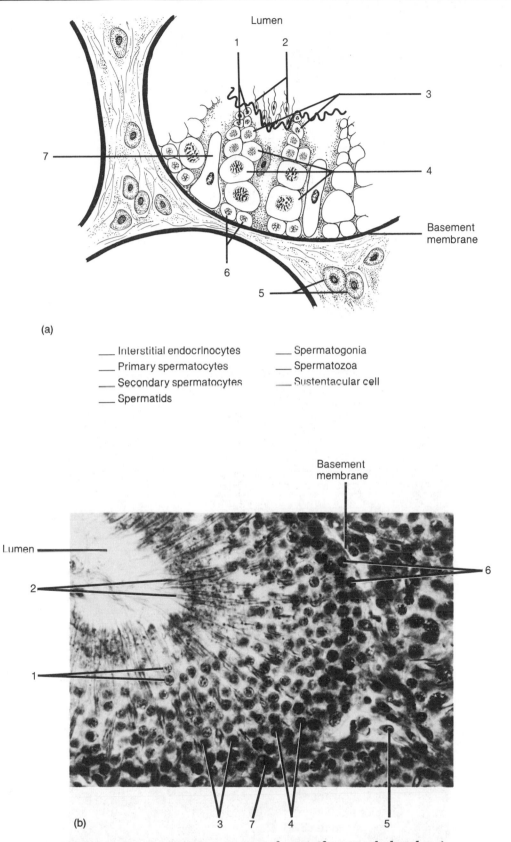

Lumen

1 2

3

7

4

Basement
membrane

6

5

(a)

___ Interstitial endocrinocytes   ___ Spermatogonia
___ Primary spermatocytes   ___ Spermatozoa
___ Secondary spermatocytes   ___ Sustentacular cell
___ Spermatids

Basement
membrane

Lumen

2

6

1

3 7 4 5

(b)

**FIGURE 24.2   Testis. Cross section of seminiferous tubules showing
various stages of spermatogenesis. (a) Diagram. (b) Photomicrograph.**

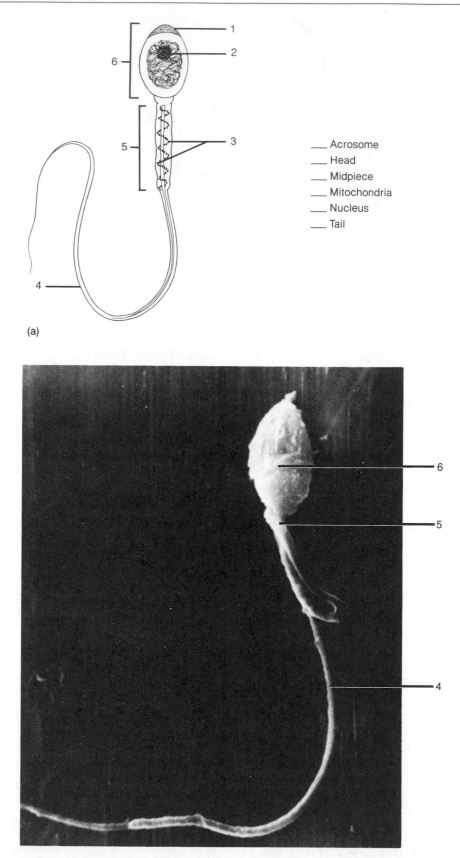

_____ Acrosome
_____ Head
_____ Midpiece
_____ Mitochondria
_____ Nucleus
_____ Tail

(a)

(b)

FIGURE 24.3 **Spermatozoa. (a) Diagram. (b) Scanning electron micrograph at magnification of 2000×.**

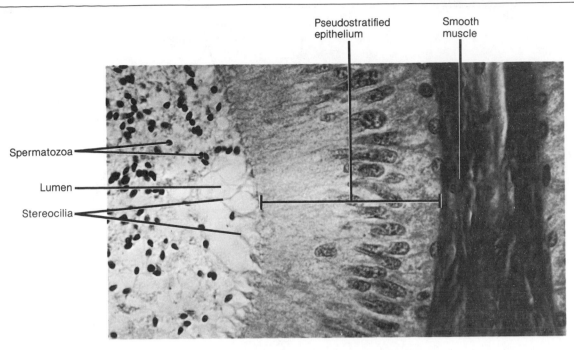

FIGURE 24.4 Histology of ductus epididymis.

Obtain a prepared slide of the ductus epi didymis showing its mucosa and muscularis. Compare your observations to Figure 24.4.

Histologically, the **ductus (vas) deferens (seminal duct)** is also lined with **pseudostratified epithelium** and its muscularis consists of three layers of smooth muscle. Peristaltic contractions of the muscularis propel spermatozoa toward the urethra during ejaculation. One method of sterilization in males, **vasectomy,** involves removal of a portion of each ductus deferens.

Obtain a prepared slide of the ductus deferens showing its mucosa and muscularis. Compare your observations to Figure 24.5.

3. Accessory Sex Glands

Whereas the ducts of the male reproductive system store or transport sperm, a series of **accessory sex glands** secrete the liquid portion of **semen (seminal fluid).** Semen is a mixture of spermatozoa and the secretions of the seminal vesicles, prostate gland, and bulbourethral glands.

The **seminal vesicles** are paired, convoluted, pouchlike structures posterior to and at the base of the urinary bladder in front of the rectum. The glands secrete the alkaline viscous component of semen into the ejaculatory duct. The seminal vesicles contribute about 60% of the volume of semen.

The **prostate gland,** a single doughnut-shaped gland inferior to the urinary bladder, surrounds the prostatic urethra. The prostate secretes an alkaline fluid into the prostatic urethra. The prostatic secretion constitutes 13% to 33% of the total semen produced.

The paired **bulbourethral** (bul´-bō-yoo-RĒ-thral) or **Cowper's glands,** located inferior to the prostate on either side of the membranous urethra, are about the size of peas. They secrete mucus for lubrication through ducts that open into the spongy (cavernous) urethra.

With the aid of your textbook, label the accessory glands and associated structures in Figure 24.6.

4. Penis

The **penis** conveys urine to the exterior and introduces spermatozoa into the vagina during copulation. Its principal parts are:

a. **Glans penis**—Slightly enlarged distal end.
b. **Corona**—Margin of glans penis.
c. **Prepuce**—Foreskin; loosely fitting skin covering glans.
d. **Corpora cavernosa penis**—Two dorsolateral masses of erectile tissue.

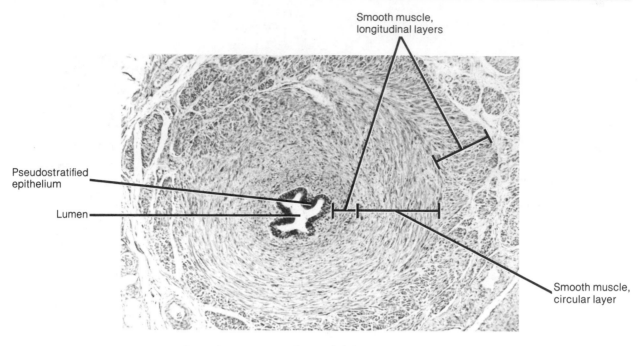

Smooth muscle,
longitudinal layers

Pseudostratified
epithelium

Lumen

Smooth muscle,
circular layer

FIGURE 24.5   Histology of ductus (vas) deferens.

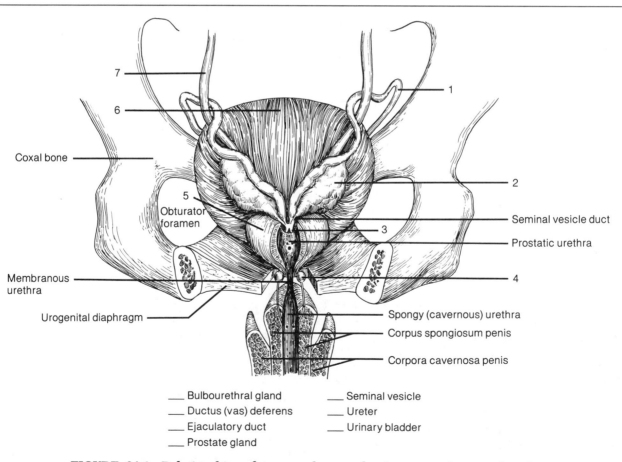

7

6

1

Coxal bone

2

5

Obturator
foramen

Seminal vesicle duct

3

Prostatic urethra

Membranous
urethra

4

Urogenital diaphragm

Spongy (cavernous) urethra

Corpus spongiosum penis

Corpora cavernosa penis

___ Bulbourethral gland   ___ Seminal vesicle

___ Ductus (vas) deferens   ___ Ureter

___ Ejaculatory duct   ___ Urinary bladder

___ Prostate gland

FIGURE 24.6   Relationships of some male reproductive organs in posterior view.

e. **Corpus spongiosum penis**—Midventral mass of erectile tissue that contains spongy (cavernous) urethra.

f. **Urethral orifice**—Opening of spongy (cavernous) urethra to exterior.

With the aid of your textbook, label the parts of the penis in Figure 24.7.

B. ORGANS OF FEMALE REPRODUCTIVE SYSTEM

The **female reproductive system** includes the female gonads (ovaries), which produce ova; uterine (fallopian) tubes, or oviducts, which transport ova to the uterus; vagina; external organs that compose the vulva; and mammary glands.

1. Ovaries

The **ovaries** are paired glands that resemble almonds in size and shape. Functionally, the ovaries produce ova (eggs), discharge them about once a month by a process called ovulation, and secrete female sex hormones (estrogens, progesterone, and relaxin). The point of entrance for blood vessels and nerves is the **hilus.** The ovaries are positioned in the upper pelvic cavity, one on each side of the uterus, by a series of ligaments:

a. **Mesovarium**—Double-layered fold of peritoneum that attaches ovaries to broad ligament of uterus.

b. **Ovarian ligament**—Anchors ovary to uterus.

c. **Suspensory ligament**—Attaches ovary to pelvic wall.

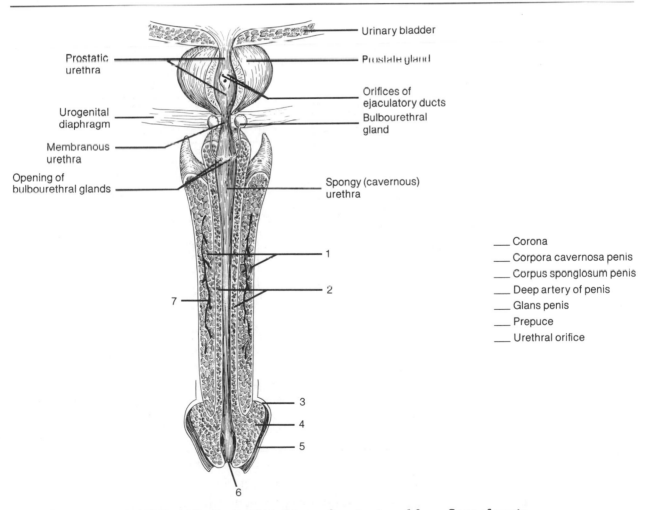

FIGURE 24.7 Internal structure of penis viewed from floor of penis.

With the aid of your textbook, label the ovarian ligaments in Figure 24.8.

Histologically, the ovaries consist of the following parts:

a. **Germinal epithelium**—Layer of simple cuboidal epithelium covering the free surface of ovary.

b. **Tunica albuginea**—Connective tissue capsule immediately deep to the germinal epithelium.

c. **Stroma**—Region of connective tissue deep to tunica albuginea. Outer region, called **cortex,** contains ovarian follicles; inner region is **medulla.**

d. **Ovarian follicles**—Ova and their surrounding tissue in various stages of development.

e. **Vesicular ovarian (graafian) follicle**—Endocrine gland consisting of a mature ovum and surrounding tissues that secrete estrogens.

f. **Corpus luteum**—Glandular body that develops from vesicular ovarian follicle after ovulation; secretes estrogens, progesterone, and relaxin.

With the aid of your textbook, label the parts of an ovary in Figure 24.9.

Obtain prepared slides of the ovary, examine them, and compare your observations to Figure 24.10.

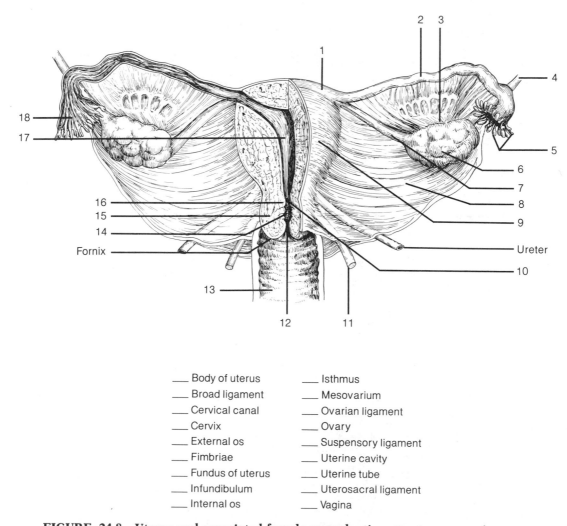

___ Body of uterus

___ Broad ligament

___ Cervical canal

___ Cervix

___ External os

___ Fimbriae

___ Fundus of uterus

___ Infundibulum

___ Internal os

___ Isthmus

___ Mesovarium

___ Ovarian ligament

___ Ovary

___ Suspensory ligament

___ Uterine cavity

___ Uterine tube

___ Uterosacral ligament

___ Vagina

FIGURE 24.8 Uterus and associated female reproductive structures seen in anterior view. Left side of figure has been sectioned to show internal structures.

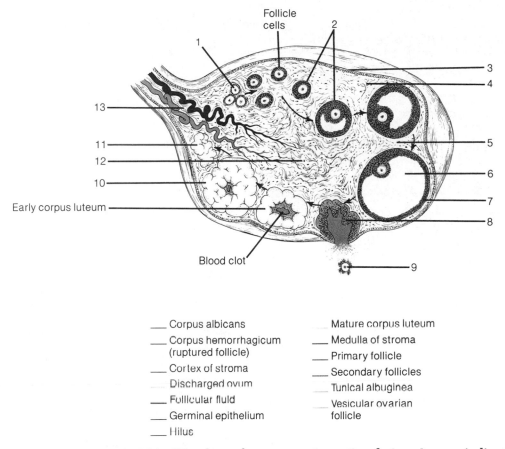

Follicle
cells

Early corpus luteum

Blood clot

___ Corpus albicans

___ Corpus hemorrhagicum
(ruptured follicle)

___ Cortex of stroma

___ Discharged ovum

___ Follicular fluid

___ Germinal epithelium

___ Hilus

___ Mature corpus luteum

___ Medulla of stroma

___ Primary follicle

___ Secondary follicles

___ Tunical albuginea

___ Vesicular ovarian
follicle

**FIGURE 24.9   Histology of ovary seen in sectional view. Arrows indicate
sequence of developmental stages that occur as part of ovarian cycle.**

2. Uterine Tubes

The **uterine (fallopian) tubes** or **oviducts** extend laterally from the uterus and transport ova from the ovaries to the uterus. Fertilization normally occurs in the uterine tubes. The tubes are positioned between folds of the broad ligaments of the uterus. The funnel-shaped, open distal end of each uterine tube, called the **infundibulum,** is surrounded by a fringe of fingerlike projections called **fimbriae** (FIM-brē-ē). The **ampulla** (am-POOL-la) of the uterine tube is the widest, longest portion, constituting about two-thirds of its length. The **isthmus** (IS-mus) is the short, narrow, thick-walled portion that joins the uterus.

With the aid of your textbook, label the parts of the uterine tubes in Figure 24.8.

Histologically, the mucosa of the uterine tubes consists of ciliated columnar cells and secretory cells. The muscularis is composed of inner circular and outer longitudinal layers of smooth muscle. Wavelike contractions of the muscularis help move the ovum down into the uterus. The serosa is the outer covering.

Examine a prepared slide of the wall of the uterine tube, and compare your observations to Figure 24.11.

3. Uterus

The **uterus** is the site of menstruation, implantation of a fertilized ovum, development of the fetus during pregnancy, and labor. Located between the urinary bladder and the rectum, the organ is shaped like an inverted pear. The uterus is subdivided into the following regions:

a. **Fundus**—Dome-shaped portion above uterine tubes.

b. **Body**—Major, tapering portion.

c. **Cervix**—Inferior narrow opening into vagina.

d. **Isthmus**—Constricted region between body and cervix.

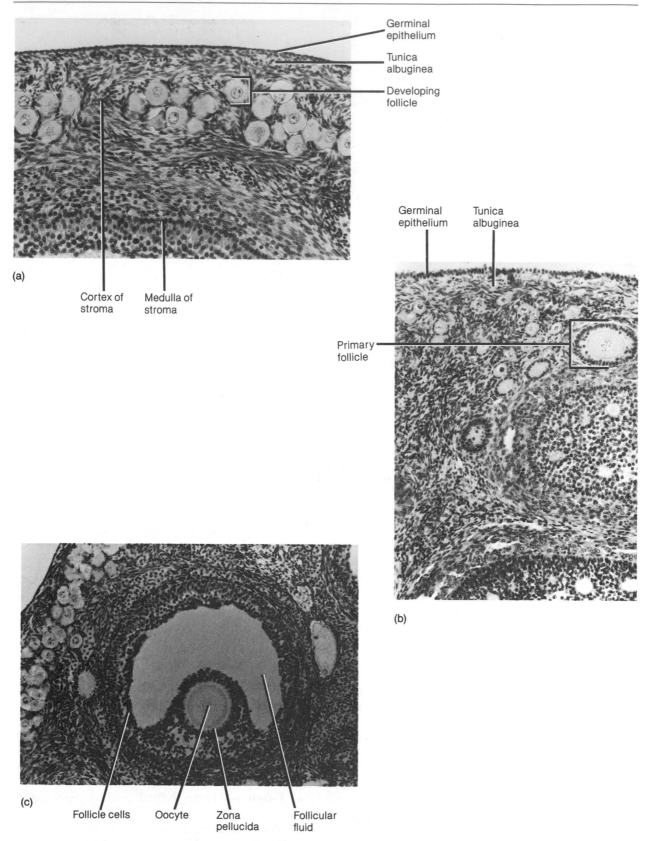

(a)

Germinal
epithelium

Tunica
albuginea

Developing
follicle

Cortex of
stroma

Medulla of
stroma

Germinal
epithelium

Tunica
albuginea

Primary
follicle

(b)

(c)

Follicle cells

Oocyte

Zona
pellucida

Follicular
fluid

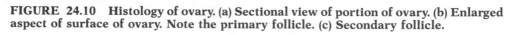

FIGURE 24.10 Histology of ovary. (a) Sectional view of portion of ovary. (b) Enlarged aspect of surface of ovary. Note the primary follicle. (c) Secondary follicle.

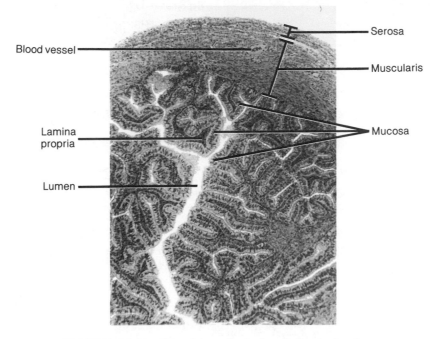

FIGURE 24.11 Histology of uterine (fallopian) tube.

e. **Uterine cavity**—Interior of the body.

f. **Cervical canal**—Interior of the cervix.

g. **Internal os**—Junction of isthmus and cervical canal.

h. **External os**—Site where cervix opens into vagina.

Label these structures in Figure 24.8.

The uterus is maintained in position by the following ligaments:

a. **Broad ligaments**—Double folds of parietal peritoneum that anchor the uterus to either side of the pelvic cavity.

b. **Uterosacral ligaments**—Parietal peritoneal extensions that connect the uterus to the sacrum.

c. **Cardinal ligaments**—Tissues containing smooth muscle, uterine blood vessels, and nerves. These ligaments extend below the bases of the broad ligaments between the pelvic wall and the cervix and vagina, and are the chief ligaments that maintain position of uterus, helping to keep it from dropping into vagina.

d. **Round ligaments**—Extend from uterus to external genitals between folds of broad ligaments.

Label the uterine ligaments in Figure 24.8.

Histologically, the uterus consists of three principal layers: endometrium, myometrium, and perimetrium (serosa). The inner **endometrium** is a mucous membrane with numerous glands and consists of two layers: (1) **stratum functionalis,** the layer closer to the uterine cavity that is shed during menstruation, and (2) **stratum basale** (bā-SAL-ē), the permanent layer that produces a new functionalis after menstruation. The middle **myometrium** forms the bulk of the uterine wall and consists of three layers of smooth muscle. During labor its coordinated contractions help to expel the fetus. The outer layer is the **perimetrium (serosa),** part of the visceral peritoneum.

As noted, the uterus is associated with menstruation. The **menstrual cycle** is a series of changes in the endometrium of a nonpregnant female that prepares the endometrium to receive a fertilized ovum each month (see Figure 24.12). The cycle is controlled by estrogens, progesterone, follicle-stimulating hormone (FSH), luteinizing hormone (LH), and gonadotropin-releasing factor (GnRF). The menstrual cycle is divided into the following stages:

1. **Menstrual phase (menstruation).** This is the periodic discharge of blood, fluid, mucus, and epithelial cells due to the sudden drop in estro-

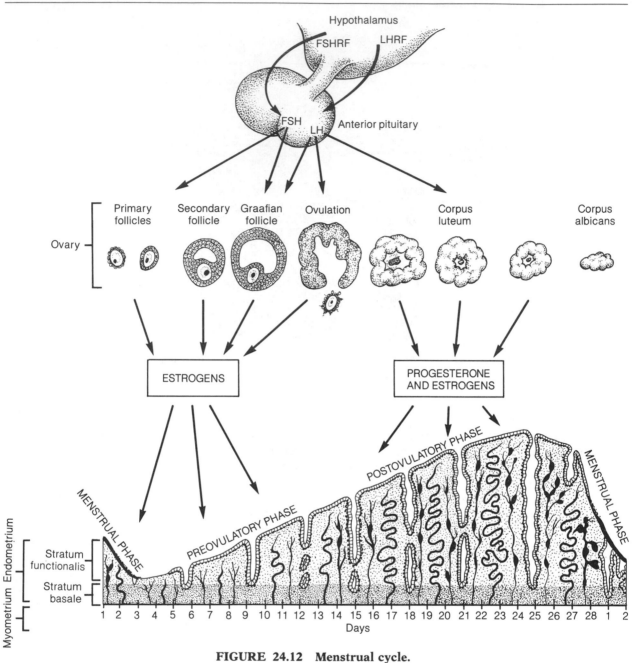

FIGURE 24.12 Menstrual cycle.

gens and progesterone. It lasts for about 5 days in an average 28-day cycle. During this phase, the stratum functionalis of the endometrium is sloughed off.

2. **Preovulatory (proliferative) phase.** This phase lasts from about day 6 through day 13 in a 28-day cycle. Rises in levels of estrogens stimulate endometrial repair, proliferation of endometrial glands and blood vessels, and result in thickening of the endometrium. Ovulation occurs on the 14th day.

3. **Postovulatory (secretory) phase.** This phase lasts from about day 15 through day 28 in a 28-day cycle. Mainly under the influence of progesterone, the vascular supply of the endometrium increases even more. Also, the endometrial glands further increase in size. These changes are greatest about one week after ovulation.

Obtain microscope slides of the endometrium showing the menstrual, preovulatory, and postovulatory phases of the menstrual cycle. See if you can note the differences in thickness of the endometrium, distribution of blood vessels, and distribution and size of endometrial glands.

4. Vagina

A muscular, tubular organ lined with a mucous membrane, the **vagina** is the passageway for menstrual flow, the receptacle for the penis during copulation, and the inferior portion of the birth canal. The vagina is situated between the urinary bladder and rectum and extends from the cervix of the uterus to the vestibule of the vulva. Recesses called **fornices** (FOR-ni-sēz′) surround the vaginal attachment to the cervix (see Figure 24.8) and make possible the use of contraceptive diaphragms. The opening of the vagina to the exterior, the **vaginal orifice**, is bordered by a thin fold of vascularized membrane, the **hymen.**

Label the vagina in Figure 24.8.

Histologically, the mucosa of the vagina consists of stratified squamous epithelium and connective tissue that lies in a series of transverse folds, the **rugae.** The muscularis is composed of a longitudinal layer of smooth muscle.

5. Vulva

The **vulva** or **pudendum** (pyoo-DEN-dum) is a collective term for the external genitals of the female. It consists of the following parts:

a. **Mons pubis**—Elevation of adipose tissue over the symphysis pubis covered by pubic hair.
b. **Labia majora** (LĀ-be-a ma-JŌ-ra)—Two longitudinal folds of skin that extend inferiorly and posteriorly from the mons pubis. The folds, covered by pubic hair on their superior lateral surfaces, contain abundant adipose tissue and sebaceous and sudoriferous glands.
c. **Labia minora**—Two folds of mucous membrane medial to labia majora. The folds have numerous sebaceous but few sudoriferous glands and no fat or pubic hair.
d. **Clitoris** (KLI-to-ris)—Small cylindrical mass of erectile tissue at anterior junction of labia minora. The exposed portion is called the **glans,** the covering is called the **prepuce.**
e. **Vestibule**—Cleft between labia minora containing vaginal orifice, hymen, urethral orifice,

and openings of ducts of lesser and greater vestibular glands.
f. **Vaginal orifice**—Opening of vagina to exterior.
g. **Hymen**—Thin fold of vascularized membrane that borders vaginal orifice.
h. **Urethral orifice**—Opening of urethra to exterior.
i. **Orifices of paraurethral (Skene's) glands**—Located on either side of urethral orifice. The glands secrete mucus.
j. **Orifices of ducts of greater vestibular** (ves-TIB-yoo-lar) or **Bartholin's glands**—Located in a groove between hymen and labia minora. These glands produce a mucoid secretion.
k. **Orifices of ducts of lesser vestibular glands**—Microscopic orifices opening into vestibule.

Using your textbook as an aid, label the parts of the vulva in Figure 24.13.

6. Mammary Glands

The **mammary glands** are modified sweat glands (branched tubuloalveolar glands) that lie over the pectoralis major muscles and are attached to them by a layer of connective tissue. They consist of the following structures:

a. **Lobes**—Around 15 to 20 separated by adipose tissue.
b. **Lobules**—Smaller compartments in lobes that contain milk-secreting cells called **alveoli.**
c. **Secondary tubules**—Receive milk from alveoli.
d. **Mammary ducts**—Receive milk from secondary tubules.
e. **Ampullae**—Expanded sinuses of mammary ducts.
f. **Lactiferous ducts**—Receive milk from ampullae.
g. **Nipple**—Projection on anterior surface of mammary gland that contains lactiferous ducts.
h. **Areola** (a-RĒ-ō-la)—Circular pigmented skin around nipple.

With the aid of your textbook, label the parts of the mammary gland in Figure 24.14.

Examine a prepared slide of alveoli of the mammary gland, and compare your observations to Figure 24.15.

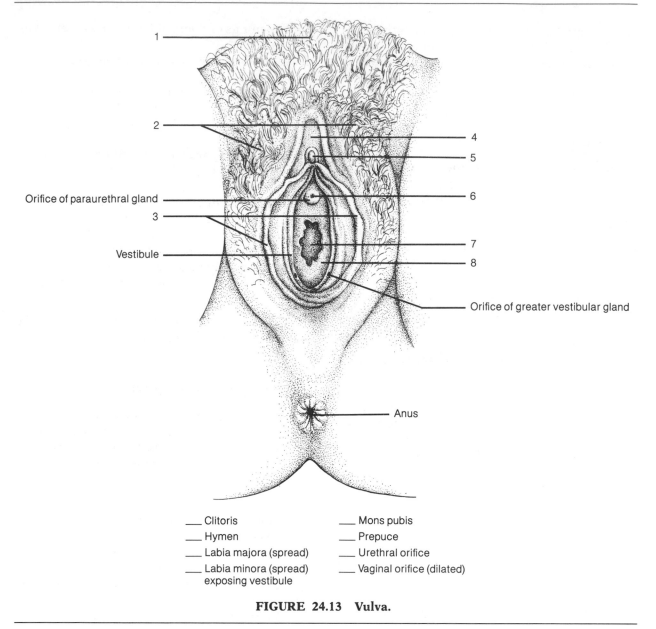

1

2

Orifice of paraurethral gland

3

Vestibule

4

5

6

7

8

Orifice of greater vestibular gland

Anus

___ Clitoris   ___ Mons pubis

___ Hymen   ___ Prepuce

___ Labia majora (spread)   ___ Urethral orifice

___ Labia minora (spread)   ___ Vaginal orifice (dilated)
exposing vestibule

FIGURE 24.13   Vulva.

C. DISSECTION OF FETUS-CONTAINING PIG UTERUS

Examination of the uterus of a pregnant pig reveals that the fetuses are equally spaced in the two uterine horns. Each fetus produces a local enlargement of the horn. The litter size normally ranges from 6 to 12. Your instructor may have you dissect the fetus-containing uterus of a pregnant pig or have one available as a demonstration (see Figure 24.16). If you do a dissection, use the following directions. Also examine a chart or model of a human fetus and pregnant uterus if they are available.

1. Using a sharp scissors, cut open one of the enlargements of the horn and you will see that each fetus is enclosed together with an elongated, sausage-shaped **chorionic vesicle.**

2. You will also notice many round bumps called **areolae** located over the chorionic surface.

3. The lining of the uterus together with the wall of the chorionic vesicle forms the **placenta.**

4. Carefully cut open the chorionic vesicle, avoiding cutting or breaking the second sac lying within that surrounds the fetus itself.

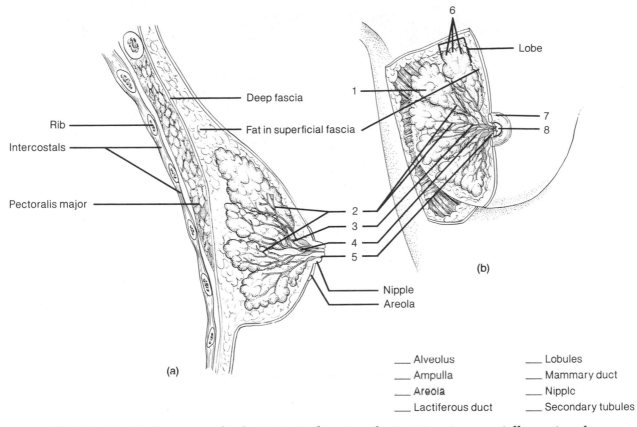

Deep fascia

Rib

Intercostals

Pectoralis major

Fat in superficial fascia

6

Lobe

1

7

8

2

3

4

5

Nipple

Areola

(b)

(a)

___ Alveolus   ___ Lobules

___ Ampulla   ___ Mammary duct

___ Areola   ___ Nipple

___ Lactiferous duct   ___ Secondary tubules

FIGURE 24.14   Mammary glands. (a) Sagittal section. (b) Anterior view, partially sectioned.

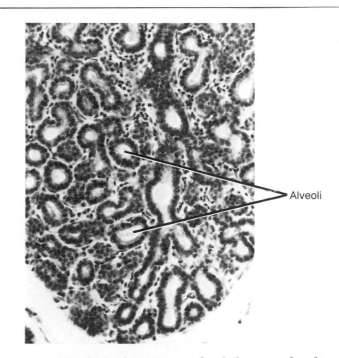

Alveoli

FIGURE 24.15   Histology of mammary gland showing alveoli.

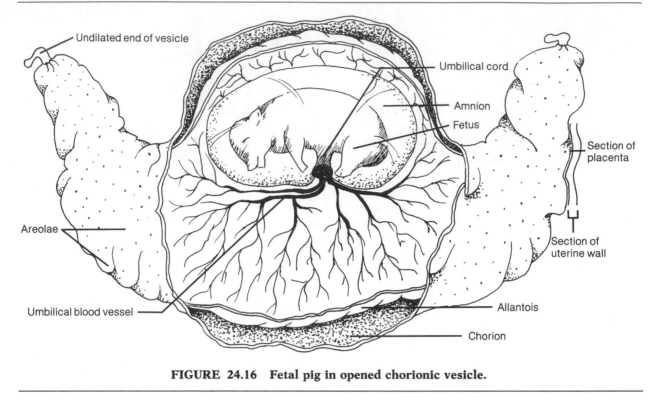

FIGURE 24.16 **Fetal pig in opened chorionic vesicle.**

5. The vesicle wall is the fusion of two extraembryonic membranes, the outer **chorion** and the inner **allantois.** The allantois is the large sac growing out from the fetus, and the umbilical cord contains its stalk.

6. The **umbilical blood vessels** are seen in the allantoic wall spreading out in all directions and are also seen entering the **umbilical cord.**

7. A thin-walled nonvascular **amnion** surrounds the fetus. This membrane is filled with **amniotic fluid,** which acts as a protective water cushion and prevents adherence of the fetus and membranes.

LABORATORY REPORT QUESTIONS (PAGE 443)

25 | DEVELOPMENT

Development refers to the sequence of events starting with fertilization and ending with the formation of a complete organism. Consideration will be given to how reproductive cells are produced and to a few developmental events associated with pregnancy.

A. GAMETOGENESIS

The two major processes by which sets of chromosomes are distributed to the daughter cells are **mitosis** and **meiosis.** Mitosis occurs in many types of cells and results in two daughter cells that have exactly the same nuclei and chromosome content and also the same amount of cytoplasm as the parent cell from which they were derived. In other words, mitosis produces two cells that are identical in every way to each other, and to the original parent cell. Mitosis accounts for the continued production of new cells needed for the growth and maintenance of the body. Review the phases of mitosis in Section G of Exercise 3, Cells.

1. Meiosis

In sexual reproduction, offspring are produced by the union and fusion of two different sex cells, one produced by each parent. Such sex cells are called **gametes.** The female gamete is the ovum produced in the ovaries and the male gamete is the spermatozoon produced in the testes. The union and fusion of ovum and spermatozoon is called fertilization and results in the formation of a zygote, or fertilized ovum. The zygote contains chromosomes from each parent. Through repeated mitotic divisions, the zygote develops into a complete organism.

Gametes are different from all other body cells, called somatic cells, with regard to the number of chromosomes in their nuclei. Somatic cell nuclei contain 46 chromosomes, of which 23 are a complete set and contain all the genes required for carrying out the activities of a cell. The other 23 chromosomes, in a sense, are a duplicate set.

The symbol n is used to represent the number of different chromosomes in a nucleus. Because somatic cells contain two sets of chromosomes, they are referred to as **diploid** (DIP-loyd) **cells** (di = two), symbolized by $2n$. In a diploid cell, two chromosomes that belong to a pair are called **homologous** (hō-MOL-ō-gus) **chromosomes.**

If gametes had the same chromosome number as somatic cells, the zygote formed from their union and fusion would have double the chromosome number ($4n$) and, with each succeeding generation of cells, the chromosome number would double ($8n$, $16n$, $32n$, and so on). This does not happen, however, because of a special nuclear division, called **meiosis,** which occurs only in the production of gametes. As a result of meiosis, an ovum or spermatozoon relinquishes its duplicate set of chromosomes so that each contains only 23 chromosomes. Thus, gametes are **haploid** (HAP-loyd) **cells,** meaning one-half, and are symbolized by n.

Formation in the testes of haploid spermatozoa by meiosis is called **spermatogenesis** (sper′-ma-tō-JEN-e-sis). Formation in the ovary of haploid ova by meiosis is known as **oogenesis** (o′-ō-JEN-e-sis).

2. Spermatogenesis

In humans, spermatogenesis takes 2 to 3 weeks. Immature cells called **spermatogonia** (SPER-ma-tō-GŌ-nē-a) develop into **primary spermatocytes** (SPER-ma-tō-sītz). Both spermatogonia and spermatocytes are diploid in chromosome number. Two nuclear divisions take place as part of the process of meiosis. In the first division, 46 duplicated chromosomes move toward the equatorial plane of the nucleus. There homologous pairs line up so that 23 pairs of chromosomes (each composed of two chromatids) are in the center of the nucleus. This pairing is called **synapsis.** Because each pair of chromosomes consists of four chromatids, the pair is now called a **tetrad.** In a tetrad, portions of one chromatid may be exchanged with portions of another. This process, called **crossing over,** permits an exchange of genes that could result in their recombination and consequently variation among humans (Figure 25.1). The cells thus formed by the first nuclear division (reduction division) are called **secondary spermatocytes,** and each secondary spermatocyte has 23 chromosomes (the haploid number). Note again that each of the 23 chromosomes is composed of two chromatids.

The second nuclear division of meiosis is an equatorial division. The chromosomes (each composed of two chromatids) line up in single file around the equatorial plane, and the chromatids of each chromosome separate from each other. The cells thus formed from the equatorial division are called **spermatids.** Each spermatid contains half the original chromosome number, or 23 chromosomes, and is haploid. Each primary spermatocyte (diploid) therefore produces four spermatids (haploid) by meiosis (reduction division and equatorial division). In the final stage of spermatogenesis, called **spermiogenesis** (sper'-me-ō-JEN-e-sis), the spermatids mature into **spermatozoa** (see Figure 25.2).

With the aid of your textbook, label Figure 25.2.

3. Oogenesis

Oogenesis occurs in essentially the same manner as spermatogenesis, and includes both meiosis and maturation. Immature cells called **oogonia** (ō-o-GŌ-nē-a) lose their ability to carry on mitosis, are diploid in chromosome number, and are called **primary oocytes** (Ō-o-sītz). Primary oocytes undergo reduction division, tetrad formation, and crossing over, and divide to form two cells of unequal size. Both cells contain 23 chromosomes (haploid) of two chromatids each. The smaller cell is called the **first polar body.** The larger cell is known as the **secondary oocyte** (see Figure 25.3). The secondary oocyte with its polar body is released in the process of ovulation, but the oocyte is not yet mature. If fertilization occurs, the second division (equatorial division) takes place. The secondary oocyte produces two cells of unequal size, both of them haploid. The larger cell is the **ootid;** the smaller is the **second polar body.** In time, the ootid develops into an **ovum,** or mature egg. Thus, in the female, one oogonium produces a single ovum, whereas each male spermatocyte produces four spermatozoa.

With the aid of your textbook, label Figure 25.3.

B. EMBRYONIC PERIOD

The **embryonic period** is the first 2 months of development, and the developing human is called an **embryo.** After the second month, it is called a **fetus.**

When a spermatozoon enters the ovum (Figure 25.4a), the male nucleus and the female nucleus fuse to produce a **segmentation nucleus**—a process termed **fertilization.** The segmentation nucleus contains 23 male chromosomes and 23 female chromosomes. Thus the fusion of the haploid nuclei restores the diploid number. The fertilized ovum, consisting of the segmentation nucleus, cytoplasm, and enveloping membrane, is called a **zygote.** The zygote undergoes rapid mitotic division immediately

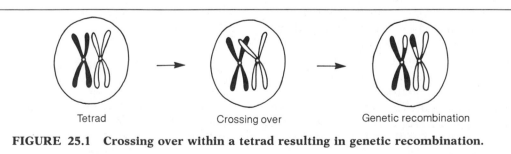

Tetrad   Crossing over   Genetic recombination

FIGURE 25.1   Crossing over within a tetrad resulting in genetic recombination.

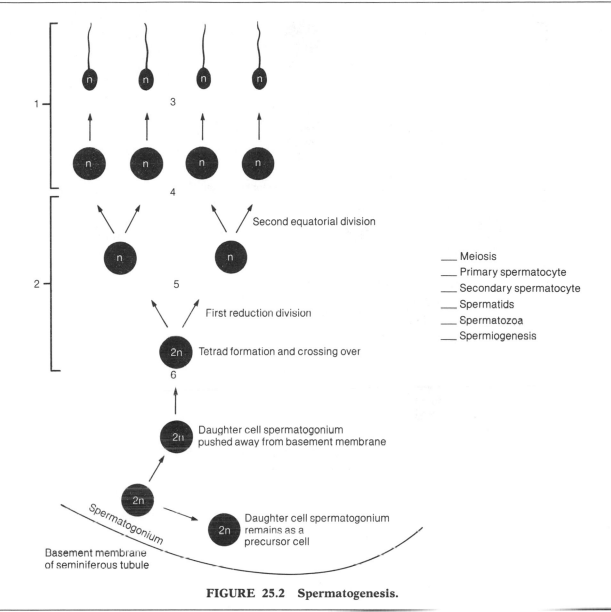

Second equatorial division

___ Meiosis
___ Primary spermatocyte
___ Secondary spermatocyte
___ Spermatids
___ Spermatozoa
___ Spermiogenesis

First reduction division

Tetrad formation and crossing over

Daughter cell spermatogonium pushed away from basement membrane

Spermatogonium

Daughter cell spermatogonium remains as a precursor cell

Basement membrane of seminiferous tubule

FIGURE 25.2 Spermatogenesis.

after fertilization. This early division of the zygote is called **cleavage** (Figure 25.4b). **Blastomeres** (BLAS-tō-mērz) are the progressively smaller cells that are produced by successive cleavages. Successive cleavages produce the **morula** (MOR-yoo-la), which is a solid mass of cells only slightly larger than the original zygote (Figure 25.4c). The morula continues dividing as it descends through the uterine tube and forms a hollow ball of cells called a **blastocyst** (Figure 25.4d). The outer covering of cells in a blastocyst is called the **trophectoderm** (trō-FEK-tō-derm), the rest of the cells the **inner cell mass,** and the cavity itself the **blastocoel** (BLAS-tō-sēl).

About the third day after fertilization, the blastocyst enters the uterine cavity. The blastocyst attaches to the endometrium 7 to 8 days after fertilization, and this process is **implantation** (Figure 25.4e).

Obtain prepared slides of the embryonic development of the sea urchin. First try to find a zygote. This will appear as a single cell surrounded by an inner fertilization membrane and an outer, jellylike membrane. Draw a zygote in the space provided.

Now find several cleavage stages. See if you can isolate two-cell, four-cell, eight-cell, and sixteen-cell stages. Draw the various stages in the spaces provided.

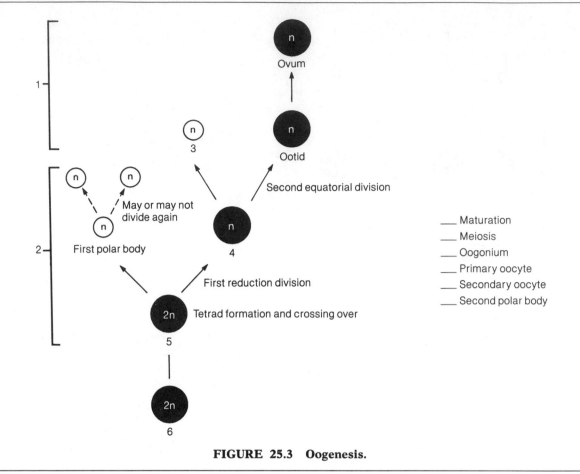

FIGURE 25.3 Oogenesis.

___ Maturation
___ Meiosis
___ Oogonium
___ Primary oocyte
___ Secondary oocyte
___ Second polar body

Zygote

Four-cell stage

Two-cell stage

Eight-cell stage

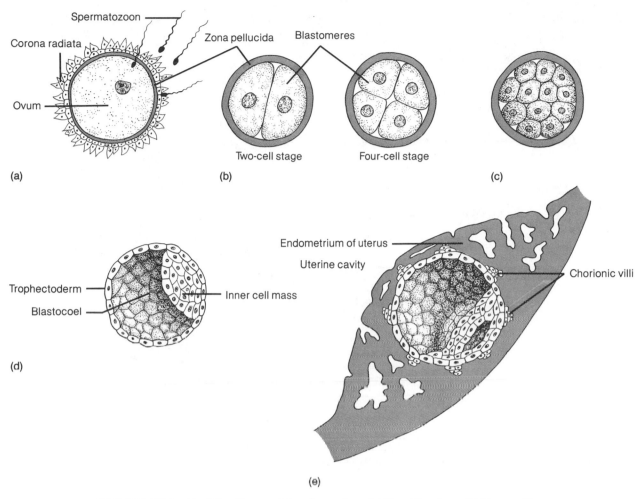

(a)

(b)

(c)

(d)

(e)

FIGURE 25.4 Fertilization and implantation. (a) Fertilization. (b) Two-cell and four-cell stages of cleavage. (c) Morula. (d) Blastocyst. (e) Implantation.

Sixteen-cell stage

Blastocyst

Try to find a blastocyst, a hollow ball of cells with a lighter center due to the presence of the blastocoel. Draw a blastocyst in the space provided.

Following implantation, the inner cell mass of the blastocyst differentiates into three **primary germ layers: ectoderm, endoderm,** and **mesoderm.** The primary germ layers are em-

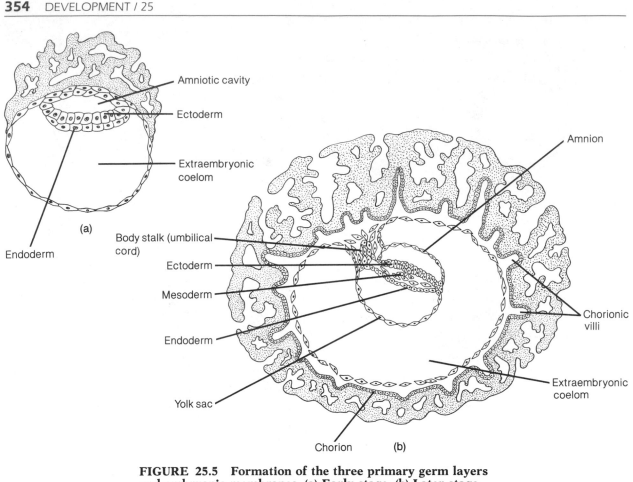

Amniotic cavity

Ectoderm

Extraembryonic coelom

(a)

Endoderm

Body stalk (umbilical cord)

Ectoderm

Mesoderm

Endoderm

Yolk sac

Chorion

(b)

Amnion

Chorionic villi

Extraembryonic coelom

FIGURE 25.5 Formation of the three primary germ layers and embryonic membranes. (a) Early stage. (b) Later stage.

bryonic tissues from which all tissues and organs of the body will develop. Various movements of groups of cells leading to establishment of primary germ layers is called **gastrulation.** Cells of the inner cell mass divide by mitosis and form two cavities: the **amniotic cavity** and **extraembryonic coelom** (Figure 25.5). In gastrulation, the layer of cells nearest the amniotic cavity is the ectoderm; the layer nearest the extraembryonic coelom is the endoderm. Within the ectoderm are cells that form mesoderm between ectoderm and endoderm.

As the embryo develops, the endoderm becomes the epithelium that lines most of the digestive tract, urinary bladder, gallbladder, liver, pharynx, larynx, trachea, bronchi, lungs, vagina, urethra, and thyroid, parathyroid, and thymus glands, among other structures. The mesoderm develops into all skeletal, all cardiac, and most smooth muscle; cartilage, bone and other connective tissues; bone marrow, lymphoid tissue, endothelium of blood and lymphatic vessels, gonads, dermis of the skin, and other structures. The ectoderm develops into the entire nervous system, epidermis of skin, epidermal derivatives of the skin, and portions of the eye and other sense organs.

During the embryonic period, the **embryonic membranes** form, lying outside of the embryo. They function to protect and nourish the embryo and later the fetus. These membranes include the **yolk sac, amnion, chorion** (KŌ-rē-on), and **allantois** (a-LAN-tō-is) (see Figures 25.5 and 25.6).

The **placenta** is a mostly vascular organ formed by the chorion of the embryo and a portion of the endometrium (decidua basalis) of the mother (see Figure 25.5). It functions to exchange nutrients and wastes between fetus and mother and secretes the hormones necessary to maintain pregnancy. When the baby is delivered, the placenta detaches from the uterus and is called the afterbirth. The scar that marks the site of the entry of the fetal umbilical

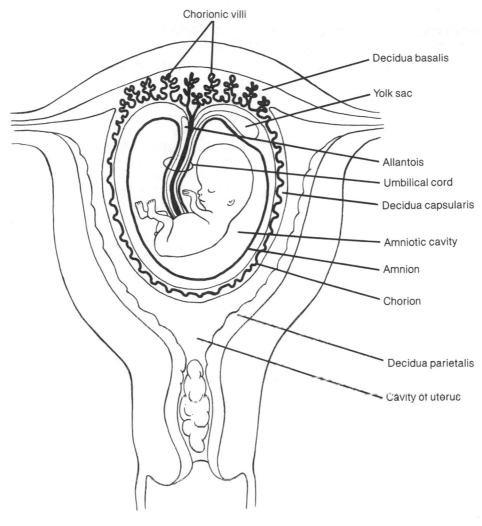

Chorionic villi

Decidua basalis

Yolk sac

Allantois

Umbilical cord

Decidua capsularis

Amniotic cavity

Amnion

Chorion

Decidua parietalis

Cavity of uterus

FIGURE 25.6   Embryonic membranes.

cord into the abdomen is called the **umbilicus.** The umbilical cord contains blood vessels that (1) deliver fetal blood containing carbon dioxide and wastes to the placenta and (2) return fetal blood containing oxygen and nutrients from the placenta.

C. FETAL PERIOD

During the **fetal period,** all the organs of the body grow rapidly from the original primary germ layers, and the organism takes on a human appearance. Some of the principal changes associated with fetal growth are summarized in Table 25.1.

LABORATORY REPORT QUESTIONS (PAGE 447)

TABLE 25.1
CHANGES ASSOCIATED WITH EMBRYONIC AND FETAL GROWTH

END OF MONTH	APPROXIMATE SIZE AND WEIGHT	REPRESENTATIVE CHANGES
1	0.6 cm (3/16 in.)	Eyes, nose, and ears not yet visible. Backbone and vertebral canal form. Small buds that will develop into arms and legs form. Heart forms and starts beating. Body systems begin to form.
2	3 cm (1 1/4 in.) 1 g (1/30 oz)	Eyes far apart, eyelids fused, nose flat. Ossification begins. Limbs become distinct as arms and legs. Digits well formed. Major blood vessels form. Many internal organs continue to develop.
3	7.5 cm (3 in.) 28 g (1 oz)	Eyes almost fully developed but eyelids still fused, nose develops bridge, external ears present. Ossification continues. Appendages fully formed, nails develop. Heartbeat can be detected. Body systems continue to develop.
4	18 cm (6 1/2–7 in.) 113 g (4 oz)	Head large in proportion to rest of body. Face takes on human features and hair appears on head. Skin bright pink. Many bones ossified, joints begin to form. Continued development of body systems.
5	25–30 cm (10–12 in.) 227–454 g (1/2–1 lb)	Head less disproportionate to rest of body. Fine hair (lanugo) covers body. Skin still bright pink. Rapid development of body systems.
6	27–35 cm (11–14 in.) 567–681 g (1 1/4–1 1/2 lb)	Head even less disproportionate to rest of body. Eyelids separate, eyelashes form. Skin wrinkled and pink.
7	32–42 cm (13–17 in.) 1,135–1,362 g (2 1/2–3 lb)	Head and body more proportionate. Skin wrinkled and pink. Seven-month fetus (premature baby) capable of survival.
8	41–45 cm (16 1/2–18 in.) 2,043–2,270 g (4 1/2–5 lb)	Subcutaneous fat deposited. Skin less wrinkled. Testes descend into scrotum. Bones of head soft. Chances of survival much greater at end of eighth month.
9	50 cm (20 in.) 3,178–3,405 g (7–7 1/2 lb)	Additional subcutaneous fat accumulates. Lanugo shed. Nails extend to tips of fingers and maybe even beyond.

26 | GENETICS

Genetics is the branch of biology that studies inheritance. **Inheritance** is the passage of hereditary traits from one generation to another. It is through the passage of hereditary traits that you acquired your characteristics from your parents and will transmit your characteristics to your children. If all individuals were brown-eyed, we could learn nothing of the hereditary basis of eye color. However, because some people are blue-eyed and marry brown-eyed people, we can gain some knowledge of how hereditary traits are transmitted. We constantly analyze the genetic bases of the *differences* between individuals. Some of these differences occur normally, such as differences in eye color, blood groups, or ability to taste PTC (phenylthiocarbamide). Other differences are abnormal, such as physical abnormalities and abnormalities in the processes of metabolism.

A. GENOTYPE AND PHENOTYPE

The vast majority of human cells, except gametes, contain 23 pairs of chromosomes (diploid number) in their nuclei. One chromosome from each pair comes from the mother, and the other comes from the father. The two chromosomes that belong to a pair are called **homologous** (hō-MOL-ō-gus) **chromosomes,** and these homologues contain genes that control the same traits. The homologue of a chromosome that contains a gene for height also contains a gene for height.

The relationship of genes to heredity can be illustrated by the disorder called phenylketonuria, or PKU (see Figure 26.1). People with the disorder PKU are unable to manufacture the enzyme phenylalanine hydroxylase. Current belief is that PKU results from the presence of an abnormal gene symbolized as *p*. The normal gene is symbolized as *P*. *P* and *p* are said to be alleles. An **allele** is one of many alternative forms of a gene, occupying the same **locus** (position of a gene on a chromosome) in homologous chromosomes. The chromosome that has the gene that directs phenylalanine hydroxylase production will either have *p* or *P* on it. Its homologue will also have either *p* or *P*. Thus every individual will have one of the following genetic makeups, or **genotypes** (JĒ-nō-tīps): *PP*, *Pp*, or *pp*. Although people with genotypes of *Pp* have the abnormal gene, only those with genotype *pp* suffer from the disorder because the normal gene masks the abnormal one. A gene that masks the expression of its allele is called the **dominant gene,** and the trait expressed is said to be a dominant trait. The homologous gene that is masked is called the **recessive gene.** The trait expressed when two recessive genes are present is called the recessive trait. Several dominant and recessive traits inherited in human beings are listed in Table 26.1.

Traditionally, the dominant gene is symbolized with a capital letter and the recessive one with a lowercase letter. When the same genes appear on homologous chromosomes, as in *PP* or *pp*, you are said to be **homozygous** for a trait. When the genes on homologous chromosomes are different, however, as in *Pp*, you are said to be **heterozygous** for the trait. **Phenotype** (FĒ-nō-tīp) refers to how the genetic composition is expressed in the body. An individual with *Pp* has a different genotype than one with *PP*, but both have the same phenotype—which in this case is normal production of phenylalanine hydroxylase.

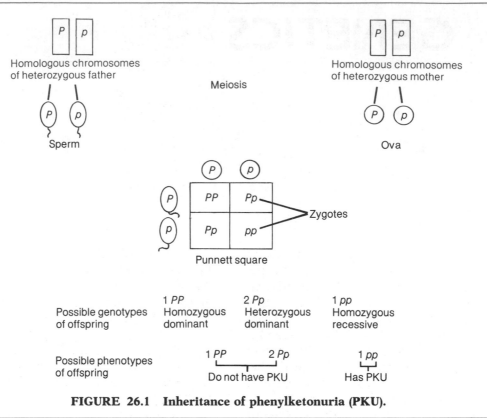

FIGURE 26.1 Inheritance of phenylketonuria (PKU).

TABLE 26.1
HEREDITARY TRAITS IN HUMAN BEINGS

DOMINANT	RECESSIVE
Curly hair	Straight hair
Dark brown hair	All other colors
Normal skin pigmentation	Albinism
Nearsightedness or farsightedness	Normal vision
Normal color vision	Color blindness
Syndactylism (webbed digits)	Normal digits
Diabetes insipidus	Normal excretion
Huntington's chorea	Normal nervous system
A or B blood factor	O blood factor
Rh blood factor	No Rh blood factor
Normalcy	Phenylketonuria (PKU)

B. PUNNETT SQUARES

To determine how gametes containing haploid chromosomes unite to form diploid fertilized eggs, special charts called **Punnett squares** are used. The Punnett square is merely a device that helps one visualize all the possible combinations of male and female gametes, and is invaluable as a learning exercise in genetics. Usually, the male gametes (sperm cells) are placed at the side of the square and the female ga-metes (ova) at the top (see Figure 26.1). The four spaces in the chart represent the possible combinations of male and female gametes that could form fertilized eggs. Possible combinations are determined simply by dropping the female gamete on the left into the two boxes below it and dropping the female gamete on the right into the two spaces under it. The upper male gamete is then moved across to the two spaces in line with it, and the lower male gamete is moved across to the two spaces in line with it.

C. SEX INHERITANCE

Lining up human chromosomes in pairs reveals that the last pair (the twenty-third pair) differs in males and in females (see Figure 26.2a). In females, the pair consists of two rod-shaped chromosomes designated as *X* chromosomes. One *X* chromosome is also present in males, but its mate is hook-shaped and called a *Y* chromosome. The *XX* pair in the female and the *XY* pair in the male are called the **sex chromosomes,** and all other pairs of chromosomes are called **autosomes.**

The sex of an individual is determined by the sex chromosomes (Figure 26.2b). When a spermatocyte undergoes meiosis to reduce its chromosome number from diploid to haploid, one daughter cell will contain the *X* chromosome and the other will contain the *Y* chromosome. When the ovum is fertilized by an *X*-bearing sperm, the offspring normally will be a female *(XX)*. Fertilization by a *Y* sperm normally produces a male *(XY)*.

D. *X*-LINKED INHERITANCE

As do the other 22 pairs of chromosomes, the sex chromosomes contain genes that are responsible for the transmission of a number of nonsexual traits. Genes for these traits appear on *X* chromosomes, but many of these genes are absent from *Y* chromosomes. Traits transmitted by genes on the *X* chromosome are called **X-linked (sex-linked) traits.** This pattern of heredity is different from the pattern described earlier. About 150 *X*-linked traits are known in humans. Examples of *X*-linked traits are color blindness and hemophilia.

1. Color Blindness

The gene for **color blindness** is a recessive one symbolized as *c*. Normal vision, symbolized *C*, dominates. The *C* and *c* genes are located on the *X* chromosome. The *Y* chromosome, however, does not contain the segment of DNA that programs color vision. Thus the ability to see colors

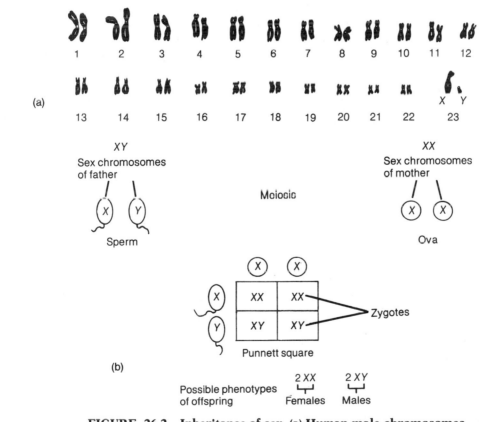

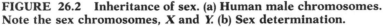

FIGURE 26.2 Inheritance of sex. (a) Human male chromosomes. Note the sex chromosomes, *X* and *Y*. (b) Sex determination.

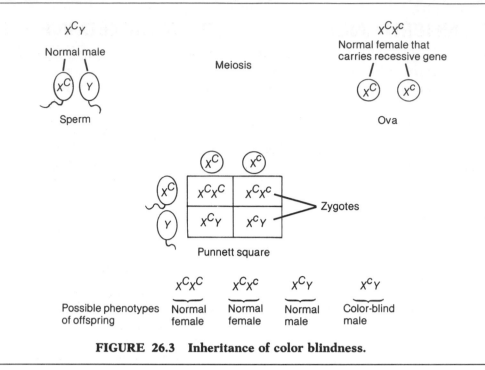

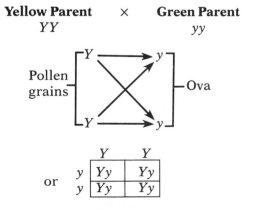

FIGURE 26.3 Inheritance of color blindness.

depends entirely on the X chromosome. The genetic possibilities and the inheritance of color blindness are shown in Figure 26.3. Only females who have two X^c chromosomes are color blind. In $X^C X^c$ females the trait for color blindness is inhibited by the normal dominant gene. Males, however, do not have a second X chromosome that would inhibit the trait. Therefore, all males with an X^c chromosome will be color blind. Their pair of sex chromosomes is $X^c Y$.

2. Hemophilia

Hemophilia is a condition in which the blood fails to clot or clots very slowly after an injury. Hemophilia is a much more serious defect than color blindness because individuals with severe hemophilia can bleed to death from even a small cut. Hemophilia is caused by a recessive gene as is color blindness. If H represents normal clotting and h represents abnormal clotting, $X^h X^h$ females will be hemophiliacs. Males with $X^H Y$ will be normal and males with $X^h Y$ will be hemophiliacs. Other X-linked traits in human beings are certain forms of diabetes, night blindness, juvenile glaucoma, and juvenile muscular dystrophy.

E. MENDELIAN LAWS

In any genetic cross, all the offspring in the first (that is, the parental, or P_1) generation are symbolized as F_1. The F is from the Latin word *filial*, which means progeny. The second generation is symbolized as F_2, the third as F_3, and continues that way. The recognized "father" of genetics is Gregor Mendel, whose basic experiments were performed on garden peas. As a result of his tests, Gregor Mendel postulated what are now called **Mendelian Laws,** or **Mendelian Principles.** The **First Mendelian Law,** or the **Law of Segregation,** asserts that, in cells of individuals, genes occur in pairs, and that when those individuals produce germ cells, each germ cell receives only one member of the pair.

This law applies equally to pollen grains (or sperm) and to ova. The genetic cross is represented as follows:

Yellow Parent	$\times$	**Green Parent**
YY		yy

Pollen grains / Ova

	Y	Y
y	Yy	Yy
y	Yy	Yy

or

All possible combinations of pollen grains and ova are indicated by the arrows. Notice that all combinations yield the genotype *Yy*. All these F_1 seeds were yellow, yellow being dominant to green, or, in genetic terms, *Y* being dominant to *y*. These F_1 individuals resembled the yellow parent in phenotype (being yellow) but not in genotype (*Yy* as opposed to *YY*). Both parents were homozygous. Both members of that pair of alleles were the same. The yellow parent was homozygous for *Y* and the green parent for *y*. The F_1 individuals were heterozygous, having one *Y* and one *y*.

When the F_1 plants were self-fertilized, the F_2 seeds appeared in the ratio of 3 yellow/1 green. Mendel found similar 3:1 ratios for the other traits he studied, and this type of result has been reported in many species of animals and plants for a variety of traits. Not only does the recessive trait reappear in the F_2, but also in a definite proportion of the individuals, one-fourth of the total. If the sample is small, the ratio may deviate considerably from 3:1, but as the progeny or sampling numbers get larger, the ratio usually comes closer and closer to an exact 3:1 ratio. The reason is that the ratio depends on the random union of gametes. The result is a 3:1 phenotypic ratio, or a 1:2:1 genotypic ratio.

F_1 Parents genotype	**Yellow** *Yy*	×	**Yellow** *Yy*

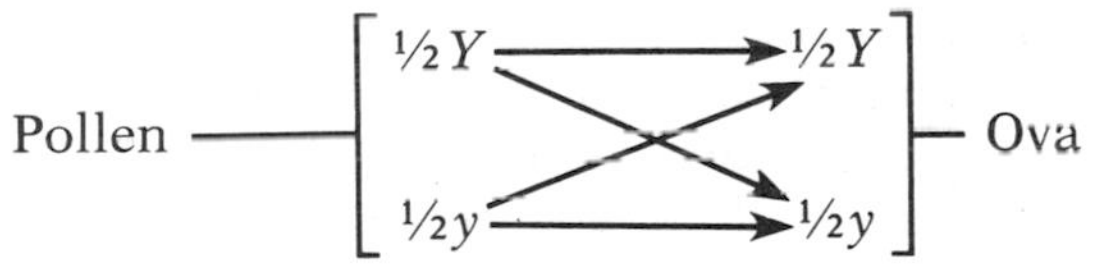

or

	Y	*y*
Y	*YY*	*Yy*
y	*Yy*	*yy*

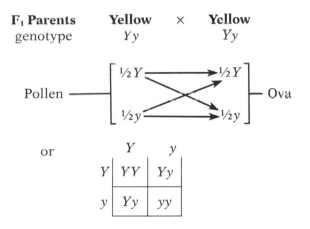

Thus, the four combinations of pollen and ova are expected to occur as follows:

¼ *YY* = yellow ⎤
¼ *Yy* = yellow ⎬ ¾
¼ *Yy* = yellow ⎦

¼ *yy* = green ⎯ ¼

It is important to realize that these fractions depend on the operation of the laws of probability. A model using coins will emphasize the point. This model consists of two coins, a nickel and a penny, tossed at the same time. The penny may represent the pollen (male parent). At any given toss, the chances are equal that the penny will come up "heads" or that it will come up "tails." Similarly, at any given fertilization the chances are equal that a *Y*-bearing pollen grain or that a *y*-bearing one will be transmitted. The nickel represents the ovum. Again, the chances are equal for "heads" or "tails," just as the chances are equal that in any fertilization a *Y*-bearing or a *y*-bearing ovum will take part. If we toss the two coins together and do it many times, we will obtain approximately the following:

¼ nickel heads; penny heads	(= *YY*)
¼ nickel heads; penny tails	(= *Yy*)
¼ nickel tails; penny heads	(= *yY*)
¼ nickel tails; penny tails	(= *yy*)

If we assume "heads" as dominant, we find that three-fourths of the time there is at least one "head" and one-fourth of the time no "heads" (both coins "tails"). Hence this gives us a model of the 3:1 ratio dependent on the laws of probability.

The genetic cross just demonstrated considered only one pair of alleles (yellow versus green or "heads" versus "tails") and is therefore called a **monohybrid cross.** Mendel's second principle applied to genetic crosses in which two traits or two pairs of alleles were considered. These were **dihybrid crosses** and they enabled him to postulate his second principle, the **Principle of Independent Assortment.** This principle stated that the segregation of one pair of traits occurred independently of the segregation of a second pair of traits. This is the case only if the traits are caused by genes located on nonhomologous chromosomes.

When Mendel crossed garden peas with round yellow seeds with garden peas with wrinkled green seeds, his F_1 generation showed that yellow and round were dominant. If self-fertilization then occurred, the F_2 generation resulted as follows:

round yellow	$\frac{3}{4} \times \frac{3}{4} = \frac{9}{16}$
round green	$\frac{3}{4} \times \frac{1}{4} = \frac{3}{16}$
wrinkled yellow	$\frac{1}{4} \times \frac{3}{4} = \frac{3}{16}$
wrinkled green	$\frac{1}{4} \times \frac{1}{4} = \frac{1}{16}$

Therefore, in a dihybrid cross, the expected phenotypic ratio was 9:3:3:1, with $\frac{9}{16}$ of the F_2 being doubly dominant, and only $\frac{1}{16}$ being doubly recessive.

F. MULTIPLE ALLELES

In the genetics examples we have considered to this point, we have discussed only two alleles of each gene. However, many, and possibly all genes, have **multiple alleles,** that is, they exist in more than two allelic forms even though a diploid cell cannot carry more than two alleles.

One example of multiple alleles in humans involves ABO blood groups (Exercise 16). The four basic blood groups of the ABO system are determined by three alleles: I^A, I^B, and i. Alleles I^A and I^B are not dominant over each other (codominant), but are dominant over allele i. These three alleles can give rise to six genotypes as follows:

Genotype	Phenotype (blood type)
$I^A I^A$ or $I^A i$	A
$I^B I^B$ or $I^B i$	B
$I^A I^B$	AB
ii	O

Given this information, is it possible for a child with type O blood to have a mother with type O blood and a father with type AB blood?

Explain. _____

_____

_____

If two children in a family have type O blood, the mother has type B blood and the father has type A blood, what is the genotype of the father? _____

What is the genotype of the mother? _____

G. GENETIC EXERCISES

1. Karyotyping

A group of cytogeneticists meeting in Denver, Colorado, in 1960 adopted a system for classifying and identifying human chromosomes. Chromosome **length** and **centromere position** were the bases for classification. The Denver classification has become a standard for human chromosome studies. By the early 1970s, most human chromosomes could be identified microscopically.

Every chromosome pair could not be identified consistently until chromosome **banding techniques** finally distinguished all 46 human chromosomes. Bands are defined as parts of chromosomes that appear lighter or darker than adjacent regions with particular staining methods.

A **karyotype** is a chart made from a photograph of the chromosomes in metaphase. The chromosomes are cut out and arranged in matched pairs according to length (see Figure 26.2a). Their comparative size, shape, and morphology are then examined to determine if they are normal or not.

The procedure for obtaining a karyotype is as follows:

1. Three drops of blood obtained by the puncture procedure outlined in Section D.1 of Exercise 16 are added to PHA (phytohemagglutin) extract and placed in a nutrient culture medium.[1]

2. This solution remains for 3 days, after which the cells, which are actively growing and dividing because of the PHA, are placed on a slide and squashed with a cover slip or another slide.

3. A photograph is made of the squashed cell and an enlarged print from the negative. Then, with a pair of sharp scissors, each chromosome is cut out, and the chromosomes are matched in pairs according to number and glued to a sheet. The individual chromosomes are then examined.

Karyotyping helps scientists to visualize chromosomal abnormalities. For example, individuals with Down's syndrome typically have 47 chromosomes, instead of the usual 46, with chromosomal 21 being represented three times rather than only twice. The syndrome is characterized by mental retardation, retarded physical development, and distinctive facial features (round head, broad skull, slanting eyes, and large tongue). With chronic myelogenous leukemia, part of the long arm of a chromosome 22 is missing, resulting in the blood disease. The chromosome is referred to as the Philadelphia chromosome, named for the city where it was first detected.

2. PKU Screening

Phenylketonuria (PKU), an inherited metabolic disorder that occurs in approximately 1 in

---

[1]The culture medium used is Bacto-phytohemagglutinin M and Bacto-phytohemagglutinin P, Codes 0528 and 3110, respectively. These culture reagents are obtained from Difco tissue culture and virus propagation reagents.

16,000 births, is transmitted by an autosomal recessive gene (see Figure 26.1). Individuals with this condition do not have the enzyme phenylalanine hydroxylase, which converts the amino acid phenylalanine to tyrosine. As a result, phenylalanine and phenylpyruvic acid accumulate in the blood and urine. These substances are toxic to the central nervous system and can produce irreversible brain damage. Most states in the United States require routine screening for this disorder at birth. The test is accomplished by a simple color change in treated urine.

The procedure for testing for PKU is as follows:

1. A Phenistix test strip is made specifically for testing urine for phenylpyruvic acid. Dip this test strip in freshly voided urine.
2. Compare the color change with the color chart on the Phenistix bottle. The test is based on the reaction of ferric ions with phenylpyruvic acid to produce a gray-green color.
3. Record your results in Section G.1 in the Laboratory Report Results.

3. PTC Inheritance

The ability to taste the chemical compound known as phenylthiocarbamide, commonly called PTC, is inherited. On the average, 7 out of 10 people, on chewing a small piece of paper treated with PTC, detect a definite bitter or sweet taste. Others do not taste anything.

Individuals who can taste something (bitter or sweet) are called "tasters" and have the dominant allele *T*, either as *TT* or *Tt*. A nontaster is a homozygous recessive and is designated as *tt*.

Determine your phenotype for tasting PTC and record your results in Section G.2 in the Laboratory Report Results.

Note: If PTC paper is not available, a 0.5% solution of phenylthiourea (PTT) can be substituted because the capacity to taste PTT is also inherited as a dominant.

4. Corn Genetics

Genetic corn may be purchased and used in this exercise. Each ear of corn represents a family of offspring. Mark a starting row with a pin to avoid repetition. Count the kernels (individuals) for each trait (color, wrinkled, or smooth). Record your results in Section G.3 in the Laboratory Report Results.

Develop a ratio by using your lowest number as "1" and dividing it into the others to determine what multiples of it they are. See how close you come to Mendel's ratios. Figure out the probable genotype and phenotype of the parent plants if you can. Monohybrid crosses, test crosses, dihybrid crosses, and trihybrid crosses are available.

5. Color Blindness

Using either Stilling or Ishihara test charts, test the entire class for color blindness. Tests for color blindness depend on the person's ability to distinguish various colors from each other and also on his or her ability to judge correctly the degree of contrast between colors.

Of all men, 2% are color blind to red and 6% to green, so 8% of all men are red-green color blind. Red-green color blindness is rare in the female, occurring in only 1 of every 250 women. Record your results in Section G.4 in the Laboratory Report Results.

6. Mendelian Laws of Inheritance

Follow the procedure outlined in the explanation of the Mendelian Law of Segregation, tossing a nickel and a penny simultaneously to prove the law and determine ratios.

1. Toss the nickel and the penny together 10 times to get the genotypes of a family of 10. Repeat this procedure for a total of five times to obtain five families of 10 offspring. Record all results on the chart in Section G.5 in the Laboratory Report Results.

Note: Use the following symbols for the following exercises.

- G = gene for yellow
- g = gene for green
- GG = the genotype of an individual pure (homozygous) for yellow
- gg = the genotype of an individual pure (homozygous) for green
- Gg = the genotype of the hybrid (heterozygous) individual, phenotypically yellow
- ♀ = symbol for female
- ♂ = symbol for male

2. Obeying the Mendelian Law of Segregation and using the Punnett square shown in Section G.6 in the Laboratory Report Results, cross yellow garden peas with green garden peas (a monohybrid cross). Show the P_1, F_1, and F_2 generations and all the different phenotypes and genotypes.

3. Obeying the Mendelian Law of Independent Assortment and using the Punnett square shown in Section G.8 in the Laboratory Report Results, cross the round yellow seeds with the wrinkled green seeds (a dihybrid cross). Show the P_1, F_1, and F_2 generations and all the different phenotypes and genotypes. The F_2 generation can be generated from a Punnett square comparable to that for the monohybrid cross, but with 16 rather than 4 squares.

LABORATORY REPORT QUESTIONS (PAGE 453)

1 | LABORATORY REPORT QUESTIONS
MICROSCOPY

Student _____   Date _____

Laboratory Section _____   Score/Grade _____

PART I. MULTIPLE CHOICE

_____ 1. The amount of light entering a microscope may be adjusted by regulating the (a) ocular (b) diaphragm (c) fine adjustment knob (d) nosepiece

_____ 2. If the ocular on a microscope is marked 10× and the low-power objective is marked 15×, the total magnification is (a) 50× (b) 25× (c) 150× (d) 1500×

_____ 3. The size of the light beam that passes through a microscope is regulated by the (a) revolving nosepiece (b) coarse adjustment knob (c) ocular (d) condenser

_____ 4. Parfocal means that (a) the microscope employs only one lens (b) final focusing can only be done with the fine adjustment knob (c) changing objectives by revolving the nosepiece will still keep the specimen in focus (d) the highest magnification attainable is 1000×

_____ 5. Which of these is *not* true when changing magnification from low power to high power? (a) the specimen should be centered (b) illumination should be decreased (c) the specimen should be in clear focus (d) the high power objective should be in line with the body tube

_____ 6. A microscope with which of the following resolving powers could distinguish the finest detail? (a) 0.01 μm (b) 1.0 Å (c) 0.001 μm (d) 0.1 Å

PART II. COMPLETION

7. The advantage of using immersion oil is that it has special _____ properties that permit the use of a powerful objective in a narrow field of vision.

8. The uniform circle of light that appears when one looks into the ocular is called the _____ .

9. In determining the position (depth) of the colored threads, the _____ (red, blue, yellow) colored thread was in the middle.

10. If you move your slide to the right, the specimen moves to the _____ as you are viewing it microscopically.

11. After switching from low power to high power, _____ (more or less) of the specimen will be visible.

12. The ability of lenses to distinguish between two points at a specified distance apart is called

_____ .

13. The wavelength of electrons is about _____ (what proportion?) that of visible white light.

14. A photograph of a specimen taken through a compound light microscope is called a(n)

_____ .

15. The type of microscope that provides three-dimensional images of nonliving specimens is the

_____ microscope.

PART III. MATCHING

_____ 16. Ocular	A. Platform on which slide is placed
_____ 17. Stage	B. Mounting for objectives
_____ 18. Arm	C. Lens below stage opening
_____ 19. Condenser	D. Brings specimen into sharp focus
_____ 20. Revolving nosepiece	E. Eyepiece
_____ 21. Low-power objective	F. An objective usually marked 43× or 45×
_____ 22. Fine adjustment knob	G. An objective usually marked 10×
_____ 23. Diaphragm	H. Angular or curved part of frame
_____ 24. Coarse adjustment knob	I. Brings specimen into general focus
_____ 25. High-power objective	J. Regulates light intensity

2 | INTRODUCTION TO THE HUMAN BODY

Student _____   Date _____

Laboratory Section _____   Score/Grade _____

PART I. MULTIPLE CHOICE

_____ 1. The directional term that best describes the eyes in relation to the nose is (a) distal (b) superficial (c) anterior (d) lateral

_____ 2. Which does *not* belong with the others? (a) right pleural cavity (b) pericardial cavity (c) vertebral cavity (d) left pleural cavity

_____ 3. Which plane divides the brain into an anterior and a posterior portion? (a) frontal (b) median (c) sagittal (d) horizontal

_____ 4. The urinary bladder lies in which region? (a) umbilical (b) hypogastric (c) epigastric (d) left iliac

_____ 5. Which is *not* a characteristic of the anatomical position? (a) the subject is erect (b) the subject faces the observer (c) the palms face backward (d) the arms are at the sides

_____ 6. The abdominopelvic region that is bordered by all four imaginary lines is the (a) hypogastric (b) epigastric (c) left hypochondriac (d) umbilical

_____ 7. Which directional term best describes the position of the phalanges with respect to the carpals? (a) lateral (b) distal (c) anterior (d) proximal

_____ 8. The pancreas is found in which body cavity? (a) abdominal (b) pericardial (c) pelvic (d) vertebral

_____ 9. The anatomical term for the leg is (a) brachial (b) tarsal (c) crural (d) sural

_____ 10. In which abdominopelvic region is the spleen located? (a) left lumbar (b) right lumbar (c) epigastric (d) left hypochondriac

_____ 11. Which of the following represents the most complex level of structural organization? (a) organ (b) cellular (c) tissue (d) chemical

_____ 12. Which body system is concerned with support, protection, leverage, blood cell production, and mineral storage? (a) cardiovascular (b) lymphatic (c) skeletal (d) digestive

_____ 13. The skin and structures derived from it, such as nails, hair, sweat glands, and oil glands, are components of which system? (a) respiratory (b) integumentary (c) muscular (d) lymphatic

_____ 14. Hormone-producing glands belong to which body system? (a) cardiovascular (b) lymphatic (c) endocrine (d) digestive

_____ 15. Which body system brings about movement, maintains posture, and produces heat? (a) skeletal (b) respiratory (c) reproductive (d) muscular

_____ 16. Which abdominopelvic quadrant contains most of the liver? (a) RUQ (b) RLQ (c) LUQ (d) LLQ

_____ 17. The physical and chemical breakdown of food for use by body cells and the elimination of solid wastes are accomplished by which body system? (a) respiratory (b) urinary (c) cardiovascular (d) digestive

PART II. COMPLETION

18. The tibia is _____ to the fibula.

19. The ovaries are found in the _____ body cavity.

20. The upper horizontal line that helps divide the abdominopelvic cavity into nine regions is the _____ line.

21. The anatomical term for the hollow behind the knee is _____ .

22. A plane that divides the stomach into a superior and an inferior portion is a(n) _____ plane.

23. The wrist is described as _____ to the elbow.

24. The heart is located in the _____ cavity within the thoracic cavity.

25. The abdominopelvic region that contains the rectum is the _____ region.

26. A plane that divides the body into unequal left and right sides is the _____ plane.

27. The spinal cord is located within the _____ cavity.

28. The body system that removes carbon dioxide from body cells, delivers oxygen to body cells, helps maintain acid-base balance, helps protect against disease, helps regulate body temperature, and prevents hemorrhage by forming clots is the _____ system.

29. The _____ abdominopelvic quadrant contains the descending colon of the large intestine.

30. Which body system returns proteins and plasma to the cardiovascular system, transports fats from the digestive system to the cardiovascular system, filters blood, protects against disease, and produces white blood cells? _____

PART III. MATCHING

_____ 31. Right hypochondriac region

_____ 32. Hypogastric region

_____ 33. Left iliac region

_____ 34. Right lumbar region

_____ 35. Epigastric region

_____ 36. Left hypochondriac region

_____ 37. Right iliac region

_____ 38. Umbilical region

_____ 39. Left lumbar region

A. Junction of descending and sigmoid colons of large intestine
B. Descending colon of large intestine
C. Spleen
D. Most of right lobe of liver
E. Appendix
F. Ascending colon of large intestine
G. Middle of transverse colon of large intestine
H. Adrenal (suprarenal) glands
I. Sigmoid colon of large intestine

PART IV. MATCHING

_____ 40. Anterior

_____ 41. Thumb

_____ 42. Transtubercular line

_____ 43. Armpit

_____ 44. Umbilical region

_____ 45. Medial

_____ 46. Cranial cavity

_____ 47. Front of knee

_____ 48. Breast

_____ 49. Chest

_____ 50. Buttock

_____ 51. Superior

_____ 52. Groin

_____ 53. Vertebral cavity

_____ 54. Cheek

_____ 55. Neck

_____ 56. Distal

_____ 57. Pericardial cavity

_____ 58. Forearm

_____ 59. Plantar

_____ 60. Mouth

A. Passes through iliac crests

B. Contains spinal cord

C. Nearer the midline

D. Thoracic

E. Cervical

F. Axillary

G. Contains the heart

H. Pollex

 I. Antebrachial

J. Gluteal

K. Mammary

L. Sole of foot

M. Contains navel

N. Buccal

O. Farther from the attachment of an extremity

P. Patellar

Q. Toward the head

R. Nearer to or at the front of the body

S. Oral

T. Contains brain

U. Inguinal

3 | CELLS
LABORATORY REPORT QUESTIONS

Student _____   Date _____

Laboratory Section _____   Score/Grade _____

PART 1. MULTIPLE CHOICE

_____   1. The portion of the cell that forms part of the mitotic spindle during division is the (a) endoplasmic reticulum (b) Golgi complex (c) cytoplasm (d) centriole

_____   2. Movement of molecules or ions from a region of higher concentration to a region of lower concentration until they are evenly distributed is called (a) phagocytosis (b) diffusion (c) active transport (d) pinocytosis

_____   3. If red blood cells are placed in a hypertonic solution of sodium chloride, they will (a) swell (b) burst (c) shrink (d) remain the same

_____   4. The reagent used to test for the presence of sugar is (a) silver nitrate (b) nitric acid (c) IKI (d) Benedict's solution

_____   5. A cell that carries on a great deal of digestion also contains a large number of (a) lysosomes (b) centrioles (c) mitochondria (d) nuclei

_____   6. Which process does *not* belong with the others? (a) active transport (b) dialysis (c) phagocytosis (d) pinocytosis

_____   7. Movement of oxygen and carbon dioxide between blood and body cells is an example of (a) osmosis (b) active transport (c) diffusion (d) pinocytosis

_____   8. Which type of solution will cause hemolysis? (a) isotonic (b) hypotonic (c) isometric (d) hypertonic

_____   9. One process by which kidneys regulate the chemical composition of blood is (a) diffusion (b) active transport (c) filtration (d) osmosis

_____   10. Engulfment of solid particles or organisms by pseudopodia is called (a) active transport (b) dialysis (c) phagocytosis (d) filtration

_____   11. Rupture of red blood cells with subsequent loss of hemoglobin into the surrounding medium is called (a) hemolysis (b) plasmolysis (c) plasmoptysis (d) hemoglobinuria

_____   12. The area of the cell between the plasma membrane and nuclear membrane where chemical reactions occur is the (a) centrosome (b) vacuole (c) peroxisome (d) cytoplasm

_____   13. The "powerhouses" of the cell where ATP is produced are the (a) ribosomes (b) mitochondria (c) centrioles (d) lysosomes

_____   14. A modified plasma membrane that insulates and protects the axon of a neuron is a (a) microvillus (b) flagellum (c) myelin sheath (d) stereocilium

_____   15. Which process does *not* belong with the others? (a) diffusion (b) phagocytosis (c) active transport (d) pinocytosis

_____   16. A cell inclusion that is a pigment in skin and hair is (a) glycogen (b) melanin (c) mucus (d) collagen

371

_____ 17. Which extracellular material is found in ligaments and tendons? (a) elastic fibers (b) chondroitin sulfate (c) collagenous fibers (d) mucus

_____ 18. The organelles that contain enzymes for the metabolism of hydrogen peroxide are (a) lysosomes (b) mitochondria (c) vacuoles (d) peroxisomes

_____ 19. The framework of cilia, flagella, centrioles, and spindle fibers is formed by (a) endoplasmic reticulum (b) collagenous fibers (c) chondroitin sulfate (d) microtubules

_____ 20. A viscous fluidlike substance that binds cells together, lubricates joints, and maintains the shape of the eyeballs is (a) elastin (b) hyaluronic acid (c) mucus (d) plasmin

PART II. COMPLETION

21. The external boundary of the cell through which substances enter and exit is called the

_____ .

22. The cytoskeleton is formed by microtubules and _____ .

23. The portion of the cell that contains hereditary information is the _____ .

24. The tail of a sperm cell is a long whiplash structure called a(n) _____ .

25. Fingerlike projections that line some cells of the small intestine and increase their surface area for absorption are called _____ .

26. The sites of protein synthesis in cells are the _____ .

27. Lipid and protein secretion, carbohydrate synthesis, and assembly of glycoproteins are functions of the _____ .

28. Storage of digestive enzymes is accomplished by the _____ of a cell.

29. Projections of cells that move substances along their surfaces are called _____ .

30. The _____ provides a surface area for chemical reactions, a pathway for transporting molecules, and a storage area for synthesized molecules.

31. _____ is a cell inclusion that represents stored glucose in the liver and skeletal muscles.

32. A jellylike substance that supports cartilage, bone, heart valves, and the umbilical cord is

_____ .

33. The framework of many soft organs is formed by _____ fibers.

34. The net movement of water through a semipermeable membrane from a region of higher concentration of water to a region of lower concentration of water is known as _____ .

35. The principle of _____ is employed in the operation of an artificial kidney.

36. In an interphase cell, DNA is in the form of a granular substance called _____ .

37. Distribution of chromosomes into separate and equal nuclei is referred to as

_____ .

PART III. MATCHING

_____ 38. Anaphase

_____ 39. Metaphase

_____ 40. Interphase

_____ 41. Telophase

_____ 42. Prophase

A. Mitotic spindle appears

B. Movement of chromosome sets to opposite poles of cell

C. Centromeres line up on equatorial plane

D. Formation of two identical nuclei

E. Phase between divisions

4 | LABORATORY REPORT QUESTIONS
TISSUES

Student _____   Date _____

Laboratory Section _____   Score/Grade _____

PART I. MULTIPLE CHOICE

_____   1. In parts of the body such as the urinary bladder, where considerable distension occurs, you can expect to find which epithelial tissue? (a) pseudostratified (b) cuboidal (c) columnar (d) transitional

_____   2. Stratified epithelium is usually found in areas of the body where the principal activity is (a) filtration (b) absorption (c) protection (d) diffusion

_____   3. Ciliated epithelium destroyed by disease would cause malfunction in which system? (a) digestive (b) respiratory (c) skeletal (d) cardiovascular

_____   4. The tissue that provides the skin with resistance to wear and tear and serves to waterproof it is (a) keratinized stratified squamous (b) pseudostratified (c) transitional (d) simple columnar

_____   5. The connective tissue cell that would most likely increase its activity during an infection is the (a) melanocyte (b) macrophage (c) mast cell (d) fibroblast

_____   6. Torn ligaments would involve damage to which tissue? (a) collagenous (b) reticular (c) elastic (d) loose

_____   7. Simple squamous tissue that lines the heart, blood vessels, and lymphatic vessels is called (a) transitional (b) adipose (c) endothelium (d) mesothelium

_____   8. Microvilli and goblet cells are associated with which tissue? (a) hyaline cartilage (b) simple columnar nonciliated (c) transitional (d) stratified squamous

_____   9. Superficial fascia contains which tissue? (a) elastic (b) reticular (c) fibrocartilage (d) loose

_____   10. Which tissue forms articular cartilage and costal cartilage? (a) fibrocartilage (b) elastic cartilage (c) adipose (d) hyaline cartilage

_____   11. Because the sublingual gland contains a branched duct and flasklike secretory portions, it is classified as (a) simple coiled tubular (b) compound acinar (c) simple acinar (d) compound tubular

_____   12. Which glands discharge an entire dead cell and its contents as their secretory products? (a) merocrine (b) apocrine (c) endocrine (d) holocrine

_____   13. Membranes that line cavities that open directly to the exterior are called (a) synovial (b) serous (c) mucous (d) cutaneous

PART II. COMPLETION

14. Single cells found in epithelium that secrete mucus are called _____ cells.

15. A type of epithelium that appears to consist of several layers but actually contains only one layer of cells is _____ .

16. The cell in connective tissue that forms new fibers is the _____ .

17. Heparin, a substance that prevents blood from clotting in vessels, is secreted by _____ cells.

18. Cartilage cells found in lacunae are called _____ .

19. The simple squamous epithelium of a serous membrane that covers viscera is called _____ .

20. The tissue that provides insulation, support, protection, and serves as a food reserve is _____ .

21. _____ tissue forms the stroma of organs such as the liver and spleen.

22. The cartilage that provides support for the larynx and external ear is _____ .

23. Collagenous fibers, elastic fibers, reticular fibers, and hyaluronic acid are associated with _____ tissue.

24. Ductless glands that secrete hormones are called _____ glands.

25. Multicellular exocrine glands that contain branching ducts are classified as _____ glands.

26. The mammary glands are classified as _____ glands because their secretory products are the pinched-off margins of cells.

27. _____ membranes consist of a parietal and visceral layer and line cavities that do not open to the exterior.

28. If the secretory portion of a gland is flasklike, it is classified as a(n) _____ gland.

29. Membranes that line joint cavities are called _____ membranes.

30. An example of a simple branched acinar gland is a(n) _____ gland.

5 | LABORATORY REPORT QUESTIONS
INTEGUMENTARY SYSTEM

Student _____   **Date** _____

Laboratory Section _____   **Score/Grade** _____

PART I. MULTIPLE CHOICE

_____   1. The waterproofing quality of skin is due to the presence of (a) melanin (b) carotene (c) keratin (d) receptors

_____   2. Sebaceous glands (a) produce a watery solution called sweat (b) produce an oily substance that prevents excessive water evaporation from the skin (c) are associated with mucous membranes (d) are part of the subcutaneous layer

_____   3. Which of the following is the proper sequence of layering of the epidermis, going from the free surface toward the underlying tissues? (a) basale, spinosum, granulosum, corneum (b) spinosum, basale, granulosum, corneum (c) corneum, lucidum, granulosum, spinosum, basale (d) corneum, granulosum, lucidum, spinosum

_____   4. Skin color is *not* determined by the (a) presence or absence of melanin (b) presence or absence of carotene (c) presence or absence of keratin (d) presence or absence of blood vessels in the dermis

_____   5. Destruction of what part of a single hair would result in its inability to grow? (a) sebaceous gland (b) arrector pili muscles (c) matrix (d) bulb

_____   6. One would expect to find relatively few, if any, sebaceous glands in the skin of the (a) palms (b) face (c) neck (d) upper chest

_____   7. Which of the following sequences is correct? (a) epidermis, reticular layer, papillary layer, subcutaneous layer (b) epidermis, subcutaneous layer, reticular layer, papillary layer (c) epidermis, reticular layer, subcutaneous layer, papillary layer (d) epidermis, papillary layer, reticular layer, subcutaneous layer

_____   8. The attached visible portion of a nail is called the (a) nail bed (b) nail root (c) nail fold (d) nail body

_____   9. Nerve endings sensitive to touch are called (a) corpuscles of touch (Meissner's corpuscles) (b) papillae (c) lamellated (pacinian) corpuscles (d) follicles

_____   10. The cuticle of a nail is referred to as the (a) matrix (b) eponychium (c) hyponychium (d) fold

_____   11. One would *not* expect to find sudoriferous glands associated with the (a) forehead (b) axilla (c) palms (d) nail beds

_____   12. Fingerlike projections of the dermis that contain loops of capillaries and receptors are called (a) dermal papillae (b) nodules (c) polyps (d) pili

_____   13. Which of the following statements about the function of skin is *not* true? (a) it helps control body temperature (b) it prevents excessive water loss (c) it synthesizes several compounds (d) it absorbs water and salts

_____ 14. Which is *not* part of the internal root sheath? (a) granular (Huxley's) layer (b) cortex (c) pallid (Henle's) layer (d) cuticle of the internal root sheath

_____ 15. Growth in the length of nails is the result of the activity of the (a) eponychium (b) nail matrix (c) hyponychium (d) nail fold

PART II. COMPLETION

16. A group of tissues that performs a definite function is called a(n) _____ .

17. The outer, thinner layer of the skin is known as the _____ .

18. The skin is attached to underlying tissues and organs by the _____ .

19. A group of organs that operate together to perform a specialized function is called a(n) _____ .

20. The epidermal layer that contains eleidin is the stratum _____ .

21. The epidermal layers that produce new cells are the stratum spinosum and stratum _____ .

22. The smooth muscle attached to a hair follicle is called the _____ muscle.

23. An inherited ability to produce melanin is called _____ .

24. Nerve endings sensitive to deep pressure are referred to as _____ corpuscles.

25. The inner region of a hair shaft and root is the _____ .

26. The portion of a hair containing loose connective tissue and blood vessels is the _____ .

27. Modified sweat glands that line the external auditory meatus are called _____ glands.

28. The whitish semilunar area at the proximal end of the nail body is referred to as the _____ .

29. The secretory product of sudoriferous glands is called _____ .

30. Melanin is synthesized in cells called _____ .

6 | LABORATORY REPORT QUESTIONS
OSSEOUS TISSUE

Student _____   Date _____

Laboratory Section _____   Score/Grade _____

PART I. COMPLETION

1. Small clusters of bones between certain cranial bones are referred to as _____ bones.

2. The technical name for a bone cell is a(n) _____ .

3. Canals that extend obliquely inward or horizontally from the bone surface and contain blood vessels and lymphatics are _____ canals.

4. The end, or extremity, of a bone is referred to as the _____ .

5. Cube-shaped bones that contain more spongy than compact bone are known as _____ bones.

6. The cavity within the shaft of a bone that contains marrow is the _____ cavity.

7. The thin layer of hyaline cartilage covering the end of a bone where joints are formed is called _____ cartilage.

8. Minute canals that radiate from lacuna to lacuna are called _____ .

9. The white fibrous covering around the surface of a bone, except for the areas covered by cartilage, is the _____ .

10. The shaft of a bone is referred to as the _____ .

11. The _____ are concentric layers of calcified intercellular substance.

12. The membrane that lines the medullary cavity and contains osteoblasts and a few osteoclasts is the _____ .

13. The technical name for bone tissue is _____ tissue.

14. In a mature bone, the region where the shaft joins the extremity is called the

_____ .

15. The microscopic structural unit of compact bone is called a(n) _____ .

16. The hardness of bone is primarily due to the mineral salt _____ .

Student _____   Date _____

Laboratory Section _____   Score/Grade _____

PART I. MULTIPLE CHOICE

_____ 1. The suture between the parietal and temporal bone is the (a) lambdoidal (b) coronal (c) squamosal (d) sagittal

_____ 2. Which bone does *not* contain a paranasal sinus? (a) ethmoid (b) maxilla (c) sphenoid (d) sacral

_____ 3. Which is the superior, concave curve in the vertebral column? (a) thoracic (b) lumbar (c) cervical (d) sacral

_____ 4. The fontanel between the parietal and occipital bones is the (a) anterolateral (b) anterior (c) posterior (d) posterolateral

_____ 5. Which is *not* a component of the upper extremity? (a) radius (b) femur (c) carpus (d) humerus

_____ 6. All are components of the appendicular skeleton *except* the (a) humerus (b) occipital bone (c) calcaneus (d) triquetral

_____ 7. Which bone does *not* belong with the others? (a) occipital (b) frontal (c) parietal (d) mandible

_____ 8. Which region of the vertebral column is closer to the skull? (a) thoracic (b) lumbar (c) cervical (d) sacral

_____ 9. Of the following bones, the one that does *not* help form part of the orbit is the (a) sphenoid (b) frontal (c) occipital (d) lacrimal

_____ 10. Which bone does *not* form a border for a fontanel? (a) maxilla (b) temporal (c) occipital (d) parietal

PART II. IDENTIFICATION

For each surface marking listed, identify the skull bone to which it belongs:

11. Glabella _____

12. Mastoid process _____

13. Sella turcica _____

14. Cribriform plate _____

15. Foramen magnum _____

16. Mental foramen _____

17. Infraorbital foramen _____

18. Crista galli _____

19. Foramen ovale _____

20. Horizontal plate _____

21. Optic foramen _____

22. Superior nasal concha _____

23. Zygomatic process

24. Styloid process _____

25. Mandibular fossa _____

PART III. MATCHING

_____ 26. Iliac crest

_____ 27. Capitulum

_____ 28. Medial malleolus

_____ 29. Laminae

_____ 30. Vertebral foramen

_____ 31. Talus

_____ 32. Olecranon

_____ 33. Pisiform

_____ 34. Acromial extremity

_____ 35. Symphysis pubis

_____ 36. Hamate

_____ 37. Costal groove

_____ 38. Xiphoid process

_____ 39. Greater trochanter

_____ 40. Transverse lines

_____ 41. Radial tuberosity

_____ 42. Greater tubercle

_____ 43. Ischium

_____ 44. Glenoid cavity

_____ 45. Lateral malleolus

A. Inferior portion of sternum
B. Medial bone of distal carpals
C. Distal projection of tibia
D. Lateral end of clavicle
E. Points where bodies of sacral vertebrae join
F. Portion of a rib that contains blood vessels
G. Prominence of elbow
H. Lateral projection of humerus
I. Medial projection for insertion of biceps muscle
J. Lower posterior portion of hipbone
K. Articulates with head of radius
L. Prominence on lateral side of femur
M. Distal projection of fibula
N. Superior border of ilium
O. Articulates with head of humerus
P. Anterior joint between hipbones
Q. Opening through which spinal cord passes
R. Form posterior wall of vertebral arch
S. Medial bone of proximal carpals
T. Component of tarsus

8 | ARTICULATIONS

Student _____   Date _____

Laboratory Section _____   Score/Grade _____

PART I. MULTIPLE CHOICE

_____ 1. A joint united by dense fibrous tissue that permits a slight degree of movement is a (a) suture (b) syndesmosis (c) symphysis (d) synchondrosis

_____ 2. A joint that contains a broad flat disc of fibrocartilage is classified as a (a) ball-and-socket joint (b) suture (c) symphysis (d) gliding joint

_____ 3. The following characteristics define what type of joint? Presence of a synovial cavity, articular cartilage, synovial membrane, and ligaments. (a) suture (b) synchondrosis (c) syndesmosis (d) hinge

_____ 4. Which joints are slightly movable? (a) diarthroses (b) amphiarthroses (c) synovial (d) synarthroses

_____ 5. Which type of joint is immovable? (a) synarthrosis (b) syndesmosis (c) symphysis (d) diarthrosis

_____ 6. What type of joint provides triaxial movement? (a) hinge (b) ball-and-socket (c) saddle (d) ellipsoidal

_____ 7. Which ligament provides strength on the medial side of the knee joint? (a) oblique popliteal (b) posterior cruciate (c) fibular collateral (d) tibial collateral

_____ 8. On the basis of structure, which joint is fibrous? (a) symphysis (b) synchondrosis (c) pivot (d) syndesmosis

_____ 9. The elbow, knee, and interphalangeal joints are examples of which type of joint? (a) pivot (b) hinge (c) gliding (d) saddle

_____ 10. Functionally, which joint provides the greatest degree of movement? (a) diarthrosis (b) synarthrosis (c) amphiarthrosis (d) syndesmosis

PART II. COMPLETION

11. The thin layer of hyaline cartilage on articulating surfaces of bones is called

_____ cartilage.

12. The synovial membrane and fibrous capsule together form the _____ capsule.

13. Pads of fibrocartilage between the articular surfaces of bones that maintain stability of the

joint are called _____ .

14. Fluid-filled connective tissue sacs that cushion movements of one body part over another are

referred to as _____ .

15. The _____ ligament supports the back of the knee and helps to prevent hyperextension.

PART III. MATCHING

_____ 16. Circumduction

_____ 17. Adduction

_____ 18. Flexion

_____ 19. Pronation

_____ 20. Elevation

_____ 21. Protraction

_____ 22. Rotation

_____ 23. Plantar flexion

_____ 24. Dorsiflexion

_____ 25. Inversion

A. Decrease in the angle, usually between the anterior surfaces of articulating bones
B. Moving a part upward
C. Extension of the foot at the ankle joint
D. Forward movement parallel to the ground
E. Movement of the sole of the foot inward at the ankle joint
F. Movement toward the midline
G. Flexion of the foot at the ankle joint
H. Turning the palm posterior
I. Movement of a bone around its own axis
J. Distal end of a bone moves in a circle while the proximal end remains relatively stable

Student _____ **Date** _____

Laboratory Section _____ **Score/Grade** _____

1. Complete the following table with the values obtained.

Stimulus Strength	Contraction Strength

The all-or-none principle states that, once threshold is reached, a muscle cell will contract maximally, and that a subthreshold stimulus will not elicit a response. Based upon the data you collected in Section G.4, did the muscle obey the all-or-none principle?

2. Attach and label the myogram obtained with a single stimulus. Label latent period, contraction period, and relaxation period. Include the average values obtained.

Attach and label the myogram obtained with a single stimulus in a fatigued muscle. Label the latent period, contraction period, and relaxation period, and include the average values obtained.

Explain the physiological reason for the differences observed between the two myograms.

3. Draw and label the myogram obtained as the stimulus frequency was increased. Label treppe and tetanus in your diagram.

4. Complete the following graph based upon your results obtained in Section G.8.

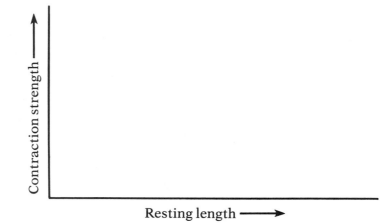

9 | MUSCLE TISSUE

Student _____   **Date** _____

Laboratory Section _____   **Score/Grade** _____

PART I. MULTIPLE CHOICE

_____   1. The ability of muscle tissue to return to its original shape after contraction or extension is called (a) excitability (b) elasticity (c) extension (d) tetanus

_____   2. Which of the following is striated and voluntary? (a) skeletal muscle tissue (b) cardiac muscle tissue (c) visceral muscle tissue (d) smooth muscle tissue

_____   3. The portion of a sarcomere composed of thin myofilaments only is the (a) H zone (b) A band (c) I band (d) Z line

_____   4. The area of contact between a motor axon terminal and a muscle cell sarcolemma is called the (a) synapse (b) myofilament (c) T tubule (d) neuromuscular junction

_____   5. The connective tissue layer surrounding bundles of muscle fibers is called the (a) perimysium (b) endomysium (c) ectomysium (d) myomysium

_____   6. Which of the following is striated and involuntary? (a) smooth muscle tissue (b) skeletal muscle tissue (c) cardiac muscle tissue (d) visceral muscle tissue

_____   7. The portion of a sarcomere where thin and thick myofilaments overlap is called the (a) H zone (b) triad (c) A band (d) I band

_____   8. The portion of a physiograph that converts nonelectrical signals into electrical signals is the (a) transducer (b) electrode (c) amplifier (d) coupler

_____   9. In a skeletal muscle twitch, which period requires the *least* amount of time? (a) relaxation (b) latent (c) contraction (d) extension

_____   10. A state of sustained muscle contraction is known as (a) tetanus (b) treppe (c) myopathy (d) hypertrophy

PART II. COMPLETION

11. The ability of muscle tissue to receive and respond to stimuli is called _____ .

12. Fibrous connective tissue located between muscle fibers is known as _____ .

13. The sections of a muscle fiber separated by Z lines are called _____ .

14. The plasma membrane surrounding a muscle cell is called the _____ .

15. The region in a sarcomere consisting of thick myofilaments only is known as the _____ .

16. Muscle tissue that is nonstriated and involuntary is _____ .

17. The ability of muscle tissue to stretch when pulled is called _____ .

18. The phenomenon by which a muscle fiber contracts to its fullest or not at all is known as the

_____ .

19. A record of muscle contraction is referred to as a(n) _____ .

20. A stimulus too weak to initiate a nerve impulse is called a(n) _____ stimulus.

10 | LABORATORY REPORT QUESTIONS
SKELETAL MUSCLES

Student _____   Date _____

Laboratory Section _____   Score/Grade _____

PART I. MULTIPLE CHOICE

_____ 1. The connective tissue covering that encloses the entire skeletal muscle is the (a) perimysium (b) endomysium (c) epimysium (d) mesomysium

_____ 2. A cord of connective tissue that attaches a skeletal muscle to the periosteum of bone is called a(n) (a) ligament (b) aponeurosis (c) perichondrium (d) tendon

_____ 3. A skeletal muscle that decreases the angle at a joint is referred to as a(n) (a) flexor (b) abductor (c) pronator (d) evertor

_____ 4. The name *abductor* means that a muscle (a) produces a downward movement (b) moves a part away from the midline (c) elevates a body part (d) increases the angle at a joint

_____ 5. Which connective tissue layer directly encircles the fasciculi of skeletal muscles? (a) epimysium (b) endomysium (c) perimysium (d) mesomysium

_____ 6. Which muscle is *not* associated with a movement of the eyeball? (a) superior rectus (b) superior oblique (c) medial rectus (d) genioglossus

_____ 7. Of the following, which muscle is involved in compression of the abdomen? (a) external oblique (b) superior oblique (c) medial rectus (d) genioglossus

_____ 8. A muscle directly concerned with breathing is the (a) sternocleidomastoid (b) mentalis (c) brachialis (d) external intercostal

_____ 9. Which muscle is *not* related to movement of the wrist? (a) extensor carpi ulnaris (b) flexor carpi radialis (c) supinator (d) flexor carpi ulnaris

_____ 10. A muscle that helps move the thigh is the (a) piriformis (b) triceps brachii (c) hypoglossus (d) peroneus tertius

389

PART II. MATCHING

Identify the criterion (or criteria) used to name the following muscles:

_____ 11. Supinator

_____ 12. Deltoid

_____ 13. Stylohyoideus

_____ 14. Flexor carpi radialis

_____ 15. Gluteus maximus

_____ 16. External oblique

_____ 17. Triceps brachii

_____ 18. Adductor longus

_____ 19. Temporalis

_____ 20. Trapezius

A. Location
B. Shape
C. Size
D. Direction of fibers
E. Action
F. Number of origins
G. Insertion and origin

PART III. COMPLETION

21. The principal cheek muscle used in compression of the cheek is the _____ .

22. The muscle that protracts the tongue is the _____ .

23. The eye muscle that rolls the eyeball downward is the _____ .

24. The _____ muscle flexes the neck on the chest.

25. The abdominal muscle that flexes the vertebral column is the _____ .

26. The muscle of the pectoral (shoulder) girdle that depresses the clavicle is the

_____ .

27. Flexion, adduction, and medial rotation of the arm are accomplished by the

_____ muscle.

28. The _____ muscle is the most important extensor of the forearm.

29. The muscle that flexes and abducts the wrist is the _____ .

30. The erect position of the spine is maintained by the _____ muscle.

31. The four muscles that extend the legs are the vastus lateralis, vastus medialis, vastus intermedius, and _____ .

32. Two muscles that dorsiflex the foot are the peroneus tertius and _____ .

11 | SURFACE ANATOMY

Student _____   **Date** _____

Laboratory Section _____   **Score/Grade** _____

PART I. MULTIPLE CHOICE

_____ 1. The term used to refer to the crown of the skull (vertex) is (a) occipital (b) mental (c) parietal (d) zygomatic

_____ 2. The laryngeal cartilage in the midline of the anterior cervical region known as the Adam's apple is the (a) cricoid (b) epiglottis (c) arytenoid (d) thyroid

_____ 3. Inflammation of which muscle is associated with "stiff neck"? (a) teres major (b) trapezius (c) deltoid (d) cervicalis

_____ 4. The skeletal muscle immediately on either side of the vetebral column is the (a) serratus anterior (b) infraspinatus (c) teres major (d) erector spinae

_____ 5. The jugular notch and xiphoid process are associated with the (a) sternum (b) scapula (c) clavicle (d) ribs

_____ 6. The expanded end of the spine of the scapula is the (a) acromion (b) linea alba (c) olecranon (d) superior angle

_____ 7. Which nerve can be palpated as a rounded cord in a groove behind the medial epicondyle? (a) median (b) radial (c) ulnar (d) brachial

_____ 8. Which carpal bone can be palpated as a projection distal to the styloid process of the ulna? (a) trapezoid (b) trapezium (c) hamate (d) pisiform

_____ 9. The lateral rounded contour on the anterior surface of the hand (at the base of the thumb) formed by the muscles of the thumb is the (a) "anatomical snuffbox" (b) thenar eminence (c) hypothenar eminence (d) dorsal venous arch

_____ 10. The superior margin of the hipbone is the (a) symphysis pubis (b) iliac spine (c) acetabulum (d) iliac crest

_____ 11. Which bony structure bears the weight of the body when a person is seated? (a) greater trochanter (b) iliac crest (c) ischial tuberosity (d) gluteal fold

_____ 12. Which muscle is *not* a component of the quadriceps femoris group? (a) biceps femoris (b) vastus lateralis (c) vastus medialis (d) rectus femoris

_____ 13. The diamond-shaped space on the posterior aspect of the knee is the (a) cubital fossa (b) posterior triangle (c) popliteal fossa (d) nuchal groove

_____ 14. The projection of the distal end of the tibia that forms the prominence on one side of the ankle is the (a) medial condyle (b) medial malleolus (c) lateral condyle (d) lateral malleolus

_____ 15. The tendon that can be seen in line with the great toe belongs to which muscle? (a) extensor digiti minimi (b) extensor digitorum longus (c) extensor hallucis longus (d) extensor carpi radialis

PART II. COMPLETION

16. The laryngeal cartilage that connects the larynx to the trachea is the _____ cartilage.

17. The _____ triangle is bordered by the mandible, sternum, cervical midline, and sternocleidomastoid muscle.

18. The depression on the superior surface of the sternum between the medial ends of the clavicle is the _____ .

19. The principal superifical chest muscle is the _____ .

20. Tendinous intersections are associated with the _____ muscle.

21. The muscle that forms the rounded prominence of the shoulder is the _____ muscle.

22. The triangular space in the anterior aspect of the elbow is the _____ .

23. The "anatomical snuffbox" is bordered by the tendons of the extensor pollicius brevis muscle and the _____ muscle.

24. The dorsal aspects of the distal ends of metacarpals II through V are commonly referred to as

_____ .

25. The tendon of the _____ muscle is in line with phalanx V.

26. The dimple that forms about 4 cm lateral to the midline just above the buttocks lies superficial to the _____ .

27. The femoral projection that can be palpated about 20 cm inferior to the iliac crest is the

_____ .

28. The continuation of the quadriceps femoris tendon inferior to the patella is the

_____ .

29. The tendon of insertion for the gastrocnemius and soleus muscles is the _____ tendon.

30. Superficial veins in the dorsum of the foot that unite to form the small and great saphenous veins belong to the _____ .

31. The prominent veins along the lateral cervical regions are the _____ veins.

32. The pronounced vertebral spine of C7 is the _____ .

33. The most reliable surface anatomy feature of the chest is the _____ .

34. A slight groove extending from the xiphoid process to the symphysis pubis is the

_____ .

35. The vein that crosses the cubital fossa and is frequently used to remove blood is the

_____ vein.

PART III. MATCHING

_____ 36. Mental region

_____ 37. Xiphoid process

_____ 38. Arm

_____ 39. Nuchal

_____ 40. Shoulder

_____ 41. Gluteus maximus muscle

_____ 42. Costal margin

_____ 43. Olecranon

_____ 44. Wrist

_____ 45. Auricular region

_____ 46. Semitendinosus muscle

_____ 47. Leg

_____ 48. Cranium

_____ 49. Ankle

_____ 50. Hand

A. Inferior edges of costal cartilages of ribs 7 through 10

B. Forms elbow

C. Inferior portion of sternum

D. Manus

E. Crus

F. Brachium

G. Tarsus

H. Anterior part of mandible

I. Brain case

J. Component of hamstrings

K. Forms main part of prominence of buttock

L. Carpus

M. Posterior neck region

N. Acromial (omos)

O. Ear

12 | NERVOUS TISSUE AND PHYSIOLOGY

Student _____   **Date** _____

Laboratory Section _____   **Score/Grade** _____

SECTION D. SPINAL REFLEXES OF FROG

Record the results of your observations of frog reflexes in the following table.

REFLEX ACTIVITY	NORMAL FROG	SINGLE-PITHED FROG	DOUBLE-PITHED FROG
1. Head and leg position			
2. Rate of respiration			
3. Righting reflex			
4. Horizon reflex			
5. Swimming			
6. Withdrawal reflex			
7. Corneal reflex			
8. Response to noise			
9. Acetic acid on leg			
10. Acetic acid on chest			

What conclusions may be drawn as to the levels of complexity of the above reflexes?

What conclusions may be drawn as to the reactivity of peripheral nerves in a single- or double-pithed frog?

12 | NERVOUS TISSUE AND PHYSIOLOGY

Student _____   Date _____

Laboratory Section _____   Score/Grade _____

PART I. MULTIPLE CHOICE

_____ 1. The portion of a neuron that conducts impulses away from the cell body is the (a) dendrite (b) axon (c) receptor (d) effector

_____ 2. The fine branching filaments of an axon are called (a) myelin sheaths (b) axolemmas (c) telodendria (d) axon hillocks

_____ 3. The component of a reflex arc that responds to a motor impulse is the (a) center (b) receptor (c) sensory neuron (d) effector

_____ 4. Which type of neuron conducts impulses toward the central nervous system? (a) afferent (b) association (c) internuncial (d) efferent

_____ 5. In a reflex arc, the impulse is transmitted directly to the effector by the (a) sensory neuron (b) motor neuron (c) center (d) receptor

_____ 6. Bulblike structures at the distal ends of telodendria that contain storage sacs for neurotransmitters are called (a) dendrites (b) synaptic end bulbs (c) axon collaterals (d) neurofibrils

_____ 7. Which neuroglial cell is phagocytic? (a) oligodendrocyte (b) protoplasmic astrocyte (c) microglial cell (d) fibrous astrocyte

PART II. COMPLETION

8. A neuron that contains several dendrites and one axon is classified as _____ .

9. The portion of a neuron that contains the nucleus and cytoplasm is the _____ .

10. The phospholipid covering around many peripheral axons is called the _____ .

11. The two types of cells that compose the nervous system are neurons and

_____ .

12. The peripheral, nucleated layer of the neurolemmocyte (Schwann cell) that encloses the myelin

sheath is the _____ .

13. The side branch of an axon is referred to as the _____ .

14. The part of a neuron that conducts impulses toward the cell body is the _____ .

15. Neurons that carry impulses between sensory neurons and motor neurons are called
_____ neurons.

16. Neurons with one dendrite and one axon are classified as _____ .

17. Unmyelinated gaps between segments of the myelin sheath are known as

_____ .

18. The neuroglial cell that produces a myelin sheath around axons of neurons of the central nervous system is called a(n) _____ .

19. In a reflex arc, the muscle or gland that responds to a motor impulse is called the

_____ .

Student _____ Date _____

Laboratory Section _____ Score/Grade _____

PART I. MULTIPLE CHOICE

_____ 1. The tapered, conical portion of the spinal cord is the (a) filum terminale (b) conus medullaris (c) cauda equina (d) lumbar enlargement

_____ 2. The outermost meninx composed of dense fibrous connective tissue is the (a) pia mater (b) arachnoid (c) dura mater (d) denticulate

_____ 3. The portion of a spinal nerve that contains motor nerve fibers only is the (a) posterior root (b) posterior root ganglion (c) lateral root (d) anterior root

_____ 4. The connective tissue covering around individual nerve fibers is the (a) endoneurium (b) epineurium (c) perineurium (d) ectoneurium

_____ 5. On the basis of organization, which does *not* belong with the others? (a) pons (b) medulla (c) thalamus (d) midbrain

_____ 6. The lateral ventricles are connected to the third ventricle by the (a) interventricular foramen (b) cerebral aqueduct (c) median aperture (d) lateral aperture

_____ 7. The vital centers for heartbeat, respiration, and blood vessel diameter regulation are found in the (a) pons (b) cerebrum (c) cerebellum (d) medulla

_____ 8. The reflex centers for movements of the head and trunk in response to auditory stimuli are located in the (a) inferior colliculi (b) medial geniculate nucleus (c) superior colliculi (d) ventral posterior nucleus

_____ 9. Which thalamic nucleus controls general sensations and taste? (a) medial geniculate (b) ventral posterior (c) ventral lateral (d) ventral anterior

_____ 10. Integration of the autonomic nervous system, secretion of regulating factors, control of body temperature, and the regulation of food intake and thirst are functions of the (a) pons (b) thalamus (c) cerebrum (d) hypothalamus

_____ 11. The left and right cerebral hemispheres are separated from each other by the (a) central sulcus (b) transverse fissure (c) longitudinal fissure (d) insula

_____ 12. Which structure does *not* belong with the others? (a) putamen (b) caudate nucleus (c) insula (d) globus pallidus

_____ 13. Which peduncles connect the cerebellum with the midbrain? (a) superior (b) inferior (c) middle (d) lateral

_____ 14. Which cranial nerve has the most anterior origin? (a) XI (b) IX (c) VII (d) IV

_____ 15. Extensions of the pia mater that suspend the spinal cord and protect against shock are the (a) choroid plexuses (b) pyramids (c) denticulate ligaments (d) superior colliculi

_____ 16. Which branch of a spinal nerve enters into formation of plexuses? (a) meningeal (b) dorsal (c) rami communicantes (d) ventral

_____ 17. Which plexus innervates the upper extremities and shoulders? (a) sacral (b) brachial (c) lumbar (d) cervical

_____ 18. How many pairs of thoracic spinal nerves are there? (a) 1 (b) 5 (c) 7 (d) 12

PART II. COMPLETION

19. The narrow, shallow groove on the posterior surface of the spinal cord is the

_____.

20. The space between the dura mater and wall of the vertebral canal is called the

_____ .

21. In a spinal nerve, the cell bodies of sensory neurons are found in the _____ .

22. The outermost connective tissue covering around a spinal nerve is the _____ .

23. The middle meninx is referred to as the _____ .

24. The nuclei of origin for cranial nerves IX, X, XI, and XII are found in the _____ .

25. The portion of the brain containing the cerebral peduncles is the _____.

26. Cranial nerves V, VI, VII, and VIII have their nuclei of origin in the _____ .

27. A shallow downfold of the cerebral cortex is called a(n) _____ .

28. The _____ separates the frontal lobe of the cerebrum from the parietal lobe.

29. White matter tracts of the cerebellum are called _____ .

30. The space between the dura mater and arachnoid is referred to as the _____ .

31. Together, the thalamus, hypothalamus, and pineal gland are called the _____ .

32. Cerebrospinal fluid passes from the third ventricle into the fourth ventricle through the

_____ .

33. The cerebrum is separated from the cerebellum by the _____ fissure.

34. The branches of a spinal nerve that are components of the autonomic nervous system are known as _____ .

35. The plexus that innervates the buttocks, perineum, and lower extremities is the

_____ plexus.

36. There are _____ pairs of spinal nerves.

37. Together, the brain and spinal cord are referred to as the _____ nervous system.

38. The cell bodies of _____ neurons of the ANS are found inside autonomic ganglia.

39. The portion of the ANS concerned with the fight-or-flight response is the _____ division.

40. The autonomic ganglia that are anterior to the vertebral column and close to large abdominal arteries are called _____ ganglia.

14 | LABORATORY REPORT QUESTIONS
SENSATIONS

Student _____ Date _____

Laboratory Section _____ Score/Grade _____

PART I. MULTIPLE CHOICE

_____ 1. The process by which the brain refers sensations to their point of stimulation is referred to as (a) modality (b) projection (c) accommodation (d) convergence

_____ 2. An awareness of the activities of muscles, tendons, and joints is known as (a) referred pain (b) adaptation (c) refraction (d) proprioception

_____ 3. The papillae located in an inverted V-shaped row at the posterior portion of the tongue are the (a) circumvallate (b) filiform (c) fungiform (d) gustatory

_____ 4. The technical name for the "white of the eye" is the (a) cornea (b) conjunctiva (c) choroid (d) sclera

_____ 5. Which is *not* a component of the vascular tunic? (a) choroid (b) macula lutea (c) iris (d) ciliary body

_____ 6. The amount of light entering the eyeball is regulated by the (a) lens (b) iris (c) cornea (d) conjunctiva

_____ 7. Which region of the eye is concerned primarily with image formation? (a) retina (b) choroid (c) lens (d) ciliary body

_____ 8. The densest concentration of cones is found at the (a) blind spot (b) macula lutea (c) central fovea (d) optic disc

_____ 9. Which region of the eyeball contains vitreous humor? (a) anterior chamber (b) posterior cavity (c) posterior chamber (d) conjunctiva

_____ 10. Among the structures found in the middle ear are the (a) vestibule (b) auditory ossicles (c) semicircular canals (d) external auditory canal

_____ 11. The receptors for dynamic equilibrium are the (a) saccules (b) utricles (c) cristae in semicircular ducts (d) spiral organs (organs of Corti)

_____ 12. The auditory ossicles are attached to the tympanic membrane, to each other, and to the (a) fenestra vestibuli (b) fenestra cochlea (c) round window (d) labyrinth

_____ 13. Another name for the internal ear is the (a) labyrinth (b) fenestra (c) cochlea (d) vestibule

_____ 14. Orientation of the body relative to the ground is termed (a) postural reflex (b) tonal reflex (c) dynamic equilibrium (d) static equilibrium

_____ 15. The inability to feel a sensation consciously even though a stimulus is still being applied is called (a) modality (b) projection (c) adaptation (d) afterimage formation

_____ 16. Which sequence best describes the normal flow of tears from the eyes into the nose? (a) lacrimal canals, lacrimal sacs, nasolacrimal ducts (b) lacrimal sacs, lacrimal canals, nasolacrimal ducts (c) nasolacrimal ducts, lacrimal sacs, lacrimal canals (d) lacrimal sacs, nasolacrimal ducts, lacrimal canals

_____ 17. A patient whose lens has lost transparency is suffering from (a) glaucoma (b) conjunctivitis (c) cataract (d) trachoma

_____ 18. The portion of the eyeball that contains aqueous humor is the (a) anterior cavity (b) lens (c) posterior chamber (d) macula lutea

_____ 19. The organ of hearing located within the inner ear is the (a) vestibule (b) fenestra cochlea (c) modiolus (d) spiral organ (organ of Corti)

_____ 20. The sense organs of static equilibrium are the (a) semicircular ducts (b) membranous labyrinths (c) maculae in the utricle and saccule (d) pinnae

_____ 21. Which receptor does _not_ belong with the others? (a) muscle spindle (b) tendon organ (Golgi tendon organ) (c) joint kinesthetic receptor (d) lamellated (pacinian) corpuscle

_____ 22. The membrane that is reflected from the eyelids onto the eyeball is the (a) retina (b) bulbar conjunctiva (c) sclera (d) choroid

_____ 23. A characteristic of sensations by which one sensation may be distinguished from another is called (a) modality (b) projection (c) adaptation (d) afterimage formation

_____ 24. Which are _not_ cutaneous receptors? (a) tactile (Merkel's) discs (b) muscle spindles (c) lamellated (pacinian) corpuscles (d) corpuscles of touch (Meissner's corpuscles)

_____ 25. Which region of the tongue reacts strongest to bitter tastes? (a) tip (b) center (c) back (d) sides

_____ 26. Which of the following values indicates the best visual acuity? (a) 20/30 (b) 20/40 (c) 20/50 (d) 20/60

_____ 27. Nearsightedness is referred to as (a) emmetropia (b) hypermetropia (c) eumetropia (d) myopia

PART II. COMPLETION

28. Receptors found in blood vessels and viscera are classified as _____ .

29. Structures that collectively produce and drain tears are referred to as the _____ .

30. The three zones of the inner nervous layer of the nervous tunic (retina) are the photoreceptor neurons, bipolar neurons, and _____ neurons.

31. The small area of the retina where no image is formed is referred to as the _____ .

32. Abnormal elevation of intraocular pressure is called _____ .

33. In the visual pathway, nerve impulses pass from the optic chiasma to the _____ before passing to the thalamus.

34. The openings between the middle and inner ears are the oval and _____ windows.

35. The fluid within the bony labyrinth is called _____ .

36. Tactile sensations include touch, pressure, and _____ .

37. Receptors for pressure are free nerve endings, type II cutaneous mechanoreceptors (end organs of Ruffini), and _____ corpuscles.

38. Proprioceptive receptors that provide information about the degree and rate of angulations of joints are _____ .

39. The neural pathway for olfaction includes olfactory cells, olfactory bulbs, _____, and cerebral cortex.

40. The posterior wall of the middle ear communicates with the mastoid air cells of the temporal bone through the _____ .

41. A thin semitransparent partition of fibrous connective tissue that separates the external auditory meatus from the inner ear is the _____ .

42. The fluid in the membranous labyrinth is called _____ .

43. The cochlear duct is separated from the scala vestibuli by the _____ .

44. The gelatinous glycoprotein layer over the hair cells in the maculae is called the _____ .

45. _____ is blurred vision caused by an irregular curvature of the surface of the cornea or lens.

46. Image formation requires refraction, accommodation, constriction of the pupil, and _____ .

15 | ENDOCRINE SYSTEM

Student _____ Date _____

Laboratory Section _____ Score/Grade _____

SECTION L. PHYSIOLOGY OF THE ENDOCRINE SYSTEM

Complete the following table based upon your calculations.

	CONTROL		HYPERTHYROID		HYPOTHYROID	
	Your Value	Class Average	Your Value	Class Average	Your Value	Class Average
Time to consume 40 ml oxygen						
Rat weight						
Oxygen consumption						

Record your observations for each of the demonstrations.

Males

Normal

Castrated

Castrated plus injections

Injections only

Females

Normal

Ovariectomized

Ovariectomized plus injections

Injections only

15 | ENDOCRINE SYSTEM

Student _____ Date _____

Laboratory Section _____ Score/Grade _____

PART I. MULTIPLE CHOICE

_____ 1. Growth hormone cells, gonadotroph cells, and cortico-lipotroph cells are associated with the (a) thyroid (b) hypophysis (c) parathyroids (d) suprarenals

_____ 2. The posterior pituitary is *not* an endocrine gland because it (a) has a rich blood supply (b) is not near the brain (c) does not make hormones (d) contains ducts

_____ 3. Which hormone assumes a role in the development and discharge of an ovum? (a) GH (b) TSH (c) LH (d) PRL

_____ 4. The endocrine gland that is probably malfunctioning if a person has a high metabolic rate is the (a) thymus (b) posterior pituitary (c) anterior pituitary (d) thyroid

_____ 5. The antagonistic hormones that regulate blood calcium level are (a) GH-TSH (b) insulin-glucagon (c) aldosterone-cortisone (d) CT-PTH

_____ 6. The endocrine gland that develops from the sympathetic nervous system is the (a) adrenal medulla (b) pancreas (c) thyroid (d) anterior pituitary

_____ 7. The hormone that aids in sodium conservation and potassium excretion is (a) hydrocortisone (b) CT (c) ADH (d) aldosterone

_____ 8. Which of the following hormones is sympathomimetic? (a) insulin (b) oxytocin (c) epinephrine (d) testosterone

_____ 9. Which hormone lowers blood sugar level? (a) glucagon (b) melatonin (c) insulin (d) cortisone

_____ 10. The endocrine gland that may assume a role in regulation of the menstrual cycle, release of aldosterone, and normal brain physiology is the (a) pineal (b) thymus (c) thryoid (d) suprarenal

PART II. COMPLETION

11. The hypophysis is attached to the hypothalamus by a stalklike structure called the

_____ .

12. A hormone that acts on another endocrine gland and causes that gland to secrete its own hormones is called a(n) _____ hormone.

13. _____ hormone is responsible for increasing skin pigmentation.

14. The hormone that helps cause contraction of the smooth muscle of the pregnant uterus is

_____ .

15. Histologically, the spherical sacs that compose the thyroid gland are called thyroid

_____ .

16. The thyroid hormones associated with metabolism are triiodothyronine and _____ .

17. Principal and oxyphil cells are associated with the _____ gland.

18. The zona glomerulosa of the adrenal cortex secretes a group of hormones called

_____ .

19. The hormones that promote normal metabolism, provide resistance to stress, and function as anti-inflammatories are _____ .

20. The pancreatic hormone that raises blood sugar level is _____ .

21. In spermatogenesis, the most immature cells near the basement membrane are called

_____ .

22. Cells within the testes that secrete testosterone are known as _____ .

23. The ovaries are attached to the uterus by means of the _____ ligament.

24. The female hormones that help cause the development of secondary sex characteristics are called _____ .

25. The endocrine gland that assumes a direct function in immunity is the _____ .

26. Any hormone that regulates the functions of the gonads is classified as a(n) _____ hormone.

27. The hormone that is stored in the neurohypophysis that prevents excessive urine production is

_____ .

28. The region of the adrenal cortex that synthesizes androgens is the _____ .

29. The hormone-producing cells of the adrenal medulla are called _____ cells.

30. Together, alpha cells, beta cells, and delta cells constitute the _____ .

31. Regulating factors from the hypothalamus reach the adenohypophysis by a network of blood vessels called the _____ portal system.

32. FSH and LH are produced by _____ cells of the adenohypophysis.

33. The portion of an ovary that produces progesterone, estrogens, and relaxin is the

_____ .

34. Calcium deposits in the pineal gland are referred to as _____ .

35. Under the influence of thymic hormones, B cells develop into antibody-producing

_____ cells.

16 | LABORATORY REPORT RESULTS
BLOOD

Student _____ **Date** _____

Laboratory Section _____ **Score/Grade** _____

SECTION D. RED BLOOD CELL TESTS

1. Red blood cell count results: _____ RBCs per cu mm.

2. Red blood cell volume (hematocrit) results: _____ %.

3. Sedimentation rate results: _____ mm per hr.

4. Hemoglobin estimation results: _____ g per 100 ml.

SECTION E. LEUKOCYTES

5. White blood cell count results: _____ WBCs per cu mm.

6. Drawings of various blood cells.

SECTION H. CLOTTING TESTS

1. Clotting time (slide method) results: _____ min., _____ sec.

2. Clotting time (capillary tube method) results: _____ min., _____ sec.

SECTION I. BLOOD GROUPINGS

1. In determining your ABO blood grouping, did you observe clumping when your blood was mixed with

_____ anti-A serum only

_____ anti-B serum only

_____ both anti-A and anti-B serums

_____ neither anti-A nor anti-B serum

2. Based on your observations, what is your ABO blood grouping?

_____ A _____ B _____ AB _____ O

3. Based on your observations, briefly explain why you identify your ABO blood grouping as you

do. _____

_____

_____

4. Record the results of the ABO blood grouping tests done by your class.

TYPE	ANTI-A (present or absent)	ANTI-B (present or absent)	NUMBER OF INDIVIDUALS	CLASS PERCENTAGE
A				
B				
AB				
O				

5. Based on your observations, are you Rh$^+$ or Rh$^-$?

_____ Rh$^+$ _____ Rh$^-$

6. Record the results of the Rh tests done by your class.

TYPE	NUMBER OF INDIVIDUALS	CLASS PERCENTAGE
Rh$^+$		
Rh$^-$		

16 BLOOD

Student _____   Date _____

Laboratory Section _____   Score/Grade _____

PART I. MULTIPLE CHOICE

_____ 1. The process by which all blood cells are formed is called (a) hemocytoblastosis (b) erythropoiesis (c) hematopoiesis (d) leucocytosis

_____ 2. An inability of body cells to receive adequate amounts of oxygen may indicate a malfunction of (a) neutrophils (b) leucocytes (c) lymphocytes (d) erythrocytes

_____ 3. Special cells of the body that have the responsibility of clearing away dead, disintegrating bodies of red and white blood cells are called (a) agranular leucocytes (b) reticuloendothelial cells (c) erythrocytes (d) thrombocytes

_____ 4. The name of the test procedure that informs the physician about the rate of erythropoiesis is called the (a) reticulocyte count (b) sedimentation rate (c) hemoglobin count (d) differential count

_____ 5. The normal red blood cell count per cubic millimeter in a male is about (a) 5.4 million (b) 7 million (c) 4 million (d) more than 9 million

_____ 6. The normal number of leucocytes per cubic millimeter is (a) 5000 to 9000 (b) 8000 to 12,000 (c) 2000 to 4000 (d) over 15,000

_____ 7. Under the microscope, red blood cells appear as (a) circular discs with centrally located nuclei (b) circular discs with lobed nuclei (c) oval discs with many nuclei (d) biconcave discs without nuclei

_____ 8. An increase in the number of white blood cells is called (a) leucopenia (b) hematocrit (c) polycythemia (d) leucocytosis

_____ 9. Thrombocytes are formed from a special large cell that breaks up into small fragments. This cell is called a(n) (a) eosinophil (b) hemocytoblast (c) megakaryocyte (d) platelet

_____ 10. The blood type showing the highest incidence in Caucasians in the United States is (a) A (b) O (c) AB (d) B

PART II. COMPLETION

11. Another name for red blood cells is _____ .

12. Blood gets its red color from the presence of _____ .

13. The life span of a red blood cell is approximately _____ .

14. A good method for routine testing for anemia is _____ .

15. The normal sedimentation rate value for adults is _____ .

411

16. The normal ratio of red blood cells to white blood cells is _____ .

17. The granular leucocytes are formed from _____ tissue.

18. The number of thrombocytes per cubic millimeter found normally in blood is

_____ .

19. The function of thrombocytes is to prevent blood loss by starting a chain of reactions resulting

in _____ .

20. In blood groupings (typing), the antigens are also called _____ .

21. The hemolysis produced by a fetal-maternal incompatability of blood cells is called

_____ .

22. The part of the cell where agglutinogens are located is _____ .

PART III. MATCHING

_____ 23. Hemocytoblast

_____ 24. Polycythemia

_____ 25. A high neutrophil count

_____ 26. A high monocyte count

_____ 27. Leucopenia

_____ 28. A high lymphocyte count

_____ 29. Plasma

_____ 30. A high eosinophil count

_____ 31. Serum

A. Tissue destruction by invading bacteria

B. An increase in the normal red blood cell count

C. Leukemia and infectious mononucleosis

D. Immature cells that develop into mature blood cells

E. Parasitic infections

F. Liquid portion of blood without the formed elements and clotting substances

G. An allergic reaction

H. A decrease in the normal white blood cell count

I. Liquid portion of blood without the formed elements

17 | LABORATORY REPORT QUESTIONS
HEART

Student _____   **Date** _____

Laboratory Section _____   **Score/Grade** _____

PART I. MULTIPLE CHOICE

_____ 1. Which of the following veins drains the blood from most of the vessels supplying the heart wall? (a) vasa vasorum (b) superior vena cava (c) coronary sinus (d) inferior vena cava

_____ 2. The atrioventricular valve on the same side of the heart as the origin of the aorta is the (a) aortic semilunar (b) tricuspid (c) bicuspid (d) pulmonary semilunar

_____ 3. Which valve does the blood go through just before entering the pulmonary trunk on the way to the lungs? (a) tricuspid (b) pulmonary semilunar (c) aortic semilunar (d) bicuspid

_____ 4. The pointed end of the heart that projects downward and to the left is the (a) costal surface (b) base (c) apex (d) coronary sulcus

_____ 5. Which of these structures is more internal? (a) fibrous pericardium (b) serous pericardium (c) visceral pericardium (d) myocardium

_____ 6. The musculature of the heart is referred to as the (a) endocardium (b) myocardium (c) epicardium (d) pericardium

_____ 7. The depression in the interatrial septum corresponding to the foramen ovale of fetal circulation is the (a) interventricular sulcus (b) musculi pectinati (c) chordae tendineae (d) fossa ovalis

PART II. COMPLETION

8. Malfunction of the _____ valve would interfere with the flow of blood from the right atrium to the right ventricle.

9. Deoxygenated blood is sent to the lungs through the _____ .

10. The loose-fitting serous membrane that encloses the heart is called the _____ .

11. The two inferior chambers of the heart are separated by the _____ .

12. The earlike flap of tissue on each atrium is called a(n) _____ .

13. The large vein that drains blood from superior parts of the body and empties into the right atrium is the _____ .

14. The cusps of atrioventricular valves are prevented from inverting by the presence of cords called _____ , which are attached to papillary muscle.

15. A groove on the surface of the heart that houses blood vessels and a variable amount of fat is called a(n) _____ .

413

PART III. SPECIAL EXERCISE

Draw a model of the heart and carefully label the four chambers, the four valves in their proper places, and the major blood vessels entering and exiting from the heart.

18 | BLOOD VESSELS

Student _____   **Date** _____

Laboratory Section _____   **Score/Grade** _____

PART I. MULTIPLE CHOICE

_____   1. The largest of the circulatory routes is (a) systemic (b) pulmonary (c) coronary (d) hepatic portal

_____   2. All arteries of systemic circulation branch from the (a) superior vena cava (b) aorta (c) pulmonary artery (d) coronary artery

_____   3. The arterial system that supplies the brain with blood is the (a) hepatic portal system (b) pulmonary system (c) cerebral arterial circle (circle of Willis) (d) hepatic system

_____   4. An obstruction in the inferior vena cava would hamper the return of blood from the (a) head and neck (b) upper extremities (c) thorax (d) abdomen and pelvis

_____   5. Which statement best describes arteries? (a) all carry oxygenated blood to the heart (b) all contain valves to prevent the backflow of blood (c) all carry blood away from the heart (d) only large arteries are lined with endothelium

_____   6. Which statement is *not* true of veins? (a) they have less elastic tissue and smooth muscle than arteries (b) they contain more fibrous tissue than arteries (c) most veins in the extremities have valves (d) they always carry deoxygenated blood

_____   7. A thrombus in the first branch of the arch of the aorta would affect the flow of blood to the (a) left side of the head and neck (b) myocardium of the heart (c) right side of the head and neck and right upper extremity (d) left upper extremity

_____   8. If a vein must be punctured for an injection, transfusion, or removal of a blood sample, the likely site would be the (a) median cubital (b) subclavian (c) hemiazygous (d) anterior tibial

_____   9. In hepatic portal circulation, blood is eventually returned to the inferior vena cava through the (a) superior mesenteric vein (b) portal vein (c) hepatic artery (d) hepatic veins

_____ 10. Which of the following are involved in pulmonary circulation? (a) superior vena cava, right atrium, and left ventricle (b) inferior vena cava, right atrium, and left ventricle (c) right ventricle, pulmonary artery, and left atrium (d) left ventricle, aorta, and inferior vena cava

_____ 11. If a thrombus in the left common iliac vein dislodged, into which arteriole system would it first find its way? (a) brain (b) kidneys (c) lungs (d) left arm

_____ 12. In fetal circulation, the blood containing the highest amount of oxygen is found in the (a) umbilical arteries (b) ductus venosus (c) aorta (d) umbilical vein

_____ 13. The greatest amount of elastic tissue found in the arteries is located in which coat? (a) tunica interna (b) tunica media (c) tunica externa (d) tunica adventitia

_____ 14. Which coat of an artery contains endothelium? (a) tunica interna (b) tunica media (c) tunica externa (d) tunica adventitia

_____ 15. Permitting the exchange of nutrients and gases between the blood and tissue cells is the primary function of (a) capillaries (b) arteries (c) veins (d) arterioles

_____ 16. The circulatory route that runs from the digestive tract to the liver is called (a) coronary circulation (b) pulmonary circulation (c) hepatic portal circulation (d) cerebral circulation

_____ 17. Which of the following statements about systemic circulation is *not* correct? (a) its purpose is to carry oxygen and nutrients to body tissues and to remove carbon dioxide (b) all systemic arteries branch from the aorta (c) it involves the flow of blood from the left ventricle to all parts of the body except the lungs (d) it involves the flow of blood from the body to the left atrium

_____ 18. The opening in the septum between the right and left atria of a fetus is called the (a) foramen ovale (b) ductus venosus (c) foramen rotundum (d) foramen spinosum

_____ 19. The branch of the umbilical vein in the fetus that connects with the inferior vena cava, bypassing the liver, is the (a) foramen ovale (b) ductus venosus (c) ductus arteriosus (d) patent ductus

_____ 20. Which of the vessels does *not* belong with the others? (a) brachiocephalic artery (b) left common carotid artery (c) celiac artery (d) left subclavian artery

PART II. MATCHING

_____ 21. aortic branch that supplies the head and associated structures

_____ 22. artery that distributes blood to the small intestine and part of the large intestine

_____ 23. vessel into which veins of the head and neck, upper extremities, and thorax enter

_____ 24. vessel into which veins of the abdomen, pelvis, and lower extremities enter

_____ 25. vein that drains the head and associated structures

_____ 26. longest vein in the body

_____ 27. vein just behind the knee

_____ 28. artery that supplies a major part of the large intestine and rectum

_____ 29. first branch off of the arch of the aorta

_____ 30. arteries supplying the heart

A. Inferior vena cava
B. Superior vena cava
C. Superior mesenteric
D. Common carotid
E. Jugular
F. Brachiocephalic
G. Coronary
H. Inferior mesenteric
I. Popliteal
J. Great saphenous

19 | CARDIOVASCULAR PHYSIOLOGY

Student _____   Date _____

Laboratory Section _____   Score/Grade _____

SECTION B. ISOLATED TURTLE HEART EXPERIMENTS

1. Cardiac cycle

2. Intrinsic control of the cardiac cycle

3. Extrinsic control of the cardiac cycle
   a. Vagal stimulation

   b. Application of acetylcholine

   c. Application of atropine sulfate

d. Application of atropine sulfate immediately followed by acetylcholine

e. Application of atropine sulfate and vagal stimulation

f. Application of epinephrine

4. Refractory period

SECTION C. HEART SOUNDS

1. Which heart sound is the loudest? _____

2. Did you hear a third sound? _____

3. Where does the first sound originate? _____

4. Where does the second sound originate? _____

5. After you exercised, how did the heart sounds differ from before? _____

_____

6. Did they differ in rate and intensity? _____

7. Did the first or second sound increase in loudness? _____

SECTION D. PULSE RATE

1. Radial pulse rate count results: _____ pulses per minute

2. Have all radial pulse rates put on the blackboard, arranging them from the highest to the lowest. The median pulse rate is found exactly halfway down from the top.

   What is the median radial pulse rate of the class? _____

   What was the highest rate? _____

   What was the lowest rate? _____

3. Compare your radial and carotid pulse rates by filling in the following table.

	RADIAL PULSE RATE	CAROTID PULSE RATE
Sitting quietly		
Standing quietly		
After walking		
After running in place		

SECTION E. CONDUCTION SYSTEM AND ELECTROCARDIOGRAM

Attach examples of the electrocardiogram strips you obtained.

LEAD I

Electrocardiogram Strip

LEAD II

Electrocardiogram Strip

LEAD III

Electrocardiogram Strip

SECTION F. BLOOD PRESSURE

Record your systolic and diastolic blood pressures in the following table.

	SYSTOLIC PRESSURE		DIASTOLIC PRESSURE		PULSE PRESSURE
	Left Arm	Right Arm	Left Arm	Right Arm	
Sitting					
Standing					
After running					

19 | LABORATORY REPORT QUESTIONS
CARDIOVASCULAR PHYSIOLOGY

Student _____   Date _____

Laboratory Section _____   Score/Grade _____

PART I. MULTIPLE CHOICE

_____ 1. During atrial systole, all of the following occur *except* (a) deoxygenated blood passes into the right ventricle (b) oxygenated blood passes into the left ventricle (c) the ventricles are in diastole (d) the semilunar valves are open

_____ 2. The two distinct heart sounds, described phonetically as lubb and dupp, represent (a) contraction of the ventricles and relaxation of the atria (b) contraction of the atria and relaxation of the ventricles (c) closing of the atrioventricular and semilunar valves (d) surging of blood into the pulmonary artery and aorta

_____ 3. When the semilunar valves are open during a cardiac cycle, which of the following occur? I—atrioventricular valves are closed; II—ventricles are in systole; III—ventricles are in diastole; IV—blood enters the aorta; V—blood enters the pulmonary artery; VI—atria contract. (a) I, II, IV, and V (b) I, II, and VI (c) II, IV, and V (d) I, III, IV, and VI

_____ 4. A pulse rate of 100 times per minute indicates (a) bradycardia (b) myocardia (c) tachycardia (d) endocardia

_____ 5. Pulse pressure provides clinical information concerning (a) condition of the arteries (b) ventricular contractions (c) state of the atrioventricular valves (d) state of the semilunar valves

PART II. COMPLETION

6. Systole and diastole of both atria plus systole and diastole of both ventricles is called

_____ .

7. Blood flow through the heart is controlled by speed of the cardiac cycle, venous return to the heart, opening and closing of the valves, and _____ .

8. Heart sounds provide valuable information about the _____ .

9. Abnormal or peculiar heart sounds are called _____ .

10. Although the pulse may be detected in most surface arteries, pulse rate is usually determined on the _____ .

11. The heart has an intrinsic regulating system called the cardiac _____ system.

12. Electrical impulses accompanying the cardiac cycle are recorded by the _____ .

13. The typical ECG produces three clearly recognizable waves. The first wave, which indicates depolarization of the atria, is called the _____ .

14. Various up-and-down impulses produced by an ECG are called _____ .

15. The instrument normally used to measure blood pressure is called a(n) _____ .

16. The artery that is normally used to evaluate blood pressure is the _____ .

17. Rapping or thumping sounds heard clinically when blood pressure is being taken are called _____ sounds.

18. The difference between systolic and diastolic pressure is called _____ .

19. An average blood pressure value for an adult is _____ .

20. An average pulse pressure is _____ .

20 LABORATORY REPORT QUESTIONS
LYMPHATIC SYSTEM

Student _____   Date _____

Laboratory Section _____   Score/Grade _____

PART I. COMPLETION

1. Small masses of lymphoid tissue located along the length of the lymphatics are called _____ .

2. Lymphatics have thinner walls than veins, but resemble veins in that they also have _____ .

3. All lymphatics converge, get larger, and eventually merge into two main channels, the thoracic duct and the _____ .

4. Lymph is processed in the lymph nodes by special cells of the _____ system.

5. These special cells are called _____ .

6. Lymph nodes produce certain cells that are responsible for the production of antibodies. These cells are called _____ .

7. The x-ray examination of lymphatic vessels and lymph organs after they are filled with a radiopaque substance is called _____ .

8. This x-ray examination is useful in detecting edema and _____ .

9. and 10. Organs that compose the lymphatic system are the tonsils, _____ , and _____ .

21 | LABORATORY REPORT RESULTS
RESPIRATORY SYSTEM

Student _____   **Date** _____

Laboratory Section _____   **Score/Grade** _____

D. LABORATORY TESTS ON RESPIRATION

1. Use of Pneumograph

   Attach a sample of any one of the following activities.

   Reading and talking
   Swallowing water
   Laughing
   Yawning
   Coughing
   Sniffing

2. Measurement of Chest and Abdomen in Respiration

   Record the results of your chest measurements in the following table.

	THORAX		ABDOMEN	
	Inspiration	Expiration	Inspiration	Expiration
Tape (normal)	in.	in.	in.	in.
Tape (forced)	in.	in.	in.	in.
Calipers (normal)	in.	in.	in.	in.
Calipers (forced)	in.	in.	in.	in.

3. Use of Collins Respirometer

   Record the results of your exercises using the Collins respirometer in the following table.

	TIDAL VOLUME (1)	EXPIRATORY RESERVE (2)	VITAL CAPACITY (3)	INSPIRATORY RESERVE (4)	FEV$_1$ (5)
First time	ml	ml	ml	ml	ml
Second time	ml	ml	ml	ml	ml
Third time	ml	ml	ml	ml	ml
Your average	ml	ml	ml	ml	ml
Normal value	ml	ml	ml	ml	ml

4. Use of Handheld Respirometer

Vital capacity _____

FEV_1 _____

Maximum breathing capacity _____

SECTION E. COMBINED RESPIRATORY AND CARDIOVASCULAR INTERACTIONS

Record the results of your exercises in the following table.

	RESPIRATORY RATE AND DEPTH	SYSTOLIC AND DIASTOLIC PRESSURE	PULSE RATE
Basal readings while sitting erect and quiet for 3 minutes			
Basal readings while standing on cycle or in front of platform for 3 minutes			
Readings after 1 minute of exercise			
Readings after 2 minutes of exercise			
Readings after 3 minutes of exercise			
Readings after 4 minutes of exercise			
Readings after 1 minute following completion of exercise			
Readings after 2 minutes following completion of exercise			
Readings after 3 minutes following completion of exercise			
Readings after 5 minutes following completion of exercise			

21 | RESPIRATORY SYSTEM

Student _____   Date _____

Laboratory Section _____   Score/Grade _____

PART I. MULTIPLE CHOICE

_____ 1. The overall exchange of gases between the atmosphere, blood, and cells is called (a) inspiration (b) respiration (c) expiration (d) none of these

_____ 2. The internal nose is formed by the ethmoid bone, the maxillae, the inferior conchae, and the (a) hyoid bone (b) nasal bone (c) palatine bone (d) none of these

_____ 3. The portion of the pharynx that contains the pharyngeal tonsils is the (a) oropharynx (b) laryngopharynx (c) nasopharynx (d) pharyngeal orifice

_____ 4. The Adam's apple is a common term for the (a) thyroid cartilage (b) cricoid cartilage (c) epiglottis (d) none of these

_____ 5. The C-shaped rings of cartilage of the trachea not only prevent the trachea from collapsing but also aid in the process of (a) lubrication (b) removing foreign particles (c) gas exchange (d) swallowing

_____ 6. Of the following structures, the smallest in diameter is the (a) left primary bronchus (b) bronchioles (c) secondary bronchi (d) alveolar ducts

_____ 7. The structures of the lung that actually contain the alveoli are the (a) respiratory bronchioles (b) fissures (c) lobules (d) terminal bronchioles

_____ 8. From superficial to deep, the structure(s) that you would encounter first among the following is (are) the (a) bronchi (b) parietal pleura (c) pleural cavity (d) secondary bronchi

PART II. COMPLETION

9. An advantage of nasal breathing is that the air is warmed, moistened, and _____ .

10. Improper fusion of the palatine and maxillary bones results in a condition called

_____ .

11. The protective lid of cartilage that prevents food from entering the trachea is the

_____ .

12. After removal of the _____ an individual would be unable to speak.

13. The upper respiratory tract is able to trap and remove dust because of its lining of

_____ .

14. The passage of a tube into the mouth and down through the larynx and trachea to bypass an obstruction is called _____ .

15. An x-ray of the bronchial tree after administration of an iodinated media is called a

_____ .

16. The sequence of respiratory tubes from largest to smallest is trachea, primary bronchi, secondary bronchi, bronchioles, _____, respiratory bronchioles, and alveolar ducts.

17. Both the external and internal nose are divided internally by a vertical partition called the

_____ .

18. The undersurface of the external nose contains two openings called the nostrils or

_____ .

19. The functions of the pharynx are to serve as a passageway for air and food and to provide a resonating chamber for _____ .

20. An inflammation of the membrane that encloses and protects the lungs is called

_____ .

21. The anterior portion of the nasal cavity just inside the nostrils is called the _____ .

22. Groovelike passageways in the nasal cavity formed by the conchae are called

_____ .

23. The portion of the pharynx that contains the palatine and lingual tonsils is the

_____ .

24. Each lobe of a lung is subdivided into compartments called _____ .

25. A(n) _____ is an outpouching lined by squamous epithelium and supported by a thin elastic membrane.

26. The _____ cartilage attaches the larynx to the trachea.

27. The portion of a lung that rests on the diaphragm is the _____ .

28. Phagocytic cells in the alveolar wall are called _____ .

29. The surface of a lung lying against the ribs is called the _____ surface.

30. The _____ is a vertical slit in the medial surface of a lung through which bronchi, blood vessels, lymphatics, and nerves pass.

PART III. MATCHING

_____ 31. Tidal volume

_____ 32. Inspiratory reserve volume

_____ 33. Inspiratory capacity

_____ 34. Expiratory reserve volume

_____ 35. Vital capacity

_____ 36. Total lung capacity

A. 1200 ml of air

B. 3600 ml of air

C. 4800 ml of air

D. 500 ml of air

E. 3100 ml of air

F. 6000 ml of air

22 | LABORATORY REPORT RESULTS
DIGESTIVE SYSTEM

Student _____   Date _____

Laboratory Section _____   Score/Grade _____

SECTION D. CHEMISTRY OF DIGESTION

1. Digestion of Starch

a. How long did it take for the starch to be digested? _____

b. Did your observation indicate the presence of maltose? _____

c. What is the meaning of this result? _____

2. Effect of Temperature on Starch Digestion

d. Record the time required for starch to disappear at the temperatures tested.

_____ 0 °C to 1 °C   _____ 40 °C   _____ Boiling

_____ 10 °C   _____ 60 °C

e. What is the optimum temperature for starch digestion? _____

3. Effect of pH on Starch Digestion

f. Record the time required for starch to disappear at the pH readings tested.

solution A: pH 4.0 _____

solution B: pH 7.0 _____

solution C: pH 9.0 _____

g. Explain your results.

A: pH 4.0 _____

B: pH 7.0 _____

C: pH 9.0 _____

4. Digestion of Fats

h. Record the results of the digestion of fats by pancreatic juice in the following table.

TUBE NO.	TEMPERATURE OF WATER BATH	CHANGE IN pH (COLOR)	EXPLANATION OF RESULTS
1			
2			

5. Action of Bile on Fats

　　i. What difference can you detect in the appearance of the mixtures in the two vials?

　　_____

　　j. How does emulsification of lipids by means of bile aid in the digestion of fat?

　　_____

6. Digestion of Protein

　　k. Record the results of the digestion of protein by pepsin in the following table.

TUBE NO.	TUBE CONTENTS	pH	DIGESTION OBSERVED (yes or no)	EXPLANATION OF RESULTS
1				
2				
3				
4				
5				

22 | DIGESTIVE SYSTEM

Student _____   Date _____

Laboratory Section _____   Score/Grade _____

PART I. MULTIPLE CHOICE

_____ 1. If an incision has to be made in the small intestine to remove an obstruction, the first layer of tissue to be cut is the (a) muscularis (b) mucosa (c) serosa (d) submucosa

_____ 2. Mesentery, lesser omentum, and greater omentum are all directly associated with the (a) peritoneum (b) liver (c) esophagus (d) mucosa of the alimentary canal

_____ 3. Chemical digestion of carbohydrates is initiated in the (a) stomach (b) small intestine (c) mouth (d) large intestine

_____ 4. A tumor of the villi and plicae circulares would interfere most directly with the body's ability to carry on (a) absorption (b) deglutition (c) mastication (d) peristalsis

_____ 5. The main chemical activity of the stomach is to begin the digestion of (a) fats (b) proteins (c) carbohydrates (d) all of the above

_____ 6. Surgical cutting of the lingual frenulum would occur in which part of the body? (a) salivary glands (b) esophagus (c) nasal cavity (d) tongue

_____ 7. To free the small intestine from the posterior abdominal wall, which of the following would have to be cut? (a) mesocolon (b) mesentery (c) lesser omentum (d) falciform ligament

_____ 8. The cells of gastric glands that produce secretions directly involved in chemical digestion are the (a) mucous (b) parietal (c) zymogenic (d) pancreatic islets (islets of Langerhans)

_____ 9. An obstruction in the hepatopancreatic ampulla (ampulla of Vater) would affect the ability to transport (a) bile and pancreatic juice (b) gastric juice (c) salivary amylase (d) succus entericus

_____ 10. The terminal portion of the small intestine is known as the (a) duodenum (b) ileum (c) jejunum (d) pyloric sphincter (valve)

_____ 11. The portion of the large intestine closest to the liver is the (a) right colic flexure (b) rectum (c) sigmoid colon (d) left colic flexure

_____ 12. The lamina propria is found in which coat? (a) serosa (b) muscularis (c) submucosa (d) mucosa

_____ 13. Which structure attaches the liver to the anterior abdominal wall and diaphragm? (a) lesser omentum (b) greater omentum (c) mesocolon (d) falciform ligament

_____ 14. The opening between the oral cavity and pharynx is called (a) vermilion border (b) fauces (c) vestibule (d) lingual frenulum

_____ 15. All of the following are parts of a tooth except the (a) crown (b) root (c) cervix (d) papilla

_____ 16. Cells of the liver that destroy worn-out white and red blood cells and bacteria are termed (a) hepatic cells (b) stellate reticuloendothelial (Kupffer) cells (c) alpha cells (d) beta cells

_____ 17. Bile is manufactured by which cells? (a) alpha (b) beta (c) hepatic (d) stellate reticuloen-dothelial (Kupffer)

_____ 18. Which part of the small intestine secretes the intestinal digestive enzymes? (a) intestinal glands (b) duodenal (Brunner's) glands (c) lacteals (d) microvilli

_____ 19. Structures that give the colon a puckered appearance are called (a) taenia coli (b) villi (c) rugae (d) haustrae

PART II. COMPLETION

20. An acute inflammation of the serous membrane lining the abdominal cavity and covering the abdominal viscera is referred to as _____ .

21. The _____ is a sphincter between the ileum and large intestine.

22. The portion of the small intestine that is attached to the stomach is the _____ .

23. The portion of the stomach closest to the esophagus is the _____ .

24. The _____ forms the floor of the oral cavity and is composed of skeletal muscle covered with mucous membrane.

25. The convex lateral border of the stomach is called the _____ .

26. The three special structures found in the wall of the small intestine that increase its efficiency in absorbing nutrients are the villi, plicae circulares, and _____ .

27. The three pairs of salivary glands are the parotids, submandibulars, and _____ .

28. The small intestine is divided into three segments: duodenum, ileum, and _____ .

29. The large intestine is divided into four main regions: the cecum, colon, rectum, and

_____ .

30. The enzyme that is present in saliva is called _____ .

31. The transition zone of the lips where the outer skin and inner mucous membrane meet is called the _____ .

32. The _____ papillae are arranged in the form of an inverted **V** on the posterior surface of the tongue.

33. The portion of a tooth containing blood vessels, lymphatics, and nerves is the

_____ .

34. The teeth present in permanent dentition, but not in deciduous dentition, that replace the deciduous molars are the _____ .

35. The portion of the GI tract that conveys food from the pharynx to the stomach is the

_____ .

36. The inferior region of the stomach connected to the small intestine is the _____ .

37. The clusters of cells in the pancreas that secrete digestive enzymes are called

_____ .

38. The caudate lobe, quadrate lobe, and central vein are all associated with the

_____ .

39. The common bile duct is formed by the union of the common hepatic duct and

_____ duct.

40. The pear-shaped sac that stores bile is the _____ .

41. _____ glands of the small intestine secrete an alkaline substance to protect the mucosa from excess acid.

42. The _____ attaches the large intestine to the posterior abdominal wall.

43. The _____ is the last 20 cm of the GI tract.

44. A midline fold of mucous membrane that attaches the inner surface of each lip to its corresponding gum is the _____ .

45. The bonelike substance that gives teeth their basic shape is called _____ .

46. The _____ anchors teeth in position and helps to dissipate chewing forces.

47. The portion of the colon that terminates at the rectum is the _____ colon.

48. The palatine tonsils are between the palatoglossal and _____ arches.

49. The teeth closest to the midline are the _____ .

50. The vermiform appendix is attached to the _____ .

PART III. MATCHING

_____ 51. Lipase

_____ 52. Benedict's solution

_____ 53. Lugol's solution

_____ 54. Salivary amylase

_____ 55. Pepsin

A. Commonly used solution in the test for starch
B. Capable of digesting starch
C. Capable of digesting protein
D. Commonly used solution for detecting reducing sugars
E. Digests fat to fatty acids and glycerol and changes the color of blue litmus to red

23 LABORATORY REPORT RESULTS
URINARY SYSTEM

Student ______________________ **Date** ______________________

Laboratory Section ______________________ **Score/Grade** ______________________

SECTION B. TUBULAR SECRETION

1. Secretion of Phenol Red

   Time required for first appearance ______________________

   Time required for maximum concentration ______________________

2. Inhibition of Secretion

   Time required for first appearance ______________________

   Time required for maximum concentration ______________________

3. Metabolic Requirements for Secretion

   Time required for first appearance ______________________

   Time required for maximum concentration ______________________

SECTION E. URINALYSIS

1. Physical Analysis

Characteristic	Normal	Your Sample
a. Color	Straw yellow to amber	______________
b. Sediment	None	______________
c. pH	5.0–7.8	______________
d. Specific gravity	1.008–1.030	______________

2. Chemical Analysis

Record your results in the spaces provided.

a. GLUCOSE

   Benedict's test ______________________

   Clinitest tablet ______________________

   Chemstrip ______________________

b. PROTEIN

Sulfosalicylic acid method _____

Albutest reagent tablets _____

Chemstrip _____

c. KETONE (ACETONE) BODIES

Acetest tablet _____

Sodium nitroprusside _____

Chemstrip _____

d. BILE PIGMENTS

Shaken tube (bile pigments) _____

Rosenbach test (biliverdin) _____

Ictotest (bilirubin) _____

Chemstrip _____

e. HEMOGLOBIN

Weber test _____

Chemstrip _____

3. Microscopic Analysis
Draw some of the substances (types of cells, types of crystals, or other elements) that you found in the microscopic examination of urinary sediment.

4. Unknown specimens
a. What substance did you find in the unknown specimen that was prepared by your instructor?

_____

b. What substance did you find in the unknown specimen that was prepared by other students?

_____

Student _____   Date _____

Laboratory Section _____   Score/Grade _____

PART I. MULTIPLE CHOICE

_____   1. Beginning at the innermost layer and moving toward the outermost layer, identify the order of tissue layers surrounding the kidney. (a) renal capsule, renal fascia, adipose capsule (b) renal fascia, adipose capsule, renal capsule (c) adipose capsule, renal capsule, renal fascia (d) renal capsule, adipose capsule, renal fascia

_____   2. The functional unit of the kidney is the (a) nephron (b) ureter (c) urethra (d) hilus

_____   3. Substances filtered by the kidney must pass through the endothelial-capsular membrane, which is composed of several parts. Which of the following choices lists the correct order of the parts as passed through by the substances? (a) epithelium of the visceral layer of glomerular (Bowman's) capsule, endothelium of the glomerulus, basement membrane of the glomerulus (b) endothelium of the glomerulus, basement membrane of the glomerulus, epithelium of the visceral layer of glomerular capsule (c) basement membrane of the glomerulus, endothelium of the glomerulus, epithelium of the visceral layer of glomerular capsule (d) epithelium of the visceral layer of glomerular capsule, basement membrane of the glomerulus, endothelium of the glomerulus

_____   4. In the glomerular capsule, the afferent arteriole divides into a capillary network called a(n) (a) glomerulus (b) interlobular artery (c) peritubular capillary (d) efferent arteriole

_____   5. Transport of urine from the renal pelvis into the urinary bladder is the function of the (a) urethra (b) calculi (c) casts (d) ureters

_____   6. The terminal portion of the urinary system is the (a) urethra (b) urinary bladder (c) ureter (d) nephron

_____   7. Damage to the renal medulla would interfere first with the functioning of which part of a juxtaglomerular nephron? (a) glomerular capsule (b) distal convoluted tubule (c) collecting ducts (d) proximal convoluted tubules

_____   8. An obstruction in the glomerulus would affect the flow of blood into the (a) renal artery (b) efferent arteriole (c) afferent arteriole (d) intralobular artery

_____   9. Urine that leaves the distal convoluted tubule passes through the following structures in which sequence? (a) collecting duct, hilus, calyces, ureter (b) collecting duct, calyces, pelvis, ureter (c) calyces, collecting duct, pelvis, ureter (d) calyces, hilus, pelvis, ureter

_____   10. The position of the kidneys behind the peritoneal lining of the abdominal cavity is described by the term (a) retroperitoneal (b) anteroperitoneal (c) ptosis (d) inferoperitoneal

_____   11. Of the following structures, the one to receive filtrate *last* as it passes through the nephron is the (a) proximal convoluted tubule (b) ascending limb (c) glomerulus (d) collecting duct

_____   12. Peristalsis of the ureter is a function of the (a) serosa (b) mucosa (c) submucosa (d) muscularis

_____ 13. The trigone and the detrusor muscle are associated with the (a) kidney (b) urinary bladder (c) urethra (d) ureters

_____ 14. The notch on the medial surface of the kidney through which blood vessels enter and exit is called the (a) medulla (b) major calyx (c) hilus (d) renal column

_____ 15. Blood is drained from the kidneys by the (a) renal arteries (b) interlobar arteries (c) interlobular veins (d) renal veins

_____ 16. The epithelium of the urinary bladder that permits distension is (a) stratified squamous (b) transitional (c) simple squamous (d) pseudostratified

_____ 17. How many times a day is the entire volume of blood in the body filtered by the kidneys? (a) 100 times (b) 5 times (c) 30 times (d) 60 times

_____ 18. The average urine capacity of the urinary bladder is (a) 1000 to 1200 ml (b) 50 to 100 ml (c) 700 to 800 ml (d) 200 to 300 ml

_____ 19. The normal pH of urine is between (a) 5.0 and 7.8 (b) 2.0 and 4.8 (c) 10.0 and 12.0 (d) none of the above

_____ 20. Normal urine has a specific gravity of approximately (a) 1.008 to 1.030 (b) 1.030 to 1.080 (c) 1.100 to 1.200 (d) none of the above

_____ 21. The special chemical that may be used to detect glucose in the urine is (a) sulfosalicylic acid (b) Benedict's solution (c) Lugol's solution (d) nitric acid

PART II. COMPLETION

22. In addition to the urinary system, other systems that help eliminate wastes are the respiratory, integumentary, and _____ systems.

23. The double-walled cup found in a nephron is called a(n) _____ .

24. The special capillary network found inside of this double-walled cup is the

_____ .

25. The major blood vessel that enters each kidney is the _____ .

26. The nerve supply to the kidneys comes from the autonomic nervous system and is called the

_____ .

27. Urine is expelled from the bladder by an act called urination, voiding, or

_____ .

28. The small tube in the urinary system that leads from the floor of the urinary bladder to the outside is the _____ .

29. The apices of renal pyramids are referred to as renal _____ .

30. The cortical substance between renal pyramids is called a renal _____ .

31. Cuplike extensions of the renal pelvis, usually two or three in number, are referred to as

_____ .

32. Epithelial cells of the visceral layer of the glomerular capsule are called _____ .

33. Distal convoluted tubules terminate by merging with _____ .

34. Long loops of blood vessels around the medullary structures of juxtaglomerulary nephrons are called _____ .

35. Which blood vessel comes next in this sequence? interlobar artery, arcuate artery, interlobular artery, _____ .

36. The abnormal condition when red blood cells are found in the urine in appreciable amounts is called _____ .

37. Various salts that solidify in the urinary tract are called _____ .

38. Various substances that have hardened and assumed the shape of the lumens of the nephron tubules are the _____ .

39. The pH of urine in individuals on high-protein diets tends to be _____ than normal.

40. The greater the concentration of solutes in urine, the greater will be its _____ .

24 | LABORATORY REPORT QUESTIONS
REPRODUCTIVE SYSTEMS

Student _____   Date _____

Laboratory Section _____   Score/Grade _____

PART I. MULTIPLE CHOICE

_____ 1. Structures of the male reproductive system responsible for production of sperm are the (a) efferent ducts (b) seminiferous tubules (c) seminal vesicles (d) rete testis

_____ 2. The superior portion of the male urethra is encircled by the (a) epididymis (b) testes (c) prostate gland (d) seminal vesicles

_____ 3. Cryptorchidism is a condition associated with the (a) prostate gland (b) testes (c) seminal vesicles (d) bulbourethral (Cowper's) glands

_____ 4. Weakening of the suspensory ligament would directly affect the position of the (a) mammary glands (b) uterus (c) uterine (fallopian) tubes (d) ovaries

_____ 5. Organs in the female reproductive system responsible for transporting ova from the ovaries to the uterus are the (a) uterine tubes (b) seminal vesicles (c) inguinal canals (d) none of the above

_____ 6. The name of the process that is responsible for the actual production of sperm is called (a) cryptorchidism (b) oogenesis (c) spermatogenesis (d) ovulation

_____ 7. Fertilization normally occurs in the (a) uterine (fallopian) tubes (b) vagina (c) uterus (d) ovaries

_____ 8. The portion of the uterus that assumes an active role during labor is the (a) serosa (b) endometrium (c) peritoneum (d) myometrium

_____ 9. Stereocilia are associated with the (a) ductus deferens (b) oviduct (c) epididymis (d) rete testis

_____ 10. The major portion of the volume of semen is contributed by the (a) bulbourethral (Cowper's) glands (b) testes (c) prostate gland (d) seminal vesicles

_____ 11. The chief ligament supporting the uterus and keeping it from dropping into the vagina is the (a) cardinal ligament (b) round ligament (c) broad ligament (d) ovarian ligament

_____ 12. Which sequence, from inside to out, best represents the histology of the uterus? (a) stratum basalis, stratum functionalis, myometrium, perimetrium (b) myometrium, perimetrium, stratum functionalis, stratum basalis (c) stratum functionalis, stratum basalis, myometrium, perimetrium (d) stratum basalis, stratum functionalis, perimetrium, myometrium

_____ 13. The white fibrous tissue layer that divides the testis into lobules is called the (a) dartos (b) raphe (c) tunica albuginea (d) germinal epithelium

_____ 14. Which sequence best represents the course taken by spermatozoa from their site of origin to the exterior? (a) seminiferous tubules, efferent ducts, epididymis, ductus deferens, ejaculatory duct, urethra (b) seminiferous tubules, efferent ducts, epididymis, ductus deferens, urethra, ejaculatory duct (c) seminiferous tubules, efferent ducts, ductus deferens, epididymis, ejaculatory duct, urethra (d) seminiferous tubules, epididymis, efferent ducts, ductus deferens, ejaculatory duct, urethra

_____ 15. The ovaries are anchored to the uterus by the (a) ovarian ligament (b) broad ligament (c) suspensory ligament (d) mesovarium

_____ 16. The terminal duct for the male reproductive system is the (a) urethra (b) vas deferens (c) inguinal canal (d) ejaculatory duct

_____ 17. The site of sperm maturation is the (a) ductus deferens (b) spermatic cord (c) epididymis (d) testes

_____ 18. Which of the following is the site of menstruation, implantation of a fertilized ovum, development of the fetus during pregnancy, and labor? (a) uterus (b) uterine (fallopian) tubes (c) vagina (d) cervix

_____ 19. Branched tubuloalveolar glands lying over the pectoralis major muscles are (a) lesser vestibular glands (b) adrenal (suprarenal) glands (c) mammary glands (d) greater vestibular glands

PART II. COMPLETION

20. Discharge of an ovum from the ovary about once each month is a process referred to as

_____ .

21. The inferior, narrow portion of the uterus that opens into the vagina is the _____ .

22. The milk-secreting cells of the mammary glands are referred to as _____ .

23. The distal end of the penis is a slightly enlarged region called the _____ .

24. Covering the slightly enlarged region of the penis is a loosely fitting skin called the

_____ .

25. The circular pigmented area surrounding each nipple of the mammary glands is the

_____ .

26. After an ovum leaves the ovary, it enters the open, funnel-shaped distal end of the uterine (fallopian) tube called the _____ .

27. The portion of a spermatozoon that contains the nucleus and acrosome is the

_____ .

28. Vasectomy refers to removal of a portion of the _____ .

29. The mass of erectile tissue in the penis that contains the spongy urethra is the

_____ .

30. Both the vesicular ovarian (graafian) follicle and _____ of the ovary secrete hormones.

31. The superior dome-shaped portion of the uterus is called the _____ .

32. The _____ anchor the uterus to either side of the pelvic cavity.

33. The passageway for menstrual flow and inferior portion of the birth canal is the

_____ .

34. Two longitudinal folds of skin that extend inferiorly and posteriorly from the mons pubis and are covered with pubic hair are the _____ .

35. The _____ is a small mass of erectile tissue at the anterior junction of the labia minora.

36. The thin fold of vascularized membrane that borders the vaginal orifice is the

_____ .

37. Complete the following sequence for the passage of milk: alveoli, secondary tubules,

_____ , ampullae, lactiferous ducts, nipple.

38. The layer of simple cuboidal epithelium covering the free surface of the ovary is the

_____ .

39. The phase of the menstrual cycle between days 6 and 13 during which endometrial repair occurs is the _____ phase.

40. During menstruation, the stratum _____ of the endometrium is sloughed off.

25 | LABORATORY REPORT QUESTIONS
25 | DEVELOPMENT

Student _____   **Date** _____

Laboratory Section _____   **Score/Grade** _____

PART I. MULTIPLE CHOICE

_____ 1. The basic difference between spermatogenesis and oogenesis is that (a) two more polar bodies are produced in spermatogenesis (b) the mature ovum contains the haploid chromosome number, whereas the mature sperm contains the diploid number (c) in oogenesis, one mature ovum is produced, and in spermatogenesis four mature sperm are produced (d) both mitosis and meiosis occur in spermatogenesis, but only meiosis occurs in oogenesis

_____ 2. The union of a sperm nucleus and an ovum nucleus resulting in formation of a zygote is referred to as (a) implantation (b) fertilization (c) gestation (d) parturition

_____ 3. The most advanced stage of development is the (a) morula (b) zygote (c) ovum (d) blastocyst

_____ 4. Damage to the mesoderm during embryological development would directly affect the formation of (a) muscle tissue (b) the nervous system (c) the epidermis of the skin (d) hair, nails, and skin glands

_____ 5. The placenta, the organ of exchange between mother and fetus, is formed by union of the endometrium with the (a) yolk sac (b) amnion (c) chorion (d) umbilicus

_____ 6. One oogonium produces (a) one ovum and three polar bodies (b) two ova and two polar bodies (c) three ova and one polar body (d) four ova

_____ 7. Implantation is defined as (a) attachment of the blastocyst to the uterine (fallopian) tube (b) attachment of the blastocyst to the endometrium (c) attachment of the embryo to the endometrium (d) attachment of the morula to the endometrium

_____ 8. Epithelium lining most of the digestive tract and a number of other organs is derived from (a) ectoderm (b) mesoderm (c) endoderm (d) mesophyll

_____ 9. The nervous system is derived from the (a) ectoderm (b) mesoderm (c) endoderm (d) mesophyll

_____ 10. Which of the following is *not* an embryonic membrane? (a) amnion (b) placenta (c) chorion (d) allantois

PART II. COMPLETION

11. A normal human sperm cell, as a result of meiosis, contains _____ chromosomes.

12. The process that permits an exchange of genes resulting in their recombination and the great variation among humans is called _____ .

13. The result of meiosis in spermatogenesis is that each primary spermatocyte produces four

_____ .

14. The stage of spermatogenesis that results in maturation of spermatids into spermatozoa is

called _____ .

15. The afterbirth expelled in the final stage of delivery is the _____ .

16. After the second month, the developing human is referred to as a(n) _____ .

17. Embryonic tissues from which all tissues and organs of the body develop are called the

_____ .

18. The cells of the inner cell mass divide to form two cavities: amniotic cavity and

_____ .

19. Somatic cells that contain two sets of chromosomes are referred to as _____
cells.

20. At the end of the _____ month of development, a heartbeat can be detected.

Student _____   Date _____

Laboratory Section _____   Score/Grade _____

SECTION G. GENETIC EXERCISES

PKU Screening

1. _____ negative—cream color

   _____ 15 mg%—light green

   _____ 40 mg%—medium green

   _____ 100 mg%—dark green

PTC Inheritance

2. _____ bitter taste

   _____ sweet taste

   _____ negative (no taste)

Corn Genetics

3. Ratio _____ monohybrid cross

   Ratio _____ test cross

   Ratio _____ dihybrid cross

   Ratio _____ trihybrid cross

Color Blindness

	Male Students	Female Students
4. Red color blind	_____	_____
Green color blind	_____	_____

Mendelian Laws of Inheritance

5. Record the results of tossing a nickel and a penny together 10 times.

	FEMALE (nickel)	MALE (penny)	1	2	3	4	5	TOTAL	CLASS TOTAL
Dominant offspring	A Heads	A Heads							
	A Heads	a Tails							
	a Tails	A Heads							
Recessive offspring	a Tails	a Tails							
Ratio dominant to recessive									

6. Complete the following monohybrid cross. Fill in genotypes (within circles) and phenotypes (under circles).

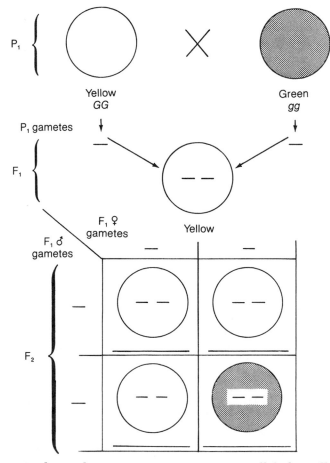

Monohybrid cross in the garden pea (*Pisum sativum*). *G* = allele for yellow, *g* = allele for green, P_1 = parental generation, F_1 = first filial generation, F_2 = second filial generation.

7. What is the phenotype ratio of the F₂ generation? _____ yellow/ _____ green.

8. Complete the following dihybrid cross. Fill in genotypes (within circles) and phenotypes (under circles).

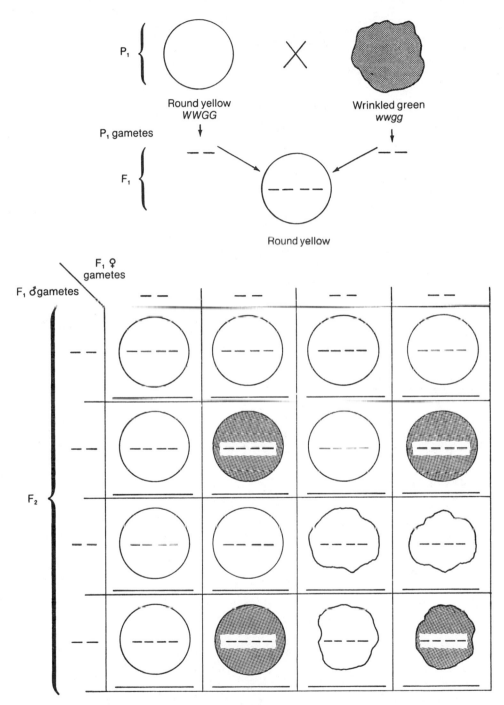

Dihybrid cross in the garden pea (*Pisum sativum*). **W** = allele for round, **w** = allele for wrinkled, **G** = allele for yellow, **g** = allele for green.

9. What is the phenotype ratio of the F₂ generation?

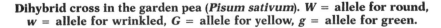
_____ round yellow/ _____ wrinkled yellow/ _____ round green/ _____ wrinkled green.

Student _____ **Date** _____

Laboratory Section _____ **Score/Grade** _____

PART I. MULTIPLE CHOICE

_____ 1. Using the symbols *Aa* to represent genes, (a) the trait is homozygous for the dominant characteristic (b) the trait is homozygous for the recessive characteristic (c) the trait is heterozygous (d) X-linked inheritance is in operation

_____ 2. Which statement concerning the normal inheritance of sex is correct? (a) all zygotes contain a *Y* chromosome (b) some ova contain a *Y* chromosome, (c) all ova and all sperm contain an *X* chromosome (d) all ova have an *X* chromosome, some sperm have an *X* chromosome, and some sperm have a *Y* chromosome

_____ 3. The genotype that will express characteristics associated with hemophilia (assume that *H* represents the gene for normal blood) is (a) $X^H X^h$ (b) $X^h Y$ (c) $X^H X^H$ (d) $X^H Y$

_____ 4. The exact position of a gene on a chromosome is called the (a) homologue (b) locus (c) triad (d) allele

PART II. COMPLETION

5. When the same genes appear on homologous chromosomes, as in *PP* or *pp*, the individual is said to be _____ for the trait.

6. If different genes appear on homologous chromosomes, as in *Pp* or *pP*, the individual is _____ for the trait.

7. Genetic composition expressed in the body or morphologically is called the body's

_____ .

8. The device that helps one visualize all the possible combinations of male and female gametes is called the _____ .

9. The twenty-third pair of human chromosomes are the sex chromosomes. All of the other pairs of chromosomes are called _____ .

10. Color blindness is an inherited trait that is specifically called _____ trait.

11. The recognized "father" of genetics is _____ .

12. A genetic cross that involves only one pair of alleles (or traits) is called a(n) _____ cross.

13. Passage of hereditary traits from one generation to another is called _____ .

14. The genetic makeup of an individual is called the person's _____ .

15. One of the many alternative forms of a gene is called its _____ .

APPENDIX A
SOME IMPORTANT UNITS
OF MEASUREMENT

ENGLISH UNITS OF MEASUREMENT

Fundamental or derived unit	Units and equivalents
Length	12 inches (in.) = 1 foot (ft) = 0.333 yard (yd)
	3 ft = 1 yd
	1760 yd = 1 mile (mi)
	5280 ft = 1 mi
Mass	1 ounce (oz) = 28.35 grams (g); 1 g = 0.0353 oz
	1 pound (lb) = 453 g = 16 oz; 1 kilogram (kg) = 2.205 lb
	1 ton = 2000 lb = 907 kg
Time	1 second (sec) = 1/86 400 of a mean solar day
	1 minute (min) = 60 sec
	1 hour (hr) = 60 min = 3600 sec
	1 day = 24 hr = 1440 min = 86 400 sec
Volume	1 fluid dram (fl dr) = 0.125 fluid ounce (fl oz)
	1 fl oz = 8 fl dr = 0.0625 quart (qt) = 0.008 gallon (gal)
	1 qt = 256 fl dr = 32 fl oz = 2 pints (pt) = 0.25 gal
	1 gal = 4 qt = 128 fl oz = 1024 fl dr

METRIC UNITS OF LENGTH AND SOME ENGLISH EQUIVALENTS

Metric unit	Meaning of prefix	Metric equivalent	English equivalent
1 kilometer (km)	kilo = 1000	1000 m	3280.84 ft or 0.62 mi; 1 mi = 1.61 km
1 hectometer (hm)	hecto = 100	100 m	328 ft
1 dekameter (dam)	deka = 10	10 m	32.8 ft
1 meter (m)		Standard unit of length	39.37 in. or 3.28 ft or 1.09 yd
1 decimeter (dm)	deci = $\frac{1}{10}$	0.1 m	3.94 in.
1 centimeter (cm)	centi = $\frac{1}{100}$	0.01 m	0.394 in.; 1 in. = 2.54 cm
1 millimeter (mm)	milli = $\frac{1}{1\,000}$	0.001 m = $\frac{1}{10}$ cm	0.0394 in.

Metric unit	Meaning of prefix	Metric equivalent	English equivalent
1 micrometer (μm) [formerly micron (μ)]	micro $= \frac{1}{1\,000\,000}$	$0.000\,001$ m $= \frac{1}{10\,000}$ cm	3.94×10^{-5} in.
1 nanometer (nm) [formerly millimicron (mμ)]	nano $= \frac{1}{1\,000\,000\,000}$	$0.000\,000\,001$ m $= \frac{1}{10\,000\,000}$ cm	3.94×10^{-8} in.
1 angstrom (Å)		$0.000\,000\,000\,1$ m $= \frac{1}{100\,000\,000}$ cm	3.94×10^{-9} in.

TEMPERATURE

Unit	K	°F	°C
1 degree Kelvin (K)	1	$\frac{9}{5}(K) - 459.7$	$K + 273.16*$
1 degree Fahrenheit (°F)	$\frac{5}{9}(°F) + 255.4$	1	$\frac{5}{9}(°F - 32)$
1 degree Celsius (°C)	$°C - 273$	$\frac{9}{5}(°C) + 32$	1

VOLUME

Unit	ml	cm³	qt	oz
1 milliliter (ml)	1	1	1.06×10^{-3}	3.392×10^{-2}
1 cubic centimeter (cm³)	1	1	1.06×10^{-3}	3.392×10^{-2}
1 quart (qt)	943	943	1	32
1 fluid ounce (fl oz)	29.5	29.5	3.125×10^{-2}	1

*Absolute zero (K) $= -273.16°C$.

APPENDIX B
PERIODIC TABLE OF THE ELEMENTS

KEY

6	← Atomic Number
C	← Symbol
12.01	← Atomic Weight
Carbon	← Name

1																	2
H 1.0080 Hydrogen																	**He** 4.003 Helium
3 **Li** 6.940 Lithium	4 **Be** 9.013 Berilium											5 **B** 10.82 Boron	6 **C** 12.011 Carbon	7 **N** 14.008 Nitrogen	8 **O** 16.000 Oxygen	9 **F** 19.00 Fluorine	10 **Ne** 20.183 Neon
11 **Na** 22.991 Sodium	12 **Mg** 24.32 Magnesium											13 **Al** 26.98 Aluminum	14 **Si** 28.09 Silicon	15 **P** 30.975 Phosphorus	16 **S** 32.066 Sulfur	17 **Cl** 35.457 Chlorine	18 **Ar** 39.944 Argon
19 **K** 39.100 Potassium	20 **Ca** 40.08 Calcium	21 **Sc** 44.96 Scandium	22 **Ti** 47.90 Titanium	23 **V** 50.95 Vanadium	24 **Cr** 52.01 Chromium	25 **Mn** 54.94 Manganese	26 **Fe** 55.85 Iron	27 **Co** 58.94 Cobalt	28 **Ni** 58.71 Nickel	29 **Cu** 63.54 Copper	30 **Zn** 65.38 Zinc	31 **Ga** 69.72 Gallium	32 **Ge** 72.60 Germanium	33 **As** 74.91 Arsenic	34 **Se** 78.96 Selenium	35 **Br** 79.916 Bromine	36 **Kr** 83.80 Krypton
37 **Rb** 85.48 Rubidium	38 **Sr** 87.63 Strontium	39 **Y** 88.92 Yttrium	40 **Zr** 91.22 Zirconium	41 **Nb** 92.91 Niobium	42 **Mo** 95.95 Molybdenum	43 **Tc** (99) Technetium	44 **Ru** 101.1 Ruthenium	45 **Rh** 102.91 Rhodium	46 **Pd** 106.4 Palladium	47 **Ag** 0Z880 Silver	48 **Cd** 112.41 Cadmium	49 **In** 114.32 Indium	50 **Sn** 118.70 Tin	51 **Sb** 121.76 Antimony	52 **Te** 127.61 Tellurium	53 **I** 126.91 Iodine	54 **Xe** 131.30 Xenon
55 **Cs** 132.91 Cesium	56 **Ba** 137.36 Barium	57 **La** 138.92 Lanthanum	72 **Hf** 178.50 Hafnium	73 **Ta** 180.95 Tantalum	74 **W** 183.86 Wolfram	75 **Re** 186.22 Rhenium	76 **Os** 190.2 Osmium	77 **Ir** 192.2 Iridium	78 **Pt** 195.09 Platinum	79 **Au** 197.0 Gold	80 **Hg** 200.61 Mercury	81 **Tl** 204.39 Thallium	82 **Pb** 207.21 Lead	83 **Bi** 209.00 Bismuth	84 **Po** (210) Polonium	85 **At** (210) Astatine	86 **Rn** (222) Radon
87 **Fr** (223) Francium	88 **Ra** (226) Radium	89 **Ac** (227) Actinium	104 (Russian Proposal Unofficial)														

58 **Ce** 140.13 Cerium	59 **Pr** 140.92 Praseodymium	60 **Nd** 144.27 Neodymium	61 **Pm** (147) Promethium	62 **Sm** 150.35 Samarium	63 **Eu** 152.0 Europium	64 **Gd** 157.26 Gadolinium	65 **Tb** 158.93 Terbium	66 **Dy** 162.51 Dysprosium	67 **Ho** 164.94 Holmium	68 **Er** 167.27 Erbium	69 **Tm** 168.94 Thulium	70 **Yb** 173.04 Ytterbium	71 **Lu** 174.99 Lutetium
90 **Th** (232) Thorium	91 **Pa** (231) Protactinium	92 **U** 238.07 Uranium	93 **Np** (237) Neptunium	94 **Pu** (242) Plutonium	95 **Am** 243 Americium	96 **Cm** (247) Curium	97 **Bk** (249) Berkelium	98 **Cf** (251) Californium	99 **Es** (254) Einsteinium	100 **Fm** (253) Fermium	101 **Md** (256) Mendelevium	102 **No** (253) Nobelium	103 **Lr** 257 Lawrencium

FIGURE CREDITS

1.1 Courtesy of Bausch & Lomb, Rochester, NY.

3.5 (a)–(f) By James R. Smail, Macalester College.

4.1 (a), (b), and (e) By Matt Iacobino and Gerard J. Tortora. (c), (d), (f), and (g) By James R. Smail and Russell A. Whitehead, Macalester College.

4.3 (a), (d), (f), (g), and (h) By James R. Smail and Russell A. Whitehead, Macalester College. (b) and (c) Courtesy of Ward's Natural Science Establishment, Inc., Rochester, NY. (e) By Matt Iacobino and Gerard J. Tortora.

5.2 From *Tissues and Organs: A Text-Atlas of Scanning Electron Microscopy* by Richard G. Kessel and Randy H. Kardon. Copyright © 1979, W. H. Freeman and Company.

6.1 (b) From *The Musculoskeletal System in Health and Disease* by Cornelius Rosse and D. Kay Clawson. Courtesy of Lippincott Publishers, 1980. (c) and (d) Courtesy of Fisher Scientific, an Allied Company, and S.T.E.M. Laboratories, copyright © 1975.

6.2 (a) Courtesy of Fisher Scientific, an Allied Company, and S.T.E.M. Laboratories, copyright © 1975. (b) From *Tissues and Organs: A Text-Atlas of Scanning Electron Microscopy* by Richard G. Kessel and Randy H. Kardon. Copyright © 1979, W. H. Freeman and Company.

7.1(a), (b), (d), (e), 7.2, 7.3, 7.4, 7.7(g), 7.8(a), 7.9–7.12 Courtesy of Matt Iacobino.

7.8 (b) Courtesy of Mayo Foundation, Rochester, MN.

8.2 (c) By John Eads.

8.3 (a)–(e) Copyright © 1983 by Gerard J. Tortora, courtesy of Matt Iacobino and Lynne Tortora. (i) and (j) Biomedical Graphics Department, University of Minnesota Hospitals. (f), (g), and (h) Courtesy of Matt Iacobino.

9.1, 9.3, 9.4 By James R. Smail and Russell A. Whitehead, Macalester College.

9.8 Courtesy of Narco BioSystems, Inc., Houston, TX.

11.2–11.8, 11.9(a), 11.10–11.12 Biomedical Graphics Department, University of Minnesota Hospitals.

11.9 (b) Courtesy of O. Richard Johnson.

13.4 (b) From *Tissues and Organs: A Text-Atlas of Scanning Electron Microscopy* by Richard G. Kessel and Randy H. Kardon. Copyright © 1979, W. H. Freeman and Company.

13.5(b), 13.8(b), 13.9(b) By James R. Smail, Macalester College.

14.2, 14.3(b) By James R. Smail and Russell A. Whitehead, Macalester College.

14.6 Biomedical Graphics Department, University of Minnesota Hospitals.

14.14 By James R. Smail and Russell A. Whitehead, Macalester College.

14.15 Copyright © 1983 by Gerard J. Tortora, courtesy of James Borghesi.

15.2 By James R. Smail and Russell A. Whitehead, Macalester College.

15.3 By James R. Smail, Macalester College.

15.4–15.6 By James R. Smail and Russell A. Whitehead, Macalester College.

16.2 Courtesy of Fisher Scientific, an Allied Company, and S.T.E.M. Laboratories, copyright © 1975.

16.6–16.8 By James R. Smail, Macalester College.

16.9 Courtesy of Lenni Patti.

17.2 From *Photographic Atlas of the Human Body*, Second Edition, by Chihiro Yokoshi and Johannes Rohen. Copyright © 1978, Igaku-Shoin Ltd., Tokyo.

17.3 (b) By John Eads.

18.1 (a), (b), and (c) By James R. Smail and Russell A. Whitehead, Macalester College. (d) From *Tissues and Organs: A Text-Atlas of Scanning Electron Microscopy* by Richard G. Kessel and Randy H. Kardon. Copyright © 1979, W. H. Freeman and Company.

19.7 Copyright © 1983 by Gerard J. Tortora, courtesy of Geraldine C. Tortora and Matt Iacobino.

20.3 From *The Essentials of Roentgen Interpretation*, Fourth Edition, by Lester W. Paul and John H. Juhl. Copyright © 1981, Harper & Row Publishers, Inc., New York.

459

21.2 (b) From *Photographic Atlas of the Human Body*, Second Edition, by Chihiro Yokoshi and Johannes Rohen. Copyright © 1978, Igaku-Shoin Ltd., Tokyo.

21.3 Copyright © 1983 by Gerard J. Tortora, courtesy of Lynne Tortora.

21.5 From *Photographic Atlas of the Human Body*, Second Edition, by Chihiro Yokoshi and Johannes Rohen. Copyright © 1978, Igaku-Shoin Ltd., Tokyo.

21.7 (a) By James R. Smail and Russell A. Whitehead, Macalester College. (b) From *Tissues and Organs: A Text-Atlas of Scanning Electron Microscopy* by Richard G. Kessel and Randy H. Kardon. Copyright © 1979, W. H. Freeman and Company.

21.8 Courtesy of the Mayo Foundation, Rochester, MN.

21.10 From *Tissues and Organs: A Text-Atlas of Scanning Electron Microscopy* by Richard G. Kessel and Randy H. Kardon. Copyright © 1979, W. H. Freeman and Company.

21.11 (a) Courtesy of Kinetix, Upper Saddle River, NJ. (b) Courtesy of Warren E. Collins, Inc., Braintree, MA.

22.3, 22.6 By James R. Smail and Russell A. Whitehead, Macalester College.

22.8 (a) From *Tissues and Organs: A Text-Atlas of Scanning Electron Microscopy* by Richard G. Kessel and Randy H. Kardon. Copyright © 1979, W. H. Freeman and Company. (b) and (c) By James R. Smail and Russell A. Whitehead, Macalester College.

22.10 By James R. Smail and Russell A. Whitehead, Macalester College.

22.11 (a) From *Tissues and Organs: A Text-Atlas of Scanning Electron Microscopy* by Richard G. Kessel and Randy H. Kardon. Copyright © 1979, W. H. Freeman and Company. (b), (c), and (d) By James R. Smail and Russell A. Whitehead, Macalester College.

22.13 (a) From *Tissues and Organs: A Text-Atlas of Scanning Electron Microscopy* by Richard G. Kessel and Randy H. Kardon. Copyright © 1979, W. H. Freeman and Company. (b) and (c) By James R. Smail and Russell A. Whitehead, Macalester College.

23.2 (b) From *Photographic Atlas of the Human Body*, Second Edition, by Chihiro Yokoshi and Johannes Rohen. Copyright © 1978, Igaku-Shoin Ltd., Tokyo.

23.3 (c) From *Tissues and Organs: A Text-Atlas of Scanning Electron Microscopy* by Richard G. Kessel and Randy H. Kardon. Copyright © 1979, W. H. Freeman and Company.

23.5 (a) and (b) By James R. Smail and Russell A. Whitehead, Macalester College. (c) Courtesy of Fisher Scientific, an Allied Company, and S.T.E.M. Laboratories, copyright © 1975.

23.7, 23.9 By James R. Smail and Russell A. Whitehead, Macalester College.

23.10 By James R. Smail, Macalester College.

24.2 (b) By James R. Smail and Russell A. Whitehead, Macalester College.

24.3 (b) Courtesy of Fisher Scientific, an Allied Company, and S.T.E.M. Laboratories, copyright © 1975.

24.4, 24.5, 24.10, 24.11, 24.15 By James R. Smail and Russell A. Whitehead, Macalester College.

INDEX